DESIGNING WITH LIGHT

Design HPU040369, see page 29F

Table of Contents

Windowscaping® 4F

Classic Beginnings
Efficient plans, stylish introductions 1

Special Details
Smart designs that shine with brilliant benefits 63

Sheer Genius
Comfortable homes that offer warm welcomes 149

Natural Beauty
Handsome styles, dramatic effects 243

Timeless Elegance
Graceful designs with a new perspective 333

Best and Brightest
Luxurious homes that reflect elegant style 417

How to Order Plans for the Homes in this Book 500

About the Pella® Window Specifications Program 512

Windowscaping®

Quality windows and doors define your personal style and make your home the special place you have in mind.

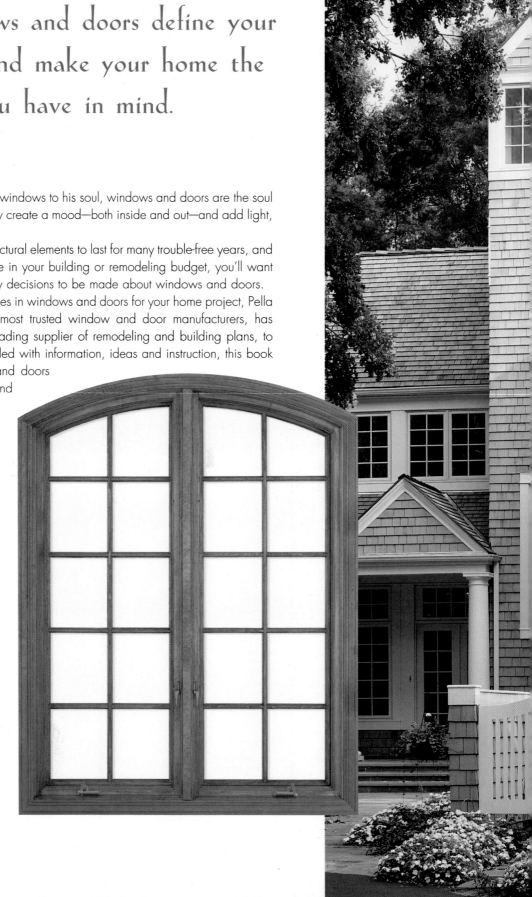

Just as a person's eyes are the windows to his soul, windows and doors are the soul of a new or remodeled home. They create a mood—both inside and out—and add light, fresh air and views to your life.

Since you'll expect these architectural elements to last for many trouble-free years, and because they are a major expense in your building or remodeling budget, you'll want to give serious thought to the many decisions to be made about windows and doors.

To help you make the best choices in windows and doors for your home project, Pella Corporation, one of the world's most trusted window and door manufacturers, has teamed with Home Planners, a leading supplier of remodeling and building plans, to bring you *Designing with Light*. Filled with information, ideas and instruction, this book explores the world of windows and doors from the design perspective and includes tips on choosing the best quality—and how to determine what quality really is. You'll need only to apply your own imagination to make the best decisions for your project.

We've also included a select group of Home Planners home plans that make beautiful use of windows and doors. Whether you intend to build a new home, or are considering remodeling an older home, these plans will help generate ideas.

Quality wood windows not only add beauty to your home, but give long-lasting performance and durability.

By choosing the right windows, your interior design scheme takes on brightness and allows fabulous views.

Windows and doors make dramatic statements and bring life to any building and remodeling project.

Pella Corporation is known for quality wood windows and doors, plus other products of unsurpassed performance and beauty. Its line incorporates the best of both worlds—the beauty of wood interiors plus the low-maintenance aspect of aluminum exteriors. Among the many convenient products developed by this Iowa-based manufacturer are between-the-glass shades and blinds, the Rolscreen® retractable window screen and patio doors with self-closing screens. Between-the-glass shades and blinds alleviate the need for constant dusting and help protect the shades and blinds from damage. Rolscreen® window screens eliminate the seasonal hassle of removing and storing screens.

Between-the-glass blinds add convenience to Pella® windows and doors by keeping the blinds free from dust and damage.

The exclusive Rolscreen® retractable window screen allows you to raise or lower the screen as you wish, eliminating the need to remove and store in winter.

Home Planners is one of the oldest and most trusted stock plans providers in the country, with a diverse portfolio of home plans. Their well-respected network of registered architects and home designers assures you of the very finest in architectural plans. Recognized for superior quality and attention to detail, their blueprints make a home building or remodeling project as precise as possible.

The Language of Windows and Doors

A proper education in windows and doors begins with learning the lingo. There are two simple sets of terms you should become familiar with—those that refer to the various parts of windows and those that refer to the types of windows.

Parts of a Window

1. **Head:** The top of the window frame.
2. **Jamb:** The side of the window frame.
3. **Sill:** The bottom of the window frame.
4. **Frame:** The combination of the head, two jambs and the sill that forms a precise opening in which a window sash fits.
5. **Sash:** An assembly of stiles (sides) and rails (top and bottom) that make up a movable frame—except, of course, on fixed windows. The sash holds the glass and fits into the frame.
6. **Glazing:** A sheet of glass or a sealed insulating glass unit.
7. **Pane:** A framed sheet of glass within a window. Often called a light.
8. **Muntin, grille, windowpane divider:** All terms for any small bar that divides a window's glass into sections. Divided lights are those with panes segmented by muntins.
9. **Aluminum Cladding:** A low-maintenance and durable exterior material found on premium-quality windows and doors.

Types of Windows

The variety of windows and doors available today would astound anyone from a previous era. Modern innovation and technology have made it possible to shape and form windows and doors into so many fabulous configurations. Start with the standards:

Casement windows swing open on a hinge through the use of a crank near the bottom of the window frame. Pella offers exclusive integrated cranks that fold away, so as not to interfere with window treatments. Or, if you prefer, Pella®

casement windows also are available with a classic handle. The Pella® SureLock® System sash lock holds the sash tight against the frame. Pella's casement windows also include an easy-clean feature—the sash moves toward the center of the frame to make reaching the exterior glass more convenient from the inside.

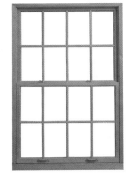

Double-hung windows feature two sash—an upper and a lower sash, both of which slide in the frame. Open the top or the bottom or both by sliding up or down. For easy cleaning, Pella's double-hung windows allow both sash to tilt—making the exteriors accessible from inside.

Fixed windows do not open. These may be plain square or rectangular windows, or they may take on any variety of shapes. (See specialty windows below.)

Awning windows swing out from the bottom and are engaged and locked in place when closed with a sash lock. The Pella® SureLock® System sash lock pulls the sash tight against the frame.

Specialty windows include **bay** and **bow windows** (see sidebar below), **circlehead windows** and other shape variations. The Pella portfolio of specialty windows is a potpourri of shapes and sizes. Full circles, partial arch heads, gothic arches, half and full chord windows, plus many others make up the full line. The professionals at Pella may also be able to create custom specialty windows to suit your needs and imagination. Pella's choices include contemporary and classic French-door styles.

Left: Pella® casement windows add a classic touch to any room. And they are available in sizes that fit almost anywhere.

Below: To create the look of historical accuracy, use Pella® Architect Series® double-hung windows with Integral Light Technology™. It allows architectural detail without sacrificing energy efficiency.

Left: Awning windows by Pella are not only gloriously unique, they have been designed so the top slides down, letting you clean the outside from inside your home.

Bay or Bow Window—How to Tell the Difference

Popular bay and bow windows are especially good choices for adding a unique touch for either a building or a remodeling project. They add space to a smaller area, allowing more glass surface. Both are elegant but have slightly different configurations.

A bow window is a combination of four or more casement windows, shaped into a gentle curve. Any (or even none) of the windows may be operable. A bay window usually consists of three windows set together at slight angles. The center piece is usually fixed. The side windows may be operable (either casement or double-hung) or fixed.

Bow Window

Bay Window

French doors may be singles or in sets of two with one side fixed or with both opening. The classic variety has paned glass with muntins, though choices abound without muntins. The Pella® French Hinged door is available in styles that swing in or swing out. These appealing doors work well as exterior doors but are also easily incorporated as interior doors to screen off a smaller room without making it seem so isolated.

Combinations of these doors and windows can invoke a period style, create an open entertainment area, pull in a view, dramatize a wall or create whatever home sense you choose. Consider some of the wonderful options.

Lifestyle and Design Choices

What makes a house a home? Of course, you have ideas about the style of home you want to build or how you want a remodeling project to change the look of an existing residence. But you may not have thought about what goes into creating what you have in mind. Windows and doors are a big part of it. They add distinctive touches that complement other architectural features and create interest in otherwise bland interiors and exteriors.

Living Areas

Consider pairing fixed, casement or double-hung windows with circleheads in a front-facing dining room or living area. Such a combination can balance the front entry on the outside and add a breathtaking focal point on the inside. Pella offers a wide variety of specialty choices from ½ circle and ¼ circle to arch head and gothic windows that can enhance the look of a traditional casement, fixed or double-hung option. Make it a bay or a bow window and you'll also have the option of installing a cozy window seat to add to the attraction. You may even want to turn the additional space gained by a bow or bay window into a minigreenhouse, where the soft natural light from the window encourages house plants to flourish.

Above: The best of both worlds, sliding doors are doors that admit light and fresh air—just like windows.

Below: Circlehead windows add a crowning touch to fixed or double-hung windows and are available in a myriad of shapes and sizes.

Above: Hinged patio doors work well as entryways to a deck or porch but may also be used to separate rooms without blocking off the light or a view.

Or maybe you want to expand the usefulness of a gathering area by adding sliding doors or French hinged doors. By gaining access to a patio or covered porch, your entertainment options spill into the great outdoors. And because these doors are mostly glass, you'll add light to the room. Add a hinged screen to the French hinged door or Pella's self-closing sliding screen to the sliding door and you'll bring in fresh air. Pella's French hinged door offers wood muntin bars, blinds that fit between the panes of glass and matching sidelights. Choose one or two doors and swing-in or swing-out styles. The Pella® Sliding Door was inspired by Japanese sliding screens—and is equally as elegant. Choose one door that slides to the side or two doors that slide apart in either contemporary or wide-frame French door styles.

The Bathroom and Kitchen

The bathroom is often one of the smallest rooms in the house. Open it up by installing casement windows with a circlehead transom above. For privacy, add sheer curtains or hang plants as a screen. Or consider Pella's between-the-glass blinds or shades.

Awning windows are the perfect complement to a gourmet kitchen. Use them above wall-hung cabinets or over countertops to ventilate your cooking space and to add natural light in places that might be difficult to brighten with artificial light. Awning windows by Pella are designed for easy cleaning: the top of the window slides down, allowing you to clean the outside of the window from the inside.

Bay and bow windows also work well in a kitchen and breakfast room setting. Choose a smaller bay window above the kitchen sink and you'll have a sunny spot for a potted herb garden. A large bay window area in the breakfast room can allow space for table and chairs—or install built-in bench seats along the window wall with a trestle table for a casual country flavor.

Above: Open a sitting area with light from a French hinged door.

Right: Casement windows with a circlehead above brighten the bath—sometimes the smallest, darkest room in the house.

Below: Everyone loves windows over the kitchen sink. They help lighten and brighten even the dreariest tasks.

Elegant Entries

Make a bold, beautiful statement on the exterior of your home with a dramatic entry. In fiberglass or steel, the Pella® entry door is both safe and stylish. Add hand-tooled decorative glass options, sidelights or transoms in a variety of styles and shapes and you'll create an entryway that is the envy of the neighborhood.

The Technology of Windows and Doors

The world of windows and doors is not only about beauty. There are serious quality and energy-efficiency issues that you'll want to address as well. These include the construction of the windows and doors, their insulation properties, their ease of maintenance and their ability to hold their good looks over time.

Construction

When it comes to window and door construction, nothing can equal the beauty and long-lasting value of wood. But as with wood furniture, there are differing degrees of craftsmanship in wood windows and doors. Look for solid wood construction with interlocking wood joints, weather-impervious glue, hardware that's built into the frame and treated wood to enhance durability. One good way to inspect the quality of construction is to check the corners and how they are joined. This will provide clues to durability and sturdiness. Pella's sash corners are joined in three ways: interlocking wood joints, metal fasteners and glue.

The exterior of a wood window or door should have some protection from moisture and other harsh weather conditions—usually accomplished with cladding of either aluminum or vinyl. Pella®'s EnduraClad® coated aluminum cladding is protected by a seven-step baked-on coating process. It resists chalking, fading and corrosion and comes in a number of standard colors and nearly unlimited custom colors to match or complement the siding on your house.

On the inside, the beauty of wood shines through with versatility and ele-

Above: First impressions are important. Create an appealing entry with an impressive entry door with sidelights and transom.

Right: Pella stores wood prior to use to ensure the moisture content is within optimum range.

Below: Pella®'s seven-step EnduraClad® coated aluminum cladding assures durability on the outside of Pella®'s clad wood windows and doors.

gance. Wood can be stained or painted to match interior décor and can easily be changed if you redecorate.

Measuring Energy Efficiency

Let's face it. Windows and doors are essentially big holes in your home. Holes that can allow the transfer of hot or cold —probably when you don't want that transfer. At one time, there were no options to help forestall this transfer of heat. But today's windows and doors are so energy-efficient, there's no reason not to include them in abundance.

First of all, how is energy efficiency measured in an opening that contains glass? It's done by the use of a standard system developed by the National Fenestration Rating Council (NFRC). The system uses U-value to show the relative ability of a window or window-type door to resist the transfer of heat and cold. The lower the U-value, the better the window or door will insulate against weather, keeping you more comfortable and keeping your heating and cooling costs down. Better quality window and door manufacturers, such as Pella, will display an NFRC label that rates their products' U-value.

Another factor is air infiltration, which most good window and door manufacturers publish for their products. A low number means less air will leak through a closed window or door. As of yet, there are no standardized ways for manufacturers to report this number. Pella, however, publishes the maximum air leakage for its products. In addition, Pella is the only manufacturer that tests most operable windows for air infiltration before they leave the factory. If they don't pass Pella's standards, they don't go out the door. Many manufacturers publish an average based

Top right: Fade protection is an important factor in choosing quality windows and doors. Pella uses standards set by Lawrence Berkeley Laboratory that measure a glazing's systems ability to protect furniture from fading.

Right: Using an abundance of windows in your home need not compromise energy efficiency, especially if you use Pella® windows with low U-value that keep your heating and cooling costs down.

on random tests. Some of their products may perform better than average; some may perform worse—but there is no true way of knowing how an individual product actually performs.

Though not an energy consideration, fade protection is an important factor in a quality window or door. Besides providing ultraviolet (UV) protection, a window or door should block the entire spectrum of solar radiation. This is measured by Lawrence Berkeley Laboratory (LBL) ratings and is the best measure of a glazing system's ability to protect furnishings from fading. Pella uses this rating system for its products.

Glazing Options

You might think that glass is just glass but it is really so much more. New technologies have made it possible to choose glass for differing climates. If you live in a colder climate, for example, you'll want glass that allows fade protection, but does not block the heat of the sun's rays in winter. Warm-climate residents need protection from the burning rays of the sun, and glass that will help keep homes cool.

Pella addresses these varying needs by producing different glazing options for windows and doors. The four most popular are:

With a virtually invisible seam, Pella®'s CornerView® window allows an unobstructed view.

Argon-filled InsulShield® Insulating Glass. This system combines Low-E coatings and argon gas. Two panes of glass are treated with Low-E coatings to decrease the heating and fading rays of the sun; argon gas in the air space between the panes decreases heat transfer. The system can reduce energy bills by up to 24% compared to single-pane wood windows.*

Standard Insulating Glass. This system utilizes two panes of glass with an air space between them. It is economical and allows some solar gain. This technology may reduce heating and cooling bills by up to 10% compared to single-pane wood windows.*

SmartSash® II. This system uses Pella®'s SmartEdge® technology to position two panes of glass so there's enough space between them to install wood muntin bars and blinds or pleated shades.

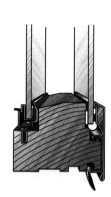

(Not all glazing and between-the-glass options are available on all products.) As an option, the interior pane may be Low-E coated. This glazing option can reduce energy bills by up to 17% compared to single-pane windows.* The addition of blinds or shades increases energy savings.

SmartSash® III. Again using the SmartEdge® technology, this system adds a third panel of glass. The two interior panels can be Low-E coated. This system may reduce energy bills by up to 28% compared to single-pane wood windows.* With SmartSash® III, you can choose one between-the-glass option: muntin bars, blinds or shades.

Care and Cleaning

Certainly one of the most hated household chores is washing windows. Though no one has invented a window that never needs cleaning, Pella provides the next best thing with an easy-does-it approach to cleaning. On double-hung windows, the top and bottom sashes pivot. On casement and awning windows, the sash moves toward the center of the frame. Choose between-the-glass muntin bars, and the chore is even easier.

Pella's double-hung windows have sashes that both tilt to make cleaning the exterior easy from the inside.

*Computer simulation average compared to single-pane wood windows. Actual savings may vary.

The Pella Advantage

In the end, the decisions to be made about window and door selection are all about budget-savvy, beautiful choices without compromising quality. You want the finest, most attractive windows you can buy, but your choices must not exceed your building budget. Pella produces three distinctive product lines to meet all of your design expectations, while incorporating the famous Pella quality—to fit every budget.

Architect Series®

This line of products offers excellent energy efficiency combined with versatile design options for the traditional home. Pella®'s Architect Series® products combine superior energy-efficient properties with a traditional divided-light appearance in a patented process called

Above: Pella® Architect Series® products offer excellent energy efficiency with versatile design options.

Above: Pella®'s between-the-glass removable muntin bars are available in standard or Colonial profiles.

Left: Pella® ProLine® windows and doors are an affordable choice with the famous Pella quality built in.

13F

Integral Light Technology™. This process re-creates the charm and historical accuracy of true divided light with modern, energy-efficient glazing. A non-glare insulating spacer is installed between insulating glass panels and under the muntins, while the muntin bars are permanently bonded on the interior and exterior glass.

Though available in standard sizes and styles, the superbly crafted windows and doors in the Architect Series® line can be customized to meet the most exacting design standards. Choose arch tops for doors as well as casement and double-hung windows. Or allow Pella to create interesting custom shapes such as triangles and trapezoids.

Three standard muntin bar patterns are available in this series: traditional style, prairie style and 9-light prairie style. However, if none of these three will meet your particular needs, Pella's design professionals will work with you to design an original muntin bar pattern that complements your home design.

Architect Series® windows and doors are also available without muntin bars or with removable wood muntin bars that snap onto the interior side of the window.

Choose wood on the exterior of the windows and doors in this series, or protect the wood with Pella's aluminum cladding with the seven-step EnduraClad® finish.

Above: Pella's Architect Series® windows and doors offer attention to detail that is unmatched and offers years of uncompromised performance.

Below: Between-the-glass shades by Pella come in 12 colors, with six featuring a special backing that increases energy efficiency.

Choose from three standard muntin patterns for Pella's Architect Series® windows—Prairie Style, 9-Lite Prairie Style or Traditional Style.

Designer Series®

If you love to redecorate or update the look of your home periodically with a new and different look, Pella®'s Designer Series® windows and doors are right for you. They can suit your style, no matter how often it changes.

The Designer Series line offers unmatched versatility. It allows you to put between-the-glass blinds or pleated shades between the interior and exterior panes of glass. Choose Pella® blinds or shades in a color that coordinates with your interior. When you decide to make an interior change, you can change the blinds or shades as well. The interior panel of glass is removable, so you can switch between blinds and shades or easily change their color.

Another option to consider: use wood muntin bars between the interior and exterior panes of glass. When your mood calls for a traditional look, install the muntin bars. When you want a wide-open, casual look, remove the muntin bars and go contemporary. It's that simple. The removable panel of glass lets you customize your windows even further by allowing you to add stained-glass overlays.

If you hate to dust (and who doesn't?), you'll love between-the-glass shades, blinds and muntin bars. Their location between panes of glass keeps them dust-free and also protects them from damage. Blinds are available in raise-and-lower styles or tilt-only for those who prefer to avoid the annoyance of hanging cords.

Products in Pella®'s Designer Series® feature aluminum cladding with Pella's seven-step EnduraClad® finish.

ProLine®

ProLine® windows and doors incorporate Pella's renowned quality characteristics at a price that fits any budget. A simplified product offering of standard sizes, colors and glazings makes ProLine products a great value.

All windows and doors in the line consist of all-wood construction, energy-efficient glazing options, superior weather-stripping and aluminum-clad exteriors with the durable EnduraClad® finish. ProLine products also include optional wood muntin bars that attach to the interior of the window for a classic look.

Don't Forget the Details

With all of the decisions to be made about doors and windows themselves, it would be easy to ignore details such as screens, hardware and locking mechanisms. But these are the tools that make the windows and doors functional and durable.

Pella offers a full line of locks, hardware and screens for all of its products. Options include:

- Fold-away handles or classic cranks for casement and awning windows.
- Corrosion-resistant hardware for casement and double-hung windows
- SureLock® System sash locks for casement windows and cam-lock sash locks for double-hung windows. Dual sash locks are standard on larger double-hung windows.
- Designer handles in brass, pewter and chrome for hinged patio doors.
- Corrosion-resistant hardware for sliding patio doors.
- A unique three-point locking system for hinged patio doors that secures the door at the head, jamb and sill.
- A standard multipoint locking system for sliding patio doors with a thumbblock on the interior and a keylock on the exterior.
- A footbolt lock, which holds a sliding door open about 3" for ventilation.
- The optional Rolscreen® retractable insect screen for casement windows that is self-storing and rolls up out of sight when not in use.
- A self-closing screen on Designer Series® sliding patio doors. It gently closes and latches after it has been opened wide enough for someone to pass through.

Above: The exclusive self-closing screen door on Pella®'s Designer Series® sliding doors means no more left-open screen doors.

Right: The SureLock® System on Pella's casement windows reaches out to engage and lift the window sash, pulling it tight against the weatherstripping.

Available for Pella's awning and casement windows—an integrated crank with a fold-away handle or the classic handle.

Standard on all Pella® Designer Series® doors (optional on ProLine® doors), a footbolt holds the door open about 3" for ventilation.

The Choice Is Yours

Finally, the decisions to be made about the perfect windows and doors for your new or remodeled home are yours. Because they are such critical decisions and because you'll live with the selections for a considerable length of time, you need to make informed choices. Pella can help you make those choices for a home you'll be proud to live in today and for years to come.

Because you want the best for your new home, choose the Pella advantage in windows and doors for beauty, durability and efficiency.

On the following pages is a specially selected

group of home plans blessed with an unparalleled complement of windows and doors arranged for balance and grace. Orient your chosen design to capture maximum light, views and ventilation, and you'll achieve what we mean by Windowscaping®.

The plans comprise a wide range of styles and sizes to fit your needs, desires and building budget. Each has been designed by a registered architect or home designer and has complete construction blueprints available separately. See page 500 for more information about the blueprint packages. Many feature complementary landscape or deck plans to make them even more special.

Other products are available for many of the plans to make your building project smoother and more efficient. These include a complete Materials List package, Construction Information packages, a Specification Outline, a Plan-A-Home® kit, and Home Planners exclusive Quote One® service that allows you to estimate the cost of building your home in your zip-code area. For more information about these products and services, turn to page 502.

With the grand number of plans shown here, you'll most likely find the perfect home for you and your family. But, if not, turn

Photo courtesy of Larry E. Belk Designs

to page 498, where we offer our full line of home plan books—with thousands of choices in home design.

With the help of Pella and Home Planners you'll have the very place you want to call home, filled with quality windows and doors and your unique design choices.

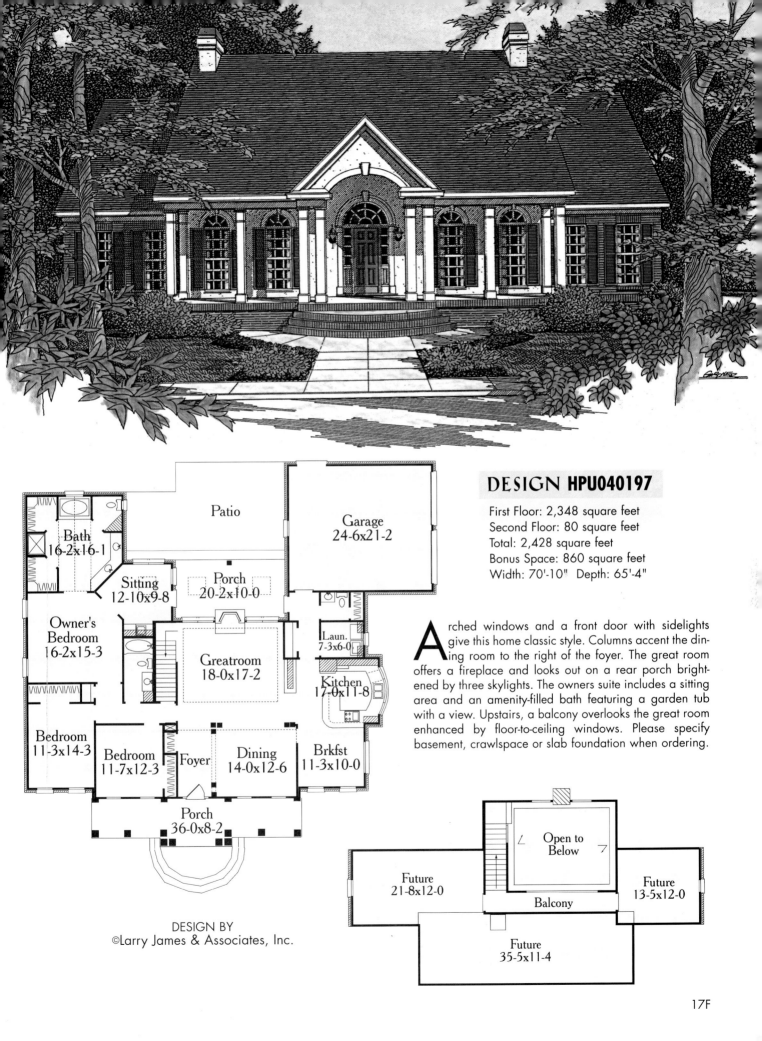

DESIGN HPU040197

First Floor: 2,348 square feet
Second Floor: 80 square feet
Total: 2,428 square feet
Bonus Space: 860 square feet
Width: 70'-10" Depth: 65'-4"

Arched windows and a front door with sidelights give this home classic style. Columns accent the dining room to the right of the foyer. The great room offers a fireplace and looks out on a rear porch brightened by three skylights. The owners suite includes a sitting area and an amenity-filled bath featuring a garden tub with a view. Upstairs, a balcony overlooks the great room enhanced by floor-to-ceiling windows. Please specify basement, crawlspace or slab foundation when ordering.

Floor Plan Labels:

- Patio
- Garage 24-6x21-2
- Bath 16-2x16-1
- Sitting 12-10x9-8
- Porch 20-2x10-0
- Owner's Bedroom 16-2x15-3
- Greatroom 18-0x17-2
- Laun. 7-3x6-0
- Kitchen 17-0x11-8
- Bedroom 11-3x14-3
- Bedroom 11-7x12-3
- Foyer
- Dining 14-0x12-6
- Brkfst 11-3x10-0
- Porch 36-0x8-2

- Future 21-8x12-0
- Open to Below
- Future 13-5x12-0
- Balcony
- Future 35-5x11-4

DESIGN BY
©Larry James & Associates, Inc.

17F

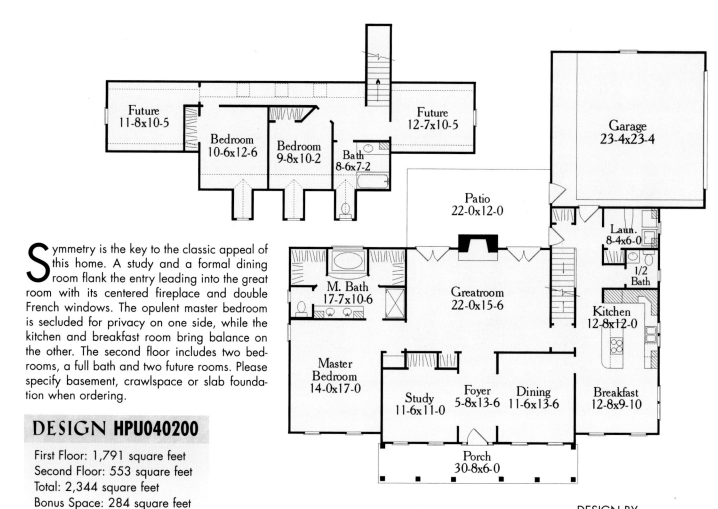

Future
11-8x10-5

Bedroom
10-6x12-6

Bedroom
9-8x10-2

Bath
8-6x7-2

Future
12-7x10-5

Garage
23-4x23-4

Patio
22-0x12-0

Laun.
8-4x6-0

1/2
Bath

M. Bath
17-7x10-6

Greatroom
22-0x15-6

Kitchen
12-8x12-0

Master
Bedroom
14-0x17-0

Study
11-6x11-0

Foyer
5-8x13-6

Dining
11-6x13-6

Breakfast
12-8x9-10

Porch
30-8x6-0

Symmetry is the key to the classic appeal of this home. A study and a formal dining room flank the entry leading into the great room with its centered fireplace and double French windows. The opulent master bedroom is secluded for privacy on one side, while the kitchen and breakfast room bring balance on the other. The second floor includes two bedrooms, a full bath and two future rooms. Please specify basement, crawlspace or slab foundation when ordering.

DESIGN HPU040200

First Floor: 1,791 square feet
Second Floor: 553 square feet
Total: 2,344 square feet
Bonus Space: 284 square feet
Width: 64'-4" Depth: 66'-1"

DESIGN BY
©Larry James & Associates, Inc.

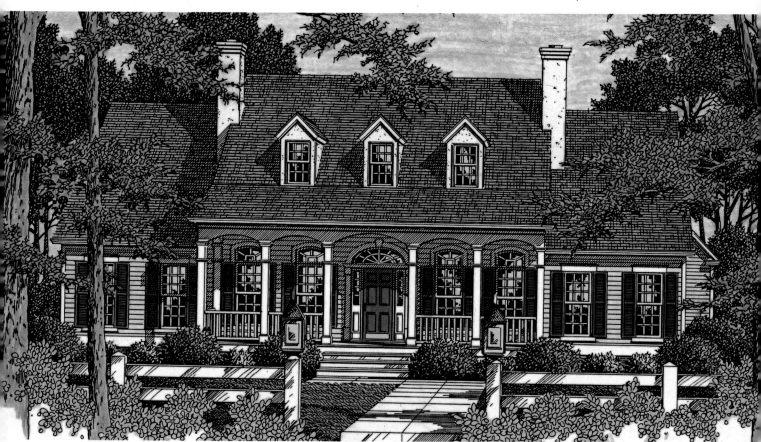

DESIGN HPU040209

First Floor: 1,813 square feet
Second Floor: 885 square feet
Total: 2,698 square feet
Width: 70'-2" Depth: 51'-4"

DESIGN BY
©Michael E. Nelson, Nelson
Design Group, LLC

Four graceful columns support a long covered porch, topped by three attractive dormers. The two-story foyer is flanked by a formal dining room and a cozy study—or make it a guest suite with the full bath nearby. The island kitchen is sure to please with a walk-in pantry and easy access to the breakfast area. A spacious great room has a balcony overlook from the second floor and a fireplace. The master bedroom boasts two walk-in closets, a whirlpool tub and a separate shower. Upstairs, three bedrooms—all with window seats—share a full hall bath. Please specify basement, crawlspace or slab foundation when ordering.

This home, as shown in the photograph, may differ from the actual blueprints. For more detailed information, please check the floor plans carefully.

Photo by Stephanie Nelson

Photo by Riley & Riley Photography, Inc.

This home, as shown in the photograph, may differ from the actual blueprints. For more detailed information, please check the floor plans carefully.

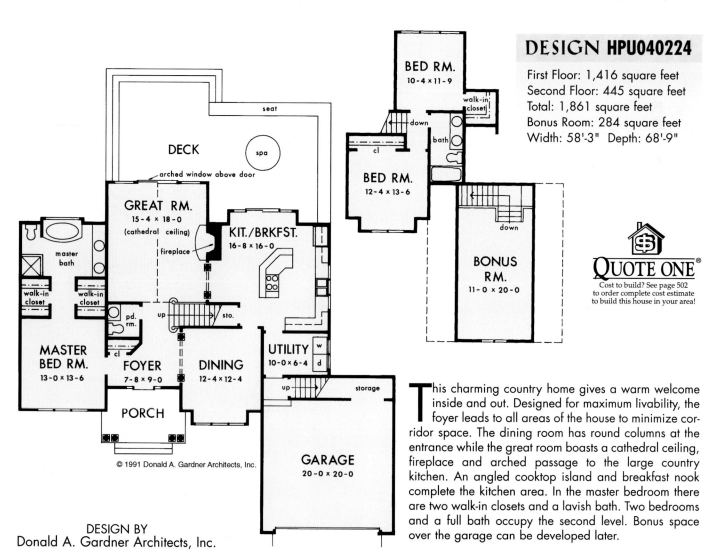

seat

DECK

spa

arched window above door

GREAT RM.
15-4 x 18-0
(cathedral ceiling)

fireplace

KIT./BRKFST.
16-8 x 16-0

master bath

walk-in closet

walk-in closet

pd. rm.

up

sto.

cl

MASTER BED RM.
13-0 x 13-6

FOYER
7-8 x 9-0

DINING
12-4 x 12-4

UTILITY
10-0 x 6-4

w
d

PORCH

up

storage

© 1991 Donald A. Gardner Architects, Inc.

GARAGE
20-0 x 20-0

BED RM.
10-4 x 11-9

walk-in closet

down

bath

cl

BED RM.
12-4 x 13-6

down

BONUS RM.
11-0 x 20-0

DESIGN **HPU040224**

First Floor: 1,416 square feet
Second Floor: 445 square feet
Total: 1,861 square feet
Bonus Room: 284 square feet
Width: 58'-3" Depth: 68'-9"

QUOTE ONE®
Cost to build? See page 502
to order complete cost estimate
to build this house in your area!

This charming country home gives a warm welcome inside and out. Designed for maximum livability, the foyer leads to all areas of the house to minimize corridor space. The dining room has round columns at the entrance while the great room boasts a cathedral ceiling, fireplace and arched passage to the large country kitchen. An angled cooktop island and breakfast nook complete the kitchen area. In the master bedroom there are two walk-in closets and a lavish bath. Two bedrooms and a full bath occupy the second level. Bonus space over the garage can be developed later.

DESIGN BY
Donald A. Gardner Architects, Inc.

Decorative pillars and a wraparound porch provide a perfect introduction to this charming bungalow. Inside, from the foyer where an angled stairway leads to the second floor, French doors lead to the den that shares a see-through fireplace with the two-story family room. The large island kitchen includes a writing desk, corner sink, breakfast nook and an efficient utility room. Upstairs, the master suite is a real treat with its French-door access, vaulted ceiling and luxurious bath. Two secondary bedrooms and a full bath complete the second floor.

DESIGN HPU040233

First Floor: 1,371 square feet
Second Floor: 916 square feet
Total: 2,287 square feet
Width: 43'-0" Depth: 69'-0"

QUOTE ONE®
Cost to build? See page 502
to order complete cost estimate
to build this house in your area!

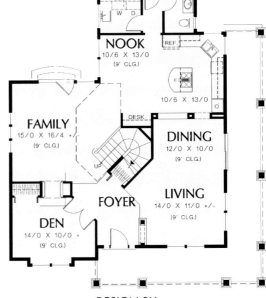

DESIGN BY
©Alan Mascord Design Associates, Inc.

This home, as shown in the photograph, may differ from the actual blueprints.
For more detailed information, please check the floor plans carefully.

Photo by Bob Greenspan

21F

Photo by Design Basics, Inc.

This home, as shown in the photograph, may differ from the actual blueprints. For more detailed information, please check the floor plans carefully.

This Colonial elevation makes a comfortable yet impressive statement. A volume entry opens to the formal dining room defined by special ceiling treatment and flooring materials. The great room with a ten-foot ceiling features a fireplace. The kitchen offers a wraparound counter with a lazy Susan, large pantry, planning desk and island. A sunny breakfast bay features sliding glass doors to the covered porch. The master bedroom includes a pampering master bath with a whirlpool tub, shower and dual lavatories, a large walk-in closet and access to a private den. Three bedrooms and a full bath occupy the second floor.

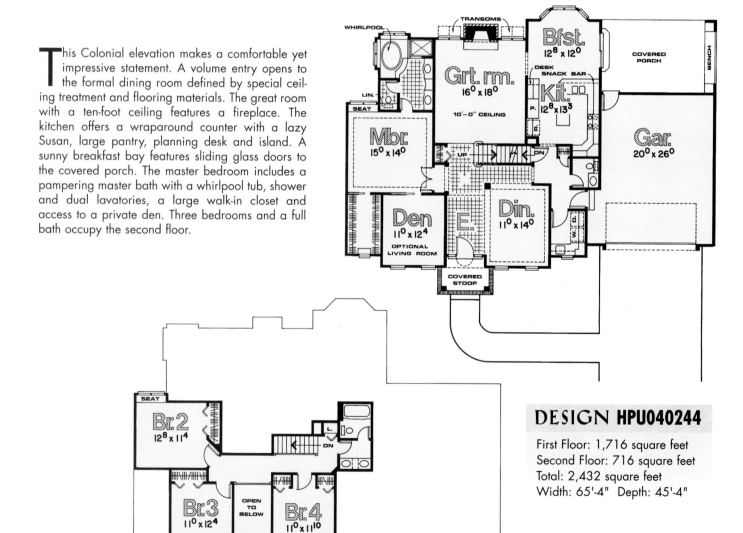

DESIGN HPU040244

First Floor: 1,716 square feet
Second Floor: 716 square feet
Total: 2,432 square feet
Width: 65'-4" Depth: 45'-4"

DESIGN BY
©Design Basics, Inc.

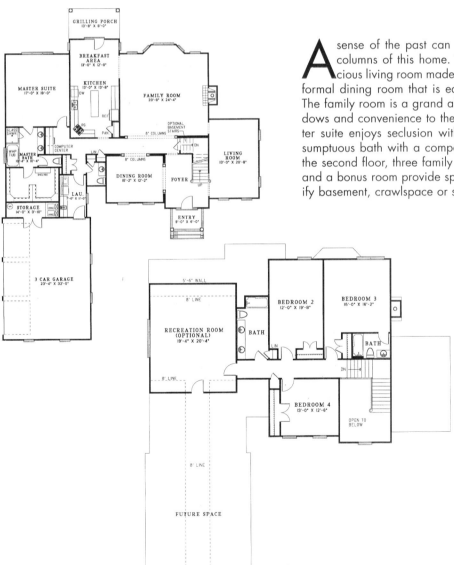

A sense of the past can be found in the stately pediment and columns of this home. The large entry foyer opens to a spacious living room made for entertaining. Across the foyer is the formal dining room that is easily served from the gourmet kitchen. The family room is a grand affair that features a fireplace, bay windows and convenience to the kitchen and breakfast area. The master suite enjoys seclusion with His and Hers walk-in closets and a sumptuous bath with a compartmented toilet and dual vanities. On the second floor, three family bedrooms—one with a private bath—and a bonus room provide space for a growing family. Please specify basement, crawlspace or slab foundation when ordering.

DESIGN HPU040261

First Floor: 2,562 square feet
Second Floor: 1,051 square feet
Total: 3,613 square feet
Bonus Room: 493 square feet
Width: 69'-4" Depth: 87'-10"

DESIGN BY
©Michael E. Nelson, Nelson
Design Group, LLC

23F

deck

porch

covered porch

porch

br. 3
11'-6" x 12'-0"
10'-0"h. clg.

fireplace
great room
15'-0" x 19'-6"
vaulted clg.

dining
11'-0" x 12'-8"
11'-0" tray clg.

built ins

kitchen
11'-0" x 12'-0"

br. 2
12'-10" x 12'-0"
10'-0"h. clg.

up

stor.

util.

up
foyer

entry

DESIGN BY
©The Sater Design Collection

2 car garage

bonus/
storage

storage

porch

master suite
12'-8" x 17'-8"
10'-0" tray clg.

open to below

w.i.c.

overlook

dn

master bath

dn

porch

The stone facade and woodwork detail give this home a Craftsman appeal. The foyer opens to a staircase up to the vaulted great room, which features a fireplace flanked by built-ins and French-door access to the rear covered porch. The open dining room with a tray ceiling offers convenience to the spacious kitchen. Two family bedrooms share a bath and enjoy private porches. An overlook to the great room below is a perfect introduction to the master suite. The second level spreads out master-suite luxury with a spacious walk-in closet, private porch and a glorious master bath with a garden tub, dual vanities and compartmented toilet.

DESIGN HPU040100

First Floor: 1,383 square feet
Second Floor: 595 square feet
Total: 1,978 square feet
Width: 48'-0" Depth: 42'-0"

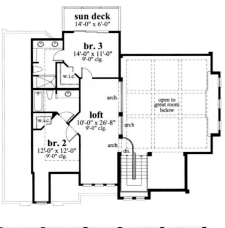

sun deck
14'-0" x 6'-0"

br. 3
14'-0" x 11'-0"
9'-0" clg.

w.i.c.

loft
10'-0" x 26'-8"
9'-0" clg.

br. 2
12'-0" x 12'-0"
9'-0" clg.

w.i.c.

arch

arch

arch

open to
great room
below

dn.

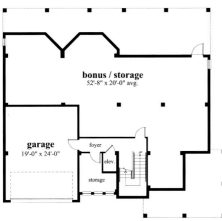

bonus / storage
52'-8" x 20'-0" avg.

garage
19'-0" x 24'-0"

foyer

elev.

storage

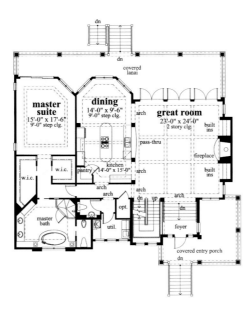

dn

dn

covered
lanai

master
suite
15'-0" x 17'-6"
9'-0" step clg.

dining
14'-0" x 9'-6"
9'-0" step clg.

great room
23'-0" x 24'-0"
2 story clg.

arch

built
ins

pass-thru

fireplace

built
ins

w.i.c.

w.i.c.

kitchen
14'-0" x 15'-0"

pantry

arch

arch

arch

dn

up

arch

opt.

arch

dn

dn

master
bath

util.

foyer

covered entry porch

dn

DESIGN HPU040290

First Floor: 2,096 square feet
Second Floor: 892 square feet
Total: 2,988 square feet
Bonus Space: 1,295 square feet
Width: 56'-0"   Depth: 54'-0"

Siding and shingles give this home a Craftsman look while columns and gables suggest a more traditional style. The foyer opens to a short flight of stairs that leads to the great room, which features a lovely coffered ceiling, a fireplace, built-ins and French doors to the rear lanai. To the left, the open, island kitchen enjoys a pass-through to the great room and easy service to the dining bay. The secluded master suite has two walk-in closets, a luxurious bath and lanai access. Upstairs, two family bedrooms enjoy their own full baths and share a loft area.

DESIGN BY
©The Sater Design Collection

25F

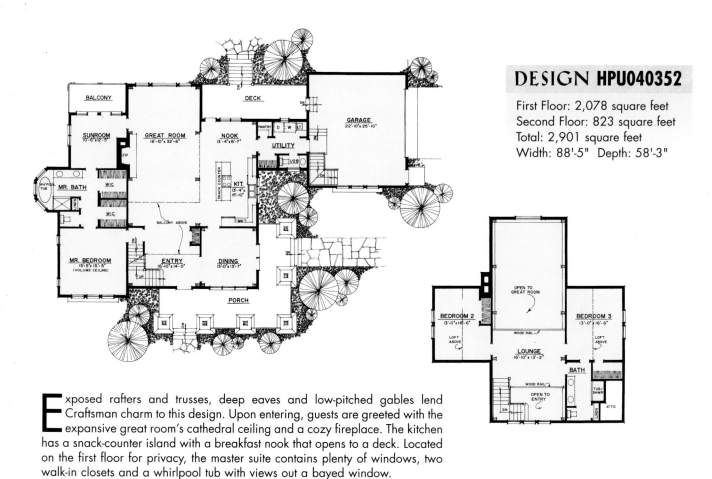

DESIGN HPU040352

First Floor: 2,078 square feet
Second Floor: 823 square feet
Total: 2,901 square feet
Width: 88'-5" Depth: 58'-3"

Exposed rafters and trusses, deep eaves and low-pitched gables lend Craftsman charm to this design. Upon entering, guests are greeted with the expansive great room's cathedral ceiling and a cozy fireplace. The kitchen has a snack-counter island with a breakfast nook that opens to a deck. Located on the first floor for privacy, the master suite contains plenty of windows, two walk-in closets and a whirlpool tub with views out a bayed window.

DESIGN BY
©R.L. Pfotenhauer

Photo by Roger Hart

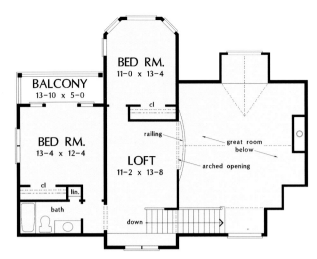

BALCONY
13-10 x 5-0

BED RM.
11-0 x 13-4

cl

BED RM.
13-4 x 12-4

railing

great room
below

LOFT
11-2 x 13-8

arched opening

cl

lin.

bath

down

First Floor: 1,650 square feet
Second Floor: 712 square feet
Total: 2,362 square feet
Width: 58'-10" Depth: 47'-4"

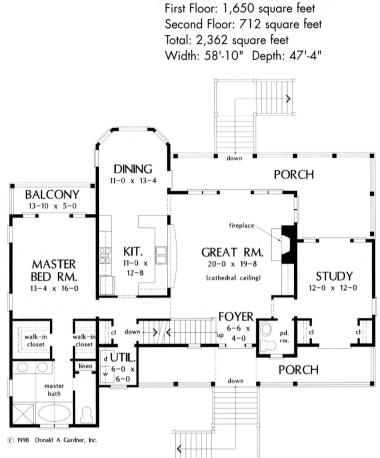

BALCONY
13-10 x 5-0

DINING
11-0 x 13-4

PORCH

down

MASTER
BED RM.
13-4 x 16-0

KIT.
11-0 x
12-8

fireplace

GREAT RM.
20-0 x 19-8
(cathedral ceiling)

STUDY
12-0 x 12-0

walk-in
closet

walk-in
closet

cl

down

FOYER
6-6 x
4-0

up

pd.
rm.

cl

cl

UTIL.
6-0 x
6-0

linen

d

w

master
bath

down

PORCH

Ⓒ 1998 Donald A Gardner, Inc.

Cedar shakes and striking gables with decorative scalloped insets adorn the exterior of this lovely coastal home. The generous great room is expanded by a rear wall of windows, with additional light from transom windows above the front door and a rear clerestory dormer. The kitchen features a pass-through to the great room that doubles as a breakfast/snack bar. The dining room, great room and study all access an inviting back porch. The master bedroom is a treat with a private balcony, His and Hers walk-in closets and an impeccable bath. Upstairs, a room-sized loft with an arched opening overlooks the great room below. Two more bedrooms, one with its own private balcony, share a hall bath.

DESIGN BY
Donald A. Gardner Architects, Inc.

Photo courtesy of Larry E. Belk Designs

This home, as shown in the photograph, may differ from the actual blueprints. For more detailed information, please check the floor plans carefully.

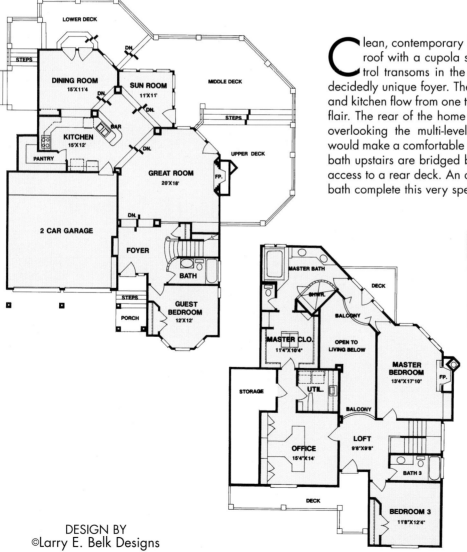

Clean, contemporary lines, a unique floor plan and a metal roof with a cupola set this farmhouse apart. Remote-control transoms in the cupola open to create an airy and decidedly unique foyer. The great room, sun room, dining room and kitchen flow from one to another for casual entertaining with flair. The rear of the home is fashioned with plenty of windows overlooking the multi-level deck. A front bedroom and bath would make a comfortable guest suite. The owners bedroom and bath upstairs are bridged by a pipe-rail balcony that also gives access to a rear deck. An additional bedroom, home office and bath complete this very special plan.

DESIGN HPU040330

First Floor: 1,309 square feet
Second Floor: 1,343 square feet
Total: 2,652 square feet
Width: 44'-4" Depth: 58'-2"

L

DESIGN BY
©Larry E. Belk Designs

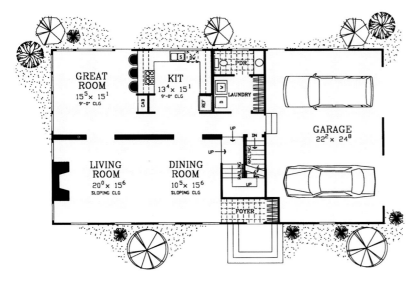

DESIGN **HPU040369**

First Floor: 1,245 square feet
Second Floor: 1,138 square feet
Total: 2,383 square feet
Width: 60'-5" Depth: 31'-8"

Dramatic windows, prominant dormers and shingles strike a harmonious cord in this Cape Cod original. The display of mutin-divided window lights through-out enhances the airy feeling of spaciousness and invites natural light into the heart of the home. Inside, an open floor plan provides ease of movement from the spacious living room, which features a fireplace, to the formal dining area and U-shpaed kitchen. Upstairs, two family bedrooms enjoy a compartmented bath and plenty of closet space. The master suite offers twin walk-in closets, dual vanities and a compartmented toilet. A two-car garage completes this plan.

DESIGN BY
Stuart Cohen & Julie Hacker
Architects

This home, as shown in the photograph, may differ from the actual blueprints. For more detailed information, please check the floor plans carefully.

Photo by Living Concepts Home Planning

This home, as shown in the photograph, may differ from the actual blueprints. For more detailed information, please check the floor plans carefully.

DESIGN HPU040372

First Floor: 2,450 square feet
Second Floor: 1,674 square feet
Total: 4,124 square feet
Width: 65'-10" Depth: 85'-2"

This sensational bungalow borrows exquisite details from the Craftsman style. The rustic texture of the building materials, broad overhangs and second-floor shingles call up a brilliant architectural era. Inside, an open arrangement of dining and living space allows shared views, impeded only by lovely decorative columns. The gourmet kitchen shares a through-fireplace with the grand room and serves a breakfast area. The master suite occupies the entire left wing, while three family bedroom suites reside upstairs.

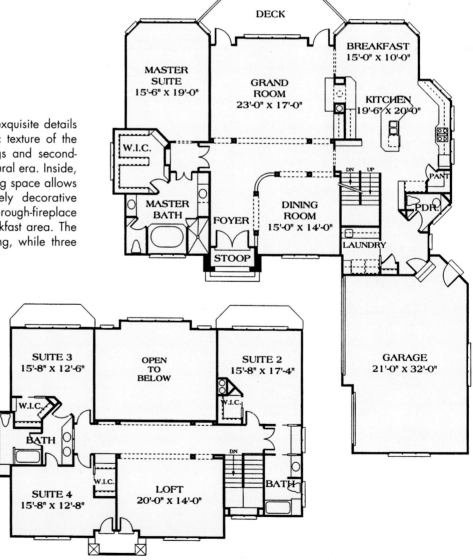

DESIGN BY
©Living Concepts Home Planning

This home, as shown in the photograph, may differ from the actual blueprints. For more detailed information, please check the floor plans carefully.

Photo by Bob Greenspan

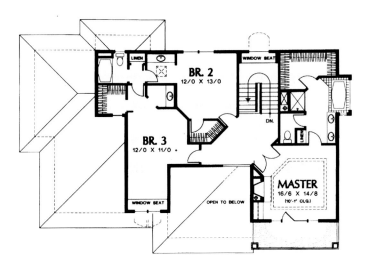

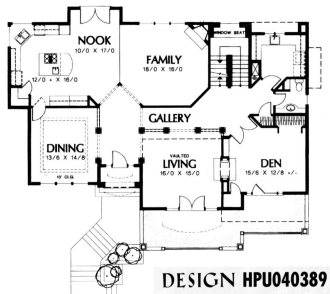

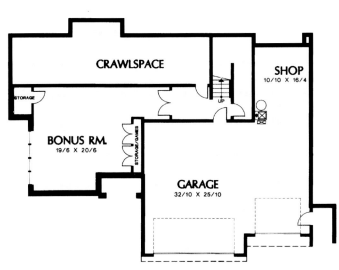

DESIGN **HPU040389**

First Floor: 1,989 square feet
Second Floor: 1,349 square feet
Finished Basement:
    105 square feet
Total: 3,443 square feet
Bonus Room: 487 square feet
Width: 63'-0" Depth: 48'-0"

QUOTE ONE®
Cost to build? See page 502
to order complete cost estimate
to build this house in your area!

Dramatic balconies and spectacular window treatment enhance this stunning luxury home. Inside, a through-fireplace warms the formal living room and a restful den. Both living spaces open to a balcony that invites quiet reflection on starry nights. The banquet-sized dining room is easily served from the adjacent kitchen. Here, space is shared with an eating nook that provides access to the rear grounds and a family room with a corner fireplace perfect for casual gatherings. The upper level contains two family bedrooms and a luxurious master suite that enjoys its own private balcony. The lower level accommodates a shop and a bonus room for future development.

DESIGN BY
©Alan Mascord Design Associates, Inc.

31F

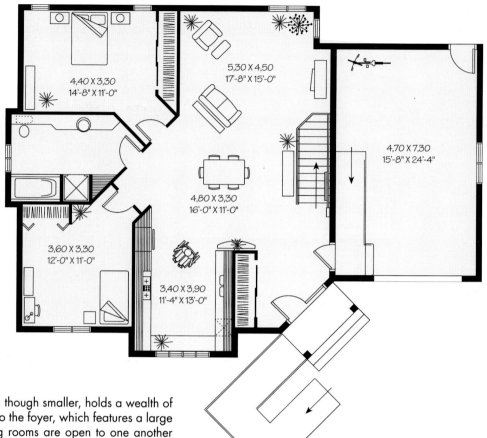

DESIGN HPU040100

Square Footage: 1,276
Width: 52'-0" Depth: 38'-0"

4,40 X 3,30
14'-8" X 11'-0"

5,30 X 4,50
17'-8" X 15'-0"

4,70 X 7,30
15'-8" X 24'-4"

4,80 X 3,30
16'-0" X 11'-0"

3,60 X 3,30
12'-0" X 11'-0"

3,40 X 3,90
11'-4" X 13'-0"

This one-story contemporary home, though smaller, holds a wealth of livability. An angled entry opens to the foyer, which features a large coat closet. The living and dining rooms are open to one another and are conveniently located near the U-shaped kitchen. The two large bedrooms share an oversized bath that features a separate shower and tub. The garage opens to the main house at a door near the entry. This home is designed with a basement foundation.

DESIGN BY
©Drummond Designs, Inc.

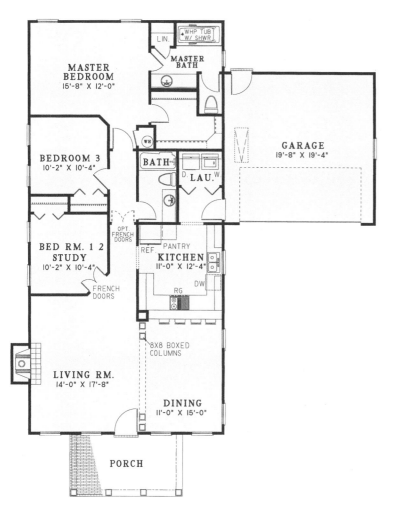

MASTER
BEDROOM
15'-8" X 12'-0"

MASTER
BATH

WHP TUB
W/ SHWR

LIN.

BEDROOM 3
10'-2" X 10'-4"

BATH

GARAGE
19'-8" X 19'-4"

OPT.
FRENCH
DOORS

BED RM. 1 2
STUDY
10'-2" X 10'-4"

REF. PANTRY

KITCHEN
11'-0" X 12'-4"

DW

RG

FRENCH
DOORS

8X8 BOXED
COLUMNS

LIVING RM.
14'-0" X 17'-8"

DINING
11'-0" X 15'-0"

PORCH

Graceful columns, reminiscent of fine Greek Revival style, adorn the covered front porch of this compact yet elegant design. The entry opens directly to the living room and its fireplace. Decorative columns define the boundary between the living and dining rooms. The kitchen has a pass-through counter to the dining room and leads to a service entry to the optional garage. The master bedroom offers a private bath and a walk-in closet. One of the family bedrooms could be used as a study. Please specify crawlspace or slab foundation when ordering.

DESIGN HPU040001

Square Footage: 1,404
Width: 48'-4" Depth: 62'-0"

DESIGN BY
©Michael E. Nelson, Nelson
Design Group, LLC

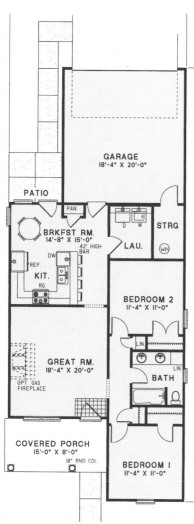

GARAGE
18'-4" X 20'-0"

PATIO

PAN

BRKFST RM.
14'-8" X 15'-0"

STRG

D W

LAU.

WH

DW

42" HIGH BAR

REF.

KIT.

RG

BEDROOM 2
11'-4" X 11'-0"

LIN.

GREAT RM.
18'-4" X 20'-0"

BATH

LIN.

OPT. GAS FIREPLACE

COVERED PORCH
15'-0" X 8'-0"

BEDROOM 1
11'-4" X 11'-0"

10" RND COL.

Round columns and muntin windows with shutters add curb appeal to this country cottage. This functional floor plan begins with the great room, which offers space for an optional gas fireplace. The U-shapaed kitchen is fully equipped with a pantry, breakfast room and high bar easily accessible to the rear patio. A full hall bath with dual vanities and two linen closets are available to both family bedrooms. Don't overlook the storage space available inside the garage and the utility room near the garage entrance. This comfortable, narrow floor plan is a perfect starter home. Please specify crawlspace or slab foundation when ordering.

DESIGN **HPU040002**

Square Footage: 985
Width: 27'-0" Depth: 65'-2"

DESIGN BY
©Michael E. Nelson, Nelson
Design Group, LLC

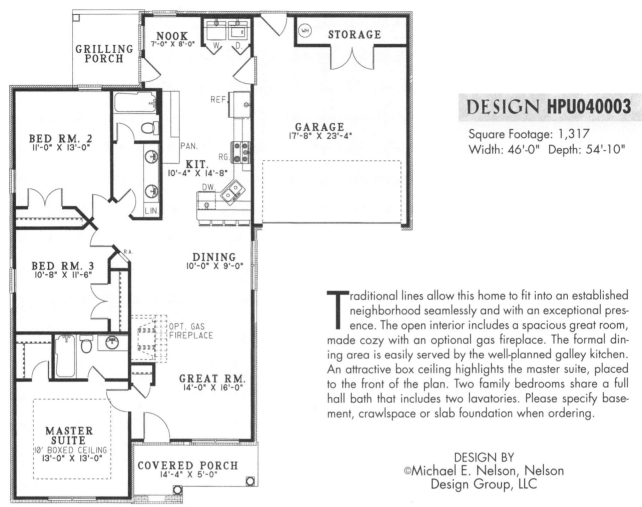

GRILLING PORCH

NOOK
7'-0" X 8'-0"

STORAGE

BED RM. 2
11'-0" X 13'-0"

REF.

PAN.

KIT.
10'-4" X 14'-8"

GARAGE
17'-8" X 23'-4"

LIN.

DW

BED RM. 3
10'-8" X 11'-6"

DINING
10'-0" X 9'-0"

OPT. GAS FIREPLACE

GREAT RM.
14'-0" X 16'-0"

MASTER SUITE
10' BOXED CEILING
13'-0" X 13'-0"

COVERED PORCH
14'-4" X 5'-0"

DESIGN HPU040003

Square Footage: 1,317
Width: 46'-0" Depth: 54'-10"

Traditional lines allow this home to fit into an established neighborhood seamlessly and with an exceptional presence. The open interior includes a spacious great room, made cozy with an optional gas fireplace. The formal dining area is easily served by the well-planned galley kitchen. An attractive box ceiling highlights the master suite, placed to the front of the plan. Two family bedrooms share a full hall bath that includes two lavatories. Please specify basement, crawlspace or slab foundation when ordering.

DESIGN BY
©Michael E. Nelson, Nelson
Design Group, LLC

3

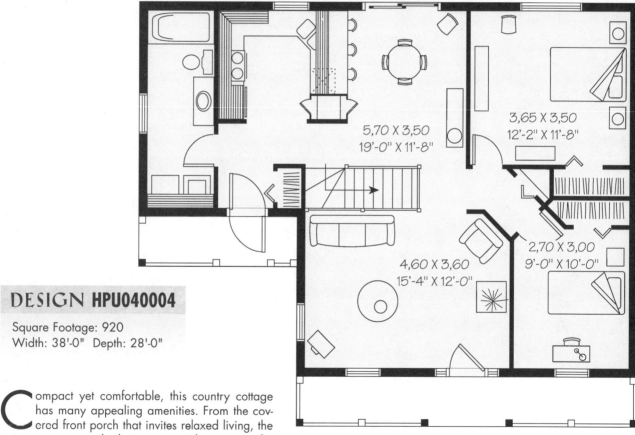

5,70 X 3,50
19'-0" X 11'-8"

3,65 X 3,50
12'-2" X 11'-8"

4,60 X 3,60
15'-4" X 12'-0"

2,70 X 3,00
9'-0" X 10'-0"

DESIGN HPU040004

Square Footage: 920
Width: 38'-0" Depth: 28'-0"

Compact yet comfortable, this country cottage has many appealing amenities. From the covered front porch that invites relaxed living, the entrance opens to the living room with access to the dining room and snack bar at the rear. Two bedrooms are secluded to the right of the plan with the kitchen and bathroom/laundry facilities located on the left side. A second porch off the kitchen provides an opportunity for more relaxation, casual dining and quiet moments. This home is designed with a basement foundation.

DESIGN BY
©Drummond Designs, Inc.

4

DESIGN HPU040005

Square Footage: 1,079
Width: 34'-0" Depth: 34'-0"

This house plan is rich in efficiency and cottage-style living. A quaint covered porch charms visitors and offers an enchanting glimpse into the spacious living room through a beautiful front window. Kitchen counter space is in abundance for the family chef. The kitchen is open to a dining area, which accesses the rear of the home. The opposite side of the home is dedicated to the family sleeping quarters. The master bedroom enjoys twin windows overlooking the backyard. An additional bedroom has a window viewing the front of the property and shares a full hall bath with the master bedroom. This home is designed with a basement foundation.

DESIGN BY
©Drummond Designs, Inc.

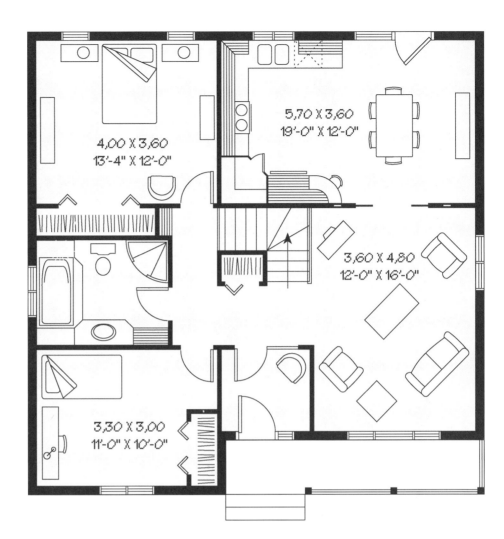

4,00 X 3,60
13'-4" X 12'-0"

5,70 X 3,60
19'-0" X 12'-0"

3,60 X 4,80
12'-0" X 16'-0"

3,30 X 3,00
11'-0" X 10'-0"

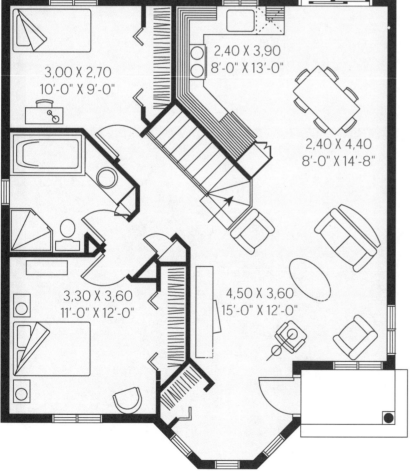

3,00 X 2,70
10'-0" X 9'-0"

2,40 X 3,90
8'-0" X 13'-0"

2,40 X 4,40
8'-0" X 14'-8"

3,30 X 3,60
11'-0" X 12'-0"

4,50 X 3,60
15'-0" X 12'-0"

This sweet Folk Victorian cottage, decorated with a bit of gingerbread trim, features a unique bay-windowed foyer with a generously sized coat closet. Additional windows—the elegant arched window in the front bedroom and four tall windows in the family room—fill this design with natural light. The family room adjoins a skylit kitchen, which provides a compact pantry and opens to a dining room with sliding glass doors to the backyard. Two bedrooms, both with long wall closets, share a bath that includes an angled vanity, corner shower and comfortable tub. This home is designed with a basement foundation.

DESIGN HPU040006

Square Footage: 958
Width: 30'-0" Depth: 35'-4"

DESIGN BY
©Drummond Designs, Inc.

An exciting floor plan and an attractive exterior with side panels and a display of muntin windows make this home a great starter. Upon entry, a coat closet resides to the left. On the right is the living area well lighted by the bayed windows under the turret and open to the dining area. A sliding door in the dining room leads to the backyard. An angled kitchen counter provides plenty of work space and features a window sink. An owners bedroom shares a full hall bath with one family bedroom. This home is designed with a basement foundation.

DESIGN HPU040007

Square Footage: 972
Width: 30'-0" Depth: 35'-0"

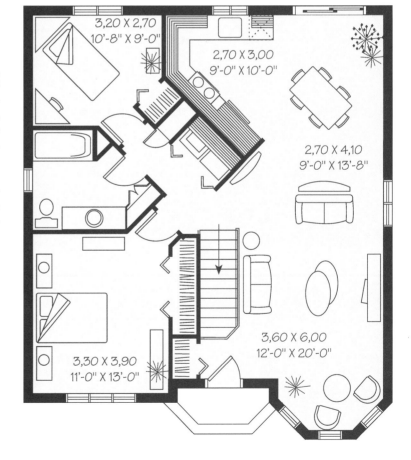

3,20 X 2,70
10'-8" X 9'-0"

2,70 X 3,00
9'-0" X 10'-0"

2,70 X 4,10
9'-0" X 13'-8"

3,30 X 3,90
11'-0" X 13'-0"

3,60 X 6,00
12'-0" X 20'-0"

This cottage, complete with sweeping rooflines, is dazzled with country allure. The covered front porch is perfect for rocking chairs on cool summer nights. Enter into the foyer, which features a coat closet. To the right, the dining room connects to an island-cooktop kitchen. To the left, the spacious living room overlooks the front yard. A laundry room is located at the rear of the plan, near a secondary coat closet and a back door to the outside. Upstairs, the master bedroom contains a large walk-in closet and a private bath. Two additional bedrooms share a hall bath. This home is designed with a basement foundation.

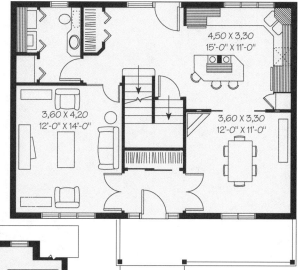

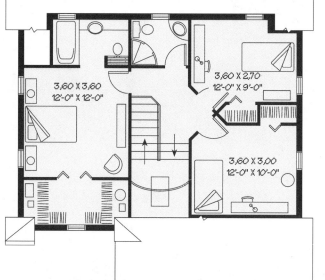

DESIGN HPU040008

First Floor: 768 square feet
Second Floor: 726 square feet
Total: 1,494 square feet
Width: 32'-0" Depth: 24'-0"

DESIGN BY
©Drummond Designs, Inc.

3,60 X 4,40
12'-0" X 14'-8"

4,80 X 4,20
16'-0" X 14'-0"

3,30 X 4,20
11'-0" X 14'-0"

3,70 X 3,80
12'-4" X 12'-8"

3,60 X 3,90
12'-0" X 13'-0"

Pillars and nested gables add style and charm to this one-story home. An open and airy floor plan allows for great versatility and creativity. Lots of windows bring sunshine in and expand the interior with wonderful views in every direction. Two bedrooms with huge closets reside on the left; the living spaces occupy the right side of the plan. A well-equipped kitchen serves the dining area with ease. A full bath sits to the left of the entry. This home is designed with a basement foundation.

DESIGN HPU040010

Square Footage: 1,387
Width: 44'-0" Depth: 34'-0"

DESIGN BY
©Drummond Designs, Inc.

DESIGN HPU040009

Square Footage: 1,064
Width: 38'-0" Depth: 28'-0"

DESIGN BY
©Drummond Designs, Inc.

Brightly lit by multiple windows, this petite home is a sunny haven for any family. Traditional siding graces the exterior. The kitchen opens to an eating area and family room. Two family bedrooms share a full hall bath that includes a tub overlooking the backyard. A side entrance to the home opens between the eating area and family room. This home is designed with a basement foundation.

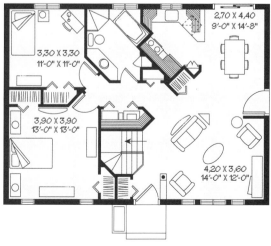

3,30 X 3,30
11'-0" X 11'-0"

2,70 X 4,40
9'-0" X 14'-8"

3,90 X 3,90
13'-0" X 13'-0"

4,20 X 3,60
14'-0" X 12'-0"

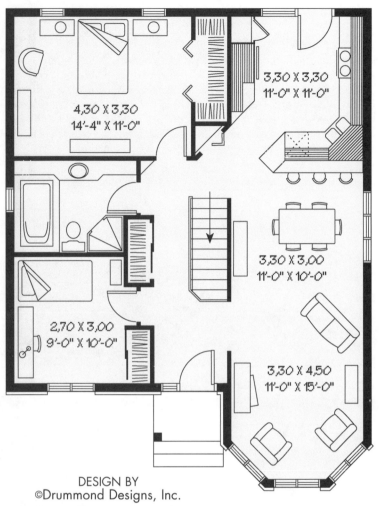

4,30 X 3,30
14'-4" X 11'-0"

3,30 X 3,30
11'-0" X 11'-0"

3,30 X 3,00
11'-0" X 10'-0"

2,70 X 3,00
9'-0" X 10'-0"

3,30 X 4,50
11'-0" X 15'-0"

DESIGN BY
©Drummond Designs, Inc.

An alluring quaint, brick exterior creates a cozy ambience inside this traditional family plan. Petite yet efficient, this plan is designed for the young family. Surrounded by brightly lit windows, the bayed sitting area is perfect for a living room setting. The dining area views the side yard, while the kitchen accesses the rear yard. The master bedroom features roomy closet space. An additional bedroom shares a full hall bath with the master bedroom. This home is designed with a basement foundation.

DESIGN HPU040011

Square Footage: 994
Width: 30'-0" Depth: 38'-0"

This design promises sunlit mornings with the panel of windows on the front bedroom, the lovely etched-glass front door and sidelights, and the sunburst on the garage. Inside, this adorable European cottage offers a generous amount of living space and well-thought-out plan. The right side of the plan is occupied by one of three family bedrooms, the living room and an L-shaped kitchen with a pantry and sliding glass doors to the backyard. A full hall bath, with a tub and separate shower, is just around the corner from the two additional bedrooms. This home is designed with a basement foundation.

DESIGN HPU040012

Square Footage: 1,089
Width: 32'-0" Depth: 45'-0"

DESIGN BY
©Drummond Designs, Inc.

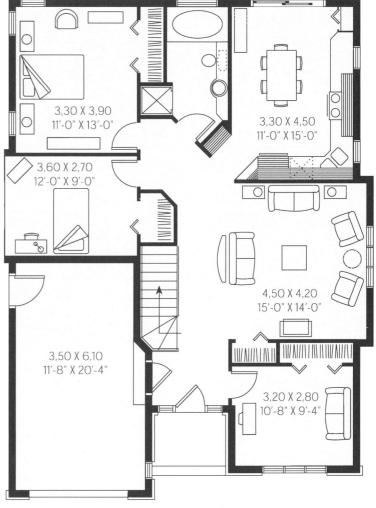

3,30 X 3,90
11'-0" X 13'-0"

3,60 X 2,70
12'-0" X 9'-0"

3,30 X 4,50
11'-0" X 15'-0"

4,50 X 4,20
15'-0" X 14'-0"

3,50 X 6,10
11'-8" X 20'-4"

3,20 X 2,80
10'-8" X 9'-4"

3,80 X 2,40
12'-8" X 8'-0"

3,00 X 3,30
10'-0" X 11'-0"

3,60 X 4,20
12'-0" X 14'-0"

This country classic boasts a traditional siding exterior, plus a two-story bay window area. Downstairs, the bay windows illuminate the living room, while upstairs they brighten the master bedroom. An open kitchen/dining area and a laundry room complete the first floor. Two additional family bedrooms share a full bath with the master bedroom and reside on the second floor. This home is designed with a basement foundation.

DESIGN HPU040013

First Floor: 643 square feet
Second Floor: 643 square feet
Total: 1,286 square feet
Width: 24'-0" Depth: 30'-0"

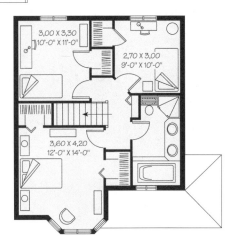

3,00 X 3,30
10'-0" X 11'-0"

2,70 X 3,00
9'-0" X 10'-0"

3,60 X 4,20
12'-0" X 14'-0"

DESIGN HPU040014

First Floor: 759 square feet
Second Floor: 735 square feet
Total: 1,494 square feet
Width: 22'-0" Depth: 36'-0"

The charming front porch and the two-story turret welcome guests to this lovely home. The turret houses the living room on the first floor and the owners suite on the second floor. The dining room is open to the living room and provides a box-bay window. The L-shaped kitchen features a breakfast room accessible to the backyard. A curved staircase next to the powder room leads upstairs to three bedrooms and a bath. Each family bedroom contains a walk-in closet. This home is designed with a basement foundation.

2,90 X 2,70
9'-8" X 9'-0"

3,30 X 2,70
11'-0" X 9'-0"

3,90 X 2,70
13'-0" X 9'-0"

3,50 X 4,80
11'-8" X 16'-0"

3,40 X 2,70
11'-4" X 9'-0"

3,50 X 3,30
11'-8" X 11'-0"

3,50 X 4,50
11'-8" X 15'-0"

DESIGN HPU040015

First Floor: 681 square feet
Second Floor: 623 square feet
Total: 1,304 square feet
Width: 28'-0" Depth: 40'-0"

DESIGN BY
©Drummond Designs, Inc.

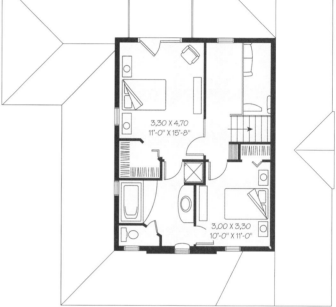

A glass-door entrance welcomes visitors into the picturesque charm of this countryside home. A large wraparound porch leads to a relaxing outdoor lounge area—perfect for summer afternoons. The island kitchen opens to an eating area, across from the living room. A powder room, laundry area and the one-car garage complete this floor. Upstairs, two family bedrooms are linked by a full bath. This home is designed with a basement foundation.

13

DESIGN BY
©Vaughn A. Lauban Designs

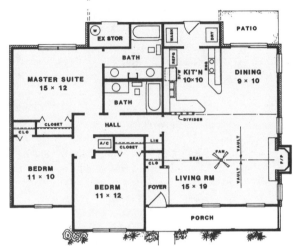

DESIGN HPU040017

Square Footage: 1,253
Width: 44'-0" Depth: 34'-0"

Rustic and efficient, this home is packed with family appeal. Enter through the foyer into the vaulted living room. This room features a ceiling fan and a fireplace. The L-shaped kitchen opens to the dining room, which overlooks the rear patio. The spacious master suite includes a private bath, while two additional bedrooms share a full hall bath. An optional two-car garage is also available.

DESIGN HPU040016

Square Footage: 1,036
Width: 37'-0" Depth: 45'-0"

DESIGN BY
©Vaughn A. Lauban Designs

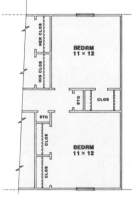

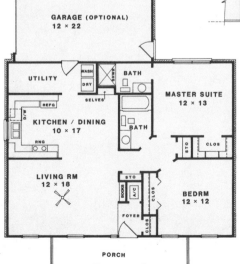

This quaint Victorian cottage offers beautiful detailing and the possibility of adding on later. Enter the spacious living room and then continue to the dining area and U-shaped kitchen. A utility room is located just off the kitchen. On the right, a family or guest bedroom is steps away from a full bath. The master suite features a full bath and walk-in closet. The future expansion offers two more secondary bedrooms and provides the owners suite with two closets instead of a walk-in for a total addition of 392 square feet. The garage is optional.

DESIGN HPU040018

Square Footage: 1,463
Width: 54'-0" Depth: 60'-0"

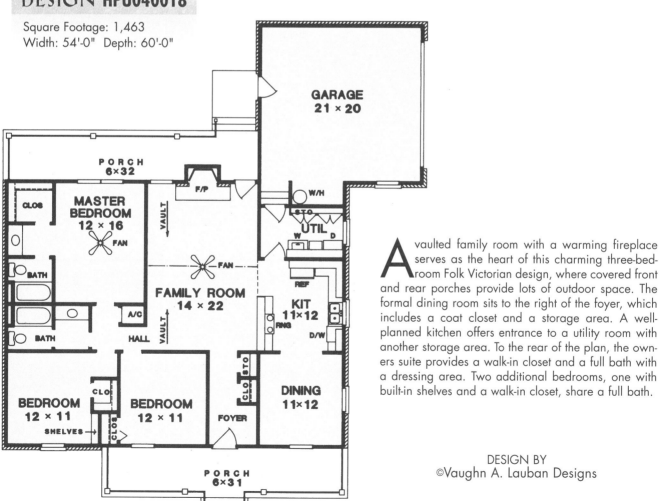

GARAGE
21 × 20

PORCH
6×32

MASTER
BEDROOM
12 × 16

FAN

VAULT

F/P

W/H

STO

UTIL

W   D

REF

FAMILY ROOM
14 × 22

FAN

A/C

BATH

BATH

HALL

VAULT

KIT
11×12

RNG

D/W

CLO
STO

DINING
11×12

BEDROOM
12 × 11

BEDROOM
12 × 11

CLO

CLO

FOYER

SHELVES →

CLOS

PORCH
6×31

A vaulted family room with a warming fireplace serves as the heart of this charming three-bedroom Folk Victorian design, where covered front and rear porches provide lots of outdoor space. The formal dining room sits to the right of the foyer, which includes a coat closet and a storage area. A well-planned kitchen offers entrance to a utility room with another storage area. To the rear of the plan, the owners suite provides a walk-in closet and a full bath with a dressing area. Two additional bedrooms, one with built-in shelves and a walk-in closet, share a full bath.

DESIGN BY
©Vaughn A. Lauban Designs

15

DESIGN HPU040019

Square Footage: 1,385
Width: 48'-0" Depth: 60'-4"

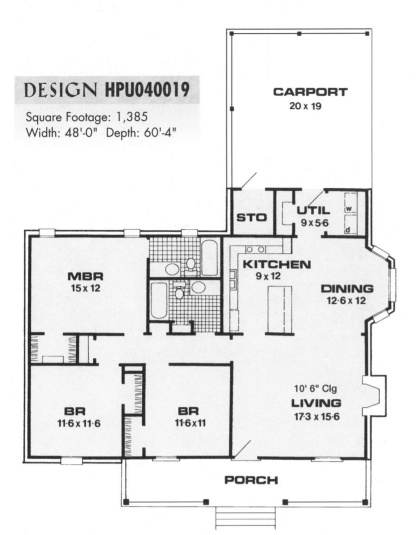

CARPORT
20 x 19

STO

UTIL
9 x 5·6

w
d

KITCHEN
9 x 12

MBR
15 x 12

DINING
12·6 x 12

BR
11·6 x 11·6

BR
11·6 x 11

10' 6" Clg
LIVING
17·3 x 15·6

PORCH

This awesome exterior starts with wide front steps under a gabled roof that lead to an extended covered porch. The brilliant floor plan provides a generous amount of space in the living room (with fireplace) and the island kitchen adjoined by a bayed dining area. Just past the kitchen is a utility room with a washer and dryer plus a utility storage area. The master bedroom features a private bath and a walk-in closet, while two additional family bedrooms share a full hall bath and a linen closet. The carport and storage room are located in the rear of the home. Please specify basement, crawlspace or slab foundation when ordering.

DESIGN BY
©Larry James & Associates, Inc.

DESIGN HPU040020

First Floor: 720 square feet
Second Floor: 203 square feet
Total: 923 square feet
Width: 32'-0" Depth: 38'-6"

DESIGN BY
©Larry James & Associates, Inc.

This compact design offers a host of extras beginning with its charming exterior. Wide country-style porches grace both the front and back of this cozy home. The focus of the interior centers on the open living area with a vaulted ceiling. Split into a great room and dining room, this area includes a large warming fireplace and lots of windows for outdoor viewing and increased natural lighting. The fully equipped kitchen is located near the rear porch for convenient outdoor dining. The owners bedroom finishes the first floor. An extra bedroom upstairs includes two closets. Storage space is located in the eaves. Please specify basement, slab or crawlspace foundation when ordering.

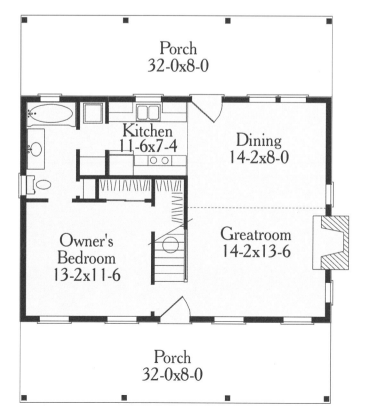

Porch
32-0x8-0

Kitchen
11-6x7-4

Dining
14-2x8-0

Owner's
Bedroom
13-2x11-6

Greatroom
14-2x13-6

Porch
32-0x8-0

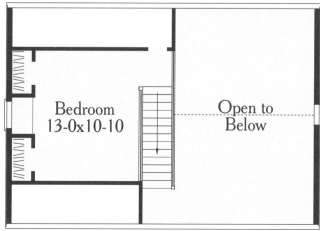

Bedroom
13-0x10-10

Open to
Below

DESIGN HPU040022

First Floor: 772 square feet
Second Floor: 411 square feet
Total: 1,183 square feet
Width: 32'-0" Depth: 28'-7"

DESIGN BY
©R.L. Pfotenhauer

This petite Gothic Revival cottage, with a steeply pitched roof, dormers and pointed-arch windows, would be perfect as a vacation or starter home. A large covered front porch is available for entertaining and relaxing, while the living room, warmed by a fireplace, offers access to a covered side porch. The U-shaped kitchen shares space with a cozy dining area. A boxed window allows natural light in to the front bedroom, which is conveniently close to a bath. Upstairs, another bedroom, this one with a walk-in closet, accesses a full bath and overlooks the living room.

DESIGN HPU040021

First Floor: 688 square feet
Second Floor: 559 square feet
Total: 1,247 square feet
Width: 27'-8" Depth: 30'-8"

Steep, soaring gables embellished with band-sawn ornamentation heightens the drama of this Gothic Revival gem. The heavy carved brackets on the front porch invite the curious into the entry foyer. The living room features a fireplace and plenty of light that filters through the casement windows. For effortless entertaining, the kitchen opens to the dining room. Upstairs, there are two bedrooms including the master bedroom and a full bath. The master bedroom features sloped ceilings and tie beams.

DESIGN BY
©R.L. Pfotenhauer

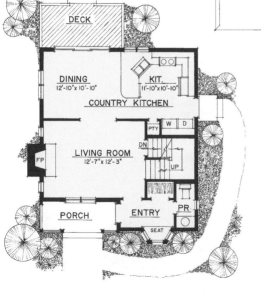

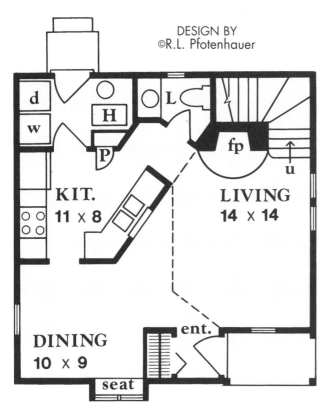

DESIGN BY
©R.L. Pfotenhauer

d
w
H
L
P
fp
u

KIT.
11 x 8

LIVING
14 x 14

DINING
10 x 9

ent.

seat

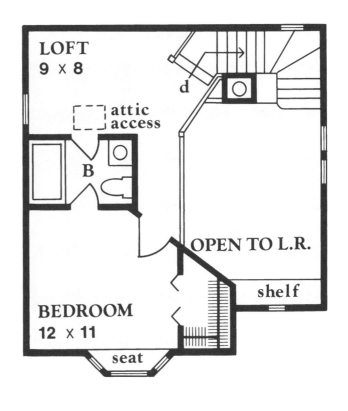

LOFT
9 x 8

attic
access

d

B

OPEN TO L.R.

shelf

BEDROOM
12 x 11

seat

Graceful, curving, gingerbread trim trans-
forms this cozy cottage into a Carpenter
Gothic-style confection. From the steep
gable roof and appropriately detailed ornamentation on the outside, to the snug yet well planned
interior, this design is packed with vintage charm.
A soaring two-story living room with a balcony
overlook dominates the first floor. The fireplace
and stair are combined into one unique architectural feature. The dining room has a cozy window
seat; the kitchen offers a handy pass-through to
the living area. Upstairs, the master bedroom
enjoys an elaborate bay window, a twelve-foot
ceiling and a walk-in closet. The sleeping loft,
which can be enclosed for a second bedroom,
shares a bathroom with the master bedroom.

DESIGN HPU040023

First Floor: 547 square feet
Second Floor: 418 square feet
Total: 965 square feet
Width: 24'-0" Depth: 25'-4"

DESIGN HPU040024

First Floor: 448 square feet
Second Floor: 448 square feet
Total: 896 square feet
Width: 16'-0" Depth: 28'-0"

DESIGN BY
©R.L. Pfotenhauer

This petite Carpenter Gothic charmer would make an ideal vacation or starter home. The exterior boasts a heavy wood-shingled roof, board-and-batten siding and scroll-sawn detailing. A well-planned interior is simplicity itself: a double-door entry leads to an open living, dining and kitchen area. The kitchen is hidden from the living room by a stairway and a half-bath. Nine-foot ceilings highlight the second floor, which contains two bedrooms—each with plenty of closet space—and a paneled bathroom.

BEDROOM 2

LIN.

BATH

DN

BEDROOM 1

KITCHEN

W/D

F

UP

LAV

LIVING ROOM

PORCH

DESIGN **HPU040025**

First Floor: 448 square feet
Second Floor: 448 square feet
Total: 896 square feet
Width: 16'-0" Depth: 41'-6"

Perfect for a lakeside, vacation or starter home, this two-story design is sure to be a favorite. A large railed porch on the first floor and the covered balcony on the second floor are available for watching the sunrise. Inside, on the first floor, the living room is spacious and convenient to the kitchen and dining area. A powder room finishes off this level. Upstairs, the sleeping zone consists of two bedrooms, each with roomy closets, and a full hall bath with a linen closet. The front bedroom accesses the balcony.

DESIGN BY
©R.L. Pfotenhauer

DESIGN HPU040026

First Floor: 1,342 square feet
Second Floor: 511 square feet
Total: 1,853 square feet
Width: 44'-0" Depth: 40'-0"

DESIGN BY
©The Sater Design Collection

Amenities abound in this delightful two-story Floridian home. Behind the extravagant exterior, the foyer opens directly to the fantastic grand room, which offers a warming fireplace and two sets of double doors to the rear deck. The dining room also accesses this deck and a second deck shared with Bedroom 2. A convenient kitchen and another bedroom also reside on this level. Upstairs, the master bedroom reigns supreme. Entered through double doors, it pampers with a luxurious bath, a walk-in closet, a morning kitchen and a private balcony.

deck
17'-0" x 9'-0"

dining
12'-8" x 11'-0"
8' clg.

deck

grand room
20'-0" x 18'-0"
vault. clg.

kitchen
11' x 12'

br. 2
12'-0" x 11'-8"
8' clg.

fireplace

up

down

foyer

br. 3
12'-0" x 10'-0"
8' clg.

down

entry porch

garage
40'-0" x 20'-0" avg.

storage
13'-0" x 18'-0" avg.

stor./bonus
20'-0" x 20'-0"

up

stor.

up

lattice work
panel walls

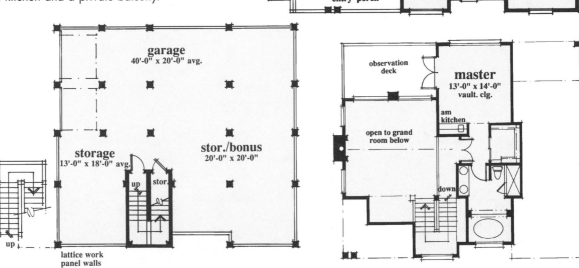

observation deck

master
13'-0" x 14'-0"
vault. clg.

am kitchen

open to grand room below

down

DESIGN HPU040027

Square Footage: 1,288
Width: 32'-4" Depth: 60'-0"

Welcome home to casual, unstuffy living with this comfortable Tidewater design. Asymmetrical lines celebrate the turn of the new century, and blend a current Gulf Coast style with vintage panache brought forward from its regional past. The heart of this home is the great room, where a put-your-feet-up atmosphere prevails, and the dusky hues of sunset can mingle with the sounds of ocean breakers. French doors open the master suite to a private area of the covered porch, where sunlight and sea breezes mingle with a spirit of bon vivant.

DESIGN BY
©The Sater Design Collection

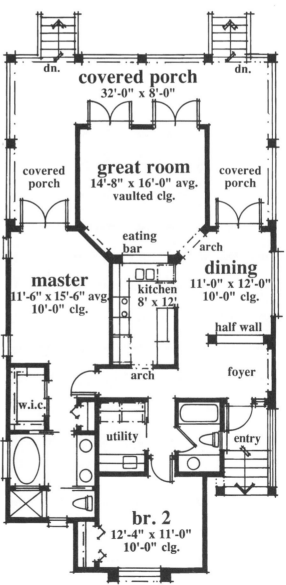

DESIGN BY
©Select Home Designs

DESIGN HPU040029

Square Footage: 1,475
Width: 44'-0" Depth: 43'-0"

mbr
12 x 13'10

brk
7' x15'

7'10 x13'

k

DW

BUTCHER BLOCK

VERANDAH

FRENCH DOOR

din
10'x11'

DESK

W D

RAILING

LIN

SHELVES

VAULTED CEILING

12' x 10'2
br2

9'6 x 10'2
br3

SKYLIGHT OVER

VERANDAH

RAILING

13'6x17'
liv

A railed veranda and turned posts complement a lovely Palladian window on the exterior of this home. The foyer is brightly lit by a skylight, and leads to the living room with a vaulted ceiling, fireplace and bookshelves. The dining room overlooks a covered veranda that opens from the breakfast room. A well-organized kitchen features a butcher-block island. Sleeping quarters include a master suite and two family bedrooms that share a full double-vanity bath.

br2
9'8 X 12'6

br3
11' X 9'2

PATIO

k/brk
15'8 X 9'2

D W

ldr

F

SKYLIGHT

12' X 14'
liv

ARCH

10'8 X 12'
din

21'6x21'
two-car garage

14'4 X 12'2
mbr

VERANDAH

DESIGN HPU040028

Square Footage: 1,399
Width: 69'-0" Depth: 35'-0"

DESIGN BY
©Select Home Designs

Classic floor planning and a worthy exterior dominate this one-story starter home. The exterior features a Palladian window and multi-pane windows. The central foyer is flanked by the living room with a fireplace and the formal dining room. Across the hall are the U-shaped kitchen and the breakfast room with sliding glass doors to the rear terrace. A laundry area accesses the two-car garage and the backyard. Two family bedrooms share a full skylit bath. The master bedroom boasts a large wall closet and private bath. A full basement can be developed at a later time, if needed.

W hat an appealing plan! Its rustic character is defined by cedar lattice, covered columned porches, exposed rafters and multi-pane, double-hung windows. The great room/dining room combination is reached through double doors off the veranda and features a fireplace towering two stories to the lofty ceiling. A U-shaped kitchen contains an angled snack counter that serves this area and loads of space for a breakfast table—or use the handy side porch for alfresco dining. To the rear resides the master bedroom with a full bath and double doors to the veranda. An additional half-bath sits just beyond the laundry room. Upstairs, two family bedrooms and a full bath finish the plan.

PORCH

mbr
12'9x13'4

DN

D
W

COATS

k
10'x10'

DN

UP

LINE OF
FLOOR OVER

din/
great rm
21'x13'6

VERANDAH

DN

DN

LINE OF
FLOOR OVER

br3
10'4x10'2

br2
10'4x11'2

DN

RAILING

OPEN TO
GREAT ROOM
BELOW

PLANT LEDGE

DESIGN HPU040030

First Floor: 995 square feet
Second Floor: 484 square feet
Total: 1,479 square feet
Width: 38'-0" Depth: 44'-0"

QUOTE ONE®

Cost to build? See page 502
to order complete cost estimate
to build this house in your area!

DESIGN BY
©Select Home Designs

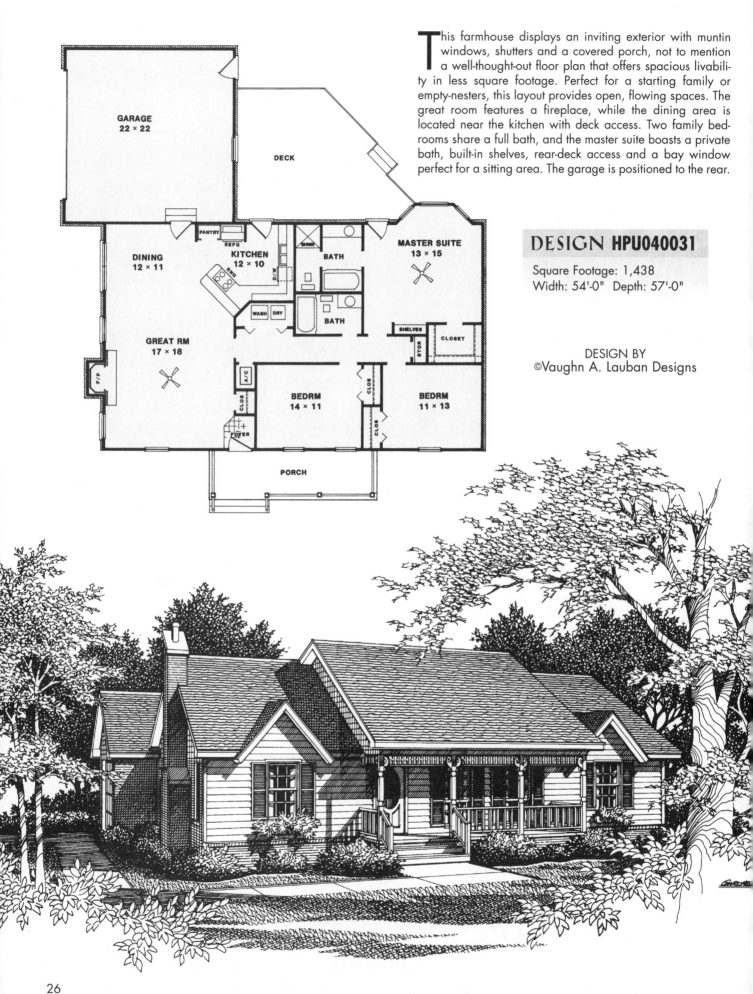

GARAGE
22 × 22

DECK

This farmhouse displays an inviting exterior with muntin windows, shutters and a covered porch, not to mention a well-thought-out floor plan that offers spacious livability in less square footage. Perfect for a starting family or empty-nesters, this layout provides open, flowing spaces. The great room features a fireplace, while the dining area is located near the kitchen with deck access. Two family bedrooms share a full bath, and the master suite boasts a private bath, built-in shelves, rear-deck access and a bay window perfect for a sitting area. The garage is positioned to the rear.

DINING
12 × 11

PANTRY
REFG

KITCHEN
12 × 10

D/W
RNG

SHWR

BATH

MASTER SUITE
13 × 15

DESIGN HPU040031

Square Footage: 1,438
Width: 54'-0" Depth: 57'-0"

WASH DRY

BATH

DESIGN BY
©Vaughn A. Lauban Designs

GREAT RM
17 × 18

SHELVES

STOR CLOSET

F/P

A/C

CLOS

BEDRM
14 × 11

CLOS

CLOS

BEDRM
11 × 13

CLOS

FOYER

PORCH

26

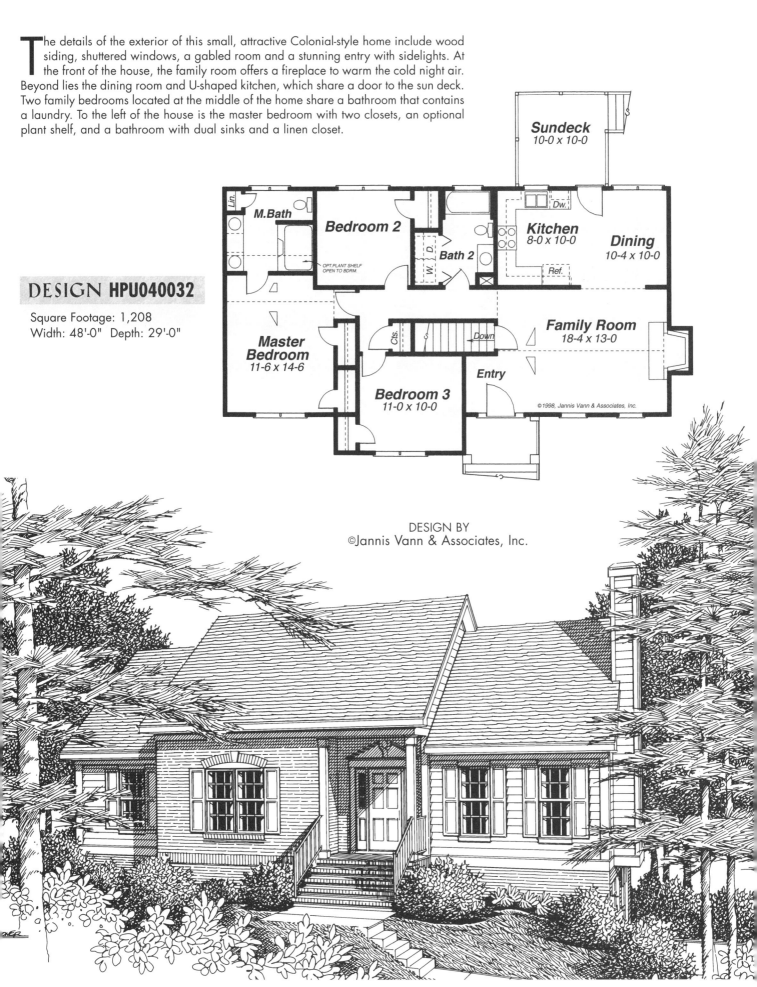

The details of the exterior of this small, attractive Colonial-style home include wood siding, shuttered windows, a gabled room and a stunning entry with sidelights. At the front of the house, the family room offers a fireplace to warm the cold night air. Beyond lies the dining room and U-shaped kitchen, which share a door to the sun deck. Two family bedrooms located at the middle of the home share a bathroom that contains a laundry. To the left of the house is the master bedroom with two closets, an optional plant shelf, and a bathroom with dual sinks and a linen closet.

Lin.

M.Bath

Bedroom 2

Dw.

Kitchen
8-0 x 10-0

Sundeck
10-0 x 10-0

Dining
10-4 x 10-0

OPT. PLANT SHELF
OPEN TO BDRM.

W. D.

Bath 2

Ref.

DESIGN HPU040032

Square Footage: 1,208
Width: 48'-0" Depth: 29'-0"

Master
Bedroom
11-6 x 14-6

Cts.

Down

Family Room
18-4 x 13-0

Bedroom 3
11-0 x 10-0

Entry

©1998, Jannis Vann & Associates, Inc.

DESIGN BY
©Jannis Vann & Associates, Inc.

Sundeck
14-0 x 10-0

Brkfst.
8-2 x 8-2

Kitchen
10-0 x 8-2

Dw.

Ref.

Cts.

W. D.

Dining
11-10 x 10-0

Slope

Sky Lt.

Bth.2

Built In Cabinet

Bdrm.3
10-0 x 11-6

Lin.

Master Bdrm.
10-8 x 16-10

Lin.

M.Bath

Living Area
13-8 x 15-0

Slope

Down

Slope

Bdrm.2
13-6 x 11-2

DESIGN HPU040033

Square Footage: 1,345
Width: 52'-0" Depth: 32'-0"

This home, with its gabled roof, covered front porch and columns with arched beam support, offers a practical floor plan. The front door opens to the living room, which has a sloped ceiling, a fireplace and built-in cabinetry. To the left is the master suite with a walk-in closet, dual-vanity bathroom, separate shower and garden tub set in a bayed window. Two more bedrooms on the other side of the house share a bathroom that includes a skylight. The dining room, kitchen and breakfast area at the back of the house enjoy views of the sun deck and backyard. The dining room features bayed windows as well as a door leading to the sun deck.

DESIGN BY
©Jannis Vann & Associates, Inc.

A brilliant display of windows decorates the siding exterior of this traditional design. Walk onto the covered front porch—perfect for stargazing at night. Inside, the living room features a ceiling fan and a fireplace. The kitchen opens to the dining area and is conveniently located near the two-car garage, which is connected by a patio. Two family bedrooms share a full hall bath. The master suite overlooks the rear deck and features a ceiling fan, private bath and spacious closet.

DESIGN HPU040034

Square Footage: 1,247
Width: 43'-0" Depth: 60'-0"

DESIGN BY
©Vaughn A. Lauban Designs

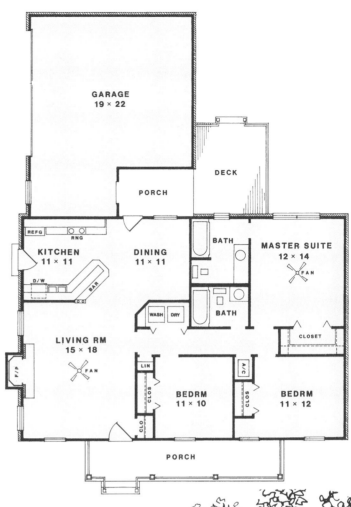

DESIGN HPU040035

Square Footage: 1,395
Width: 44'-11" Depth: 50'-1"

A combination of muntin windows with lintels, side paneling and brick add flavor to this traditional home. Surrounding the foyer is a full hall bath separating two family suites. The master bedroom is located to the rear of the plan and boasts a private bath, linen closet and a huge walk-in closet. The self-sufficient kitchen includes plenty of work space, a breakfast bar and a pantry. Adjacent to the dining room, the family room provides an area for an optional fireplace. The garage entrance is conveniently placed near the laundry room and the kitchen.

DESIGN BY
©Living Concepts Home Planning

B eyond the luminous exterior of hipped and gabled roofs, you can enter this traditional home through a covered porch with a railing—perfect for a rocking chair to sit and enjoy the weather! The master suite includes a vast walk-in closet and a master bath with two linen closets. A full hall bath is available to the occupants of the two additional suites; each suite presents angled entries and wall closets. The kitchen provides a serving bar, an entire wall of cabinet space and direct access to the laundry room and garage. A fireplace is optional in the family room. The dining area includes sliding glass doors to the rear patio.

DESIGN HPU040036

Square Footage: 1,395
Width: 44'-11" Depth: 50'-1"

DESIGN BY
©Living Concepts Home Planning

DESIGN HPU040037

Square Footage: 1,204
Width: 43'-1"   Depth: 47'-1"

A welcoming porch leads to an entry that features a sidelight and transom. Inside, the foyer carries guests past a utility closet and niche, to the island kitchen with a snack bar. The kitchen opens to the eating area and the family room (with an optional fireplace) accessible to the rear patio. The secluded master suite provides privacy and features a master bath and walk-in closet. Suites 2 and 3 are separated from the living area and share a full hall bath. The well-placed garage entrance opens to the foyer.

DESIGN BY
©Living Concepts Home Planning

MASTER SUITE
12'-0" x 12'-0"

FAMILY ROOM
15'-0" x 15'-4"

PATIO

EATING AREA
7'-0" x 8'-0"

BATH

NICHE

KITCHEN
12'-0" x 10'-0"

SUITE 2
9'-8" x 9'-10"

FOYER

SUITE 3
9'-8" x 9'-0"

PORCH

GARAGE
20'-0" x 20'-0"

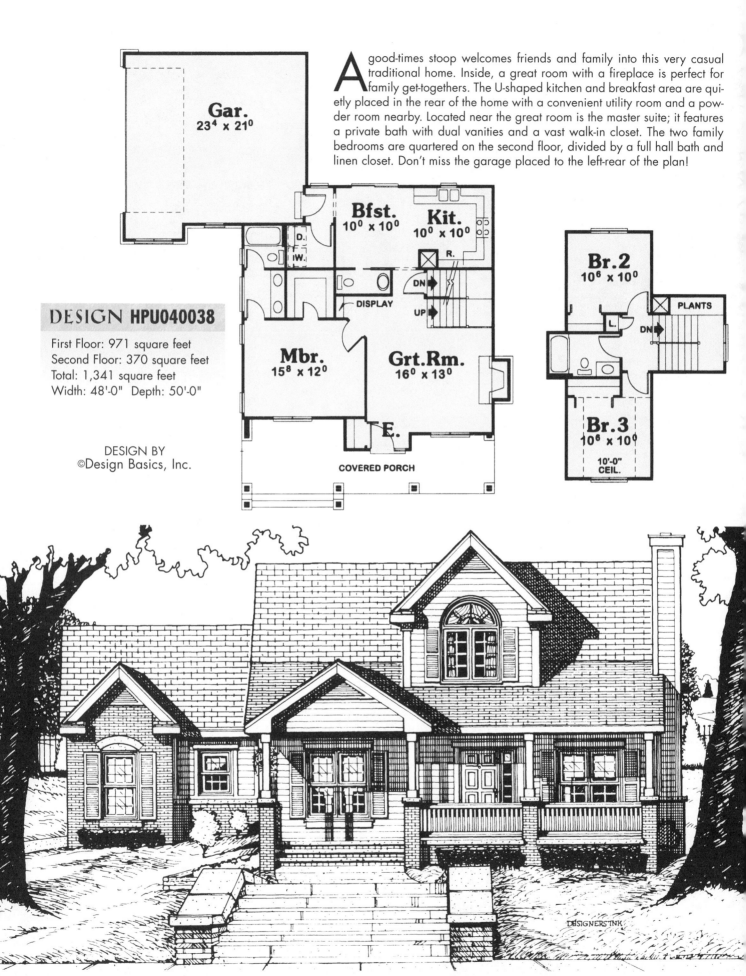

Gar.
23⁴ x 21⁰

A good-times stoop welcomes friends and family into this very casual traditional home. Inside, a great room with a fireplace is perfect for family get-togethers. The U-shaped kitchen and breakfast area are quietly placed in the rear of the home with a convenient utility room and a powder room nearby. Located near the great room is the master suite; it features a private bath with dual vanities and a vast walk-in closet. The two family bedrooms are quartered on the second floor, divided by a full hall bath and linen closet. Don't miss the garage placed to the left-rear of the plan!

Bfst.
10⁰ x 10⁰

Kit.
10⁰ x 10⁰

D.

W.

R.

DN

UP

DISPLAY

DESIGN HPU040038

First Floor: 971 square feet
Second Floor: 370 square feet
Total: 1,341 square feet
Width: 48'-0" Depth: 50'-0"

Br. 2
10⁶ x 10⁰

PLANTS

L.

DN

DESIGN BY
©Design Basics, Inc.

Mbr.
15⁸ x 12⁰

Grt. Rm.
16⁰ x 13⁰

E.

Br. 3
10⁶ x 10⁰

10'-0"
CEIL.

COVERED PORCH

DESIGNERS INK

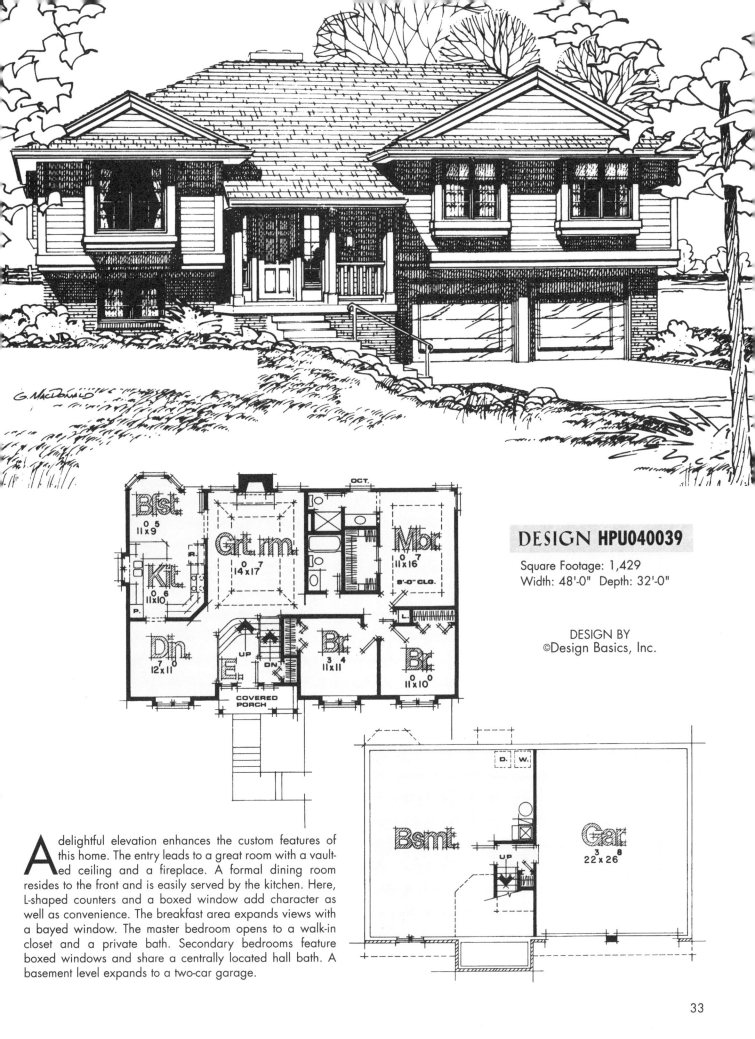

G. MACDONALD

Bfst.
0 5
11 x 9

Kit.
0 6
11 x 10

P.

Dn.
7 0
12 x 11

E

Grt. rm.
0 7
14 x 17

OCT.

UP

DN

Mbr
0 7
11 x 16

8'-0" CLG.

L

Br
3 4
11 x 11

Br
0 0
11 x 10

COVERED PORCH

DESIGN HPU040039

Square Footage: 1,429
Width: 48'-0" Depth: 32'-0"

DESIGN BY
©Design Basics, Inc.

Bsmt.

D. W.

UP

Gar
3 8
22 x 26

A delightful elevation enhances the custom features of this home. The entry leads to a great room with a vaulted ceiling and a fireplace. A formal dining room resides to the front and is easily served by the kitchen. Here, L-shaped counters and a boxed window add character as well as convenience. The breakfast area expands views with a bayed window. The master bedroom opens to a walk-in closet and a private bath. Secondary bedrooms feature boxed windows and share a centrally located hall bath. A basement level expands to a two-car garage.

33

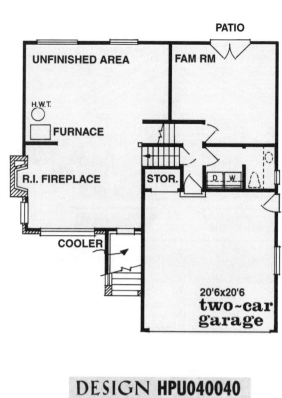

UNFINISHED AREA

PATIO

FAM RM

H.W.T.

FURNACE

R.I. FIREPLACE

STOR.

D W

COOLER

20'6x20'6
two~car
garage

DESIGN HPU040040

Square Footage: 1,211
Unfinished Basement:
  742 square feet
Width: 38'-0" Depth: 42'-5"

DESIGN BY
©Select Home Designs

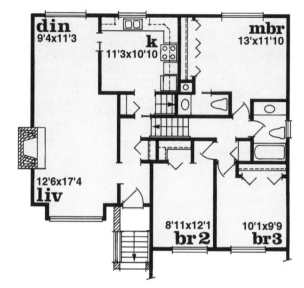

din
9'4x11'3

k
11'3x10'10

mbr
13'x11'10

12'6x17'4
liv

8'11x12'1
br 2

10'1x9'9
br 3

Adorned with horizontal siding and brick, the exterior of this home sports details for a rustic, country appeal. The entry is deep-set for weather protection and opens directly to the airy living and dining room area of the home. A fireplace and box-bay window here are added features. The kitchen's L-shaped configuration is made for convenience and allows space for a breakfast table. Up a few steps sit two family bedrooms and a master suite with a full bath. One family bedroom boasts a walk-in closet. Space on the lower level can be developed into a family room with double-door access to the rear patio, a den or recreation room with a fire-place, and bedrooms, if you choose. Rough-in plumbing is included for a half-bath and the laundry room.

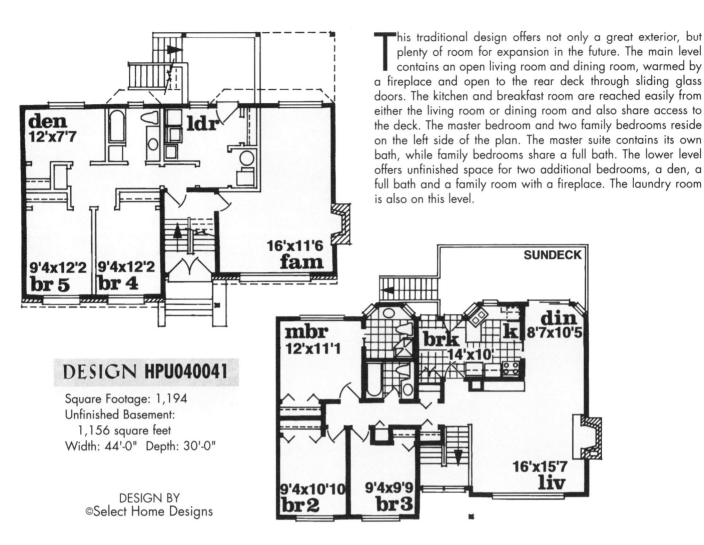

den
12'x7'7

ldr

9'4x12'2
br 5

9'4x12'2
br 4

16'x11'6
fam

This traditional design offers not only a great exterior, but plenty of room for expansion in the future. The main level contains an open living room and dining room, warmed by a fireplace and open to the rear deck through sliding glass doors. The kitchen and breakfast room are reached easily from either the living room or dining room and also share access to the deck. The master bedroom and two family bedrooms reside on the left side of the plan. The master suite contains its own bath, while family bedrooms share a full bath. The lower level offers unfinished space for two additional bedrooms, a den, a full bath and a family room with a fireplace. The laundry room is also on this level.

SUNDECK

mbr
12'x11'1

brk
14'x10'

k

din
8'7'x10'5

9'4x10'10
br 2

9'4x9'9
br 3

16'x15'7
liv

DESIGN HPU040041

Square Footage: 1,194
Unfinished Basement:
1,156 square feet
Width: 44'-0" Depth: 30'-0"

DESIGN BY
©Select Home Designs

DESIGN HPU040042

Square Footage: 1,458
Bonus Room: 256 square feet
Width: 47'-7" Depth: 46'-5"

A multitude of windows fills this home with an abundance of natural light. The foyer leads you and your guests into the inviting living room, which can be furnished with an optional warming fireplace and built-ins. A short hallway to the left of the living room takes you to the family sleeping quarters where a full bath is shared by two suites. The master suite is secluded for privacy on the far right. The private bath here includes a walk-in closet and Hollywood tub. Additional space above the garage can be developed at a later date.

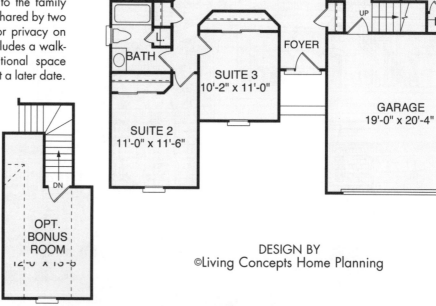

OPT. BONUS ROOM
12'-0 x 15'-6

DINING ROOM
11'-0" x 9'-10"

KITCHEN
11'-0" x 10'-6"

BATH

SUITE 2
11'-0" x 11'-6"

SUITE 3
10'-2" x 11'-0"

FOYER

LIVING ROOM
16'-2" x 18'-4"

MASTER SUITE
12'-0" x 15'-0"

W.I.C.

MASTER BATH

UP

GARAGE
19'-0" x 20'-4"

DESIGN BY
©Living Concepts Home Planning

DESIGN HPU040043

Square Footage: 1,395
Width: 44'-11" Depth: 50'-1"

A double-gabled roof and garage lead you to admire the welcoming porch and front muntin window with shutters. Inside, two bedroom suites are divided by a full hall bath. The L-shaped kitchen includes a pantry and snack bar and opens to the family room with an optional fireplace. The dining area provides sliding glass doors to the rear patio. The master suite boasts a vast walk-in closet and a grand private bath. The garage entrance is located in the utility room.

DESIGN BY
©Living Concepts Home Planning

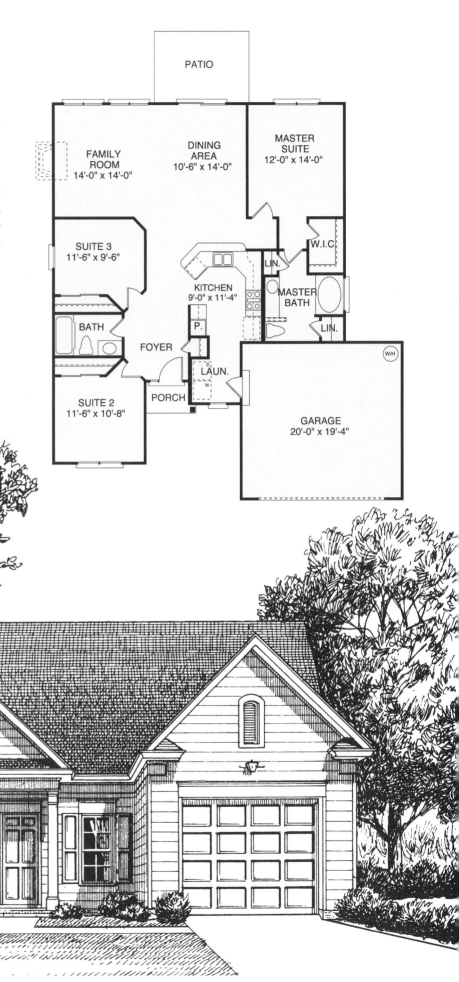

PATIO

FAMILY ROOM
14'-0" x 14'-0"

DINING AREA
10'-6" x 14'-0"

MASTER SUITE
12'-0" x 14'-0"

W.I.C

SUITE 3
11'-6" x 9'-6"

LIN.

KITCHEN
9'-0" x 11'-4"

MASTER BATH

LIN.

BATH

P.

FOYER

LAUN.

PORCH

SUITE 2
11'-6" x 10'-8"

GARAGE
20'-0" x 19'-4"

W/H

E. NATHAN
© 1995 Donald A. Gardner Architects, Inc.

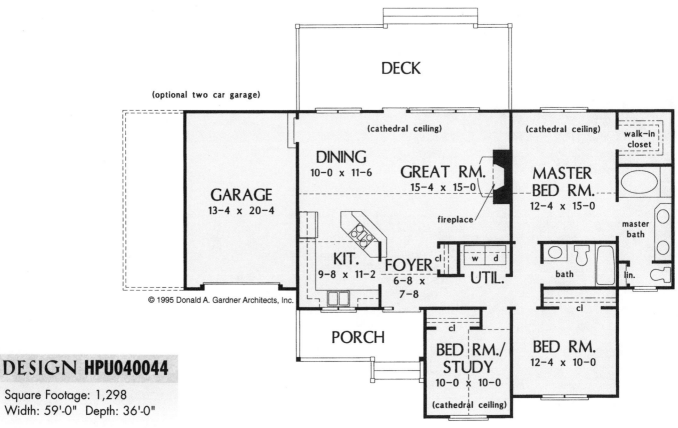

DECK

(optional two car garage)

(cathedral ceiling)

(cathedral ceiling)

walk-in
closet

DINING
10-0 x 11-6

GREAT RM.
15-4 x 15-0

MASTER
BED RM.
12-4 x 15-0

GARAGE
13-4 x 20-4

fireplace

master
bath

KIT.
9-8 x 11-2

FOYER
6-8 x
7-8

cl

w | d

UTIL.

bath

lin.

© 1995 Donald A. Gardner Architects, Inc.

cl

PORCH

cl

BED RM./
STUDY
10-0 x 10-0

BED RM.
12-4 x 10-0

(cathedral ceiling)

DESIGN HPU040044

Square Footage: 1,298
Width: 59'-0" Depth: 36'-0"

This design possesses plenty of curb appeal. From its gable roof and covered front porch, to its large rear deck, this home will brighten any neighborhood. Inside, open planning is the theme in the dining room/great room area, with a cathedral ceiling combining the two areas into a comfortable unit. The kitchen contributes to the openness with its snack bar/work island. Three bedrooms—or two bedrooms and a study—complete this attractive second home.

DESIGN BY
Donald A. Gardner Architects, Inc.

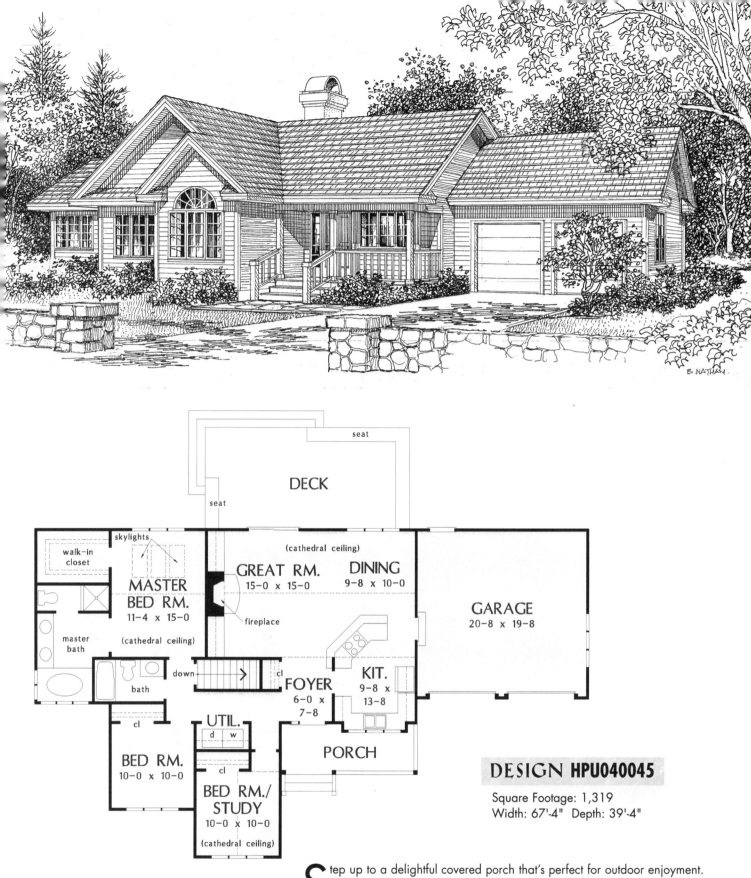

DECK

seat

seat

skylights

walk-in closet

MASTER BED RM.
11-4 x 15-0

(cathedral ceiling)

GREAT RM.
15-0 x 15-0

DINING
9-8 x 10-0

(cathedral ceiling)

fireplace

master bath

bath

down

cl

FOYER
6-0 x 7-8

KIT.
9-8 x 13-8

GARAGE
20-8 x 19-8

cl

UTIL.
d   w

cl

BED RM.
10-0 x 10-0

BED RM./ STUDY
10-0 x 10-0

(cathedral ceiling)

PORCH

DESIGN HPU040045

Square Footage: 1,319
Width: 67'-4" Depth: 39'-4"

DESIGN BY
Donald A. Gardner Architects, Inc.

Step up to a delightful covered porch that's perfect for outdoor enjoyment. A full basement almost doubles the square footage of this starter family home, which is as efficient as it is attractive. The floor plan features a cooktop-island kitchen, which opens to the great room with a fireplace and the dining area. French doors lead from the master bedroom to a deluxe private bath with a double-bowl vanity, separate shower and garden tub. The master bedroom also boasts skylights and a walk-in closet. One bedroom and a bedroom/study each include spacious closets and share a full hall bath.

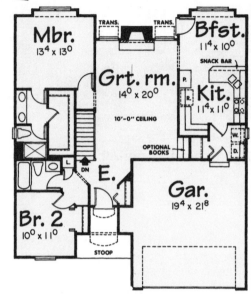

DESIGN HPU040048

Square Footage: 1,212
Width: 40'-0" Depth: 47'-8"

Attractive and uncomplicated, this two-bedroom home is perfect for first-time or empty-nest builders. Living, eating and cooking areas are designated as the center of activity in an open and unrestricted space. The master bedroom offers plenty of closet space and a private bath. Other features include a front coat closet for guests, a closet in the laundry room and, in the great room, a fireplace flanked by transom windows.

The wide, covered stoop is substantial enough for a chair. The great-room fireplace is flanked by transom windows and shares its warmth with the adjacent breakfast room. The kitchen, open to the breakfast room via a snack bar, also accesses the laundry room that leads to the garage. On the other side of the plan, two family bedrooms share a hall bath, and the master suite enjoys the luxury of a walk-in closet and a private bath with a double-bowl vanity and separate tub and shower.

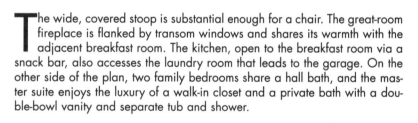

DESIGN HPU040047

Square Footage: 1,360
Width: 52'-0" Depth: 46'-0"

DESIGN HPU040049

Square Footage: 1,400
Width: 39'-4" Depth: 50'-0"

Look closely at this smaller plan, and you'll be amazed at the livability it contains. Three bedrooms, two with a shared bath, are separated by the common areas. The family room and dining room form one open area with a sliding glass door to the rear for patio access—or choose the fireplace option for this area. The L-shaped kitchen has an attached nook with another sliding glass door to the patio. A well-appointed master suite contains a walk-in closet and full bath. The bath may be reconfigured to include a spa tub and separate shower. A laundry room connects the main house to the two-car garage.

DESIGN BY
©Lucia Custom Home Designers, Inc.

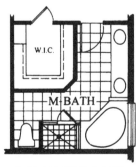

OPT. MASTER BATH

FIREPLACE OPTION

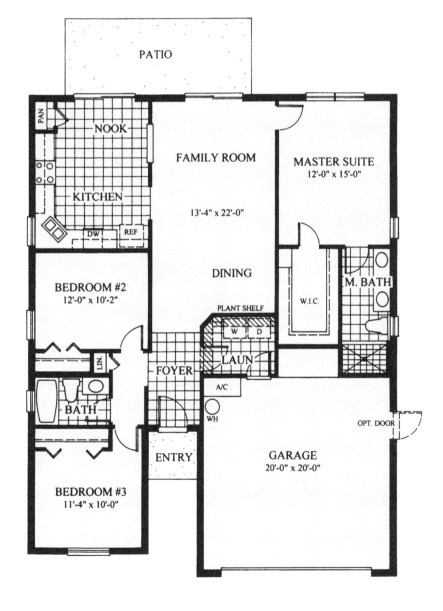

PATIO

NOOK

PAN

KITCHEN

DW   REF

FAMILY ROOM
13'-4" x 22'-0"

MASTER SUITE
12'-0" x 15'-0"

DINING

PLANT SHELF

W.I.C.

M. BATH

BEDROOM #2
12'-0" x 10'-2"

LIN.

W   D

LAUN

FOYER

A/C

BATH

WH

ENTRY

OPT. DOOR

GARAGE
20'-0" x 20'-0"

BEDROOM #3
11'-4" x 10'-0"

DESIGN HPU040050

Square Footage: 1,392
Width: 42'-0" Depth: 54'-0"

With an unusually narrow footprint, this one-story home will fit on most slender lots and still provide a great floor plan. The entry is graced with a handy coat closet and leads back to the spacious great room (note the ten-foot ceiling here) and to the right to two family bedrooms and a full bath. Stairs to the basement level are found just beyond the entry hall. The breakfast room and kitchen dominate the left side of the plan. Separating them is a snack-bar counter for quick meals. Pampered amenities in the secluded master bedroom include a walk-in closet, windowed corner whirlpool tub, dual sinks and separate shower. A service entrance through the kitchen to the garage leads to a convenient laundry area and broom closet.

DESIGN BY
©Design Basics, Inc.

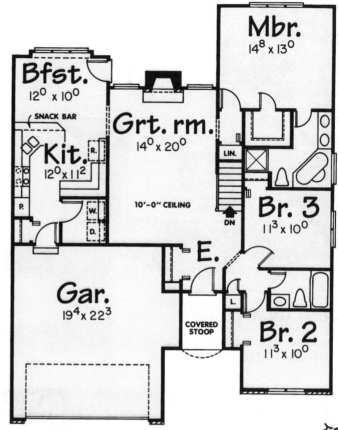

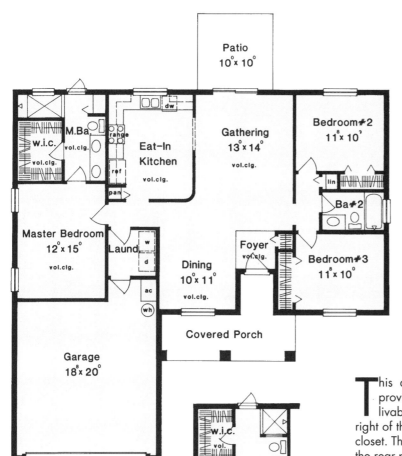

Patio
10⁰ x 10⁰

M.Ba.
w.i.c.
vol.clg.
vol.clg.

Eat-In Kitchen
vol.clg.

range
ref
pan
dw

Gathering
13⁰ x 14⁰
vol.clg.

Bedroom#2
11⁸ x 10³

lin

Ba#2

Master Bedroom
12⁰ x 15⁰
vol.clg.

Laund.
w
d
ac
wh

Dining
10⁰ x 11⁰
vol.clg.

Foyer
vol.clg.

Bedroom#3
11⁸ x 10⁰

Covered Porch

Garage
18⁸ x 20⁰

w.i.c.
vol.

M.Ba.
vol.clg.

Master Bedroom
12⁰ x 14⁰
vol.clg.

Optional
Master Suite

DESIGN HPU040051

Square Footage: 1,390
Width: 50'-0" Depth: 48'-0"

This attractive bungalow with multi-pane windows provides three bedrooms and an awesome plan for livability. The two family bedrooms reside to the far right of the plan and share a full hall bath and hall linen closet. The gathering room features sliding glass doors to the rear patio, and easily accesses the eat-in kitchen and dining area. On the far left of the plan is the laundry room and the master suite. The master suite features two options for a private bath; each option includes dual vanities, a walk-in closet and separate shower.

DESIGN BY
©Lucia Custom Home Designers, Inc.

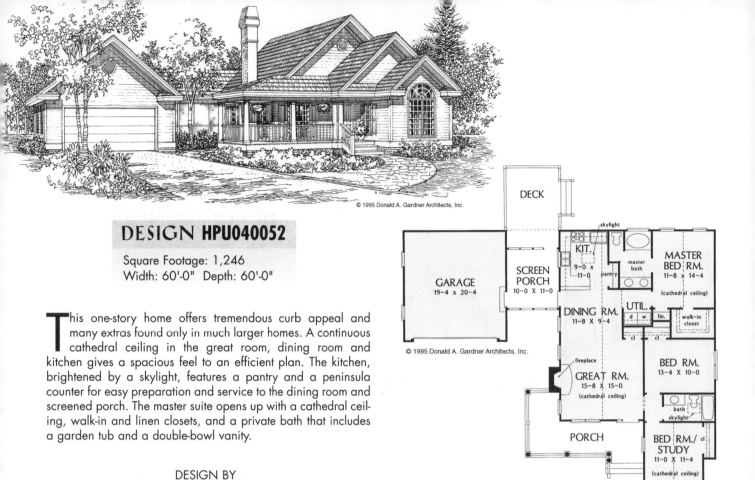

© 1995 Donald A. Gardner Architects, Inc.

DESIGN HPU040052

Square Footage: 1,246
Width: 60'-0" Depth: 60'-0"

This one-story home offers tremendous curb appeal and many extras found only in much larger homes. A continuous cathedral ceiling in the great room, dining room and kitchen gives a spacious feel to an efficient plan. The kitchen, brightened by a skylight, features a pantry and a peninsula counter for easy preparation and service to the dining room and screened porch. The master suite opens up with a cathedral ceiling, walk-in and linen closets, and a private bath that includes a garden tub and a double-bowl vanity.

DESIGN BY
Donald A. Gardner Architects, Inc.

DECK

SCREEN PORCH
10-0 X 11-0

GARAGE
19-4 x 20-4

skylight

KIT.
9-0 x
11-0

master bath

pantry

MASTER BED RM.
11-8 x 14-4
(cathedral ceiling)

DINING RM.
11-8 X 9-4

UTIL.
d w lin.

walk-in closet

fireplace

GREAT RM.
15-8 X 15-0
(cathedral ceiling)

BED RM.
13-4 X 10-0

bath
skylight

PORCH

BED RM./
STUDY
11-0 X 11-4
(cathedral ceiling)

© 1995 Donald A. Gardner Architects, Inc.

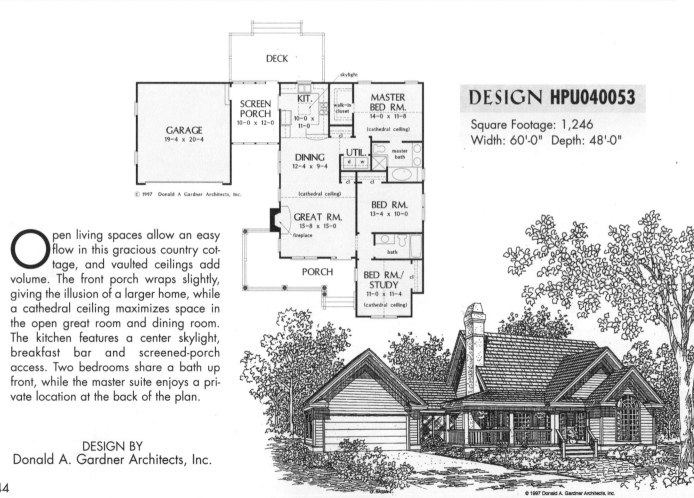

DECK

skylight

SCREEN PORCH
10-0 x 12-0

KIT.
10-0 x
11-0

walk-in closet

MASTER BED RM.
14-0 x 11-8
(cathedral ceiling)

GARAGE
19-4 x 20-4

DINING
12-4 x 9-4

UTIL.
d w

master bath

(cathedral ceiling)

BED RM.
13-4 X 10-0

GREAT RM.
15-8 x 15-0
fireplace

bath

PORCH

BED RM./
STUDY
11-0 x 11-4
(cathedral ceiling)

© 1997 Donald A Gardner Architects, Inc.

DESIGN HPU040053

Square Footage: 1,246
Width: 60'-0" Depth: 48'-0"

Open living spaces allow an easy flow in this gracious country cottage, and vaulted ceilings add volume. The front porch wraps slightly, giving the illusion of a larger home, while a cathedral ceiling maximizes space in the open great room and dining room. The kitchen features a center skylight, breakfast bar and screened-porch access. Two bedrooms share a bath up front, while the master suite enjoys a private location at the back of the plan.

DESIGN BY
Donald A. Gardner Architects, Inc.

© 1997 Donald A. Gardner Architects, Inc.

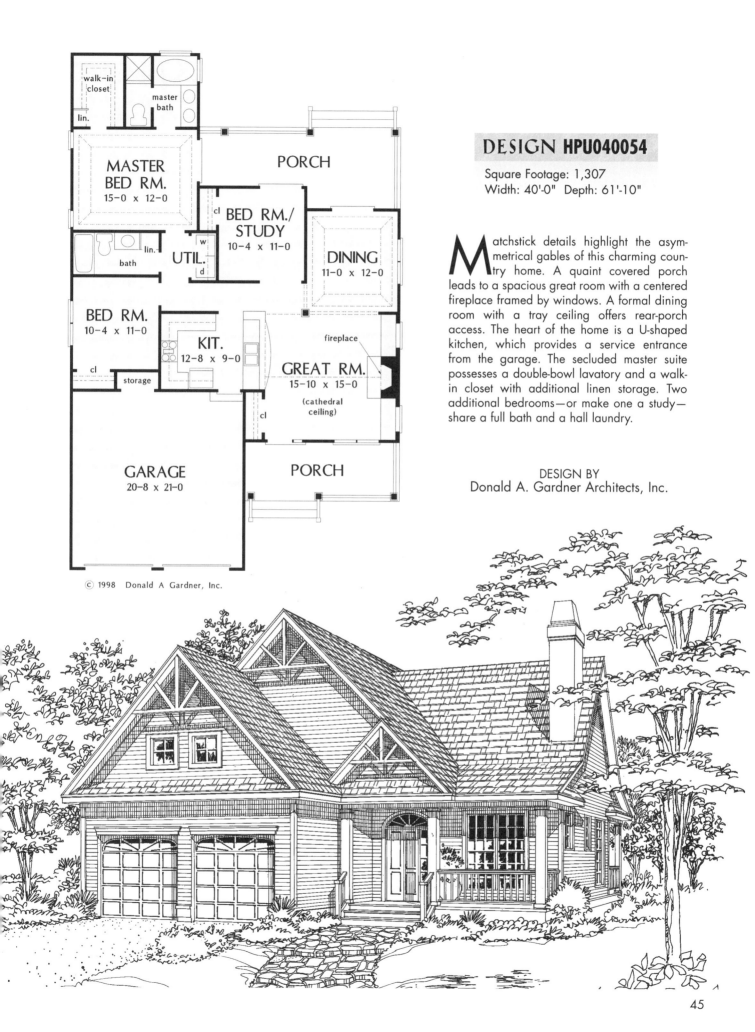

walk-in
closet

lin.

master
bath

MASTER
BED RM.
15-0 x 12-0

PORCH

cl

BED RM./
STUDY
10-4 x 11-0

UTIL.

w

d

DINING
11-0 x 12-0

bath

lin.

BED RM.
10-4 x 11-0

cl

KIT.
12-8 x 9-0

fireplace

storage

GREAT RM.
15-10 x 15-0

(cathedral
ceiling)

cl

GARAGE
20-8 x 21-0

PORCH

© 1998   Donald A Gardner, Inc.

DESIGN HPU040054

Square Footage: 1,307
Width: 40'-0" Depth: 61'-10"

Matchstick details highlight the asymmetrical gables of this charming country home. A quaint covered porch leads to a spacious great room with a centered fireplace framed by windows. A formal dining room with a tray ceiling offers rear-porch access. The heart of the home is a U-shaped kitchen, which provides a service entrance from the garage. The secluded master suite possesses a double-bowl lavatory and a walk-in closet with additional linen storage. Two additional bedrooms—or make one a study—share a full bath and a hall laundry.

DESIGN BY
Donald A. Gardner Architects, Inc.

45

© 1996 Donald A. Gardner Architects, Inc.

B. NATHAN

Square Footage: 1,306
Width: 43'-0" Depth: 49'-0"

arched window above

MASTER
BED RM.
14-0 x 12-0
(cathedral ceiling)

master
bath

skylight

walk-in
closet

plant shelf

BED RM.
11-0 x 10-0

walk-in
closet

lin.

KIT.
9-0 x 10-8

BED RM.
11-0 x 10-0

cl

cl

lin.

bath

d   w

GREAT RM.
14-0 x 16-0

fireplace

7' wall

DINING
11-4 x 12-0
(cathedral ceiling)

GARAGE
14-8 x 20-0

PORCH

© 1996 Donald A. Gardner Architects, Inc.

A central kitchen acts as the focal point for this country ranch home. It includes a snack bar and is conveniently close to both the living and the sleeping areas. The great room and dining area are combined, offering a fireplace, a cathedral ceiling and access to the front porch. Notice that the washer and dryer are handy to the kitchen as well as the family bedrooms and the shared full bath. The master bedroom and bath include a cathedral ceiling, a walk-in closet and a skylit whirlpool tub.

DESIGN BY
Donald A. Gardner Architects, Inc.

A spacious cathedral ceiling expands the open great room, dining room and kitchen. The versatile bedroom/study features a cathedral ceiling and shares a full skylit bath with another bedroom. The master bedroom is highlighted by a cathedral ceiling for extra volume and light. The private bath opens up with a skylight and includes a double-bowl vanity, garden tub and separately located toilet. A walk-in closet adjacent to the bedroom completes the suite.

DESIGN BY
Donald A. Gardner Architects, Inc.

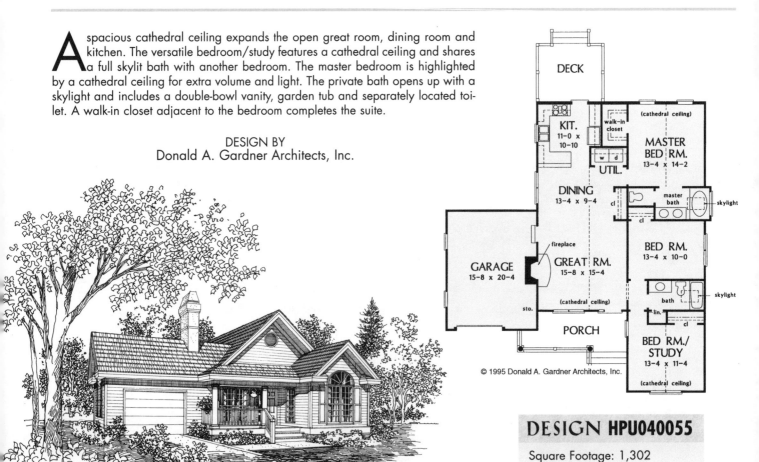

DECK

KIT.
11-0 x
10-10

walk-in
closet

(cathedral ceiling)

MASTER
BED RM.
13-4 x 14-2

w d

UTIL.

master
bath

skylight

DINING
13-4 x 9-4

cl

GARAGE
15-8 x 20-4

fireplace

GREAT RM.
15-8 x 15-4

BED RM.
13-4 x 10-0

(cathedral ceiling)

bath

skylight

sto.

PORCH

lin.

cl

BED RM./
STUDY
13-4 x 11-4

(cathedral ceiling)

© 1995 Donald A. Gardner Architects, Inc.

B NATHAN · © 1995 Donald A. Gardner Architects, Inc.

Square Footage: 1,302
Width: 47'-0" Depth: 50'-4"

© 1992 Donald A. Gardner Architects, Inc.

B. NATHAN

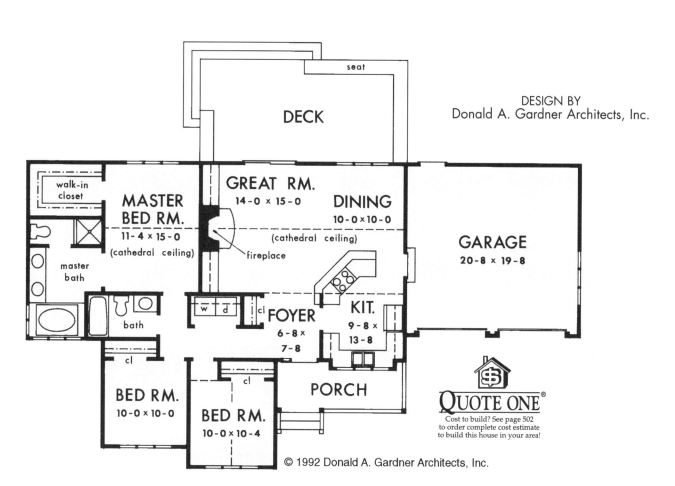

DESIGN BY
Donald A. Gardner Architects, Inc.

DECK

seat

GREAT RM.
14-0 × 15-0

DINING
10-0 × 10-0

(cathedral ceiling)

fireplace

GARAGE
20-8 × 19-8

walk-in closet

MASTER
BED RM.
11-4 × 15-0
(cathedral ceiling)

master bath

bath

w d   cl

FOYER
6-8 ×
7-8

KIT.
9-8 ×
13-8

cl

cl

BED RM.
10-0 × 10-0

BED RM.
10-0 × 10-4

PORCH

Quote One®
Cost to build? See page 502
to order complete cost estimate
to build this house in your area!

© 1992 Donald A. Gardner Architects, Inc.

DESIGN HPU040057

Square Footage: 1,287
Width: 66'-4" Depth: 48'-0"

This economical plan makes an impressive visual statement with its comfortable and well-proportioned appearance. The entrance foyer leads to all areas of the house. The great room, dining area and kitchen are all open to one another, allowing visual interaction. The great room and dining area share a dramatic cathedral ceiling and feature a grand fireplace flanked by bookshelves and cabinets. The owners suite has a cathedral ceiling, walk-in closet and bath with double-bowl vanity, whirlpool tub and shower. Two family bedrooms and a full hall bath complete this cozy home.

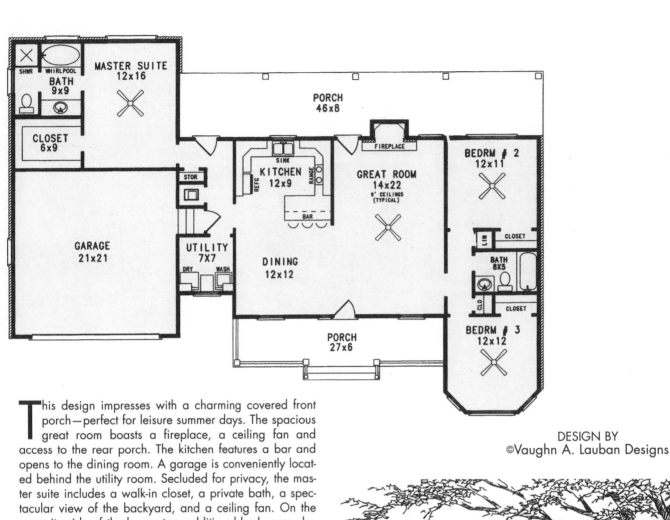

This design impresses with a charming covered front porch—perfect for leisure summer days. The spacious great room boasts a fireplace, a ceiling fan and access to the rear porch. The kitchen features a bar and opens to the dining room. A garage is conveniently located behind the utility room. Secluded for privacy, the master suite includes a walk-in closet, a private bath, a spectacular view of the backyard, and a ceiling fan. On the opposite side of the home, two additional bedrooms also feature ceiling fans and share a full hall bath.

DESIGN BY
©Vaughn A. Lauban Designs

DESIGN HPU040058

Square Footage: 1,455
Width: 67'-0" Depth: 46'-0"

DESIGN HPU040059

Square Footage: 1,372
Width: 38'-0" Depth: 65'-0"

Petite and efficiently impressive, this home is perfect for any average-sized family. A covered front porch welcomes visitors into the foyer. The living room is cooled by a ceiling fan in the summer and warmed by a corner fireplace in the winter. The kitchen, which features a utility room, is conveniently located between the garage and the dining room. A porch located off the dining area is perfect for outdoor grilling. The master suite is also cooled by a ceiling fan, and features a private bath and a walk-in closet with shelves. Two additional bedrooms share a full hall bath between them.

DESIGN BY
©Vaughn A. Lauban Designs

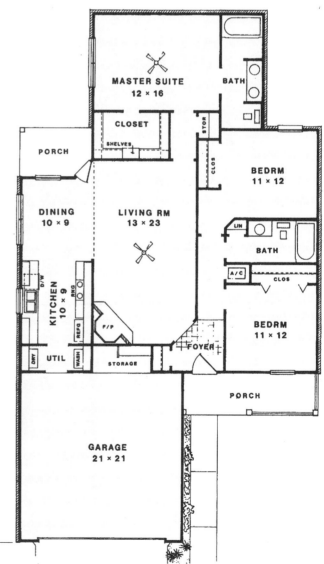

DESIGN HPU040060

Square Footage: 1,345
Width: 56'-6"
Depth: 62'-2"

A dormer above the great room and a round-top window add special features to this cozy traditional plan. The great room also contains a fireplace and a sloped ceiling. Elegant round columns define the dining and kitchen areas while creating an openness with the great room. Ceilings in the dining room, kitchen and great room all slope up to a ridge above the columns. A bedroom adjacent to the foyer can double as a study. The master bedroom has a fine bath which includes a double bowl vanity, shower and whirlpool tub. The garage is connected to the house with a breezeway for flexibility. The plan is available with a crawlspace foundation.

DESIGN BY
Donald A. Gardner Architects, Inc.

©1992 Donald A. Gardner Architects, Inc.

©1992 Donald A. Gardner Architects, Inc.

50

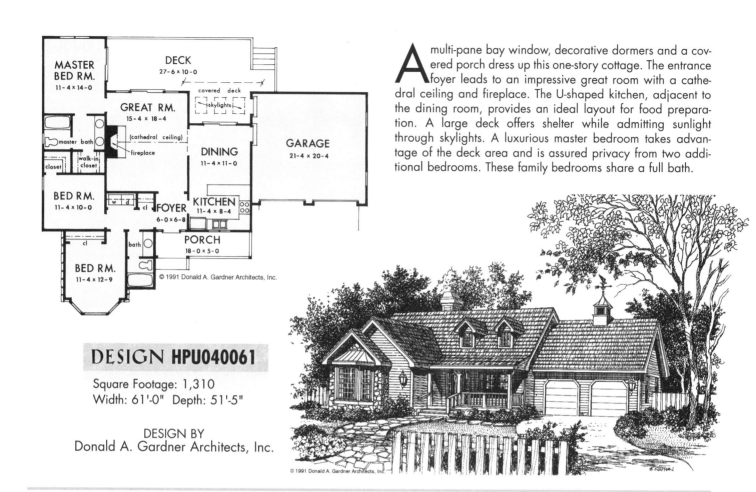

A multi-pane bay window, decorative dormers and a covered porch dress up this one-story cottage. The entrance foyer leads to an impressive great room with a cathedral ceiling and fireplace. The U-shaped kitchen, adjacent to the dining room, provides an ideal layout for food preparation. A large deck offers shelter while admitting sunlight through skylights. A luxurious master bedroom takes advantage of the deck area and is assured privacy from two additional bedrooms. These family bedrooms share a full bath.

DESIGN HPU040061

Square Footage: 1,310
Width: 61'-0" Depth: 51'-5"

DESIGN BY
Donald A. Gardner Architects, Inc.

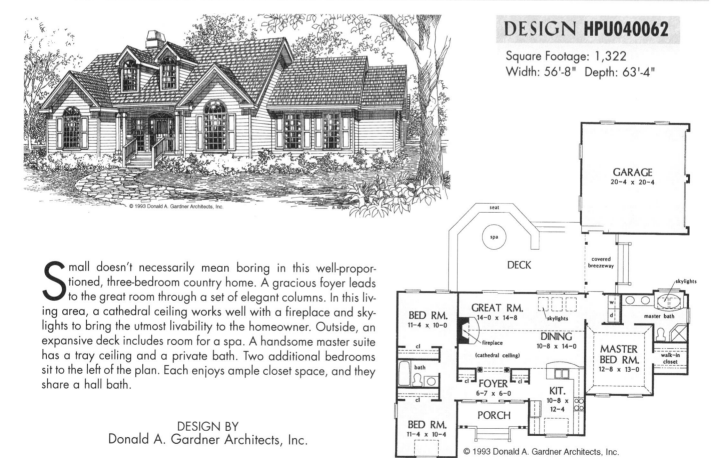

DESIGN HPU040062

Square Footage: 1,322
Width: 56'-8" Depth: 63'-4"

Small doesn't necessarily mean boring in this well-proportioned, three-bedroom country home. A gracious foyer leads to the great room through a set of elegant columns. In this living area, a cathedral ceiling works well with a fireplace and skylights to bring the utmost livability to the homeowner. Outside, an expansive deck includes room for a spa. A handsome master suite has a tray ceiling and a private bath. Two additional bedrooms sit to the left of the plan. Each enjoys ample closet space, and they share a hall bath.

DESIGN BY
Donald A. Gardner Architects, Inc.

DESIGN **HPU040063**

Square Footage: 1,142
Width: 48'-10" Depth: 35'-8"

This one-story traditional home caters to family living. The efficient, U-shaped kitchen opens to an adjacent bayed breakfast area. The family room features a corner fireplace and access to the rear yard. Two family bedrooms share a full bath, while the master bedroom offers a private bath with a walk-in closet. Please specify slab or crawlspace foundation when ordering.

DESIGN BY
©Larry E. Belk Designs

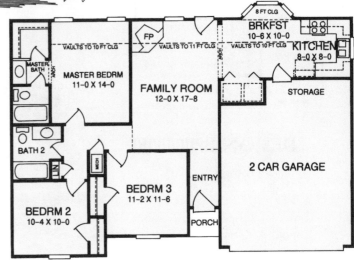

Well suited for the countryside, this rustic design features a multitude of amenities within. The covered front porch welcomes visitors inside to the great room, which offers a fireplace and ceiling fan. The master suite also features a ceiling fan and, in addition, a walk-in closet and private bath. Two other family bedrooms are located on the opposite side of the home.

DESIGN **HPU040064**

Square Footage: 1,458
Width: 67'-0" Depth: 40'-0"

DESIGN BY
©Vaughn A. Lauban Designs

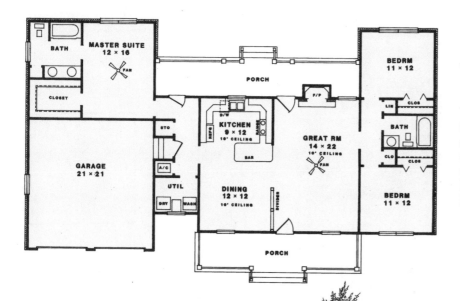

DESIGN HPU040065

Square Footage: 1,267
Width: 52'-0" Depth: 49'-0"

This design is rich in traditional American appeal. Enter from a charming covered porch. A vaulted ceiling, a fireplace and a ceiling fan enhance the great room. Straight ahead, the dining room accesses the rear patio. The kitchen features a snack bar and a side utility room with a door to the master bath. The master suite is secluded for privacy and includes a private bath, a walk-in closet and a wide view to the backyard. On the other side of the home, two additional bedrooms share a hall bath. A two-car garage with storage space completes the plan.

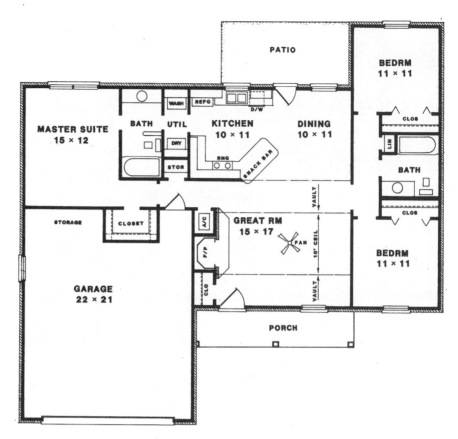

DESIGN BY
©Vaughn A. Lauban Designs

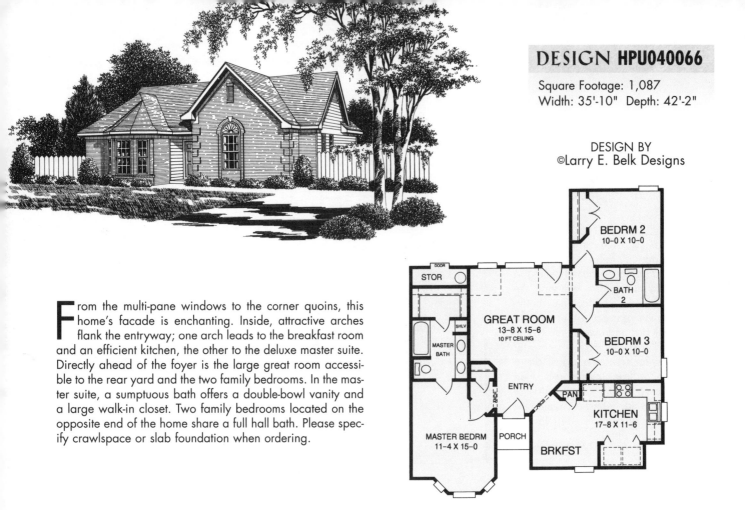

DESIGN HPU040066

Square Footage: 1,087
Width: 35'-10" Depth: 42'-2"

DESIGN BY
©Larry E. Belk Designs

From the multi-pane windows to the corner quoins, this home's facade is enchanting. Inside, attractive arches flank the entryway; one arch leads to the breakfast room and an efficient kitchen, the other to the deluxe master suite. Directly ahead of the foyer is the large great room accessible to the rear yard and the two family bedrooms. In the master suite, a sumptuous bath offers a double-bowl vanity and a large walk-in closet. Two family bedrooms located on the opposite end of the home share a full hall bath. Please specify crawlspace or slab foundation when ordering.

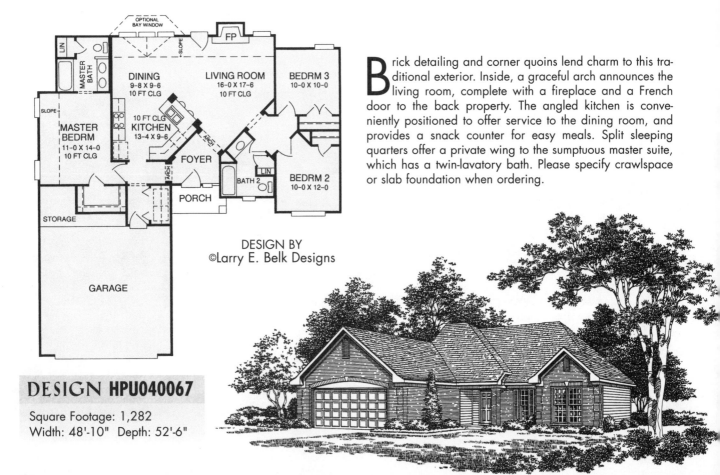

Brick detailing and corner quoins lend charm to this traditional exterior. Inside, a graceful arch announces the living room, complete with a fireplace and a French door to the back property. The angled kitchen is conveniently positioned to offer service to the dining room, and provides a snack counter for easy meals. Split sleeping quarters offer a private wing to the sumptuous master suite, which has a twin-lavatory bath. Please specify crawlspace or slab foundation when ordering.

DESIGN BY
©Larry E. Belk Designs

DESIGN HPU040067

Square Footage: 1,282
Width: 48'-10" Depth: 52'-6"

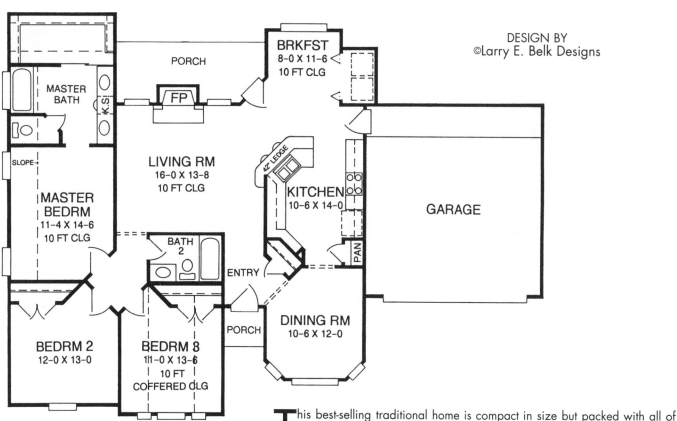

DESIGN BY
©Larry E. Belk Designs

BRKFST
8-0 X 11-6
10 FT CLG

PORCH

FP

MASTER
BATH

W.S.

LIVING RM
16-0 X 13-8
10 FT CLG

42" LEDGE

KITCHEN
10-6 X 14-0

GARAGE

SLOPE

MASTER
BEDRM
11-4 X 14-6
10 FT CLG

BATH
2

PAN

ENTRY

BEDRM 2
12-0 X 13-0

BEDRM 3
11-0 X 13-6
10 FT
COFFERED CLG

PORCH

DINING RM
10-6 X 12-0

DESIGN HPU040068

Square Footage: 1,500
Width: 59'-10"   Depth: 44'-4"

This best-selling traditional home is compact in size but packed with all of the amenities you'd expect in a larger home. The foyer opens to a formal dining room with a classic bay window. The adjacent kitchen opens to a breakfast nook and shares an angled eating bar with the living room, which offers a cozy fireplace flanked by picture windows. The master suite features His and Hers vanities, a whirlpool tub/shower combination and a walk-in closet. Ten-foot ceilings in the major living areas as well as in two of the bedrooms contribute an aura of spaciousness to this plan. Please specify crawlspace or slab foundation when ordering.

55

DESIGN HPU040070

Square Footage: 1,405
Width: 40'-0" Depth: 60'-8"

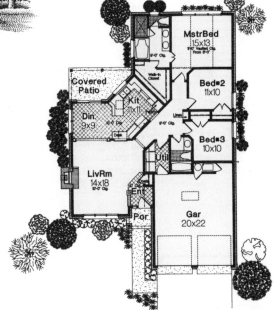

This traditional brick home flaunts a touch of European flavor with its corner quoins. It also presents great curb appeal from the wide muntin window to the sidelight and transom in the entry. The spacious living room includes a warming fireplace. The dining room and U-shaped kitchen are connected by the snack bar and easily access a covered patio. Two family bedrooms reside along the extended hallway. At the end of the hall is the master bedroom, which presents a deluxe private bath and a walk-in closet. The utility room acts as a passage to the two-car garage.

DESIGN BY
©Fillmore Design Group

DESIGN HPU040069

First Floor: 748 square feet
Second Floor: 705 square feet
Total: 1,453 square feet
Width: 49'-8" Depth: 28'-4"

DESIGN BY
©Studer Residential Designs, Inc.

This two-story brick features siding accents and gabled rooflines. The front porch is perfect for welcoming guests or spending an evening on a porch swing. Inside, a long great room is a wonderful space for multiple uses. With access to the rear yard, the great room provides outdoor interaction. A breakfast bay accompanies the roomy kitchen, which features plenty of work space. Upstairs, two family bedrooms share a hall bath. The master bedroom features a walk-in closet and a private bath. This home is designed with a basement foundation.

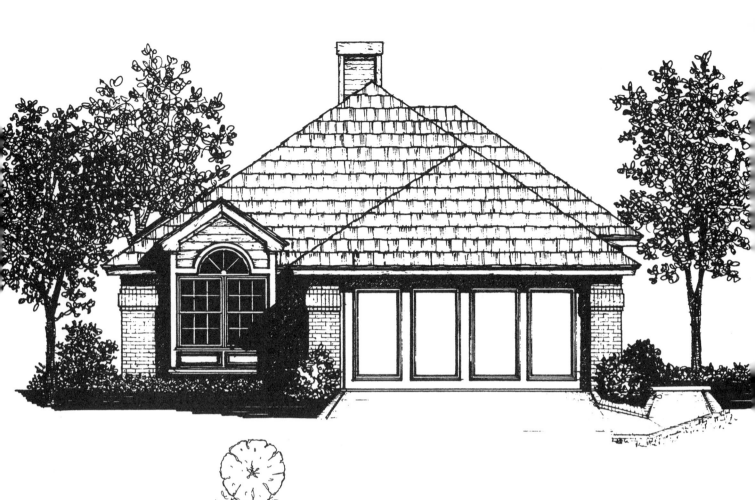

DESIGN HPU040071

Square Footage: 1,285
Width: 32'-10"   Depth: 52'-10"

This traditional-style home with decorative brick begins with a ten-foot entry ceiling and a closet. The living room also features a ten-foot ceiling as well as a warming fireplace. The U-shaped kitchen and dinette area highlights a sloping ceiling. The master bedroom opens to a patio and includes a sloping ceiling, a bath with a skylight and a walk-in closet. A second bedroom also includes a sloping ceiling.

DESIGN BY
©Fillmore Design Group

Patio

Sloping Clg.

MstrBed
14x13

Sloping Clg.

Kit/Din
9x11   9x11

LivRm
16x16

10'Clg.

Skylite

Util

Ent
10'Clg.

Por

Bed#2
12x13

Sloping Clg.

Gar
20x20

DESIGN HPU040072

Square Footage: 1,317
Width: 45'-0" Depth: 52'-4"

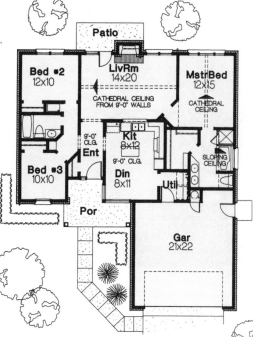

This unique home has many attractive features, including a sidelight and sunburst. The living room offers a cathedral ceiling with a wood-burning fireplace. The kitchen boasts an island counter and a dining area, which then leads to the utility room. The master suite enjoys a cathedral ceiling, garden tub, walk-in closet and separate shower. Two bedrooms share a bath on the opposite side of the house.

DESIGN BY
©Fillmore Design Group

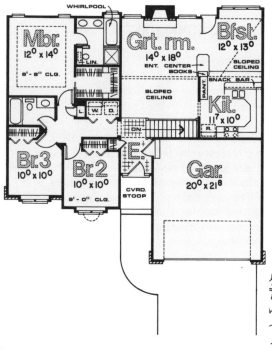

For great livability, this one-story home places its living areas to the back of the plan. The foyer leads directly to the great room and its focal-point fireplace. Extras include a built-in entertainment center and bookcase in the great room and a snack bar separating the sunny breakfast room from the U-shaped kitchen. The master bedroom includes a large walk-in closet and a pampering bath with a whirlpool tub, separate shower and dual-bowl vanity. Two front-facing family bedrooms share a full hall bath.

DESIGN BY
©Design Basics, Inc.

DESIGN HPU040073

Square Footage: 1,341
Width: 47'-4" Depth: 45'-8"

DESIGN HPU040074

Square Footage: 1,451
Width: 50'-0" Depth: 50'-0"

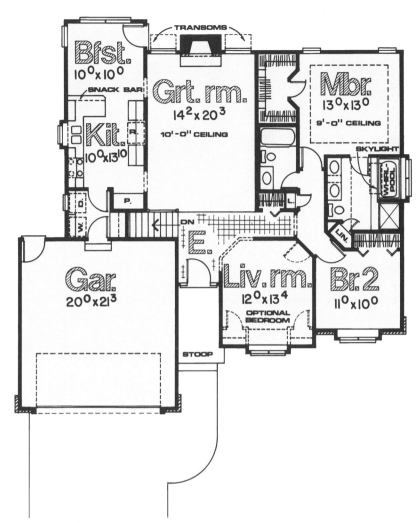

A bright volume entry with a transom opens to the great room with a fireplace and tall windows. The kitchen features a generous pantry and a snack bar adjoining the breakfast room. The spacious master bedroom contains a large walk-in closet, a boxed ceiling and a delightful master bath filled with amenities such as dual vanities and a whirlpool tub. The private second bedroom features a boxed window. Note how the angles used throughout the home enhance architectural interest. A versatile front room with an optional transom and second entrance from the foyer may be used as a living room or third bedroom.

DESIGN BY
©Design Basics, Inc.

DESIGN HPU040075

Square Footage: 1,310
Width: 49'-10" Depth: 40'-6"

DESIGN BY
©Larry E. Belk Designs

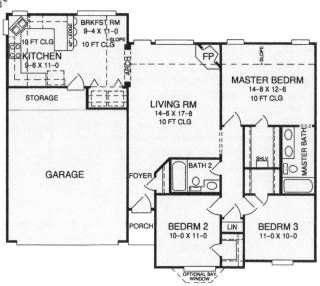

This charming plan is perfect for families just starting out or for the empty-nester looking to pare down. Every room is designed for maximum livability, from the living room with a corner fireplace to the efficient kitchen with a snack bar and hidden washer and dryer. The master bedroom is fashioned with a dual-vanity bath and a walk-in closet equipped with shelves. Two additional bedrooms each have a walk-in closet and share a hall bath. Please specify crawlspace or slab foundation when ordering.

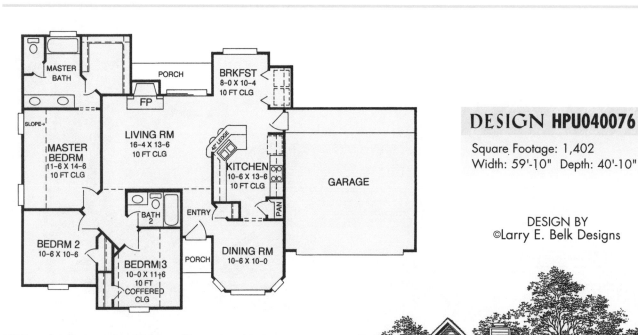

DESIGN HPU040076

Square Footage: 1,402
Width: 59'-10" Depth: 40'-10"

DESIGN BY
©Larry E. Belk Designs

Fine detailing and multiple rooflines give this home plenty of curb appeal. A large living room with a fireplace is the focal point for this lovely home. The dining room and sunny breakfast room provide complementary eating areas. The master bedroom features a large walk-in closet and a bath with a combination whirlpool tub and shower. Two additional bedrooms and a full hall bath complete this livable plan. Please specify crawlspace or slab foundation when ordering.

DESIGN HPU040077

Square Footage: 1,453
Width: 48'-8" Depth: 44'-0"

With two gables, a hipped roof and a covered front porch, this petite three-bedroom home is sure to please. A spacious great room features a warming fireplace flanked by transom windows. In the kitchen, an island counter is available for added space to prepare meals. A large breakfast area sits adjacent to this room. Two secondary bedrooms share a full bath as well as easy access to the laundry room. The master bedroom offers a walk-in closet and a private bath. Note the option for a second closet in this bedroom.

DESIGN BY
©Design Basics, Inc.

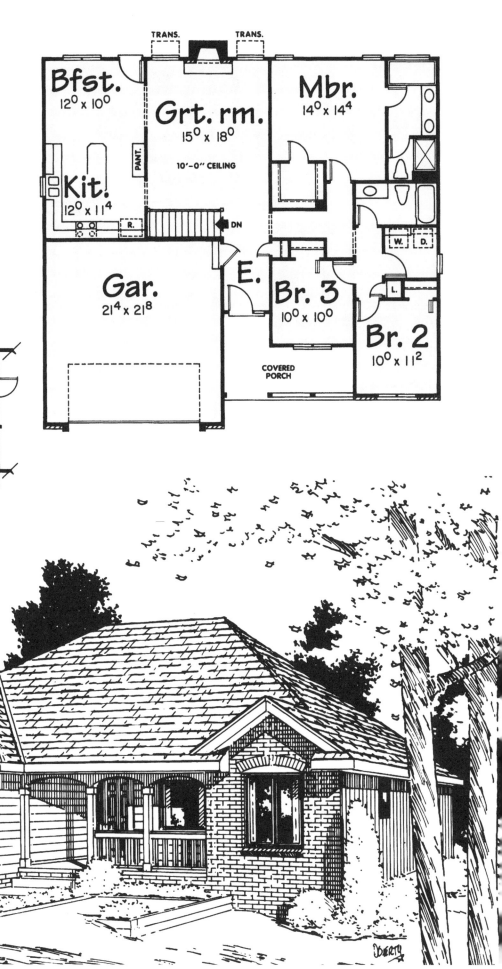

Optional Master Bedroom

Mbr.
14⁰ x 12⁰

Bfst.
12⁰ x 10⁰

Grt. rm.
15⁰ x 18⁰

10'-0" CEILING

Mbr.
14⁰ x 14⁴

TRANS.   TRANS.

PANT.

Kit.
12⁰ x 11⁴

R.   DN

Gar.
21⁴ x 21⁸

E.

Br. 3
10⁰ x 10⁰

W.   D.

L.

Br. 2
10⁰ x 11²

COVERED PORCH

DESIGN HPU040078

Square Footage: 1,434
Width: 70'-0" Depth: 44'-0"

With the exterior facade of a large elegant home, this super-efficient design creates not only an exterior that looks much larger than it is, but the room sizes are impressive too! The isolated and spacious master suite provides a grand bath and a walk-in closet. The secondary bedrooms are located at the far right of the plan; each features walk-in closets, and they share a full hall bath. The living room opens to porches via French doors to the front and back. The kitchen is the heart of the home and includes a pantry. Please specify crawlspace or slab foundation when ordering.

DESIGN BY
©Breland & Farmer Designers, Inc.

WIC

MASTER SUITE
18' x 12'

LINEN

BATH

SHVS

DRY WASH

STORAGE

WH

PORCH
13' x 6'

WIC

BEDROOM
12' x 11'

HALL

DINETTE
9' x 9'

DISP. STAIRS

DW

KITCHEN
12' x 10'

RANGE

HALL

BATH

SINK

LIVING ROOM
17' x 16'

GARAGE
21' x 21'

REF.

WIC

DINING ROOM
12' x 12'

PORCH
16' x 6'

BEDROOM
12' x 11'

SPECIAL DETAILS

Smart designs that shine with brilliant benefits

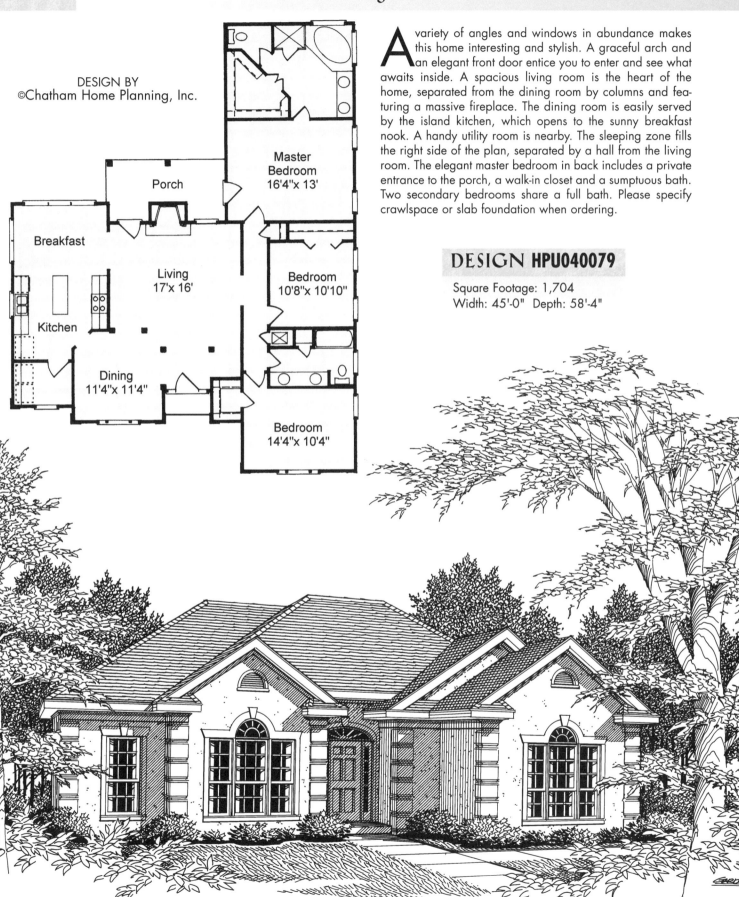

DESIGN BY
©Chatham Home Planning, Inc.

Master Bedroom
16'4"x 13'

Porch

Breakfast

Living
17'x 16'

Kitchen

Bedroom
10'8"x 10'10"

Dining
11'4"x 11'4"

Bedroom
14'4"x 10'4"

A variety of angles and windows in abundance makes this home interesting and stylish. A graceful arch and an elegant front door entice you to enter and see what awaits inside. A spacious living room is the heart of the home, separated from the dining room by columns and featuring a massive fireplace. The dining room is easily served by the island kitchen, which opens to the sunny breakfast nook. A handy utility room is nearby. The sleeping zone fills the right side of the plan, separated by a hall from the living room. The elegant master bedroom in back includes a private entrance to the porch, a walk-in closet and a sumptuous bath. Two secondary bedrooms share a full bath. Please specify crawlspace or slab foundation when ordering.

DESIGN HPU040079

Square Footage: 1,704
Width: 45'-0" Depth: 58'-4"

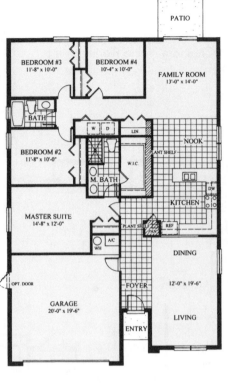

The unique exterior of this home presents a volume entry with a transom. The floor plan is designed in a symmetrical pattern, arranged around a center hall. The formal areas, the kitchen, the breakfast nook and the family room are aligned along the right side of the plan. A patio to the rear of the plan is accessed through a sliding glass door in the family room. Or, if you choose, install the fireplace instead. Three family bedrooms share a full hall bath, while the master suite enjoys its own private bath with a walk-in closet.

DESIGN HPU040080

Square Footage: 1,855
Width: 39'-4" Depth: 59'-4"

Optional
Master Bath

DESIGN BY
©Lucia Custom Home Designers, Inc.

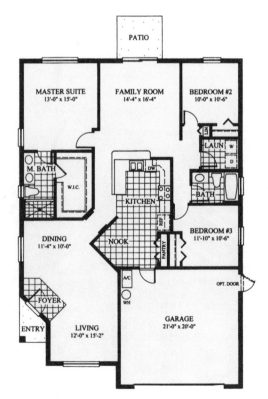

Though only just over 1,600 square feet, the choices you have with this design are astounding. The master bedroom suite includes optional sliding glass doors and a private bath configuration. At the heart of all these spaces is a U-shaped kitchen with an adjoining breakfast nook. A laundry room and a hall bath separate the two family bedrooms. A door to the side yard is optional in the garage.

DESIGN HPU040081

Square Footage: 1,666
Width: 39'-4" Depth: 56'-8"

DESIGN BY
©Lucia Custom Home Designers, Inc.

Optional
Master Bath

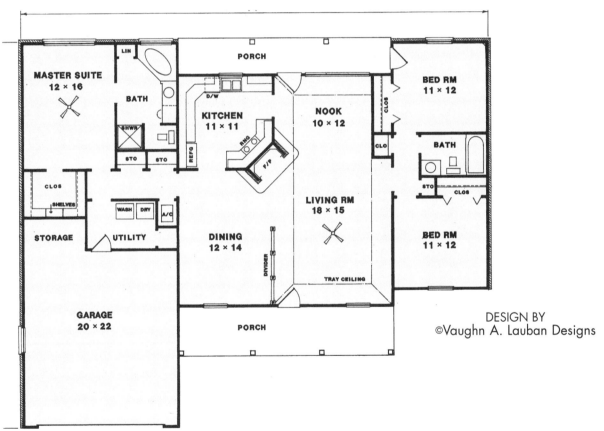

MASTER SUITE
12 × 16

LIN

BATH

SHWR

STO   STO

REFG

CLOS

SHELVES

STORAGE

WASH DRY   A/C

UTILITY

GARAGE
20 × 22

PORCH

KITCHEN
11 × 11

D/W

RNG

F/P

NOOK
10 × 12

CLOS

CLO

LIVING RM
18 × 15

DINING
12 × 14

DIVIDER

TRAY CEILING

PORCH

BED RM
11 × 12

BATH

CLOS

STO

BED RM
11 × 12

DESIGN BY
©Vaughn A. Lauban Designs

DESIGN HPU040082

Square Footage: 1,646
Width: 59'-0" Depth: 48'-0"

This design embraces French accents with a Southern feel. Corner quoins, a covered porch and a hipped roof define elegance. The open living room enjoys a tray ceiling and easy flow to the breakfast nook and kitchen. A fireplace is perfect for cozy evenings with guests. The dining room is just a few steps from the super-efficient kitchen. Two family bedrooms share a full bath and are split to the right. The master suite is secluded to the left and is pampered with a private bath and walk-in closet. A two-car garage completes this design.

DESIGN HPU040083

Square Footage: 1,920
Width: 38'-10" Depth: 74'-4"

The entry courtyard creates an impressive introduction to this lovely European-style home. Double doors lead to the foyer, which opens through decorative columns to the formal dining room. A view of the enchanting rear garden and fountain enhances the heart of the home and invites guests to linger. Casual living space includes a breakfast nook with a view of the rear courtyard, and a family room with a fireplace and access to a private porch. A secluded master bedroom offers a whirlpool tub.

DESIGN BY
©Andy McDonald Design Group

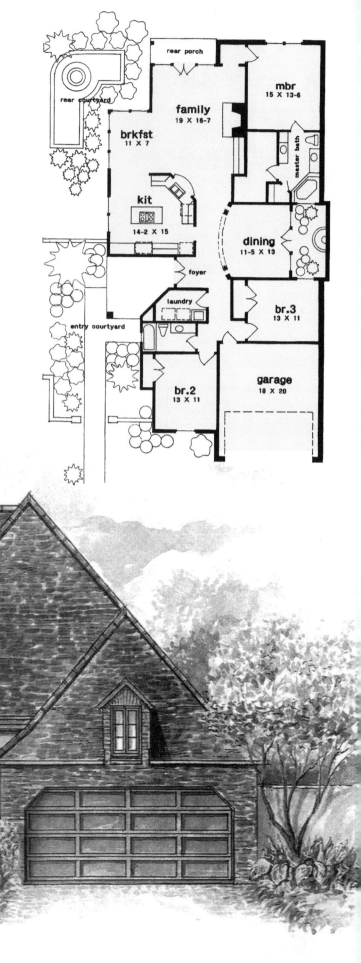

DESIGN HPU040084

Square Footage: 1,804
Width: 49'-10" Depth: 74'-9"

Extraordinary rooflines complement this brick-and-stucco home. Through the foyer, the family room enjoys a central position with a fireplace—the warm spot in the house. The family room provides rear views through double doors and windows. The dining area is conveniently located near the island kitchen and adjoining breakfast room, which is surrounded by natural light and accesses the rear covered porch. Two family bedrooms can be found to the front right of the plan and share a full bath. The master bedroom features a walk-in closet, compartmented toilet and accommodating bath. A two-car garage completes this design.

DESIGN BY
©Andy McDonald Design Group

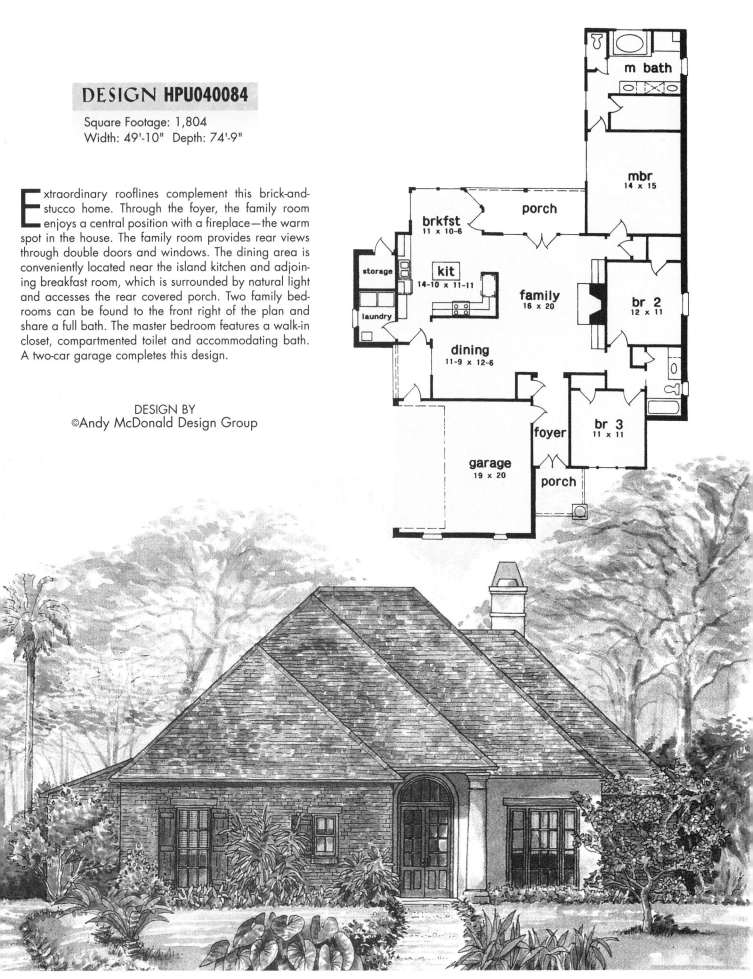

m bath

mbr
14 x 15

porch

brkfst
11 x 10-6

storage

kit
14-10 x 11-11

family
16 x 20

br 2
12 x 11

laundry

dining
11-9 x 12-6

br 3
11 x 11

foyer

garage
19 x 20

porch

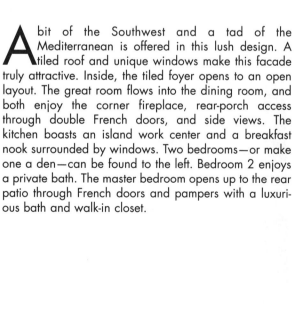

DESIGN HPU040085

Square Footage: 1,992
Width: 44'-0" Depth: 92'-0"

A bit of the Southwest and a tad of the Mediterranean is offered in this lush design. A tiled roof and unique windows make this facade truly attractive. Inside, the tiled foyer opens to an open layout. The great room flows into the dining room, and both enjoy the corner fireplace, rear-porch access through double French doors, and side views. The kitchen boasts an island work center and a breakfast nook surrounded by windows. Two bedrooms—or make one a den—can be found to the left. Bedroom 2 enjoys a private bath. The master bedroom opens up to the rear patio through French doors and pampers with a luxurious bath and walk-in closet.

DESIGN BY
©Lucia Custom Home Designers, Inc.

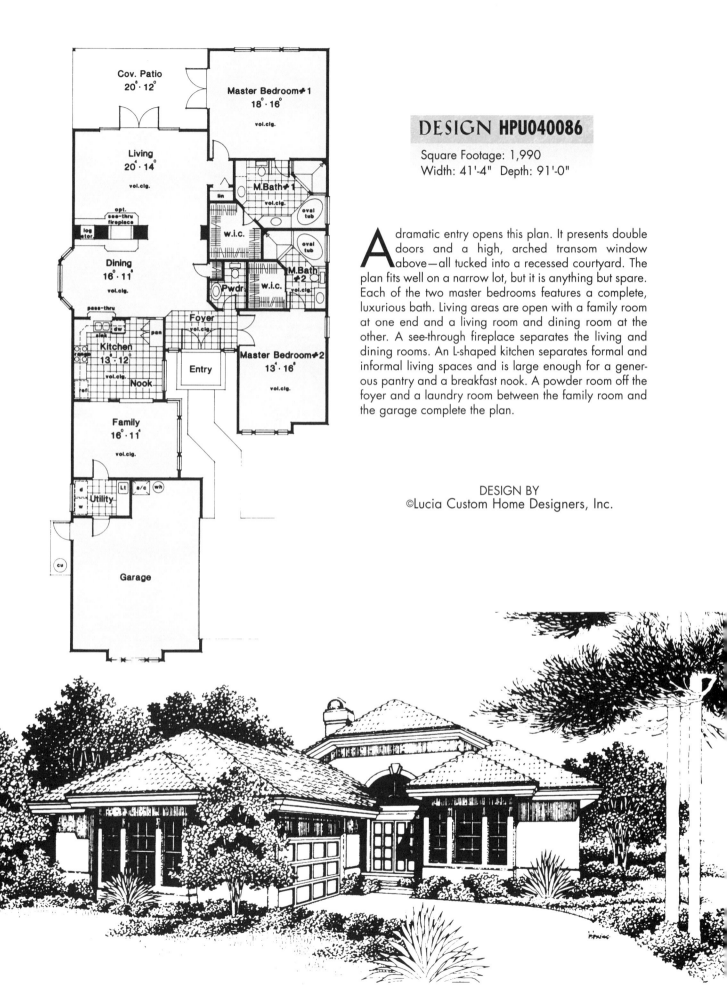

Cov. Patio
20⁸·12⁰

Master Bedroom≠1
18⁰·16⁰
vol.clg.

Living
20⁴·14⁰
vol.clg.

M.Bath≠1
vol.clg.

oval tub

oval tub

w.i.c.

opt. see-thru fireplace

log stor.

Dining
16⁰·11⁸
vol.clg.

M.Bath ≠2

Pwdr.

w.i.c.

w.i.c.

pass-thru

sink

dw

Foyer
vol.clg.

pan

Kitchen
13⁰·12⁰
vol.clg.

range

Entry

Master Bedroom≠2
13⁴·16⁰
vol.clg.

ref.

Nook

Family
16⁰·11⁴
vol.clg.

d

Lt

a/c

wh

Utility

w

cu

Garage

DESIGN HPU040086

Square Footage: 1,990
Width: 41'-4" Depth: 91'-0"

A dramatic entry opens this plan. It presents double doors and a high, arched transom window above—all tucked into a recessed courtyard. The plan fits well on a narrow lot, but it is anything but spare. Each of the two master bedrooms features a complete, luxurious bath. Living areas are open with a family room at one end and a living room and dining room at the other. A see-through fireplace separates the living and dining rooms. An L-shaped kitchen separates formal and informal living spaces and is large enough for a generous pantry and a breakfast nook. A powder room off the foyer and a laundry room between the family room and the garage complete the plan.

DESIGN BY
©Lucia Custom Home Designers, Inc.

DESIGN BY
©Chatham Home Planning, Inc.

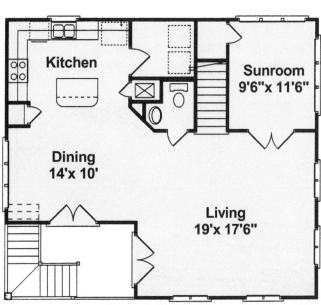

Kitchen

Sunroom
9'6"x 11'6"

Dining
14'x 10'

Living
19'x 17'6"

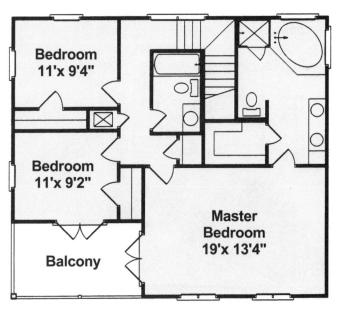

Bedroom
11'x 9'4"

Bedroom
11'x 9'2"

Balcony

Master
Bedroom
19'x 13'4"

DESIGN HPU040087

First Floor: 907 square feet
Second Floor: 872 square feet
Total: 1,779 square feet
Width: 34'-0" Depth: 30'-0"

Two stories and still up on a pier foundation! A covered front porch leads to two sets of French doors—one to the spacious living room and one to the dining area. An L-shaped kitchen features a work island, a nearby utility room and plenty of counter and cabinet space. A sun room finishes off this floor with class. Upstairs, the sleeping zone consists of two family bedrooms—one with access to a balcony—a full bath and a master bedroom. Here, the homeowner will surely be pleased with a walk-in closet, a corner tub and a separate shower, as well as balcony access.

DESIGN BY
©Chatham Home Planning, Inc.

Kitchen

Living
14'2"x 19'6"

Dining
11'4"x 12'

Porch

Bedroom
11'x 10'

Bedroom
10'6"x 10'6"

Study
9'x 7'3"

Master
Bedroom
13'x 14'

Balcony

With a pier foundation, this two-story home is perfect for an oceanfront lot. The main level consists of an open living area that flows into the dining area adjacent to the kitchen. Here, a walk-in pantry and plenty of counter and cabinet space will please the gourmet of the family. A full bath and a utility room complete this floor. Upstairs, the sleeping zone is complete with two family bedrooms sharing a linen closet and a full hall bath, as well as a deluxe master bedroom. Features here include a private balcony, a walk-in closet and a dual-vanity bath.

DESIGN HPU040088

First Floor: 912 square feet
Second Floor: 831 square feet
Total: 1,743 square feet
Width: 34'-0" Depth: 32'-0"

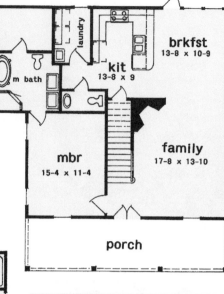

brkfst
13-8 x 10-9

laundry

kit
13-8 x 9

m bath

family
17-8 x 13-10

mbr
15-4 x 11-4

porch

This adorable abode could serve as a vacation cottage, guest house, starter home or in-law quarters. The side-gabled design allows for a front porch with a "down-South" feel. Despite the small size, this home is packed with all the necessities. The first-floor master bedroom has a large bathroom—with a clawfoot tub!—and a walk-in closet and is ideal for older guests or family members. An open, functional floor plan includes a powder room, a kitchen/breakfast nook area and a family room with a corner fireplace. Upstairs, two additional bedrooms share a bath. One could be used as a home office.

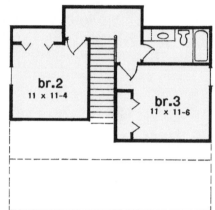

br.2
11 x 11-4

br.3
11 x 11-6

DESIGN HPU040090

First Floor: 1,050 square feet
Second Floor: 458 square feet
Total: 1,508 square feet
Width: 35'-6" Depth: 39'-9"

DESIGN BY
©Andy McDonald Design Group

Run up a flight of stairs to an attractive four-bedroom home! With a traditional flavor, this fine pier design is sure to please. The living room features a fireplace and easy access to the L-shaped kitchen. Here, a work island makes meal preparation a breeze. Two family bedrooms share a full bath and access to the laundry facilities. Upstairs, a third bedroom offers a private bath and two walk-in closets. The master suite is complete with a pampering bath, two walk-in closets and a large private balcony.

DESIGN BY
©Chatham Home Planning, Inc.

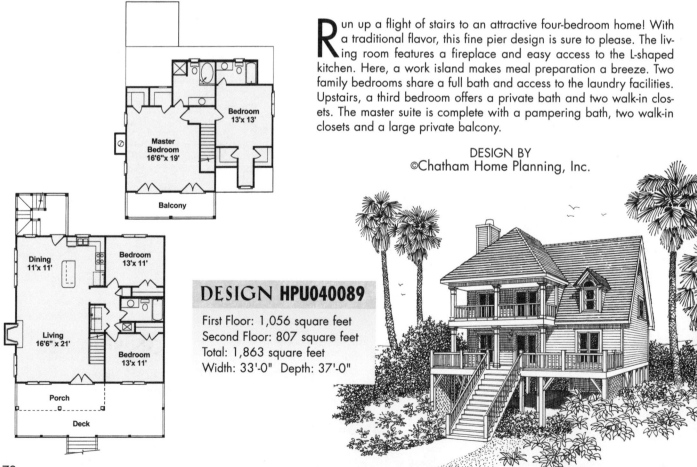

Bedroom
13'x 13'

Master
Bedroom
16'6"x 19'

Balcony

Dining
11'x 11'

Bedroom
13'x 11'

Living
16'6"x 21'

Bedroom
13'x 11'

Porch

Deck

DESIGN HPU040089

First Floor: 1,056 square feet
Second Floor: 807 square feet
Total: 1,863 square feet
Width: 33'-0" Depth: 37'-0"

DESIGN HPU040091

First Floor: 1,189 square feet
Second Floor: 575 square feet
Total: 1,764 square feet
Width: 46'-0"   Depth: 44'-6"

An abundance of porches and a deck encourage year-round indoor/outdoor relationships in this classic two-story home. The spacious great room, with its cozy fireplace, and the adjacent dining room both offer access to the screened porch/deck area through French doors. The private master suite accesses both front and rear porches and leads into a relaxing private bath complete with dual vanities and a walk-in closet. An additional family bedroom and a loft/bedroom are also available.

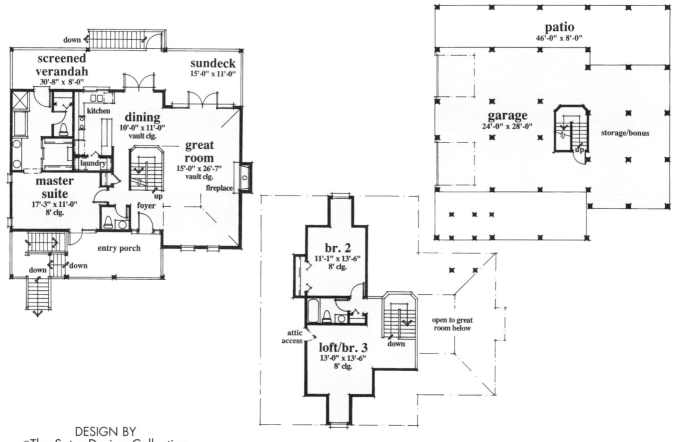

DESIGN HPU040092

First Floor: 1,007 square feet
Second Floor: 869 square feet
Total: 1,876 square feet
Width: 43'-8" Depth: 53'-6"

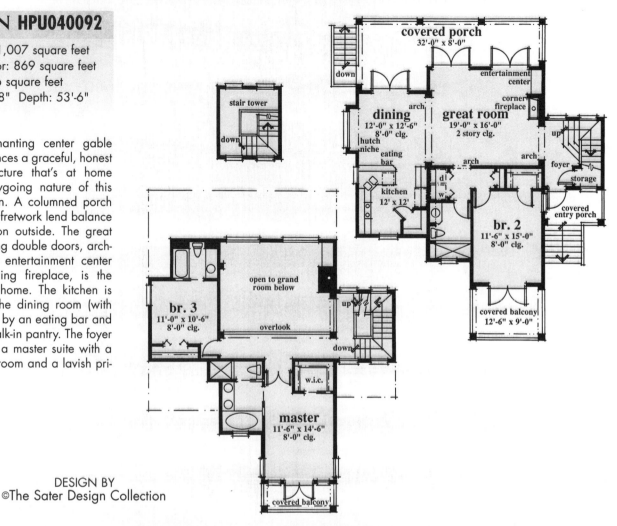

stair tower
down

covered porch
32'-0" x 8'-0"
down

entertainment center

dining
12'-0" x 12'-6"
8'-0" clg.
arch
hutch niche
eating bar

corner fireplace

great room
19'-0" x 16'-0"
2 story clg.

up

foyer

storage

kitchen
12' x 12'
d
w

arch

arch

arch

br. 2
11'-6" x 15'-0"
8'-0" clg.

covered entry porch

covered balcony
12'-6" x 9'-0"

br. 3
11'-0" x 10'-6"
8'-0" clg.

open to grand room below

overlook

up

down

w.i.c.

master
11'-6" x 14'-6"
8'-0" clg.

covered balcony

DESIGN BY
©The Sater Design Collection

An enchanting center gable announces a graceful, honest architecture that's at home with the easygoing nature of this coastal design. A columned porch and romantic fretwork lend balance and proportion outside. The great room, featuring double doors, arches, a built-in entertainment center and a warming fireplace, is the heart of this home. The kitchen is adjoined to the dining room (with French doors) by an eating bar and provides a walk-in pantry. The foyer stairs lead to a master suite with a spacious bedroom and a lavish private bath.

This cozy retreat offers bright and airy living areas and covered porches. Built-ins and a media niche frame the great-room fireplace. Four sets of French doors in the great room access the covered wraparound porch. The gourmet kitchen shares an eating bar with the great room and is open to the dining room through a hallway with arches. A first-floor bedroom with a built-in desk easily accesses the full hall bath. The second floor contains an observation deck, the master suite with a grand private bath and walk-in closet, plus a third bedroom with a private bath and window seat.

DESIGN HPU040093

First Floor: 1,046 square feet
Second Floor: 638 square feet
Total: 1,684 square feet
Width: 25'-0" Depth: 65'-6"

DESIGN BY
©The Sater Design Collection

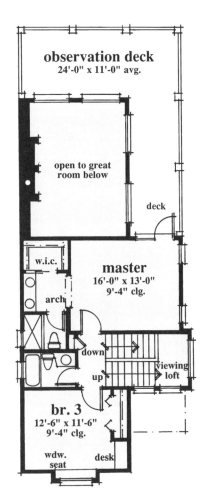

observation deck
24'-0" x 11'-0" avg.

open to great room below

deck

w.i.c.

arch

master
16'-0" x 13'-0"
9'-4" clg.

down

up

viewing loft

br. 3
12'-6" x 11'-6"
9'-4" clg.

wdw. seat

desk

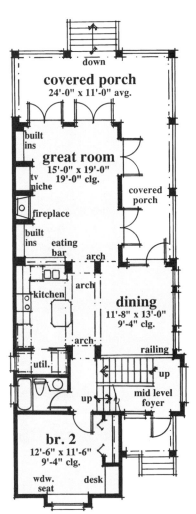

down

covered porch
24'-0" x 11'-0" avg.

built ins

great room
15'-0" x 19'-0"
19'-0" clg.

tv niche

fireplace

built ins

eating bar

arch

arch

covered porch

kitchen

arch

dining
11'-8" x 13'-0"
9'-4" clg.

util.

arch

railing

up

up

mid level foyer

br. 2
12'-6" x 11'-6"
9'-4" clg.

wdw. seat

desk

DESIGN HPU040094

First Floor: 938 square feet
Second Floor: 1,034 square feet
Total: 1,972 square feet
Width: 30'-0" Depth: 74'-0"

The wide steps of this inviting farmhouse greet all who approach with a warm welcome. Encircled by sidelights and a transom, the front door leads to an extra-spacious great room. Just beyond, a secluded rear porch also touches the breakfast room, providing a convenient transition to the backyard. Any accomplished cook would deeply appreciate the long angled kitchen with its abundant counter space and storage capabilities. A covered cooking porch will protect those who want to grill outdoors despite inclement weather conditions. In the bedroom area above, the master suite has an interesting nook for either a desk or a sitting area. A garden tub is well placed away from the double vanities, to give the couple who share the bath a spacious area in which to dress. All bedrooms contain large walk-in closets. Each bedroom enjoys its own long, private vanity area.

DESIGN BY
©Authentic Historical Designs, Inc.

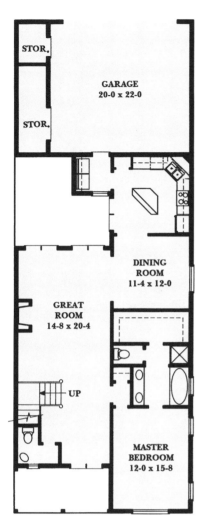

STOR.

GARAGE
20-0 x 22-0

STOR.

DINING
ROOM
11-4 x 12-0

GREAT
ROOM
14-8 x 20-4

UP

MASTER
BEDROOM
12-0 x 15-8

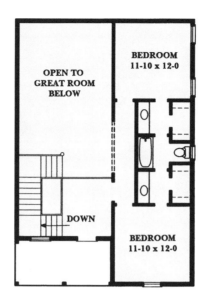

OPEN TO
GREAT ROOM
BELOW

BEDROOM
11-10 x 12-0

DOWN

BEDROOM
11-10 x 12-0

DESIGN HPU040095

First Floor: 1,270 square feet
Second Floor: 630 square feet
Total: 1,900 square feet
Width: 28'-0" Depth: 76'-0"

DESIGN BY
©Authentic Historical Designs, Inc.

Possessing an irresistible charm, this electric French design will elicit accolades from all who pass by. The double front porch provides a shady spot for a cool drink and a moment of relaxation. A spacious foyer, ample enough for a cherished antique, greets those who enter. Just beyond, the great room with its soaring ceiling gives additional flair to this open and inviting plan. An open-railed stairwell leads to a dramatic landing that overlooks the great room below. Access the second-floor porch easily from this landing. Two spacious bedrooms share a compartmented bath; each has a separate vanity and a walk-in closet.

DESIGN HPU040096

First Floor: 1,340 square feet
Second Floor: 651 square feet
Total: 1,991 square feet
Width: 30'-0" Depth: 74'-0"

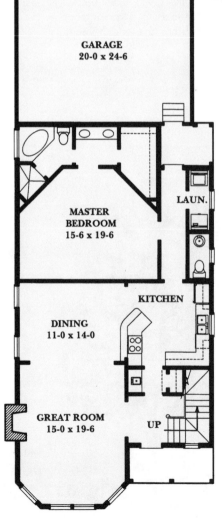

This pleasing Victorian design, with its double-stacked front bay, will meet your requirements. A multitude of windows admits the sun into this glittering home, drenching the house with light. The handsome great room showcases an old-fashioned fireplace and leads into a semi-formal dining room. The kitchen is partially separated from the dining room by a raised breakfast bar. A separate wet bar will assist in entertaining and could open to the great room, if desired. The first-floor master bedroom, with its intriguing angles, repeats the bays on the front facade of the house. A step-in laundry room is conveniently located near the master bedroom and is also in close proximity to the kitchen. A graceful, open stairway rises to the well-apportioned family bedrooms above.

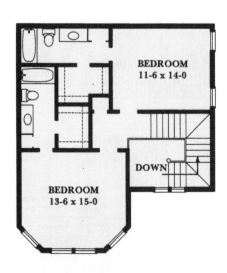

DESIGN BY
©Authentic Historical Designs, Inc.

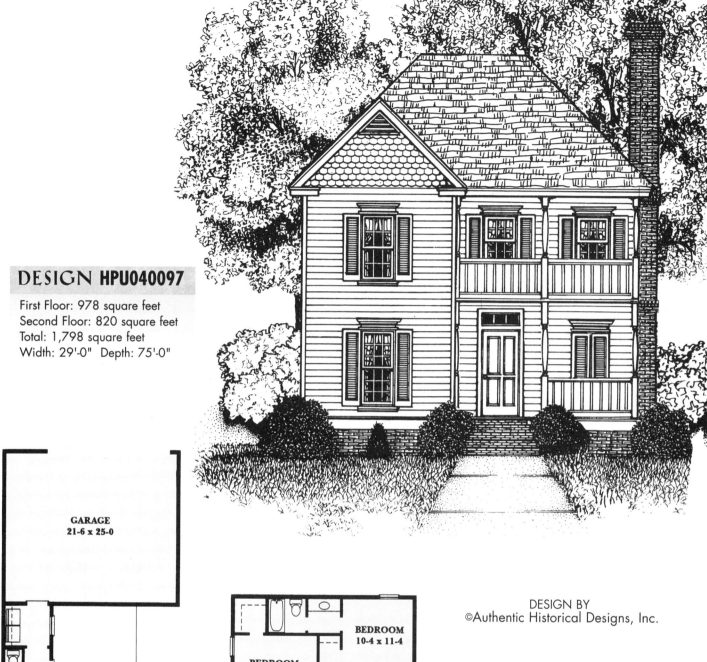

DESIGN HPU040097

First Floor: 978 square feet
Second Floor: 820 square feet
Total: 1,798 square feet
Width: 29'-0" Depth: 75'-0"

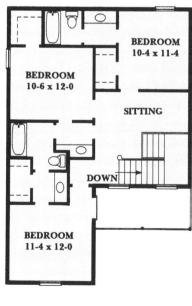

GARAGE
21-6 x 25-0

DINING

GREAT
ROOM
13-8 x 17-6

UP

MASTER
BEDROOM
12-0 x 13-8

BEDROOM
10-6 x 12-0

BEDROOM
10-4 x 11-4

SITTING

DOWN

BEDROOM
11-4 x 12-0

DESIGN BY
©Authentic Historical Designs, Inc.

The clapboard siding and double-stacked porches of this simple Victorian residence give warmth and appeal to this inviting design. Fish-scale shingles provide additional architectural ornamentation. Inside, an open-railed stairway rises from the foyer. The first-floor master suite is located off a vestibule adjacent to the foyer, providing privacy from family activities. The master suite has a roomy bath and a large walk-in closet. The L-shaped kitchen makes space for a dining table, which will be the center of family activities. The great room, with a wood-burning fireplace, opens to a large covered porch. Above, the open stairs rise to a sitting area, perfect for a computer or play center. Each of the three ample family bedrooms has a walk-in closet. Additionally, each bedroom also accesses to its own private vanity. One of the bedrooms opens directly to the second-floor porch; this bedroom could also serve as a second-floor den, if desired.

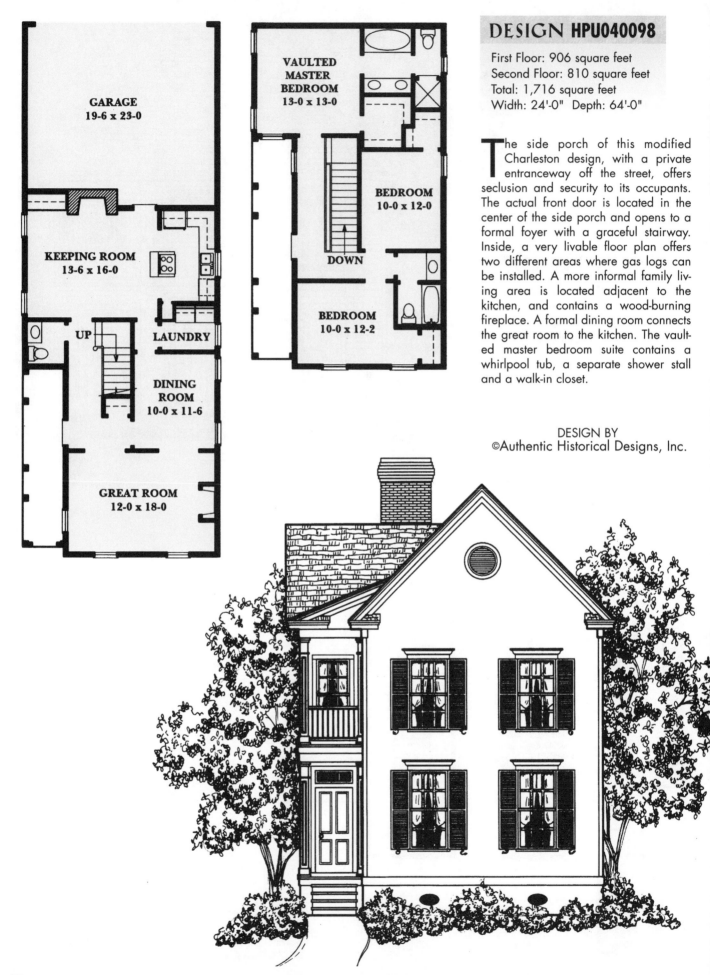

GARAGE
19-6 x 23-0

KEEPING ROOM
13-6 x 16-0

UP

LAUNDRY

DINING ROOM
10-0 x 11-6

GREAT ROOM
12-0 x 18-0

VAULTED MASTER BEDROOM
13-0 x 13-0

BEDROOM
10-0 x 12-0

DOWN

BEDROOM
10-0 x 12-2

DESIGN HPU040098

First Floor: 906 square feet
Second Floor: 810 square feet
Total: 1,716 square feet
Width: 24'-0" Depth: 64'-0"

The side porch of this modified Charleston design, with a private entranceway off the street, offers seclusion and security to its occupants. The actual front door is located in the center of the side porch and opens to a formal foyer with a graceful stairway. Inside, a very livable floor plan offers two different areas where gas logs can be installed. A more informal family living area is located adjacent to the kitchen, and contains a wood-burning fireplace. A formal dining room connects the great room to the kitchen. The vaulted master bedroom suite contains a whirlpool tub, a separate shower stall and a walk-in closet.

DESIGN BY
©Authentic Historical Designs, Inc.

DESIGN HPU040099

First Floor: 900 square feet
Second Floor: 1,081 square feet
Total: 1,981 square feet
Width: 26'-0" Depth: 66'-0"

There is not an area in this country where this classic Greek Revival home would not feel instantly at home. A friendly front-facing gable with an elegant spider-web window accentuates the openness of the front facade. The double tier of galleries proclaims a house that will play a predominant role in a vibrant urban streetscape. Transom-topped windows lend additional grandeur to the ample great room. The bayed dining room can be handled with as much or as little formality as the owners desire. An adjacent breakfast bar provides a more casual setting for sandwiches and snacks. Conveniently located, a covered porch is readily accessible for a summer barbecue. The large walk-in laundry has a separate sink and pantry for the cook who likes to stock up on both staples and gourmet items. The sleeping quarters reside upstairs.

DESIGN BY
©Authentic Historical Designs, Inc.

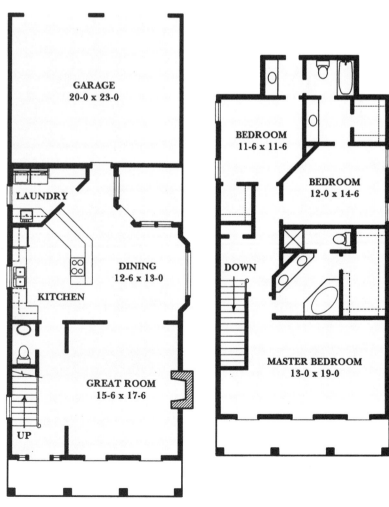

GARAGE
20-0 x 23-0

LAUNDRY

DINING
12-6 x 13-0

KITCHEN

GREAT ROOM
15-6 x 17-6

UP

BEDROOM
11-6 x 11-6

BEDROOM
12-0 x 14-6

DOWN

MASTER BEDROOM
13-0 x 19-0

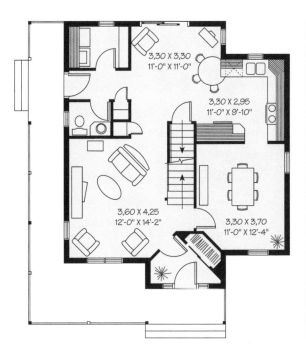

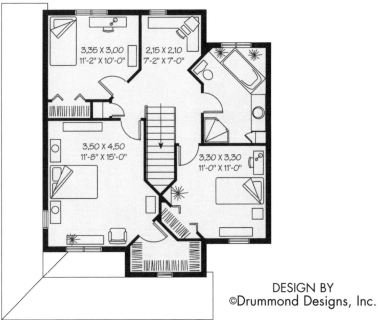

DESIGN BY
©Drummond Designs, Inc.

DESIGN HPU040101

First Floor: 802 square feet
Second Floor: 802 square feet
Total: 1,604 square feet
Width: 28'-0" Depth: 32'-0"

Here's a sophisticated country design with a few gently European details and a wrap-around porch. A stylish interior starts with a separate entrance hall with a closet. The breakfast nook features a sitting area, brightened by windows and served by an L-shaped kitchen. Sleeping quarters include a master bedroom with a walk-in closet, plus two additional bedrooms. The second-floor bath has a corner tub and a separate shower. This home is designed with a basement foundation.

DESIGN BY
©Drummond Designs, Inc.

Quaint details give this country home a lemonade and porch swing feel. The foyer leads to the living room with a corner fireplace. Just steps away is the dining room with double French doors to the rear yard. The kitchen provides plenty of space to prepare for large or intimate parties. The laundry room and a half-bath are placed near the kitchen for making chores easier. Upstairs, the master bedroom features plenty of closet space. Across the hall, two secondary bedrooms and a loft round out the upper level. This home is designed with a basement foundation.

DESIGN HPU040102

First Floor: 781 square feet
Second Floor: 720 square feet
Total: 1,501 square feet
Width: 29'-4" Depth: 30'-0"

Farmhouse fresh with a touch of Victorian style best describes this charming home. A covered front porch wraps around the dining room's bay window and leads the way to the entrance. To the right of the entry is a living room that features a wet bar and a warming fireplace. At the rear of the plan, an L-shaped kitchen is equipped with an island cooktop, making meal preparation a breeze. Casual meals can be enjoyed in a dining area that which merges with the kitchen and accesses the rear patio. A powder room and utility room complete the first floor. Sleeping quarters contained on the second floor include a relaxing master suite with a large walk-in closet, two family bedrooms and a connecting bath.

DESIGN HPU040103

First Floor: 1,082 square feet
Second Floor: 838 square feet
Total: 1,920 square feet
Width: 66'-10" Depth: 29'-5"

DESIGN BY
©Fillmore Design Group

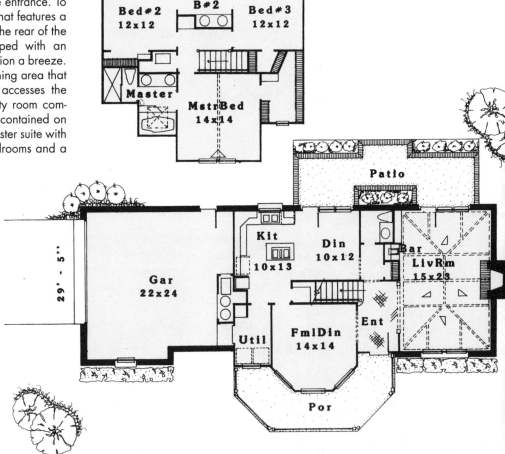

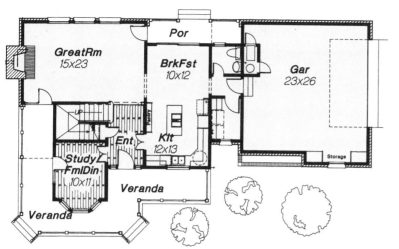

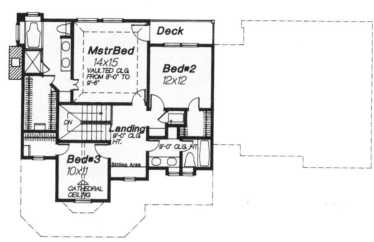

Fish-scale shingles, a weather vane, a cupola and a covered wraparound veranda complete with Victorian touches make this farmhouse a truly memorable sight. The great room includes a fireplace for those chilly evenings and accesses the porch—perfect for warmer nights. The island kitchen and breakfast area access the great room, entertainment area and a passage to the garage. All three bedrooms reside on the second floor. The master suite has a vaulted ceiling, private bath, walk-in closet and access to a private deck. A unique sitting area is located on the landing between Bedrooms 2 and 3. A full hall bath with dual vanities is also shared between the two bedrooms.

DESIGN HPU040104

First Floor: 1,024 square feet
Second Floor: 904 square feet
Total: 1,928 square feet
Width: 65'-0"   Depth: 35'-5"

DESIGN BY
©Fillmore Design Group

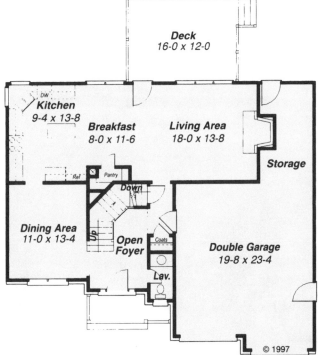

Deck
16-0 x 12-0

Kitchen
9-4 x 13-8

DW

Breakfast
8-0 x 11-6

Living Area
18-0 x 13-8

Storage

Rel. Pantry

Down

Dining Area
11-0 x 13-4

Open Foyer

Coats

Lav.

Double Garage
19-8 x 23-4

© 1997

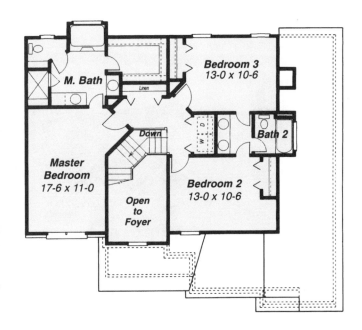

M. Bath

Linen

Bedroom 3
13-0 x 10-6

W D

Bath 2

Down

Master Bedroom
17-6 x 11-0

Open to Foyer

Bedroom 2
13-0 x 10-6

DESIGN HPU040105

First Floor: 869 square feet
Second Floor: 963 square feet
Total: 1,832 square feet
Width: 44'-0" Depth: 38'-0"

Under this quaint covered porch resides an inviting entry with sidelights and a six-panel door. Inside, the openness of the rear rooms—the living area, breakfast area and island kitchen—provide a feeling of spaciousness. The kitchen serves a formal dining room as well as the breakfast room. A rear sun deck is accessible from the main living area. Upstairs, secondary bedrooms share a vanity area that opens to a private toilet and tub room. A comfortable master suite offers a walk-in closet and a lavish bath with separate vanities.

The livability of this narrow home is great. Well worth mentioning is the veranda and the screened porch, which both highlight the relaxing outdoor design. The foyer directs traffic to the far rear of the home, where open living and dining rooms can be enjoyed. The U-shaped kitchen easily services both the dining room and the breakfast room. Three bedrooms reside on the second floor. The master suite features a private bath and walk-in closet. The third floor provides storage space.

DESIGN BY
©Home Planners

DESIGN HPU040106

First Floor: 911 square feet
Second Floor: 861 square feet
Total: 1,772 square feet
Attic: 884 square feet
Width: 38'-0" Depth: 52'-0"

L

Quote One®

Cost to build? See page 502
to order complete cost estimate
to build this house in your area!

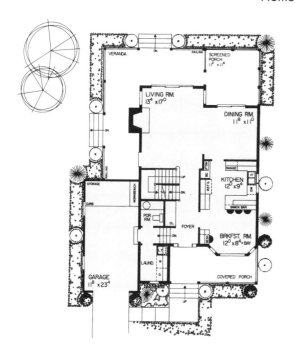

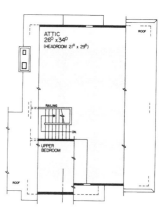

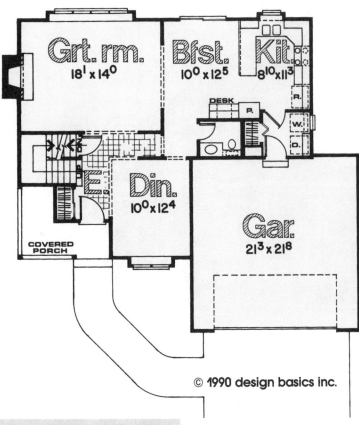

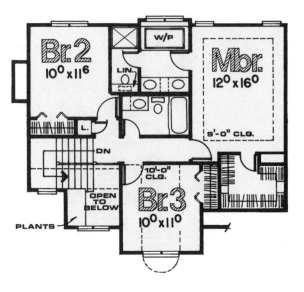

© 1990 design basics inc.

DESIGN HPU040107

First Floor: 891 square feet
Second Floor: 759 square feet
Total: 1,650 square feet
Width: 44'-0"   Depth: 40'-0"

DESIGN BY
©Design Basics, Inc.

This modest-sized home provides a quaint covered front porch that opens to a two-story foyer. The formal dining room features a boxed window that can be seen from the entry. A fireplace in the great room adds warmth and coziness to the attached breakfast room and the well-planned kitchen. Sliding glass doors lead from the breakfast room to the rear yard. A washer and dryer reside in a nearby utility room, where a closet provides ample storage. A powder room is provided nearby for guests. Three bedrooms are on the second floor; one of these includes an arched window under a vaulted ceiling. The deluxe owners suite provides a large walk-in closet and a dressing area with a double vanity and a whirlpool tub.

DESIGN BY
©Design Basics, Inc.

DESIGN HPU040108

First Floor: 1,421 square feet
Second Floor: 578 square feet
Total: 1,999 square feet
Width: 52'-0"   Depth: 47'-4"

Victorian details and a covered veranda lend a peaceful flavor to the elevation of this popular home. A volume entry hall views the formal dining room and luxurious great room. Imagine the comfort of relaxing in the great room, which features a volume ceiling and abundant windows. The kitchen and breakfast area includes a through-fireplace, snack bar, walk-in pantry and wrapping counters. The secluded master suite features a vaulted ceiling, luxurious dressing/bath area and corner whirlpool tub. Upstairs, the family sleeping quarters contain special amenities unique to each.

DECK

Great Room
15³ × 19⁹

12'-10" Ceiling

Breakfast
12⁶ × 13⁷

Kitchen
10⁰ × 11³

SNACK BAR

W/P

DESK

R.

P.

11'-6" Ceiling

Master
Sleeping
Quarters
13⁰ × 16³

UP

DN

D. W.

ENTRANCE
HALL

Dining
Room
12³ × 12⁸

HUTCH

Garage
20⁸ × 23⁰

COVERED
VERANDA

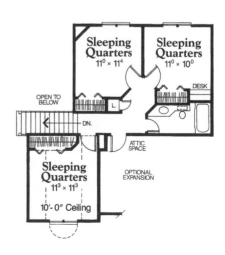

Sleeping
Quarters
11⁰ × 11⁴

Sleeping
Quarters
11⁰ × 10⁰

DESK

OPEN TO
BELOW

L

DN

ATTIC
SPACE

Sleeping
Quarters
11³ × 11³

10'-0" Ceiling

OPTIONAL
EXPANSION

89

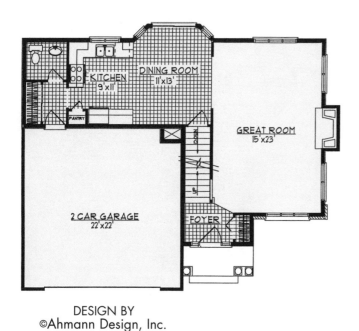

KITCHEN
9'x11'

DINING ROOM
11'x13'

PANTRY

GREAT ROOM
15'x23'

2 CAR GARAGE
22'x22'

DOWN

UP

FOYER

DESIGN BY
©Ahmann Design, Inc.

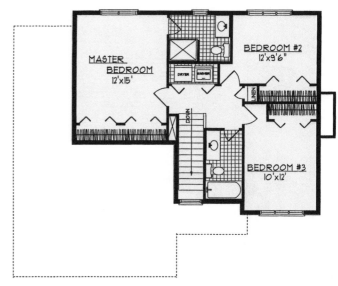

MASTER
BEDROOM
12'x15'

DRYER

WASHER

BEDROOM #2
12'x9'6"

LINEN

DOWN

BEDROOM #3
10'x12'

DESIGN HPU040109

First Floor: 811 square feet
Second Floor: 741 square feet
Total: 1,552 square feet
Width: 44'-0" Depth: 36'-0"

This two-story home features traditional details blended with a touch of contemporary flare. With three bedrooms on the second floor, this home becomes the perfect choice for a family's first home. Enjoy cozy evenings in the great room in front of the fireplace. The large windows on the front of this home allow plenty of sunlight to stream in, making this a warm and inviting place on most any day. The three bedrooms upstairs include a master bedroom with two closets.

DESIGN BY
©Living Concepts Home Planning

DESIGN HPU040110

First Floor: 760 square feet
Second Floor: 742 square feet
Total: 1,502 square feet
Bonus Room: 283 square feet
Width: 39'-1" Depth: 36'-9"

Made for a narrow footprint or in-fill lot, this home offers traditional lines with a farmhouse flavor. A welcoming porch ushers family and guests into the foyer. The large U-shaped kitchen is just to the right with a nearby laundry room for convenience. The dining area is found to the rear and enjoys rear views and porch access. The family room is perfect for a fireplace and entertaining guests or spending a quiet night at home. The master suite features a coffered ceiling, walk-in closets and a full bath. Two family suites share a full bath, and a bonus room is found just across the hall.

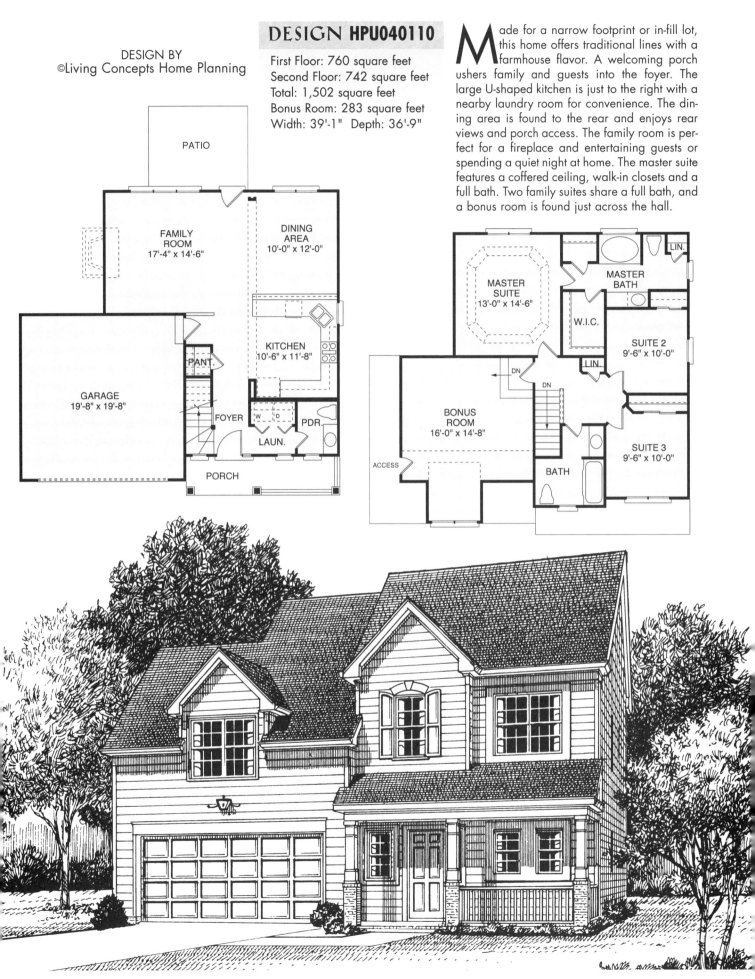

PATIO

FAMILY ROOM
17'-4" x 14'-6"

DINING AREA
10'-0" x 12'-0"

KITCHEN
10'-6" x 11'-8"

GARAGE
19'-8" x 19'-8"

PANT.

FOYER

W D

LAUN.

PDR.

PORCH

MASTER SUITE
13'-0" x 14'-6"

MASTER BATH

W.I.C.

LIN.

LIN.

SUITE 2
9'-6" x 10'-0"

BONUS ROOM
16'-0" x 14'-8"

DN

DN

ACCESS

BATH

SUITE 3
9'-6" x 10'-0"

Garage
19'-2" X 23'-8"

Stor.

Cov. Porch

Patio

Utility

Living
20' X 12'-6"

Breakfast
13' X 8'-8"

Bath

Ba.

Kitchen
11' X 10'-6"

Master Bedroom
13' X 16'

Foyer

Dining
11' X 11'-6"

Porch

DESIGN HPU040111

First Floor: 1,185 square feet
Second Floor: 617 square feet
Total: 1,802 square feet
Width: 36'-6" Depth: 69'-9"

This perfectly charming country home features amenities to complement both quiet and active family lifestyles. The foyer opens to the warmth and hospitality of the expansive living area, complete with a fireplace and double doors leading to the rear patio. A convenient U-shaped kitchen easily serves both the formal dining room and the informal bay-windowed breakfast area. The main-floor master suite sports a plush private bath and a great walk-in closet. Two large bedrooms upstairs each have their own access to a uniquely designed full bath with twin lavatories—separated by a compartmented toilet and tub. Please specify crawlspace or slab foundation when ordering.

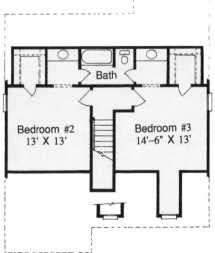

Bath

Bedroom #2
13' X 13'

Bedroom #3
14'-6" X 13'

DESIGN BY
©Chatham Home Planning, Inc.

DECK/
PATIO

KITCHEN
11'-4" x 11'-0"

BREAKFAST
9'-6" x 9'-6"

GREAT
ROOM
18'-4" x 13'-8"

PANT.

DINING
ROOM
11'-4" x 12'-0"

UP

FOYER

PDR.

GARAGE
20'-0" x 22'-4"

LOGGIA

DESIGN HPU040112

First Floor: 844 square feet
Second Floor: 875 square feet
Total: 1,719 square feet
Bonus Room: 242 square feet
Width: 45'-0" Depth: 37'-0"

SUITE 3
10'-0" x 11'-0"

BATH

MASTER
BATH

MASTER
SUITE
11'-6" x 18'-0"

DN

SUITE 2
11'-4" x 10'-0"

LAUNDRY

W.I.C.

OPEN
TO
BELOW

STOR.

UNFIN.
BONUS
ROOM
12'-0" x 18'-0"

STOR.

A Palladian window adds interest to the modified-gable roofline of this livable three-bedroom design. Columns and tall glass panels flank the covered entryway. A hall closet and a powder room line the foyer. The great room includes a warming fireplace, and the kitchen and the breakfast area with patio access sit across the back. The master suite with a deluxe private bath and walk-in closet, plus the two family bedrooms, resides on the second floor. Please specify crawlspace or slab foundation when ordering.

DESIGN BY
©Living Concepts Home Planning

DESIGN HPU040114

Square Footage: 1,544
Bonus Room: 320 square feet
Width: 63'-0" Depth: 24'-6"

DESIGN BY
Donald A. Gardner Architects, Inc.

© 1998 Donald A. Gardner, Inc.

This home would look good in any neighborhood. From the covered front porch to the trio of gables, this design has a lot of appeal. Inside, the Craftsman styling continues in the manner of built-in shelves and a warming fireplace in the great room and plenty of windows to bring in the outdoors. The U-shaped kitchen offers easy access to the formal dining area. Expansion is possible with an optional bonus room, adding a second level. A tray ceiling adorns the owners suite and the owner will enjoy a His and Hers walk-in closets and a pampering bath complete with a twin-sink vanity and a separate shower and garden tub.

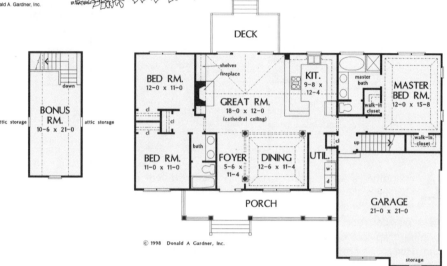

BONUS RM.
10-6 x 21-0

attic storage   attic storage

DECK

BED RM.
12-0 x 11-0

shelves
fireplace

KIT.
9-8 x 12-4

master bath

MASTER BED RM.
12-0 x 15-8

walk-in closet

GREAT RM.
18-0 x 12-0
(cathedral ceiling)

BED RM.
11-0 x 11-0

bath

FOYER
5-6 x 11-4

DINING
12-6 x 11-4

UTIL.

walk-in closet

up

GARAGE
21-0 x 21-0

PORCH

© 1998 Donald A Gardner, Inc.

storage

The foyer opens to a spacious great room with a fireplace and a cathedral ceiling in this lovely traditional home. Sliding doors open to a rear deck from the great room, posing a warm welcome to enjoy the outdoors. The U-shaped kitchen features an angled peninsula counter with a cooktop. A private hall leads to the family sleeping quarters, which includes two bedrooms and a full bath with a double-bowl lavatory. On the other side of the house, the master bedroom enjoys a tray ceiling and spacious bath. Sizable bonus space above the garage provides a skylight.

DECK

master bath

lin.

GREAT RM.
15-0 x 17-10

(cathedral ceiling)
fireplace

DINING
12-0 x 12-0

walk-in closet

BED RM.
11-0 x 11-0

bath
lin.

MASTER BED RM.
13-0 x 15-0

walk-in closet

FOYER
6-2 x 6-0

KIT.
12-0 x 12-2

UTIL.
6-4 x 6-0

BED RM.
11-0 x 11-0

up

storage

PORCH

GARAGE
20-0 x 20-4

© 1997 Donald A Gardner Architects, Inc.

BONUS RM.
12-8 x 18-4

attic storage   attic storage

down

skylight

DESIGN HPU040113

Square Footage: 1,517
Bonus Room: 287 square feet
Width: 61'-4" Depth: 48'-6"

DESIGN BY
Donald A. Gardner Architects, Inc.

© 1994 Donald A. Gardner Architects, Inc.

The intricate window treatment and stately columns give this home magnificent curb appeal. Inside, the columns continue from the foyer into the spacious great room. A fireplace is flanked by windows with a view to the rear deck and the spa. The great room opens to the large island kitchen and the formal dining room. The master suite is to the left of the foyer. The remaining bedrooms, a shared full bath and a conveniently placed utility room are located in the right wing of the house.

DESIGN HPU040115

Square Footage: 1,537
Width: 59'-2" Depth: 55'-0"

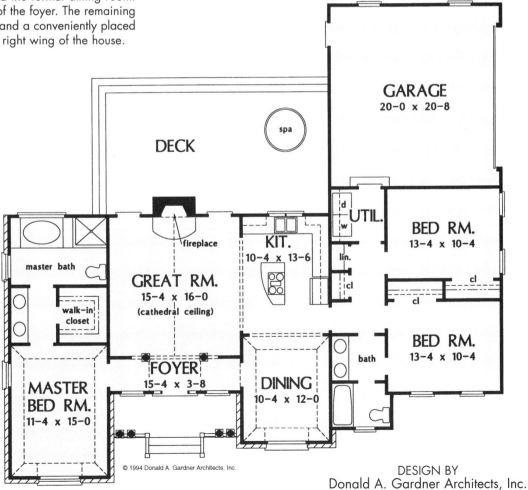

master bath

walk-in closet

DECK

spa

GARAGE
20-0 x 20-8

fireplace

KIT.
10-4 x 13-6

UTIL.

lin.

cl

BED RM.
13-4 x 10-4

cl

cl

GREAT RM.
15-4 x 16-0
(cathedral ceiling)

bath

BED RM.
13-4 x 10-4

MASTER
BED RM.
11-4 x 15-0

FOYER
15-4 x 3-8

DINING
10-4 x 12-0

© 1994 Donald A. Gardner Architects, Inc.

DESIGN BY
Donald A. Gardner Architects, Inc.

95

DESIGN HPU040116

First Floor: 1,330 square feet
Second Floor: 496 square feet
Total: 1,826 square feet
Width: 48'-0" Depth: 54'-10"

DESIGN BY
©Fillmore Design Group

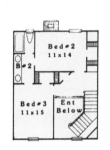

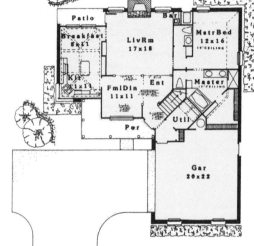

A brick exterior with wooden lap-sided gable accents proves that tradition and custom design blend nicely in this unique home. A covered porch with old-fashioned woodwork precedes an entry that offers a view of the stairs and balcony above. The first floor features a beautiful formal dining room with cedar posts and an enormous living room with a brick fireplace flanked by tall windows. The split sleeping arrangement locates the two family bedrooms upstairs, away from the secluded master bedroom downstairs.

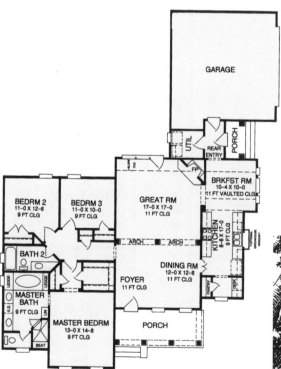

Twin dormers and double gables adorn the exterior of this pleasing three-bedroom home. The foyer opens to the formal dining area and arches leading to the great room, which offers a warming corner fireplace. Add the optional greenhouse to the kitchen-sink window for a beautiful glass display or herb garden location. Keep household records and dry goods well organized with the desk and pantry room just off the galley kitchen. The vaulted breakfast room is brightened by three lovely windows. A lovely master retreat features a whirlpool tub, separate shower and knee-space vanity. Two additional bedrooms share a full bath. Please specify crawlspace or slab foundation when ordering.

DESIGN BY
©Larry E. Belk Designs

DESIGN HPU040117

Square Footage: 1,725
Width: 56'-4" Depth: 72'-8"

DESIGN HPU040118

Square Footage: 1,654
Width: 54'-10" Depth: 69'-10"

Twin dormers perch above a welcoming covered front porch in this three-bedroom home. Inside, a formal dining room on the right is defined by pillars, while the spacious great room lies directly ahead. This room is enhanced by a fireplace, plenty of windows, access to the rear yard, and a forty-two-inch ledge looking into the angular kitchen. Nearby, a bayed breakfast room awaits casual mealtimes. The sleeping zone consists of two family bedrooms sharing a full hall bath and a luxurious master bedroom suite with a huge walk-in closet and a sumptuous private bath. Please specify crawlspace or slab foundation when ordering.

DESIGN BY
©Larry E. Belk Designs

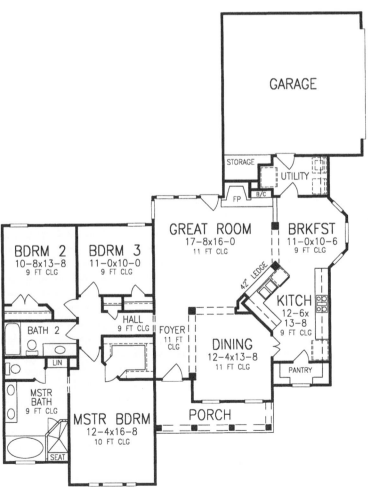

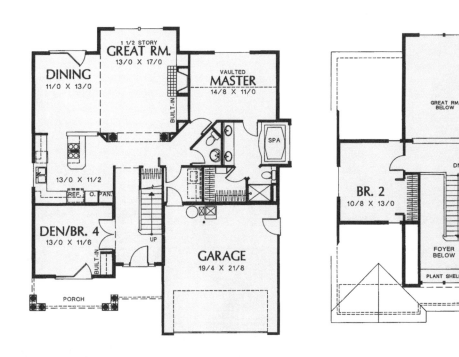

DESIGN HPU040119

First Floor: 1,396 square feet
Second Floor: 523 square feet
Total: 1,919 square feet
Width: 44'-0" Depth: 51'-0"

L

Double pillars herald the entry to this charming design. They are offset from the front door and introduce a porch that leads to the den (or make it a fourth bedroom). Living areas center on the casual life and include a great room, with a fireplace, that opens directly to the dining room. The kitchen is L-shaped for convenience and features an island cooktop. The master suite on the first floor sports a vaulted ceiling and bath with spa tub and separate shower. The upper floor holds two secondary bedrooms and a full bath. The open staircase is decorated with a plant shelf that receives light from double windows over the foyer.

DESIGN BY
©Alan Mascord Design Associates, Inc.

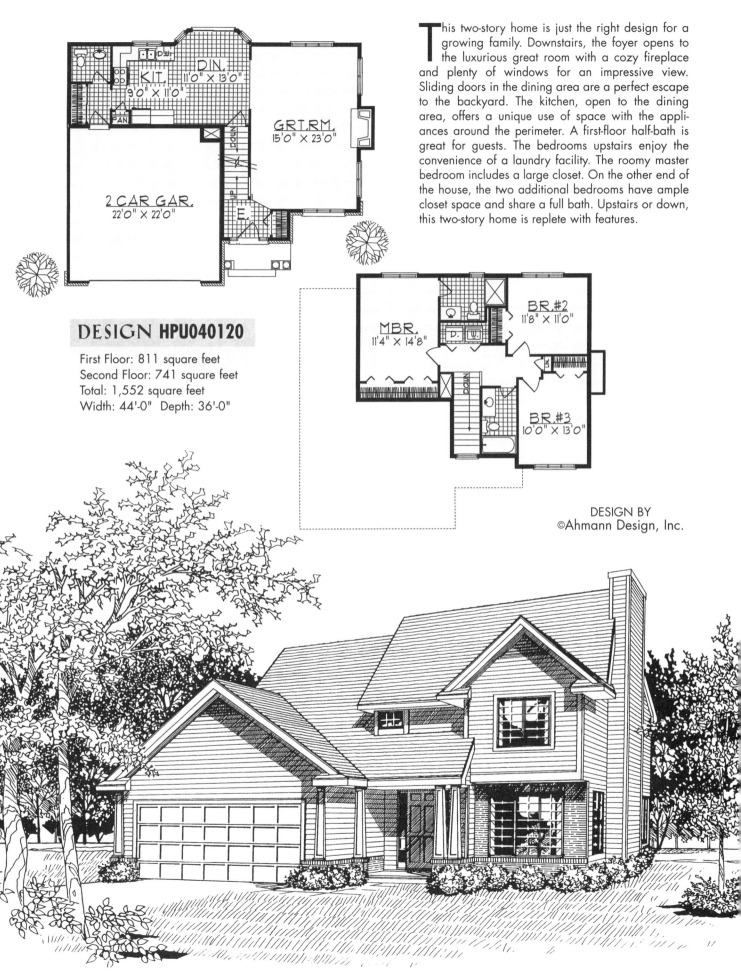

KIT.
9'0" X 11'0"

DIN.
11'0" X 13'0"

GRT. RM.
15'0" X 23'0"

DOWN

UP

PAN.

2 CAR GAR.
22'0" X 22'0"

DESIGN **HPU040120**

First Floor: 811 square feet
Second Floor: 741 square feet
Total: 1,552 square feet
Width: 44'-0" Depth: 36'-0"

MBR.
11'4" X 14'8"

BR. #2
11'8" X 11'0"

BR. #3
10'0" X 13'0"

DOWN

This two-story home is just the right design for a growing family. Downstairs, the foyer opens to the luxurious great room with a cozy fireplace and plenty of windows for an impressive view. Sliding doors in the dining area are a perfect escape to the backyard. The kitchen, open to the dining area, offers a unique use of space with the appliances around the perimeter. A first-floor half-bath is great for guests. The bedrooms upstairs enjoy the convenience of a laundry facility. The roomy master bedroom includes a large closet. On the other end of the house, the two additional bedrooms have ample closet space and share a full bath. Upstairs or down, this two-story home is replete with features.

DESIGN BY
©Ahmann Design, Inc.

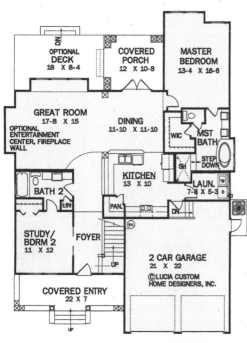

OPTIONAL DECK 18 X 8-4

COVERED PORCH 12 X 10-8

MASTER BEDROOM 13-4 X 16-6

GREAT ROOM 17-8 X 15

OPTIONAL ENTERTAINMENT CENTER, FIREPLACE WALL

DINING 11-10 X 11-10

WIC

MST BATH

STEP DOWN

SH

KITCHEN 13 X 10

LAUN. 7-8 X 5-3

BATH 2

LIN

PAN.

DN

STUDY/ BDRM 2 11 X 12

FOYER

UP

2 CAR GARAGE 21 X 22

©Lucia Custom Home Designers, Inc.

COVERED ENTRY 22 X 7

UP

DESIGN HPU040121

First Floor: 1,553 square feet
Second Floor: 391 square feet
Total: 1,944 square feet
Bonus Room: 183 square feet
Width: 44'-0" Depth: 62'-8"

DESIGN BY
©Lucia Custom Home Designers, Inc.

This floor plan offers a modern approach to today's needs. The study to the left of the foyer could be a third bedroom with an adjoining bath. The great room, dining room and kitchen make up the central open area. An entertainment center and fireplace are optional. From this area, access a covered porch and an optional deck through French doors. A bedroom and bath reside on the second floor, along with a loft area and an overlook to the great room below. There's also an optional closet and unfinished bonus space, perfect for future expansion.

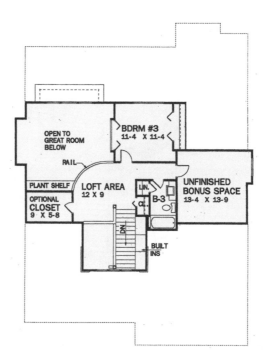

OPEN TO GREAT ROOM BELOW

BDRM #3 11-4 X 11-4

RAIL

PLANT SHELF

LOFT AREA 12 X 9

LIN.

B-3

UNFINISHED BONUS SPACE 13-4 X 13-9

OPTIONAL CLOSET 9 X 5-8

CL.

DN

BUILT INS

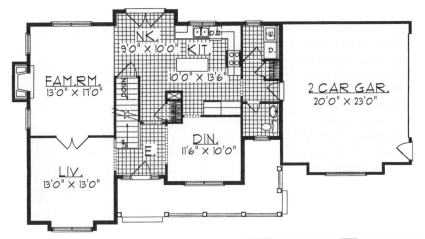

Brick-and-siding, dormered windows, open gables and circle-top windows highlight this modern farmhouse design. The tiled entry leads to the dining room on the right and the breakfast nook and island kitchen straight back. The laundry and half-bath are nearby for convenience. The family room can be found at the left rear and features a cozy fireplace and rear views. The formal living room enjoys a bumped-out bay and double doors that open onto the family room. Upstairs, two family bedrooms share a hall bath—one bedroom features a tray ceiling. The master bedroom boasts a cathedral ceiling, walk-in closet, dual vanities and separate tub and shower.

DESIGN HPU040122

First Floor: 1,065 square feet
Second Floor: 921 square feet
Total: 1,986 square feet
Width: 60'-0" Depth: 34'-0"

DESIGN BY
©Ahmann Design, Inc.

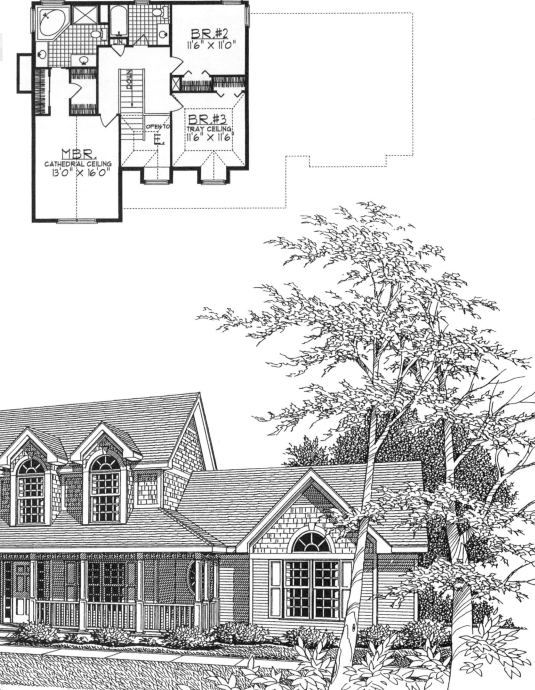

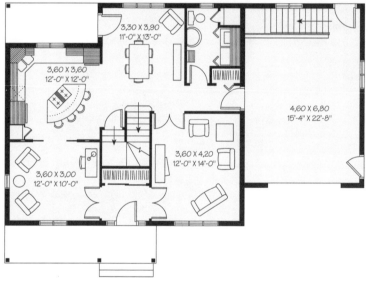

3,30 X 3,90
11'-0" X 13'-0"

3,60 X 3,60
12'-0" X 12'-0"

4,60 X 6,80
15'-4" X 22'-8"

3,60 X 4,20
12'-0" X 14'-0"

3,60 X 3,00
12'-0" X 10'-0"

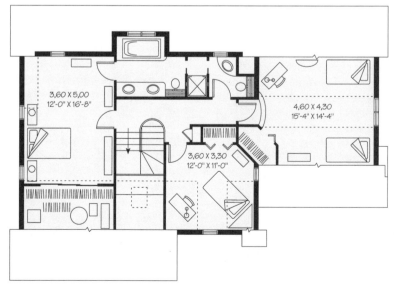

3,60 X 5,00
12'-0" X 16'-8"

4,60 X 4,30
15'-4" X 14'-4"

3,60 X 3,30
12'-0" X 11'-0"

DESIGN HPU040123

First Floor: 866 square feet
Second Floor: 998 square feet
Total: 1,864 square feet
Width: 48'-0" Depth: 29'-0"

A beautifully offset double-gabled dormer adds a playful touch to this Craftsman home. With open gables and a covered porch, an inviting atmosphere takes family and guests into the foyer. Double doors flank the entry; to the left is the media room with pocket doors to the island kitchen. On the right, a living room features double doors to the dining room. A laundry and half-bath complete this level. Upstairs, the master suite is pampered with a private bath. Two secondary bedrooms share a hall bath. This home is designed with a basement foundation.

DESIGN BY
©Drummond Designs, Inc.

A sturdy and attractive design, this fine three-bedroom home will look good in any neighborhood. The raised foyer overlooks a spacious living room, where a through-fireplace and a wall of windows add to the already abundant charm. In the L-shaped kitchen, a cooktop work island/snack bar benefits from the through-fireplace, while the adjacent dining room offers access and views to the rear yard via sliding glass doors. Upstairs, a small balcony overlooks the living room. Three bedrooms—one with a walk-in closet—share a lavish bath. This home is designed with a basement foundation.

DESIGN BY
©Drummond Designs, Inc.

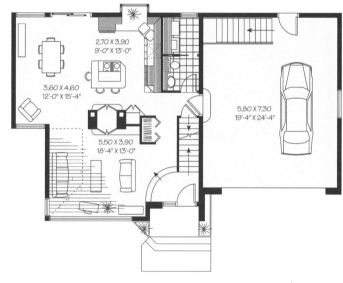

DESIGN HPU040124

First Floor: 760 square feet
Second Floor: 752 square feet
Total: 1,512 square feet
Width: 48'-0" Depth: 30'-0"

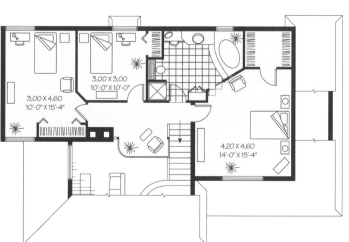

DESIGN HPU040126

Square Footage: 1,656
Bonus Room: 427 square feet
Width: 52'-8" Depth: 54'-6"

DESIGN BY
©Larry James & Associates, Inc.

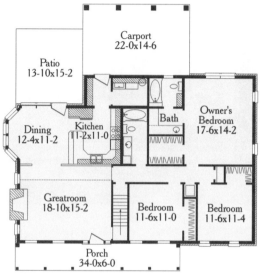

Sit and watch the sunset on this relaxing front porch, or go inside for intimate conversations by the fireplace in the great room. A bay window in the dining area will adorn any meal with sun or moonlight. A spacious owners bedroom has a large walk-in closet and a full bath. Two secondary bedrooms share a full bath with the main living areas. A bonus room upstairs allows room for expansion later. Please specify basement, crawlspace or slab foundation when ordering.

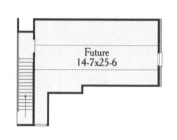

DESIGN HPU040125

First Floor: 1,159 square feet
Second Floor: 711 square feet
Total: 1,870 square feet
Width: 44'-4" Depth: 38'-0"

DESIGN BY
©Jannis Vann & Associates, Inc.

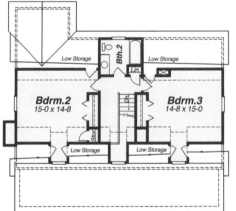

Wherever you live, this country-style home will be a winner! Dormers and an inviting covered porch lend this home enormous appeal. Inside, the main living area offers a cheery fireplace. To the rear of the plan, a dining area overlooks the sun deck. The adjacent kitchen and sunny breakfast area are just a step away. Master-bedroom luxury awaits on the other side of the plan. The large bedroom is complemented by a roomy bath with a corner tub, walk-in closet and twin vanities. Upstairs, two family bedrooms with dormer windows share a bumped-out full bath.

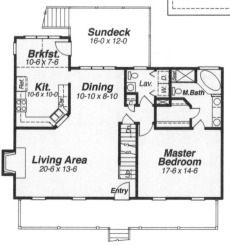

A beautiful half-circle window tops a covered front porch on this fine three-bedroom home. Inside, the main-level amenities start with the large, open great room and a warming fireplace. A uniquely shaped dining room is adjacent to the efficient kitchen, which offers a small bay window over the sink. The deluxe master suite is complete with a cathedral ceiling, bay sitting area and a private bath with laundry facilities. On the lower level, a two-car garage shelters the family fleet, while two bedrooms—or make one a study/home office—share a full hall bath.

DESIGN BY
©Jannis Vann & Associates, Inc.

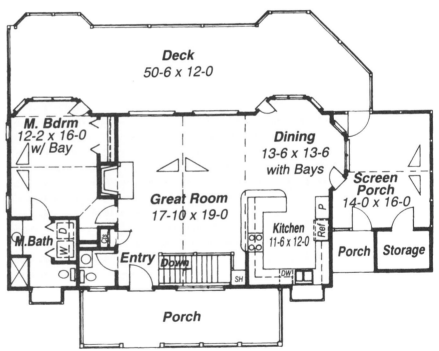

Deck
50-6 x 12-0

M. Bdrm
12-2 x 16-0
w/ Bay

Dining
13-6 x 13-6
with Bays

Great Room
17-10 x 19-0

Screen
Porch
14-0 x 16-0

Kitchen
11-6 x 12-0

M.Bath

Entry   Down

Porch   Storage

Porch

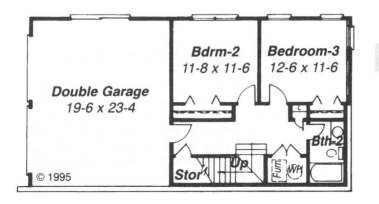

Double Garage
19-6 x 23-4

Bdrm-2
11-8 x 11-6

Bedroom-3
12-6 x 11-6

Bth-2

Stor   Up   Furn   WH

© 1995

DESIGN HPU040127

Main Floor: 1,128 square feet
Lower Floor: 604 square feet
Total: 1,732 square feet
Width: 59'-0" Depth: 46'-0"

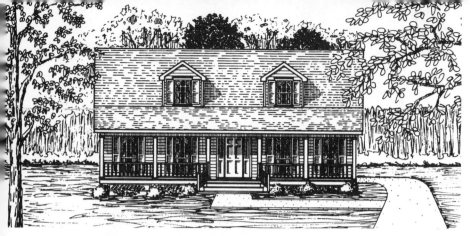

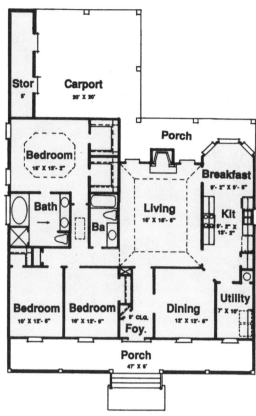

DESIGN HPU040129

Square Footage: 1,704
Width: 47'-0" Depth: 66'-0"

Old-fashioned Southern style is offset by the innovative floor plan of this charming home. Full-height windows line the front porch, drawing natural light and generous views into the front rooms. The foyer leads past the formal dining room on the right to the spacious living room with a sloped ceiling and fireplace. The large galley kitchen is open to the bay-windowed breakfast area and serves the dining room. The owners suite features an octagonal tray ceiling, His and Hers walk-in closets, a garden tub and separate shower. Please specify crawlspace or slab foundation when ordering.

DESIGN BY
©Chatham Home Planning, Inc.

DESIGN HPU040128

Square Footage: 1,689
Width: 67'-0" Depth: 43'-0"

Southern country comfort is at its finest in this three-bedroom home. The great room features a central fireplace and built-ins—perfect for entertaining friends and family. The dining room boasts double French doors to the rear patio and enjoys natural light streaming through surrounding windows. Two family bedrooms to the right share a full bath. The owners bedroom finds privacy on the left and is complemented with a full bath and walk-in closet. Please specify basement, crawlspace or slab foundation when ordering.

Basement Stair
Location

1

Owner's Bedroom

DESIGN BY
©Larry James & Associates, Inc.

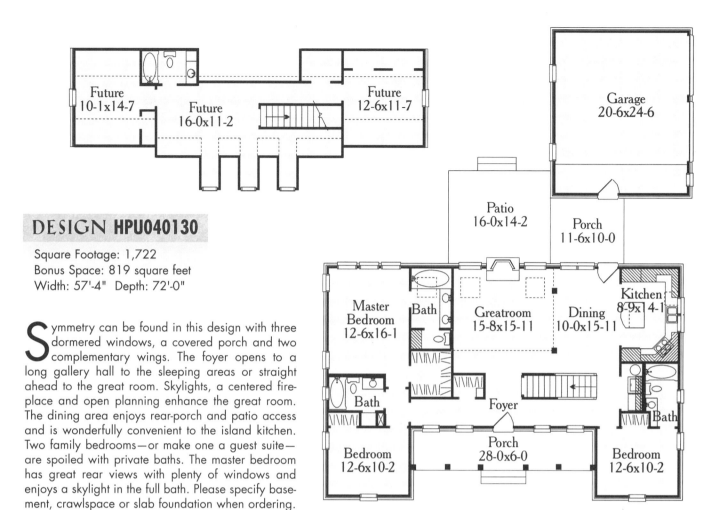

Future
10-1x14-7

Future
16-0x11-2

Future
12-6x11-7

Garage
20-6x24-6

Patio
16-0x14-2

Porch
11-6x10-0

DESIGN HPU040130

Square Footage: 1,722
Bonus Space: 819 square feet
Width: 57'-4" Depth: 72'-0"

Symmetry can be found in this design with three
dormered windows, a covered porch and two
complementary wings. The foyer opens to a
long gallery hall to the sleeping areas or straight
ahead to the great room. Skylights, a centered fireplace and open planning enhance the great room.
The dining area enjoys rear-porch and patio access
and is wonderfully convenient to the island kitchen.
Two family bedrooms—or make one a guest suite—
are spoiled with private baths. The master bedroom
has great rear views with plenty of windows and
enjoys a skylight in the full bath. Please specify basement, crawlspace or slab foundation when ordering.

Master
Bedroom
12-6x16-1

Bath

Greatroom
15-8x15-11

Dining
10-0x15-11

Kitchen
8-9x 4-1

Bath

Bath

Foyer

Bath

Bedroom
12-6x10-2

Porch
28-0x6-0

Bedroom
12-6x10-2

DESIGN BY
©Larry James & Associates, Inc.

DESIGN HPU040132

Square Footage: 1,751
Width: 64'-0" Depth: 40'-6"

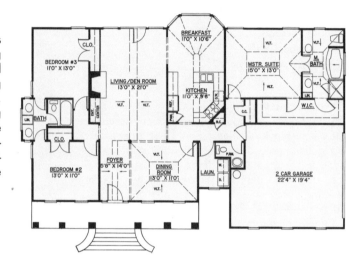

This raised-porch farmhouse holds all the charisma of others of its style, but boasts a one-story floor plan. A huge living area dominates the center of the plan. It features a vaulted ceiling, built-ins and a warming fireplace. The formal dining room across the hall opens to the foyer and the living area, which is defined by a single column at its corner. Casual dining takes place in a light-filled breakfast room attached to the designer kitchen. A spectacular master suite sits behind the two-car garage. It has a tray ceiling, walk-in closet and well-appointed bath. Family bedrooms at the other end of the hallway share a jack-and-jill bath that includes a separate vanity area.

DESIGN BY
©Archival Designs, Inc.

DESIGN HPU040131

First Floor: 1,296 square feet
Second Floor: 468 square feet
Total: 1,764 square feet
Bonus Room: 169 square feet
Width: 49'-0" Depth: 46'-0"

DESIGN BY
©Archival Designs, Inc.

This tidy Southern cottage design opens with a covered front porch that protects the entry and adds a touch of downhome flavor. A central foyer is defined by columns that separate it from the formal dining room and the grand salon. In the vaulted great room, note the fireplace and the snack bar, which it shares with the kitchen. The master bedroom on the first floor features a vaulted ceiling and a bath with a separate tub and shower. Two family bedrooms on the second floor share a full bath. One of the bedrooms has a dormer window. Bonus space can be developed later to include a home office or an additional bedroom.

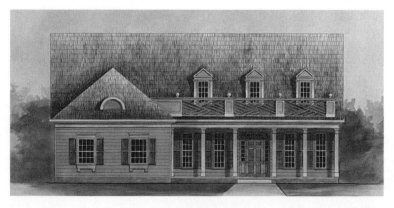

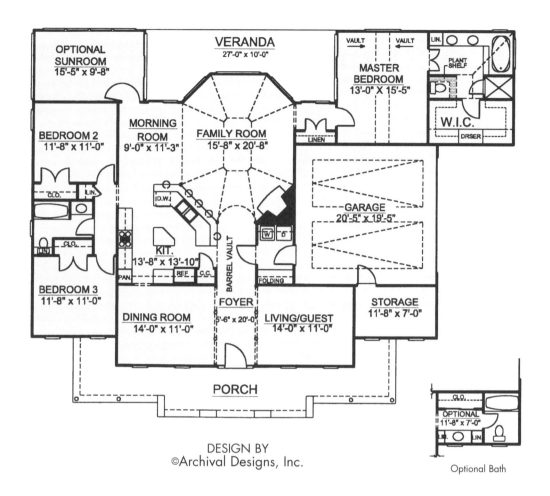

OPTIONAL
SUNROOM
15'-5" x 9'-8"

VERANDA
27'-0" x 10'-0"

VAULT   VAULT   LIN.

MASTER
BEDROOM
13'-0" X 15'-5"

PLANT
SHELF

W.I.C.

DRSER

BEDROOM 2
11'-8" x 11'-0"

MORNING
ROOM
9'-0" x 11'-3"

FAMILY ROOM
15'-8" x 20'-8"

LINEN

CLO.   LIN.

GARAGE
20'-5" x 19'-5"

D.W.

BEDROOM 3
11'-8" x 11'-0"

CLO.

KIT.
13'-8" x 13'-10"

BARREL VAULT

W

PAN.   REF. C.C.

FOLDING

DINING ROOM
14'-0" x 11'-0"

FOYER
5'-6" x 20'-0"

LIVING/GUEST
14'-0" x 11'-0"

STORAGE
11'-8" x 7'-0"

PORCH

DESIGN BY
©Archival Designs, Inc.

CLO.

OPTIONAL
11'-8" x 7'-0"

LIN

Optional Bath

S tately arches topped with a pediment make this home a comfortable fit into an elegant lifestyle. The foyer is flanked by the formal dining and living rooms. A hall with a barrel-vaulted ceiling leads to the vaulted family room, which features a corner fireplace and convenience to the kitchen, morning room and rear veranda. This area provides a spectacular space for family get-togethers. Two secondary bedrooms with a full bath can be found to the left of the kitchen. An optional sun room is a delight just off the morning room. The master suite accommodates the discerning homeowner. It highlights a vaulted ceiling, dual vanities, a separate tub and shower, and an oversized walk-in closet.

DESIGN HPU040133

Square Footage: 1,928
Bonus Room: 160 square feet
Width: 58'-0" Depth: 47'-0"

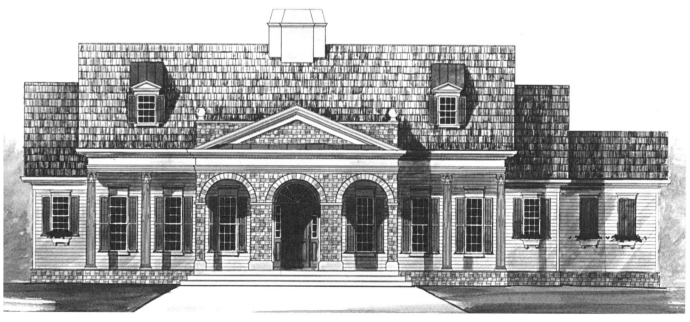

DESIGN HPU040135

First Floor: 1,247 square feet
Second Floor: 521 square feet
Total: 1,768 square feet
Width: 36'-6" Depth: 57'-0"

DESIGN BY
©Chatham Home Planning, Inc.

This Creole cottage possesses the feel of a much bigger house. Natural light streams through the full-length windows that span the entire front wall. This home has the convience of two full baths and one powder room. The master bedroom includes a walk-in closet and a deluxe bath with an oversized tub and separate shower. Two bedrooms and a balcony—that opens to the living area—occupy the second floor. Please specify crawlspace or slab foundation when ordering.

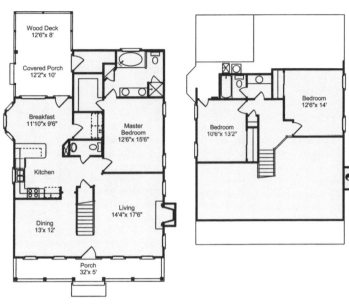

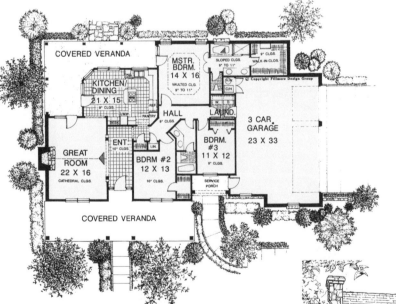

DESIGN HPU040134

Square Footage: 1,830
Width: 75'-0" Depth: 52'-3"

DESIGN BY
©Fillmore Design Group

A lovely front porch and decorative cupola give this home extra sparkle. Characteristics that include the cupola, shutters, arched transoms and an exterior of stone and lap siding mark this as a Colonial design. To the left of the entry, the great room is complete with a cathedral ceiling and fireplace. A hall leads to sleeping quarters that include two secondary bedrooms and a luxurious master bedroom.

110

A deep wraparound porch trimmed with square pillars, a wood balustrade and traditional lattice adds character and interest to this Cape Cod design. Floor-to-ceiling double-hung windows with true divided glass light the downstairs, while dormers upstairs complete the rustic look. The main floor includes a fireplace in the living room, a bay window in the dining room and a master suite with a walk-in closet. The dining room and kitchen are divided by a peninsula with seating for informal dining. The peninsula contains the sink, in keeping with one of the latest trends in kitchen design. There is also a powder room off the kitchen. Upstairs, two bedrooms, each with a walk-in closet, share a bath. Please specify crawlspace or slab foundation when ordering.

Kitchen
13'6"x 12'

Dining
11'8"x 12'

Master
Bedroom
12'x 16'

Living
14'2"x 16'

Porch

Bedroom
10'x 13'2"

Bedroom
14'x 13'2"

DESIGN HPU040136

First Floor: 1,046 square feet
Second Floor: 572 square feet
Total: 1,618 square feet
Width: 44'-0" Depth: 39'-0"

DESIGN BY
©Chatham Home Planning, Inc.

DESIGN HPU040138

Square Footage: 1,770
Width: 64'-0" Depth: 48'-0"

This traditional design boasts a large entry porch and free-flowing interior spaces. The spacious living room is open to the adjacent dining room and offers a built-in fireplace and entertainment center. The entry, breakfast area, kitchen, and dining and living areas have twelve-foot ceilings. The master suite is secluded for privacy and conveniently located only steps away from the kitchen. Please specify crawlspace or slab foundation when ordering.

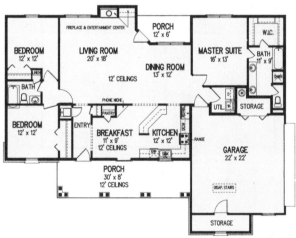

Utilizing wood and stone for the exterior facade, this home boasts a large receiving porch and free-flowing interior spaces. The spacious living room opens to the dining room and offers a built-in fireplace and entertainment center. The entry, breakfast area, kitchen and the dining and living areas all enjoy twelve-foot ceilings, while other rooms have traditional eight-foot ceilings. The master suite is secluded for privacy and features a bath with a separate tub and shower and a walk-in closet. Please specify crawlspace or slab foundation when ordering.

DESIGN HPU040137

Square Footage: 1,770
Width: 64'-0" Depth: 48'-0"

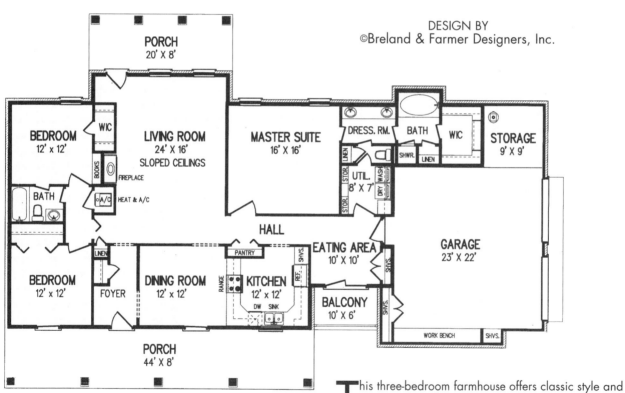

DESIGN BY
©Breland & Farmer Designers, Inc.

PORCH
20' X 8'

BEDROOM
12' x 12'

WIC

LIVING ROOM
24' X 16'
SLOPED CEILINGS

MASTER SUITE
16' X 16'

DRESS. RM.

BATH

WIC

STORAGE
9' X 9'

BOOKS

FIREPLACE

HEAT & A/C

A/C

BATH

LINEN

LINEN

SHWR.

STOR.

UTIL.
8' X 7'

DRY WASH

HALL

EATING AREA
10' X 10'

GARAGE
23' X 22'

BEDROOM
12' x 12'

LINEN

FOYER

DINING ROOM
12' X 12'

PANTRY

KITCHEN
12' X 12'

RANGE

DW SINK

REF

SHVS.

BALCONY
10' X 6'

SHVS.

SHVS.

PORCH
44' X 8'

WORK BENCH

SHVS.

DESIGN HPU040139

Square Footage: 1,925
Width: 78'-0" Depth: 52'-0"

This three-bedroom farmhouse offers classic style and an up-to-date floor plan. The slope-ceilinged living room offers a fireplace and French-door access to a covered rear porch. The kitchen features a large pantry and is located between the casual eating area and the formal dining room. Two family bedrooms, one with built-in bookshelves and a walk-in closet, share a full bath to the left of the living room. To the right, the owners suite includes a dressing room and a full bath with a walk-in closet. Please specify crawlspace or slab foundation when ordering.

DESIGN HPU040140

First Floor: 1,230 square feet
Second Floor: 477 square feet
Total: 1,707 square feet
Bonus Room: 195 square feet
Width: 40'-0" Depth: 53'-0"

L

With sunny windows throughout and a wonderfully open living space, this plan appears larger than its modest square footage. The great room is highlighted with a corner window, a fireplace and a soaring ceiling. The dining room continues the open feeling and is easily served from the kitchen. A bayed nook complements the island kitchen that also has a stylish wraparound counter. The owners bedroom suite has a lofty vaulted ceiling. Upstairs there are two family bedrooms that share a full hall bath—plus a bonus room that can be developed as needed.

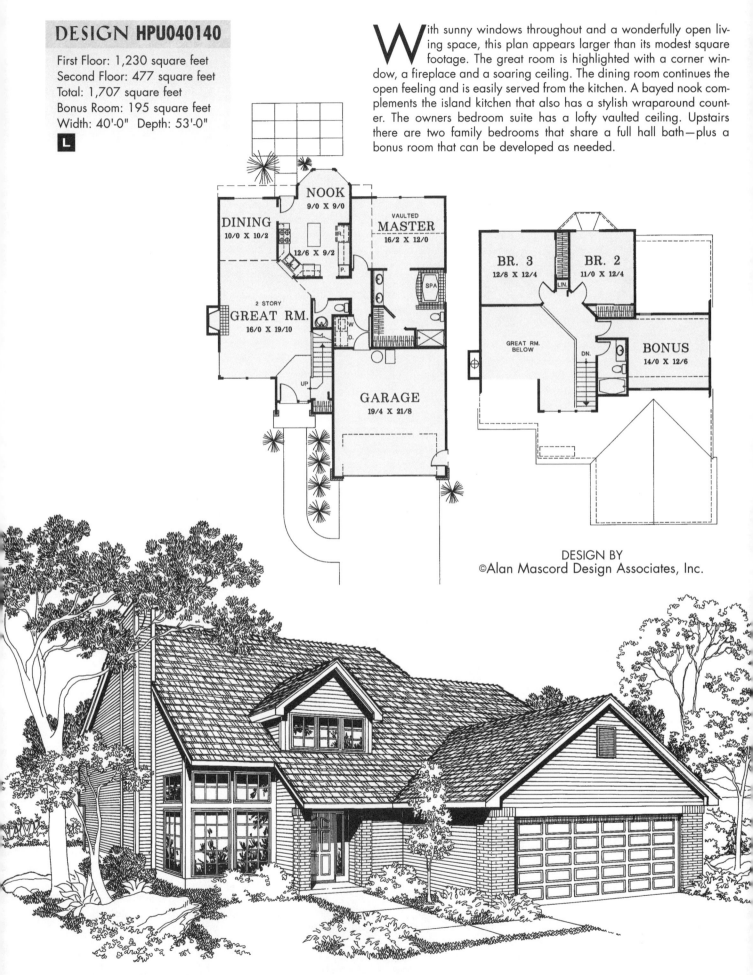

NOOK
9/0 X 9/0

DINING
10/0 X 10/2

VAULTED
MASTER
16/2 X 12/0

12/6 X 9/2

2 STORY
GREAT RM.
16/0 X 19/10

SPA

UP

GARAGE
19/4 X 21/8

BR. 3
12/8 X 12/4

BR. 2
11/0 X 12/4

LIN.

GREAT RM.
BELOW

DN.

BONUS
14/0 X 12/6

DESIGN BY
©Alan Mascord Design Associates, Inc.

DESIGN HPU040141

Square Footage: 1,687
Width: 50'-0" Depth: 52'-0"

L

Intriguing rooflines create a dynamic exterior for this home. The interior floor plan is equally attractive. Toward the rear, a wide archway forms the entrance to the spacious family living area with its centrally placed fireplace and bay-windowed nook. An island counter, mitered corner window and walk-in pantry complete the efficient kitchen. This home also boasts a terrific master suite complete with a walk-in wardrobe, spa tub with corner windows, and a compartmented shower and toilet area. Two family bedrooms share a hall bath.

DESIGN BY
©Alan Mascord Design Associates, Inc.

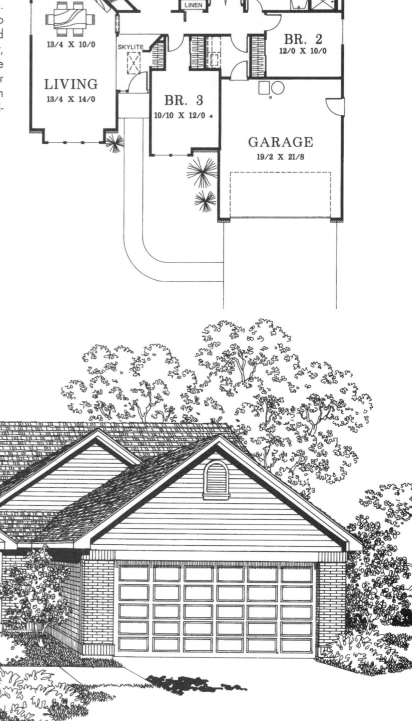

FAMILY
13/0 X 17/0

MASTER
12/0 X 15/0

SPA

10/0 X 13/0

PANTRY

LINEN

13/4 X 10/0

SKYLITE

BR. 2
12/0 X 10/0

LIVING
13/4 X 14/0

BR. 3
10/10 X 12/0 +

GARAGE
19/2 X 21/8

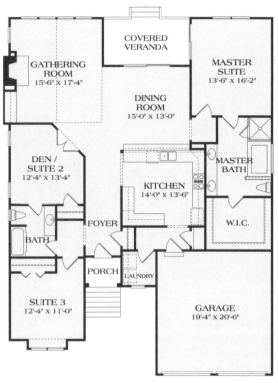

DESIGN HPU040143

Square Footage: 1,915
Width: 46'-0" Depth: 60'-2"

A sunny bay window and a shady recessed entry create an elegant impression in this lovely design. The sleeping quarters are arranged for privacy along the perimeter of the spacious living areas. The kitchen provides generous work space, and the dining room is open to the gathering room with fireplace. To the rear, a covered veranda is accessible from the dining room and the master suite. Note the lavish bath and huge walk-in closet in the master suite.

DESIGN BY
©Living Concepts Home Planning

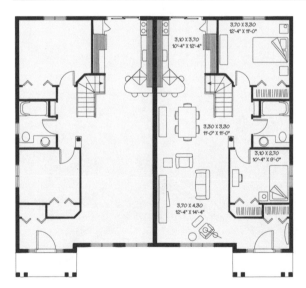

E legant living can be found in this duplex home. Enhanced with columns and a lovely pediment just above the entryway, this design offers slight differences in facade and window treatments. One side enjoys a circle-top window and an open gable, while the other is understated with a gable roofline. Inside, the floor plans are identical. The open living area provides space for a dining area and entertaining space. The kitchen features a breakfast bar and plenty of counter space. Two bedrooms and a full bath complete this efficient design. This home is designed with a basement foundation.

DESIGN HPU040142

Total: 1,893 square feet
Width: 48'-0" Depth: 40'-0"

DESIGN BY
©Drummond Designs, Inc.

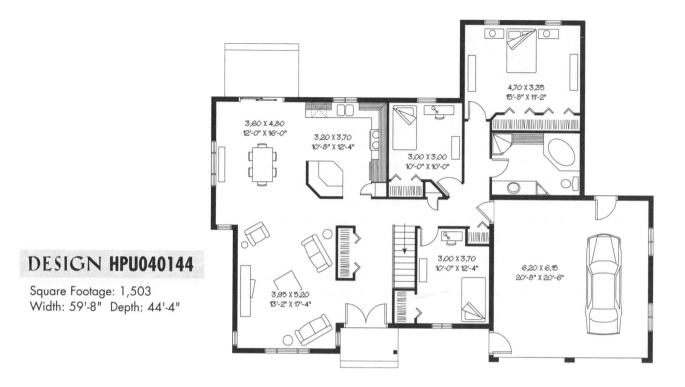

DESIGN HPU040144

Square Footage: 1,503
Width: 59'-8" Depth: 44'-4"

Traditional lines and an elegant double-door entry give this home curb appeal. In front, a large picture window is accented by a slight arch and keystone. The living room just to the left of the foyer is open to the dining room, which features a bumped-out bay flooding the area with natural light and ambience. The L-shaped kitchen boasts an island and services the dining and living rooms with ease. Two family bedrooms are down the hall. The owners suite enjoys plenty of closet space. The spacious full bath features a separate tub and shower. This home is designed with a basement foundation.

DESIGN BY
©Drummond Designs, Inc.

A lovely front porch invites family and friends into the great room that features a fireplace and open, flowing planning. The dining area enjoys an open view of the great room and the rear porch—perfect for entertaining. An island kitchen serves both areas with ease. The owners suite is positioned at the rear with a walk-in closet, dual vanities, compartmented toilet, and separate tub and shower. Two family bedrooms to the left share a full bath. Please specify basement, crawlspace or slab foundation when ordering.

Garage
20-6x21-0

Porch
15-2x8-8

Stor.
6-7x5-11

Laun.
7-11x6-2

Kitchen
13-0x12-0

Dining
14-9x12-0

Owner's
Bedroom
13-5x17-1

Bedroom
10-1x13-0

Bath

Greatroom
16-0x16-4

Bath

Foyer

Bedroom
13-10x11-1

Porch
22-3x7-2

DESIGN HPU040145

Square Footage: 1,709
Bonus Space: 710 square feet
Width: 54'-6" Depth: 62'-8"

DESIGN BY
©Larry James & Associates, Inc.

Future
19-4x16-2

Future
16-3x13-7

Future
13-4x10-6

©1999 Donald A. Gardner, Inc.

B. NATHAN

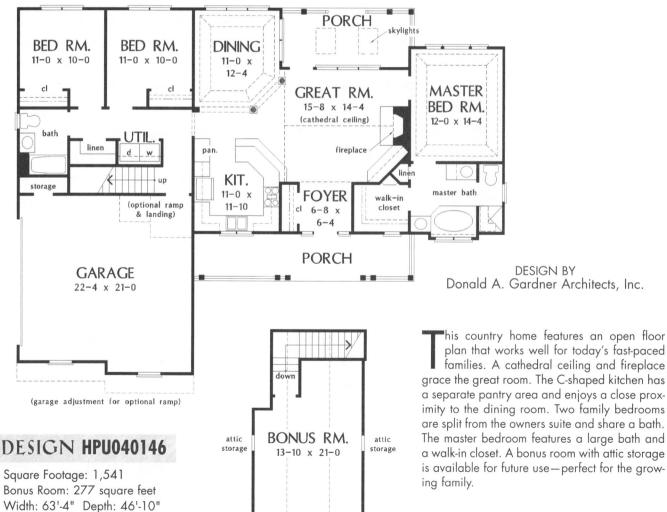

PORCH

skylights

BED RM.
11-0 x 10-0

BED RM.
11-0 x 10-0

DINING
11-0 x
12-4

GREAT RM.
15-8 x 14-4
(cathedral ceiling)

MASTER
BED RM.
12-0 x 14-4

cl

cl

bath

UTIL.

linen

d   w

pan.

fireplace

linen

storage

up

KIT.
11-0 x
11-10

FOYER
6-8 x
6-4

cl

walk-in
closet

master bath

(optional ramp
& landing)

GARAGE
22-4 x 21-0

PORCH

DESIGN BY
Donald A. Gardner Architects, Inc.

(garage adjustment for optional ramp)

down

attic
storage

BONUS RM.
13-10 x 21-0

attic
storage

DESIGN HPU040146

Square Footage: 1,541
Bonus Room: 277 square feet
Width: 63'-4" Depth: 46'-10"

This country home features an open floor plan that works well for today's fast-paced families. A cathedral ceiling and fireplace grace the great room. The C-shaped kitchen has a separate pantry area and enjoys a close proximity to the dining room. Two family bedrooms are split from the owners suite and share a bath. The master bedroom features a large bath and a walk-in closet. A bonus room with attic storage is available for future use—perfect for the growing family.

119

DESIGN BY
Donald A. Gardner Architects, Inc.

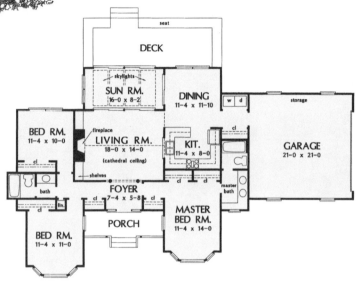

DESIGN HPU040147

Square Footage: 1,506
Width: 71'-0" Depth: 42'-4"

A lovely facade, adorned with multi-pane windows, shutters, dormers, bay windows and a covered porch, gives way to a truly livable floor plan. The living room, with a cathedral ceiling, fireplace, paddle fan, built-in cabinets and bookshelves, directly accesses the sun room through two sliding glass doors. Sleeping accommodations include a master bedroom with ample closet space and two family bedrooms. Note the split-bedroom plan configuration—providing utmost privacy.

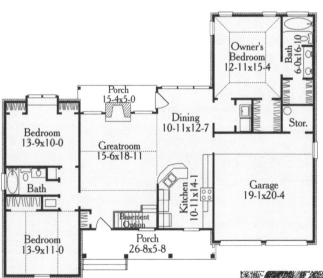

Two covered porches lend a relaxing charm to this ranch home. Inside, windows frame the focal-point fireplace. The vaulted ceiling in the great room adds spaciousness to the adjoining kitchen and dining areas. A tray ceiling decorates the owners suite, which also sports two walk-in closets and a full bath with two vanities. Two family bedrooms sit on the other side of the plan and share a full bath. Please specify basement, crawlspace or slab foundation when ordering.

DESIGN HPU040148

Square Footage: 1,643
Width: 62'-2" Depth: 51'-4"

DESIGN BY
©Larry James & Associates, Inc.

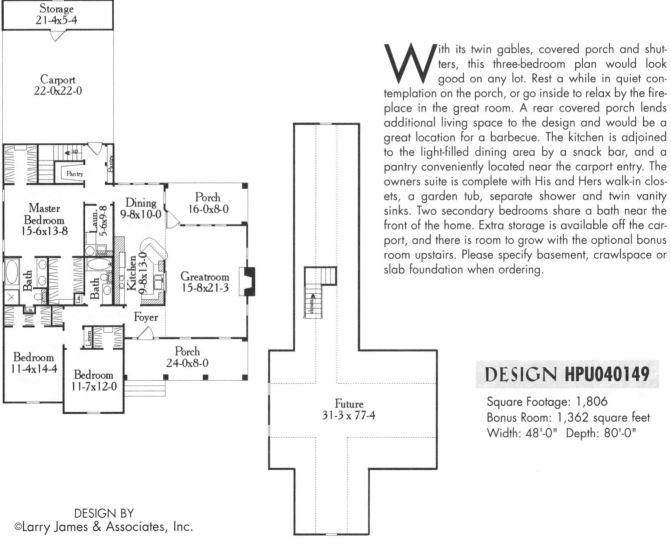

Storage
21-4x5-4

Carport
22-0x22-0

Pantry

Master
Bedroom
15-6x13-8

Laun.
5-6x9-8

Dining
9-8x10-0

Porch
16-0x8-0

Bath

Bath

Kitchen
9-8x13-0

Greatroom
15-8x21-3

Foyer

Bedroom
11-4x14-4

Linen

Bedroom
11-7x12-0

Porch
24-0x8-0

Future
31-3 x 77-4

With its twin gables, covered porch and shutters, this three-bedroom plan would look good on any lot. Rest a while in quiet contemplation on the porch, or go inside to relax by the fireplace in the great room. A rear covered porch lends additional living space to the design and would be a great location for a barbecue. The kitchen is adjoined to the light-filled dining area by a snack bar, and a pantry conveniently located near the carport entry. The owners suite is complete with His and Hers walk-in closets, a garden tub, separate shower and twin vanity sinks. Two secondary bedrooms share a bath near the front of the home. Extra storage is available off the carport, and there is room to grow with the optional bonus room upstairs. Please specify basement, crawlspace or slab foundation when ordering.

DESIGN HPU040149

Square Footage: 1,806
Bonus Room: 1,362 square feet
Width: 48'-0" Depth: 80'-0"

DESIGN BY
©Larry James & Associates, Inc.

DESIGN HPU040151

First Floor: 1,168 square feet
Second Floor: 498 square feet
Total: 1,666 square feet
Width: 44'-0" Depth: 44'-0"

DESIGN BY
©Ahmann Design, Inc.

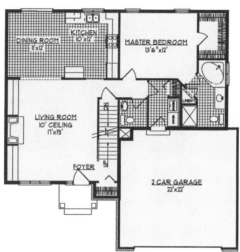

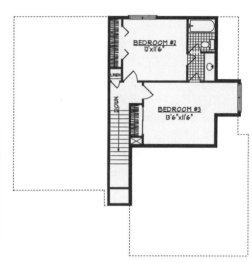

To begin this home, the foyer opens to the luxurious living room with a cozy fireplace surrounded by built-in cabinets. Sliding doors in the dining area are a perfect escape to the backyard. A first-floor master bedroom is ideal for privacy. Two additional bedrooms occupy the second floor; they have ample closet space and share a full bath. Upstairs or down, this two-story home is packed with features.

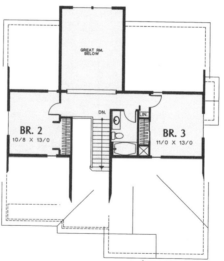

DESIGN HPU040150

First Floor: 1,396 square feet
Second Floor: 523 square feet
Total: 1,919 square feet
Width: 44'-0" Depth: 51'-0"

A covered porch flanked with double columns provides special interest for this lovely traditional home. A separate entry through the den creates a perfect opportunity for use as an office or home-operated business. The foyer leads to all areas of the house, maximizing livability. The split bedrooms, with the master suite on the first floor and two secondary bedrooms upstairs, make this an ideal design for empty-nesters or active retired couples.

DESIGN BY
©Alan Mascord Design Associates, Inc.

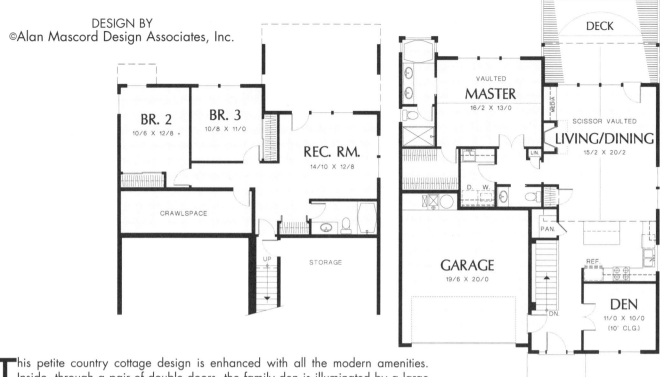

BR. 2
10/6 X 12/8 +

BR. 3
10/8 X 11/0

REC. RM.
14/10 X 12/8

CRAWLSPACE

STORAGE

UP

VAULTED
MASTER
16/2 X 13/0

MEDIA

SCISSOR VAULTED
LIVING/DINING
15/2 X 20/2

DECK

LIN.

D. W.

PAN.

GARAGE
19/6 X 20/0

REF.

DN.

DEN
11/0 X 10/0
(10' CLG.)

This petite country cottage design is enhanced with all the modern amenities. Inside, through a pair of double doors, the family den is illuminated by a large window. The kitchen, which features efficient pantry space, opens to the living/dining area. This spacious room is highlighted by a scissor vaulted ceiling, and features a warming fireplace and nook space. The living/dining room also overlooks a large rear deck, which is accessed through a back door. Secluded on the ground level for extra privacy, the vaulted master bedroom includes a private full bath and a walk-in closet. A laundry room, two-car garage and powder room all complete this floor. Downstairs, two additional family bedrooms share a hall bath. The recreation room is an added bonus. Extra storage space is also available on this floor.

DESIGN HPU040152

Main Level: 1,230 square feet
Lower Level: 769 square feet
Total: 1,999 square feet
Width: 40'-0" Depth: 52'-6"

DESIGN HPU040153

Square Footage: 1,550
Width: 62'-8" Depth: 36'-0"

DESIGN BY
©R.L. Pfotenhauer

A handsome porch dressed up with Greek Revival details greets visitors warmly in this early American home. The foyer opens to the airy and spacious living room and dining room with vaulted ceilings. The secluded master bedroom also sports a vaulted ceiling and is graced with a dressing area, private bath and walk-in closet. Two decks located at the rear of the plan are accessed via the master bedroom, kitchen and living room. A full bath serves the two family bedrooms.

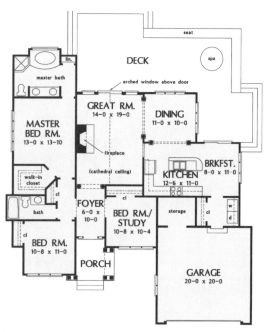

E nter through a beautiful arched entrance into the enchantment of modern American tradition. Straight beyond the foyer, the great room is spaciously enhanced by a cathedral ceiling and features a fireplace and an illuminating arched window. The island kitchen/breakfast area is open to the dining room, which overlooks a large rear deck with a spa. A complete master suite and two other bedrooms are accommodating sleeping areas for the family.

DESIGN HPU040154

Square Footage: 1,542
Width: 52'-8" Depth: 65'-2"

DESIGN BY
Donald A. Gardner Architects, Inc.

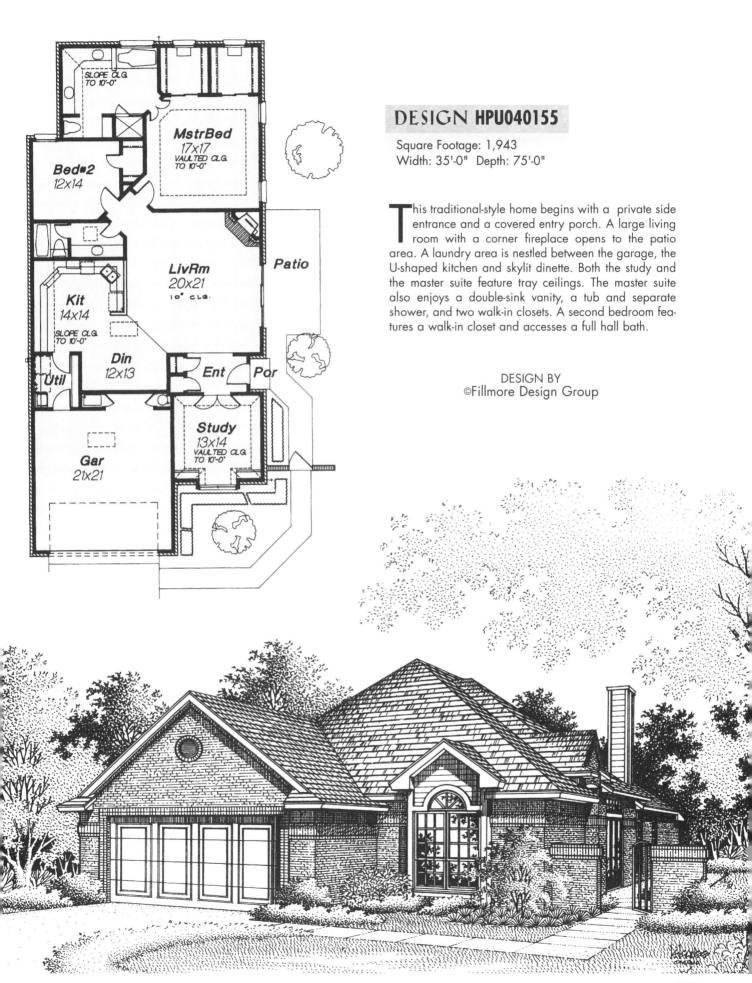

DESIGN HPU040155

Square Footage: 1,943
Width: 35'-0" Depth: 75'-0"

This traditional-style home begins with a private side entrance and a covered entry porch. A large living room with a corner fireplace opens to the patio area. A laundry area is nestled between the garage, the U-shaped kitchen and skylit dinette. Both the study and the master suite feature tray ceilings. The master suite also enjoys a double-sink vanity, a tub and separate shower, and two walk-in closets. A second bedroom features a walk-in closet and accesses a full hall bath.

DESIGN BY
©Fillmore Design Group

Floor plan labels:

- SLOPE CLG. TO 10'-0"
- MstrBed 17x17 VAULTED CLG. TO 10'-0"
- Bed#2 12x14
- LivRm 20x21 10° CLG.
- Patio
- Kit 14x14 SLOPE CLG. TO 10'-0"
- Din 12x13
- Util
- Ent
- Por
- Study 13x14 VAULTED CLG. TO 10'-0"
- Gar 21x21

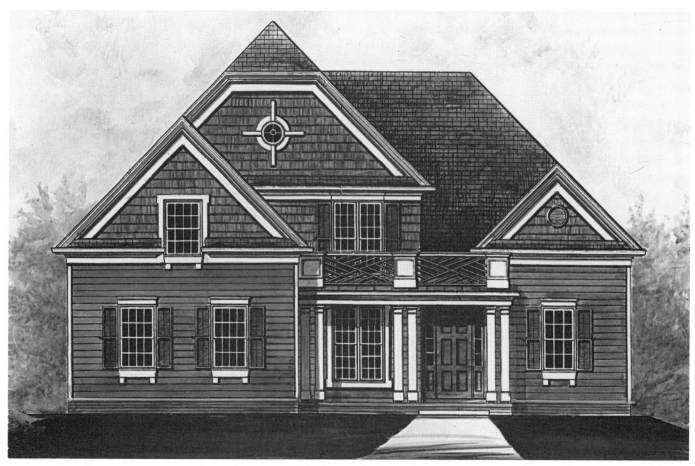

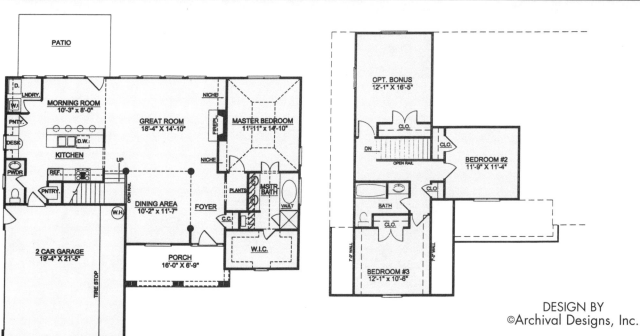

PATIO

D.
LNDRY.
W.
MORNING ROOM
10'-3" x 8'-0"
PNTY.
DESK
PWDR
REF.
KITCHEN
D.W.
PNTRY.
2 CAR GARAGE
19'-4" X 21'-5"
TIRE STOP
W.H.
UP
OPEN RAIL
GREAT ROOM
18'-4" X 14'-10"
NICHE
FIREPL.
NICHE
PLANTS
MSTR.
BATH
C.C.
VAULT
DINING AREA
10'-2" x 11'-7"
FOYER
PORCH
16'-0" X 6'-9"
W.I.C.
MASTER BEDROOM
11'-11" x 14'-10"

OPT. BONUS
12'-1" X 16'-5"
CLO.
DN
OPEN RAIL
CLO.
BEDROOM #2
11'-9" X 11'-4"
CLO.
BATH
CLO.
BEDROOM #3
12'-1" x 10'-6"
7'-0" WALL
7'-0" WALL

DESIGN BY
©Archival Designs, Inc.

DESIGN HPU040156

First Floor: 1,234 square feet
Second Floor: 458 square feet
Total: 1,692 square feet
Bonus Room: 236 square feet
Width: 48'-6" Depth: 42'-4"

With New England charm, this early American Cape Cod is a quaint haven for any family. Enter from the porch into the foyer, which opens to the dining area and great room. The great room is illuminated by a wall of windows, and features a fireplace with two built-in niches on either side. An efficient kitchen is brightened by the morning room, which accesses an outdoor porch. The opposite side of the home is dedicated to the master suite, which includes a vaulted master bath and a spacious walk-in closet. A two-car garage completes this floor. Two secondary bedrooms reside upstairs and share a full hall bath. An optional bonus room can be used as a fourth bedroom, a playroom or a home office.

DESIGN BY
©Archival Designs, Inc.

DESIGN HPU040157

First Floor: 1,638 square feet
Second Floor: 1,763 square feet
Total: 3,401 square feet
Width: 74'-0" Depth: 46'-0"

MSTR. BATH

12'0" CEILING
MSTR. BEDROOM
18'0" X 17'6"

STUDY
7'6" X 14'6" BATH

W.I.C.
16'6" X 6'0"

DRESSER

W.I.C.

CLO.

BEDROOM #2
12'0" X 13'8"

CLO.

BEDROOM #3
13'6" X 11'4"

UPPER
FOYER

BEDROOM #4
12'4" X 17'0"

LIN.

CLO.

BATH

PORCH

BREAKFAST ROOM
15'3" X 11'10"

COVERED
VERANDA

KITCHEN

VLT.

VLT.

OPT.
VEG.
SINK

FAMILY ROOM
14'8" X 24'4"

VLT.

3 CAR GARAGE
21'4" X 33'4"

LAUN.

PWR.
RM.

COATS

ARCH

NICHE   NICHE   NICHE

BALCONY ABOVE

REF.

UP

PARLOUR
11'8" X 14'6"

FOYER
10'0" X 10'4"

DINING ROOM
12'4" X 15'8"

VLT.

Double doors open to a two-story foyer in this elegant home. Flanking the foyer on the right is the formal dining room and on the left, the formal parlor. A spacious kitchen features an island for easy meal preparation and also access-es the breakfast and family rooms. Upstairs, the master bedroom is luxurious; it features a fire-place, walk-in closet and master bath. Bedrooms 2 and 3—each with walk-in closets—share a full bath, while Bedroom 4 offers a private bath as well as a study area.

127

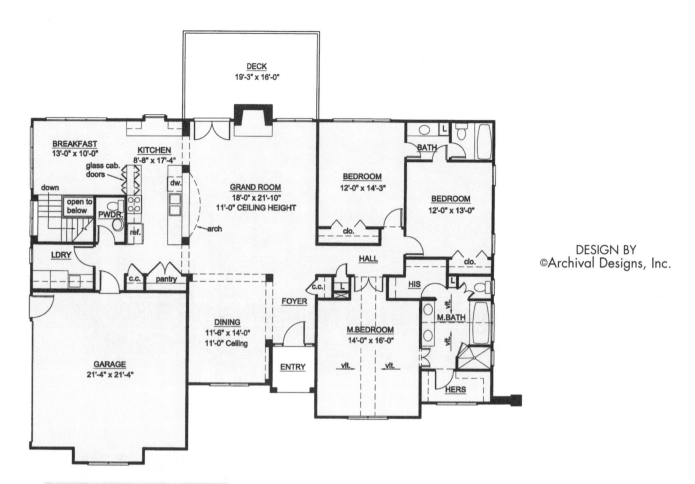

DECK
19'-3" x 16'-0"

BREAKFAST
13'-0" x 10'-0"

KITCHEN
8'-8" x 17'-4"

glass cab.
doors

down

open to
below

PWDR.

ref.

arch

LDRY

c.c. pantry

GRAND ROOM
18'-0" x 21'-10"
11'-0" CEILING HEIGHT

BATH

BEDROOM
12'-0" x 14'-3"

BEDROOM
12'-0" x 13'-0"

clo.

HALL

clo.

c.c.

HIS

FOYER

M.BATH

DINING
11'-6" x 14'-0"
11'-0" Ceiling

M.BEDROOM
14'-0" x 16'-0"

vlt.

vlt.

ENTRY

vlt.

vlt.

HERS

GARAGE
21'-4" x 21'-4"

DESIGN BY
©Archival Designs, Inc.

DESIGN HPU040158

Square Footage: 1,751
Width: 64'-0" Depth: 40'-6"

Fine detailing gives this European home a classic exterior. Beyond the foyer, columns define the dining room, and the grand room includes a fireplace and French doors accessible to the rear deck. The kitchen is filled with amenities such as glass cabinet doors, a large pantry and a view of the grand room over the sink. Easily accessible from the kitchen is the breakfast room, laundry room and powder room. Three spacious bedrooms reside on the right side of the plan. The master suite features a deluxe master bath with His and Hers closets, a whirlpool tub, separate shower and dual vanities. The two additional family bedrooms each include private access to a full compartmented bath.

DESIGN HPU040159

Square Footage: 1,670
Width: 50'-0" Depth: 45'-0"

With an offset entrance, this home adds interest and charm to any neighborhood. Enter into a spacious family room, with a galley kitchen nearby offering easy access to the sunny breakfast room. Bedrooms 2 and 3 each have walk-in closets and share a full hall bath. Bedroom 2, which opens off the family room, could also be used as a den. The formal dining room separates the master bedroom from the rest of the home, providing pleasant privacy. The master suite features many amenities, including a walk-in closet, a private bath and access to a private courtyard.

W.I.C.
plant shelf above

MASTER BEDROOM
16'-11" x 13'-5"
11'-0" CEILING

built in table

BREAKFAST
8'-0" x 7'-11"
11'-0" CEILING

M. BATH

FAMILY ROOM
15'-11" x 21'-9"
11'-0" CEILING

KITCHEN
8'-0" x 10'-1"
11'-0" CEILING

arch w/ plant shelf above

COURTYARD
12'-2" x 11'-0"

DINING ROOM
13'-1" x 11'-0"
11'-0" CEILING

pantry

c.c.

BATH

BEDROOM 2
12'-6" x 11'-2"
10'-0" CEILING

PORCH
12'-0" x 22'-4"

GARAGE
19'-5" x 19'-5"

linen

W.I.C.

LNDRY.

BEDROOM 2
13'-6" x 11'-0"
8'-0" CEILING

W.I.C.

DESIGN BY
©Archival Designs, Inc.

129

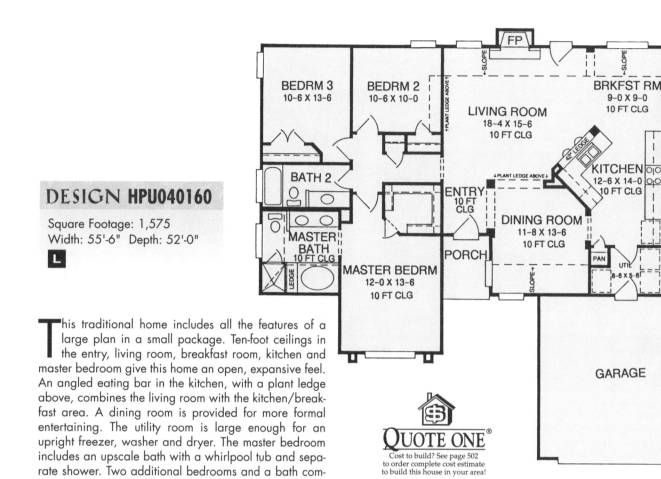

DESIGN HPU040160

Square Footage: 1,575
Width: 55'-6" Depth: 52'-0"

L

BEDRM 3
10-6 X 13-6

BEDRM 2
10-6 X 10-0

LIVING ROOM
18-4 X 15-6
10 FT CLG

BRKFST RM
9-0 X 9-0
10 FT CLG

BATH 2

KITCHEN
12-6 X 14-0
10 FT CLG

MASTER BATH
10 FT CLG

ENTRY
10 FT CLG

DINING ROOM
11-8 X 13-6
10 FT CLG

MASTER BEDRM
12-0 X 13-6
10 FT CLG

PORCH

PAN

UTIL
8-6 X 5-6

GARAGE

This traditional home includes all the features of a large plan in a small package. Ten-foot ceilings in the entry, living room, breakfast room, kitchen and master bedroom give this home an open, expansive feel. An angled eating bar in the kitchen, with a plant ledge above, combines the living room with the kitchen/breakfast area. A dining room is provided for more formal entertaining. The utility room is large enough for an upright freezer, washer and dryer. The master bedroom includes an upscale bath with a whirlpool tub and separate shower. Two additional bedrooms and a bath complete this comfortable home.

QUOTE ONE®
Cost to build? See page 502
to order complete cost estimate
to build this house in your area!

DESIGN BY
©Larry E. Belk Designs

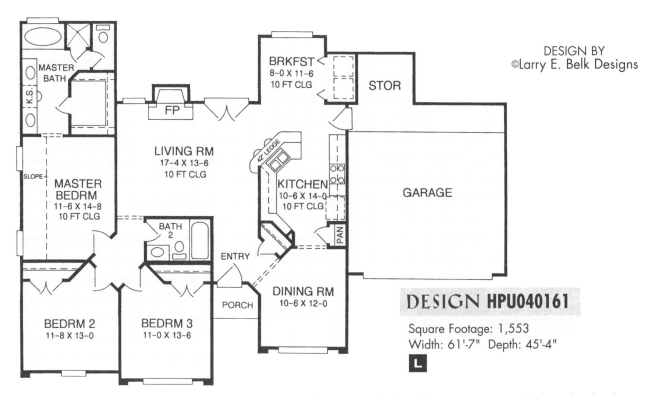

MASTER BATH

K.S.

MASTER BEDRM
11-6 X 14-8
10 FT CLG

SLOPE

FP

LIVING RM
17-4 X 13-6
10 FT CLG

BRKFST
8-0 X 11-6
10 FT CLG

STOR

42" LEDGE

KITCHEN
10-6 X 14-0
10 FT CLG

PAN

GARAGE

DESIGN BY
©Larry E. Belk Designs

BATH 2

ENTRY

BEDRM 2
11-8 X 13-0

BEDRM 3
11-0 X 13-6

PORCH

DINING RM
10-6 X 12-0

DESIGN HPU040161

Square Footage: 1,553
Width: 61'-7" Depth: 45'-4"

L

Two dominating brick gables give a unique look to this lovely starter home. Inside, the foyer opens to a great room with ten-foot ceilings. A dining room for formal entertaining is located to the right. Ten-foot ceilings continue throughout the kitchen and breakfast room and give the home an open, spacious feel. An angled kitchen sink and a bar open the kitchen to the living room and breakfast room, thus allowing the cook to be part of all family gatherings. As an added bonus, the angled design brings the fireplace into view from the kitchen. The master suite features a master bath loaded with all the amenities, including double vanities, a whirlpool tub and a separate shower. Bedrooms 2 and 3 and the second bath are located close by. Please specify crawlspace or slab foundation when ordering.

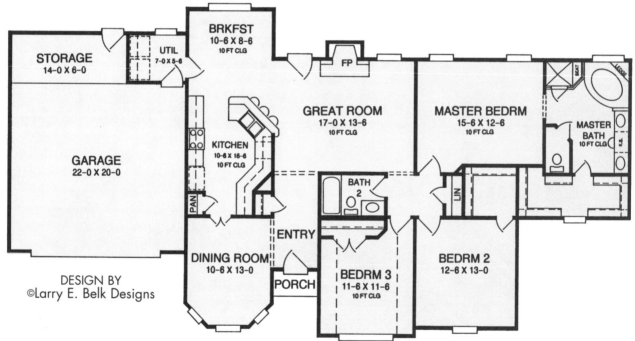

DESIGN BY
©Larry E. Belk Designs

DESIGN HPU040162

Square Footage: 1,742
Width: 78'-0" Depth: 40'-10"

This traditional design warmly welcomes both family and visitors with a delightful bay window, a Palladian window and shutters. The entry introduces a beautiful interior plan, starting with the formal dining room, the central great room with a fireplace, views and access to outdoor spaces. Ten-foot ceilings in the major living areas give the home an open, spacious feel. The kitchen features an angled eating bar, a pantry and lots of cabinet and counter space. Comfort and style abound in the distinctive master suite, offering a high ceiling, corner whirlpool tub, knee-space vanity and compartmented toilet. An ample walk-in closet with a window for natural light completes this retreat. Nearby, Bedrooms 2 and 3 share a hall bath, and Bedroom 3 offers a raised ceiling. Please specify crawlspace or slab foundation when ordering.

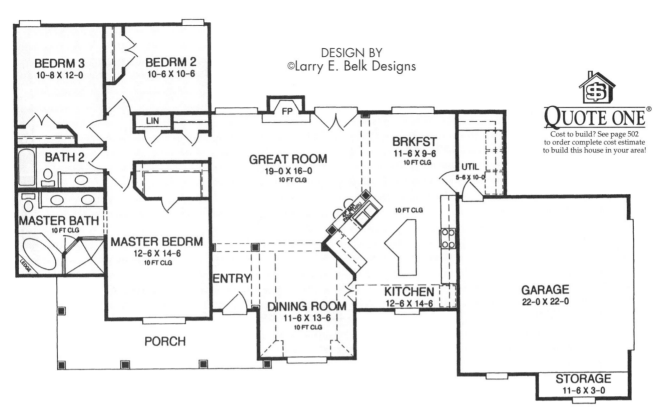

DESIGN BY
©Larry E. Belk Designs

BEDRM 3
10-8 X 12-0

BEDRM 2
10-6 X 10-6

LIN

GREAT ROOM
19-0 X 16-0
10 FT CLG

FP

BRKFST
11-6 X 9-6
10 FT CLG

UTIL
5-6 X 10-0

BATH 2

10 FT CLG

MASTER BATH
10 FT CLG

MASTER BEDRM
12-6 X 14-6
10 FT CLG

LEDGE

ENTRY

KITCHEN
12-6 X 14-6

GARAGE
22-0 X 22-0

DINING ROOM
11-6 X 13-6
10 FT CLG

PORCH

STORAGE
11-6 X 3-0

A traditional brick-and-siding elevation with a lovely wraparound porch sets the stage for a plan that incorporates features demanded by today's lifestyle. The entry opens to the great room and dining room. The use of square columns to define the areas gives the plan the look and feel of a much larger home. The kitchen features loads of counter space and a large work island. The angled sink features a pass-through to the great room. Washer, dryer and freezer space are available in the utility room along with cabinets and countertops. The master bedroom includes a walk-in closet with ample space for two. The master bath features all the amenities: a corner whirlpool tub, a shower and His and Hers vanities. Bedrooms 2 and 3 are located nearby and complete the plan. Please specify slab or crawlspace foundation when ordering.

DESIGN HPU040163

Square Footage: 1,789
Width: 78'-0" Depth: 47'-0"

L

DESIGN HPU040165

First Floor: 1,250 square feet
Second Floor: 534 square feet
Total: 1,784 square feet
Width: 42'-0" Depth: 49'-0"

From the foyer to the breakfast nook and formal dining room, this two-story home has it all. To the left of the foyer sits an elegant formal dining room. Straight ahead is the great room with a central fireplace and two large rear-facing windows to bring the outdoors in. The master suite located on the main floor offers a large walk-in closet and a private bath with a double vanity. Upstairs, two additional spacious bedrooms share a full bath.

DESIGN BY
©Ahmann Design, Inc.

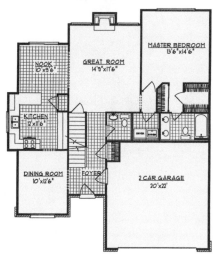

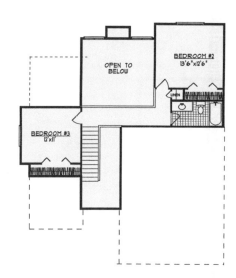

This spacious two-story home is designed for the family who needs functionality but doesn't want to sacrifice the eye-catching design. On the main floor, an open great room invites you to evenings around the fireplace. The open plan on this floor allows free circulation of guests and family from the great room to the nook to the island/snack-bar kitchen. Upstairs, the master suite is spacious and the master bath has His and Hers vanities. Two additional bedrooms share a full bath. No matter which room is your favorite, this stunning home is sure to be the home of your dreams.

DESIGN HPU040164

First Floor: 1,026 square feet
Second Floor: 726 square feet
Total: 1,752 square feet
Width: 60'-4" Depth: 43'-0"

DESIGN BY
©Ahmann Design, Inc.

DESIGN BY
©Fillmore Design Group

DESIGN HPU040166

First Floor: 1,368 square feet
Second Floor: 492 square feet
Total: 1,860 square feet
Width: 50'-0" Depth: 47'-1"

This narrow-lot, two-story home shows an abundance of exterior charm. Of particular note is the transom above the front door with glass sidelights. The two-story brick gable in front creates a massive appearance. Inside, the foyer opens directly to a formal dining room and a large great room that offers windows to the rear and a fireplace and built-in TV shelf. The family dining area features a cone ceiling and fantastic view of the rear yard. The first-floor master suite has a cathedral ceiling and two walk-in closets in the bath area. There is a covered patio off the master suite and also off the casual dining room. Two family bedrooms and a full bath complete the second floor.

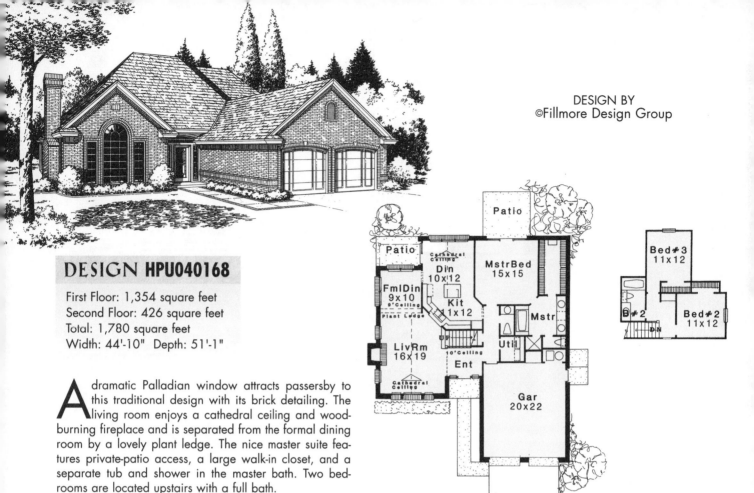

DESIGN HPU040168

First Floor: 1,354 square feet
Second Floor: 426 square feet
Total: 1,780 square feet
Width: 44'-10" Depth: 51'-1"

A dramatic Palladian window attracts passersby to this traditional design with its brick detailing. The living room enjoys a cathedral ceiling and wood-burning fireplace and is separated from the formal dining room by a lovely plant ledge. The nice master suite features private-patio access, a large walk-in closet, and a separate tub and shower in the master bath. Two bedrooms are located upstairs with a full bath.

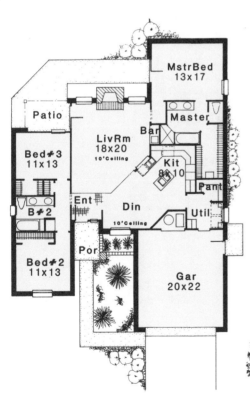

DESIGN HPU040167

Square Footage: 1,664
Width: 48'-0" Depth: 63'-1"

Soaring round-top windows lend excitement to the brick exterior of this traditional design. A spacious living room, with a grand fireplace flanked by windows, opens to the kitchen and dining areas on the right and an appealing covered patio on the left. The large master bedroom features a double-vanity bath and an oversized walk-in closet. The utility area directly accesses the garage and a walk-in pantry.

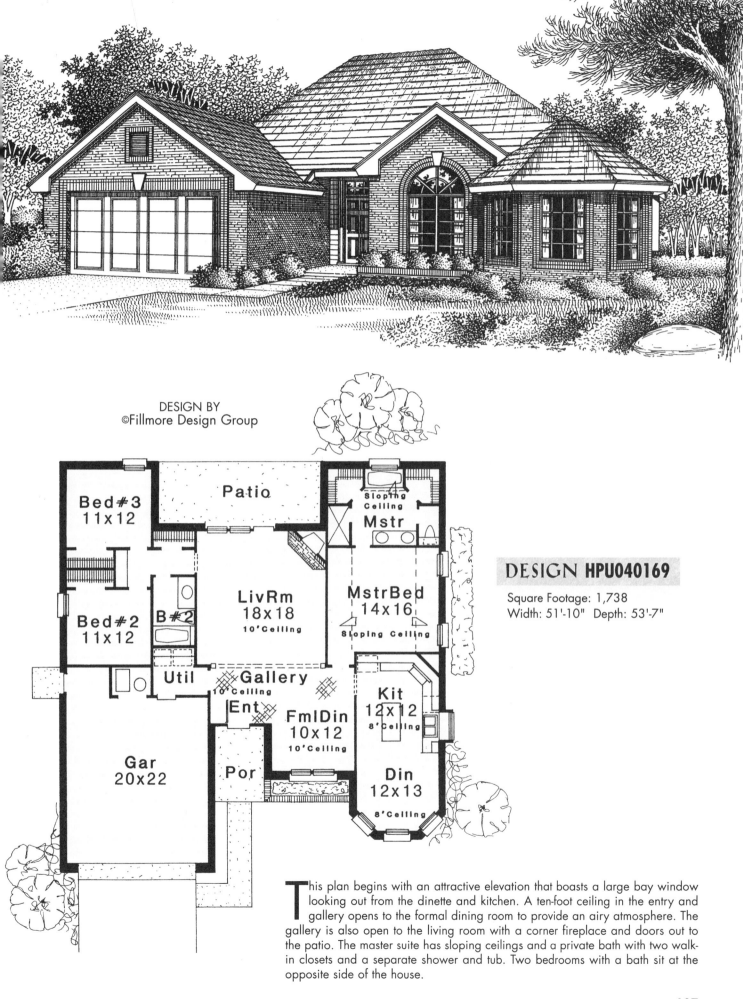

DESIGN BY
©Fillmore Design Group

Bed #3
11x12

Patio

Sloping
Ceiling

Mstr

DESIGN HPU040169

Square Footage: 1,738
Width: 51'-10" Depth: 53'-7"

LivRm
18x18
10'Ceiling

B #2

Bed #2
11x12

MstrBed
14x16
Sloping Ceiling

Util

Gallery
10'Ceiling

Ent

Kit
12x12
8'Ceiling

FmlDin
10x12
10'Ceiling

Gar
20x22

Por

Din
12x13
8'Ceiling

This plan begins with an attractive elevation that boasts a large bay window looking out from the dinette and kitchen. A ten-foot ceiling in the entry and gallery opens to the formal dining room to provide an airy atmosphere. The gallery is also open to the living room with a corner fireplace and doors out to the patio. The master suite has sloping ceilings and a private bath with two walk-in closets and a separate shower and tub. Two bedrooms with a bath sit at the opposite side of the house.

137

Arched lintels, shutters and a welcoming covered entryway lend this three-bedroom home country charm. Inside, the foyer leads directly to the great room with a fireplace and built-ins along two walls. Nearby, the kitchen joins the dining area, which has a built-in pantry and window seat. Keeping household records organized will be easy with the built-in desk by the laundry room. The sleeping quarters all reside on the left of this design. The master bedroom includes a lavish bath with a garden tub, separate shower, dual vanity sinks and compartmented toilet. Two secondary bedrooms share a bath. Homeowners will sigh with relief when they see the large storage off the carport. Please specify basement, crawlspace or slab foundation when ordering.

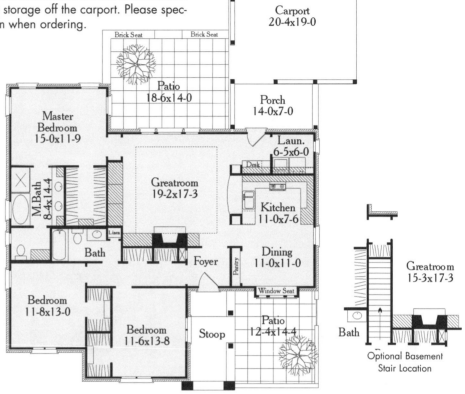

DESIGN HPU040170

Square Footage: 1,702
Width: 55'-0" Depth: 76'-4"

DESIGN BY
©Larry James & Associates, Inc.

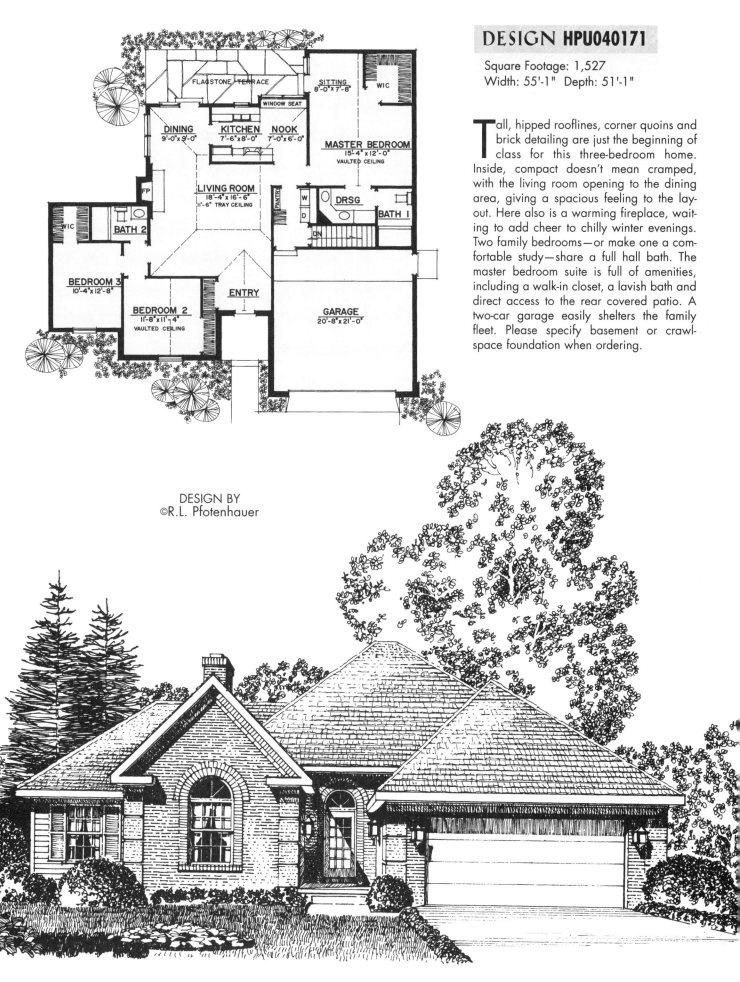

DESIGN HPU040171

Square Footage: 1,527
Width: 55'-1" Depth: 51'-1"

Tall, hipped rooflines, corner quoins and brick detailing are just the beginning of class for this three-bedroom home. Inside, compact doesn't mean cramped, with the living room opening to the dining area, giving a spacious feeling to the lay-out. Here also is a warming fireplace, waiting to add cheer to chilly winter evenings. Two family bedrooms—or make one a comfortable study—share a full hall bath. The master bedroom suite is full of amenities, including a walk-in closet, a lavish bath and direct access to the rear covered patio. A two-car garage easily shelters the family fleet. Please specify basement or crawl-space foundation when ordering.

FLAGSTONE TERRACE

SITTING
8'-0" x 7'-8"

WIC

DINING
9'-0" x 9'-0"

KITCHEN
7'-6" x 8'-0"

NOOK
7'-0" x 6'-0"

WINDOW SEAT

MASTER BEDROOM
15'-4" x 12'-0"
VAULTED CEILING

FP

LIVING ROOM
18'-4" x 16'-6"
11'-6" TRAY CEILING

W
D

PANTRY

DRSG

BATH 1

WIC

BATH 2

DN

BEDROOM 3
10'-4" x 12'-8"

BEDROOM 2
11'-8" x 11'-4"
VAULTED CEILING

ENTRY

GARAGE
20'-8" x 21'-0"

DESIGN BY
©R.L. Pfotenhauer

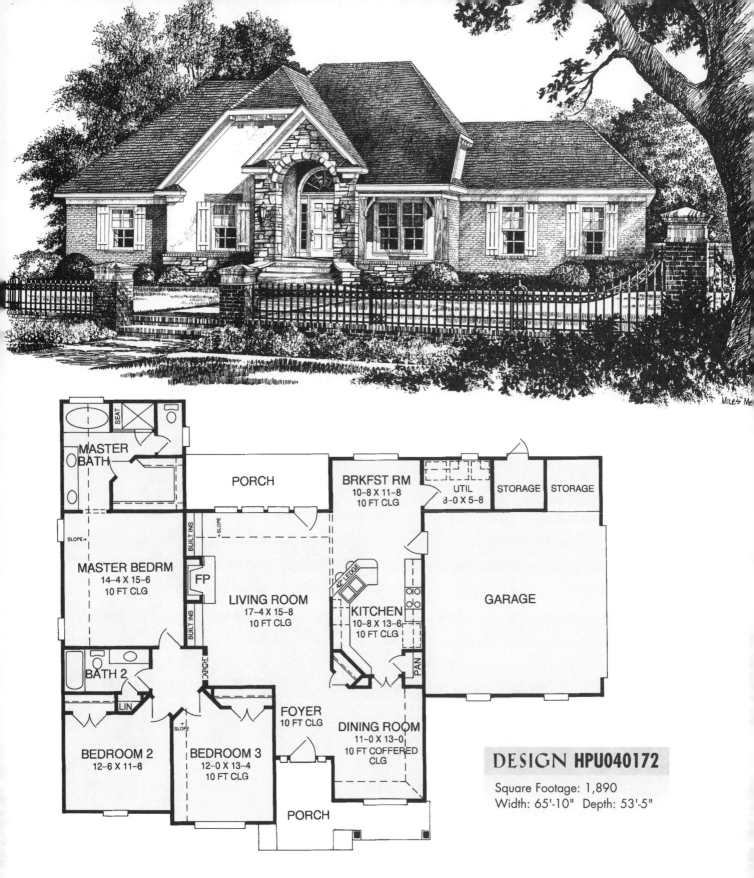

MASTER
BATH

SEAT

PORCH

BRKFST RM
10-8 X 11-8
10 FT CLG

UTIL
8-0 X 5-8

STORAGE STORAGE

SLOPE→

MASTER BEDRM
14-4 X 15-6
10 FT CLG

BUILT INS

SLOPE

FP

BUILT INS

LIVING ROOM
17-4 X 15-8
10 FT CLG

42 LEDGE

KITCHEN
10-8 X 13-6
10 FT CLG

PAN

GARAGE

BATH 2

LIN

PORCH

BEDROOM 2
12-6 X 11-6

SLOPE

BEDROOM 3
12-0 X 13-4
10 FT CLG

FOYER
10 FT CLG

DINING ROOM
11-0 X 13-0
10 FT COFFERED
CLG

PORCH

DESIGN HPU040172

Square Footage: 1,890
Width: 65'-10" Depth: 53'-5"

DESIGN BY
©Larry E. Belk Designs

This charming country home possesses a heart of gold. Wide views invite natural light and provide a sense of spaciousness in the living room. A fireplace with an extended hearth is framed by built-in bookcases and complemented by a sloped ceiling. A well-organized kitchen has wrapping counters and a serving ledge, which overlooks the breakfast area. Bright light fills the casual dining space through a wide window. The formal dining room has a coffered ceiling and enjoys easy service from the kitchen through double doors. The master suite contains a garden tub and a separate shower with a seat. Please specify crawlspace or slab foundation when ordering.

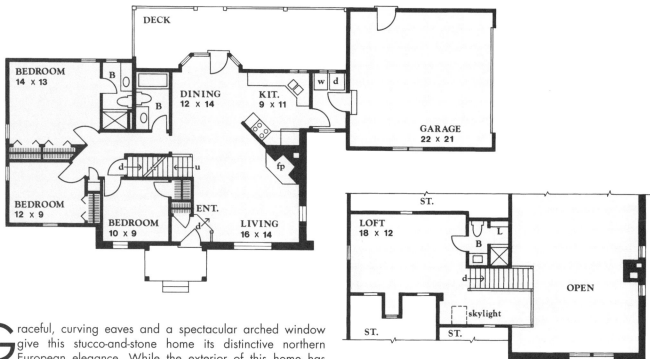

Graceful, curving eaves and a spectacular arched window give this stucco-and-stone home its distinctive northern European elegance. While the exterior of this home has abundant Old World charm, the interior is filled with contemporary amenities. From the entrance, an expansive open area comprised of the living room, dining room and kitchen—all with beam ceilings—provides a dramatic centerpiece. The angled bay from the dining room opens conveniently to the rear deck, furnishing options for dining alfresco. Sleeping quarters located on the left wing of the first floor include a master bedroom with a private bath. A full bath serves both family bedrooms and is readily accessible to guests. Upstairs, a spacious loft has its own bathroom and a balcony overlooking the living room.

DESIGN HPU040173

First Floor: 1,277 square feet
Second Floor: 378 square feet
Total: 1,655 square feet
Width: 74'-8" Depth: 42'-8"

DESIGN BY
©R.L. Pfotenhauer

Though this home gives the impression of the Northwest, it will be the winner of any neighborhood. Craftsman style is evident both on the outside and the inside of this three-bedroom home. From the foyer, the two-story living room is just a couple of steps up and features a through-fireplace. The U-shaped kitchen has a cooktop work island, an adjacent nook and easy access to the formal dining room. A spacious family room shares the fireplace with the living room, is enhanced by built-ins and also offers a quiet deck for stargazing. The upstairs consists of two family bedrooms sharing a full bath and a vaulted master suite complete with a walk-in closet and sumptuous bath. A two-car, drive-under garage has plenty of room for storage. Please specify basement or slab foundation when ordering.

DESIGN BY
©Alan Mascord Design Associates, Inc.

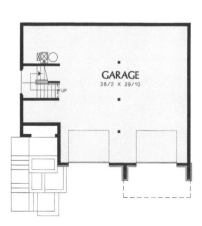

DESIGN HPU040174

Main Floor: 1,106 square feet
Upper Floor: 872 square feet
Total: 1,978 square feet
Width: 38'-0" Depth: 35'-0"

DESIGN HPU040175

First Floor: 1,097 square feet
Second Floor: 807 square feet
Total: 1,904 square feet
Width: 40'-0" Depth: 45'-0"

The combination of rafter tails, stone-and-siding and gabled rooflines gives this home plenty of curb appeal. The Craftsman styling on this three-bedroom bungalow is highly attractive. Inside, enter a cozy vaulted den through double doors, just to the left of the foyer. A spacious, vaulted great room features a fireplace and is near the formal dining room, providing entertaining ease. The kitchen offers an octagonal island, a corner sink with a window, and a pantry. Up the angled staircase is the sleeping zone. Here two secondary bedrooms share a hall bath, while the master suite is enhanced with a private bath and a walk-in closet. The three-car garage easily shelters the family fleet.

DESIGN BY
©Alan Mascord Design Associates, Inc.

This adapted Tudor-style design will fit a narrow lot and offers an efficient and stylish floor plan. A family room to the rear of the plan invites informal gatherings and casual conversation with its cozy fireplace. A nearby nook provides access to the outdoors and opens to an island-cooktop kitchen with an angled sink and a generous pantry. Living and dining rooms to the front of the plan create a spacious area for more formal entertaining, with a vaulted ceiling and a fireplace with an extended hearth in the living room. Two family bedrooms and a sumptuous master suite share a connecting balcony hall upstairs. Double doors open to the master bedroom, which offers comfort to spare with a garden tub, separate shower, twin lavatories and a walk-in closet.

DESIGN HPU040176

First Floor: 1,062 square feet
Second Floor: 838 square feet
Total: 1,900 square feet
Width: 46'-0" Depth: 48'-0"

L

DESIGN BY
©Alan Mascord Design Associates, Inc.

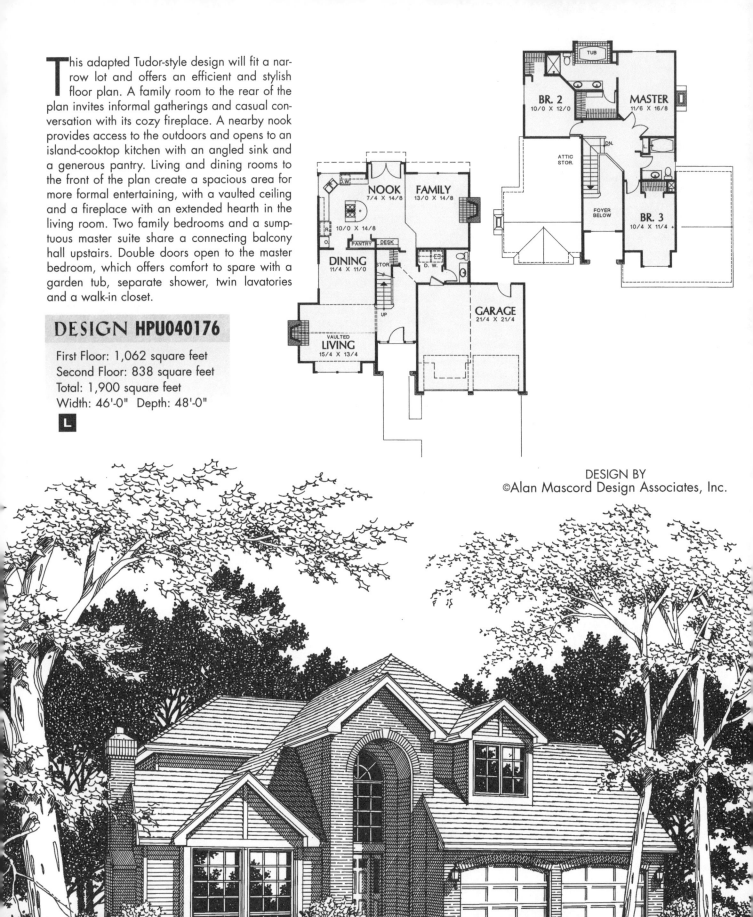

A brick arch and a two-story bay window adorn the facade of this comfortable family home. Inside, the formal bayed living room and dining room combine to make entertaining a breeze. At the rear of the home, family life is easy with the open floor plan of the family room, nook and efficient kitchen. A fireplace graces the family room, and sliding glass doors access the outdoors from the nook. A powder room is conveniently located in the entry hall to make it easily accessible. Upstairs, three bedrooms include the master suite with a pampering bath. A full hall bath with twin vanities is shared by the family bedrooms. A bonus room is available for future development as a study, library or fourth bedroom.

DESIGN HPU040177

First Floor: 972 square feet
Second Floor: 843 square feet
Total: 1,815 square feet
Bonus Room: 180 square feet
Width: 45'-0" Depth: 37'-0"

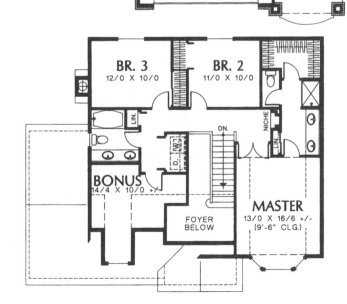

DESIGN BY
©Alan Mascord Design Associates, Inc.

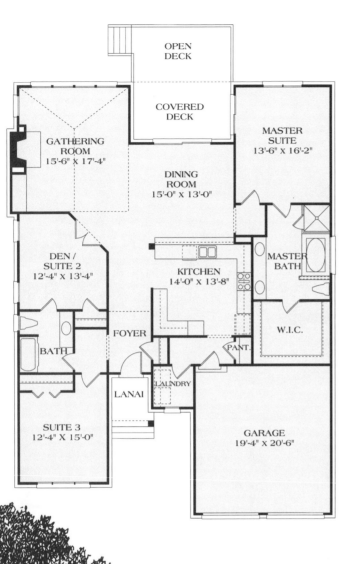

OPEN
DECK

COVERED
DECK

GATHERING
ROOM
15'-6" x 17'-4"

MASTER
SUITE
13'-6" x 16'-2"

DINING
ROOM
15'-0" X 13'-0"

DEN /
SUITE 2
12'-4" x 13'-4"

KITCHEN
14'-0" X 13'-8"

MASTER
BATH

BATH

FOYER

W.I.C.

PANT.

LANAI

LAUNDRY

SUITE 3
12'-4" X 15'-0"

GARAGE
19'-4" x 20'-6"

This cottage-style home is the picture of enchantment. The plan begins with a stylish columned lanai, which leads to a spacious foyer and hall that opens to all areas. An open, spacious gathering room shares the glow of an extended-hearth fireplace with the dining area and kitchen. The owners suite opens from a private vestibule and offers a deluxe bath with a garden tub, separate shower and U-shaped walk-in closet. Two secondary bedrooms share a full bath—one enjoys a Palladian window!

DESIGN HPU040178

Square Footage: 1,913
Width: 46'-10" Depth: 61'-0"

DESIGN BY
©Living Concepts Home Planning

A dramatic entry introduces this hillside design and offers an arched window over the door to add light to the foyer. A split staircase leads up to the main level of the home where there are formal living and dining rooms decorated with columns. A family room with a fireplace and built-in media center adjoins the island kitchen and breakfast nook at the rear. A door in the nook leads out to a rear deck. The master suite on the main level holds a walk-in closet and bath with a spa tub and separate shower. The lower level accesses the two-car garage and allows for two additional bedrooms and a full bath. A large storage space may also be used as a den, if you choose.

DESIGN BY
©Alan Mascord Design Associates, Inc.

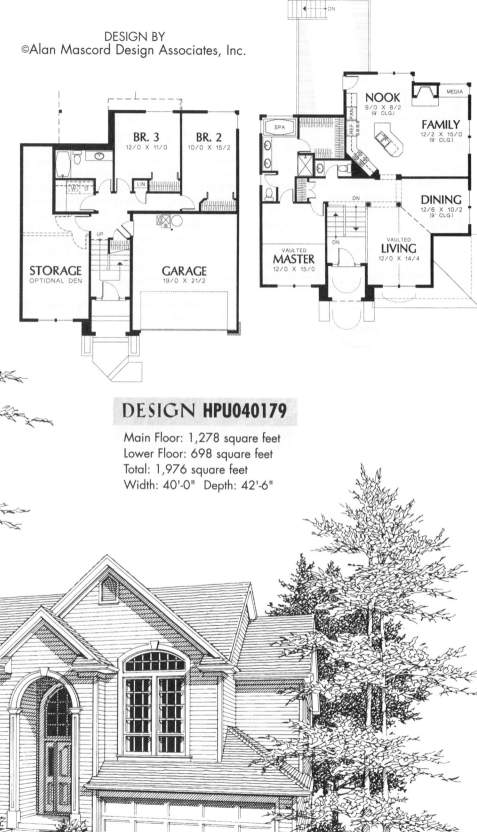

DESIGN HPU040179

Main Floor: 1,278 square feet
Lower Floor: 698 square feet
Total: 1,976 square feet
Width: 40'-0" Depth: 42'-6"

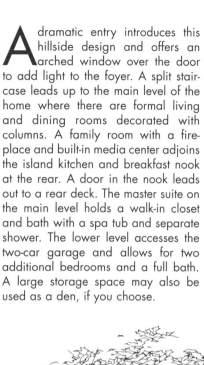

147

DESIGN BY
©Living Concepts Home Planning

This open, airy design is one that seems much larger than it actually is. A large, two-story great room, which can be viewed from the balcony above, opens into the dining room. The roomy master suite boasts a terrific walk-in closet and bath with dual lavatories. A breakfast area that opens to a deck, and corner windows at the kitchen sink help bring the outdoors in. There's plenty of storage, including an ample pantry, a two-car garage and a bonus room that can double as a fourth suite. Special features include a plant ledge over the great room and an arched, copper dormer. Please specify slab or crawlspace foundation when ordering.

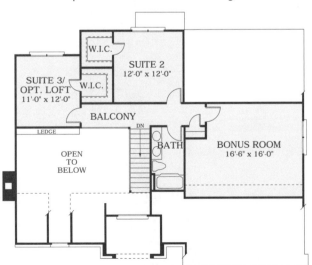

DESIGN HPU040180

First Floor: 1,383 square feet
Second Floor: 546 square feet
Total: 1,929 square feet
Bonus Room: 320 square feet
Width: 50'-6" Depth: 42'-10"

SHEER GENIUS

Comfortable homes that offer warm welcomes

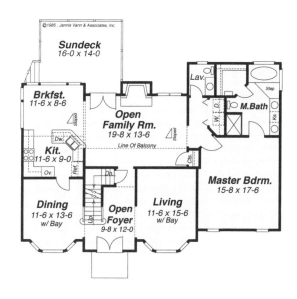

©1985 , Jannis Vann & Associates, Inc.

Sundeck 16-0 x 14-0

Brkfst. 11-6 x 8-6

Open Family Rm. 19-8 x 13-6

Lav.

M.Bath

Line Of Balcony

Kit. 11-6 x 9-0

Dining 11-6 x 13-6 w/ Bay

Open Foyer 9-8 x 12-0

Living 11-6 x 15-6 w/ Bay

Master Bdrm. 15-8 x 17-6

DESIGN HPU040181

First Floor: 1,560 square feet
Second Floor: 834 square feet
Total: 2,394 square feet
Width: 50'-0" Depth: 47'-0"

This French-style home is designed for a sloping lot, with the garage at basement level. The stone-and-stucco exterior is highlighted by interesting windows, corner quoins and a variety of gables. Inside, the two-story foyer is flanked by the formal living and dining rooms, both of which are lighted by bay windows. The family room features a fireplace and access to the sun deck. An efficient kitchen opens to a glass-walled breakfast room and provides a snack bar that serves the entire informal living area. Completing the first floor, the master suite includes a compartmented bath with a walk-in closet and twin vanities. Upstairs, three family bedrooms share a good-sized bath and views of much of the first floor.

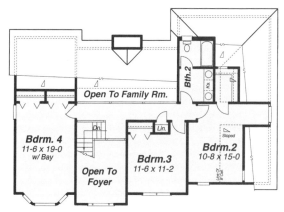

Open To Family Rm.

Bth.2

Bdrm. 4 11-6 x 19-0 w/ Bay

Open To Foyer

Bdrm.3 11-6 x 11-2

Bdrm.2 10-8 x 15-0

DESIGN BY
©Jannis Vann & Associates, Inc.

DESIGN HPU040183

Square Footage: 2,289
Width: 66'-0" Depth: 77'-0"

A striking facade with plenty of windows and column accents gives this home a regal appeal. Stucco works together with a handsome tiled roof to define a Mediterranean exterior. A see-through fireplace opens to the receiving room and graces the great room. The kitchen sits between the dining room and the great room and offers a cooktop island. The master suite provides a lounging area, a vaulted ceiling, two closets and a bath.

DESIGN BY
©Vaughn A. Lauban Designs

The dramatic entry with an arched opening leads to the comfortable interior of this delightful one-story home. Volume ceilings highlight the main living areas, which include a formal dining room and a great room with access to one of the verandas. In the turreted study, quiet time is assured. The master suite features a bath with a double-bowl vanity and a bumped-out whirlpool tub. The secondary bedrooms reside on the other side of the house.

DESIGN BY
©The Sater Design Collection

DESIGN HPU040182

Square Footage: 2,214
Width: 63'-0" Depth: 72'-0"

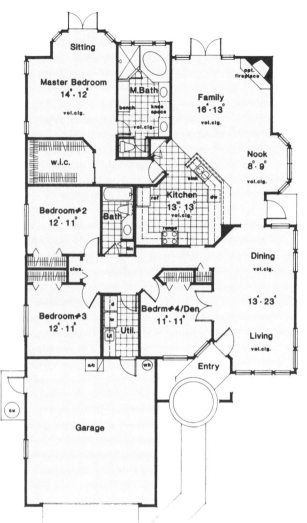

Looking for plenty of bedrooms? This design offers four, including a grand master suite with a sitting room and private bath. Bedroom 4 may be used as a den; both the foyer and the main hall access this room. The central kitchen features a pass-through counter overlooking a breakfast nook. The nearby family room highlights a corner fireplace and double-door access to the rear yard. Formal living and dining rooms are offset to the front of the plan, but open to one another. All common areas have volume ceilings, as does the master bedroom and its bath. The laundry room connects the main house to the two-car garage.

DESIGN HPU040184

Square Footage: 2,202
Width: 45'-0" Depth: 77'-4"

DESIGN BY
©Lucia Custom Home Designers, Inc.

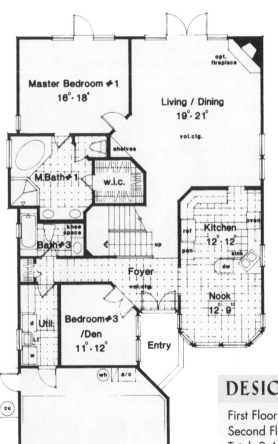

Master Bedroom #1
16⁰·18⁴

Living / Dining
19⁰·21⁰

opt. fireplace

vol.clg.

shelves

M.Bath #1

w.i.c.

knee space

Bath #3

oven

Kitchen
12·12

ref

pan

sink

dw

up

Foyer
vol.clg.

Nook
12⁰·9¹⁰

Util.

d

Lt

Bedroom #3
/Den
11⁰·12⁰

Entry

wh

a/c

cu

Garage

Generous bay windows give this home an opulent look. From the foyer, you can enter the kitchen and breakfast nook, which is housed in one of the wide bay windows. Or you can enter the den through French doors on the left—this could be a third bedroom. Or continue past the den to the laundry room and a hall bath. If you walk straight ahead from the foyer, you will end up in the combination living/dining room, which offers an optional corner fireplace and French doors to the outside. The master bedroom off this area includes a compartmented bath and a walk-in closet. The second floor houses another master suite—this one with a private balcony—and a secondary bedroom with a smaller walk-in closet and private bath.

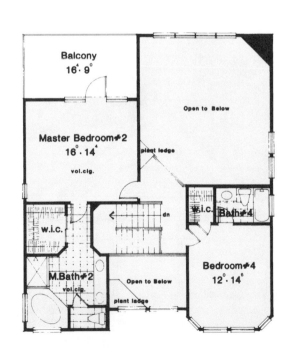

Balcony
16⁰·9⁰

Open to Below

Master Bedroom #2
16⁰·14⁴

vol.clg.

plant ledge

w.i.c.

Bath #4

dn

w.i.c.

M.Bath #2
vol.clg.

Open to Below

plant ledge

Bedroom #4
12⁰·14⁶

DESIGN HPU040185

First Floor: 1,619 square feet
Second Floor: 846 square feet
Total: 2,465 square feet
Width: 37'-4" Depth: 69'-0"

DESIGN BY
©Lucia Custom Home Designers, Inc.

Born as sunny stucco and bred in warm-weather climates, this one-story, two-bedroom home is the perfect choice for starters or empty-nesters. The living room and dining room form an open area near the gourmet kitchen. An attached breakfast nook has a wall of glass for bright casual meals. Generous outdoor access includes double doors in the master bedroom, the living room, the den and the nook all leading to outdoor spaces. Other special features include an optional wet bar, an outdoor grill and sink, an optional pool bath and built-in shelves in the den.

DESIGN HPU040186

Square Footage: 2,150
Width: 42'-0" Depth: 75'-0"

DESIGN BY
©Lucia Custom Home Designers, Inc.

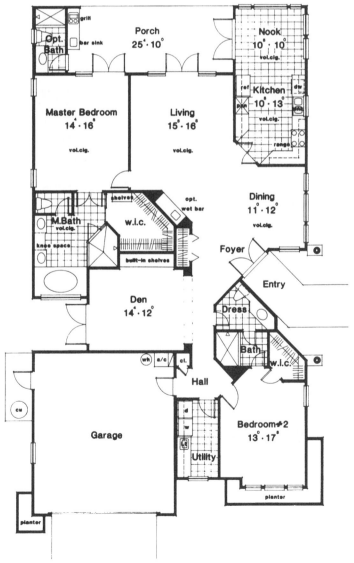

153

PATIO

MASTER SUITE
17'-8" x 12'-0"
VOL. CLG.

FAMILY ROOM
20'-0" x 14'-0"
VOL. CLG.

W.I.C.

STOR

LAZY
SUSAN

DW

M. BATH

KITCHEN

NOOK

STOR

REF

LAUN

DINING
14'-0" x 11'-8"
OPEN ABOVE

PWD

W   D

PANTRY

WH
OPT. DOOR

A/C

FOYER

GARAGE
20'-4" x 22'-0"

ENTRY

LIVING
11'-8" x 12'-4"
VOL. CLG.

Three designs give options for the exterior of this home—all three come with the same floor plan. The entry leads into a small foyer, and opens to the living room and a two-story dining room. A powder room and a U-shaped stairway are on the way to the kitchen, which offers a large work island, walk-in pantry, breakfast nook and laundry room. The family room at the rear of the plan accesses the rear patio through sliding glass doors. The master bath features a double-bowl vanity, corner window tub and walk-in closet. Three second-floor bedrooms share a bath that has a double-bowl vanity. A fifth bedroom may be added over the dining room.

BEDROOM #5
13'-0" x 11'-4"

Optional 5th
Bedroom

Alternate Elevation A

DESIGN HPU040187

First Floor: 1,514 square feet
Second Floor: 632 square feet
Total: 2,146 square feet
Width: 39'-4" Depth: 53'-4"

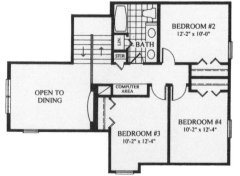

BEDROOM #2
12'-2" x 10'-0"

LIN

BATH

STOR

OPEN TO
DINING

COMPUTER
AREA

BEDROOM #3
10'-2" x 12'-4"

BEDROOM #4
10'-2" x 12'-4"

Alternate Elevation B

DESIGN BY
©Lucia Custom Home Designers, Inc.

Modern gables define this plan's dramatic exterior. A covered front porch welcomes visitors into the foyer. To the left, the great room features a warming fireplace. The dining room is highlighted by a beautiful display of bayed windows. The kitchen opens to a breakfast area, which also features a bayed window area. This split-bedroom design allows for a private first-floor master bedroom, which includes its own private bath and walk-in closet. Throughout this plan, bay-window accents, a rear deck and a screened porch provide a fresh, indoor/outdoor livability. A two-car garage completes this floor. Bonus space on the second level makes this plan an intriguing option for the growing family.

DESIGN HPU040188

First Floor: 1,563 square feet
Second Floor: 736 square feet
Total: 2,299 square feet
Bonus Room: 280 square feet
Width: 44'-0" Depth: 72'-0"

L

DESIGN BY
©Home Planners

Alternate Plan for
Crawlspace

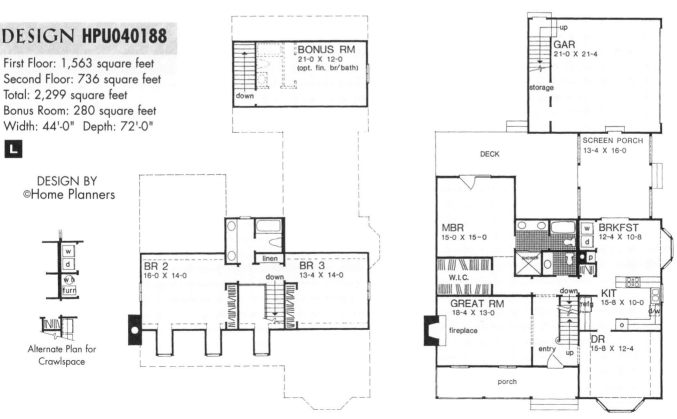

Lattice walls, pickets and horizontal siding complement a relaxed Key West design that's perfect for waterfront properties. The grand room with a fireplace, the dining room and Bedroom 2 open through French doors to the veranda. The master suite occupies the entire second floor and features access to a private balcony through double doors. This pampering suite also includes a spacious walk-in closet and a full bath with a whirlpool tub. Enclosed storage/bonus space and a garage are available on the lower level. This home is designed with a pier foundation.

DESIGN HPU040189

First Floor: 1,586 square feet
Second Floor: 601 square feet
Total: 2,187 square feet
Width: 50'-0" Depth: 44'-0"

DESIGN BY
©The Sater Design Collection

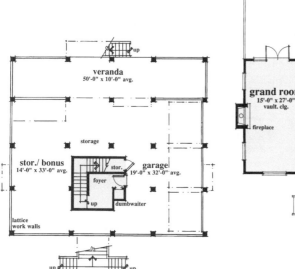

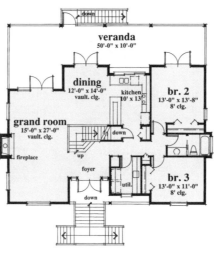

Lattice door panels, shutters, a balustrade and a metal roof add character to this delightful coastal home. Double doors flanking a fireplace open to the side sun deck from the spacious great room. Access to the rear veranda is also provided from this room. An adjacent dining room provides views of the rear grounds and space for formal and informal entertaining. The glassed-in nook shares space with the L-shaped kitchen containing a center work island. Bedrooms 2 and 3, a full bath and a utility room complete this floor. Upstairs, a sumptuous master suite awaits. Double doors extend to a private deck from the master bedroom. His and Hers walk-in closets lead the way to a grand bath featuring an arched whirlpool tub, a double-bowl vanity and a separate shower.

DESIGN BY
©The Sater Design Collection

DESIGN HPU040190

First Floor: 1,736 square feet
Second Floor: 640 square feet
Total: 2,376 square feet
Bonus Space: 840 square feet
Width: 54'-0" Depth: 44'-0"

L

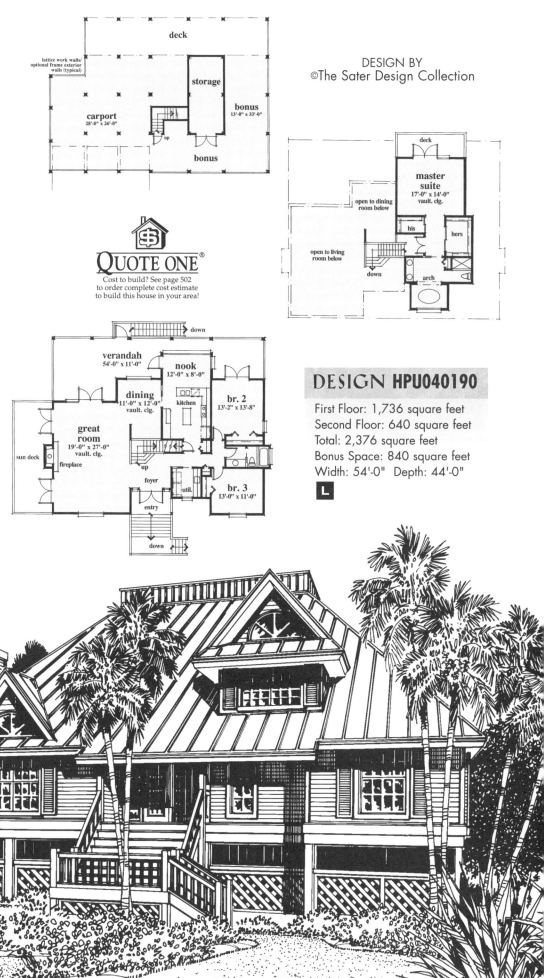

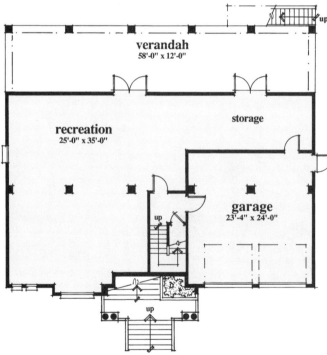

verandah
58'-0" x 12'-0"

recreation
25'-0" x 35'-0"

storage

garage
23'-4" x 24'-0"

up

up

The dramatic arched entry of this Southampton-style cottage borrows freely from its Southern coastal past. The foyer and central hall open to the grand room. The kitchen is flanked by the dining room and morning nook, which opens to the lanai. On the left side of the plan, the master suite also accesses the lanai. Two walk-in closets, a compartmented bath with separate tub and shower and a double-bowl vanity complete this opulent retreat. The right side of the plan includes two secondary bedrooms and a full bath.

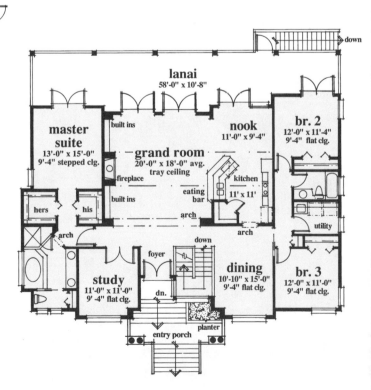

down

lanai
58'-0" x 10'-8"

master suite
13'-0" x 15'-0"
9'-4" stepped clg.

built ins

fireplace

built ins

grand room
20'-0" x 18'-0" avg.
tray ceiling

nook
11'-0" x 9'-4"

br. 2
12'-0" x 11'-4"
9'-4" flat clg.

eating bar

kitchen
11' x 11'

hers

his

arch

arch

arch

utility

down

foyer

dining
10'-10" x 15'-0"
9'-4" flat clg.

br. 3
12'-0" x 11'-0"
9'-4" flat clg.

study
11'-0" x 11'-0"
9'-4" flat clg.

dn.

planter

entry porch

DESIGN HPU040191

Square Footage: 2,190
Width: 58'-0"   Depth: 54'-0"

158

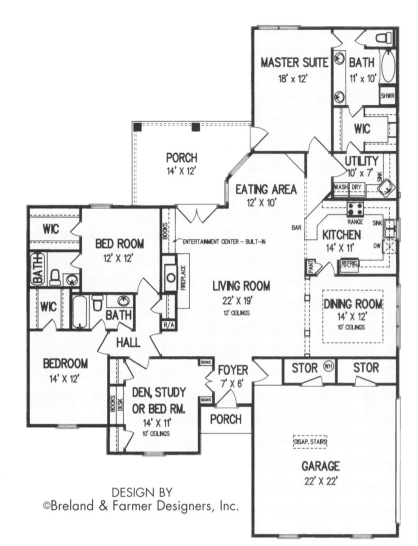

A versatile swing room is a highlight of this compact and charming French-style home. Using the optional door to the entry, the swing room makes a perfect office, or it can be used as a bedroom or study. The king-size master suite is isolated for privacy and has a spacious bath and walk-in closet with passage to the utility room. The open and spacious living room features twelve-foot ceilings. Two secondary bedrooms offer walk-in closets and private baths. Please specify crawlspace or slab foundation when ordering.

DESIGN HPU040192

Square Footage: 2,200
Width: 56'-0" Depth: 74'-0"

MASTER SUITE
18' X 12'

BATH
11' x 10'

WIC

UTILITY
10' x 7'

PORCH
14' X 12'

EATING AREA
12' X 10'

WIC

BED ROOM
12' X 12'

ENTERTAINMENT CENTER – BUILT-IN

KITCHEN
14' X 11'

BATH

WIC

LIVING ROOM
22' X 19'
12' CEILINGS

DINING ROOM
14' X 12'
10' CEILINGS

BATH

HALL

BEDROOM
14' X 12'

FOYER
7' X 6'

STOR

STOR

DEN, STUDY
OR BED RM.
14' X 11'
10' CEILINGS

PORCH

DISAP. STAIRS

GARAGE
22' X 22'

DESIGN BY
©Breland & Farmer Designers, Inc.

S huttered windows encompass-
ing the breadth of this lovely
home recall the easy-living
feeling of the Southern Plantation
style. Perfect for warm climates, this
home includes a large rear porch,
punctuated with skylights, that
enlarges the capacity for entertaining. Two family bedrooms share a
full bath and complement the master suite. The two-car garage has a
compartmented storage area and is
situated near the kitchen and laundry room. Please specify basement,
crawlspace or slab foundation
when ordering.

DESIGN BY
©Larry James & Associates, Inc.

M.Bath
17-8x10-6

Master
Bedroom
19-2x13-7

Porch
22-0x12-0

Greatroom
22-0x15-2

Garage
20-4x21-4

1/2
Bath

Stor.
5-0x6-1

Laun.
8-4x5-8

Kitchen
12-8x12-0

Bath

Bedroom
10-8x12-0

Bedroom
11-6x11-0

Foyer

Dining
11-6x13-6

Breakfast
12-8x9-10

Porch
30-8x6-0

Future
14-0x12-0

Future
29-4x16-0

Future
12-8x12-0

DESIGN HPU040193

Square Footage: 2,089
Bonus Space: 878 square feet
Width: 63'-10" Depth: 64'-7"

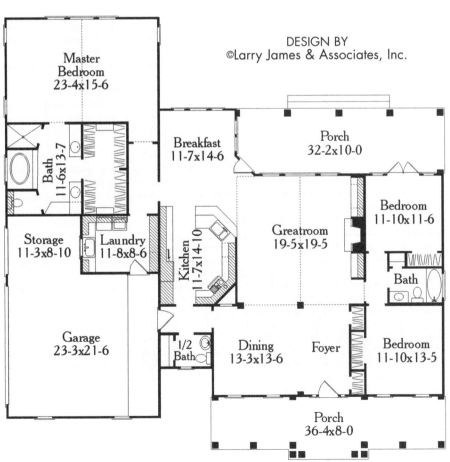

DESIGN BY
©Larry James & Associates, Inc.

Master Bedroom 23-4x15-6

Bath 11-6x13-7

Breakfast 11-7x14-6

Porch 32-2x10-0

Storage 11-3x8-10

Laundry 11-8x8-6

Kitchen 11-7x14-10

Greatroom 19-5x19-5

Bedroom 11-10x11-6

Bath

Garage 23-3x21-6

1/2 Bath

Dining 13-3x13-6

Foyer

Bedroom 11-10x13-5

Porch 36-4x8-0

Beyond this home's beautiful columned porch and keystone arches is a successful plan. Enter the foyer to find the formal dining room and two convenient closets. Straight ahead lies the great room, which includes a fireplace and built-ins. Between the spacious kitchen and the breakfast area is the hallway leading to the master bedroom. The private bath here provides convenience with dual vanities, a separate shower and an enormous walk-in closet. Two additional bedrooms to the far right of the plan share a full bath that includes a linen closet. The rear bedroom has French doors, which access the covered porch. Please specify crawlspace or slab foundation when ordering.

DESIGN HPU040194

Square Footage: 2,424
Width: 68'-2" Depth: 67'-6"

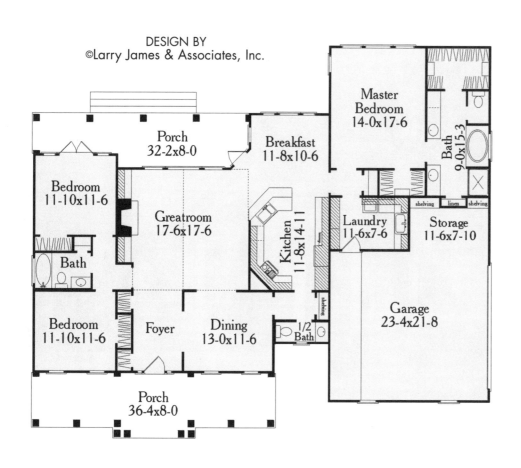

Porch
32-2x8-0

Breakfast
11-8x10-6

Master
Bedroom
14-0x17-6

Bath
9-0x15-3

Bedroom
11-10x11-6

Greatroom
17-6x17-6

Kitchen
11-8x14-11

Laundry
11-6x7-6

Storage
11-6x7-10

shelving   linen   shelving

Bath

Bedroom
11-10x11-6

Foyer

Dining
13-0x11-6

1/2
Bath

Garage
23-4x21-8

shelving

Porch
36-4x8-0

Curb appeal abounds in this three-bedroom farmhouse with its columned porch, keystone lintel windows and stucco facade. A warming fireplace with adjacent built-ins in the great room can be viewed from the foyer and breakfast area. Light pours in from the rear porch with windows at every turn. Counter space abounds in this interesting kitchen adjoining the breakfast area. The private master suite enjoys a luxury bath with twin vanity sinks, a garden tub and separate shower. At the opposite end of the home, two secondary bedrooms share a bath. One features French-door access to the rear porch. Please specify basement, crawlspace or slab foundation when ordering.

DESIGN HPU040195

Square Footage: 2,046
Width: 68'-2" Depth: 57'-4"

This elegant, symmetrical home features a gabled porch complemented by columns. The breakfast room, adjacent to the kitchen, opens to a rear porch. The spacious great room provides a fireplace and a view of the patio. A lovely bayed window brightens the master bedroom, which includes a walk-in closet and a bath with a garden tub and a separate shower. Two secondary bedrooms each offer a private bath. A winding staircase leads to second-level future space. Please specify basement, crawlspace or slab foundation when ordering.

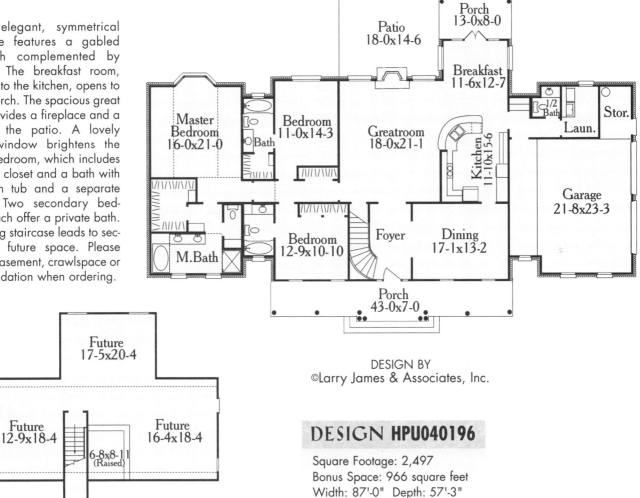

Patio
18-0x14-6

Porch
13-0x8-0

Breakfast
11-6x12-7

Master Bedroom
16-0x21-0

Bath

Bedroom
11-0x14-3

Greatroom
18-0x21-1

Kitchen
11-10x15-6

1/2 Bath

Laun.

Stor.

M.Bath

Bedroom
12-9x10-10

Foyer

Dining
17-1x13-2

Garage
21-8x23-3

Porch
43-0x7-0

Future
17-5x20-4

Future
12-9x18-4

Future
16-4x18-4

6-8x8-11
(Raised)

DESIGN BY
©Larry James & Associates, Inc.

DESIGN HPU040196

Square Footage: 2,497
Bonus Space: 966 square feet
Width: 87'-0" Depth: 57'-3"

Garage
20-4x23-4

Storage
12-8x5-8

M.Bath
17-8x11-2

Porch
21-6x12-2

1/2
Bath

Laundry
8-5x12-2

Master
Bedroom
17-8x16-8

Greatroom
21-9x17-2

Kitchen
12-9x13-0

Bath
10-9x5-8

Bedroom
11-0x12-0

Bedroom
11-0x13-6

Foyer

Dining
11-0x16-4

Breakfast
12-9x11-6

Porch
29-8x6-2

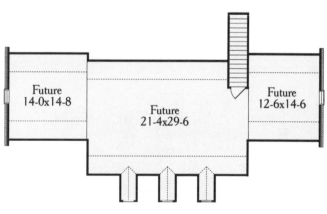

Future
14-0x14-8

Future
21-4x29-6

Future
12-6x14-6

DESIGN BY
©Larry James & Associates, Inc.

Three dormers in a row bring charm while the porch colonnade adds elegance to this home. The dining room has plenty of room for formal gatherings and provides ease of service with the island kitchen close by. A bumped-out sitting bay, twin walk-in closets, dual vanities and a compartmented toilet highlight the spacious master suite. Please specify basement, crawlspace- or slab foundation when ordering.

DESIGN HPU040198

Square Footage: 2,410
Bonus Space: 1,123 square feet
Width: 64'-4" Depth: 77'-4"

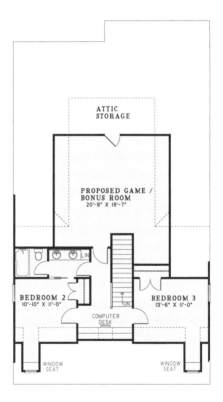

DESIGN BY
©Michael E. Nelson, Nelson Design Group, LLC

DESIGN HPU040199

First Floor: 1,698 square feet
Second Floor: 533 square feet
Total: 2,231 square feet
Bonus Room: 394 square feet
Width: 35'-4" Depth: 71'-6"

For the homeowner who wants luxury on a narrow lot, this design is the way. Walk into the formal spaces—a study with French doors and a dining room with shapely columns. From there, step into the voluminous kitchen with a hefty pantry and angled snack bar. The great room and breakfast room flow from this point into the rear master suite and garage. The secondary bedrooms are tucked away upstairs along with a large proposed game/bonus room. Please specify crawlspace or slab foundation when ordering.

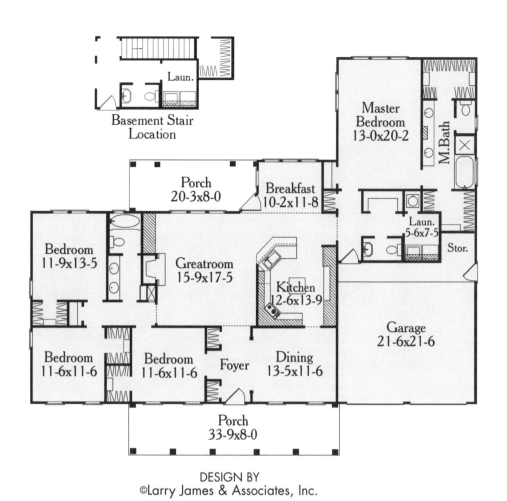

Basement Stair
Location

Laun.

Porch
20-3x8-0

Breakfast
10-2x11-8

Master
Bedroom
13-0x20-2

M.Bath

Bedroom
11-9x13-5

Greatroom
15-9x17-5

Kitchen
12-6x13-9

Laun.
5-6x7-5

Stor.

Bedroom
11-6x11-6

Bedroom
11-6x11-6

Foyer

Dining
13-5x11-6

Garage
21-6x21-6

Porch
33-9x8-0

DESIGN BY
©Larry James & Associates, Inc.

Six columns and a steeply pitched roof lend elegance to this four-bedroom home. To the right of the foyer, the dining area sits conveniently near the efficient kitchen. The kitchen island and serving bar add plenty of work space to the food-preparation zone. Natural light will flood the breakfast nook through a ribbon of windows facing the rear yard. Escape to the relaxing master bedroom, with its luxurious bath set between His and Hers walk-in closets. The great room occupies the center of this L-shaped plan, and is complete with a warming fireplace and built-ins. Three family bedrooms enjoy private walk-in closets and share a fully appointed bath. Please specify basement, crawlspace or slab foundation when ordering.

DESIGN HPU040201

Square Footage: 2,267
Width: 71'-2" Depth: 62'-0"

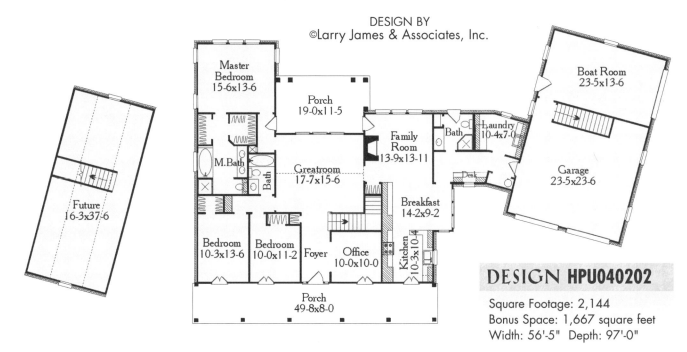

DESIGN BY
©Larry James & Associates, Inc.

Master
Bedroom
15-6x13-6

Porch
19-0x11-5

Boat Room
23-5x13-6

Laundry
10-4x7-0

Bath

Family
Room
13-9x13-11

M.Bath

Garage
23-5x23-6

Greatroom
17-7x15-6

Bath

Desk

Future
16-3x37-6

Breakfast
14-2x9-2

Bedroom
10-3x13-6

Bedroom
10-0x11-2

Foyer

Office
10-0x10-0

Kitchen
10-3x10-4

DESIGN HPU040202

Square Footage: 2,144
Bonus Space: 1,667 square feet
Width: 56'-5" Depth: 97'-0"

Porch
49-8x8-0

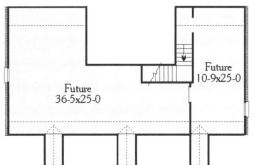

Future
36-5x25-0

Future
10-9x25-0

There is plenty of space to be developed on the second levels of both the house and the garage, making this an ideal country home. An office to the right of the foyer is another added bonus. The great room and family room are separated by a warming fireplace, and the family room accesses the rear porch. The wing bridging the garage and the central block houses a laundry room, a desk and a half-bath. The breakfast area features a bank of windows, while the kitchen, office and two family bedrooms each have French doors accessing the front porch. Please specify basement, crawlspace or slab foundation when ordering.

Welcome your family home to this wonderful four-bedroom cottage. Step through the entry door with its transom and sidelights to a well-lit foyer. A ribbon of windows greets the eye in the great room, and a warming fireplace spreads comfort. A pass-through window to the kitchen is an added convenience. The master suite enjoys a private wing, luxurious bath and His and Hers walk-in closets. On the opposite side of the plan, three secondary bedrooms—all with walk-in closets!—share a full bath. Please specify basement, crawlspace or slab foundation when ordering.

DESIGN BY
©Larry James & Associates, Inc.

DESIGN HPU040203

Square Footage: 2,093
Width: 71'-2" Depth: 56'-4"

Laundry
11-6x7-0

Basement Stair
Location

Bedroom
11-9x13-6

Greatroom
15-0x17-5

Porch
16-0x10-0

Master
Bedroom
13-0x20-0

M.Bath

Dining
13-9x11-0

Laundry
11-6x7-0

Stor.

Bedroom
11-6x11-6

Bedroom
11-4x11-2

Foyer

Kitchen
11-6x12-4

Garage
21-6x21-6

Porch
21-6x6-7

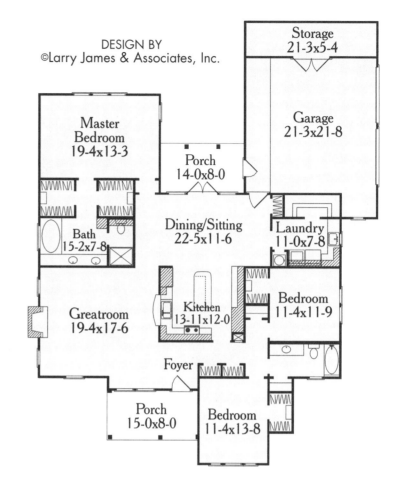

DESIGN BY
©Larry James & Associates, Inc.

Shutters, multi-pane glass windows and cross-hatched railing on the front porch make this a beautiful country cottage. To the left of the foyer is a roomy great room and a warming fireplace, framed by windows. To the right of the foyer, two family bedrooms feature walk-in closets and share a fully appointed bath. The efficient kitchen centers around a long island workstation and opens to the large dining/sitting room. The rear porch adds living space to view the outdoors. French doors, a fireplace and columns complete this three-bedroom design. Please specify basement, crawlspace or slab foundation when ordering.

DESIGN HPU040204

Square Footage: 2,053
Width: 57'-8" Depth: 71'-10"

Storage
21-3x5-4

Garage
21-3x21-8

Master
Bedroom
19-4x13-3

Porch
14-0x8-0

Bath
15-2x7-8

Dining/Sitting
22-5x11-6

Laundry
11-0x7-8

Greatroom
19-4x17-6

Kitchen
13-11x12-0

Bedroom
11-4x11-9

Foyer

Porch
15-0x8-0

Bedroom
11-4x13-8

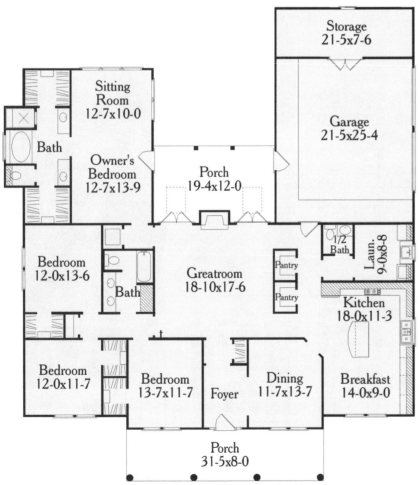

This home boasts a well-laid-out design that promotes comfort and flow. The great room offers two sets of French doors to the rear porch, a fireplace, and a spacious layout perfect for entertaining. The open island kitchen shares an area with the breakfast room and connects to the dining room. The owners suite delights in a room-sized sitting area, His and Hers walk-in closets and vanities, a compartmented toilet, and a separate tub and shower. Please specify basement, crawlspace or slab foundation when ordering.

DESIGN HPU040205

Square Footage: 2,465
Width: 65'-1" Depth: 64'-2"

DESIGN BY
©Larry James & Associates, Inc.

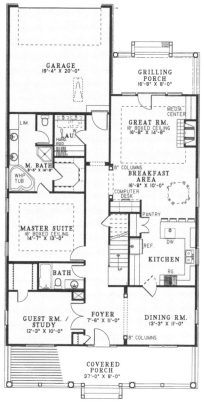

GARAGE
19'-4" X 20'-0"

GRILLING
PORCH
16'-8" X 8'-0"

MEDIA
CENTER

GREAT RM.
10' BOXED CEILING
16'-8" X 14'-8"

LIN

D.W.

LAU.
HANG.
ROD

M. BATH
8'-6" X 14'-8"

WHP
TUB

8" COLUMNS

BREAKFAST
AREA
16'-8" X 10'-0"

COMPUTER
DESK

MASTER SUITE
10' BOXED CEILING
14'-7" X 13'-0"

PANTRY

REF.

DW

KITCHEN

BATH

RG.

GUEST RM. /
STUDY
12'-3" X 10'-0"

FOYER
7'-6" X 11'-0"

DINING RM.
13'-3" X 11'-0"

8" COLUMNS

COVERED
PORCH
37'-0" X 8'-0"

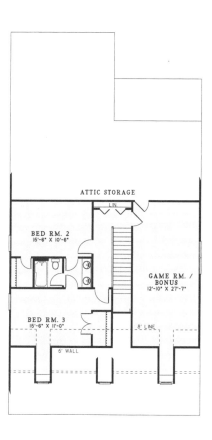

ATTIC STORAGE

LIN

BED RM. 2
15'-6" X 10'-6"

GAME RM. /
BONUS
12'-10" X 27'-7"

BED RM. 3
15'-6" X 11'-0"

8' LINE

6' WALL

DESIGN BY
©Michael E. Nelson, Nelson Design Group, LLC

This inviting country home includes a covered front porch with columns and railings, double-hung casement windows, wood and brick siding, and dormer windows. The formal dining room at the front of the house begins with an entrance flanked by two columns. The U-shaped kitchen has a pantry and a snack bar. A built-in computer desk lies adjacent to the breakfast room, and a box-ceilinged great room with a fireplace and media center sits at the back of the home. The master suite also has a boxed ceiling and a luxurious master bath with all of the amenities. Use the front bedroom as a study or guest room. On the second floor are two bedrooms, each with its own walk-in closet. The bonus room can be used as a game or hobby room, or as a spare bedroom. Please specify basement, crawlspace or slab foundation when ordering.

DESIGN HPU040206

First Floor: 1,713 square feet
Second Floor: 610 square feet
Total: 2,323 square feet
Bonus Room: 384 square feet
Width: 37'-0" Depth: 73'-0"

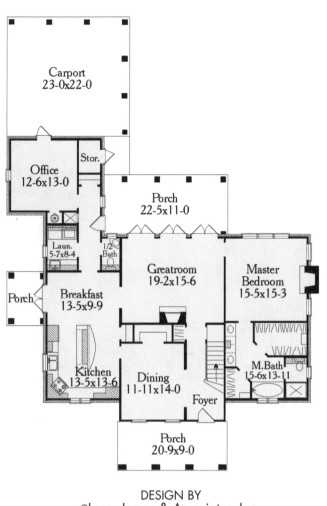

Carport
23-0x22-0

Office
12-6x13-0

Stor.

Laun.
5-7x8-4

Porch

Breakfast
13-5x9-9

Kitchen
13-5x13-6

Porch
22-5x11-0

1/2
Bath

Greatroom
19-2x15-6

Dining
11-11x14-0

Foyer

Master
Bedroom
15-5x15-3

M.Bath
15-6x13-11

Porch
20-9x9-0

DESIGN BY
©Larry James & Associates, Inc.

eep in the South, this home sets a country tone. This Southern Colonial design boasts decorative two-story columns and large windows that enhance the front porch and balcony. Enter through the foyer—notice that the formal dining room on the left connects to an island kitchen. The kitchen opens to a breakfast room, which accesses a side porch perfect for outdoor grilling. The great room features a warming fireplace and accesses a rear porch. The master bedroom also includes a fireplace, as well as a private bath with a whirlpool tub and a walk-in closet. A home office, laundry room and carport complete the first floor. Upstairs, two additional bedrooms share a full hall bath. One bedroom opens through two glass doors to a private balcony. Please specify crawlspace or slab foundation when ordering.

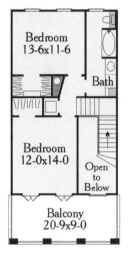

Bedroom
13-6x11-6

Bath

Bedroom
12-0x14-0

Open
to
Below

Balcony
20-9x9-0

DESIGN HPU040207

First Floor: 1,663 square feet
Second Floor: 551 square feet
Total: 2,214 square feet
Width: 58'-10" Depth: 83'-7"

STORAGE

GARAGE
19-10 x 21-6

STORAGE

PANTRY

LAUNDRY

BEDROOM
11-0 x 11-4

BREAKFAST
9-10 x 10-10

DINING
ROOM
10-8 x 14-2

GREAT ROOM
16-0 x 21-10

UP

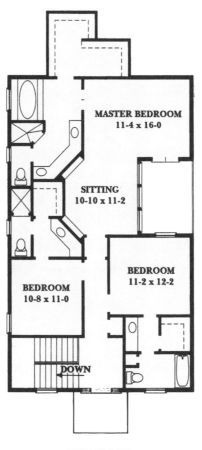

MASTER BEDROOM
11-4 x 16-0

SITTING
10-10 x 11-2

BEDROOM
10-8 x 11-0

BEDROOM
11-2 x 12-2

DOWN

DESIGN BY
©Authentic Historical Designs, Inc.

This stately home is striking in its simplicity and grandeur. Within, the high-ceilinged rooms retain the grandeur of the original homes of the late 19th Century. An expansive great room flows into a formal dining room, separated only by elegant interior columns. Beyond, a spacious kitchen features a snack bar and breakfast area, which overlooks the secluded courtyard. A downstairs bedroom can function as an office or cozy den.

DESIGN HPU040208

First Floor: 1,190 square feet
Second Floor: 1,220 square feet
Total: 2,410 square feet
Width: 30'-0" Depth: 72'-0"

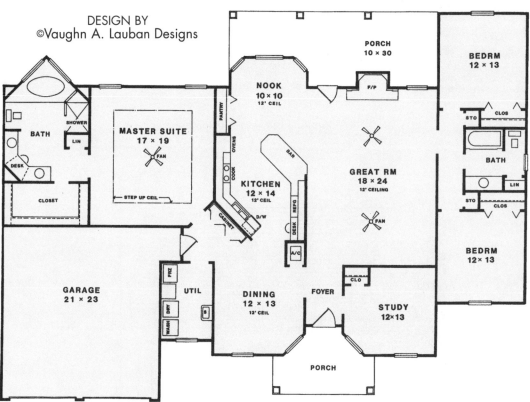

PORCH
10 × 30

BEDRM
12 × 13

NOOK
10 × 10
12' CEIL

F/P

STO   CLOS

MASTER SUITE
17 × 19

FAN

PANTRY

OVENS

COOK

KITCHEN
12 × 14
12' CEIL

BAR

GREAT RM
18 × 24
12' CEILING

FAN

BATH

LIN

SHOWER

LIN

BATH

DESK

CLOSET

STEP UP CEIL

CABINET

D/W

DESK

REFG

STO   CLOS

BEDRM
12 × 13

A/C

GARAGE
21 × 23

FRZ

UTIL

DRY

WASH

DINING
12 × 13
12' CEIL

FOYER

CLO

STUDY
12×13

PORCH

A striking facade with corner quoins and a two-story porch entry define a layout that marries elegance and comfort. With a defined but open dining room and convenient great room, the gourmet in the kitchen will be able to entertain while preparing the meal. The great room features a fireplace and rear-porch access, which makes this spot perfect for family gatherings and outdoor activities. Two secondary bedrooms share a full bath and enjoy plenty of closet and storage space. The master suite is bound to pamper the owner, with a step-up ceiling, spacious walk-in closet, dual vanities, bumped-out triangular tub space and separate shower.

DESIGN HPU040210

Square Footage: 2,256
Width: 72'-0" Depth: 52'-0"

The inspiration for this plan came directly from the 1878 edition of Bicknell's *Victorian Buildings*. At that time, the estimated building cost for this appealing residence was only $2,500. Though the cost of constructing this home has changed, its charm remains! Multiple windows brighten the living room, which opens to a small side porch. The kitchen boasts a walk-in pantry and adjoins a sunny breakfast area and a spacious keeping room with built-ins and a fireplace. The second floor features an inviting master suite with a relaxing bath that includes a raised corner tub. Three additional bedrooms, one with a walk-in closet, share a bath. The laundry area is conveniently close to the bedrooms.

DESIGN HPU040211

First Floor: 1,184 square feet
Second Floor: 1,093 square feet
Total: 2,277 square feet
Width: 28'-0" Depth: 74'-0"

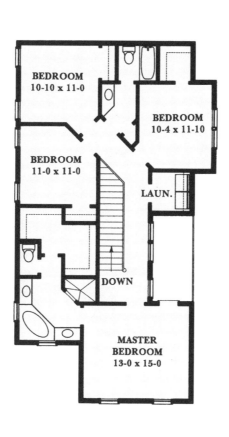

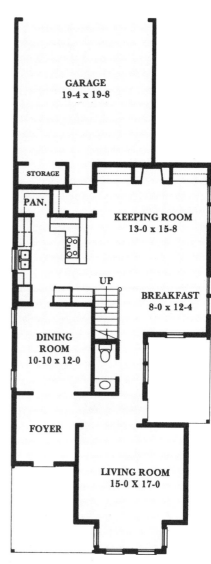

DESIGN BY
©Authentic Historical Designs, Inc.

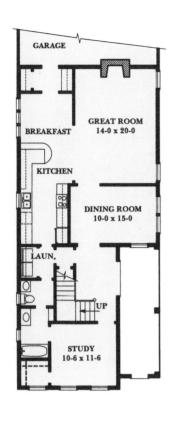

GARAGE

GREAT ROOM
14-0 x 20-0

BREAKFAST

KITCHEN

DINING ROOM
10-0 x 15-0

LAUN.

UP

STUDY
10-6 x 11-6

DESIGN BY
©Authentic Historical Designs, Inc.

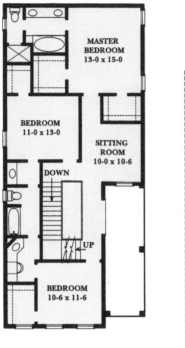

MASTER
BEDROOM
13-0 x 15-0

BEDROOM
11-0 x 13-0

SITTING
ROOM
10-0 x 10-6

DOWN

UP

BEDROOM
10-6 x 11-6

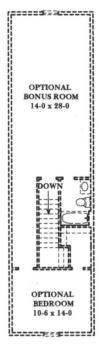

OPTIONAL
BONUS ROOM
14-0 x 28-0

DOWN

OPTIONAL
BEDROOM
10-6 x 14-0

Distinctive design features of the Charleston single house make it a perfect candidate for the narrow urban lot. Since its narrow end faces the street and its two-story piazza faces the side yard, the plan affords its occupants much more privacy than a house with a front-facing porch. The street entry leads to a porch, providing a secluded, but graceful transition from the neighborhood. A grand foyer with an open stairwell opens to a formal dining room and the great room beyond. The front study could serve as an office or guest room. Bedrooms reside on the second floor—note the sitting room in the master suite. For more space, develop the bonus space on the upper level.

DESIGN HPU040212

First Floor: 1,227 square feet
Second Floor: 1,133 square feet
Total: 2,360 square feet
Bonus Room: 792 square feet
Width: 25'-0" Depth: 77'-0"

The romantic character of the hacienda is captured in this appealing residence. The barrel-tile roof, smooth stucco exterior and rope columns are other characteristics of the Spanish Colonial style. The front door is shielded from the weather; within, a foyer welcomes all who enter. The great room is generously sized; a downstairs guest room can also double as a study or office. A sunny dining room opens to a spacious kitchen with a large island and breakfast bar. Above, there is a sitting area large enough for a computer and desk area. A luxurious master suite privately accesses an upstairs deck. Note all the walk-in closets, which provide excellent storage spaces. The front bedroom also has walkout access to the front balcony. Please specify basement or crawlspace foundation when ordering.

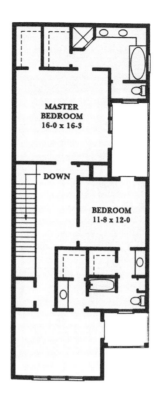

MASTER BEDROOM
16-0 x 16-3

DOWN

BEDROOM
11-8 x 12-0

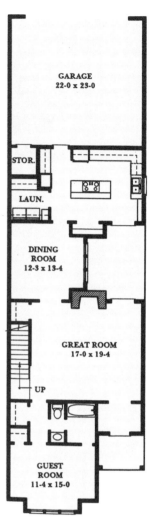

GARAGE
22-0 x 23-0

STOR.

LAUN.

DINING ROOM
12-3 x 13-4

GREAT ROOM
17-0 x 19-4

UP

GUEST ROOM
11-4 x 15-0

DESIGN BY
©Authentic Historical Designs, Inc.

DESIGN HPU040213

First Floor: 1,247 square feet
Second Floor: 1,221 square feet
Total: 2,468 square feet
Width: 24'-0" Depth: 86'-0"

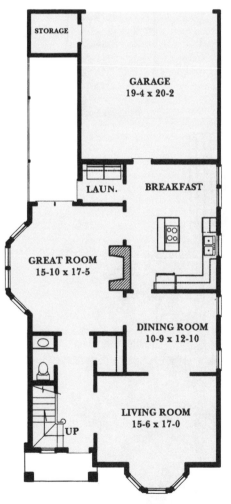

STORAGE

GARAGE
19-4 x 20-2

LAUN.   BREAKFAST

GREAT ROOM
15-10 x 17-5

DINING ROOM
10-9 x 12-10

LIVING ROOM
15-6 x 17-0

UP

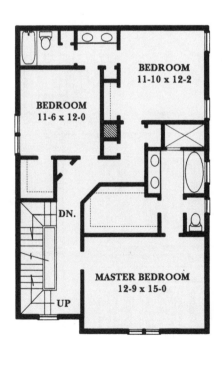

BEDROOM
11-10 x 12-2

BEDROOM
11-6 x 12-0

DN.

MASTER BEDROOM
12-9 x 15-0

UP

DESIGN BY
©Authentic Historical Designs, Inc.

The facade of this enticing Victorian was taken from Bicknell's *Detail Cottage and Construction Architecture*, published in 1873, while the floor plan has been modified to suit modern lifestyles. The living room, with a lovely bay window, leads to the dining room. The great room, also with a bay window, opens to the covered side porch, and the island kitchen adjoins a sunlit breakfast area. An open staircase with an overlook leads to the family sleeping zone, composed of a master suite and two additional bedrooms. The master suite offers a large walk-in closet and a full bath with dual vanities; the two family bedrooms, one of which features a walk-in closet, share another full bath, this one with two linen closets.

DESIGN HPU040214

First Floor: 1,131 square feet
Second Floor: 1,038 square feet
Total: 2,169 square feet
Width: 30'-0" Depth: 66'-0"

This timeless Georgian design will provide enduring approval. The expansive great room features a wood-burning fireplace and opens to a dining room of ample proportions with a niche under the stairs that can accommodate a small piano or desk. Serious cooks will appreciate the ample cabinet space, the pantry and the breakfast bar. A two-car garage completes the first floor. Upstairs, a luxurious master suite includes a sitting area, private bath and walk-in closet. Three additional family bedrooms share access to another full bath.

DESIGN HPU040215

First Floor: 940 square feet
Second Floor: 1,088 square feet
Total: 2,028 square feet
Width: 22'-0"   Depth: 70'-0"

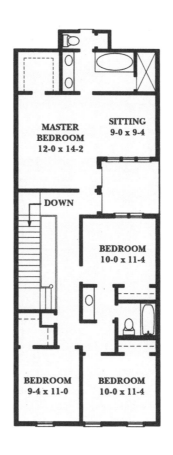

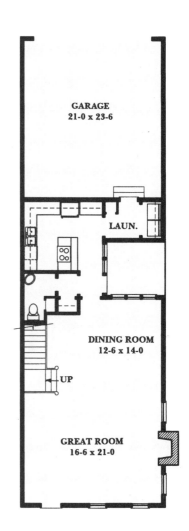

DESIGN BY
©Authentic Historical Designs, Inc.

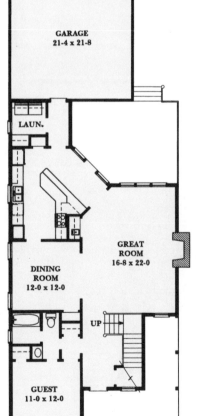

Adapted from George Barber's *The Cottage Souvenir #2*, published in 1890, this Victorian design possesses an irresistible charm and an updated floor plan. Elegant columns define the dining room, which adjoins a large great room with a fireplace. The nearby kitchen features a long, angled work counter and opens to an expansive rear deck. A front bedroom serves as a guest suite with an adjacent bath. Three additional bedrooms, one a roomy master suite, are found upstairs. The master bedroom includes a dramatic bath with an angled tub, dual vanities and two walk-in closets. The two family bedrooms feature walk-in closets and private vanities.

DESIGN HPU040216

First Floor: 1,274 square feet
Second Floor: 1,178 square feet
Total: 2,452 square feet
Width: 30'-0" Depth: 80'-0"

DESIGN BY
©Authentic Historical Designs, Inc.

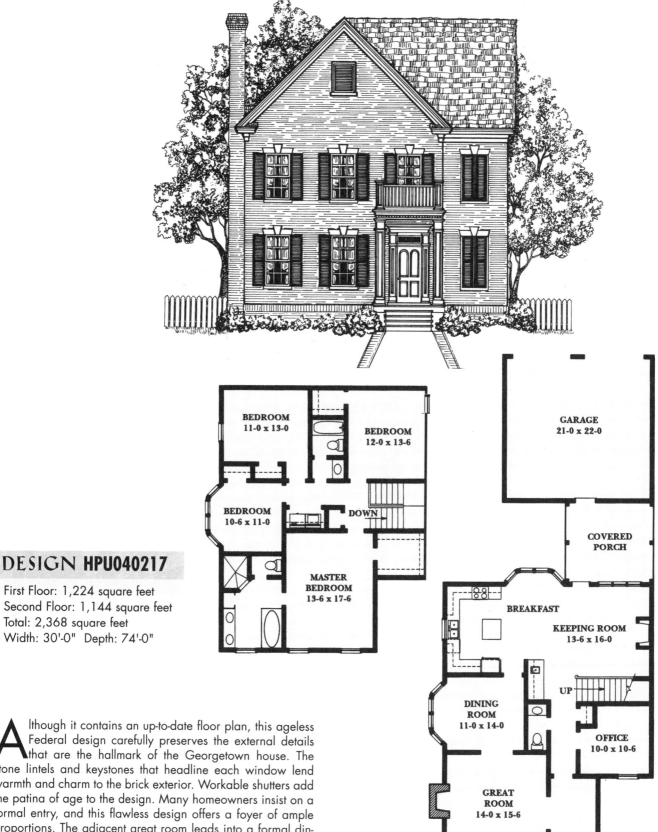

DESIGN HPU040217

First Floor: 1,224 square feet
Second Floor: 1,144 square feet
Total: 2,368 square feet
Width: 30'-0" Depth: 74'-0"

Although it contains an up-to-date floor plan, this ageless Federal design carefully preserves the external details that are the hallmark of the Georgetown house. The stone lintels and keystones that headline each window lend warmth and charm to the brick exterior. Workable shutters add the patina of age to the design. Many homeowners insist on a formal entry, and this flawless design offers a foyer of ample proportions. The adjacent great room leads into a formal dining room. The U-shaped kitchen provides a central island, an angled breakfast bay and a keeping room with a fireplace. The sleeping quarters—including the luxurious master bedroom—reside upstairs.

DESIGN BY
©Authentic Historical Designs, Inc.

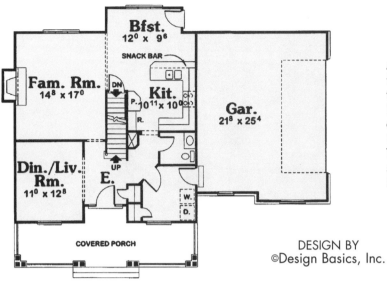

Bfst.
12⁰ x 9⁶

SNACK BAR

Fam. Rm.
14⁸ x 17⁰

DN

Kit.
10¹¹ x 10⁰

P.

R.

Gar.
21⁸ x 25⁴

Din./Liv.
Rm.
11⁰ x 12⁸

UP

E.

W.
D.

COVERED PORCH

DESIGN BY
©Design Basics, Inc.

Br.2
11⁰ x 13⁸

LINEN

WHIRLPOOL

Mbr.
17⁸ x 14⁰

DN

Br.3
11⁰ x 12⁸

Br.4
10¹¹ x 12⁸

A gabled roof, shutters and the covered porch translate to traditional family living. Inside, the floor plan results in a convenient traffic pattern. The family room is removed from the wear-and-tear of through-traffic, while the placement of the formal dining/living room avoids kitchen clatter. A two-car garage completes the first floor. Upstairs, the master suite includes a private bath and generous walk-in closet. Three family bedrooms—one with a walk-in closet—share a bath that has a double vanity. Please specify basement or slab foundation when ordering.

DESIGN HPU040218

First Floor: 952 square feet
Second Floor: 1,272 square feet
Total: 2,224 square feet
Width: 52'-0" Depth: 34'-8"

DESIGNERS INK

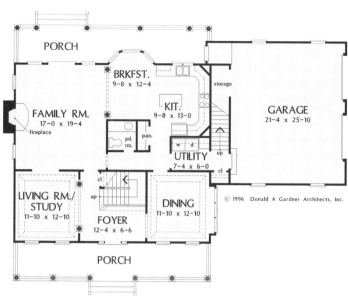

A large center gable with a Palladian window and a gently vaulted portico make this two-story home stand out from the typical farmhouse. A formal dining room and a living room/study, both highlighted by tray ceilings, flank the foyer, which leads into a spacious family room. Nine-foot ceilings add volume to the entire first floor, including the efficient kitchen with a center work island and large pantry. Upstairs, the gracious master suite features a tray ceiling, a generous walk-in closet, and a skylit bath with a double-bowl vanity, linen closet and garden tub. Three additional bedrooms share a full bath.

DESIGN BY
Donald A. Gardner Architects, Inc.

DESIGN HPU040219

First Floor: 1,299 square feet
Second Floor: 1,176 square feet
Total: 2,475 square feet
Bonus Room: 464 square feet
Width: 64'-8" Depth: 47'-2"

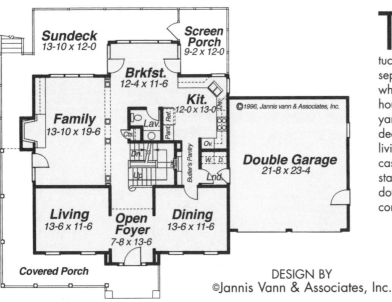

Sundeck
13-10 x 12-0

Screen Porch
9-2 x 12-0

Brkfst.
12-4 x 11-6

Kit.
12-0 x 13-0

© 1996, Jannis vann & Associates, Inc.

Family
13-10 x 19-6

Lav.

Pant. Ref.

Cts.

Dn.

Up

Butler's Pantry

W.D.

Lndy.

Double Garage
21-8 x 23-4

Living
13-6 x 11-6

Open Foyer
7-8 x 13-6

Dining
13-6 x 11-6

Covered Porch

Τhis home is reminiscent of Main Street, USA with its classic features. The two-story foyer is flanked by the formal living and dining rooms, while the stairs are tucked back in the center of the house. Columns create a separation from the family room to the breakfast area, while keeping that open feeling across the entire rear of the house. Corner windows in the kitchen look into the side yard and rear screened porch. The porch leads to the rear deck, which also ties into the side porch, creating outdoor living on three sides of the house. As you ascend the staircase to the second floor, you will pass a lighted panel of stained glass on the landing, creating the illusion of a window wall. The second floor features four bedrooms and a compartmented hall bath.

DESIGN BY
©Jannis Vann & Associates, Inc.

DESIGN HPU040220

First Floor: 1,250 square feet
Second Floor: 1,166 square feet
Total: 2,416 square feet
Width: 64'-0" Depth: 52'-0"

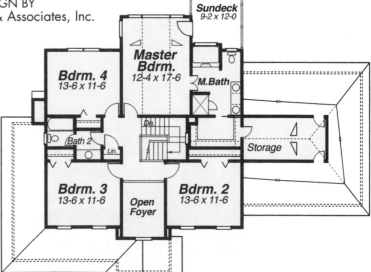

Sundeck
9-2 x 12-0

Master Bdrm.
12-4 x 17-6

M.Bath

Bdrm. 4
13-6 x 11-6

Bath 2

Lin.

Dn.

Storage

Bdrm. 3
13-6 x 11-6

Open Foyer

Bdrm. 2
13-6 x 11-6

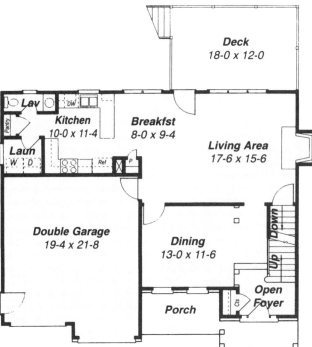

Deck
18-0 x 12-0

Lav

Kitchen
10-0 x 11-4

DW

Pantry

Breakfst
8-0 x 9-4

Laun
W D

Ref

P

Living Area
17-6 x 15-6

Double Garage
19-4 x 21-8

Dining
13-0 x 11-6

Up

Down

Open Foyer

Cls

Porch

The metal-roofed porch and multiple gables create added curb appeal to this traditional brick and siding design. Inside, a spacious living area flows into the breakfast room, which leads to the efficient kitchen with plenty of cabinets and counter space. The back deck is perfect for outdoor grilling or entertaining. A double garage completes the first floor. Upstairs, the three bedrooms feature a deluxe master suite, two family bedrooms that share a bath, and a loft available for a fourth bedroom, home office or play area. Please specify basement, crawlspace or slab foundation when ordering.

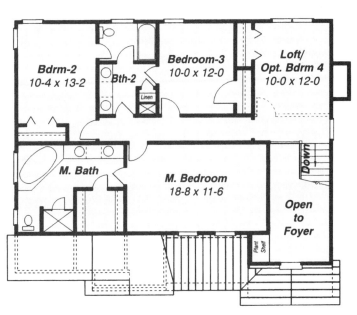

Bdrm-2
10-4 x 13-2

Bth-2

Bedroom-3
10-0 x 12-0

Linen

Loft/ Opt. Bdrm 4
10-0 x 12-0

M. Bath

M. Bedroom
18-8 x 11-6

Down

Plant Shelf

Open to Foyer

DESIGN HPU040221

First Floor: 905 square feet
Second Floor: 1,120 square feet
Total: 2,025 square feet
Width: 44'-4" Depth: 36'-5"

DESIGN BY
©Jannis Vann & Associates, Inc.

COVERED PORCH

MASTER
BEDRM
13⁴ x 18⁰

FAMILY
ROOM
15⁴ x 11⁶

MASTER
BATH

BREAKFAST ROOM
15⁴ x 11⁸

DESK

LINEN

KIT
13⁰ x 11⁴

WET
BAR

DINING
RM
13⁴ x 11⁰

SINK

DW

5' HIGH SHELVES

LIVING
RM
13⁴ x 11⁴

UP

OPEN ABOVE

FOYER

PDR

COVERED PORCH

This handsome bungalow is designed for easy living with a floor plan that puts the owner's comfort first. A quaint living and dining room is separated with a half-wall of built-in shelves. The large kitchen provides an open wet bar to the dining room and a snack bar to the combination breakfast/family room. The extra-large family room has sliding glass doors off the breakfast area and a door opening to the covered rear porch. The master suite offers privacy and convenience thanks to thoughtful first-floor planning. The two spacious bedrooms upstairs share a twin-basin bath.

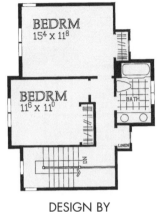

BEDRM
15⁴ x 11⁸

BEDRM
11⁶ x 11⁰

BATH

LINEN

DN

DESIGN BY
©Home Planners

DESIGN HPU040222

First Floor: 1,581 square feet
Second Floor: 592 square feet
Total: 2,173 square feet
Width: 35'-4"   Depth: 66'-0"

QUOTE ONE®
Cost to build? See page 502
to order complete cost estimate
to build this house in your area!

Craftsman detailing adorns the exterior of this fine hillside home. Its cozy nature includes horizontal and shingle siding and a covered porch at the entry with a wide-based column. The great room is warmed by a hearth surrounded by built-ins. Columns define the dining room, which separates the great room and the U-shaped kitchen. A wide deck at the side of the home is accessed through the dining room or the great room. A cozy den sits at the back of this level and has double doors to the rear portion of the deck. Three bedrooms on the upper level include two family bedrooms with a shared full bath, and a master bedroom with a sitting area, private bath and walk-in closet. The lower level has space for a game room and a guest bedroom with a bath.

DESIGN HPU040223

First Floor: 1,158 square feet
Second Floor: 1,038 square feet
Total: 2,196 square feet
Bonus Space: 760 square feet
Width: 34'-6" Depth: 42'-0"

DESIGN BY
©Alan Mascord Design Associates, Inc.

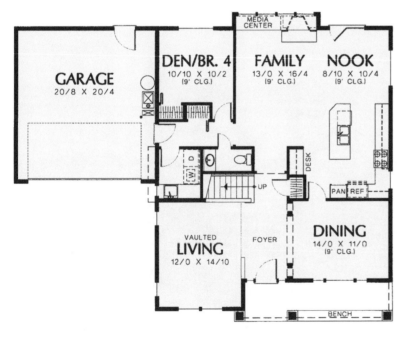

GARAGE
20/8 X 20/4

DEN/BR. 4
10/10 X 10/2
(9' CLG.)

FAMILY
13/0 X 16/4
(9' CLG.)

NOOK
8/10 X 10/4
(9' CLG.)

MEDIA
CENTER

DESK

UP

PAN. REF

VAULTED
LIVING
12/0 X 14/10

FOYER

DINING
14/0 X 11/0
(9' CLG.)

BENCH

DESIGN HPU040225

First Floor: 1,300 square feet
Second Floor: 933 square feet
Total: 2,233 square feet
Width: 54'-0" Depth: 43'-0"

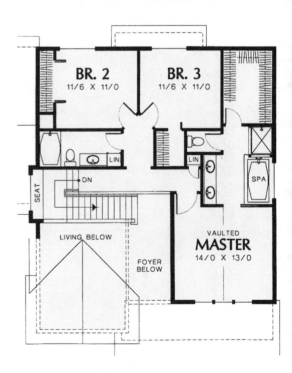

BR. 2
11/6 X 11/0

BR. 3
11/6 X 11/0

LIN

LIN

SEAT

DN

LIVING BELOW

FOYER
BELOW

VAULTED
MASTER
14/0 X 13/0

SPA

Subtle Craftsman style is evident in this three-bedroom home. From its rafter-tails poking out from under the roof overhang to the pillars supporting the shed roof over the porch, this attractive design is sure to be a favorite. Inside, there is room enough for all family pursuits. Formal entertaining is easy in the formal dining room, with a vaulted living room just across the hall for after-dinner conversations. Casual times will be fun in the family room, with a fireplace, built-in media center and nearby L-shaped kitchen and sunny nook. A den—or make it a fourth bedroom—completes this floor. Upstairs, two family bedrooms share a hall bath, while the vaulted master suite features a spacious private bath. Note also the large walk-in closet.

DESIGN BY
©Alan Mascord Design Associates, Inc.

NOOK
10/0 X 10/8
(9' CLG.)

FAMILY
13/2 X 15/0
(9' CLG.)

DINING
11/2 X 10/0
(9' CLG.)

9/10 X 10/4

RANGE

REF. PAN

TWO STORY
LIVING
15/2 X 17/8 +/-

D W

UP

GARAGE
19/6 X 21/6

10/2 X 21/6

DEN
11/0 X 10/0
(11'-7" CLG.)

DESIGN HPU040226

First Floor: 1,255 square feet
Second Floor: 1,141 square feet
Total: 2,396 square feet
Width: 40'-0" Depth: 50'-0"

A two-story living room greets family and friends in this fine four-bedroom Craftsman home. A cozy den is isolated toward the front of the home, assuring privacy. The angled kitchen reigns in the center of the home, with easy access to the formal dining room, sunny nook and spacious family room. A fireplace in the family room promises warmth and welcome. The master bedroom, which includes a private bath with a spa tub and a walk-in closet, resides on the second floor. Three additional bedrooms share a full hall bath.

SPA TUB

BR. 2
10/2 X 11/0

MASTER
15/0 X 13/8

PLANT SHELF

LIN

BR. 3
10/6 X 10/8

LIVING RM. BELOW

DN

BR. 4
14/0 X 9/0+

FOYER
BELOW

PLANT SHELF

DEN
BELOW

DESIGN BY
©Alan Mascord Design Associates, Inc.

189

DESIGN HPU040227

Square Footage: 2,085
Width: 70'-0" Depth: 61'-0"

This traditional home offers a front covered porch to welcome family and friends. The foyer provides access to the study and dining room. A galley kitchen features a snack bar, built-in planning desk and a breakfast bay. The living room enjoys a corner fireplace and rear-porch access. The master suite boasts a bay sitting area, dressing area with dual vanities, and a walk-in closet. On the other side of the house, two family bedrooms share a full bath between them.

DESIGN BY
©Vaughn A. Lauban Designs

The facade of this home speaks of country lemonade and rocking chairs. The living room features a fireplace and front-porch views. The master suite enjoys its seclusion with a sumptuous bath and walk-in closet. An open dining room is reached through the living room and is served from the L-shaped island kitchen. A breakfast nook takes in the outdoors with an adjoining screened porch.

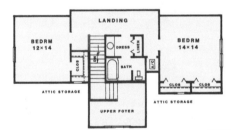

DESIGN BY
©Vaughn A. Lauban Designs

DESIGN HPU040228

First Floor: 1,677 square feet
Second Floor: 683 square feet
Total: 2,360 square feet
Width: 46'-0" Depth: 67'-0"

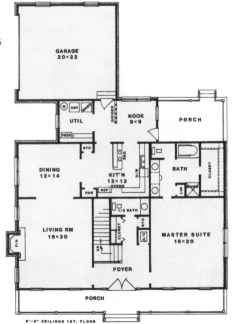

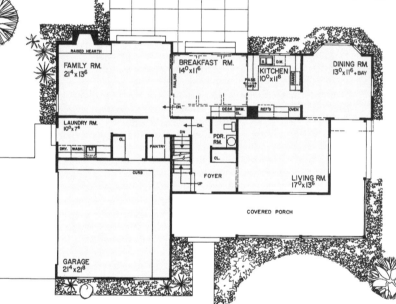

TERRACE

RAISED HEARTH

FAMILY RM.
21⁴ x 13⁶

BREAKFAST RM.
14⁰ x 11⁶

KITCHEN
10⁰ x 11⁸

DINING RM.
13⁰ x 11⁶ + BAY

LAUNDRY RM.
10⁰ x 7⁶

DRY. WASH. LT.

PANTRY

DESK BRM. CL.

REF'G

OVEN

PASS THRU

CURB

DN.

PDR. RM.

CL.

UP

FOYER

LIVING RM.
17⁰ x 13⁶

COVERED PORCH

GARAGE
21⁴ x 21⁸

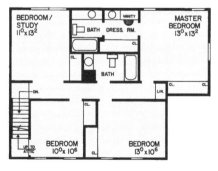

BEDROOM/
STUDY
11⁰ x 13²

BATH DRESS. RM.

VANITY

MASTER
BEDROOM
13⁰ x 13²

CL.

BATH

CL.

CL.

LIN.

CL.

DN.

UP TO
ATTIC

BEDROOM
10⁰ x 10⁶

CL.

BEDROOM
13⁰ x 10⁶

DESIGN BY
©Home Planners

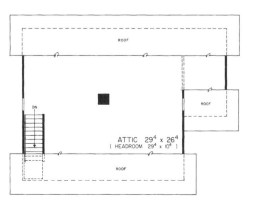

ROOF

ROOF

DN.

ATTIC 29⁴ x 26⁴
(HEADROOM 29⁴ x 10⁴)

ROOF

Here's a great farmhouse adaptation with all the most up-to-date features. There is the quiet corner living room, which has an opening to the sizable dining room. This room will enjoy plenty of natural light from the delightful bay window overlooking the rear yard and is conveniently located near the efficient U-shaped kitchen. The kitchen features many built-ins and a pass-through to the beam-ceilinged nook. Sliding glass doors to the terrace are found in both the family room and the nook. The service entrance to the garage is flanked by a clothes closet and a large, walk-in pantry. Recreational activities and hobbies can be pursued in the basement area. Four bedrooms and two baths are located on the second floor. The master bedroom includes a dressing room and double vanity.

DESIGN HPU040229

First Floor: 1,366 square feet
Second Floor: 969 square feet
Total: 2,335 square feet
Attic: 969 square feet
Width: 59'-6" Depth: 46'-0"

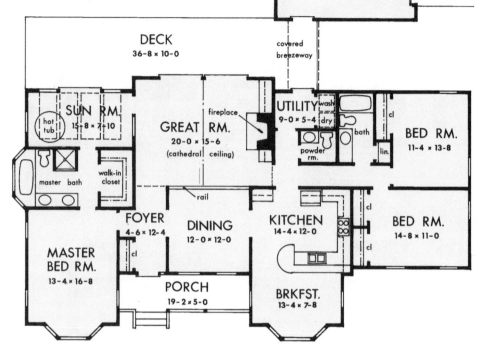

ulti-pane windows, dormers, bay windows and a delightful covered porch provide a neighborly welcome into this delightful country cottage. The great room contains a fireplace, a cathedral ceiling and sliding glass doors with an arched window above to allow for natural illumination. A sun room with a hot tub leads to an adjacent deck. This space can also be reached from the master bath. The generous master suite is filled with amenities that include a walk-in closet and a spacious bath with a double-bowl vanity, shower and garden tub. Two additional bedrooms are located at the other end of the house for privacy. The garage is connected to the house by a breezeway.

DESIGN HPU040230

Square Footage: 2,021
Width: 67'-6" Depth: 67'-4"

DESIGN BY
Donald A. Gardner Architects, Inc.

GARAGE
20-4 × 20-4

DECK
36-8 × 10-0

covered breezeway

SUN RM.
15-8 × 7-10

hot tub

GREAT RM.
20-0 × 15-6
(cathedral ceiling)

fireplace

UTILITY
9-0 × 5-4

wash
dry

cl

BED RM.
11-4 × 13-8

powder rm.

bath

lin.

master bath

walk-in closet

rail

FOYER
4-6 × 12-4

DINING
12-0 × 12-0

KITCHEN
14-4 × 12-0

cl

BED RM.
14-8 × 11-0

MASTER BED RM.
13-4 × 16-8

cl

PORCH
19-2 × 5-0

BRKFST.
13-4 × 7-8

cl

This brightly lit country home is enhanced by dormers and a welcoming entry porch. Inside the foyer, a formal living room leads to the dining room. The kitchen is conveniently set between the dining room and bayed breakfast nook. A laundry room and sewing room are set behind the two-car garage. The beam-ceilinged family room—the heart of the home—features a fireplace and access to a rear covered porch. The right side of the home is dedicated to the family's sleeping quarters. The beam-ceilinged master bedroom includes a spacious master bath and private access to the back porch. Three additional bedrooms share a full hall bath.

DESIGN HPU040231

Square Footage: 2,173
Width: 73'-4" Depth: 51'-4"

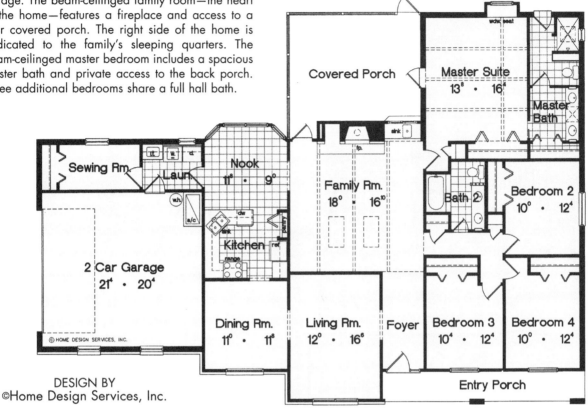

Covered Porch

Master Suite
13⁸ · 16⁴

Master Bath

Sewing Rm.

Laun.

Nook
11⁸ · 9⁰

Family Rm.
18⁰ · 16¹⁰

Bath 2

Bedroom 2
10⁰ · 12⁴

w.h.

a/c

Kitchen

dw

range

ref

2 Car Garage
21⁴ · 20⁴

© HOME DESIGN SERVICES, INC.

Dining Rm.
11⁰ · 11⁸

Living Rm.
12⁰ · 16⁶

Foyer

Bedroom 3
10⁴ · 12⁴

Bedroom 4
10⁰ · 12⁴

Entry Porch

DESIGN BY
©Home Design Services, Inc.

N. HANSEN S.D.G.

193

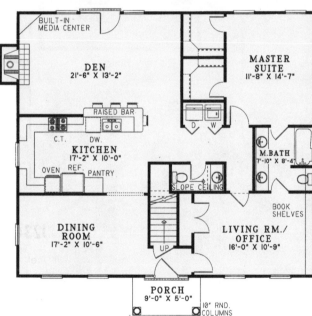

DESIGN BY
©Michael E. Nelson, Nelson Design Group, LLC

DESIGN HPU040232

First Floor: 1,400 square feet
Second Floor: 644 square feet
Total: 2,044 square feet
Width: 42'-4" Depth: 40'-0"

This attractive two-story traditional home is filled with all the modern-day amenities. A columned front porch leads inside to the living room/office, which features a closet and book shelves. The master bedroom, which boasts two walk-in closets, accesses the living room/office through the master bath. On the other side of the home, the efficient kitchen features a raised bar, a pantry and open access to the dining room. The den boasts a warming fireplace, a built-in media center and a back door. Upstairs, dormers enhance two additional family bedrooms, which both feature walk-in closets and share access to a bath. Please specify basement, crawlspace or slab foundation when ordering.

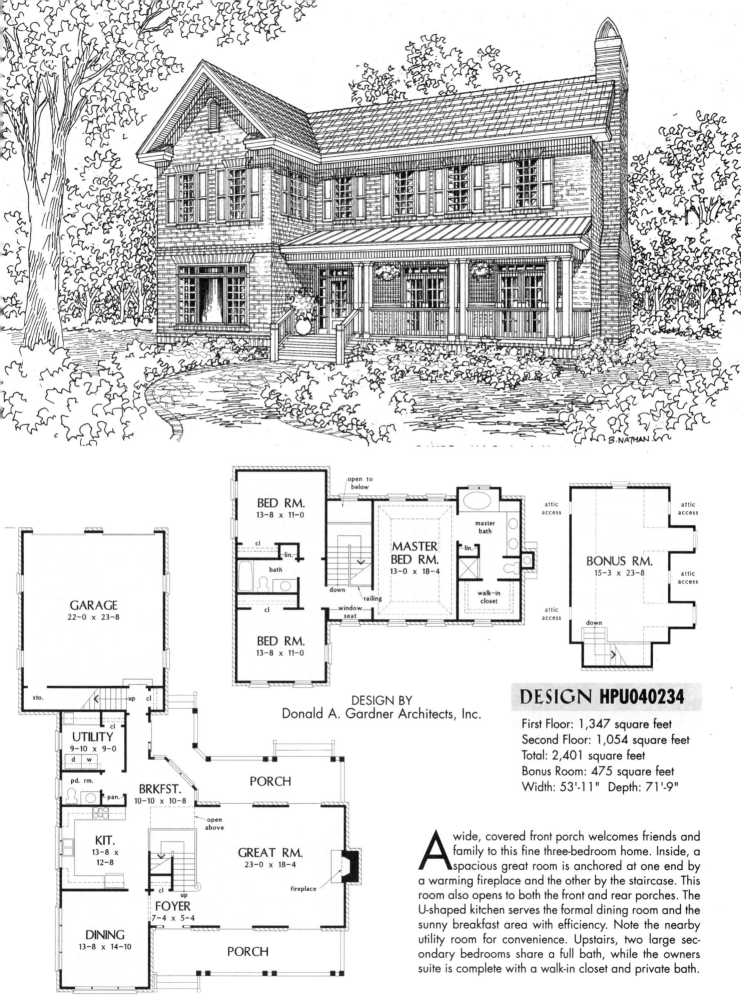

DESIGN BY
Donald A. Gardner Architects, Inc.

GARAGE
22-0 x 23-8

UTILITY
9-10 x 9-0

BRKFST.
10-10 x 10-8

PORCH

KIT.
13-8 x 12-8

GREAT RM.
23-0 x 18-4

fireplace

open above

FOYER
7-4 x 5-4

DINING
13-8 x 14-10

PORCH

BED RM.
13-8 x 11-0

open to below

master bath

MASTER BED RM.
13-0 x 18-4

walk-in closet

down

railing

window seat

BED RM.
13-8 x 11-0

attic access

attic access

BONUS RM.
15-3 x 23-8

attic access

attic access

down

DESIGN HPU040234

First Floor: 1,347 square feet
Second Floor: 1,054 square feet
Total: 2,401 square feet
Bonus Room: 475 square feet
Width: 53'-11" Depth: 71'-9"

A wide, covered front porch welcomes friends and family to this fine three-bedroom home. Inside, a spacious great room is anchored at one end by a warming fireplace and the other by the staircase. This room also opens to both the front and rear porches. The U-shaped kitchen serves the formal dining room and the sunny breakfast area with efficiency. Note the nearby utility room for convenience. Upstairs, two large secondary bedrooms share a full bath, while the owners suite is complete with a walk-in closet and private bath.

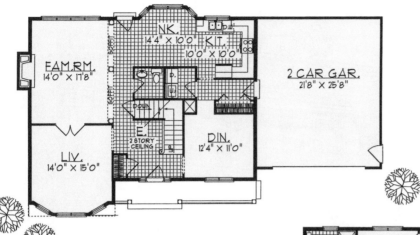

DESIGN HPU040235

First Floor: 1,228 square feet
Second Floor: 1,142 square feet
Total: 2,370 square feet
Bonus Room: 253 square feet
Width: 62'-0" Depth: 36'-0"

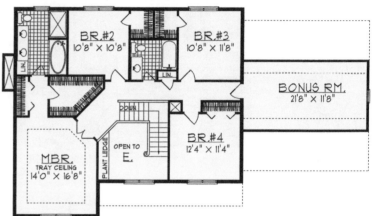

The front covered porch is perfect for reading the evening paper. Inside, the large kitchen has everything your family cook needs. The bayed nook has sliding glass doors, which open to the backyard. The family room contains a fireplace and large rear-facing windows. The formal living room sits off the foyer and has French doors, which can be open or closed for privacy. The formal dining room—off the foyer to the right—provides a perfect setting for holiday gatherings. Upstairs, the master bedroom boasts a tray ceiling, two closets and a private bath. The private bath includes a spa tub, shower and double vanity for couples on the go. The remaining bedrooms share a full bath.

DESIGN BY
©Ahmann Design, Inc.

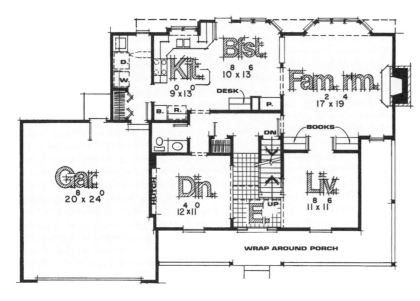

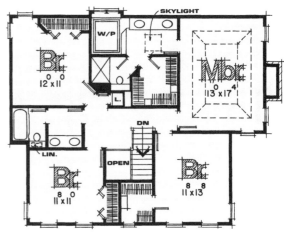

DESIGN HPU040236

First Floor: 1,188 square feet
Second Floor: 1,172 square feet
Total: 2,360 square feet
Width: 58'-0" Depth: 40'-0"

Beginning with the interest of a wraparound porch, there's a feeling of country charm in this two-story plan. Formal dining and living rooms, visible from the entry, offer ample space for gracious entertaining. The large family room is truly a place of warmth and welcome with its gorgeous bay window, fireplace and French doors to the living room. The kitchen, with an island counter, pantry and desk, makes cooking a delight. Upstairs, the secondary bedrooms share an efficient compartmented bath. The expansive master suite has its own luxury bath with a double vanity, whirlpool tub, walk-in closet and dressing area.

DESIGN BY
©Design Basics, Inc.

The grand foyer leads to a two-story great room with an extended-hearth fireplace and access to the rear deck and spa. Open planning allows the bayed breakfast nook and gourmet kitchen to enjoy the view of the fireplace, while the secluded formal dining room basks in natural light from two multi-pane windows. The master suite offers deck access and a bath that includes twin vanities and a windowed, whirlpool tub.

DESIGN HPU040238

First Floor: 1,499 square feet
Second Floor: 665 square feet
Total: 2,164 square feet
Bonus Room: 380 square feet
Width: 69'-8" Depth: 40'-6"

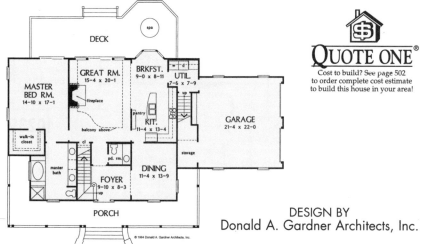

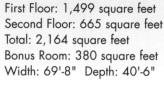

QUOTE ONE®
Cost to build? See page 502
to order complete cost estimate
to build this house in your area!

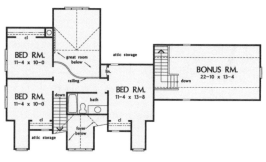

DESIGN BY
Donald A. Gardner Architects, Inc.

© 1994 Donald A. Gardner Architects, Inc.

DESIGN BY
©Home Planners

DESIGN HPU040237

First Floor: 1,655 square feet
Second Floor: 515 square feet
Total: 2,170 square feet
Width: 68'-6" Depth: 66'-5"

L D

QUOTE ONE®
Cost to build? See page 502
to order complete cost estimate
to build this house in your area!

A peaked roof with a wide-arch decorative window provides a commanding entrance to this design. The foyer leads directly into the great room with a wall of windows facing the rear porch. The dining room with a bay window, the island kitchen and the breakfast room line up to provide maximum flexibility. The master suite offers a sitting area and a bath. Two bedrooms occupy the second floor.

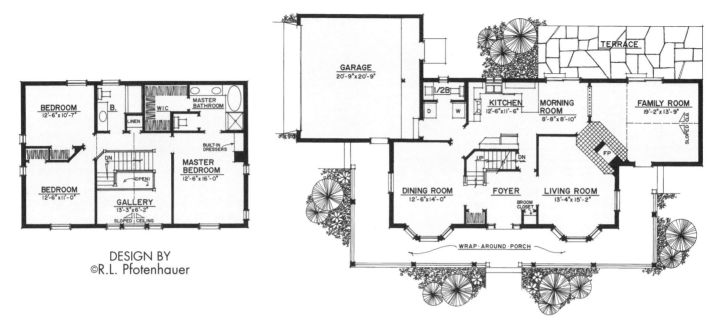

BEDROOM
12'-6"x10'-7"

B.

WIC

MASTER BATHROOM

LINEN

BUILT-IN DRESSERS

DN

(OPEN)

BEDROOM
12'-6"x11'-0"

MASTER BEDROOM
12'-6"x16'-0"

GALLERY
13'-3"x6'-2"
SLOPED CEILING

DESIGN BY
©R.L. Pfotenhauer

GARAGE
20'-9"x20'-9"

TERRACE

1/2B

D   W

KITCHEN
12'-6"x11'-6"

MORNING ROOM
8'-8"x8'-10"

FAMILY ROOM
19'-2"x13'-9"

SLOPED CLG.

UP   DN

FP

DINING ROOM
12'-6"x14'-0"

FOYER

LIVING ROOM
13'-4"x15'-2"

BROOM CLOSET

WRAP·AROUND·PORCH

A covered wraparound porch welcomes you into this updated farmhouse. A traditional floor plan puts work and gathering areas downstairs and bedrooms upstairs. The living room and dining room stand at the front of the house, while the casual living areas at the back include the open kitchen with a breakfast nook and the family room with a double-facing fireplace shared with the living room. Close by is the half-bath and the laundry area. Sliding doors open from the family room and the breakfast nook to a terrace. Upstairs, the master bedroom has a walk-in closet and a bath with a separate tub and shower. Two more bedrooms share a second full bath.

DESIGN HPU040239

First Floor: 1,308 square feet
Second Floor: 992 square feet
Total: 2,300 square feet
Width: 70'-8" Depth: 42'-8"

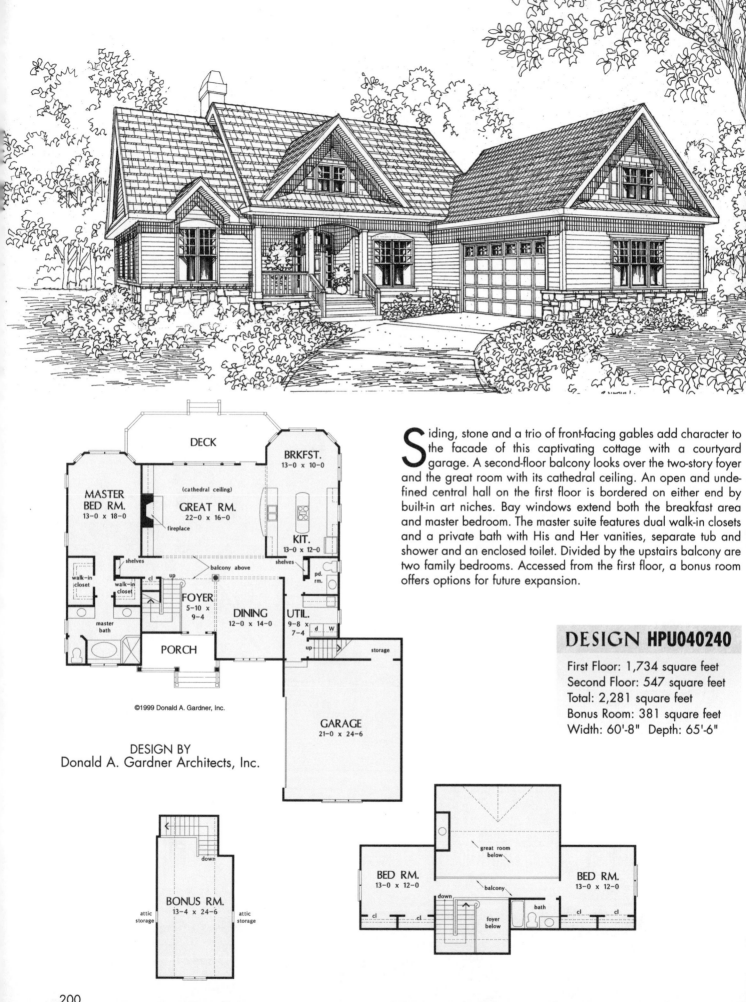

DECK

BRKFST.
13-0 x 10-0

(cathedral ceiling)

MASTER
BED RM.
13-0 x 18-0

GREAT RM.
22-0 x 16-0

fireplace

KIT.
13-0 x 12-0

shelves

walk-in
closet

walk-in
closet

shelves

balcony above

cl

up

pd.
rm.

FOYER
5-10 x
9-4

DINING
12-0 x 14-0

UTIL.
9-8 x
7-4

master
bath

PORCH

d   w

up

storage

©1999 Donald A. Gardner, Inc.

DESIGN BY
Donald A. Gardner Architects, Inc.

GARAGE
21-0 x 24-6

BONUS RM.
13-4 x 24-6

down

attic
storage

attic
storage

great room
below

BED RM.
13-0 x 12-0

BED RM.
13-0 x 12-0

balcony

down

cl

cl

cl

cl

bath

foyer
below

Siding, stone and a trio of front-facing gables add character to the facade of this captivating cottage with a courtyard garage. A second-floor balcony looks over the two-story foyer and the great room with its cathedral ceiling. An open and undefined central hall on the first floor is bordered on either end by built-in art niches. Bay windows extend both the breakfast area and master bedroom. The master suite features dual walk-in closets and a private bath with His and Her vanities, separate tub and shower and an enclosed toilet. Divided by the upstairs balcony are two family bedrooms. Accessed from the first floor, a bonus room offers options for future expansion.

DESIGN HPU040240

First Floor: 1,734 square feet
Second Floor: 547 square feet
Total: 2,281 square feet
Bonus Room: 381 square feet
Width: 60'-8" Depth: 65'-6"

Breakfast
12' x 10'4"

Dining Room
11'8" x 14'

Master Bedroom
16'11" x 14'9"

Bath

walk-in closet

Kitchen
13'3" x 10'

Laun.

Hall

Bath

Foyer

Great Room
17' x 18'8"

Two-car Garage
24'4" x 26'3"

Porch

DESIGN BY
©Studer Residential Designs, Inc.

This home is enhanced by a beautiful brick exterior. Inside, the foyer features a coat closet and opens to the great room. This room is brightened by a huge window overlooking the front yard and is warmed in the winter by a fireplace. The kitchen is conveniently set between the formal dining room and breakfast room, which accesses the rear property. Secluded on the first floor for privacy, the master bedroom includes a spacious walk-in closet and a private bath. The laundry room and a two-car garage complete this first floor. Upstairs, three additional family bedrooms share access to a full hall bath and a computer loft.

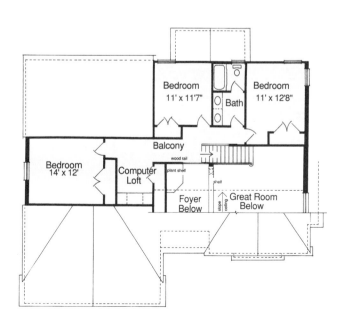

Bedroom
11' x 11'7"

Bath

Bedroom
11' x 12'8"

Balcony

Bedroom
14' x 12'

wood rail

Computer
Loft

plant shelf

shelf

Foyer
Below

slope
ceiling

Great Room
Below

DESIGN HPU040241

First Floor: 1,540 square feet
Second Floor: 808 square feet
Total: 2,348 square feet
Width: 55'-8" Depth: 50'-8"

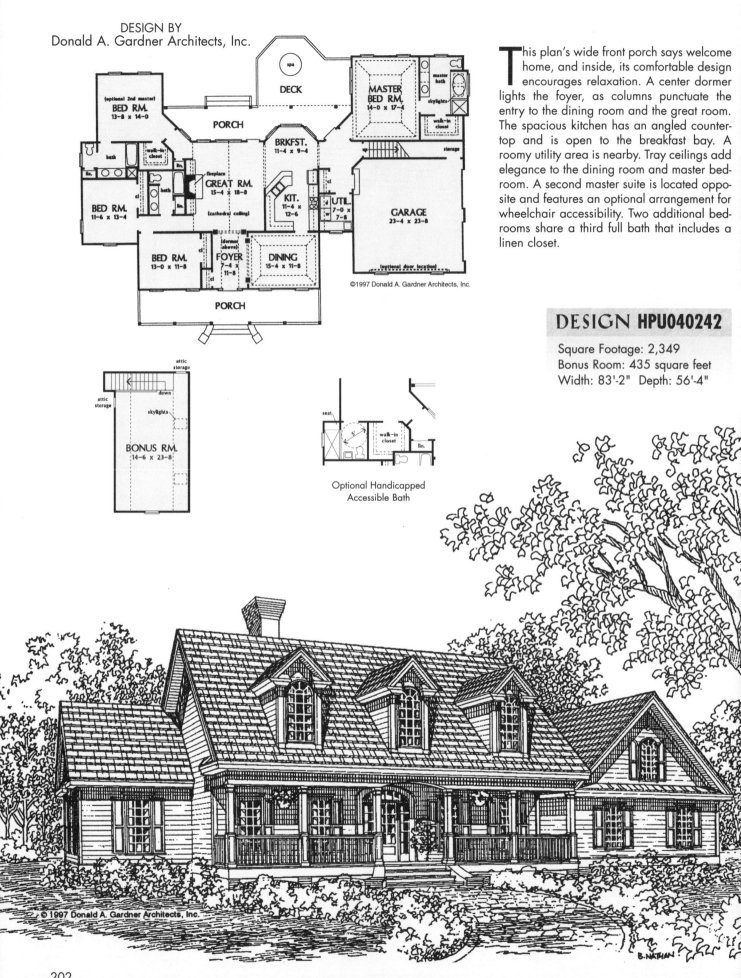

DESIGN BY
Donald A. Gardner Architects, Inc.

BED RM.
(optional 2nd master)
13-8 x 14-0

PORCH

DECK

spa

MASTER
BED RM.
14-0 x 17-4

master
bath

skylights

walk-in
closet

bath

walk-in
closet

BRKFST.
11-4 x 9-4

up

storage

GREAT RM.
15-4 x 18-8

fireplace

BED RM.
11-6 x 13-4

bath

(cathedral ceiling)

KIT.
11-4 x
12-6

UTIL.
7-0 x
7-8

GARAGE
23-4 x 23-8

w

BED RM.
13-0 x 11-8

FOYER
7-4 x
11-8

(dormer
above)

DINING
15-4 x 11-8

(optional door location)

©1997 Donald A. Gardner Architects, Inc.

PORCH

attic
storage

down

attic
storage

skylights

BONUS RM.
14-6 x 23-8

seat

walk-in
closet

lin.

Optional Handicapped
Accessible Bath

This plan's wide front porch says welcome home, and inside, its comfortable design encourages relaxation. A center dormer lights the foyer, as columns punctuate the entry to the dining room and the great room. The spacious kitchen has an angled countertop and is open to the breakfast bay. A roomy utility area is nearby. Tray ceilings add elegance to the dining room and master bedroom. A second master suite is located opposite and features an optional arrangement for wheelchair accessibility. Two additional bedrooms share a third full bath that includes a linen closet.

DESIGN HPU040242

Square Footage: 2,349
Bonus Room: 435 square feet
Width: 83'-2" Depth: 56'-4"

B. NATHAN

This board-and-batten farmhouse design carries down-home country charm with a dash of uptown New England flavor. Warm weather will invite friends and family out to the large, front covered porch to enjoy the outdoors. Just off the front entrance is a spacious living room that opens to the formal dining room, which enjoys a bay window and easy service from the U-shaped kitchen. The family room offers casual living space warmed by a raised-hearth fireplace and extended by double-door access to the rear terrace. The second floor houses two family bedrooms, which share a full bath, and a generous master suite with a walk-in closet and a private bath.

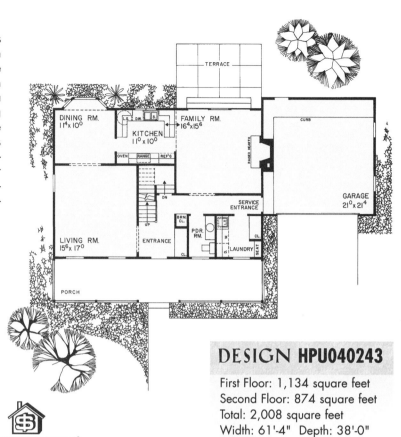

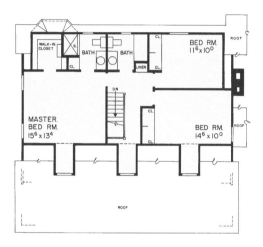

DESIGN BY
©Home Planners

DESIGN HPU040243

First Floor: 1,134 square feet
Second Floor: 874 square feet
Total: 2,008 square feet
Width: 61'-4"   Depth: 38'-0"

L D

© 1993 Donald A. Gardner Architects, Inc.

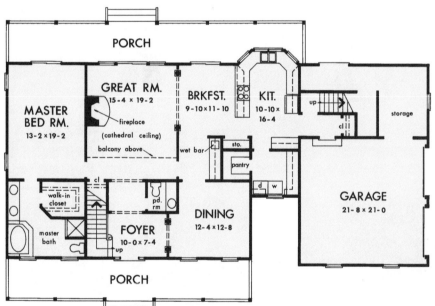

PORCH

GREAT RM.
15-4 × 19-2

BRKFST.
9-10 × 11-10

KIT.
10-10 ×
16-4

up

storage

MASTER
BED RM.
13-2 × 19-2

fireplace
(cathedral ceiling)

balcony above

cl

wet bar

sto.

pantry

walk-in
closet

cl

pd.
rm.

d   w

master
bath

FOYER
10-0 × 7-4

up

DINING
12-4 × 12-8

GARAGE
21-8 × 21-0

PORCH

© 1993 Donald A. Gardner Architects, Inc.

This open country plan boasts front and rear covered porches and a bonus room for future expansion. The slope-ceilinged foyer has a Palladian window clerestory to let in natural light. The spacious great room presents a fireplace, cathedral ceiling and clerestory with arched windows. The second-floor balcony overlooks the great room. A U-shaped kitchen provides the ideal layout for food preparation. For flexibility, access is provided to the bonus room from both the first and second floors. The first-floor master bedroom features a bath with dual lavatories, a separate tub and shower and a walk-in closet. Two large bedrooms and a full bath are located on the second floor.

DESIGN HPU040245

First Floor: 1,632 square feet
Second Floor: 669 square feet
Total: 2,301 square feet
Bonus Room: 528 square feet
Width: 72'-6" Depth: 46'-10"

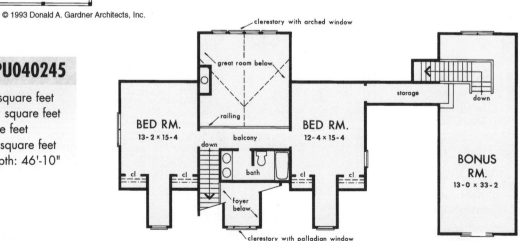

clerestory with arched window

great room below

storage

down

railing

BED RM.
13-2 × 15-4

balcony

BED RM.
12-4 × 15-4

BONUS
RM.
13-0 × 33-2

down

bath

cl

cl

cl

cl

foyer
below

clerestory with palladian window

DESIGN BY
Donald A. Gardner Architects, Inc.

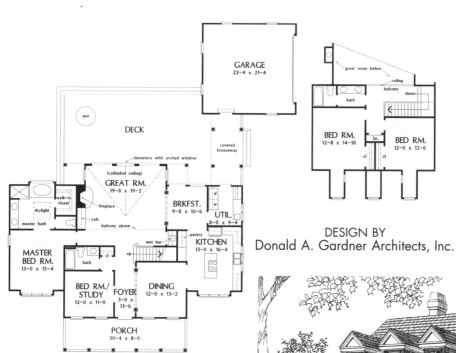

DESIGN HPU040247

First Floor: 1,783 square feet
Second Floor: 611 square feet
Total: 2,394 square feet
Width: 70'-0" Depth: 79'-2"

DESIGN BY
Donald A. Gardner Architects, Inc.

Onlookers will delight in the symmetry of this facade's arched windows and dormers. The interior offers a great room with a cathedral ceiling. This open plan is also packed with the latest design features, including an island kitchen, wet bar, bedroom/study combo on the first floor and a gorgeous master suite with a spa-style bath. Upstairs, two family bedrooms share a compartmented hall bath.

Inside this lovely rustic design, an efficient family floor plan creates a relaxing ambience. The foyer opens to the dining room on the right, which connects to the kitchen. The great room is enhanced by a cathedral ceiling and features a fireplace. The master bedroom is placed on the first floor for extra privacy and includes a walk-in closet and master bath with a whirlpool tub. Upstairs, a second-floor balcony overlooks the great room.

DESIGN BY
Donald A. Gardner Architects, Inc.

DESIGN HPU040246

First Floor: 1,467 square feet
Second Floor: 661 square feet
Total: 2,128 square feet
Bonus Room: 341 square feet
Width: 52'-2" Depth: 74'-0"

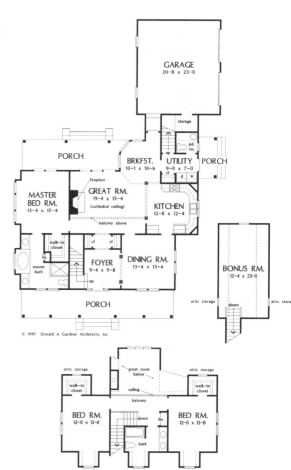

Traditional detailing such as the covered porch with a metal roof and brick steps gives this relaxed farmhouse extra finesse. A Palladian window, transoms over French doors, and large windows brighten the rooms, while nine-foot ceilings add volume and drama throughout the first floor. The master suite features a tray ceiling, and two second-floor bedrooms enjoy ample closet space and share a roomy bath.

DESIGN BY
Donald A. Gardner Architects, Inc.

© 1995 Donald A Gardner Architects, Inc.

DESIGN HPU040249

First Floor: 1,561 square feet
Second Floor: 642 square feet
Total: 2,203 square feet
Bonus Room: 324 square feet
Width: 68'-0" Depth: 50'-4"

© 1997 Donald A. Gardner Architects, Inc.

The grand foyer leads to a great room with a centered fireplace, a wall of windows and access to the rear porch. The breakfast room has its own door to the porch and shares its natural light with the kitchen. Twin walk-in closets introduce a lavish private bath in the master suite. Additional bedrooms reside on the second floor and share a full bath. A skylit bonus room offers extra storage space.

DESIGN HPU040248

First Floor: 1,489 square feet
Second Floor: 534 square feet
Total: 2,023 square feet
Bonus Room: 393 square feet
Width: 59'-4" Depth: 58'-7"

DESIGN BY
Donald A. Gardner Architects, Inc.

DESIGN HPU040250

Square Footage: 2,078
Bonus Room: 339 square feet
Width: 62'-2" Depth: 47'-8"

A n enchanting L-shaped front porch lends charm and grace to this country home with dual dormers and gables. Bay windows expand both of the home's dining areas, while the great room and kitchen are amplified by a shared cathedral ceiling. The generous great room features a fireplace with flanking built-ins, skylights and access to a marvelous back porch. A cathedral ceiling enhances the master bedroom, which enjoys a large walk-in closet and luxurious bath. Two more bedrooms, one with a cathedral ceiling, share a generous hall bath that has a dual-sink vanity.

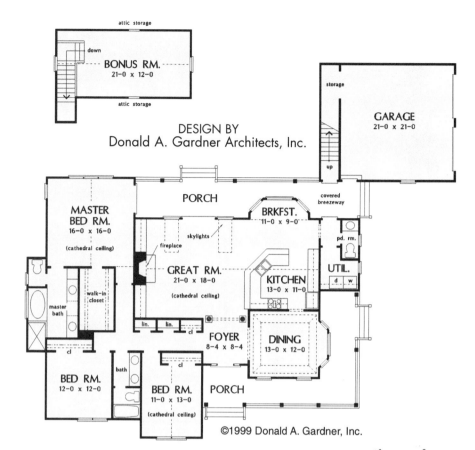

DESIGN BY
Donald A. Gardner Architects, Inc.

©1999 Donald A. Gardner, Inc.

©1999 Donald A. Gardner, Inc.   B. NATHAN

This country facade sports twin dormers, a bumped-out bay and gabled rooflines. Inside, the foyer invites you into either the dining room on the left or the study on the right. The great room features a fireplace and rear-porch access. A kitchen provides a breakfast bar, pantry and sink window. The master suite is secluded to the rear left of the plan and behind the garage for protection from street noise. Two family bedrooms share a full bath.

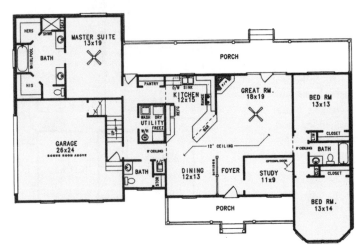

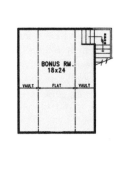

Twin dormers and a covered porch add to the relaxed country exterior of this home. The foyer opens to a study on the right and the dining room on the left. The galley-style kitchen services the dining room, breakfast nook and living room. The nook enjoys a bay window that overlooks the rear porch and yard. The master suite enjoys seclusion at the left rear of the home behind the two-car garage.

DESIGN BY
©Vaughn A. Lauban Designs

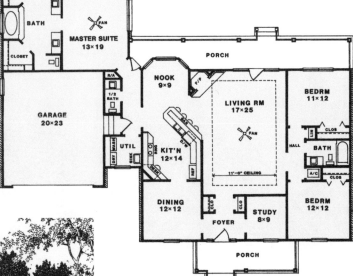

T his quaint four-bedroom home with front and rear porches reinforces its beauty with arched windows and dormers. The pillared dining room opens on your right, while a study that could double as a guest room is available on your left. Straight ahead lies the massive great room with its cathedral ceiling, enchanting fireplace and access to the private rear porch and the deck with a spa and seat. Within steps of the dining room is the efficient kitchen and the sunny breakfast nook. The master suite enjoys a cathedral ceiling, rear-deck access and a master bath with a skylit whirlpool tub, walk-in closet and double vanity. Two additional bedrooms located at the opposite end of the house share a full bath that includes dual vanities.

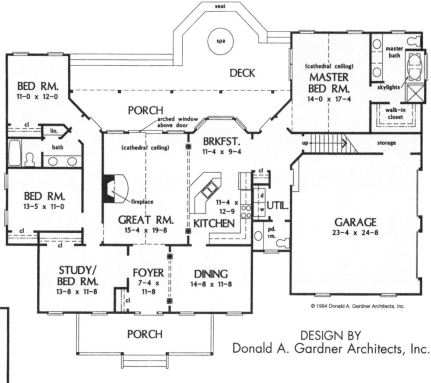

Quote One®

Cost to build? See page 502 to order complete cost estimate to build this house in your area!

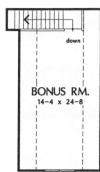

DESIGN BY
Donald A. Gardner Architects, Inc.

DESIGN HPU040253

Square Footage: 2,207
Bonus Room: 435 square feet
Width: 76'-1" Depth: 50'-0"

DESIGN HPU040254

Square Footage: 2,192
Bonus Room: 390 square feet
Width: 74'-10" Depth: 55'-8"

DESIGN BY
Donald A. Gardner Architects, Inc.

Exciting volumes and nine-foot ceilings add elegance to a comfortable and open plan. Sunlight fills the airy foyer from a vaulted dormer and streams into the great room. A dining room, delineated from the foyer by columns, features a tray ceiling. Family bedrooms share a full bath complete with a linen closet. The front bedroom doubles as a study for extra flexibility. The master bedroom suite sits to the left rear of the plan.

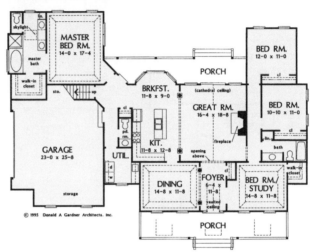
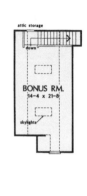

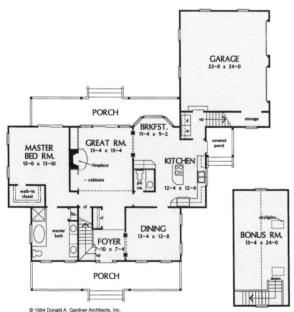

With a casually elegant exterior, this three-bedroom farmhouse celebrates sunlight with a Palladian window dormer, a skylit screened porch and a rear arched window. The clerestory window in the two-story foyer throws natural light across the loft to the great room with a fireplace and a cathedral ceiling. The master suite is a calm retreat opening to the screened porch through a bay area. Two family bedrooms and a bonus room are located upstairs.

DESIGN HPU040255

First Floor: 1,506 square feet
Second Floor: 513 square feet
Total: 2,019 square feet
Bonus Room: 397 square feet
Width: 65'-4" Depth: 67'-10"

DESIGN BY
Donald A. Gardner Architects, Inc.

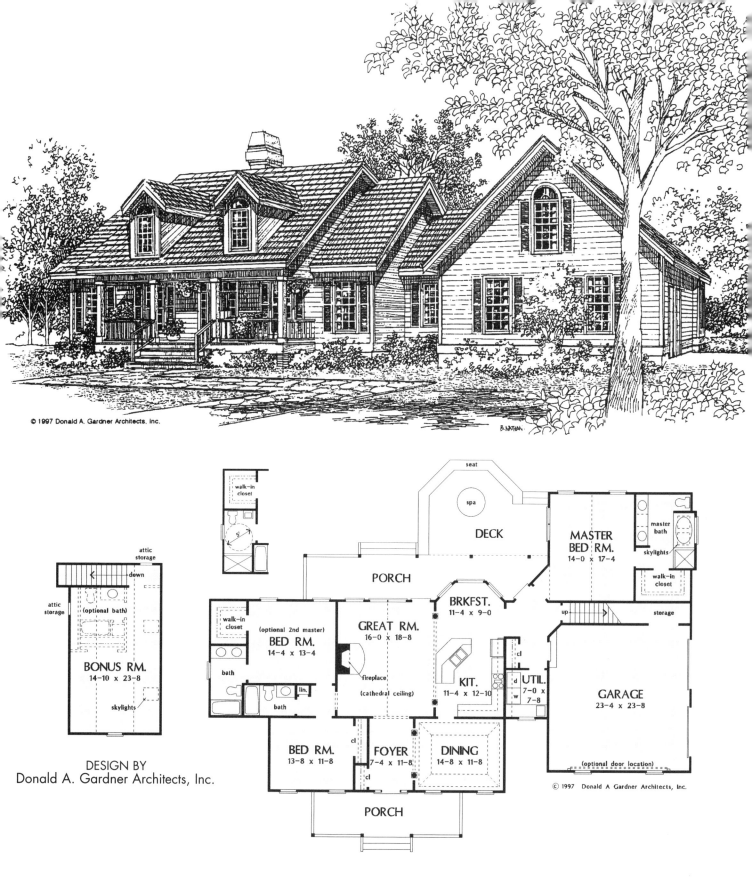

© 1997 Donald A. Gardner Architects, Inc.

B. NATHAN

walk-in closet

seat

spa

DECK

MASTER BED RM.
14-0 x 17-4

master bath

skylights

walk-in closet

PORCH

BRKFST.
11-4 x 9-0

up

storage

attic storage

down

attic storage

(optional bath)

BONUS RM.
14-10 x 23-8

skylights

walk-in closet

BED RM.
(optional 2nd master)
14-4 x 13-4

bath

bath

lin.

GREAT RM.
16-0 x 18-8

fireplace

(cathedral ceiling)

KIT.
11-4 x 12-10

cl

UTIL.
7-0 x 7-8

d
w

GARAGE
23-4 x 23-8

BED RM.
13-8 x 11-8

cl

FOYER
7-4 x 11-8

cl

DINING
14-8 x 11-8

(optional door location)

© 1997   Donald A Gardner Architects, Inc.

PORCH

DESIGN BY
Donald A. Gardner Architects, Inc.

With its clean lines and symmetry, this home radiates grace and style. Inside, cathedral and tray ceilings add volume and elegance. The L-shaped kitchen includes an angled snack bar to the breakfast bay and great room. Secluded at the back of the house, the vaulted master suite includes a skylit bath. Of the two secondary bedrooms, one acts as a "second" master suite with its own private bath, and an alternate bath design creates a wheelchair-accessible option. The bonus room makes a great craft room, playroom, office or optional fourth bedroom with a bath. The two-car garage loads to the side.

DESIGN HPU040256

Square Footage: 2,057
Bonus Room: 444 square feet
Width: 80'-10"   Depth: 61'-6"

DESIGN HPU040257

Square Footage: 2,042
Bonus Room: 475 square feet
Width: 75'-11" Depth: 56'-7"

DESIGN BY
Donald A. Gardner Architects, Inc.

A pleasing mixture of styles, this home combines a traditional brick veneer with an otherwise country home appearance. Built-ins flank the fireplace in the great room, while a soaring cathedral ceiling expands the room visually. The kitchen's angled counter opens the room to both the breakfast bay and great room. The screened porch is accessed from both the great room and the master suite.

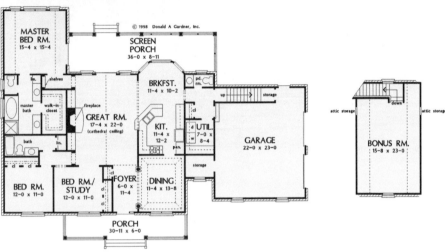

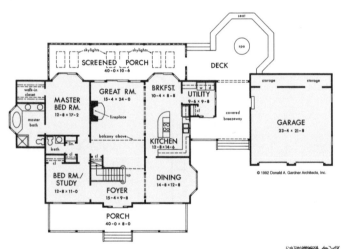

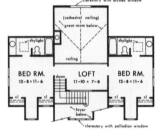

Quote One®
Cost to build? See page 502
to order complete cost estimate
to build this house in your area!

This farmhouse celebrates sunlight with a Palladian window dormer, a skylit screened porch and a rear arched window. The clerestory window in the foyer throws natural light across the loft to a great room with a fireplace and a cathedral ceiling. The central island kitchen and the breakfast area are open to the great room. The master suite is a calm retreat and opens to the screened porch through a bay area. Upstairs, a loft overlooking the great room connects two family bedrooms, each with a private bath.

DESIGN HPU040258

First Floor: 1,766 square feet
Second Floor: 670 square feet
Total: 2,436 square feet
Width: 93'-10" Depth: 62'-0"

DESIGN BY
Donald A. Gardner Architects, Inc.

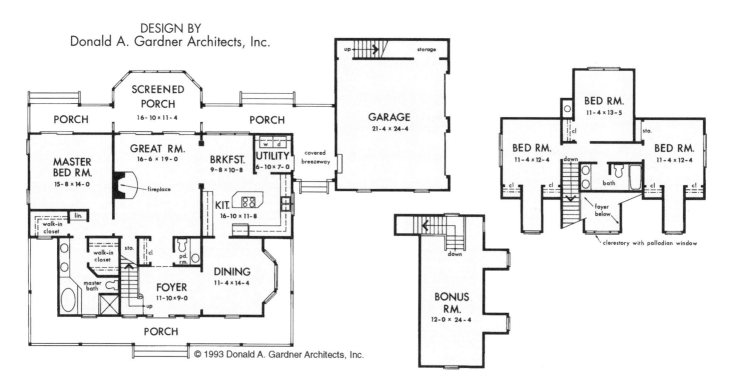

DESIGN BY
Donald A. Gardner Architects, Inc.

SCREENED PORCH
16-10 x 11-4

PORCH

GARAGE
21-4 x 24-4

BED RM.
11-4 x 13-5

PORCH

GREAT RM.
16-6 x 19-0

BRKFST.
9-8 x 10-8

UTILITY
6-10 x 7-0

covered breezeway

BED RM.
11-4 x 12-4

BED RM.
11-4 x 12-4

MASTER BED RM.
15-8 x 14-0

fireplace

KIT.
16-10 x 11-8

bath

foyer below

lin.

walk-in closet

sto.

cl

pd. rm.

DINING
11-4 x 14-4

clerestory with palladian window

walk-in closet

master bath

FOYER
11-10 x 9-0

up

BONUS RM.
12-0 x 24-4

down

PORCH

© 1993 Donald A. Gardner Architects, Inc.

DESIGN HPU040259

First Floor: 1,585 square feet
Second Floor: 723 square feet
Total: 2,308 square feet
Bonus Room: 419 square feet
Width: 80'-4" Depth: 58'-0"

This complete farmhouse projects an exciting and comfortable feeling with its wraparound porch, arched windows and dormers. A Palladian window in the clerestory above the entrance foyer allows for an abundance of natural light. The large kitchen with a cooking island easily services the breakfast area and dining room. The generous great room with a fireplace offers access to the spacious screened porch for carefree outdoor living. The master bedroom suite, located on the first level for privacy and convenience, has a luxurious master bath. The second level allows for three bedrooms and a full bath. Don't miss the garage with a bonus room—both meet the main house via a covered breezeway.

Amenities fill this two-story country home, beginning with a full wraparound porch that offers access to each room on the first floor. Formal living and dining rooms border the central foyer, each with French-door access to the covered porch. At the rear of the first floor, a U-shaped kitchen, a bayed breakfast or morning room, and a large family room with a fireplace make up the living area. Upstairs, three family bedrooms share a centrally located utility room and a full hall bath that has dual sinks. The master suite features a box-bay window seat and a private bath with separate sinks and a walk-in closet. An additional half-bath on the first floor completes this exquisite design.

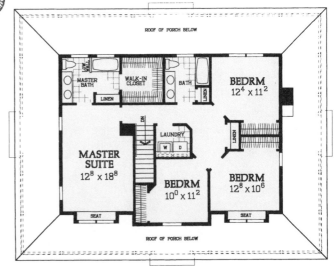

DESIGN HPU040260

First Floor: 1,160 square feet
Second Floor: 1,135 square feet
Total: 2,295 square feet
Width: 54'-0" Depth: 42'-0"

DESIGN BY
©Home Planners

QUOTE ONE®

Cost to build? See page 502 to order complete cost estimate to build this house in your area!

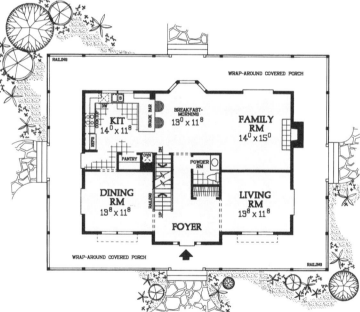

Symmetrical gables and clapboard siding lend a Midwestern style to this prairies-and-plains farmhouse. A spacious foyer opens to formal rooms and leads to a casual living area with a tiled-hearth fireplace and a breakfast bay. The U-shaped kitchen enjoys an easy-care ceramic tile floor and a walk-in pantry. The second-floor sleeping quarters include a generous master suite with a window-seat dormer and a private bath with a whirlpool tub, walk-in closet, twin vanities and linen storage. Three family bedrooms share a full bath and a central hall that leads to additional storage and a laundry.

QUOTE ONE®

Cost to build? See page 502
to order complete cost estimate
to build this house in your area!

DESIGN HPU040262

First Floor: 1,216 square feet
Second Floor: 1,191 square feet
Total: 2,407 square feet
Width: 56'-0" Depth: 42'-0"

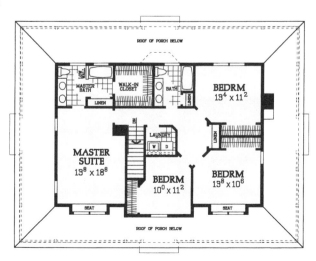

DESIGN BY
©Home Planners

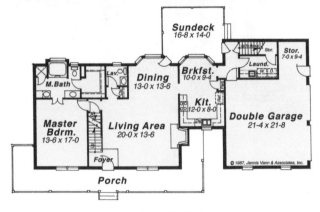

DESIGN HPU040264

First Floor: 1,362 square feet
Second Floor: 729 square feet
Total: 2,091 square feet
Bonus Room: 384 square feet
Width: 72'-0" Depth: 38'-0"

This design's open flow leads you through the living room to the dining room, where access through the bay opens to a sun deck. A kitchen connects to a bayed breakfast area. The master bedroom features a master bath suite with all the amenities. The second floor provides two spacious bedrooms with a shared study or computer room. Please specify basement, crawlspace or slab foundation when ordering.

DESIGN BY
©Jannis Vann & Associates, Inc.

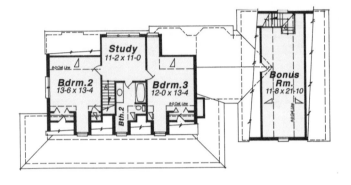

DESIGN BY
©Home Planners

This classic farmhouse enjoys a wraparound porch that's perfect for enjoyment of the outdoors. The dining room is defined by graceful archways set off by decorative columns. The tiled kitchen has a center island counter with a snack bar. Two family bedrooms reside to the side of the plan; each enjoys private access to the covered porch. A secluded master suite features a sitting area with access to the rear terrace and spa.

DESIGN HPU040263

Square Footage: 2,090
Width: 84'-6" Depth: 64'-0"

L D

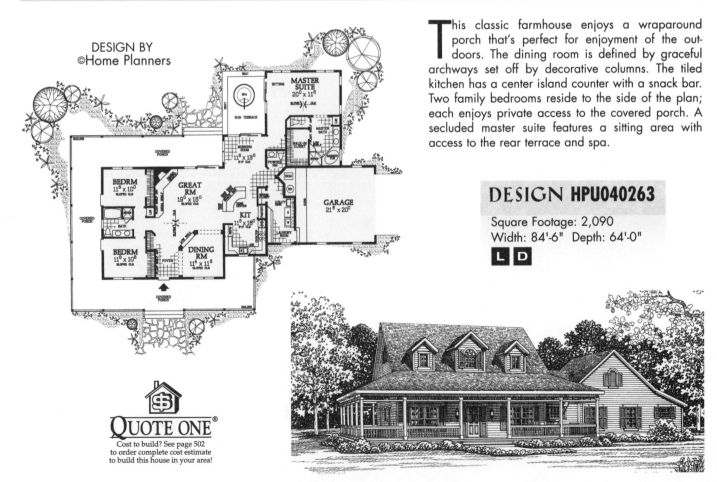

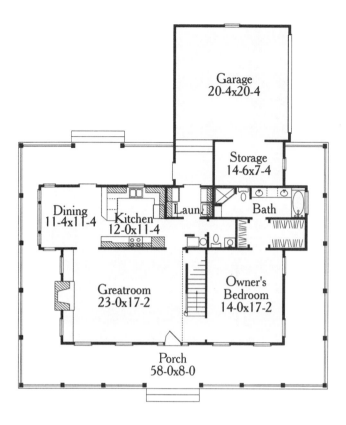

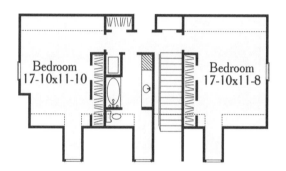

Charming dormer windows and a wraparound porch make this country home a prize. The great room offers porch views and a fireplace to warm guests and family alike. The dining room features a bumped-out wall of windows and easy service from the nearby kitchen. The owners suite is pampered by a walk-in closet and lavish bath. Upstairs, two family bedrooms enjoy plenty of closet space and share a full bath. Please specify basement, crawlspace or slab foundation when ordering.

DESIGN HPU040265

First Floor: 1,339 square feet
Second Floor: 823 square feet
Total: 2,162 square feet
Width: 58'-0" Depth: 67'-2"

DESIGN BY
©Larry James & Associates, Inc.

DESIGN HPU040267

First Floor: 1,526 square feet
Second Floor: 635 square feet
Total: 2,161 square feet
Bonus Room: 355 square feet
Width: 76'-4" Depth: 74'-2"

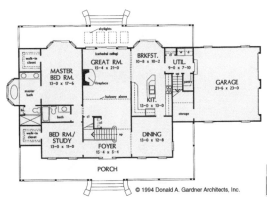

Quote One®
Cost to build? See page 502
to order complete cost estimate
to build this house in your area!

Clerestory windows with arched tops enhance the exterior both front and back, as well as allowing natural light to penetrate into the foyer and the great room. A kitchen with an island counter and a breakfast area is open to the great room. The master suite includes a walk-in closet and a lush master bath. The second level contains two bedrooms sharing a full bath and a loft/study area overlooking the great room.

DESIGN BY
Donald A. Gardner Architects, Inc.

© 1992 Donald A. Gardner Architects, Inc.

Spaciousness and lots of amenities earmark this design as a family favorite. The front wraparound porch leads to the foyer where a bedroom/study and dining room open. The central great room presents a warming fireplace, a cathedral ceiling and access to the rear porch. In the master suite, a walk-in closet and a private bath with a bumped-out tub are extra enhancements. Bonus space over the garage could become a home office.

© 1994 Donald A. Gardner Architects, Inc.

Quote One®
Cost to build? See page 502
to order complete cost estimate
to build this house in your area!

DESIGN HPU040266

First Floor: 1,841 square feet
Second Floor: 594 square feet
Total: 2,435 square feet
Bonus Room: 391 square feet
Width: 82'-2" Depth: 48'-10"

DESIGN BY
Donald A. Gardner Architects, Inc.

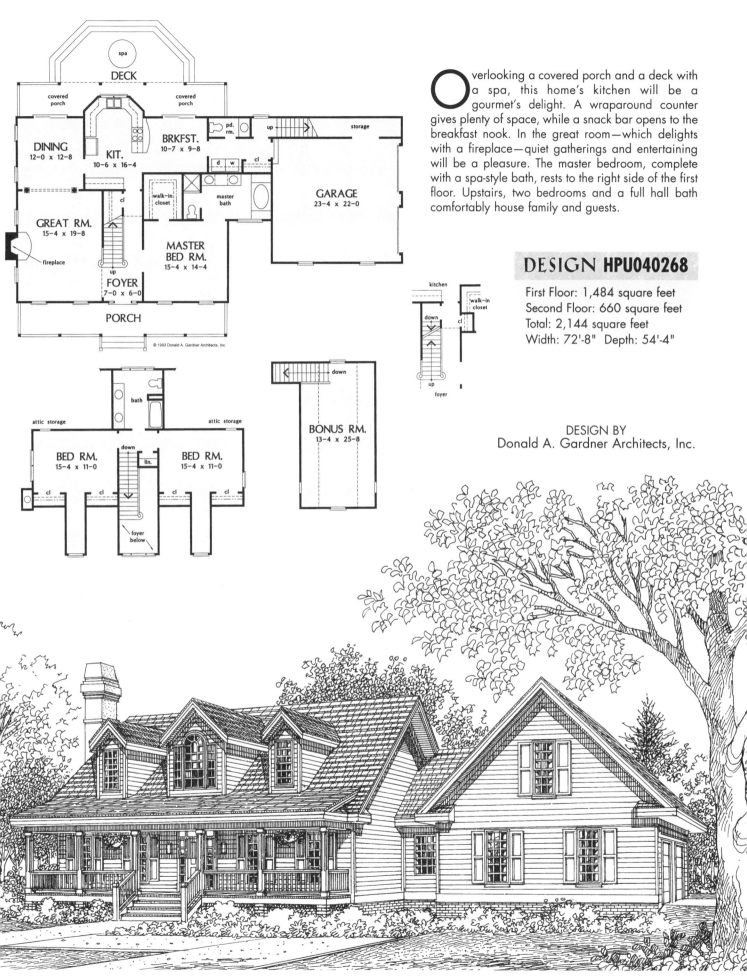

spa

DECK

covered porch

covered porch

DINING
12-0 x 12-8

KIT.
10-6 x 16-4

BRKFST.
10-7 x 9-8

pd. rm.

up

storage

d   w

cl

GARAGE
23-4 x 22-0

walk-in closet

master bath

cl

GREAT RM.
15-4 x 19-8

fireplace

MASTER BED RM.
15-4 x 14-4

up

FOYER
7-0 x 6-0

PORCH

© 1993 Donald A. Gardner Architects, Inc.

bath

attic storage

attic storage

BED RM.
15-4 x 11-0

down

lin.

BED RM.
15-4 x 11-0

cl   cl

cl   cl

foyer below

down

BONUS RM.
13-4 x 25-8

kitchen

walk-in closet

down

cl

up

foyer

O verlooking a covered porch and a deck with a spa, this home's kitchen will be a gourmet's delight. A wraparound counter gives plenty of space, while a snack bar opens to the breakfast nook. In the great room—which delights with a fireplace—quiet gatherings and entertaining will be a pleasure. The master bedroom, complete with a spa-style bath, rests to the right side of the first floor. Upstairs, two bedrooms and a full hall bath comfortably house family and guests.

DESIGN HPU040268

First Floor: 1,484 square feet
Second Floor: 660 square feet
Total: 2,144 square feet
Width: 72'-8"   Depth: 54'-4"

DESIGN BY
Donald A. Gardner Architects, Inc.

DESIGN HPU040269

First Floor: 1,756 square feet
Second Floor: 565 square feet
Total: 2,321 square feet
Width: 56'-8" Depth: 54'-4"

DESIGN BY
Donald A. Gardner Architects, Inc.

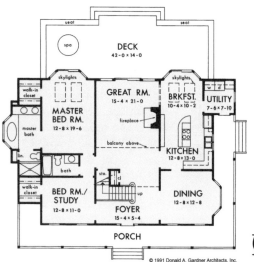

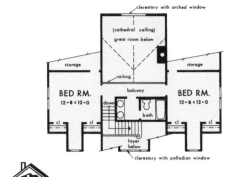

© 1991 Donald A. Gardner Architects, Inc.

QUOTE ONE®
Cost to build? See page 502
to order complete cost estimate
to build this house in your area!

A wraparound covered porch at the front and sides of this house and an open deck at the back provide plenty of outside living area. The spacious great room features a fireplace, cathedral ceiling and clerestory with an arched window. The first-floor master bedroom contains a generous closet and a bath with a garden tub, double-bowl vanity and shower. The second floor sports two bedrooms and a full bath with a double-bowl vanity.

© 1990 Donald A. Gardner Architects, Inc.

QUOTE ONE®
Cost to build? See page 502
to order complete cost estimate
to build this house in your area!

A wraparound porch at the front and sides of this house and a deck with a built-in spa provide outside living area. The great room is appointed with a fireplace, cathedral ceiling and clerestory with an arched window. The kitchen is centrally located for maximum flexibility in layout and features a food-preparation island. Besides the first-floor master bedroom, which offers access to the sun room, there are two second-floor bedrooms that share a full bath.

DESIGN HPU040270

First Floor: 1,651 square feet
Second Floor: 567 square feet
Total: 2,218 square feet
Width: 55'-0" Depth: 53'-10"

DESIGN BY
Donald A. Gardner Architects, Inc.

© 1993 Donald A. Gardner Architects, Inc.

B. NATHAN

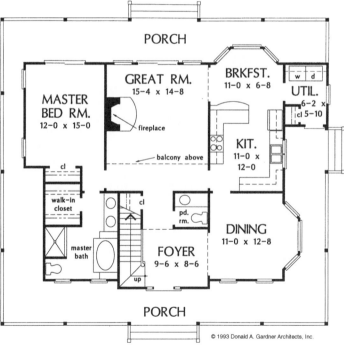

PORCH

GREAT RM.
15-4 x 14-8

BRKFST.
11-0 x 6-8

UTIL.

w | d

6-2 x
cl 5-10

MASTER
BED RM.
12-0 x 15-0

fireplace

cl

balcony above

KIT.
11-0 x
12-0

walk-in
closet

cl

pd.
rm.

master
bath

FOYER
9-6 x 8-6

up

DINING
11-0 x 12-8

PORCH

© 1993 Donald A. Gardner Architects, Inc.

DESIGN HPU040271

First Floor: 1,346 square feet
Second Floor: 836 square feet
Total: 2,182 square feet
Width: 49'-5" Depth: 45'-4"

DESIGN BY
Donald A. Gardner Architects, Inc.

This classy, two-story home with a wraparound covered porch offers a dynamic open floor plan. The entrance foyer and the spacious great room both rise to two stories—a Palladian window at the second level floods these areas with natural light. The kitchen is centrally located for maximum flexibility in layout and, as an added feature, also has a breakfast bar. The large dining room delights with a bay window. The generous master suite has plenty of closet space as well as a bath with a whirlpool tub, a shower and a double-bowl vanity. On the second level, three bedrooms branch off the balcony that overlooks the great room. One large bedroom contains a private bath and a walk-in closet, while the other bedrooms share a full bath.

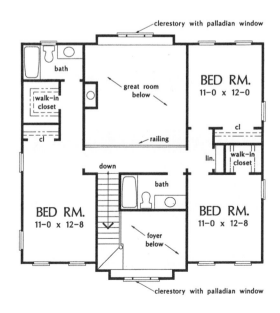

clerestory with palladian window

bath

walk-in
closet

cl

great room
below

railing

BED RM.
11-0 x 12-0

cl

lin.

walk-in
closet

down

bath

BED RM.
11-0 x 12-8

foyer
below

BED RM.
11-0 x 12-8

clerestory with palladian window

DESIGN HPU040272

First Floor: 1,471 square feet
Second Floor: 577 square feet
Total: 2,048 square feet
Bonus Room: 368 square feet
Width: 75'-5" Depth: 52'-0"

DESIGN BY
Donald A. Gardner Architects, Inc.

For the family that enjoys outdoor living, this wraparound porch that becomes a screened porch and then turns into a deck is the best of all worlds! At the front, the dining room features a bay window and mirrors the breakfast bay at the back, with the kitchen in between. On the opposite side of the plan, the master suite, with two walk-in closets and a deluxe bath, accesses the rear porch. Two family bedrooms share a full bath on the second floor.

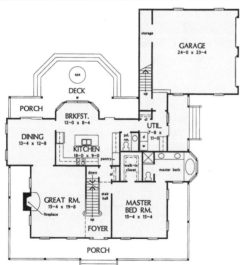

This charming farmhouse begins with a two-story entrance foyer with a Palladian window in a clerestory dormer above for natural light. The master suite, with its large walk-in closet, is on the first level for privacy and accessibility. The master bath includes a whirlpool tub, a shower and a double-bowl vanity. The second level has two bedrooms, a full bath and plenty of storage.

QUOTE ONE®
Cost to build? See page 502
to order complete cost estimate
to build this house in your area!

DESIGN HPU040273

First Floor: 1,537 square feet
Second Floor: 641 square feet
Total: 2,178 square feet
Bonus Room: 418 square feet
Width: 65'-8" Depth: 70'-0"

DESIGN BY
Donald A. Gardner Architects, Inc.

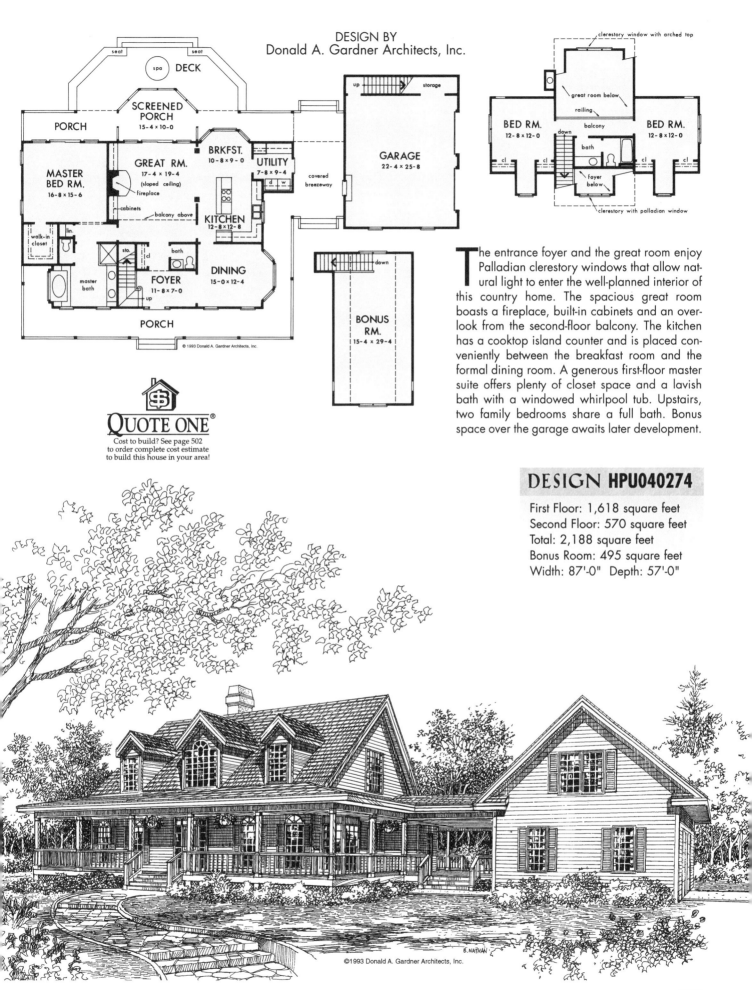

DESIGN BY
Donald A. Gardner Architects, Inc.

PORCH

SCREENED PORCH
15-4 x 10-0

DECK
seat · spa · seat

MASTER BED RM.
16-8 x 15-6

GREAT RM.
17-4 x 19-4
(sloped ceiling)
fireplace

cabinets

balcony above

BRKFST.
10-8 x 9-0

UTILITY
7-8 x 9-4
d w

covered breezeway

GARAGE
22-4 x 25-8

up · storage

KITCHEN
12-8 x 12-8

walk-in closet

lin.

master bath

sto.

cl

bath

FOYER
11-8 x 7-0
up

DINING
15-0 x 12-4

PORCH

© 1993 Donald A. Gardner Architects, Inc.

down

BONUS RM.
15-4 x 29-4

clerestory window with arched top

great room below

railing

BED RM.
12-8 x 12-0

balcony

down

bath

BED RM.
12-8 x 12-0

cl · cl · cl · cl

foyer below

clerestory with palladian window

The entrance foyer and the great room enjoy Palladian clerestory windows that allow natural light to enter the well-planned interior of this country home. The spacious great room boasts a fireplace, built-in cabinets and an overlook from the second-floor balcony. The kitchen has a cooktop island counter and is placed conveniently between the breakfast room and the formal dining room. A generous first-floor master suite offers plenty of closet space and a lavish bath with a windowed whirlpool tub. Upstairs, two family bedrooms share a full bath. Bonus space over the garage awaits later development.

DESIGN HPU040274

First Floor: 1,618 square feet
Second Floor: 570 square feet
Total: 2,188 square feet
Bonus Room: 495 square feet
Width: 87'-0" Depth: 57'-0"

S. NATHAN

©1993 Donald A. Gardner Architects, Inc.

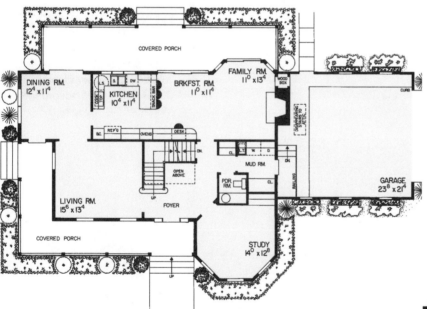

COVERED PORCH

DINING RM.
12⁴ x 11⁴

KITCHEN
10⁴ x 11⁴

BRKFST. RM.
11⁰ x 11⁴

FAMILY RM.
11⁰ x 13⁴

WOOD BOX

DISAPPEARING STAIRS TO ATTIC

CURB

REF'G

OVENS

DESK

OPEN ABOVE

UP

MUD RM.

W D

ON

RAILING

GARAGE
23⁸ x 21⁴

LIVING RM.
15⁶ x 13⁴

FOYER

PDR RM

CL

COVERED PORCH

STUDY
14⁰ x 12⁸

UP

DESIGN HPU040275

First Floor: 1,269 square feet
Second Floor: 1,227 square feet
Total: 2,496 square feet
Width: 70'-0" Depth: 44'-5"

L

QUOTE ONE®

Cost to build? See page 502
to order complete cost estimate
to build this house in your area!

The most popular feature of the Victorian house has always been its covered porches. The two finely detailed outdoor living spaces found on this home add much to formal and informal entertaining options. However, in addition to its wonderful Victorian facade, this home provides a myriad of interior features that cater to the active, growing family. Living and dining areas include a formal living room and dining room, a family room with fireplace, a study and a kitchen with an attached breakfast nook. The second floor contains three family bedrooms and a luxurious master suite with a whirlpool spa and His and Hers walk-in closets.

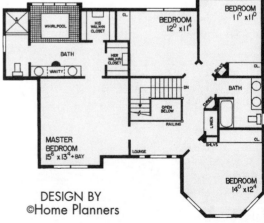

WHIRLPOOL

HIS WALK-IN CLOSET

CL

BEDROOM
12⁰ x 11⁴

BEDROOM
11⁰ x 11⁰

BATH

HER WALK-IN CLOSET

VANITY

DN

OPEN BELOW

RAILING

BATH

CL

LINEN

MASTER BEDROOM
15⁶ x 13⁴ +BAY

LOUNGE

SHLVS.

CL

BEDROOM
14⁰ x 12⁴

DESIGN BY
©Home Planners

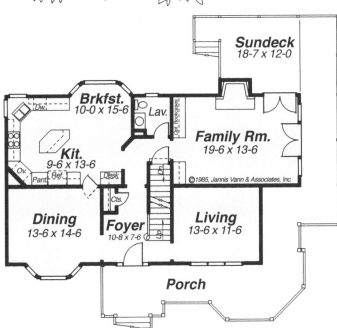

Sundeck
18-7 x 12-0

Brkfst.
10-0 x 15-6

Lav.

Kit.
9-6 x 13-6

Opt. Bookcases

Family Rm.
19-6 x 13-6

Ov.

Ref.

Desk

Pant.

Cts.

©1985, Jannis Vann & Associates, Inc.

Dining
13-6 x 14-6

Foyer
10-8 x 7-6

Living
13-6 x 11-6

Porch

DESIGN BY
©Jannis Vann & Associates, Inc.

DESIGN HPU040276

First Floor: 1,155 square feet
Second Floor: 1,209 square feet
Total: 2,364 square feet
Width: 46'-0" Depth: 36'-8"

Victorian charm is displayed at its best with fish-scale siding, bay windows, a turret roof and gingerbread trim all featured on this design. The front porch features an expanded sitting area perfect for the porch swing or a table and chairs, as the porch roof wraps around the second-floor turret. Bay windows expand space in both the formal dining room and the breakfast area. The kitchen carries on the bay-window feel as the cabinets angle at the corners, creating a bright sink corner plus an angled island for extra work space. Outside living is enhanced by the deck that connects the rear deck with the front porch. The glass wall on the side of the family room floods the room with light. The second-floor turret creates a cozy sitting area in the master suite, which accesses a balcony. Three bedrooms share a hall bath located across from the second-floor laundry closet.

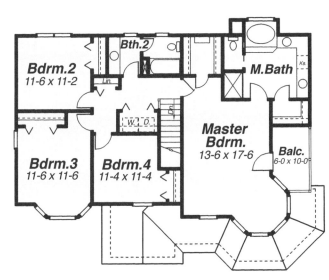

Bth.2

Bdrm.2
11-6 x 11-2

Lin.

M.Bath

Bdrm.3
11-6 x 11-6

W. D.

Bdrm.4
11-4 x 11-4

Master Bdrm.
13-6 x 17-6

Balc.
6-0 x 10-0

DESIGN HPU040277

First Floor: 1,186 square feet
Second Floor: 988 square feet
Total: 2,174 square feet
Width: 72'-4" Depth: 51'-2"

L D

DESIGN BY
©Home Planners

This Victorian-style exterior—a wrap-around porch, mullion windows and turret-style bays—offers you a wonderful floor plan. Inside, an impressive tiled entry opens to the formal rooms, which nestle to the left side of the plan and enjoy natural light from an abundance of windows. More than just a pretty face, the turret houses a secluded study on the first floor and provides a sunny bay window for a family bedroom upstairs. The second-floor master suite boasts its own fireplace, a dressing area with a walk-in closet, and a lavish bath with a garden tub and twin vanities. The two-car garage offers space for a workshop or extra storage.

QUOTE ONE®
Cost to build? See page 502 to order complete cost estimate to build this house in your area!

Victorian style is highly evident on this beautiful four-bedroom, two-story home. With fish-scale trim, a turret skirted by an octagonal porch, and varied window treatments, this home is a true winner. The interior continues with a cozy octagonal study, a spacious living room complete with a warming fireplace, a formal dining room that offers access to the rear porch, and a large efficient kitchen that shares a snack bar with the comfortable family room. The sleeping zone is contained upstairs and consists of three secondary bedrooms—one at the top of the tower—that shares a full hall bath, and a lavish master suite.

DESIGN HPU040278

First Floor: 1,186 square feet
Second Floor: 988 square feet
Total: 2,174 square feet
Width: 72'-0" Depth: 50'-10"

L D

DESIGN BY
©Home Planners

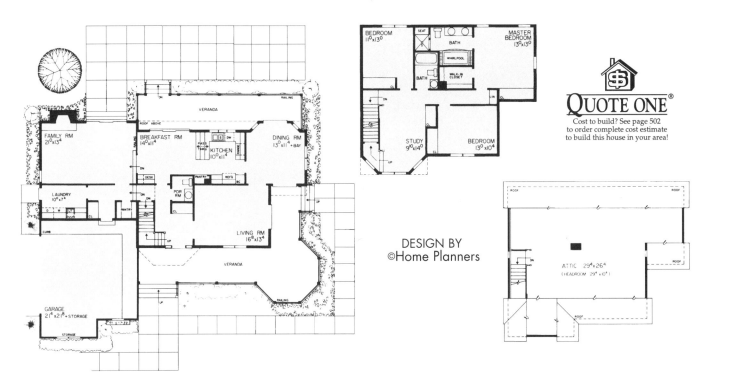

QUOTE ONE®
Cost to build? See page 502
to order complete cost estimate
to build this house in your area!

DESIGN BY
©Home Planners

DESIGN HPU040279

First Floor: 1,375 square feet
Second Floor: 1,016 square feet
Total: 2,391 square feet
Attic: 303 square feet
Width: 62'-7" Depth: 54'-0"

L

Covered porches, front and back, are a fine preview to the livable nature of this Victorian design. Living areas are defined in a family room with a fireplace, formal living and dining rooms, and a kitchen with a breakfast room. An ample laundry room, a garage with a storage area, and a powder room round out the first floor. Three second-floor bedrooms are joined by a study and two full baths. The master suite on this floor has two closets, including a spacious walk-in, as well as a relaxing bath with a tile-rimmed whirlpool tub and a separate shower with a seat.

DESIGN HPU040280

Square Footage: 2,250
Width: 84'-10" Depth: 62'-4"

DESIGN BY
Donald A. Gardner Architects, Inc.

A lovely courtyard precedes a grand French-door entry with an arched transom, while stone and stucco accent the exterior of this dignified Country French home. The foyer, great room and dining room feature stately eleven-foot ceilings, and interior columns mark boundaries for the great room and dining room. The spacious kitchen features a pass-through to the great room, where built-in shelves flank the fireplace. Cozy side decks and a large back porch add to the home's appeal. The master suite is magnificent with a double-door entry, an elegant tray ceiling, dual walk-in closets and an extravagant bath. Nearby, two additional bedrooms share their own hall bath.

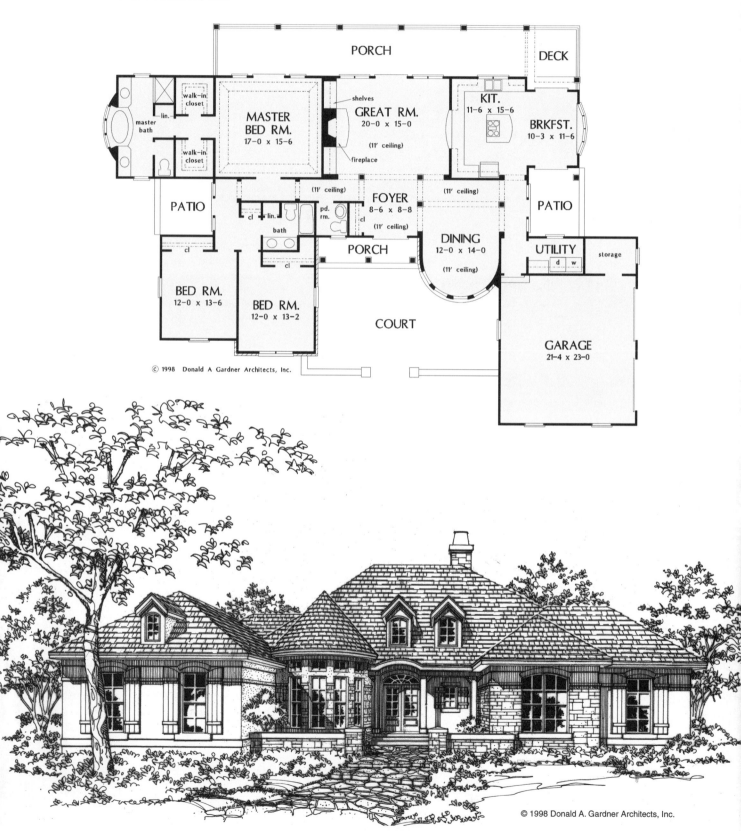

PORCH

DECK

walk-in closet

lin.

master bath

MASTER BED RM.
17-0 x 15-6

shelves

GREAT RM.
20-0 x 15-0

(11' ceiling)

fireplace

KIT.
11-6 x 15-6

BRKFST.
10-3 x 11-6

walk-in closet

(11' ceiling)

FOYER
8-6 x 8-8

(11' ceiling)

(11' ceiling)

PATIO

PATIO

cl   lin.

bath

pd. rm.

cl

DINING
12-0 x 14-0

UTILITY

storage

cl

PORCH

(11' ceiling)

d   w

BED RM.
12-0 x 13-6

cl

BED RM.
12-0 x 13-2

COURT

GARAGE
21-4 x 23-0

© 1998 Donald A Gardner Architects, Inc.

© 1998 Donald A. Gardner Architects, Inc.

228

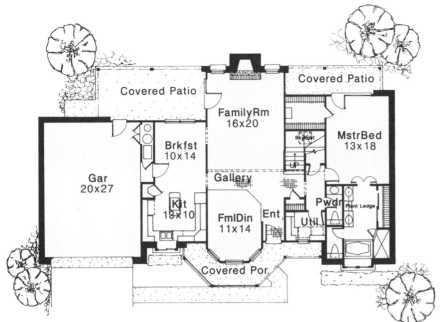

DESIGN HPU040281

First Floor: 1,572 square feet
Second Floor: 700 square feet
Total: 2,272 square feet
Bonus Room: 212 square feet
Width: 70'-0" Depth: 38'-5"

DESIGN BY
©Fillmore Design Group

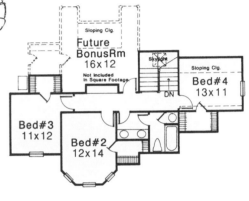

A charming porch wraps around the front of this farmhouse, whose entry opens to a formal dining room. Country and Victorian elements give this home a down-home feel. The island kitchen and sun-filled breakfast area are located nearby. The family room is warmed by a fireplace flanked by windows. Located for privacy, the first-floor master bedroom features its own covered patio and a private bath designed for relaxation. The second floor contains three family bedrooms—each with a walk-in closet—a full bath and a future bonus room.

DESIGN HPU040283

First Floor: 1,006 square feet
Second Floor: 1,099 square feet
Total: 2,105 square feet
Width: 47'-0" Depth: 43'-0"

DESIGN BY
©Design Basics, Inc.

This siding-and-brick traditional home focuses on the family. A charming covered porch welcomes guests, while inside, a formal dining area and great room with a fireplace are perfect for entertaining. A large efficient kitchen with an easy-access island and a bayed breakfast area is handy for those easy meals. Three family bedrooms and a comfortable master suite with a whirlpool bath and separate shower are located on the second floor. A loft area is a popular family retreat.

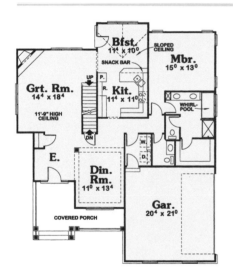

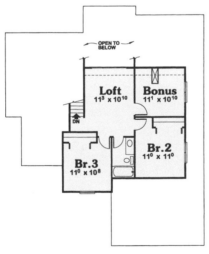

Brick and stone go hand-in-hand to create a pleasing exterior for this home. But the appeal doesn't remain only on the outside. The interior floor plan has many amenities and provides great traffic flow. The offset entry opens to a small hall and is distinguished by columns that separate it from the formal dining room. The great room boasts an eleven-foot ceiling and a corner fireplace. Just beyond is a U-shaped kitchen with an attached breakfast nook—note the snack counter that separates them. The master bedroom on the first floor features a private bath and walk-in closet. Family bedrooms on the second floor share a full bath. Bonus space and a loft area on the second floor expand its usefulness.

DESIGN HPU040282

First Floor: 1,457 square feet
Second Floor: 686 square feet
Total: 2,143 square feet
Bonus Room: 445 square feet
Width: 45'-4" Depth: 54'-0"

DESIGN BY
©Design Basics, Inc.

© 1992 Donald A. Gardner Architects, Inc.

B. NATHAN

DECK

seat

spa

PORCH
37-0 × 6-0

KITCHEN
11-0 × 13-2

BRKFST.
9-0 × 11-4

DINING
13-0 × 11-8

GREAT RM.
18-0 × 17-4

fireplace

bath

sto.

up

LIVING RM.
13-0 × 16-10

fireplace

FOYER
8-8 × 14-4

BED RM./STUDY
12-4 × 11-0

d w

UTIL.
6-8 × 7-8

up

storage

GARAGE
22-4 × 22-4

PORCH
26-4 × 6-0

© 1992 Donald A. Gardner Architects, Inc.

DESIGN HPU040284

First Floor: 1,569 square feet
Second Floor: 929 square feet
Total: 2,498 square feet
Bonus Room: 320 square feet
Width: 65'-8" Depth: 61'-4"

DESIGN BY
Donald A. Gardner Architects, Inc.

BED RM.
10-8 × 10-10

bath

master bath

MASTER BED RM.
13-8 × 17-4

down

down

foyer below

linen

BED RM.
11-0 × 11-8

BONUS RM.
12-4 × 22-4

This home's striking exterior is reinforced by its gables and arched glass window. The central foyer leads to all spaces in the home's open layout. Both the living room and great room boast fireplaces and round columns. The efficient U-shaped kitchen offers a cooking island for added luxury to serve both the dining room and breakfast area. The master bedroom holds a large walk-in closet and generous bath with a whirlpool tub, separate shower and double-bowl vanity. Two additional bedrooms share a full bath. A bedroom on the first level can easily double as a study.

DESIGN HPU040286

First Floor: 1,653 square feet
Second Floor: 700 square feet
Total: 2,353 square feet
Width: 54'-0" Depth: 50'-0"

DESIGN BY
©Design Basics, Inc.

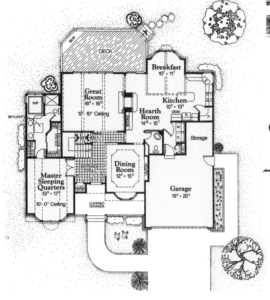

QUOTE ONE®

Cost to build? See page 502
to order complete cost estimate
to build this house in your area!

Beautiful arches and elaborate detail give the elevation of this four-bedroom, 1½-story home an unmistakable elegance. Inside, the floor plan is equally appealing. Note the formal dining room with a bay window, visible from the entrance hall. The large great room has a fireplace and a wall of windows with views of the rear property. A hearth room with a built-in bookcase adjoins the kitchen, which boasts a corner walk-in pantry and a spacious breakfast nook with a bay window. The first-floor master suite features His and Hers wardrobes, a large whirlpool tub and double lavatories. Upstairs, the family sleeping quarters share a full bath that includes compartmented sinks.

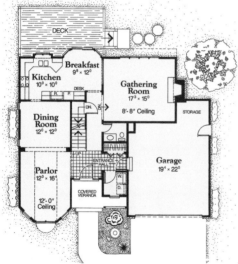

Elegant detail, a charming veranda and a tall brick chimney make a pleasing facade on this four-bedroom, two-story Victorian home. Yesterday's simpler lifestyle is reflected throughout this plan. From the large bayed parlor with its sloped ceiling to the sunken gathering room with a fireplace, there's plenty to appreciate about the floor plan. The L-shaped kitchen with its attached breakfast room has plenty of storage space and easily serves the dining room through a discreet doorway. Sleeping quarters include a master suite with a private dressing area and a whirlpool bath, and three family bedrooms arranged to share a hall bath.

DESIGN HPU040285

First Floor: 1,113 square feet
Second Floor: 965 square feet
Total: 2,078 square feet
Width: 46'-0" Depth: 41'-5"

DESIGN BY
©Design Basics, Inc.

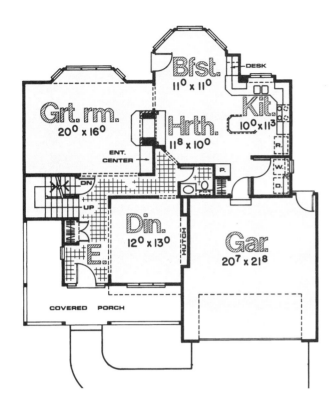

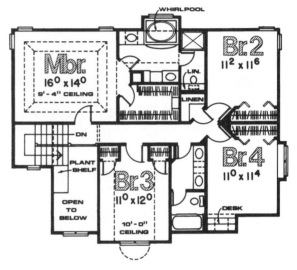

ap siding, special windows and a covered porch enhance the elevation of this popular style. The spacious two-story entry surveys the formal dining room with hutch space. An entertainment center, through-fireplace and bayed windows add appeal to the great room. Families will love the spacious kitchen with its breakfast and hearth room. Comfortable secondary bedrooms and a sumptuous master suite feature privacy by design. Bedroom 3 is highlighted by a half-round window, volume ceiling and double closets, while Bedroom 4 features a built-in desk. The master suite contains a vaulted ceiling, large walk-in closet, His and Hers vanities and an oval whirlpool tub.

DESIGN BY
©Design Basics, Inc.

DESIGN HPU040287

First Floor: 1,150 square feet
Second Floor: 1,120 square feet
Total: 2,270 square feet
Width: 46'-0" Depth: 48'-0"

As attractive on the inside as it is on the outside, this hipped-roof design is sure to be a favorite for any growing family. A covered entry porch leads inside to an attractive living room and dining area. The efficient island kitchen is conveniently located near the two-car garage, the laundry room, the breakfast nook and the family room. The family room is warmed by a large fireplace. The master bedroom has private access through double doors to the rear porch, and also features a master bath with a walk-in closet. Two additional family bedrooms are located on the other side of the home. Bedroom 2 accesses a hall bath, and Bedroom 3 features its own private bath.

DESIGN HPU040288

Square Footage: 2,384
Width: 64'-0" Depth: 69'-4"

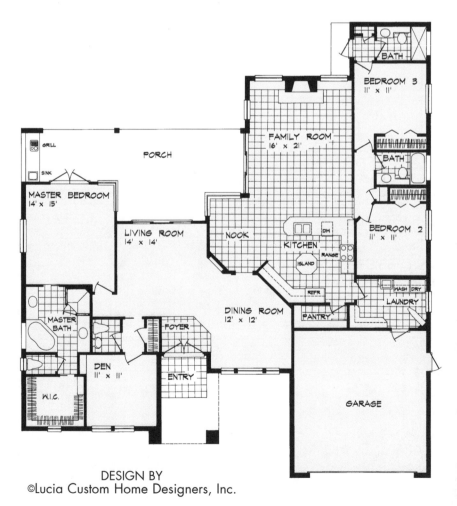

DESIGN BY
©Lucia Custom Home Designers, Inc.

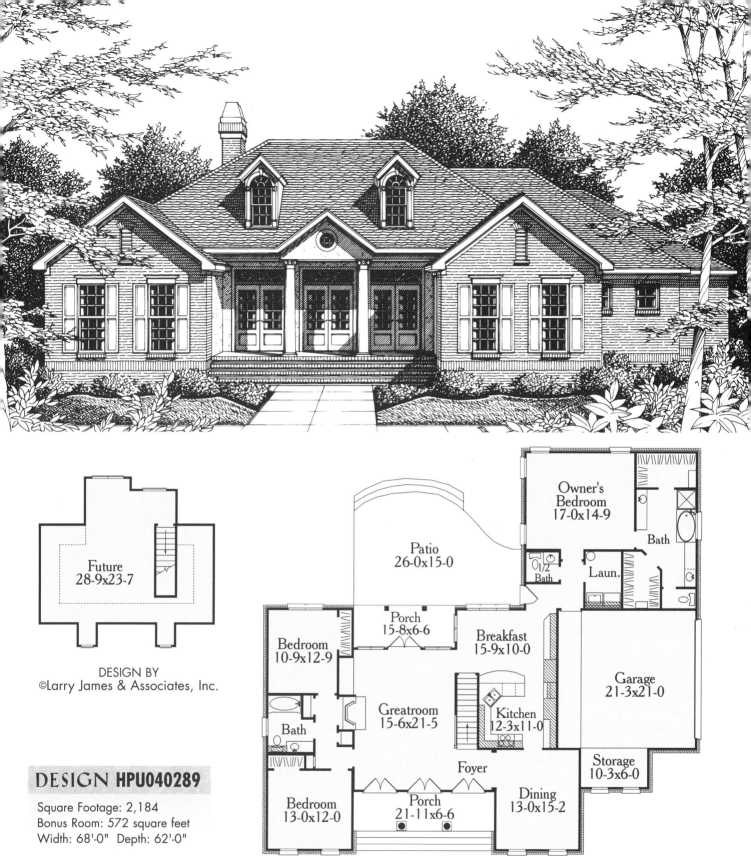

Future
28-9x23-7

DESIGN BY
©Larry James & Associates, Inc.

Patio
26-0x15-0

Owner's
Bedroom
17-0x14-9

Bath

1/2
Bath

Laun.

Porch
15-8x6-6

Breakfast
15-9x10-0

Garage
21-3x21-0

Bedroom
10-9x12-9

Bath

Greatroom
15-6x21-5

Kitchen
12-3x11-0

Foyer

Storage
10-3x6-0

DESIGN HPU040289

Square Footage: 2,184
Bonus Room: 572 square feet
Width: 68'-0" Depth: 62'-0"

Bedroom
13-0x12-0

Porch
21-11x6-6

Dining
13-0x15-2

The front porch is accented with stately columns and graceful full-length stairs. Three sets of French doors make the entry a stunning display of style. The great room features a central fireplace and rear-porch access. The breakfast room offers patio views and convenient kitchen service. The formal dining room, with the kitchen nearby, is perfect for entertaining guests. The secluded master suite enjoys two walk-in closets, a compartmented toilet, His and Hers vanities, and a separate tub and shower. Two secondary bedrooms, to the left of the great room, share a bath. Please specify basement, crawlspace or slab foundation when ordering.

DESIGN HPU040291

First Floor: 1,505 square feet
Second Floor: 610 square feet
Total: 2,115 square feet
Width: 64'-0" Depth: 52'-0"

DESIGN BY
©Design Basics, Inc.

QUOTE ONE®
Cost to build? See page 502
to order complete cost estimate
to build this house in your area!

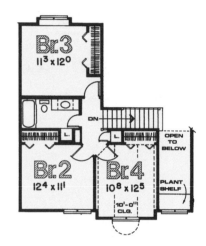

Farmhouse style is updated and improved by a high roofline and a central arched window. Many windows, lap siding and a covered porch give this elevation a welcoming country flair. The formal dining room with hutch space is conveniently located near the island kitchen. A main-floor laundry room with a sink is discreetly located next to the bright breakfast area with a desk and pantry. Highlighting the spacious great room are a raised-hearth fireplace, a cathedral ceiling and trapezoid windows. Special features in the master suite include a large dressing area with a double vanity, a skylight, a step-up corner whirlpool tub and a generous walk-in closet. Upstairs, the three secondary bedrooms are well separated from the master bedroom and share a hall bath.

PORCH

GREAT RM.
22-0 x 20-2

fireplace

shelves

DINING
12-0 x 14-0

MASTER
BED RM.
14-0 x 18-0

UTIL.
5-8 x
8-4

w
d

GALLERY
8-0 x 9-0

down

KITCHEN

BRKFST.
9-2 x 9-4

12-0 x 14-0

FOYER
12-8 x 10-0

niche

lin.

master
bath

bath

bath

cl   cl   lin.

PORCH

lin.   cl   cl

walk-in
closet

BED RM.
12-0 x 14-0

© 2000 DAG
All rights reserved

BED RM./
STUDY
12-0 x 14-0

DESIGN BY
Donald A. Gardner Architects, Inc.

An impressive hipped roof and unique, turret-style roofs top the two front bedrooms of this extraordinary coastal home. An arched window in an eyebrow dormer crowns the double-door front entrance. A remarkable foyer creates quite a first impression and leads into the generous great room via a distinctive gallery with columns and a tray ceiling. The great room, master bedroom and bath also boast tray ceilings—as well as numerous windows and back-porch access. The master bedroom not only provides a substantial amount of space in the walk-in closet, but also features a garden tub and roomy shower. A delightful bayed breakfast area complements the kitchen, and the island makes cooking much less crowded.

DESIGN HPU040292

Square Footage: 2,413
Width: 66'-4"   Depth: 62'-10"

237

DESIGN BY
©Breland & Farmer Designers, Inc.

Courtyards set the mood for this country cottage, beginning with the entry court. The narrow design of this three-bedroom plan makes it perfect for high-density areas where the owner still wants privacy. A spacious high-ceilinged living room offers a fireplace and a built-in entertainment center; these special amenities are also found in the master suite, along with two walk-in closets and a full bath. Two secondary bedrooms, one with a tray ceiling, feature walk-in closets and share a full bath. Double doors in the kitchen open to the formal dining room, which offers access to the center courtyard. Please specify crawlspace or slab foundation when ordering.

DESIGN HPU040293

Square Footage: 2,259
Width: 56'-0" Depth: 93'-0"

DESIGN HPU040294

First Floor: 1,150 square feet
Second Floor: 939 square feet
Total: 2,089 square feet
Width: 45'-10" Depth: 56'-5"

The exterior of this cottage has a distinctive European feel that will fit in almost anywhere. The combination of brick and stucco give it a country look, as do the stickwork detailing, the cupola and the massive chimneys. Formal living and dining rooms fill the right side of the plan, enhanced by a bay window, a fireplace and decorative columns. In addition to a second fireplace, the family room boasts two French doors to the side patio. The kitchen is L-shaped, with a cooktop island, a breakfast room and access to a rear patio. A laundry room and a half-bath are located off the family room. The second floor holds three bedrooms, including a master suite with a compartmented bath and two closets.

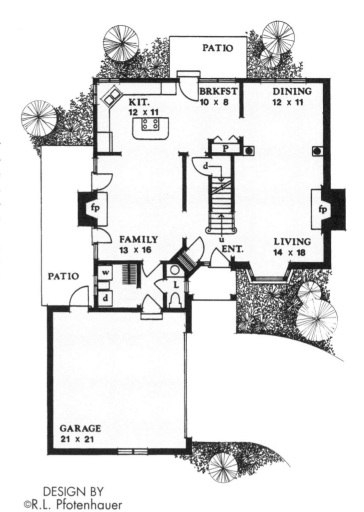

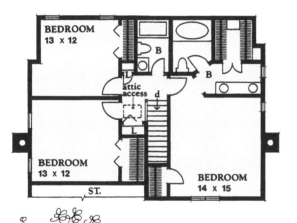

DESIGN BY
©R.L. Pfotenhauer

239

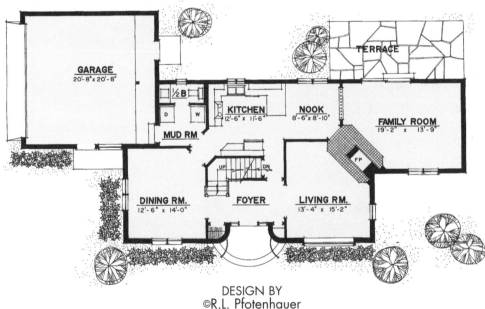

DESIGN BY
©R.L. Pfotenhauer

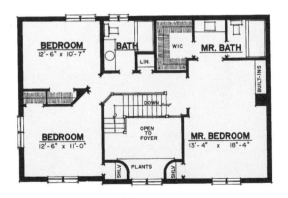

DESIGN HPU040295

First Floor: 1,159 square feet
Second Floor: 944 square feet
Total: 2,103 square feet
Width: 70'-8" Depth: 36'-0"

Shutters, a chimney, a railed semi-circular stoop and a weathervane combine to give this cottage its Old World charm. The openness and balance of the floor plan create simple comfort and livability. The centrally located L-shaped stairway rises from the two-story foyer, which is accented by a plant shelf and flanked by the formal living and dining rooms. Adjacent to the living room is a spacious family room with which it shares a through-fireplace. The kitchen, accessed from the dining room by an angled hall through double doors, is equipped with extra counter space and a bar to the breakfast room. The master bedroom is located at the top of the stairs and features double doors and a walk-in closet. Two secondary bedrooms upstairs share a full bath.

DESIGN HPU040296

First Floor: 1,132 square feet
Second Floor: 968 square feet
Total: 2,100 square feet
Width: 70'-6" Depth: 37'-1"

DESIGN BY
©R.L. Pfotenhauer

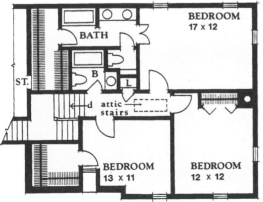

Brick and stucco, tall shutters and interesting roof details create a picturesque European-style cottage. A front terrace and a rear patio provide extra space for entertaining and relaxing, and the massive arch welcomes you in style. To the right of the entry, the formal living and dining rooms center on an imposing fireplace, one of two in the home. The other is in the family room, which offers a secondary front door as well as access to the patio. Casual meals will be enjoyed in the breakfast area, which is convenient to the kitchen. The master suite and two family bedrooms reside on the second floor; stairs lead to additional storage in the attic.

241

A stucco-and-brick facade declares the Old World influence used in this design. The steeply pitched roofline adds airiness to the interior spaces. The central entry opens to living spaces: a dining room on the left and the family room with fireplace on the right. The kitchen and breakfast nook are nearby. The kitchen features an island cooktop and a huge pantry. A door in the breakfast room leads out to the rear porch. The bedrooms include three family bedrooms—one of which could be used as a study—and a master suite. Note the double closets in the master bath.

DESIGN HPU040297

Square Footage: 2,322
Width: 68'-11" Depth: 74'-0"

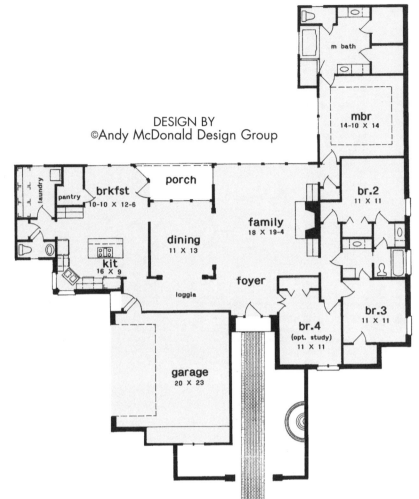

DESIGN BY
©Andy McDonald Design Group

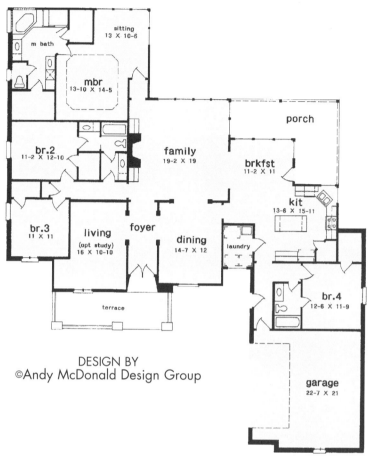

sitting
13 X 10-6

m bath

mbr
13-10 X 14-5

br.2
11-2 X 12-10

family
19-2 X 19

porch

brkfst
11-2 X 11

kit
13-6 X 15-11

br.3
11 X 11

living
(opt study)
16 X 10-10

foyer

dining
14-7 X 12

laundry

terrace

br.4
12-6 X 11-9

garage
22-7 X 21

DESIGN BY
©Andy McDonald Design Group

In true French country style, this home begins with a fenced terrace that protects the double-door entry. The main foyer separates formal living and dining areas and leads back to a large family room with a fireplace and built-ins. The breakfast room overlooks a wrapping porch and opens to the island kitchen. Three bedrooms are found on the left side of the plan—two family bedrooms sharing a full bath and a master suite with a sitting area. A fourth bedroom is tucked behind the two-car garage and features a private bath.

DESIGN HPU040298

Square Footage: 2,678
Width: 69'-4"   Depth: 84'-8"

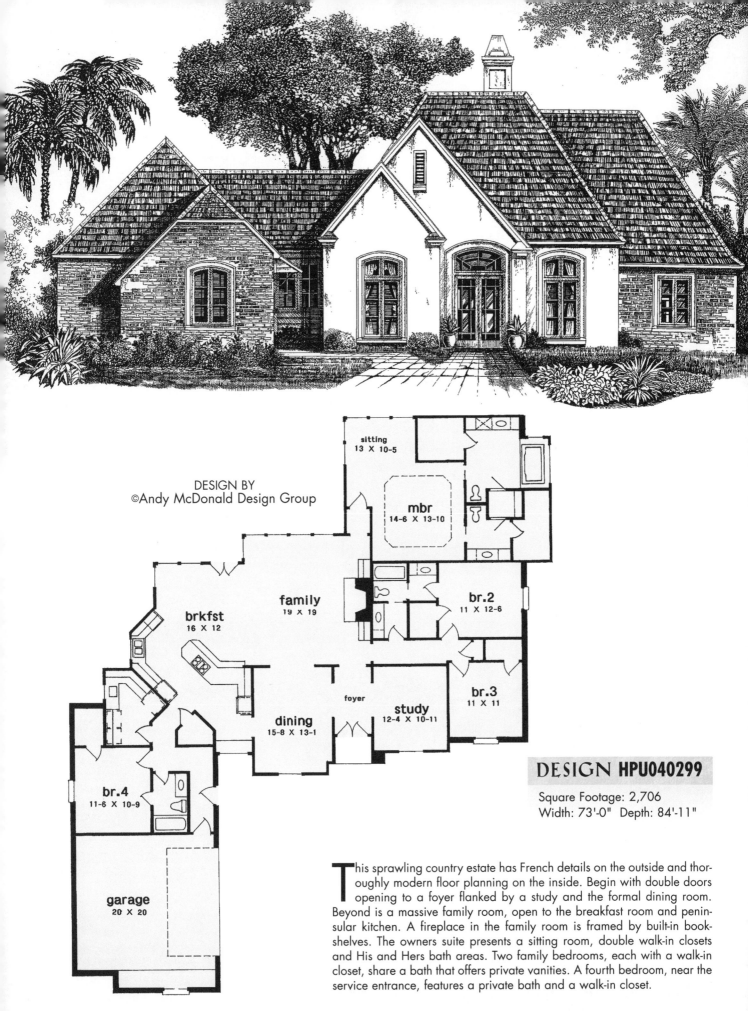

sitting
13 X 10-5

mbr
14-6 X 13-10

DESIGN BY
©Andy McDonald Design Group

family
19 X 19

brkfst
16 X 12

br.2
11 X 12-6

foyer

study
12-4 X 10-11

br.3
11 X 11

dining
15-8 X 13-1

br.4
11-6 X 10-9

DESIGN HPU040299

Square Footage: 2,706
Width: 73'-0" Depth: 84'-11"

garage
20 X 20

This sprawling country estate has French details on the outside and thoroughly modern floor planning on the inside. Begin with double doors opening to a foyer flanked by a study and the formal dining room. Beyond is a massive family room, open to the breakfast room and peninsular kitchen. A fireplace in the family room is framed by built-in bookshelves. The owners suite presents a sitting room, double walk-in closets and His and Hers bath areas. Two family bedrooms, each with a walk-in closet, share a bath that offers private vanities. A fourth bedroom, near the service entrance, features a private bath and a walk-in closet.

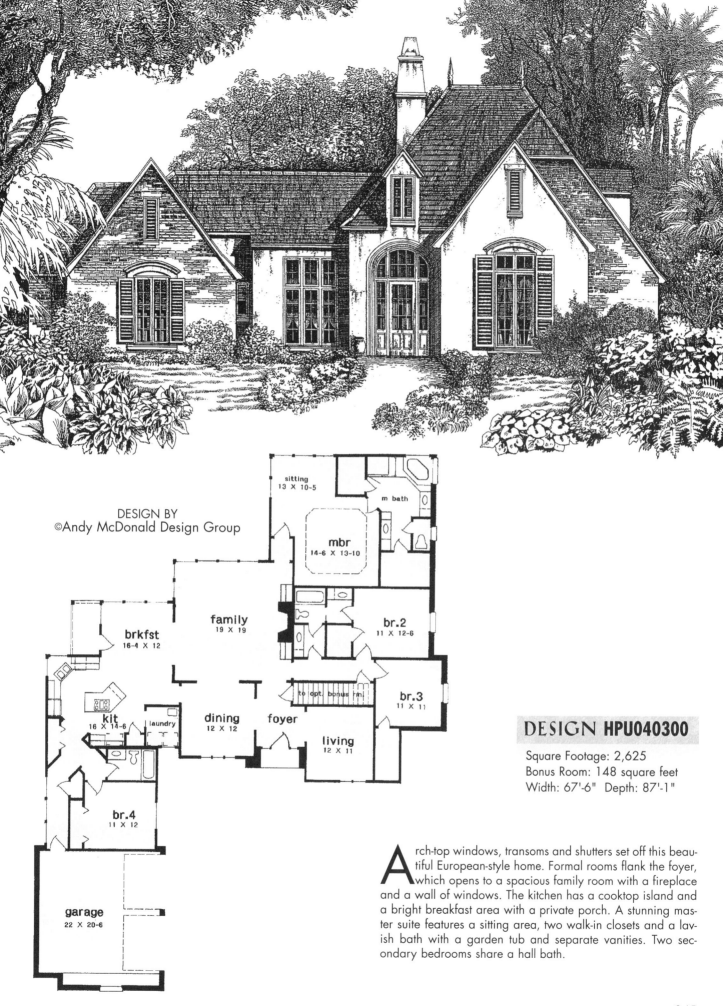

sitting
13 X 10-5

m bath

mbr
14-6 X 13-10

brkfst
16-4 X 12

family
19 X 19

br.2
11 X 12-6

to opt. bonus rm.

br.3
11 X 11

kit
16 X 14-6

laundry

dining
12 X 12

foyer

living
12 X 11

br.4
11 X 12

garage
22 X 20-6

DESIGN HPU040300

Square Footage: 2,625
Bonus Room: 148 square feet
Width: 67'-6" Depth: 87'-1"

Arch-top windows, transoms and shutters set off this beautiful European-style home. Formal rooms flank the foyer, which opens to a spacious family room with a fireplace and a wall of windows. The kitchen has a cooktop island and a bright breakfast area with a private porch. A stunning master suite features a sitting area, two walk-in closets and a lavish bath with a garden tub and separate vanities. Two secondary bedrooms share a hall bath.

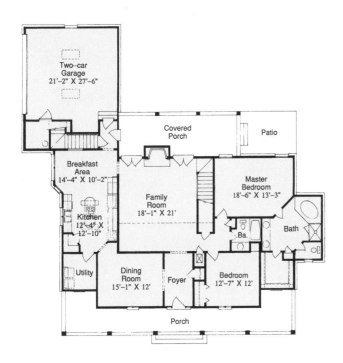

DESIGN HPU040301

First Floor: 1,977 square feet
Second Floor: 687 square feet
Total: 2,664 square feet
Width: 69'-6" Depth: 69'-9"

DESIGN BY
©Chatham Home Planning, Inc.

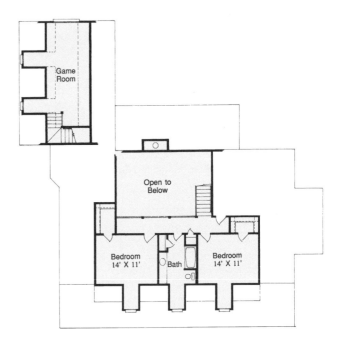

The game room above the garage of this four-bedroom, 1½-story Southern traditional home features a separate entrance and could make a convenient home office. The wraparound porch adds charm and function to the exterior. A formal dining room and a large family room with a fireplace and double doors to the rear-covered porch are accessed from the foyer. The master suite has a large offset bath with a corner tub, and across the hall is a second bedroom that could easily double as a study. Two additional bedrooms and a full bath are on the second level. Please specify crawlspace or slab foundation when ordering.

DESIGN HPU040302

First Floor: 2,155 square feet
Second Floor: 522 square feet
Total: 2,677 square feet
Width: 44'-0" Depth: 96'-2"

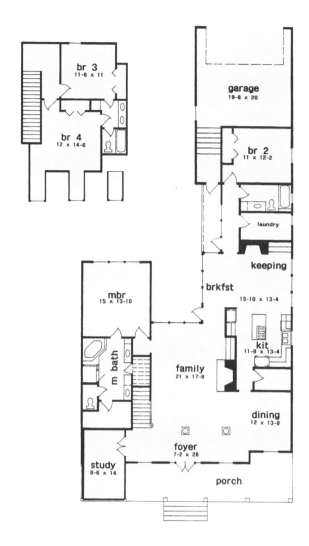

More than twice as long as it is wide, this plan presents a charming and deceptive facade. From the front gallery, the open family room provides a spacious area for gathering. To the side are a study and a master suite that includes a private bath. Behind the family room, you'll find a keeping room with a fireplace and built-in shelves, and a breakfast area that opens to the courtyard. A second bedroom and bath are located at the rear of the plan, while a third and fourth bedroom (sharing a bath) are on the second floor.

DESIGN BY
©Andy McDonald Design Group

247

DESIGN HPU040304

Square Footage: 2,607
Width: 75'-4" Depth: 81'-0"

This charming home has columned porches in both the front and back. To the left of the entry are the living and dining rooms, both defined by columns. The large open kitchen has a snack bar and breakfast area, and flows into the great room, which has a fireplace as the focal point. The bedrooms are grouped to the right, including two family bedrooms sharing a compartmented bath, and the master suite with a whirlpool tub. Please specify slab or crawlspace foundation when ordering.

DESIGN BY
©Michael E. Nelson,
Nelson Design Group, LLC

DESIGN HPU040303

First Floor: 1,976 square feet
Second Floor: 634 square feet
Total: 2,610 square feet
Width: 91'-10" Depth: 54'-0"

DESIGN BY
©Michael E. Nelson,
Nelson Design Group, LLC

This unique home is sure to be an eye-catcher on any property. The bungalow-type roof adds a bit of rustic flavor, with its overhang useful in keeping the sun from the windows. With the bedrooms separated from the main living areas, there is truly a sense of privacy achieved. The living areas include a great room with a fireplace, a studio area with deck access, a dining area and an efficient kitchen full of amenities. Here, the family gourmet will be pleased with tons of counter and cabinet space and a wall of pantry space. The sleeping structure is accessible via an enclosed bridge. Here one can either go up to the lavish master suite—complete with a private deck—or downstairs to a huge bedroom, also with a deck. Please specify crawlspace or pier foundation when ordering.

DESIGN HPU040305

First Floor: 1,623 square feet
Second Floor: 978 square feet
Total: 2,601 square feet
Width: 48'-0" Depth: 57'-0"

Offering a large wraparound porch, this fine two-story pier home is full of amenities. The living room has a warming fireplace and plenty of windows to enjoy the view. The galley kitchen features unique angles, with a large island/peninsula separating this room from the dining area. Two bedrooms share a bath and easy access to the laundry facilities. Upstairs, a lavish owners suite is complete with a detailed ceiling, a private covered porch, a walk-in closet and a pampering bath. A secondary bedroom—or make it a study—with a large walk-in closet finishes off this floor.

DESIGN BY
©Chatham Home Planning, Inc.

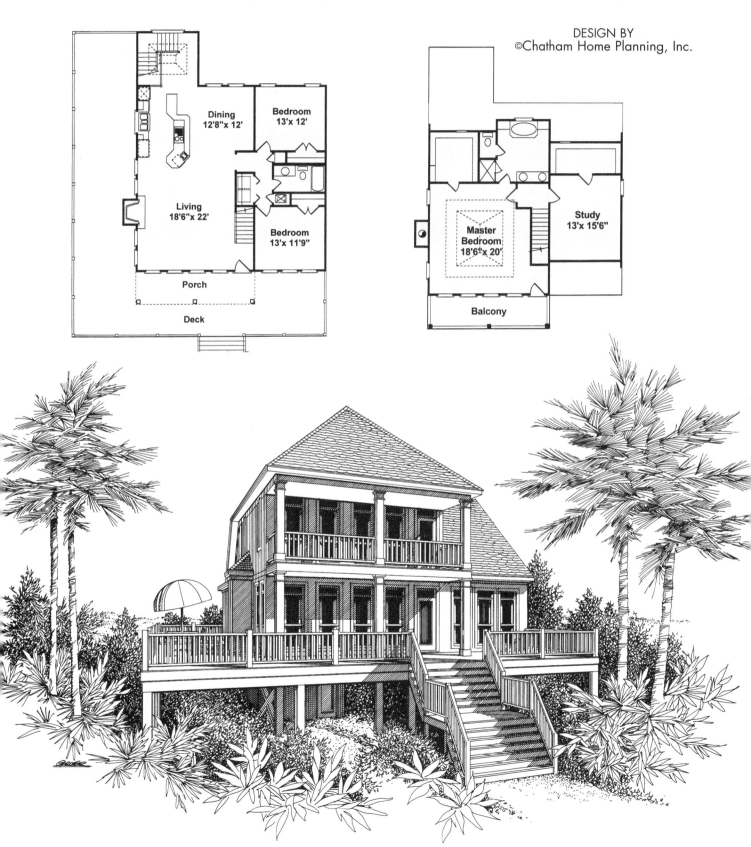

Dining
12'8"x 12'

Bedroom
13'x 12'

Living
18'6"x 22'

Bedroom
13'x 11'9"

Porch

Deck

Master
Bedroom
18'6"x 20'

Study
13'x 15'6"

Balcony

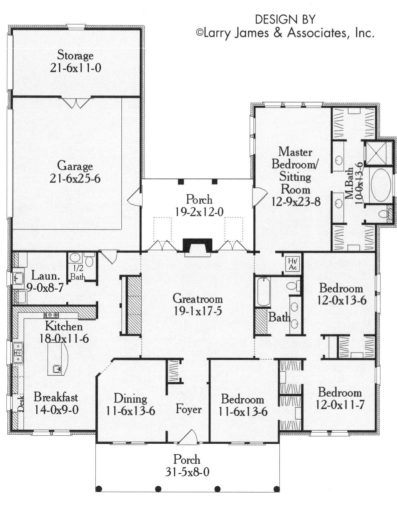

DESIGN BY
©Larry James & Associates, Inc.

Storage
21-6x11-0

Garage
21-6x25-6

Porch
19-2x12-0

Master
Bedroom/
Sitting
Room
12-9x23-8

M.Bath
10-0x13-6

Laun.
9-0x8-7

1/2
Bath

Greatroom
19-1x17-5

Bath

Bedroom
12-0x13-6

Ht/
Ac

Kitchen
18-0x11-6

Breakfast
14-0x9-0

Dining
11-6x13-6

Foyer

Bedroom
11-6x13-6

Bedroom
12-0x11-7

Porch
31-5x8-0

A steeply pitched roof and transoms over multi-pane windows give this house great curb appeal. To the left of the foyer is the formal dining room with through access to the kitchen and breakfast area. A large island/snack bar adds plenty of counter space to the food-preparation area. Double French doors frame the fireplace in the great room, leading to the skylit covered porch at the rear of the home. The owners suite has a light-filled sitting room and luxurious bath with two walk-in closets, a garden tub and separate shower. At the front, three secondary bedrooms all have walk-in closets. Please specify basement, crawl-space or slab foundation when ordering.

DESIGN HPU040306

Square Footage: 2,555
Width: 66'-1" Depth: 77'-7"

Basement
Stair Location

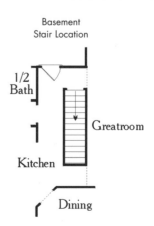

1/2
Bath

Greatroom

Kitchen

Dining

A porch full of columns gives a relaxing emphasis to this country home. To the right of the foyer, the dining area resides conveniently near the efficient kitchen. The kitchen island, walk-in pantry and serving bar add plenty of work space to the food-preparation zone. Natural light will flood the breakfast nook through a ribbon of windows facing the rear yard. Escape to the relaxing owners suite featuring a private sun room/retreat and a luxurious bath set between His and Hers walk-in closets. The great room at the center of this L-shaped plan is complete with a warming fireplace and built-ins. Three family bedrooms enjoy private walk-in closets and share a fully appointed bath. The two-car garage also has a storage area for family treasures. Please specify basement, crawlspace or slab foundation when ordering.

DESIGN HPU040307

Square Footage: 2,506
Width: 72'-2" Depth: 66'-4"

DESIGN BY
©Larry James & Associates, Inc.

Basement
Stair Location

1/2
Bath

Greatroom

Kitchen

Dining

Storage
21-6x11-0

Garage
21-6x25-6

Porch
19-2x12-0

Master
Bedroom/
Sitting
Room
12-9x23-8

M.Bath
10-0x13-6

Laun.
9-0x8-7

1/2
Bath

Greatroom
19-1x17-5

Hr
Ac

Bath

Bedroom
12-0x13-6

Kitchen
18-0x11-6

Breakfast
14-0x9-0

Dining
11-6x13-6

Foyer

Bedroom
11-6x13-6

Bedroom
12-0x11-7

Porch

DESIGN HPU040308

Square Footage: 2,585
Width: 66'-1" Depth: 77'-7"

Classical columns give the entrance of this floor plan a graceful appeal. The great room leads through two sets of double doors onto the rear porch. This porch can also be accessed by a door connected to the garage and another private door to the master bedroom. The master suite is brilliantly lit by multiple window views to the outdoors. Three additional bedrooms complete the family sleeping quarters. Please specify basement, crawlspace or slab foundation when ordering.

DESIGN HPU040309

Square Footage: 2,570
Width: 73'-0" Depth: 71'-0"

This well-planned design offers the benefits of simplicity nicely embellished with well-chosen details. A gorgeous array of window accents provides an elegant facade with the eye-candy of natural light. The spacious great room is the centerpiece of the floor plan, with a fireplace set between built-ins. The sleeping quarters include an owners suite that offers a private study. Two secondary bedrooms share a full bath. Please specify basement, crawlspace or slab foundation when ordering.

Study
8-10x9-4

M.Bath
8-4x23-5

Master
Bedroom
15-3x12-9

Porch
17-0x10-6

Breakfast
12-8x10-8

Laundry
12-0x10-0

Bedroom
11-6x13-0

Greatroom
14-9x19-4

Kitchen
12-8x14-2

1/2
Bath

Garage
23-10x23-6

Pantry

Desk

Bedroom
11-6x11-4

Living
11-6x11-6

Foyer

Dining
11-6x11-6

Storage
15-6x5-8

Porch
33-0x9-8

Master
Bedroom

Laundry
12-0x6-6

Basement
Stair Location

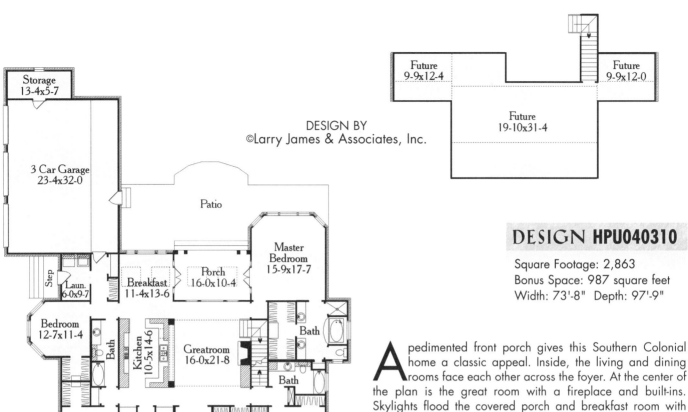

Storage
13-4x5-7

3 Car Garage
23-4x32-0

DESIGN BY
©Larry James & Associates, Inc.

Future
9-9x12-4

Future
9-9x12-0

Future
19-10x31-4

Patio

Step

Laun.
6-0x9-7

Breakfast
11-4x13-6

Porch
16-0x10-4

Master
Bedroom
15-9x17-7

Bedroom
12-7x11-4

Bath

Kitchen
10-5x14-6

Greatroom
16-0x21-8

Bath

Bath

Bedroom
12-0x13-5

Dining
13-6x11-4

Foyer

Living
11-4x13-6

Bedroom
12-0x13-5

Porch
32-11x10-6

DESIGN HPU040310

Square Footage: 2,863
Bonus Space: 987 square feet
Width: 73'-8" Depth: 97'-9"

A pedimented front porch gives this Southern Colonial home a classic appeal. Inside, the living and dining rooms face each other across the foyer. At the center of the plan is the great room with a fireplace and built-ins. Skylights flood the covered porch and breakfast room with light. Escape the busy world in the owners suite with a bay window in the main room and its luxurious bath. Two secondary bedrooms are placed on the opposite side of the home—one with a beautiful bay window—and a third is at the front right. The three-car garage provides plenty of room for family autos and a storage area for seasonal items. Expansion is also possible with bonus space on the second floor. Please specify basement, crawlspace or slab foundation when ordering.

NOOK
9/8 X 10/6
(9' CLG.)

FAMILY
16/2 X 15/6
(9' CLG.)

MASTER
13/0 X 15/2
(9' CLG.)

SPA

SHELVES

13/0 X 11/6

REF PAN

UP

STOR

D W

STOR
9/10 X 7/4

VAULTED
DINING
13/0 X 11/2

GARAGE
21/4 X 20/8

OPTIONAL FIREPLACE

VAULTED
LIVING
13/0 X 15/0

DEN
10/0 X 10/6
(9' CLG.)

DESIGN HPU040311

First Floor: 1,769 square feet
Second Floor: 893 square feet
Total: 2,662 square feet
Width: 50'-0" Depth: 50'-0"

DESIGN BY
©Alan Mascord Design Associates, Inc.

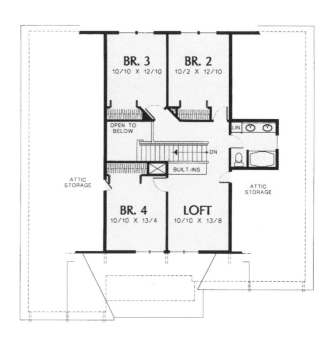

BR. 3
10/10 X 12/10

BR. 2
10/2 X 12/10

OPEN TO BELOW

LIN

ATTIC STORAGE

DN

BUILT-INS

ATTIC STORAGE

BR. 4
10/10 X 13/4

LOFT
10/10 X 13/8

Shingles, gables, window detail and rafter tails all combine to give this home plenty of curb appeal. The entrance opens right next to the vaulted living and dining area, with a cozy den to the right. The unique kitchen features a peninsula, pantry and easy access to the formal dining room and sunny nook. The nearby family room is warmed by a corner fireplace. Located on the first floor for privacy, the master bedroom suite is complete with a walk-in closet—with built-in shelves—and a pampering bath. The second floor consists of three family bedrooms sharing a full bath and an open study loft with built-ins.

Shingles and stone combine to present a highly attractive facade on this spacious three-bedroom home. The Craftsman-style influence is very evident and adds charm. The two-story foyer is flanked by a large, yet cozy, den on the right and on the left, beyond the staircase, is the formal dining room with built-ins. The vaulted great room also offers built-ins, as well as a fireplace. The U-shaped kitchen will surely please the gourmet of the family with its planning desk, corner sink, cooktop island and plenty of counter and cabinet space. The vaulted master suite is complete with a plant shelf, a walk-in closet and a lavish bath. Two secondary bedrooms make up the sleeping zone upstairs, each with a walk-in closet and having access to the full bath. A large bonus room is available for use as a guest suite.

DESIGN HPU040312

First Floor: 2,005 square feet
Second Floor: 689 square feet
Total: 2,694 square feet
Bonus Room: 356 square feet
Width: 68'-0" Depth: 73'-6"

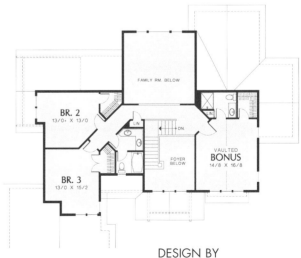

DESIGN BY
©Alan Mascord Design Associates, Inc.

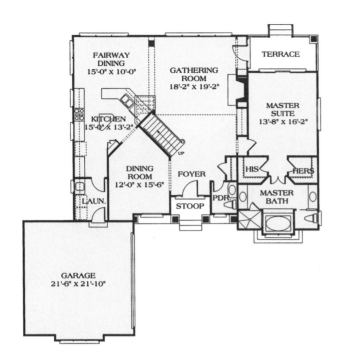

Gables, rafter tails, pillars supporting the shed roof over the porch, and window detailing all bring the flavor of Craftsman styling to your neighborhood with a touch of grace. This spacious home has a place for everyone. The angled kitchen, with a work island, peninsular sink and plenty of counter and cabinet space, will offer the family many a gourmet treat. The spacious gathering room offers a warming fireplace, built-ins and access to a rear terrace. Filled with amenities, the first-floor master suite is designed to pamper. Upstairs, two suites, each with a private bath, share an open area known as the linkside retreat. Here, access is available to a small veranda, perfect for watching sunsets.

DESIGN HPU040313

First Floor: 1,662 square feet
Second Floor: 882 square feet
Total: 2,544 square feet
Width: 59'-0" Depth: 59'-6"

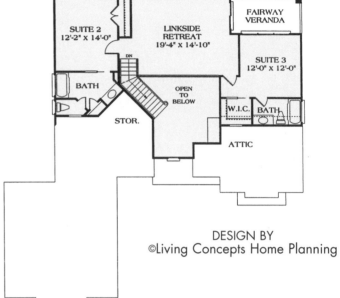

DESIGN BY
©Living Concepts Home Planning

With rustic rafter tails, sturdy pillars and a siding-and-shingle facade, this welcoming bungalow offers plenty of curb appeal. Inside, the formal dining room is to the left of the foyer, and gives easy access to the angled kitchen. A spacious gathering room offers a fireplace, built-ins, a gorgeous wall of windows and access to a covered terrace. Located on the first floor for privacy, the owners suite is lavish with its amenities. Upstairs, two suites offer private baths and share a linkside retreat that includes a covered veranda.

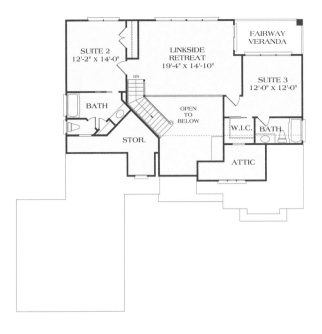

DESIGN HPU040314

First Floor: 1,661 square feet
Second Floor: 882 square feet
Total: 2,543 square feet
Width: 59'-0" Depth: 58'-11"

DESIGN BY
©Living Concepts Home Planning

DESIGN HPU040315

First Floor: 1,326 square feet
Second Floor: 1,257 square feet
Total: 2,583 square feet
Width: 30'-0" Depth: 78'-0"

DESIGN BY
©Authentic Historical Designs, Inc.

The steeply pitched pavilion roof is a distinctive feature that identifies this house as a classic French design. Inside, a long foyer ushers visitors into a generous great room, which is separated from the kitchen by a wide cased opening. An L-shaped breakfast bar provides a place for a quick snack. The computer room/office off the great room could be eliminated and used as a breakfast area. Above, a lavish master suite has separate His and Hers walk-in closets and an oversized shower. Please specify basement or crawlspace foundation when ordering.

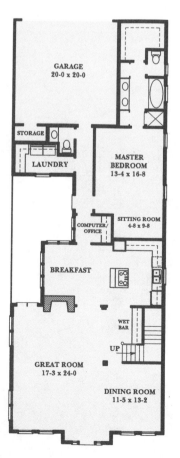

DESIGN HPU040316

First Floor: 1,767 square feet
Second Floor: 1,079 square feet
Total: 2,846 square feet
Width: 30'-0" Depth: 82'-0"

DESIGN BY
©Authentic Historical Designs, Inc.

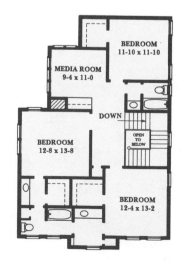

With its formal symmetry, balanced proportion and classical detailing, this Georgian design will maintain its appeal for those who value timeless architecture. Once inside, its open floor plan will entice those who realize that modern families enjoy a different lifestyle. The entrance is open to a spacious great room and formal dining room. The column-encircled stairway wraps itself around a built-in wet bar, with easy access to kitchen, dining and living areas of the home. Yet, even though the plan is very open, there are many private spaces provided. There is a computer/desk area between the kitchen and the first-floor master suite. This roomy master suite contains a secluded and separate sitting area. Note the convenient location of the walk-in closet. A second-floor media room will provide additional living space.

At the turn of the century, the growing number of railroads and automobiles made suburban living possible as an alternative to living in the city. The bungalow home was America's first response to the need for affordable single-family housing in these first new suburbs. The gently pitched street-facing gable is a dominant characteristic of the bungalow style, as well as its wide overhanging roof, deep porch and simplified interior. A century later, our updated version of the bungalow is well-suited to the needs of modern families. It provides a wide-open family room, with a large keeping room and breakfast room, as well as a separate living room and dining room. Easy access to the long side porch provides additional living space. Upstairs, four bedrooms, each with walk-in closets, provide ample space for a busy family. Please specify basement or crawlspace foundation when ordering.

DESIGN HPU040317

First Floor: 1,718 square feet
Second Floor: 1,021 square feet
Total: 2,739 square feet
Width: 33'-0" Depth: 80'-0"

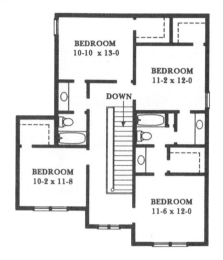

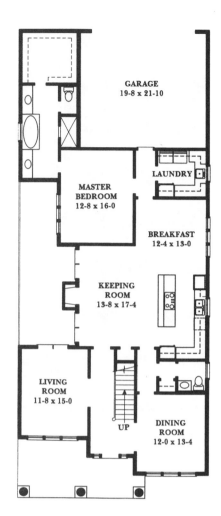

DESIGN BY
©Authentic Historical Designs, Inc.

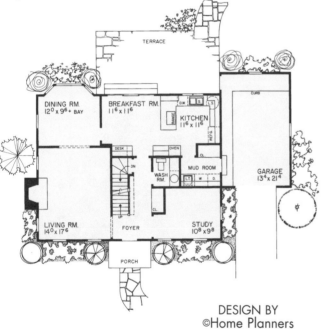

DESIGN BY
©Home Planners

The facade of this three-story, pitch-roofed house has a symmetrical placement of windows and a restrained but elegant central entrance. The central hall, or foyer, expands midway through the house to a family kitchen. Off the foyer are two rooms—a living room with a fireplace and a study. Three bedrooms are housed on the second floor, including a deluxe master suite with a pampering bath. The windowed third-floor attic can be used as a study and a studio.

DESIGN HPU040319

First Floor: 1,023 square feet
Second Floor: 1,008 square feet
Third Floor: 476 square feet
Total: 2,507 square feet
Width: 49'-8" Depth: 32'-0"

L D

QUOTE ONE®
Cost to build? See page 502
to order complete cost estimate
to build this house in your area!

Two one-story wings flank the two-story center section of this design, which echoes the architectural forms of 18th-Century Tidewater Virginia. The left wing offers a spacious living room, perfect for entertaining guests and for family events; the right wing houses the master bedroom suite, service area and garage. The heart of the home provides casual living with the kitchen, dining room and family room. Upstairs, three family bedrooms—one is perfect for a nursery or game room—share a full hall bath that includes twin vanities.

DESIGN HPU040320

First Floor: 1,827 square feet
Second Floor: 697 square feet
Total: 2,524 square feet
Width: 72'-0" Depth: 54'-0"

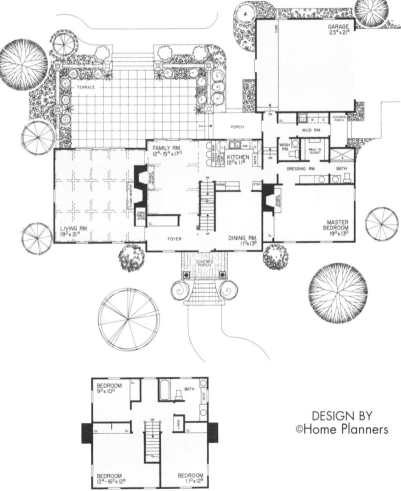

DESIGN BY
©Home Planners

DESIGN HPU040322

First Floor: 1,581 square feet
Second Floor: 1,344 square feet
Total: 2,925 square feet
Width: 74'-0" Depth: 46'-0"

L D

DESIGN BY
©Home Planners

Here's a traditional farmhouse design that's made for down-home hospitality, casual conversation and the good grace of pleasant company. The star attractions are the large covered porch and terrace, perfectly relaxing gathering points for family and friends. Inside, the design is truly a hard worker: separate living and family rooms, each with its own fireplace; a formal dining room; a large kitchen and breakfast area with bay windows; a private study; a workshop and a mudroom. The second floor contains a spacious master suite with twin closets and three family bedrooms that share a full bath.

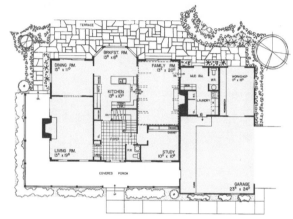

Quote One®
Cost to build? See page 502
to order complete cost estimate
to build this house in your area!

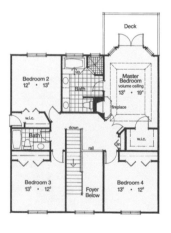

A beautiful covered porch wraps around the welcoming entrance of this country home. Sunlit, bayed areas at the rear of the plan—in the great room and breakfast nook—illuminate this efficient family floor plan. Upstairs, the pampering master suite is enhanced by a fireplace, a volume ceiling and double doors, which lead to a private sun deck. Three family bedrooms share a full hall bath.

DESIGN HPU040321

First Floor: 1,267 square feet
Second Floor: 1,327 square feet
Total: 2,594 square feet
Width: 58'-8" Depth: 38'-0"

DESIGN BY
©Home Design Services, Inc.

DESIGN HPU040323

First Floor: 1,286 square feet
Second Floor: 1,675 square feet
Total: 2,961 square feet
Width: 35'-0" Depth: 64'-0"

The Southern plantation comes to mind when looking at this two-story home complete with a porch and terrace. Formal elegance is the order of the day as you enter the foyer flanked by the living and dining rooms. The family room features a full window wall overlooking the deck, which is also accessible from the rear entry of the garage. Corner cabinets house the sink and surface unit, keeping everything within a few steps of each other. Rear stairs lead to the master suite, located over the garage, providing privacy from the rest of the second floor. Four additional bedrooms—one with its own private bath—are also on the second floor. Please specify basement or slab foundation when ordering.

DESIGN BY
©Jannis Vann & Associates, Inc.

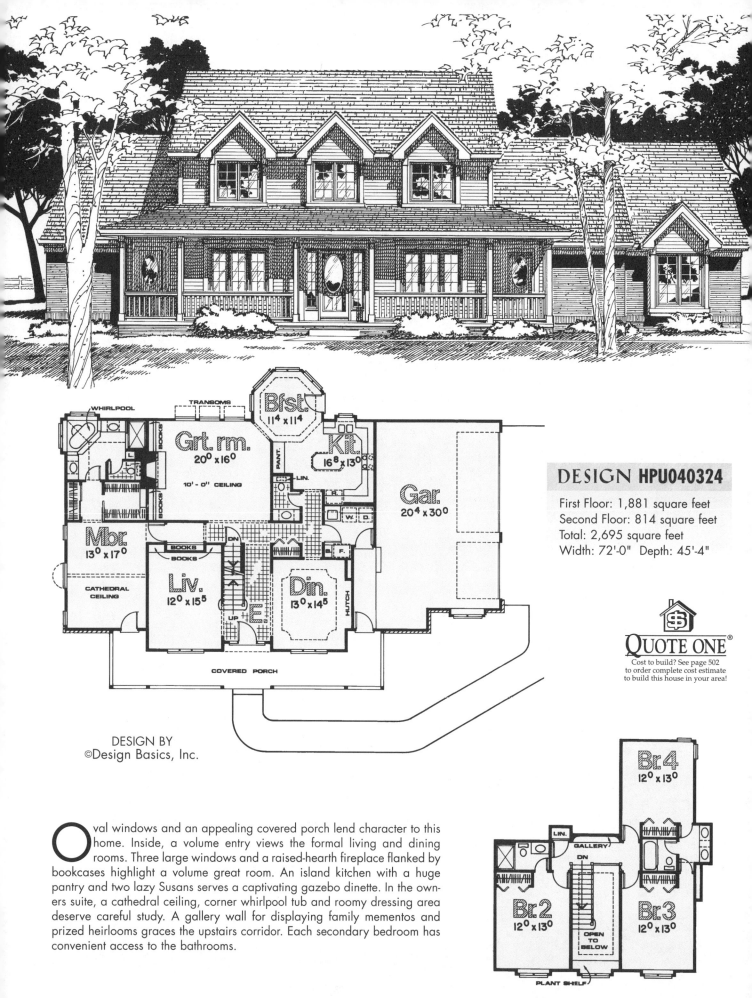

DESIGN HPU040324

First Floor: 1,881 square feet
Second Floor: 814 square feet
Total: 2,695 square feet
Width: 72'-0" Depth: 45'-4"

QUOTE ONE®
Cost to build? See page 502
to order complete cost estimate
to build this house in your area!

DESIGN BY
©Design Basics, Inc.

O val windows and an appealing covered porch lend character to this home. Inside, a volume entry views the formal living and dining rooms. Three large windows and a raised-hearth fireplace flanked by bookcases highlight a volume great room. An island kitchen with a huge pantry and two lazy Susans serves a captivating gazebo dinette. In the owners suite, a cathedral ceiling, corner whirlpool tub and roomy dressing area deserve careful study. A gallery wall for displaying family mementos and prized heirlooms graces the upstairs corridor. Each secondary bedroom has convenient access to the bathrooms.

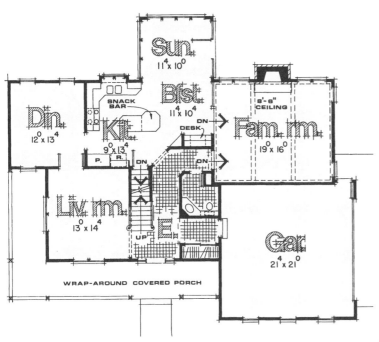

WRAP-AROUND COVERED PORCH

Sun.
11 x 10⁰

Bfst.
11 x 10⁴

Dn.
12 x 13⁴

SNACK BAR

Kit.
9⁰ x 13⁴

P.R.

DESK

Fam. rm.
19⁰ x 16⁰

8'-6" CEILING

Liv. rm.
13⁰ x 14⁴

UP

DN

DN

E.

Gar.
21 x 21

Here's the luxury you've been looking for—from the wraparound covered front porch to the bright sun room off the breakfast room. A sunken family room with a fireplace serves everyday casual gatherings, while the more formal living and dining rooms are reserved for special entertaining situations. The kitchen has a central island with a snack bar and is located most conveniently for serving and cleaning up. Upstairs are four bedrooms, one a lovely master suite with French doors to the pirvate bath and a whirlpool tub with a dramatic bay window. A double vanity in the shared bath easily serves the three family bedrooms.

DESIGN HPU040325

First Floor: 1,322 square feet
Second Floor: 1,272 square feet
Total: 2,594 square feet
Width: 56'-0"   Depth: 48'-0"

Quote One®
Cost to build? See page 502
to order complete cost estimate
to build this house in your area!

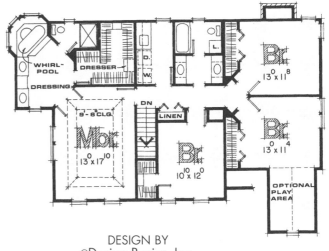

WHIRL-POOL

DRESSING

DRESSER

D.

W.

L.

Br.
13⁰ x 11⁸

9'-6 CLG.

Mbr.
13⁰ x 17⁰

DN

LINEN

Br.
10¹⁰ x 12⁰

Br.
13⁰ x 11⁴

OPTIONAL PLAY AREA

DESIGN BY
©Design Basics, Inc.

265

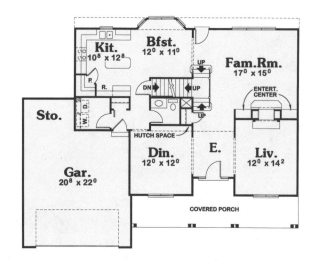

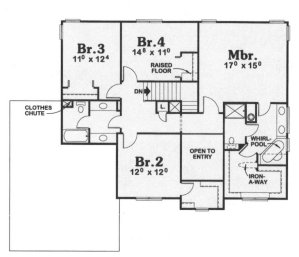

This classic American two-story home borrows details from farmhouse, Craftsman and Colonial styles to add up to a beautiful facade. The covered front porch is a lovely introduction to both formal and informal living spaces on the interior. The living room features a see-through fireplace to the family room and is complemented by a formal dining room with hutch space. The U-shaped island kitchen and bayed breakfast nook combine to form an open area for casual dining. A stairway to the second level boasts twin accesses—in the foyer and in the family room. Four bedrooms are situated on the second floor. They include three family bedrooms with a shared bath and walk-in closets. The master suite has a private bath with a whirlpool tub, separate shower, fold-away iron and huge walk-in closet.

DESIGN HPU040326

First Floor: 1,266 square feet
Second Floor: 1,292 square feet
Total: 2,558 square feet
Bonus Room: 531 square feet
Width: 54'-0"   Depth: 44'-0"

DESIGN BY
©Design Basics, Inc.

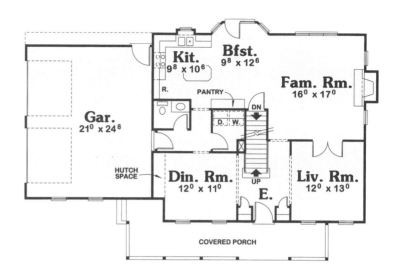

Finials, scalloped shingles and a covered front porch with spiderweb trim enhance the exterior of this home. Inside, the formal living and dining rooms flank the foyer; the dining room offers space for a hutch or china cabinet. The family room, accessed by double doors in the living room, includes a fireplace and a wall of windows. The snug island kitchen serves a breakfast bay that opens to the backyard. Upstairs, a tray ceiling adds drama to the owners suite, which features a full bath with double vanities and a whirlpool tub. All three of the secondary bedrooms include walk-in closets and access a full hall bath.

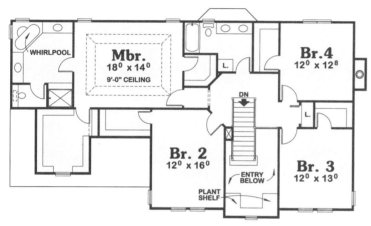

DESIGN HPU040327

First Floor: 1,120 square feet
Second Floor: 1,411 square feet
Total: 2,531 square feet
Width: 57'-4" Depth: 33'-0"

DESIGN BY
©Design Basics, Inc.

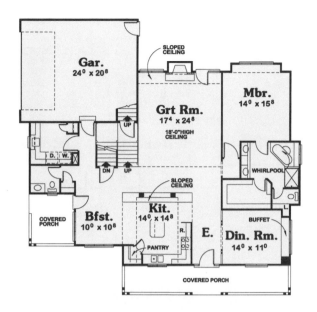

This home's fine window detailing, two front porches and rafter tails lend the feel of true Craftsman styling. The airiness of the kitchen is enhanced with openings to the second floor, entry and breakfast area. A built-in buffet and two half-railings warmly welcome passersby into the formal dining room. A tall ceiling in the great room is further dramatized when viewed from an open railing on the second floor. Also of interest in this room is the fireplace centered on the outside wall. A computer area on the second floor accompanies the second-floor bedrooms as a homework area. A large storage area accessed from the mid-level staircase landing offers a place for a playroom. Note the first-floor master suite with its lavish bath.

DESIGN HPU040328

First Floor: 1,823 square feet
Second Floor: 858 square feet
Total: 2,681 square feet
Width: 56'-8" Depth: 50'-8"

DESIGN BY
©Design Basics, Inc.

It's hard to beat the charm of this country home, which features bright bays of windows in the dining room and breakfast nook, plus a shady covered front porch. The kitchen with its cooktop island is convenient to both formal and casual dining areas. The spacious living room offers a fireplace, built-in bookshelves and access to the rear patio. The rest of the main floor is granted to the master suite, which includes a double-vanity bath with an oval tub and a separate shower. Two of the three family bedrooms upstairs have dormers.

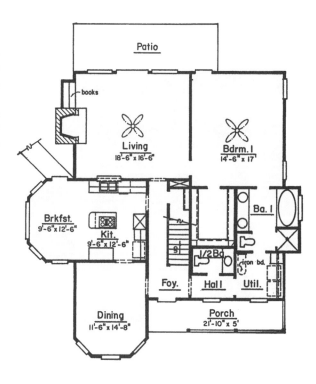

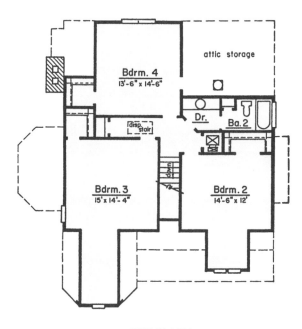

DESIGN BY
©Chatham Home Planning, Inc.

DESIGN HPU040329

First Floor: 1,499 square feet
Second Floor: 1,012 square feet
Total: 2,511 square feet
Width: 41'-6" Depth: 45'-0"

DESIGN HPU040331

Square Footage: 2,519
Width: 75'-0" Depth: 59'-0"

DESIGN BY
©Vaughn A. Lauban Designs

Porch railing, siding and twin dormered windows reflect the easy-on-the-eyes quality of country style. Walk inside to discover a very comfortable floor plan that serves family or friends well. The foyer boasts two coat closets, with the dining room to the left and the study to the right. The galley-style kitchen functions as the hub of the home, able to handle the dining room, breakfast nook and living room without fuss. The owners suite revels in its privacy with features like twin walk-in closets, a bayed tub, separate shower and dual vanities. Three family bedrooms are situated at the right of the plan. Two bedrooms share a compartmented bath, while the third enjoys its own full bath.

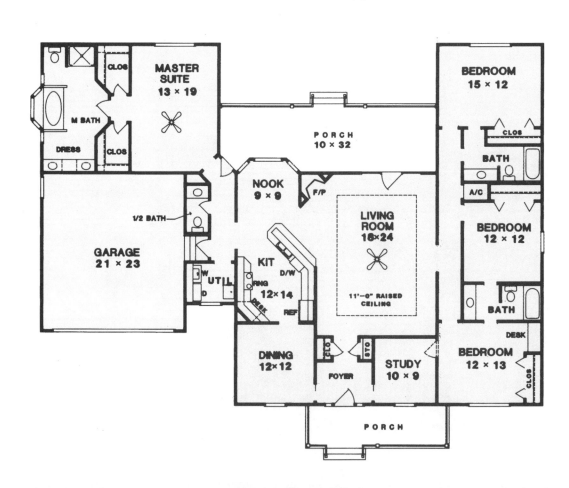

Graceful French doors and tall, shuttered windows combined with a sprawling country front porch give this charming home its unique appeal. Nine-foot ceilings expand the main floor. Walk through the elegant foyer to a grand living area, with a centered fireplace and built-in bookcase. This living space opens to the rear covered porch. The private master suite with a walk-in closet features a luxurious bath with a separate shower and compartmented toilet. A guest room (or make it a study) also has access to a full bath. Just off the formal dining area is a gourmet kitchen with an island cooktop counter. A bay-windowed breakfast area adds informal eating space. Two second-floor family bedrooms share an expansive full bath, just off the balcony hallway, and boast private dressing areas and walk-in closets. Please specify crawlspace or slab foundation when ordering.

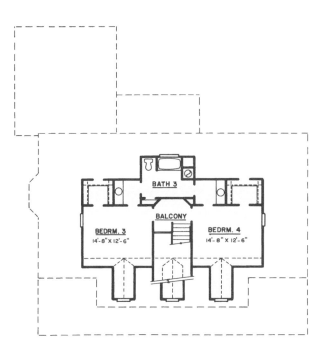

DESIGN HPU040332

First Floor: 1,916 square feet
Second Floor: 749 square feet
Total: 2,665 square feet
Width: 63'-0" Depth: 63'-9"

DESIGN BY
©Chatham Home Planning, Inc.

DESIGN HPU040333

First Floor: 1,614 square feet
Second Floor: 892 square feet
Total: 2,506 square feet
Bonus Room: 341 square feet
Width: 71'-10" Depth: 50'-0"

DESIGN BY
Donald A. Gardner Architects, Inc.

A t the front of this farmhouse design, the master suite includes a sitting bay, two walk-in closets, a door to the front porch and a compartmented bath with a double-bowl vanity. The formal dining room is in the second bay, also with a door to the front porch. Access to the rear porch is from the great room, which is open under a balcony to the breakfast room. On the second floor, three family bedrooms share a bath that has a double-bowl vanity. One of the family bedrooms offers a walk-in closet. A bonus room over the garage could be used as a study or game room.

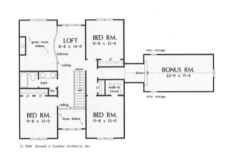

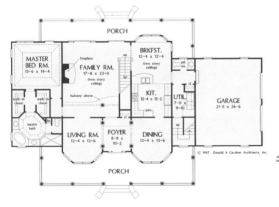

DESIGN BY
Donald A. Gardner Architects, Inc.

F illed with the charm of farmhouse details, such as twin dormers and bay windows, this design begins with a classic covered porch. The entry leads to a foyer flanked by columns that separate it from the formal dining and living rooms. The U-shaped kitchen separates the dining room from the bayed breakfast room. The first-floor owners suite features a bedroom with a tray ceiling and a luxurious private bath.

DESIGN HPU040334

First Floor: 1,914 square feet
Second Floor: 597 square feet
Total: 2,511 square feet
Bonus Room: 487 square feet
Width: 79'-2" Depth: 51'-6"

FAMILY RM.
19-0 x 15-0
fireplace

BRKFST.
12-0 x 9-6

SCREEN
PORCH
13-0 x 9-4

PATIO

KIT.
12-0 x
12-10

LIVING RM.
15-0 x 16-0
fireplace

MASTER
BED RM.
14-0 x 16-0

UTIL.
6-0 x
10-8

up

sto.

storage

pd. rm.

cl

DINING
11-0 x 13-0

FOYER
6-8 x
11-0

cl

walk-in
closet

master bath

lin.

SITTING
9-0 x 9-8

GARAGE
23-0 x 22-0

PORCH

storage

© 1998 Donald A Gardner, Inc.

This charming country-style plan includes a screened porch that opens from the breakfast nook and living room. Entertaining is simple with the dining room and living room convenient to each other. Both the formal living room and the cozy family room have a fireplace. A private homeowner's wing features a rambling master suite with a lavish bath featuring a separate tub and shower, dual vanities, a spacious walk-in closet and a private sitting room for quiet moments. Two secondary bedrooms, a full bath and a bonus room reside upstairs.

BED RM.
12-0 x 13-0

cl

cl

BED RM.
11-0 x 13-4

bath

down

storage

lin.

attic
storage

BONUS RM.
14-6 x 22-0

attic
storage

DESIGN HPU040335

First Floor: 2,010 square feet
Second Floor: 600 square feet
Total: 2,610 square feet
Bonus Room: 378 square feet
Width: 68'-2" Depth: 54'-8"

DESIGN BY
Donald A. Gardner Architects, Inc.

DESIGN HPU040336

First Floor: 1,463 square feet
Second Floor: 1,244 square feet
Total: 2,707 square feet
Bonus Room: 300 square feet
Width: 53'-0" Depth: 66'-0"

DESIGN BY
Donald A. Gardner Architects, Inc.

A stunning combination of country and traditional exterior elements forms an exciting facade for this four-bedroom home. Generous formal and informal living areas create great spaces for entertaining large parties as well as intimate gatherings. Fireplaces add warmth to both the living room and the great room, while front and back porches expand living space outside. All four bedrooms are located on the second floor, which features a marvelous balcony overlooking the foyer. The owners suite boasts a tray ceiling, two walk-in closets and a luxurious private bath.

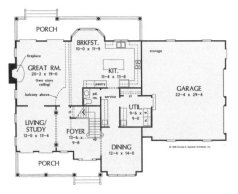

Quote One®

Cost to build? See page 502
to order complete cost estimate
to build this house in your area!

Here's an upscale country home with down-home comfort. The two-story great room is warmed by a rounded-hearth fireplace. French doors brighten the formal living room, while wide counters, a food-preparation island and a bayed breakfast nook create a dreamy kitchen area. The second floor includes a master suite, two bedrooms that share a full bath, and a skylit bonus room. The master suite boasts a sitting area and a private bath with twin vanities and a whirlpool tub.

DESIGN HPU040337

First Floor: 1,484 square feet
Second Floor: 1,061 square feet
Total: 2,545 square feet
Bonus Room: 486 square feet
Width: 66'-10" Depth: 47'-8"

DESIGN BY
Donald A. Gardner Architects, Inc.

© 1995 Donald A. Gardner Architects, Inc.

With two covered porches to encourage outdoor living, multi-pane windows and an open layout, this farmhouse has plenty to offer. Columns define the living room/study area. The family room is accented by a fireplace and has access to the rear porch. An adjacent sunny, bayed breakfast room is convenient to the oversized island kitchen. Four bedrooms upstairs include a deluxe master suite with a lush bath and walk-in closet. Three family bedrooms have plenty of storage space and share a full hall bath.

DESIGN HPU040338

First Floor: 1,483 square feet
Second Floor: 1,349 square feet
Total: 2,832 square feet
Bonus Room: 486 square feet
Width: 66'-10" Depth: 47'-8"

QUOTE ONE®

Cost to build? See page 502
to order complete cost estimate
to build this house in your area!

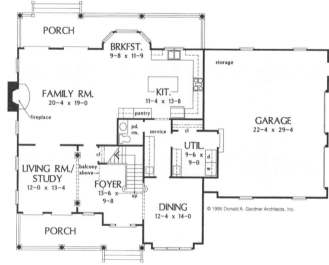

PORCH

BRKFST.
9-8 x 11-9

storage

FAMILY RM.
20-4 x 19-0

KIT.
11-4 x 13-8

GARAGE
22-4 x 29-4

fireplace

pantry

pd. rm.

service

UTIL.
9-6 x 9-0

LIVING RM./
STUDY
12-0 x 13-4

balcony above

FOYER
13-6 x 9-8

up

DINING
12-4 x 14-0

© 1995 Donald A. Gardner Architects, Inc.

PORCH

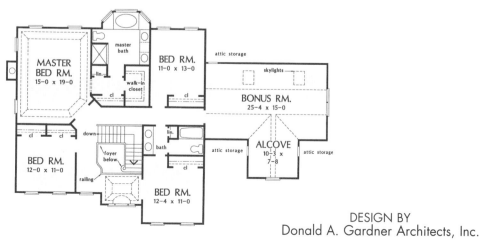

MASTER
BED RM.
15-0 x 19-0

master bath

lin.

walk-in closet

cl

BED RM.
11-0 x 13-0

attic storage

skylights

BONUS RM.
25-4 x 15-0

cl

cl

down

foyer below

bath

lin.

ALCOVE
10-3 x 7-8

attic storage

attic storage

BED RM.
12-0 x 11-0

railing

BED RM.
12-4 x 11-0

cl

DESIGN BY
Donald A. Gardner Architects, Inc.

275

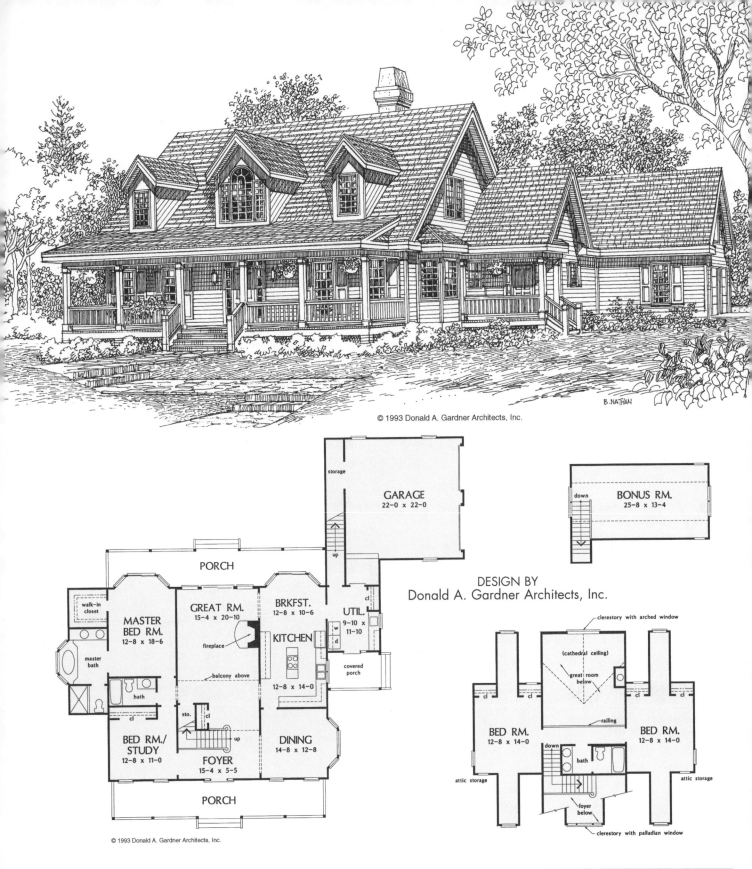

© 1993 Donald A. Gardner Architects, Inc.

GARAGE
22-0 x 22-0

storage

up

BONUS RM.
25-8 x 13-4

down

DESIGN BY
Donald A. Gardner Architects, Inc.

PORCH

walk-in
closet

**MASTER
BED RM.**
12-8 x 18-6

master
bath

bath

cl

**BED RM./
STUDY**
12-8 x 11-0

sto.

cl

up

FOYER
15-4 x 5-5

GREAT RM.
15-4 x 20-10

fireplace

balcony above

KITCHEN

12-8 x 14-0

DINING
14-8 x 12-8

BRKFST.
12-8 x 10-6

cl

UTIL.
9-10 x
11-10

w
d

covered
porch

PORCH

clerestory with arched window

(cathedral ceiling)

great room
below

railing

BED RM.
12-8 x 14-0

cl   cl

attic storage

down

bath

BED RM.
12-8 x 14-0

cl   cl

attic storage

foyer
below

clerestory with palladian window

© 1993 Donald A. Gardner Architects, Inc.

This fetching four-bedroom country home has porches and dormers at both front and rear to offer a welcoming touch. The spacious great room enjoys a large fireplace, a cathedral ceiling and an arched clerestory window. An efficient kitchen is centrally located in order to provide service to the dining room and bayed breakfast area and includes a cooktop island. The expansive owners suite is located on the first floor with a generous walk-in closet and a luxurious private bath. A front bedroom would make a lovely study or guest room. The second level is highlighted by a balcony hall that leads to two family bedrooms sharing a full bath.

DESIGN HPU040339

First Floor: 1,871 square feet
Second Floor: 731 square feet
Total: 2,602 square feet
Bonus Room: 402 square feet
Width: 77'-6" Depth: 70'-0"

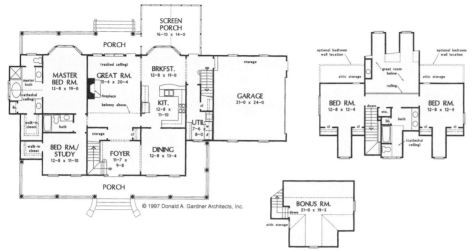

This farmhouse offers an inviting wraparound porch for comfort and three gabled dormers for style. The foyer leads to a generous great room with an extended-hearth fireplace, a cathedral ceiling and access to the back covered porch. The first-floor master suite enjoys a sunny bay window and features a private bath. Upstairs, two family bedrooms share an elegant bath that has a cathedral ceiling.

DESIGN HPU040340

First Floor: 1,939 square feet
Second Floor: 657 square feet
Total: 2,596 square feet
Bonus Room: 386 square feet
Width: 80'-10" Depth: 55'-8"

DESIGN BY
Donald A. Gardner Architects, Inc.

DESIGN HPU040341

First Floor: 1,907 square feet
Second Floor: 656 square feet
Total: 2,563 square feet
Bonus Room: 467 square feet
Width: 89'-10" Depth: 53'-4"

DESIGN BY
Donald A. Gardner Architects, Inc.

Sunny bay windows splash this favorite farmhouse with style, and create a charming facade that's set off by an old-fashioned country porch. Inside, the two-story foyer opens to a formal dining room and to a study, which could be used as a guest suite. The casual living area enjoys a fireplace with an extended hearth and access to an expansive screened porch. The sensational master suite offers a walk-in closet and a bath with a bumped-out bay tub, twin vanities and a separate shower. The two family bedrooms share a full bath upstairs.

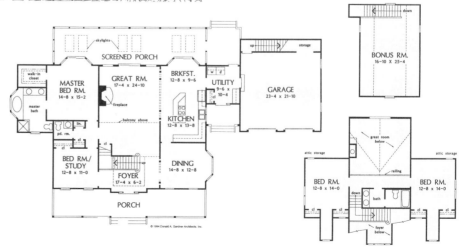

277

DESIGN HPU040342

First Floor: 1,357 square feet
Second Floor: 1,204 square feet
Total: 2,561 square feet
Width: 80'-0" Depth: 57'-0"

DESIGN BY
Donald A. Gardner Architects, Inc.

This grand farmhouse features a double-gabled roof, a Palladian window and an intricately detailed brick chimney. The living room opens to the foyer for formal entertaining, while the family room offers a fireplace, wet bar and direct access to the porch. The lavish kitchen boasts a cooking island and serves the dining room, breakfast nook and porch. The master suite on the second level has a large walk-in closet and a master bath with a whirlpool tub, separate shower and double-bowl vanity. Three additional bedrooms share a full bath.

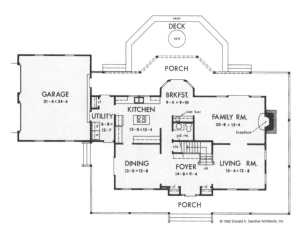

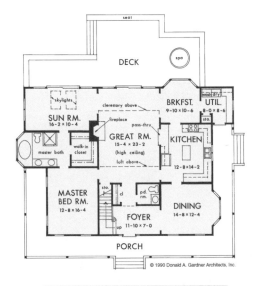

DESIGN HPU040343

First Floor: 1,734 square feet
Second Floor: 943 square feet
Total: 2,677 square feet
Width: 55'-0" Depth: 59'-10"

DESIGN BY
Donald A. Gardner Architects, Inc.

A wraparound covered porch at the front and sides of this home and the open deck with a spa and seating provide plenty of outside living area. A central great room features a vaulted ceiling, fireplace and clerestory windows above. The loft/study on the second floor overlooks this gathering area. Besides a formal dining room, kitchen, breakfast room and sun room on the first floor, there is also a generous owners suite with a garden tub. Three second-floor bedrooms complete the sleeping accommodations.

BED RM.
11-0 x 12-0

skylight

attic storage

bath

walk-in closet

walk-in closet

cl

down

BED RM.
12-0 x 11-8

lin.

master bath

cl

cl

MASTER BED RM.
15-0 x 13-0

attic storage

palladian window

BONUS RM.
26-4 x 14-0

skylights

down

DESIGN BY
Donald A. Gardner Architects, Inc.

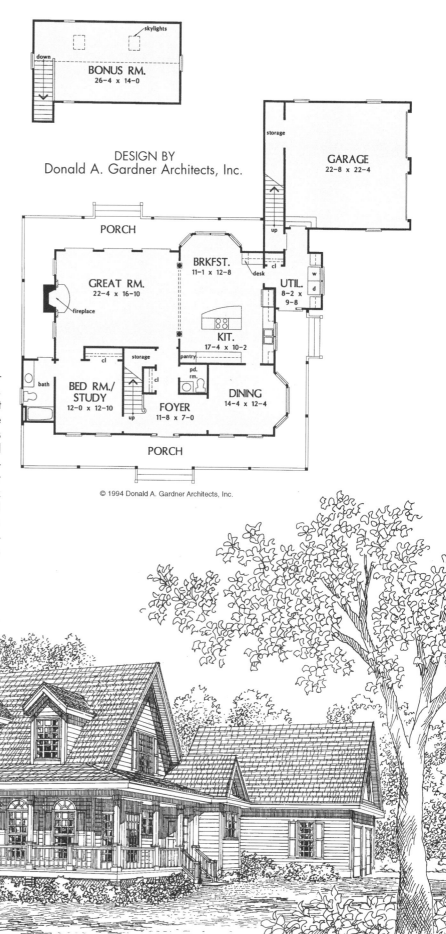

PORCH

GREAT RM.
22-4 x 16-10

fireplace

BRKFST.
11-1 x 12-8

desk

GARAGE
22-8 x 22-4

storage

up

UTIL.
8-2 x 9-8

w

d

KIT.
17-4 x 10-2

cl

storage

pantry

cl

BED RM./ STUDY
12-0 x 12-10

cl

pd. rm.

bath

FOYER
11-8 x 7-0

up

DINING
14-4 x 12-4

PORCH

© 1994 Donald A. Gardner Architects, Inc.

DESIGN HPU040344

First Floor: 1,576 square feet
Second Floor: 947 square feet
Total: 2,523 square feet
Bonus Room: 405 square feet
Width: 71'-4" Depth: 66'-0"

Enjoy balmy breezes as you relax on the wrap-around porch of this delightful country farmhouse. The foyer introduces a dining room to the right and a bedroom or study to the left. The expansive great room—with its cozy fireplace—has direct access to the rear porch. Columns define the kitchen and breakfast area. The house gourmet will enjoy preparing meals at the island cooktop, which also allows for additional eating space. A built-in pantry and a desk are additional popular features in the well-planned kitchen/breakfast room combination. A powder room and a utility room are located nearby. The master bedroom features a tray ceiling and a luxurious bath. Two additional bedrooms share a skylit bath.

© 1994 Donald A. Gardner Architects, Inc. B. NATHAN.

DESIGN HPU040346

First Floor: 1,878 square feet
Second Floor: 739 square feet
Total: 2,617 square feet
Bonus Room: 383 square feet
Width: 79'-8" Depth: 73'-4"

DESIGN BY
Donald A. Gardner Architects, Inc.

This is Southern farmhouse living at its finest. From its wraparound porch and dormer windows to its open and spacious floor plan, this home allows families to live in comfort and style. Illuminating the vaulted foyer is an arched clerestory window within the large center dormer. A cathedral ceiling crowns the generous great room, while the kitchen with a center work island offers easy service to the great room by way of a convenient pass-through. The master suite leaves nothing to chance with screened-porch access and a splendid bath with an oversized walk-in closet. The first floor bedroom/study, with its own entrance, makes an ideal home office or guest room, and two more bedrooms located upstairs are separated by a balcony over-looking the great room.

Classic country character complements this home, complete with rustic stone corners, a covered front porch and interesting gables. The entry opens to the formal living areas that include a large dining room to the right, and straight ahead to a spacious living room warmed by a fireplace. A gallery leads the way to the efficient kitchen enhanced with a snack bar and large pantry. Casual meals can be enjoyed overlooking the covered veranda and rear grounds from the connecting breakfast room. The other side of the gallery accesses the luxurious owners suite and three second bedrooms—all with walk-in closets. The opulent owners suite enjoys a private covered porch in the rear of the plan.

DESIGN HPU040345

First Floor: 2,539 square feet
Second Floor: 170 square feet
Total: 2,709 square feet
Bonus Room: 469 square feet
Width: 98'-0" Depth: 53'-11"

DESIGN BY
©Fillmore Design Group

A wraparound porch makes this unique Victorian farmhouse stand out with style and grace, as does the lovely detailing of this plan. This design is versatile enough to accommodate either a small or large family. The entry is flanked on the left side by a large kitchen/breakfast area with an island, and on the right side by a parlor/music room. The family room is enhanced with a bar ledge, fireplace and built-in entertainment center. The owners suite has access to a covered deck. The upstairs level is shared by three bedrooms, two full baths and a bonus room.

DESIGN BY
©Fillmore Design Group

DESIGN HPU040347

First Floor: 2,023 square feet
Second Floor: 749 square feet
Total: 2,772 square feet
Apartment: 448 square feet
Width: 77'-2" Depth: 57'-11"

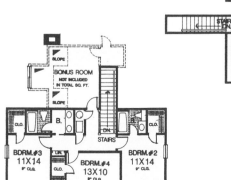

Spectacular Victorian details offer the romantic look of a bygone era. A wrap-around porch, fish-scaling, turrets and intricate woodwork are just the beginning of this fine home. Inside, the living and dining areas are open and provide an excellent space for entertaining. With the breakfast nook tucked into a windowed bay, the kitchen serves up plenty of cabinet and counter space for the family gourmet. The nearby family room will be a favorite spot for casual evenings with friends. A den/study enjoys a quiet front bay with front-porch views. Three family bedrooms share a bath, while the master bedroom enjoys lush accommodations.

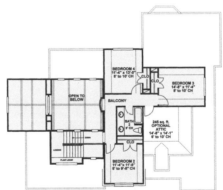

From the veranda, you can enter this home through the front entry or through the sun room. The family and sun-room combination is the high point of this design. The adjacent kitchen features a walk-in pantry and a breakfast area that opens to the back porch. A bay window highlights the first-floor master bedroom, and both the bedroom and its private bath are warmed by a through-fireplace. On the second floor, three bedrooms share a bath that has a double-bowl vanity. A balcony overlooks the family room below. There's optional attic storage plus storage space in the two-car garage. Please specify basement or slab foundation when ordering.

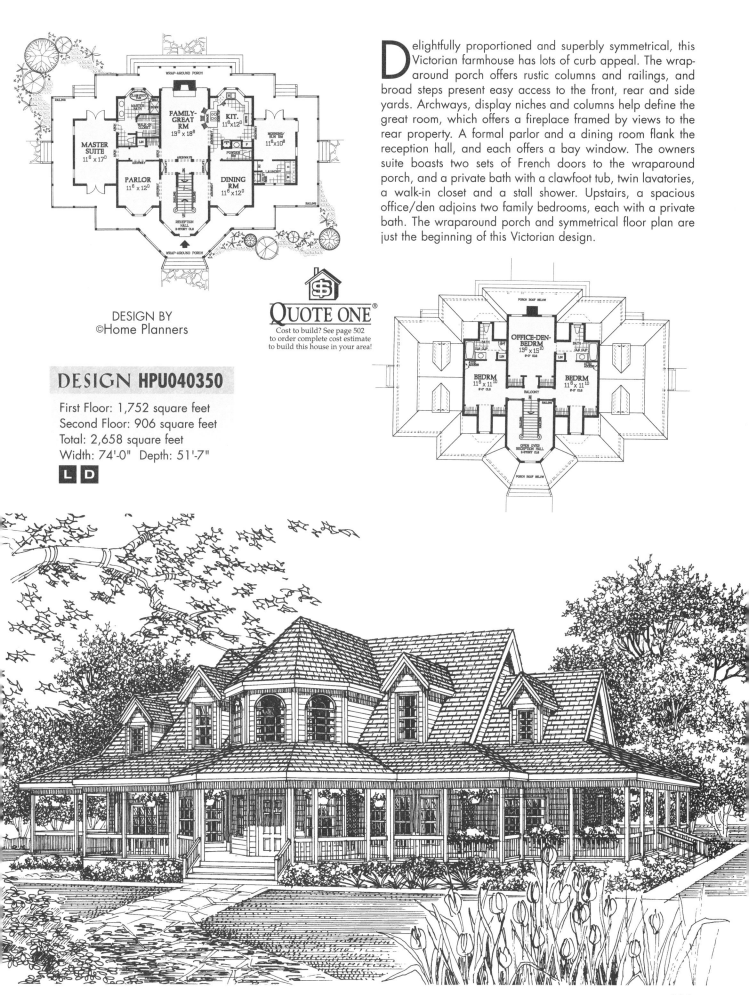

Delightfully proportioned and superbly symmetrical, this Victorian farmhouse has lots of curb appeal. The wraparound porch offers rustic columns and railings, and broad steps present easy access to the front, rear and side yards. Archways, display niches and columns help define the great room, which offers a fireplace framed by views to the rear property. A formal parlor and a dining room flank the reception hall, and each offers a bay window. The owners suite boasts two sets of French doors to the wraparound porch, and a private bath with a clawfoot tub, twin lavatories, a walk-in closet and a stall shower. Upstairs, a spacious office/den adjoins two family bedrooms, each with a private bath. The wraparound porch and symmetrical floor plan are just the beginning of this Victorian design.

DESIGN BY
©Home Planners

QUOTE ONE®
Cost to build? See page 502
to order complete cost estimate
to build this house in your area!

DESIGN HPU040350

First Floor: 1,752 square feet
Second Floor: 906 square feet
Total: 2,658 square feet
Width: 74'-0" Depth: 51'-7"

L D

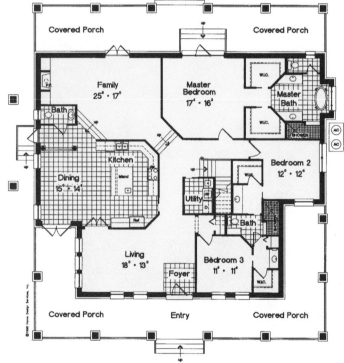

Covered Porch

Covered Porch

Family
25⁴ · 17⁰

Master
Bedroom
17⁴ · 16⁰

W.I.C.

Master
Bath

Bath

Porte Cochere

Kitchen

Dining
15⁰ · 14⁰

Island

W.I.C.

AC

AC

Ref

Utility

Bedroom 2
12⁰ · 12⁴

W.I.C.

Bath

Living
18⁰ · 13⁰

Foyer

Bedroom 3
11⁸ · 11⁸

W.I.C.

Covered Porch

Entry

Covered Porch

DESIGN HPU040351

Square footage: 2,842
Bonus Space: 1,172 square feet
Width: 91'-0" Depth: 69'-4"

DESIGN BY
©Home Design Services, Inc.

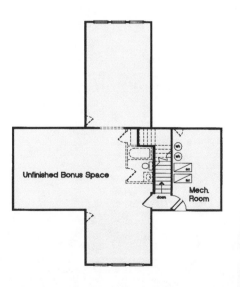

Unfinished Bonus Space

Mech.
Room

A cozy wraparound porch hugs the exterior of this quaint country home. Inside, a spacious island kitchen/dining area is connected to a sunken family room. The master bedroom privately accesses the rear porch and features a master bath with two walk-in closets and a bumped out whirlpool tub. Two additional family bedrooms are available, plus an unfinished bonus area with an optional bath.

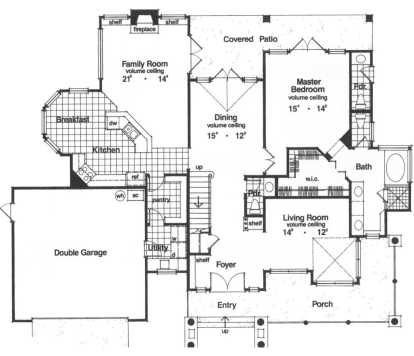

Expansive interior space, a porch and a patio are found in this country-style plan. Front-to-back views begin at the double doors that open to the foyer and extend through the dining room to the covered patio. To the right, the foyer spreads into the living room, which opens to a tower. The pass-through kitchen is linked to the sunny bayed breakfast area and has a large walk-through pantry nearby. The family room includes a fireplace flanked by windows and built-in shelves. French doors provide access to the covered patio from the family room, the dining room, and the master bedroom. A lower-level master bedroom includes a private full bath a walk-in closet, double vanity and spa tub. Three additional bedrooms and a loft are located upstairs.

DESIGN HPU040353

First Floor: 1,820 square feet
Second Floor: 700 square feet
Total: 2,520 square feet
Width: 67'-0" Depth: 55'-3"

DESIGN BY
©Home Design Services, Inc.

DESIGN HPU040355

Square Footage: 2,758
Width: 81'-4" Depth: 76'-0"

L D

DESIGN BY
©Home Planners

This comfortable traditional home offers plenty of modern livability. A clutter room off the two-car garage is an ideal space for a workbench, sewing or hobbies. Across the hall one finds a media room, the perfect place for a stereo, VCR and more. A spacious country kitchen to the right of the greenhouse (great for fresh herbs) is a cozy gathering place for family and friends, as well as a convenient work area. Both the formal living room, with its friendly fireplace, and the dining room provide access to the rear grounds. A spacious, amenity-filled master suite features His and Hers walk-in closets, a relaxing whirlpool tub and access to the rear terrace. Two large secondary bedrooms share a full bath.

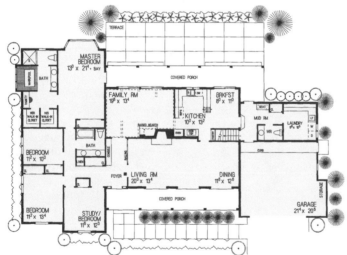

Covered porches to the front and rear will be the envy of the neighborhood when this house is built. The interior plan meets family needs perfectly in well-zoned areas: a sleeping wing with four bedrooms and two baths, a living zone with formal and informal gathering space, and a work zone with a U-shaped kitchen and laundry with a powder room. The two-car garage has a huge storage area.

DESIGN HPU040354

Square Footage: 2,549
Width: 88'-8" Depth: 53'-6"

L

DESIGN BY
©Home Planners

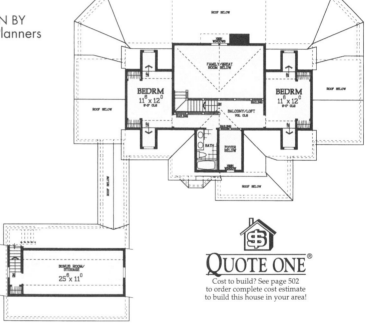

Varying roof planes, gables and dormers help create the unique character of this house. Inside, the family/great room gains attention with its high ceiling, fireplace/media-center wall, view of the upstairs balcony and French doors to the sun room. In the U-shaped kitchen, an island work surface, a planning desk and pantry are added conveniences. The spacious owners suite can function with the home office, library or private sitting room. Its direct access to the huge raised veranda provides an ideal private outdoor haven for relaxation. The second floor highlights two bedrooms and a bath. Bonus space can be found above the garage with its workshop area and stairway to a second-floor storage or multi-purpose room.

DESIGN BY
©Home Planners

DESIGN HPU040356

First Floor: 1,969 square feet
Second Floor: 660 square feet
Total: 2,629 square feet
Bonus Room: 360 square feet
Width: 90'-8" Depth: 80'-4"

L **D**

Quote One®
Cost to build? See page 502
to order complete cost estimate
to build this house in your area!

Walk-in Closet

M.Bath

Porch
13-0x10-0

Master
Bedroom
17-10x15-6

Storage
8-2x9-10

Laun.
7-5x9-10

1/2
Bath

Breakfast
11-5x14-0

Greatroom
17-3x19-6

Bedroom
15-6x11-6

Kitchen
11-5x12-0

Garage
21-0x26-0

Bath

Dining
11-5x15-2

Foyer

Bedroom
11-5x13-6

Bedroom
11-7x13-6

DESIGN HPU040358

Square Footage: 2,670
Width: 70'-6" Depth: 72'-4"

A lovely brick facade is decorated with shutters, arched and straight lintels and a transom with side-lights on the entry of this comforting cottage. At the center of the house, the great room holds a fireplace sided with built-ins. Four bedrooms and lots of storage give this house long-lasting appeal with any family. Please specify crawlspace or slab foundation when ordering.

DINING
12-0 x 15-0

PORCH

PORCH

MASTER
BED RM.
14-0 x 18-0

fireplace

GREAT RM.
22-0 x 18-8
(cathedral ceiling)

BRKFST.
9-8 x 10-0

KITCHEN
12-0 x 15-0

walk-in
closet

walk-in
closet

UTIL.
5-8 x
6-8

pantry

storage

railing

down

FOYER
6-8 x
10-0

pd.
rm.

master
bath

seat

PORCH

GARAGE
21-8 x 23-4

storage

A rched windows and arches in the covered front porch complement the gabled peaks on the facade of this stylish Craftsman home with a stone-and-siding exterior and partial, finished walkout basement. Designed for sloping lots, this home positions its common living areas and master suite on the main floor and a generous recreation room and two family bedrooms on the lower level. An exciting cathedral ceiling expands the foyer and great room, while the dining room and master bedroom and bath enjoy elegant tray ceilings. With a bay window and back-porch access, the master suite boasts dual walk-ins and a luxurious bath.

PATIO

BED RM.
11-6 x 13-4

wet bar

fireplace

REC. RM.
19-8 x 18-8

BED RM.
13-6 x 11-0

bath

up

sto.

bath

DESIGN HPU040357

Main Level: 1,725 square feet
Lower Level: 1,090 square feet
Total: 2,815 square feet
Width: 59'-0" Depth: 59'-4"

seat

spa

DECK

arched window above door

fireplace

master bath

lin

MASTER BED RM.
14-0 x 19-4

walk-in closet

SUN RM.
15-8 x 10-0
(cathedral ceiling)

BRKFST.
12-0 x 11-0

VESTIBULE UTIL.
9-0 x 6-8

d w

storage

up

BED RM.
13-0 x 12-0

GREAT RM.
18-0 x 21-0
(cathedral ceiling)

bath

fireplace

cabinets

GARAGE
21-0 x 23-0

BED RM.
11-8 x 11-0

KITCHEN
12-0 x 16-0

storage

cl

sto.

cl

FOYER
12-0 x 5-8

pd. rm.

cl

PORCH
15-0 x 5-2

DINING
12-0 x 14-0

BED RM./ STUDY
12-0 x 12-0

© 1993 Donald A. Gardner Architects, Inc.

DESIGN BY
Donald A. Gardner Architects, Inc.

skylights

attic storage

BONUS RM.
33-3 x 17-10

down

down

DESIGN HPU040359

Square Footage: 2,663
Bonus Room: 653 square feet
Width: 72'-7"   Depth: 78'-0"

This home's personality is reflected in charming arch-top windows, set off with keystones and decorative shutters. A columned foyer enjoys natural light from a clerestory window, and opens to the great room, which boasts a cathedral ceiling and sliding glass doors to the sun room. An extended-hearth fireplace adds warmth to the living area. Open planning allows the nearby gourmet kitchen to share the glow of the hearth. The breakfast room really lets the sunshine in with a triple window to the rear property. The master suite offers private access to the rear deck with a spa, and features a cozy fireplace, a relaxing bath and a generous walk-in closet. Three family bedrooms—or make one a study—share a full bath and a powder room on the other side of the plan.

© 1993 Donald A. Gardner Architects, Inc.

B. NATHAN

DESIGN HPU040361

First Floor: 1,870 square feet
Second Floor: 767 square feet
Total: 2,637 square feet
Width: 59'-4" Depth: 61'-4"

DESIGN BY
©Design Basics, Inc.

This charming facade sports a winning combination of brick and siding, set off by many lovely windows. An arched portico leads to a comfortable interior that's both traditional and casual. The great room opens to a spacious breakfast area with a side porch. The kitchen also serves the formal dining room, which offers a convenient powder room nearby. Upstairs, three secondary bedrooms share a bath that includes two lavatories.

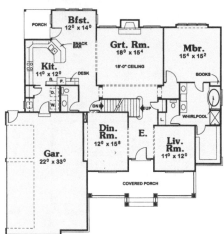

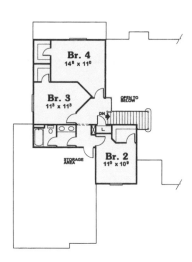

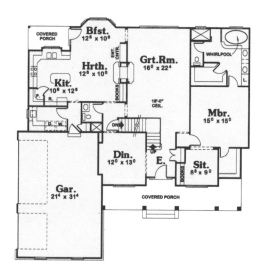

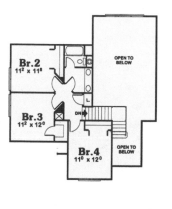

Multiple gables, shuttered windows and a covered front porch define the exterior of this farmhouse. The luxury-filled interior includes a great room that shares a through-fireplace with the hearth room, which offers a built-in entertainment center and bookshelves. A nearby breakfast bay opens to a small covered porch. The island kitchen boasts a walk-in pantry and easy access to the formal dining room. The owners suite provides a sitting room with built-in bookshelves, a large walk-in closet and an opulent bath with a whirlpool tub and double vanities. A full bath serves three secondary bedrooms upstairs, one of which features a walk-in closet. Please specify basement or block foundation when ordering.

DESIGN HPU040360

First Floor: 1,955 square feet
Second Floor: 660 square feet
Total: 2,615 square feet
Width: 60'-0" Depth: 60'-4"

DESIGN BY
©Design Basics, Inc.

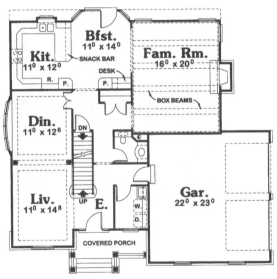

Kit.
11⁰ x 12⁰

Bfst.
11⁰ x 14⁰

SNACK BAR

Fam. Rm.
16⁰ x 20⁰

DESK

R.   P.   P.

BOX BEAMS

Din.
11⁰ x 12⁶

DN

Liv.
11⁰ x 14⁸

UP   E.   W.   D.

Gar.
22⁰ x 23⁰

COVERED PORCH

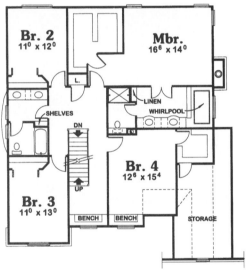

Br. 2
11⁰ x 12⁰

Mbr.
16⁶ x 14⁰

L.

SHELVES

LINEN

WHIRLPOOL

DN

Br. 4
12⁶ x 15⁴

UP

Br. 3
11⁰ x 13⁰

BENCH   BENCH

STORAGE

French country accents highlight the exterior of this spacious, traditional home. The foyer opens to an interesting hall that partly encircles the octagonal living room. The family room opens from one end of the hallway, and the master suite is reached through the opposite end. The dining room, open to the foyer, is just off the kitchen and breakfast room. The laundry room, with access to outside and to the garage, completes this floor. Upstairs, two bedrooms offer walk-in closets and share a compartmented bath. An unfinished bonus room could be used for storage.

DESIGN HPU040362

First Floor: 1,304 square feet
Second Floor: 1,504 square feet
Total: 2,808 square feet
Bonus Room: 209 square feet
Width: 48'-0"   Depth: 46'-0"

DESIGN BY
©Design Basics, Inc.

Unfinished
Attic
24⁸ x 16⁸

DN

DOWNDRAFT
FURNACE

OPTIONAL
STORAGE

Patio Area

BrkfstRm
13x10
10'Clg.

Patio Area

3-Car-Gar
24x32

MstrBed
17x14

LivRm
17x15
10'Clg.

Kit
13x14
10'Clg.

FamilyRm
16x17
10'Clg.

Util
8'Clg.

Study
11x11

Ent/Gallery
11'Clg.

Bed#4
12x12
8'Clg.

FmlDin
12x13
11'Clg.

Bed#3
12x12
10'Clg.

Bed#2
14x11

DESIGN BY
©Fillmore Design Group

DESIGN HPU040363

Square Footage: 2,858
Width: 89'-7"   Depth: 68'-4"

Multiple front gables, multi-pane windows and a recessed entry make up the front exterior of this attractive home. Ten-foot ceilings are featured throughout the sprawling main living areas. A massive fireplace and built-in bookshelves or entertainment units distinguish the spacious family room. The area containing the open kitchen and breakfast room boasts a large bay window facing the patio. The master bedroom suite features a luxurious bath and walk-in closet, plus an adjacent wood-paneled study.

DESIGN BY
©Fillmore Design Group

A brick archway covers the front porch of this European-style home, creating a truly grand entrance. Situated beyond the entry, the living room takes center stage with a fireplace flanked by tall windows overlooking the backyard. To the right is a bayed eating area reserved for casual meals and an efficient kitchen. Steps away is the formal dining room for holidays and special occasions. Skillful planning creates flexibility for the owners suite. If you wish, use Bedroom 2 as a secondary bedroom or guest room, with the adjacent study accessible to everyone. Or if you prefer, combine the owners suite with the study and use it as a private retreat with Bedroom 2 as a nursery, creating a wing that provides complete privacy. Completing this clever plan are two family bedrooms—each with a walk-in closet—a powder room and a utility room.

DESIGN HPU040364

Square Footage: 2,696
Width: 80'-0" Depth: 64'-1"

This home's heart lies in its large, circular kitchen, where an island worktop is the focal point. The kitchen blends easily with the breakfast nook, the family room—with its outdoor access and fireplace—and to the living and dining areas. Both rooms provide access to the backyard via sliding glass doors. Upstairs, three family bedrooms share a full bath and a handy writing desk—big enough for a computer. Also located on the second floor is the master bedroom, which features a fireplace and a splendid bath. A deck with room to relax completes this floor.

DESIGN HPU040365

First Floor: 1,228 square feet
Second Floor: 1,285 square feet
Total: 2,513 square feet
Width: 36'-8" Depth: 66'-2"

DESIGN BY
©Home Planners

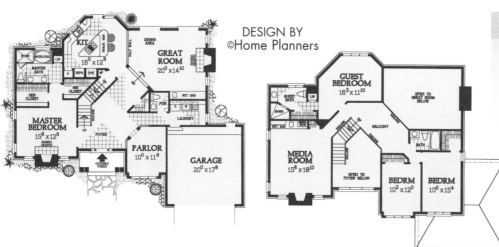

DESIGN BY
©Home Planners

DESIGN HPU040366

First Floor: 1,620 square feet
Second Floor: 1,266 square feet
Total: 2,886 square feet
Width: 60'-4" Depth: 48'-8"

L D

Massive chimneys and large-pane windows in a variety of shapes add interest to the exterior of this elegant home. A parlor to the right of the foyer is optimally located for formal gatherings, but most of the family's activities will take place in the sunken great room, with its dining area, raised-hearth fireplace and wet bar. The second floor offers a well-appointed guest suite with a large bath, two family bedrooms and a media room with a fireplace.

DESIGN HPU040367

First Floor: 1,825 square feet
Second Floor: 842 square feet
Total: 2,667 square feet
Width: 59'-0" Depth: 54'-6"

DESIGN BY
©Living Concepts Home Planning

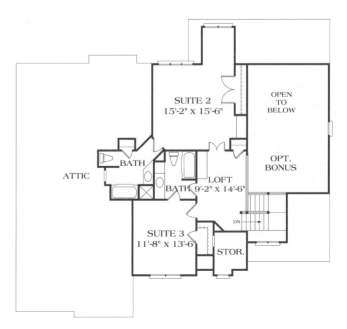

Stone and siding lend a rustic nature to this traditional home. A covered stoop is enhanced by a graceful arch and a glass-paneled entry. A formal dining room is served by a gourmet kitchen through a butler's pantry with a wet bar. The great room provides a fireplace and a French door to a golf porch. An angled tub and an oversized shower highlight the master bath, while a box-bay window and a tray ceiling enhance the homeowner's bedroom. Each of the second-floor suites has a generous bath. The loft overlooks the great room.

A brick exterior, cast-stone trim and corner quoins make up this attractive single-living-area design. The large living area opens to the kitchen/breakfast room, all with ten-foot ceilings. A large bay window enhances the breakfast room with a full glass door to the covered patio. A large master suite with vaulted ceilings features a luxurious master bath with double lavatories and an oversized walk-in closet.

DESIGN HPU040368

Square Footage: 2,504
Width: 65'-0" Depth: 59'-10"

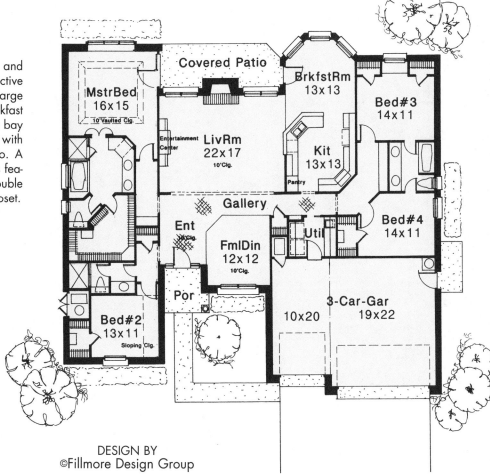

DESIGN BY
©Fillmore Design Group

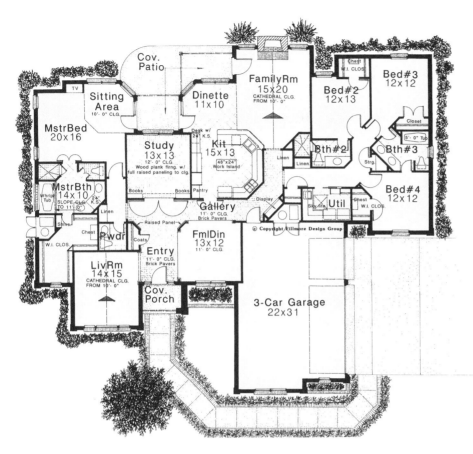

Varying rooflines, a stately brick exterior and classic window treatment accentuate the beauty of this traditional one-story home. Inside, formal living areas flank the entry—living room to the left and dining room to the right—presenting a fine introduction. Double French doors provide an elegant entrance to the centrally located study. To the right, you will find the casual living areas: a U-shaped kitchen, a dinette and a large family room with a cathedral ceiling. Three secondary bedrooms and two full baths complete this side of the plan. Tucked behind the living room is the owners suite. Amenities enhancing this private getaway include a sitting area with built-in space for a TV, a huge walk-in closet, and a private bath with a whirlpool tub and a separate shower.

DESIGN HPU040370

Square Footage: 2,985
Width: 80'-0"   Depth: 68'-0"

DESIGN BY
©Fillmore Design Group

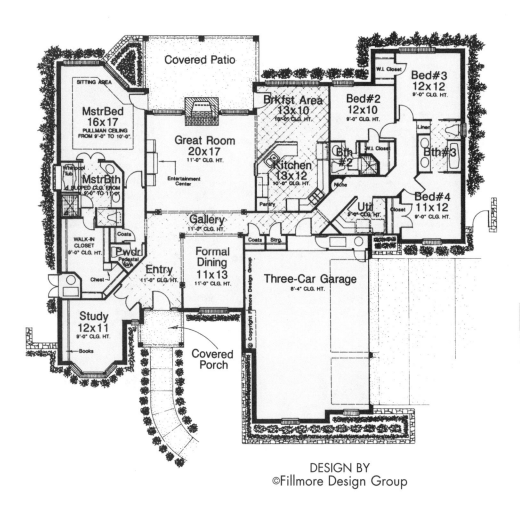

Covered Patio

MstrBed
16x17
PULLMAN CEILING
FROM 9'-0" TO 10'-0"

SITTING AREA

Great Room
20x17
11'-0" CLG. HT.

Brkfst Area
13x10
10'-0" CLG. HT.

Bed#2
12x10
9'-0" CLG. HT.

Bed#3
12x12
9'-0" CLG. HT.

W.I. Closet

MstrBth
SLOPED CLG. FROM
9'-0" TO 11'-0"

Whirlpool
Tub

Kitchen
13x12
10'-0" CLG. HT.

Entertainment
Center

Bth
#2

Bth#3

Liner

W.I. Closet

WALK-IN
CLOSET
9'-0" CLG. HT.

Pantry

Niche

Bed#4
11x12
9'-0" CLG. HT.

Coats

Gallery
11'-0" CLG. HT.

Util
9'-0" CLG. HT.

Closet

Pwdr.

Pedestal
Sink

Chest

Coats

Strg.

Entry
11'-0" CLG. HT.

Formal
Dining
11x13
11'-0" CLG. HT.

Three-Car Garage
8'-4" CLG. HT.

Study
12x11
9'-0" CLG. HT.

Books

Covered
Porch

© Copyright Fillmore Design Group

DESIGN BY
©Fillmore Design Group

With a solid exterior of rough cedar and stone, this new French country design will stand the test of time. A wood-paneled study on the front features a large bay window. The heart of the house is found in a large, open great room with a built-in entertainment center. The spacious master bedroom features a corner reading area and access to an adjacent covered patio. A three-car garage and three additional bedrooms complete this generous family home.

DESIGN HPU040371

Square Footage: 2,590
Width: 73'-6" Depth: 64'-10"

Walk-In Closet
9'-0" Clg.
Shelves

Covered Patio

FamilyRm
16x16³
Cathedral Ceiling

Walk In Closet

Whirl
Pool Tub

Ledge

Covered Patio

Din
10x15
9'-0" Clg.
Brick Pavers

Kit
12⁹x12⁶
Brick Pavers

Bed#3
12x13³
8'-0" Clg.

Ledge

MstrBed
15x17
Vaulted Ceiling
9'-0" To 10'-6"

FmlLiv
14x14

Display

Oven

Linen

Hall
Clg.

W.
D.

Util

Linen

Bed#2
12x13
8'-0" Clg.

Pantry

Brick Pavers

Gallery
9'-0" Clg.
Brick Pavers

Hall
9'-0" Clg.

Walk-In Closet

Ent
9'-0" Clg.
Brick Pavers

FmlDin
10³x12
9'-0" Clg.

Bed#4
/Study
11x12
9'-0" Clg.

Walk-In Closet

Cov Por

3-Car Gar
22⁶x30
9'-4" Clg.

Interesting angles and creative detailing characterize the exterior of this brick cottage. The island kitchen opens to an informal dining area with access to two covered patios. Formal rooms are closer to the front door for ease in entertaining. Sleeping quarters include two family bedrooms to the right of the plan and another bedroom, which could be used as a study, on the left. The left wing is home to a lavish owners suite.

DESIGN HPU040373

Square Footage: 2,526
Width: 64'-0" Depth: 81'-7"

DESIGN BY
©Fillmore Design Group

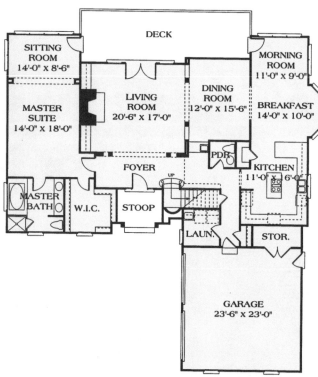

A gallery-style foyer leads to all areas of the plan, both formal and casual. The morning room is enhanced with five windows and access to the rear deck. A well-planned gourmet kitchen has an island cooktop counter, a walk-in pantry and a breakfast area with a bay window. Walls of glass brighten the sitting room, which provides French-door access to the deck. Upper-level sleeping quarters include two family bedrooms, which share a full bath that contains linen storage.

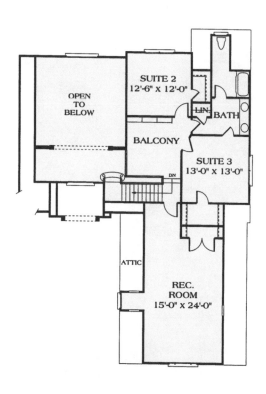

DESIGN HPU040374

First Floor: 2,100 square feet
Second Floor: 756 square feet
Total: 2,856 square feet
Bonus Room: 482 square feet
Width: 63'-5"   Depth: 65'-8"

DESIGN BY
©Living Concepts Home Planning

300

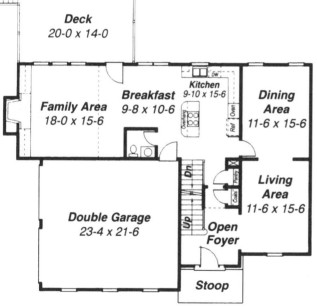

Deck
20-0 x 14-0

Family Area
18-0 x 15-6

Breakfast
9-8 x 10-6

Kitchen
9-10 x 15-6

Dining Area
11-6 x 15-6

Double Garage
23-4 x 21-6

Living Area
11-6 x 15-6

Open Foyer

Stoop

DESIGN HPU040375

First Floor: 1,183 square feet
Second Floor: 1,571 square feet
Total: 2,754 square feet
Width: 52'-4" Depth: 38'-0"

DESIGN BY
©Jannis Vann & Associates, Inc.

Classic quoins and multi-pane windows dress up this perfect blend of stone and stucco, which creates a fresh look for French country style. A glass-paneled door and clerestory window bathe the two-story foyer in natural light. The formal living and dining areas are set apart on one side of the plan. A family room enjoys a centered fireplace flanked by built-in bookcases and is conveniently open to the breakfast area, kitchen and sun deck outside. Upstairs, a tray ceiling highlights the master suite, which offers a bath and generous walk-in closet. Two family bedrooms share a full bath; a third bedroom and a loft, or fifth bedroom, share a third full bath.

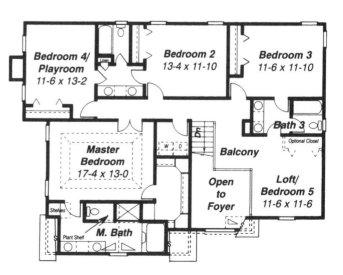

Bedroom 4/ Playroom
11-6 x 13-2

Bedroom 2
13-4 x 11-10

Bedroom 3
11-6 x 11-10

Bath 3

Optional Closet

Master Bedroom
17-4 x 13-0

Balcony

Open to Foyer

Loft/ Bedroom 5
11-6 x 11-6

Shelves

M. Bath

Plant Shelf

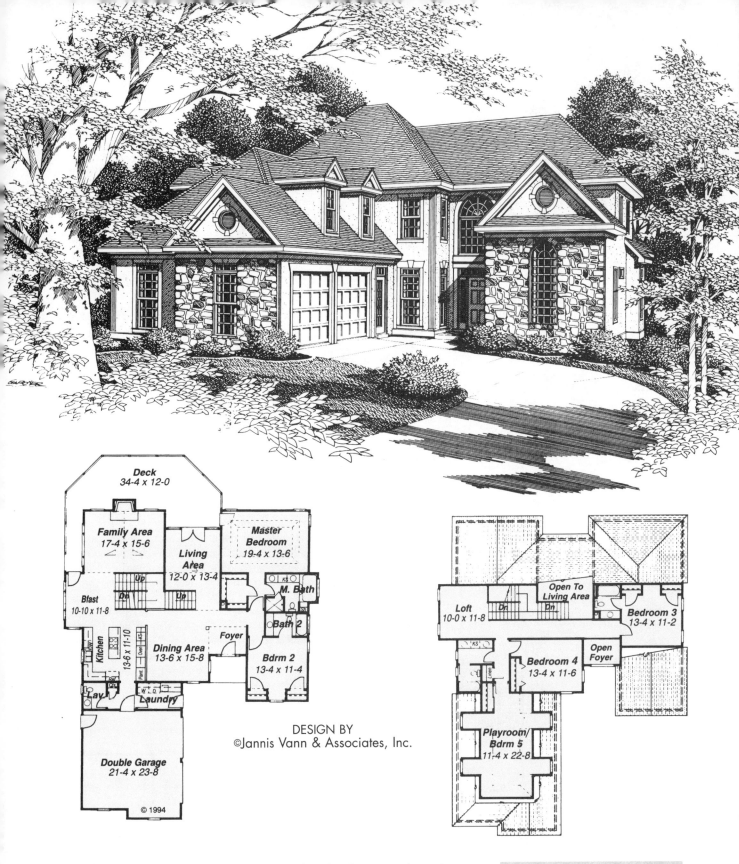

Deck
34-4 x 12-0

Family Area
17-4 x 15-6

Living Area
12-0 x 13-4

Master Bedroom
19-4 x 13-6

Up

Dn

Up

M. Bath

KS

Bfast
10-10 x 11-8

Kitchen
13-6 x 11-10

Bath 2

Pant.

Oven

Dining Area
13-6 x 15-8

Foyer

Bdrm 2
13-4 x 11-4

W

D

Lav.

Laundry

Double Garage
21-4 x 23-8

© 1994

Loft
10-0 x 11-8

Dn

Dn

Open To Living Area

Bedroom 3
13-4 x 11-2

KS

Bedroom 4
13-4 x 11-6

Linen

Open Foyer

Playroom/ Bdrm 5
11-4 x 22-8

DESIGN BY
©Jannis Vann & Associates, Inc.

An L-shaped plan and fine brick-and-siding detail present a home that is sure to please. The floor plan is designed to accommodate both formal and informal entertaining, with the formal dining and living rooms perfect for dinner parties. Toward the rear, a spacious family room offers a fireplace for cheery, casual get-togethers. A guest suite is located to the right of the foyer, near the lavish master suite. The second floor consists of two bedrooms—one with its own bath—a loft and a huge playroom over the garage.

DESIGN HPU040376

First Floor: 2,055 square feet
Second Floor: 898 square feet
Total: 2,953 square feet
Bonus Room: 358 square feet
Width: 56'-0"   Depth: 80'-0"

A combination of stacked river stone and cedar shakes gives warmth and character to this English country facade. A vaulted ceiling adds height and spaciousness to the great room, which opens to the dining room for effortless entertaining. A fireplace and a built-in wet bar are welcome additions to the area, as is easy access to a covered deck. A side door near the kitchen opens to a breezeway leading to the garage. A study with a fireplace is a quiet spot, conveniently close to the master suite, which boasts a deluxe bath and a private door to the deck. A guest suite is located to the left of the foyer, where stairs lead up to the second floor and two more bedroom suites. There's plenty of storage on this level, as well as a loft that can serve many purposes.

DESIGN HPU040377

First Floor: 2,122 square feet
Second Floor: 719 square feet
Total: 2,841 square feet
Bonus Room: 535 square feet
Width: 117'-0" Depth: 57'-2"

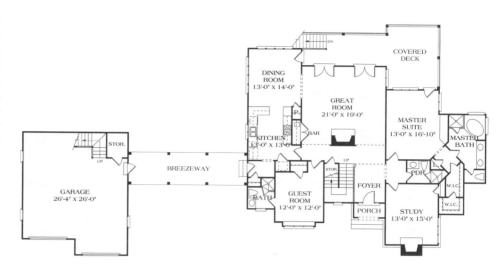

DESIGN BY
©Living Concepts Home Planning

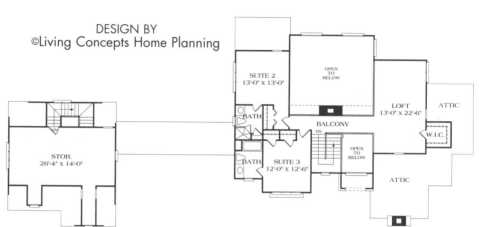

This home is designed to be a homeowner's dream come true. A formal living area opens from the gallery foyer through graceful arches and looks out to the veranda, which hosts an outdoor grill and service counter, perfect for outdoor entertaining. The leisure room offers a private veranda, a cabana bath and a wet bar just off the gourmet kitchen. Walls of windows and a bayed breakfast nook let in natural light and set a bright tone for this area. The master suite opens to the rear property through French doors, and boasts a lavish bath with a corner whirlpool tub that overlooks a private garden. An art niche off the gallery hall, a private dressing area and a secluded study complement the master suite. Two family bedrooms occupy the opposite wing of the plan, and share a full bath and private hall.

DESIGN HPU040378

Square Footage: 2,978
Width: 84'-0" Depth: 90'-0"

DESIGN BY
©The Sater Design Collection

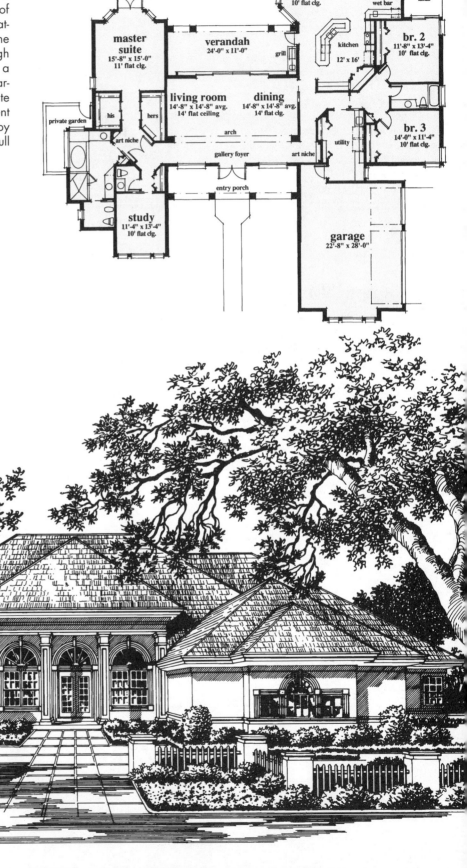

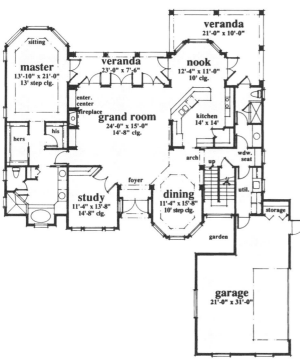

veranda
21'-0" x 10'-0"

veranda
23'-0" x 7'-6"

master
13'-10" x 21'-0"
13' step clg.

sitting

nook
12'-4" x 11'-0"
10' clg.

enter.
center
fireplace

grand room
24'-0" x 15'-0"
14'-8" clg.

kitchen
14' x 14'

hers

his

wdw.
seat

arch

up

foyer

study
11'-4" x 13'-8"
14'-8" clg.

dining
11'-4" x 15'-8"
10' step clg.

util.

storage

garden

garage
21'-0" x 31'-0"

DESIGN HPU040379

First Floor: 2,181 square feet
Second Floor: 710 square feet
Total: 2,891 square feet
Width: 66'-4" Depth: 79'-0"

DESIGN BY
©The Sater Design Collection

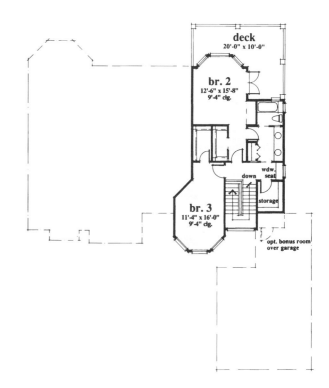

deck
20'-0" x 10'-0"

br. 2
12'-6" x 15'-8"
9'-4" clg.

down

wdw.
seat

br. 3
11'-4" x 16'-0"
9'-4" clg.

storage

opt. bonus room
over garage

An arched, covered porch presents fine double doors leading to a spacious foyer in this decidedly European home. A two-story tower contains an elegant formal dining room on the first floor and a spacious bedroom on the second floor. The grand room is aptly named with a fireplace, a built-in entertainment center and three sets of doors opening onto the veranda. A large kitchen is ready to please the gourmet of the family with a big walk-in pantry and a sunny, bay-windowed eating nook. The secluded master suite is luxury in itself. A bay-windowed sitting area, access to the rear veranda, His and Hers walk-in closets and a lavish bath are all set to pamper you. Upstairs, two bedrooms, both with walk-in closets, share a full hall bath that includes twin vanities. Please specify basement or slab foundation when ordering.

DESIGN HPU040380

First Floor: 1,920 square feet
Second Floor: 912 square feet
Total: 2,832 square feet
Width: 70'-0"   Depth: 40'-0"

DESIGN BY
©Archival Designs, Inc.

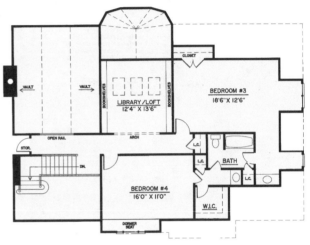

The impressive facade of this classic design previews an elegant floor plan. To the left of the large foyer, French doors open to a study filled with natural light. The open dining room, to the right of the foyer, is defined by a single column. To the rear of the plan, the living room/den and kitchen—with a bowed breakfast area—provide space for the family to gather. Also at the rear of the plan, a guest room features its own bath and private access to the outside through a garage entrance. On the left side of the plan, the master suite offers a walk-in closet, a luxurious bath and private access to the study. Upstairs, two bedrooms—each with a private compartmented vanity—share a bath. Bookshelves line the library loft, which is lighted by three skylights.

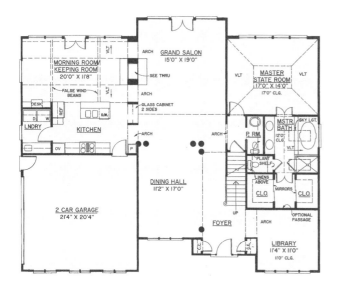

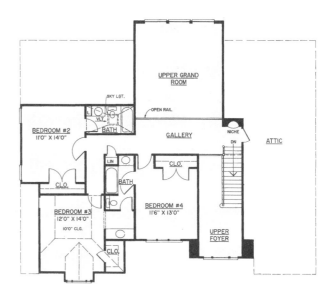

Nested, hipped gables create a dramatic effect in this beautiful two-story brick home. The arched doorway is echoed in the triple clerestory window that lights the two-story foyer. Columns decorate the formal dining room, which is open to the two-story grand room with fireplace. The master suite is located downstairs for privacy, while upstairs, three secondary bedrooms are joined by a gallery overlooking the grand room.

DESIGN HPU040381

First Floor: 1,809 square feet
Second Floor: 898 square feet
Total: 2,707 square feet
Width: 54'-4"   Depth: 46'-0"

DESIGN BY
©Archival Designs, Inc.

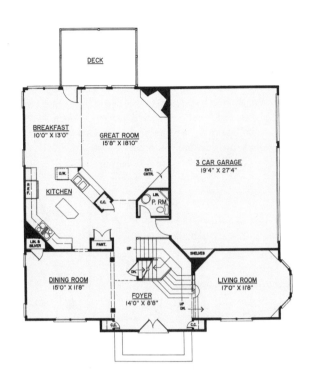

If ever a home was designed with a Fifth Avenue address in mind, this is it. The grand entry opens to a wide foyer that presents two coat closets and angled stairs to the second floor. Through a pair of columns to the left, enter the dining room. Or go to the right into the formal living room that has an elegant bay window. The angled kitchen opens to the breakfast room and two-story great room. Stairs to the second floor go up to the wide loft that overlooks the great room. The laundry room on this floor serves the three family bedrooms with their two baths and the master suite.

DESIGN HPU040382

First Floor: 1,332 square feet
Second Floor: 1,331 square feet
Total: 2,663 square feet
Width: 48'-0" Depth: 42'-0"

DESIGN BY
©Archival Designs, Inc.

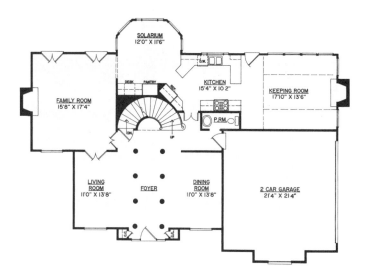

DESIGN HPU040383

First Floor: 1,431 square feet
Second Floor: 1,519 square feet
Total: 2,950 square feet
Width: 60'-0" Depth: 44'-0"

DESIGN BY
©Archival Designs, Inc.

Stunning stucco detailing, attractive gabled rooflines and an elegant, arched entrance are elements of traditional style that dress up this fine four-bedroom home. Inside, columns define a graceful foyer and separate the formal dining room and formal living room. The spacious family room, off to the left, features a warming fireplace and direct access to the rear grounds. A solarium is near the efficient kitchen, providing a warm and sunny place to relax. The keeping room is another gathering spot that will surely be a favorite of your family. Talk about lavish! When it comes to the master suite, the homeowner will have a hard time leaving this wonderful room. Two walk-in closets, a separate octagonal sitting room and a fabulous bath are sure to please.

DESIGN HPU040385

First Floor: 1,465 square feet
Second Floor: 1,349 square feet
Total: 2,814 square feet
Bonus Room: 319 square feet
Width: 72'-4" Depth: 38'-4"

DESIGN BY
©Jannis Vann & Associates, Inc.

A massive arch guards the entrance to this French-style stucco home, its keystone accent repeated over the windows in several different combinations. Inside, symmetrical dining and living rooms flank the two-story foyer. A swinging door leads from the dining room to the island kitchen, which offers a choice of a snack bar or a breakfast nook for casual meals. The laundry room and a powder room are nearby. A sunken family room boasts a fireplace and access to a sun deck that stretches across the rear of the house. The second floor offers four bedrooms, including a deluxe master suite. Please specify basement, crawlspace or slab foundation when ordering.

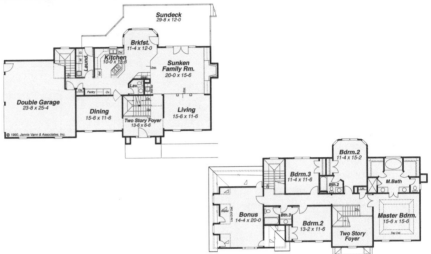

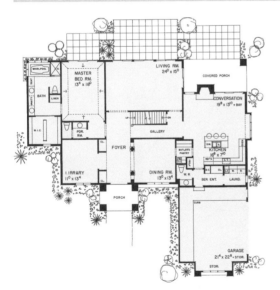

QUOTE ONE®
Cost to build? See page 502
to order complete cost estimate
to build this house in your area!

This home will keep even the most active family from feeling cramped. Adjacent to the kitchen is a conversation area with additional access to the covered porch, a snack bar, fireplace and a window bay. A butler's pantry leads to the formal dining room. Placed conveniently on the first floor, the master suite features a roomy bath with a huge walk-in closet and dual vanities. Two large bedrooms are found on the second floor.

DESIGN HPU040384

First Floor: 2,328 square feet
Second Floor: 603 square feet
Total: 2,931 square feet
Width: 69'-4" Depth: 66'-0"

DESIGN BY
©Home Planners

Intricate details make the most of this lovely one-story design. Besides the living room/dining room area to the rear, there is a large conversation area with a fireplace and plenty of windows. The kitchen is separated from living areas by an angled snack-bar counter. Three bedrooms grace the right side of the plan. The master suite features a tray ceiling and sliding glass doors to the rear terrace. The dressing area is graced by His and Hers walk-in closets, a double-bowl lavatory and a compartmented toilet. The shower area is highlighted with glass block and is sunken down one step. A garden whirlpool tub finishes off this area.

DESIGN HPU040386

Square Footage: 2,916
Width: 77'-10" Depth: 73'-10"

L **D**

DESIGN BY
©Home Planners

QUOTE ONE®
Cost to build? See page 502
to order complete cost estimate
to build this house in your area!

Sundeck
32-0 x 20-0

Privacy Deck
14-4 x 12-0

Sitting
9-8 x 11-6

Dining
13-8 x 13-4

Kitchen
13-8 x 13-6

Brkfst.
9-8 x 8-0

Master Bdrm.
13-8 x 15-6

Living
12-4 x 13-6

Open Foyer

Pant. Ov. Desk

Family Rm.
17-4 x 15-4

Lav.

Laund.
W D

M.Bath

Triple Garage
23-4 x 33-4

A rches and gables contrast and complement in a recurring theme on this impressive French exterior. Note particularly the clerestory window over the foyer. Formal living and dining rooms open off the foyer, providing a large area for entertaining. A sun deck expands outdoor living possibilities, with access from the breakfast room and the family room. A fireplace in the family room spreads cheer throughout the informal area. To the left of the plan, the master wing includes a deluxe bath, two walk-in closets and a sitting room with access to a privacy deck. The second floor offers three bedrooms, two baths and a bonus room for future use.

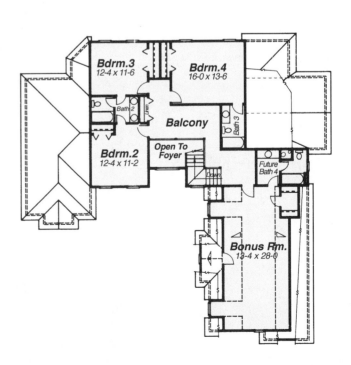

Bdrm.3
12-4 x 11-6

Bdrm.4
16-0 x 13-6

Bath 2

Balcony

Bath 3

Bdrm.2
12-4 x 11-2

Open To Foyer

Down

Future Bath 4

Bonus Rm.
13-4 x 28-0

DESIGN HPU040387

First Floor: 1,967 square feet
Second Floor: 1,014 square feet
Total: 2,981 square feet
Bonus Room: 607 square feet
Width: 66'-0" Depth: 65'-8"

DESIGN BY
©Jannis Vann & Associates, Inc.

Visual delight in this European-style home includes a high, hipped roof, multi-pane windows and a glass entry with a transom. Formal elegance is captured in the two-story living area featuring a warming fireplace and deck entry. The open space of the kitchen and breakfast area is well accented by a bay window. One family bedroom with a full bath resides on the first floor; the remaining two bedrooms and luxurious master suite are located on the second floor.

DESIGN HPU040388

First Floor: 1,268 square feet
Second Floor: 1,333 square feet
Total: 2,601 square feet
Width: 50'-0" Depth: 50'-4"

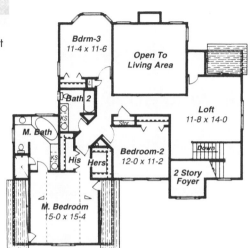

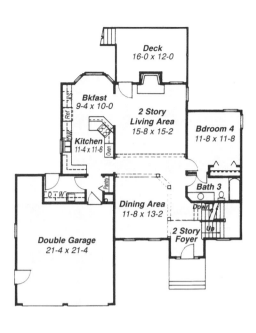

DESIGN BY
©Jannis Vann & Associates, Inc.

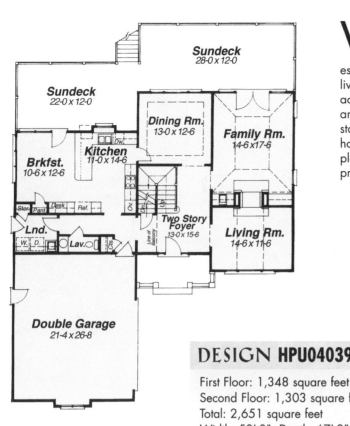

Sundeck
28-0 x 12-0

Sundeck
22-0 x 12-0

Dining Rm.
13-0 x 12-6

Family Rm.
14-6 x 17-6

Kitchen
11-0 x 14-6

Brkfst.
10-6 x 12-6

Stor. Pant Desk Ref.

Lnd.

W. D.   **Lav.**   Chs.

Two Story Foyer
13-0 x 15-6

Line of Balcony

Dn. Up

Ov.

Living Rm.
14-6 x 11-6

Double Garage
21-4 x 26-8

W ith the wonderful sun deck across the back of this home, you won't have to move to the Mediterranean to get your fill of sunshine. The stucco exterior, keystone arches and hipped roof add to the European flavor of the design. The living room opens off the two-story foyer, which also provides access to the family room and the dining room. A through-fireplace and built-ins separate and enhance the family and living rooms. A stairway in the two-story foyer leads to the second floor, which houses three family bedrooms and a master suite that's sure to please with a whirlpool tub, twin vanities, two closets and a small private balcony.

Bdrm. 4
13-0 x 10-2

Bdrm.3
11-6 x 12-6

Bath 2

Dn.

Open to Foyer

Bdrm.2
11-6 x 11-0

Balcony

Master Bdrm.
21-4 x 14-6

M.Bath
w/ Barrel Ceil.

DESIGN HPU040390

First Floor: 1,348 square feet
Second Floor: 1,303 square feet
Total: 2,651 square feet
Width: 50'-0"   Depth: 67'-0"

DESIGN BY
©Jannis Vann & Associates, Inc.

Ornate European exterior detailing creates a unique and timeless design in this fabulous French country classic home. Inside the house are open formal areas for living and dining. The kitchen, featuring a cooktop/utility island and built-in pantry, opens into the breakfast area and a cozy keeping den. The enormous walk-in closet in the master retreat allows access from both the bedroom and the bath. The bath itself offers the convenience of dual vanities. Upstairs, a balcony that overlooks the gathering room leads to two additional suites and a bonus room over the garage. A private courtyard at the rear of the house adds privacy to family outdoor living.

DESIGN HPU040391

First Floor: 2,061 square feet
Second Floor: 695 square feet
Total: 2,756 square feet
Bonus Room: 377 square feet
Width: 55'-0" Depth: 79'-10"

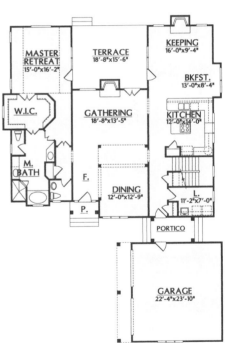

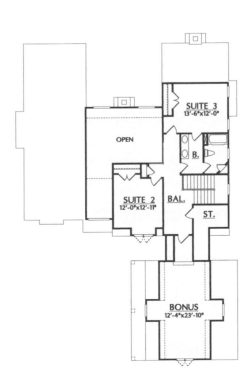

DESIGN BY
©Living Concepts Home Planning

315

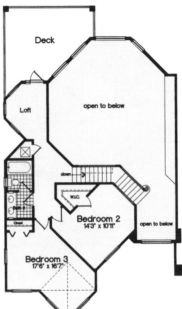

Covered Patio
17'10" x 37'0"

Master Suite
19'3" x 18'6"

Family Room
25'-0" x 21'0"

Nook
11'1" x 10'7"

Master Bath

Kitchen
14'2" x 14'8"

W.I.C.

Dining Room
12'3" x 14'3"

Foyer

Living Room
13'0" x 12'6"

Entry

1/2 Bath

Utility

W

D

2 Car Garage
19'3" x 19'3"

Deck

Loft

open to below

down

W.I.C.

Bath 2

Closet

Bedroom 2
14'3" x 10'11"

open to below

Bedroom 3
17'6" x 16'7"

DESIGN BY
©Home Design Services, Inc.

DESIGN **HPU040392**

First Floor: 2,051 square feet
Second Floor: 749 square feet
Total: 2,800 square feet
Width: 50'-0" Depth: 74'-0"

At only 50 feet in width, this fabulous design will fit anywhere! From the moment you enter the home from the foyer, this floor plan explodes in every direction with huge living spaces. Flanking the foyer are the living and dining rooms, and the visual impact of the staircase is breathtaking. Two-story ceilings adorn the huge family room with double-stacked glass walls. Sunlight floods the breakfast nook, and the kitchen is a gourmet's dream, complete with cooking island and loads of overhead cabinets. Tray ceilings grace the owners suite, which also offers a well-designed private bath. Here, a large soaking tub, doorless shower, private toilet chamber and a huge walk-in closet are sure to please. Upstairs, two oversized bedrooms and a loft space—perfect for the home computer—share a full bath.

J.N. HANSEN S.D.G.

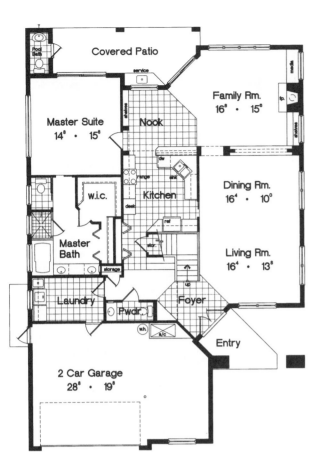

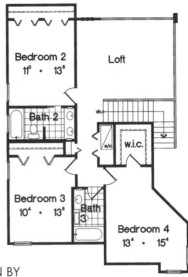

DESIGN BY
©Home Design Services, Inc.

The excitement begins upon entering the foyer of this home, where an impressive staircase is its focal point. From there you view the formal spaces of the living and dining room with vaulted ceilings. Passing through an archway, you enter the family room with its impressive media/fireplace wall. Just off the nook is a sliding glass door to the covered patio, where a wet bar can be found as well as a pool bath. The kitchen is a gourmet's dream, with loads of pantry storage and a planning desk. A built-in wall of shelves and arches just off the nook welcome you to the master wing. The suite is generously sized and has a wonderful wall of high transom glass, as well as sliding glass doors to the patio. The second floor is impressive with three large bedrooms, two of which share a bath, and one bedroom with a private bath.

DESIGN HPU040393

First Floor: 1,844 square feet
Second Floor: 1,017 square feet
Total: 2,861 square feet
Width: 45'-0" Depth: 67'-8"

DESIGN HPU040395

Square Footage: 2,718
Width: 63'-8" Depth: 64'-4"

DESIGN BY
©Home Design Services, Inc.

H ere's an exciting contemporary design that's more than just a pretty face. A tiled foyer leads to an open family room with a volume ceiling and a wall of glass that brings in a sense of the outdoors. The master wing provides a guest suite, complete with its own full bath. An oversized spa-style tub highlights the homeowner's retreat, which includes a generous walk-in closet, a soaking tub enclosed in a curved wall of glass block, and a tray ceiling in the bedroom. The kitchen features a walk-in pantry and a mitered-glass nook for casual meals. Three secondary bedrooms share a cabana bath, which opens to the covered patio.

A walkout basement adds to the total living space of this one-of-a-kind hillside home. The entry is flanked by the formal living and dining rooms and then opens to a massive great room with a covered porch beyond. The kitchen and breakfast nook are open to the great room; the kitchen features an island work center. Two family bedrooms and a den are on the left side of the plan. Bedroom 3 has a private bath. The den is a focal point, seen through arches and double doors from the great room. The master suite is on the right side and has a walk-in closet, porch access and sumptuous bath.

DESIGN HPU040394

Square Footage: 2,742
Width: 66'-8" Depth: 67'-0"

DESIGN BY
©Home Design Services, Inc.

fireplace

Family Room
vaulted ceiling
16⁰ · 19⁴

Covered Patio

wet bar

Master Bedroom
19⁰ · 18⁰

Breakfast

dw

Bedroom 3
volume ceiling
12⁴ · 11⁰

Kitchen

pantry

ref

Living Room
volume ceiling
14⁴ · 13⁶

Bath

linen

w.i.c.

w.i.c.

desk

Bath

lin

desk

Dining
volume ceiling
10⁸ · 13⁰

Foyer

Study
volume ceiling
10⁰ · 14⁶

Bath

Bedroom 4
volume ceiling
11⁰ · 11⁰

Utility

w

d

down

Entry

up

Double Garage

DESIGN BY
©Home Design Services, Inc.

ac

Bonus
11⁰ · 20⁴

DESIGN HPU040396

Square Footage: 2,551
Bonus Room: 287 square feet
Width: 69'-8" Depth: 71'-4"

Shutters and multi-pane windows dress up the exterior of this lovely stucco home. Formal and informal areas flow easily, beginning with the dining room sized to accommodate large parties and function with the adjacent living room. A gourmet kitchen is complete with a walk-in pantry and a cozy breakfast nook. Double doors lead to the spacious master suite. The lavish master bath features His and Hers walk-in closets, a tub framed by a columned archway, and an oversized shower. Off the angular hallway are two bedrooms that share a Pullman-style bath and a study desk. A bonus room over the garage provides additional space.

319

DESIGN HPU040398

Square Footage: 2,962
Width: 70'-0" Depth: 76'-0"

DESIGN BY
©Home Design Services, Inc.

Enter the formal foyer of this home and you are greeted with a traditional split living-room/dining-room layout. But the family room is where the real living takes place. It expands onto the outdoor living space, which features a summer kitchen. The ultimate master suite contains coffered ceilings, a "boomerang" vanity and angular mirrors that reflect the bayed soaking tub and shower. Efficient use of space creates a huge closet with little dead center space.

The angles in this home create unlimited views and spaces that appear larger. Majestic columns of brick add warmth to a striking elevation. Inside, the foyer commands special perspective on living areas including the living room, dining room and den. The island kitchen serves the breakfast nook and the family room. A large pantry provides ample space for food storage. Nearby, in the owners suite, mitered glass and a private bath set the tone for simple luxury. Two secondary bedrooms share privacy and quiet at the front of the house. The den may also convert to a fourth bedroom, if desired.

DESIGN HPU040397

Square Footage: 2,597
Width: 96'-6" Depth: 50'-0"

DESIGN BY
©Home Design Services, Inc.

DESIGN BY
©Home Design Services, Inc.

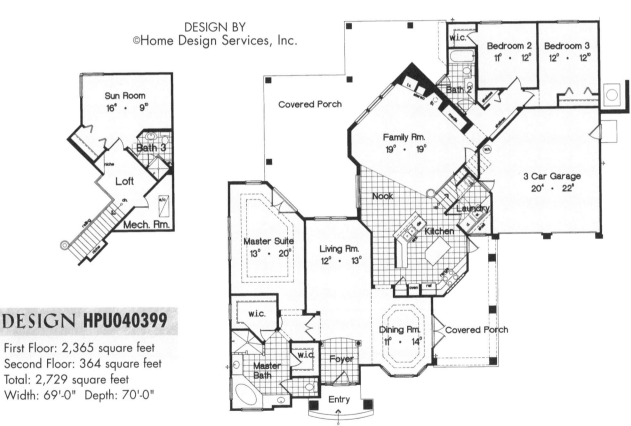

Sun Room
16⁸ · 9¹⁰

Bath 3

niche

Loft

cl.

Mech. Rm.

a/c

Covered Porch

w.i.c.

Bedroom 2
11⁰ · 12⁰

Bedroom 3
12⁰ · 12⁰

Bath 2

Family Rm.
19⁰ · 19⁰

3 Car Garage
20⁴ · 22⁸

Nook

Laundry

Kitchen

Master Suite
13⁰ · 20⁰

Living Rm.
12⁰ · 13⁰

oven ref

w.i.c.

w.i.c.

Foyer

Dining Rm.
11⁰ · 14⁰

Covered Porch

Master Bath

Entry

up

DESIGN HPU040399

First Floor: 2,365 square feet
Second Floor: 364 square feet
Total: 2,729 square feet
Width: 69'-0" Depth: 70'-0"

The columned foyer welcomes you into a series of spaces that reach out in all directions. The living room has a spectacular view of the huge covered patio area that's perfect for summer entertaining. The dining room has a tray ceiling and French doors that lead to a covered porch. A secluded owners suite affords great views through French doors and also has a tray ceiling. The private master bath is complete with His and Hers walk-in closets and a soaking tub. The family wing combines an island kitchen, nook and family gathering space, with the built-in media/fireplace wall the center of attention. Two secondary bedrooms share a bath. A staircase overlooking the family room takes you up to the sun room complete with a full bath, making this a very desirable kids' space.

DESIGN HPU040401

Square Footage: 2,656
Width: 92'-0" Depth: 69'-0"

DESIGN BY
©Home Design Services, Inc.

A graceful design sets this charming home apart from the ordinary and transcends the commonplace. From the foyer, the dining room branches off the sunny living room, setting a lovely backdrop for entertaining. Casual living is the focus in the oversized family room, where sliding doors open to the patio and the eat-in, gourmet kitchen is open for easy conversation. Two family bedrooms and a cabana bath are just off the family room. The master suite has a cozy fireplace in the sitting area, twin closets and a compartmented bath. A large covered patio adds to the living area.

Quoins and keystone accents lend a French country flavor to this stucco exterior, but brick contrasts and a glass-paneled entry give it a fresh face. A tiled foyer leads to a gracefully curved gallery hall. The heart of the plan is the vaulted living room, which overlooks the covered patio and rear grounds, but friends may want to gather in the family room, where a centered fireplace offers cozy niches. A gourmet kitchen is designed to handle casual meals as well as planned occasions, with a service kitchen on the patio for outdoor events.

DESIGN HPU040400

Square Footage: 2,931
Width: 70'-8" Depth: 83'-0"

DESIGN BY
©Home Design Services, Inc.

DESIGN HPU040402

Square Footage: 2,636
Width: 68'-8" Depth: 76'-0"

A towering entry welcomes you to the foyer of this soaring contemporary design. Interior glass walls give openness to the den/study, and mirror the arches to the formal dining room. The sunken living room has a bayed window wall, which views the patio. The master-suite wing also holds the den/study, which can access the powder room/patio bath. Sliding glass doors from the master suite access the patio. The master bath features dual closets, a sunken vanity/bath area and a doorless shower. The family wing holds the gourmet kitchen, nook and family room with a fireplace.

Floor plan labels:

- summer kitchen
- Family Room 18⁸ • 16⁴ volume ceiling
- fireplace
- Covered Patio
- Breakfast volume ceiling
- Master Bedroom 18⁰ • 15⁰ volume ceiling
- Living Room 16² • 16⁰ volume ceiling
- Bath
- coats
- ref
- dw
- Kitchen
- bar
- pan
- Bedroom 2 11¹⁰ • 11⁰ volume ceiling
- w.i.c.
- w.i.c.
- down
- down
- dn
- linen
- w.i.c.
- Bath
- Bath
- lin
- sh
- up
- Den Study 14⁰ • 11² volume ceiling
- Foyer
- Dining 13⁰ • 12⁰ volume ceiling
- Bedroom 3 13⁰ • 11⁰ volume ceiling
- Utility
- w
- d
- wh
- ac
- Entry
- up
- ac
- Double Garage

DESIGN BY
©Home Design Services, Inc.

DESIGN HPU040403

First Floor: 2,249 square feet
Second Floor: 620 square feet
Total: 2,869 square feet
Bonus Room: 308 square feet
Width: 69'-6" Depth: 52'-0"

DESIGN BY
Donald A. Gardner Architects, Inc.

An impressive two-story entrance welcomes you to this stately home. Massive chimneys and pillars and varying rooflines add interest to the stucco exterior. The foyer, lighted by a clerestory window, opens to the formal living and dining room. The living room—which could also serve as a study—features a fireplace, as does the family room. Both rooms access the patio. The L-shaped island kitchen opens to a bay-windowed breakfast nook, which is echoed by the sitting area in the master suite. A room next to the kitchen could serve as a bedroom or a home office. The second floor contains two family bedrooms plus a bonus room for future expansion.

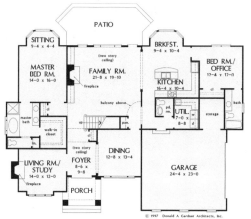

This stucco home contrasts gently curved arches with gables, and uses large multi-pane windows to flood the interior with natural light. Square pillars form an impressive entry, leading to a two-story foyer. The living room is set apart from the informal area of the house, and could serve as a cozy study instead. The back patio can be reached from both the breakfast nook and the family room, which features a cathedral ceiling and a fireplace. The owners suite offers two walk-in closets and a bath with twin vanities, garden tub and separate shower.

DESIGN HPU040404

First Floor: 1,904 square feet
Second Floor: 645 square feet
Total: 2,549 square feet
Bonus Room: 434 square feet
Width: 71'-2" Depth: 45'-8"

DESIGN BY
Donald A. Gardner Architects, Inc.

Square columns flank the entry to this contemporary three-bedroom home. The two-story great room provides a fireplace and a wall of windows. A formal dining room, located at the front of the plan, offers a tray ceiling and works well with the kitchen. A bayed den is available for quiet study. The owners suite is located on the first floor for privacy and features many amenities. Upstairs, two family bedrooms share a full bath.

DESIGN HPU040405

First Floor: 1,818 square feet
Second Floor: 698 square feet
Total: 2,516 square feet
Width: 50'-0"   Depth: 53'-0"

DESIGN BY
©Alan Mascord Design Associates, Inc.

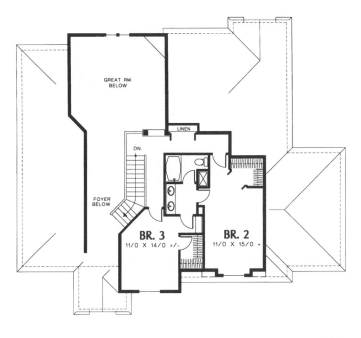

DESIGN HPU040407

Square Footage: 2,529
Width: 78'-2" Depth: 50'-2"

DESIGN BY
©R.L. Pfotenhauer

This charming home attracts notice with a beautiful facade including corner quoins, a symmetrical design and a lovely roofline. The floor plan provides comfortable livability. A central great room connects to the breakfast room and galley-style kitchen. A formal dining room, just off the foyer, has a huge wall of windows for elegant dining. A complementary room to the left of the foyer serves as a den or guest bedroom as needed. The owners bedroom features a tray ceiling and wonderfully appointed bath. A family bedroom to the front of the plan has a vaulted ceiling. The plan is completed by a screened porch in the rear.

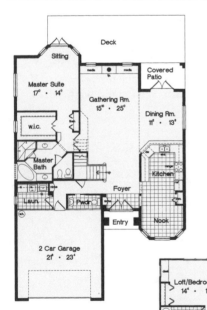

DESIGN HPU040406

First Floor: 1,698 square feet
Second Floor: 848 square feet
Total: 2,546 square feet
Width: 44'-0" Depth: 64'-8"

DESIGN BY
©Home Design Services, Inc.

The gathering room is the heart of this design, and all other spaces move from its core. The large kitchen with a sunny, bayed nook is bathed in light through walls of glass, while the formal dining room has French doors that open onto a private patio. The hub of family activity is the gathering room. It comes complete with a fireplace media wall, which soars two stories with niches and glass transoms. The master suite features a bay-windowed sitting area with a view to the deck area. The bath boasts loads of closet space, and His and Hers vanities flank a soaking tub and shower.

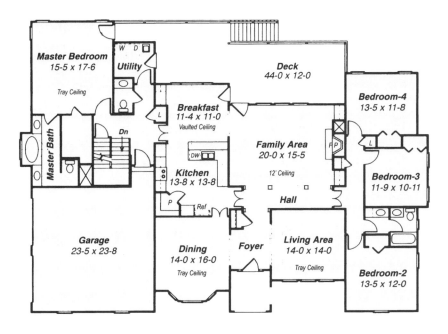

Master Bedroom
15-5 x 17-6

Tray Ceiling

W   D

Utility

Master Bath

Dn

Deck
44-0 x 12-0

Breakfast
11-4 x 11-0

Vaulted Ceiling

L

DW

Kitchen
13-8 x 13-8

P   Ref

Garage
23-5 x 23-8

Family Area
20-0 x 15-5

12' Ceiling

Hall

Bedroom-4
13-5 x 11-8

L

Bedroom-3
11-9 x 10-11

Dining
14-0 x 16-0

Tray Ceiling

Foyer

Living Area
14-0 x 14-0

Tray Ceiling

Bedroom-2
13-5 x 12-0

Inside this stylish stucco home, elegant columns separate front-facing, formal living and dining areas from rear-facing, informal living areas. The family room features a twelve-foot ceiling, a fireplace and a door leading to an expansive deck. The kitchen, breakfast room and family room flow together for entertaining ease. Bedrooms are separated for privacy. The secondary bedrooms share a full bath. The secluded master suite features a tray ceiling, large walk-in closet and bumped-out tub with dual vanities.

DESIGN HPU040408

Square Footage: 2,720
Width: 78'-0" Depth: 56'-0"

DESIGN BY
©Jannis Vann & Associates, Inc.

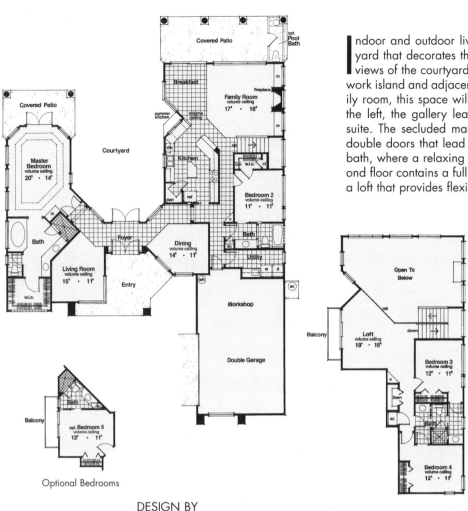

Covered Patio

opt. Pool Bath

Breakfast

Family Room
volume ceiling
17⁴ · 16⁰

fireplace

Covered Patio

summer kitchen

Master Bedroom
volume ceiling
20⁰ · 14⁰

Courtyard

volume ceiling

Kitchen

dw

Bedroom 2
volume ceiling
11⁴ · 11⁰

pan

ref

Bath

Foyer

Dining
volume ceiling
14⁰ · 11⁰

Bath

Utility

Living Room
volume ceiling
15⁴ · 11⁰

w.i.c.

Entry

wh

w d

Workshop

Double Garage

ac

Open To Below

Balcony

Loft
volume ceiling
18⁴ · 16⁰

rail

down

Bedroom 3
volume ceiling
12⁴ · 11⁰

linen

Bath

Bedroom 4
volume ceiling
12⁴ · 11⁰

Bath

Balcony

opt. Bedroom 5
volume ceiling
13⁰ · 11⁰

Optional Bedrooms

DESIGN BY
©Home Design Services, Inc.

Indoor and outdoor living are enhanced by the beautiful court-yard that decorates the center of this home. A gallery provides views of the courtyard and leads to a kitchen featuring a center work island and adjacent breakfast room. Combined with the family room, this space will be a favorite for informal gatherings. To the left, the gallery leads to the formal living room and master suite. The secluded master bedroom features a tray ceiling and double doors that lead to a covered patio. Retreat to the master bath, where a relaxing tub awaits to pamper and enjoy. The second floor contains a full bath shared by two family bedrooms and a loft that provides flexible space for an additional bedroom.

DESIGN HPU040409

First Floor: 2,254 square feet
Second Floor: 608 square feet
Total: 2,862 square feet
Width: 66'-0" Depth: 78'-10"

J.N. HANSEN

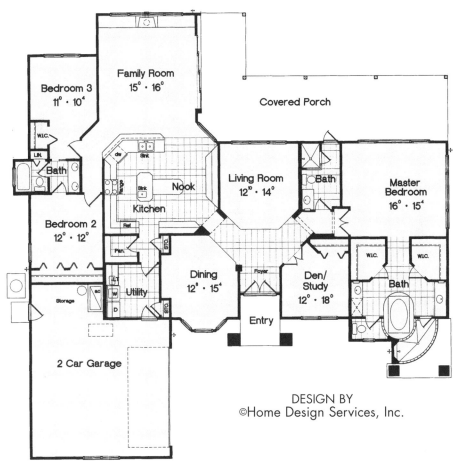

Bedroom 3
11⁰ · 10⁴

Family Room
15⁰ · 16⁰

Covered Porch

W.I.C.

Bath

Nook

Kitchen

Living Room
12¹⁰ · 14⁰

Bath

Master Bedroom
16⁰ · 15⁴

Bedroom 2
12⁰ · 12⁰

Pan.

W.I.C.

W.I.C.

Utility

Dining
12⁸ · 15⁴

Foyer

Den/Study
12⁰ · 18⁰

Bath

Storage

Entry

2 Car Garage

DESIGN BY
©Home Design Services, Inc.

rand Palladian windows create a classic look for this sensational stucco home. A magnificent view from the living room provides unlimited vistas of the rear grounds through a wall of glass, with the nearby dining room completing the formal area. The kitchen, breakfast nook and family room comprise the family wing, coming together to create the perfect place for casual gatherings. Two secondary bedrooms share a bath and provide complete privacy to the master suite, located on the opposite side of the plan. The master bedroom sets the mood for relaxation, and the lavish master bath pampers with a sumptuous soaking tub flanked by a step-down shower and compartmented toilet. Bonus space may be completed at a later date to accommodate additional space requirements.

DESIGN HPU040411

Square Footage: 2,530
Width: 71'-10"   Depth: 72'-8"

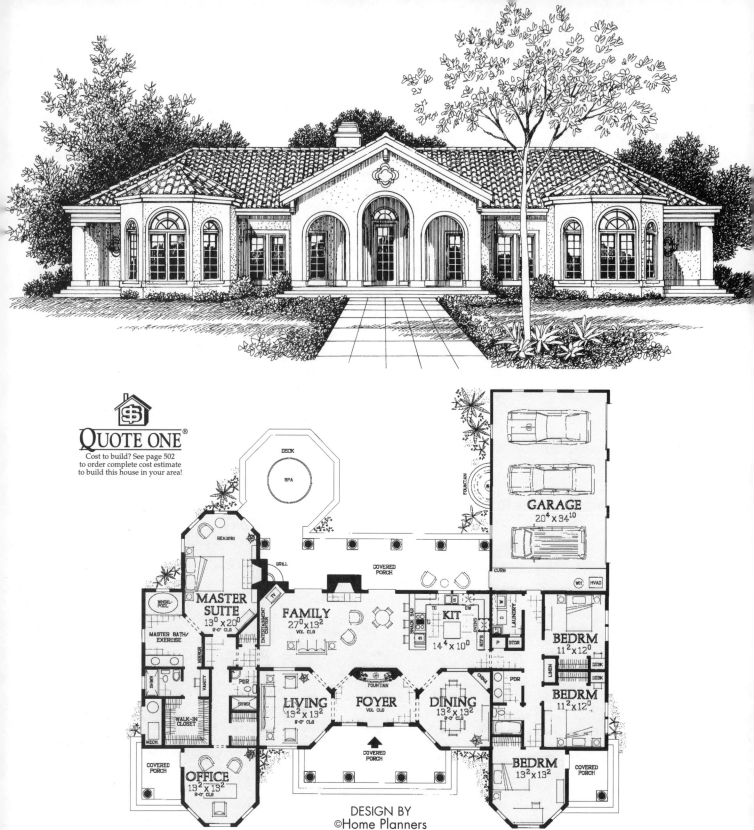

DESIGN BY
©Home Planners

B esides great curb appeal, this home has a wonderful floor plan. The foyer features a fountain that greets visitors and leads to a formal dining room on the right and a living room
on the left. A large family room at the rear has a built-in entertainment center and a fireplace. The U-shaped kitchen is perfectly located for servicing all living and dining areas. To the
right of the plan, away from the central entertaining spaces, are three family bedrooms sharing
a full bath. On the left side, with solitude and comfort for the owners suite are a large sitting
area, an office and an amenity-filled bath. Outside the owners suite is a deck with a spa.

DESIGN HPU040412

Square Footage: 2,831
Width: 84'-0" Depth: 77'-0"

MASTER
SUITE
24² x 12⁰
SITTING
AREA
SLOPED CEILING

COVERED
ARBOR

GARAGE
24² x 24²

WALK-IN
CLOSET

DRY
WALL

LINEN

OPEN
COURTYARD

UTILITY
SINK

LAUNDRY
ROOM

W   D

BATH

REFG

BEDRM
10⁴ x 11¹⁰
VOL CLG

PLANT SHELF ABV

COUNTRY
KIT
18⁸ x 17⁴
SLOPED CLG

ISLAND
SNACK BAR

COVERED
PORCH

BEDRM
10⁴ x 11⁸
VOL CLG

PLANT SHELF ABV

FAMILY-GREAT
RM
24¹⁰ x 14⁰
SLOPED CLG

PANTRY

COVERED
PORCH

PANTRY   OVEN

DINING
RM
18⁸ x 11⁸
SLOPED CEILING

OFFICE-
DEN
9⁸ x 11⁶
VOL CLG

POWDER
ROOM

RAISED HEARTH

MEDIA   MEDIA

ENTRY
ART GALLERY
SLOPED CLG

COVERED
PORCH

DESIGN BY
©Home Planners

QUOTE ONE®
Cost to build? See page 502
to order complete cost estimate
to build this house in your area!

Exposed rafter tails, arched porch detailing, massive paneled front doors and stucco exterior walls enhance the western character of this U-shaped ranch house. Double doors open to a spacious, slope-ceilinged art gallery. The quiet sleeping zone is comprised of an entire wing. The extra room at the front of this wing may be used for a den or an office. The family dining and kitchen activities are located at the opposite end of the plan. Indoor-outdoor living relationships are outstanding. The large, open courtyard is akin to the fabled Greek atrium. It is accessible from each of the zones and functions with a covered arbor, which looks out over the rear landscape. The master suite has a generous sitting area, a walk-in closet, twin lavatories, a whirlpool tub and a stall shower.

DESIGN HPU040413

Square Footage: 2,539
Width: 75'-2"   Depth: 68'-8"

L

DESIGN BY
©Home Planners

QUOTE ONE®
Cost to build? See page 502
to order complete cost estimate
to build this house in your area!

PRIVACY WALL

SPA

PRIVACY WALL

PRIVATE
PATIO

ENTERTAINMENT
PATIO

MASTER
SUITE
17⁰ x 13¹⁰
10'-0" CLG

MASTER
BATH

HVAC

SHWR.

BEDRM
12⁶ x 10⁰
10'-0" CLG

KIT
ISLAND
VEG SINK
11⁶ x 14⁸

MORNING
RM
13⁰ x 16⁰
14'-0" CLG

DN

SUNKEN
FAMILY
RM
18⁰ x 12⁶
VOL CLG

SLOPING

MEDIA CENTER

WALK-IN
CLOSET

ARCHWAY

BATH

PANTRY
OVN

ARCHED COLONNADE

DN

OFFICE-
DEN
12² x 12⁰

BEDRM
12⁶ x 10⁰
10'-0" CLG

WET BAR

HVAC
BATH

LINEN

LAUNDRY ROOM

WH

UTILITY
SINK

D W

BROOM
CLOSET

ARCHED COLONNADE

DINING
RM
11¹⁰ x 12⁰
12'-0" CLG

FOYER
14'-0" CLG

LIVING
RM
14⁰ x 12¹⁰
14'-0" CLG

GARAGE
23¹⁰ x 21⁶

CURB

GUEST
RM
12⁰ x 10²
12'-0" CLG

COVERED
PORCH

DESIGN HPU040414

Square Footage: 2,861
Width: 93'-4" Depth: 66'-6"

L

Double columns and an arched entry create a grand entrance to this elegant one-story home. Inside, arched colonnades add grace and definition to the formal living and dining rooms, as well as the family room. The master suite occupies a separate wing, providing a private retreat. Treat yourself to luxury in the master bath, which includes a bumped-out whirlpool tub, a separate shower and twin vanities. An office/den located nearby easily converts to a nursery. A snack bar provides space for quick meals and separates the island kitchen from the bay-windowed morning room. Three additional bedrooms—one a guest room with an adjacent bath—share two baths.

TIMELESS ELEGANCE

Graceful designs with a new perspective

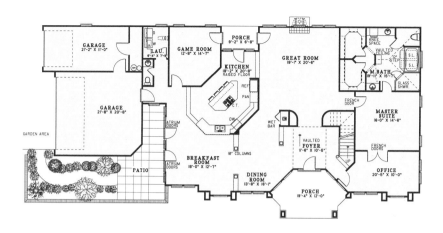

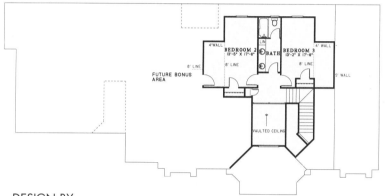

DESIGN BY
©Michael E. Nelson,
Nelson Design Group, LLC

This three-bedroom house was designed to fulfill a passion for windows and columns. Inside, the foyer streams with light from the sunburst transom over the door. To the right is an office with French-door access to the master suite. A sumptuous bath adorns the master suite, complete with His and Hers closets, a glass shower, a garden tub with two skylights and twin-vanity sinks. The great room features a fireplace and views of the rear yard. Columns lend elegant detail to the dining room and separate it from the nearby breakfast room. Beautiful atrium doors in the breakfast room allow views of the side patio. The kitchen and game room feature access to a rear porch, perfect for an outdoor grill. Two bedrooms share a full bath on the second level. Expansion is possible on the second floor. Please specify basement, crawlspace or slab foundation when ordering.

DESIGN HPU040415

First Floor: 2,634 square feet
Second Floor: 757 square feet
Total: 3,391 square feet
Width: 95'-0" Depth: 47'-9"

QUOTE ONE®

Cost to build? See page 502
to order complete cost estimate
to build this house in your area!

lanai

leisure
23'-0" x 17'-8"
12'-6" flat clg.

fireplace   built ins

lanai
30'-0" x 10'-0"

nook
10'-8" x 10'-8"
12' step clg.

grill

kitchen

bedroom
13'-4" x 13'-8"
9'-4" flat clg.

wetbar

master
suite
17'-0" x 20'-4"
14' flat clg.

living
15'-0" x 17'-2"
14' flat clg.

gallery

am kitchen

2 view fireplace

dining
17'-0" x 13'-0"
14' flat clg.

his

utility

hers

bedroom
13'-4" x 12'-0"
9'-4" flat clg.

foyer

gallery

entry

planter

study
13'-0" x 15'-8"
14' vault clg.

garage
23'-4" x 29'-8"

© 1990 The Sater Group, Inc.

DESIGN HPU040416

Square Footage: 3,477
Width: 95'-0" Depth: 88'-8"

L

Make dreams come true with this fine sunny design. An octagonal study provides a nice focal point both inside and outside. The living areas remain open to each other and access outdoor areas. A wet bar makes entertaining a breeze, especially with a window pass-through to a grill area on the lanai. The kitchen enjoys shared space with a lovely breakfast nook and a bright leisure room. Two bedrooms are located near the family living center. In the master bedroom suite, luxury abounds with a two-way fireplace, a morning kitchen, two walk-in closets and a compartmented bath. Another full bath accommodates a pool area.

DESIGN BY
©The Sater Design Collection

DESIGN HPU040417

Square Footage: 3,273
Width: 71'-4"
Depth: 77'-0"

This house is in a class all its own. The entry gives way to an impressive living room with a dining room and study radiating from it. The master bedroom suite rests to one side of the plan and includes His and Hers walk-in closets and a luxury bath. A second full bath leads from the sitting area to the outdoors. At the other side of the house, informal living areas open with a kitchen, a breakfast nook and a family leisure area. Two bedrooms here share a full bath and will provide ample space for children or guests.

DESIGN BY
©The Sater Design Collection

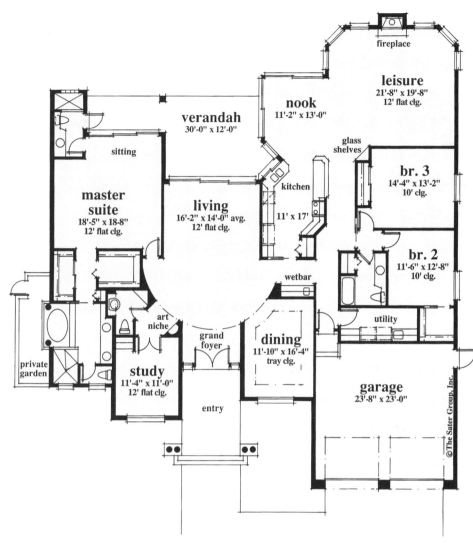

fireplace

leisure
21'-8" x 19'-8"
12' flat clg.

nook
11'-2" x 13'-0"

verandah
30'-0" x 12'-0"

glass shelves

br. 3
14'-4" x 13'-2"
10' clg.

sitting

kitchen

11' x 17'

master suite
18'-5" x 18'-8"
12' flat clg.

living
16'-2" x 14'-0" avg.
12' flat clg.

br. 2
11'-6" x 12'-8"
10' clg.

wetbar

utility

private garden

art niche

study
11'-4" x 11'-0"
12' flat clg.

grand foyer

dining
11'-10" x 16'-4"
tray clg.

garage
23'-8" x 23'-0"

entry

©The Sater Group, Inc.

DESIGN BY
©The Sater Design Collection

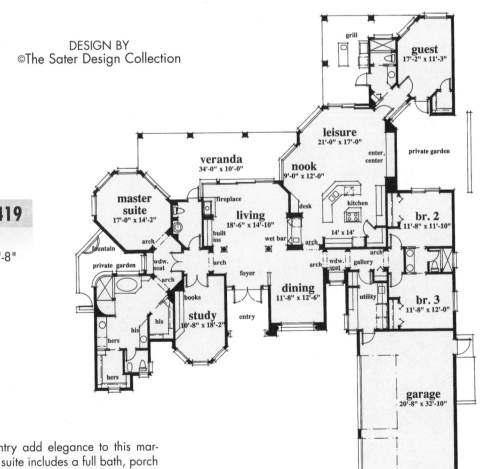

DESIGN HPU040419

Square Footage: 3,265
Width: 80'-0" Depth: 103'-8"

A turret study and a raised entry add elegance to this marvelous stucco home. A guest suite includes a full bath, porch access and a private garden entry, making it perfect for use as an in-law suite. Secondary bedrooms share a full bath. The owners suite has a foyer with a window seat overlooking another private garden and fountain area; the private owners bath holds dual closets, a garden tub and a walk-in shower with curved glass.

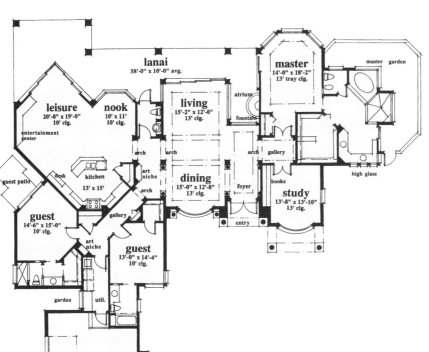

DESIGN HPU040420

Square Footage: 3,244
Width: 90'-0" Depth: 105'-0"

A high, hipped roof and contemporary fanlight windows set the tone for this elegant plan. The grand foyer opens to the formal dining and living rooms that are set apart with arches, highlighted with art niches and framed with walls of windows. Featuring a gourmet kitchen, breakfast nook and leisure room with a built-in entertainment center, the living area has full view of and access to the lanai. Secondary bedrooms are privately situated through a gallery hall, and both include private baths and walk-in closets. The main wing houses a full study and an owners suite with a private garden.

DESIGN BY
©The Sater Design Collection

Sand-finished stucco, distinctive columns and oversized circle-top windows grace this luxurious three-bedroom home. A sunken living room features a two-sided gas fireplace that it shares with the formal dining room. The family room is also sunken and shares a two-sided fireplace with an indoor spa and a glazed roof overhead. Two secondary bedrooms and a master suite are on the second floor. The master suite enjoys a through-fireplace between the bath and the bedroom.

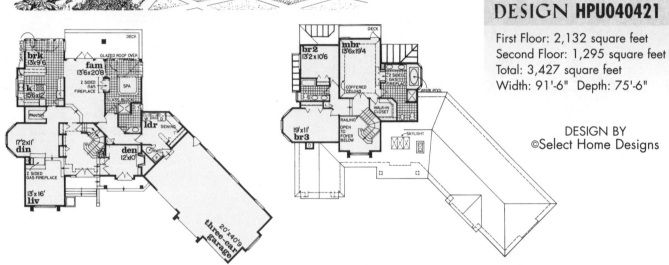

DESIGN HPU040421

First Floor: 2,132 square feet
Second Floor: 1,295 square feet
Total: 3,427 square feet
Width: 91'-6" Depth: 75'-6"

DESIGN BY
©Select Home Designs

This award-winning design has been recognized for its innovative use of space while continuing to keep family living areas combined for maximum enjoyment. The formal spaces separate the master suite and den/study from family space. The master retreat contains a master bath with His and Hers vanities, a private toilet room and walk-in closet. The perfect touch in this two-story design is the placement of two bedrooms downstairs with two extra bedrooms on the second floor.

DESIGN BY
©Home Design Services, Inc.

DESIGN HPU040422

First Floor: 2,624 square feet
Second Floor: 540 square feet
Total: 3,164 square feet
Width: 66'-0" Depth: 83'-0"

Varying rooflines, arches and corner quoins adorn the facade of this magnificent home. A porte cochere creates a stunning prelude to the double-door entry. A wet bar serves the sunken living room and overlooks the pool area. The dining room has a tray ceiling and is located near the gourmet kitchen with its preparation island and angled counter. A guest room opens off the living room. The generous family room, warmed by a fireplace, opens to the screened patio. The master bedroom has a sitting room and a fireplace that's set into an angled wall. Its luxurious bath includes a step-up tub. Upstairs, two bedrooms share the oversized balcony and nearby observation room.

DESIGN HPU040423

First Floor: 2,669 square feet
Second Floor: 621 square feet
Total: 3,290 square feet
Width: 78'-0" Depth: 84'-6"

DESIGN BY
©Home Design Services, Inc.

339

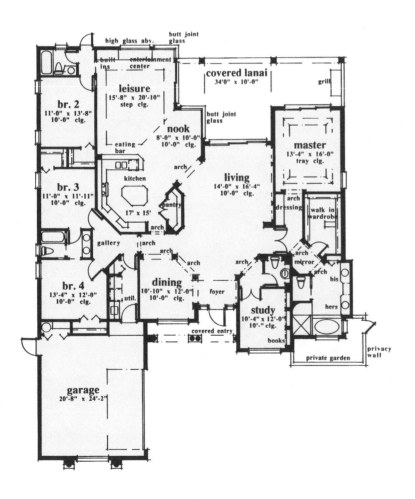

Filled with luxury and special amenities, this stucco beauty offers the best in upscale living. A recessed entry opens to the formal areas: a living room and dining room separated by columns and an arch. For more casual times, look to the leisure room near the island kitchen and nook. A covered lanai lies just outside the living room and the leisure room. The master suite is separated from the three family bedrooms. It contains outstanding closet space and a fine bath with a garden tub. A nearby study has the use of a half-bath. Note that Bedroom 2 has a private bath.

DESIGN HPU040424

Square Footage: 3,036
Width: 63'-10" Depth: 84'-0"

DESIGN BY
©The Sater Design Collection

340

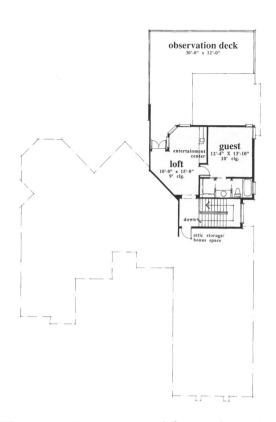

observation deck
30'-0" x 12'-0"

guest
12'-4" X 13'-10"
10' clg.

entertainment center

loft
10'-0" x 15'-0"
9' clg.

down

attic storage/
bonus space

lanai
30'-0" x 10'-0"

outdoor kitchen

leisure
15'-10" x 18'-0"
stepped clg.

fireplace

lanai
31'-0" x 10'-0"

nook
8' x 10'
10' clg.

dry bar

master
17'-0" x 14'-9"
13'-4" tray clg.

living
15'-0" x 15'-0"
14'-4" clg.

kitchen

12' x 14'

w.i.c.

arch

arch

up

stor.

mir.

nooks

dining
11'-0" x 14'-0"
15'-0" tray clg.

arch

study
10' x 11
13'-4" clg.

foyer

arch

guest
12'-0" x 11'-0"
10' clg.

his   hers

entry

master garden

glass
shwr.

planter

planter

util.

storage

garage
21'-0" x 28'-6"

Two guest suites—one on each floor—enhance the interior of this magnificent stucco home. A grand entrance provides passage to a foyer that opens to the study on the left, the formal dining room on the right and the formal living room straight ahead. The casual living area combines a kitchen with an island cooktop, a sun-filled breakfast nook and a spacious leisure room. Arched openings lead into the owners bedroom and a lavish bath that enjoys a private garden. The second-floor guest suite includes a loft and a large observation deck.

DESIGN HPU040425

First Floor: 2,894 square feet
Second Floor: 568 square feet
Total: 3,462 square feet
Width: 67'-0" Depth: 102'-0"

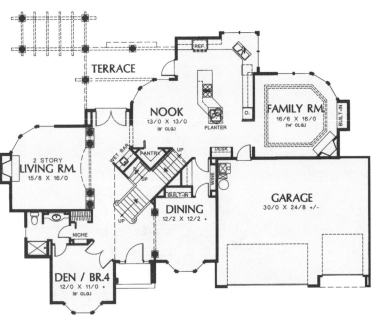

This stucco exterior with shutters and keystone lintels over the entry and windows lends a fresh European charm to this four-bedroom home. A great area for formal entertaining, the two-story living room pleases with its columns, large windows and fireplace. A wet bar furthers the ambience here. Double doors open to a terrace. Informal living takes off in the breakfast nook, kitchen and family room. The upstairs master suite enjoys lots of privacy and a luxurious bath with twin-vanity sinks, a walk-in closet, spa tub and separate shower. The second-floor stairway is exquisite, with three flights joining into one landing and space for plants.

DESIGN HPU040426

First Floor: 1,920 square feet
Second Floor: 1,552 square feet
Total: 3,472 square feet
Bonus Room: 252 square feet
Width: 72'-0" Depth: 55'-0"

L

DESIGN BY
©Alan Mascord Design
Associates, Inc.

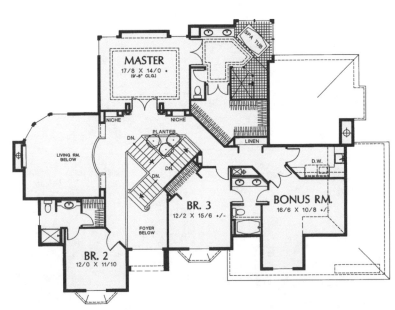

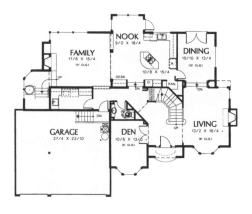

If you have a lot that slopes slightly to the front, this design will accommodate with a garage that is sunken from the main house. The entry is opulent and inviting and opens to a den with a bay window on the left and a formal living room with a fireplace on the right. The family room connects directly to the kitchen and features another fireplace. Three family bedrooms join the master suite on the second floor.

DESIGN HPU040428

First Floor: 1,740 square feet
Second Floor: 1,477 square feet
Total: 3,217 square feet
Bonus Room: 382 square feet
Width: 63'-0" Depth: 52'-0"

DESIGN BY
©Alan Mascord Design
Associates, Inc.

Formal entertaining occurs in the front of this home where the living room, dining room, butler's pantry and powder room are located, while the family enjoys the den and vaulted family room at the rear. The family room features a fireplace, built-in shelves and access to the rear yard. Upstairs, the master suite offers a walk-in closet, a luxurious bath and its own fireplace. Two secondary bedrooms share a compartmented bath and a vaulted loft.

DESIGN BY
©Alan Mascord Design
Associates, Inc.

DESIGN HPU040427

First Floor: 1,698 square feet
Second Floor: 1,644 square feet
Total: 3,342 square feet
Width: 56'-0" Depth: 54'-6"

DESIGN HPU040429

First Floor: 2,375 square feet
Second Floor: 762 square feet
Total: 3,137 square feet
Width: 73'-0" Depth: 64'-6"

L

DESIGN BY
©Alan Mascord Design
Associates, Inc.

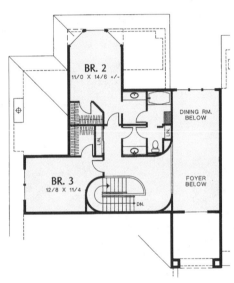

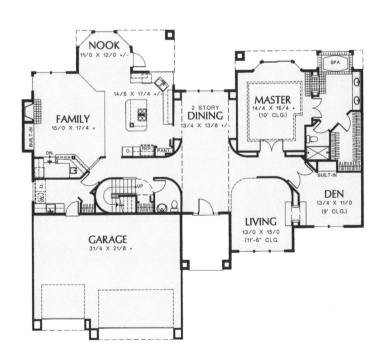

Clean lines, a hipped roof and a high, recessed entry define this sleek, contemporary home. Inside, curved lines add a twist to the well-designed floor plan. For informal entertaining, gather in the multi-windowed family room with its step-down wet bar and warming fireplace. The open kitchen will delight everyone with its center cooktop island, a corner sink and an adjacent breakfast nook. A formal dining room enjoys views of the rear grounds and separates the informal living area from the master wing. Enter the grand master suite through double doors and take special note of the see-through fireplace between the bedroom and bath. A large walk-in closet, a relaxing spa and dual vanities complete the master bath. An additional see-through fireplace is located between the living room and den. Upstairs, two family bedrooms (each with walk-in closets) share a full bath.

DESIGN HPU040430

Main Level: 2,300 square feet
Lower Level: 1,114 square feet
Total: 3,414 square feet
Width: 56'-0" Depth: 61'-6"

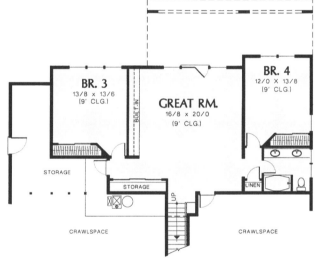

DESIGN BY
©Alan Mascord Design
Associates, Inc.

Looking for all the world like a one-story plan, this elegant hillside design has a surprise on the lower level. The main level is reached through an arched, recessed entry that opens to a twelve-foot ceiling. The formal dining room is on the right, next to a cozy den or Bedroom 3. Columns decorate the hall and separate it from the dining room and great room, which contains a tray ceiling and a fireplace flanked by built-ins. The breakfast nook and kitchen are just steps away, on the left. Lower-level space includes another great room with built-ins and two family bedrooms sharing a full bath.

A private guest suite, loft and large bonus room on the second floor enhance the floor plan of this magnificent brick home. A dormered entry featuring a large Palladian window opens the two-story foyer to the dining room on the left. A sunken living area framed by columns is located at the rear of the house. This fire-warmed family space flows into the kitchen and bayed breakfast area opening out to a rear deck. A master suite features a walk-in closet and lavish private bath. Two family bedrooms share a full bath to complete the first floor.

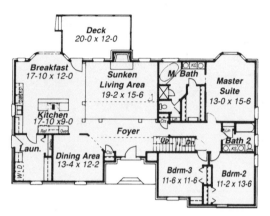

DESIGN BY
©Jannis Vann &
Associates, Inc.

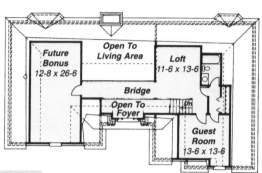

DESIGN HPU040431

First Floor: 2,697 square feet
Second Floor: 360 square feet
Total: 3,057 square feet
Width: 64'-10" Depth: 41'-2"

DESIGN BY
©Larry E. Belk Designs

DESIGN HPU040432

First Floor: 2,469 square feet
Second Floor: 1,025 square feet
Total: 3,494 square feet
Width: 67'-8" Depth: 74'-2"
L

QUOTE ONE®
Cost to build? See page 502
to order complete cost estimate
to build this house in your area!

A lovely double arch gives this European-style home a commanding presence. Once inside, a two-story foyer provides an open view directly through the formal living room to the rear grounds beyond. The private owners suite features dual sinks, twin walk-in closets, a corner garden tub and a separate shower. A second bedroom and a full bath are located nearby. Please specify basement, crawlspace or slab foundation when ordering.

Flower boxes, arches and multi-pane windows all combine to create the elegant facade of this four-bedroom home. Inside, the two-story foyer has a formal dining room to its right and leads to a two-story living room that is filled with light. An efficient kitchen has a bayed breakfast room and shares a snack bar with a cozy family room. Located on the first floor for privacy, the master suite is graced with a luxurious bath. Upstairs, three secondary bedrooms share two full baths and have access to a large game room. For future growth, there is an expandable area accessed through the game room. Please specify basement, crawlspace or slab foundation when ordering.

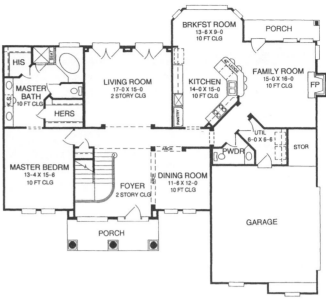

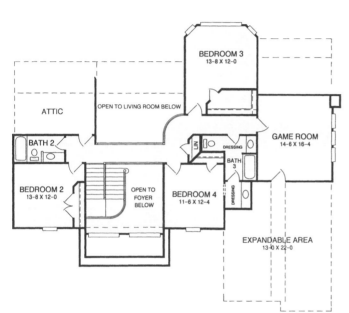

DESIGN HPU040433

First Floor: 1,919 square feet
Second Floor: 1,190 square feet
Total: 3,109 square feet
Width: 64'-6" Depth: 55'-10"

DESIGN BY
©Larry E. Belk Designs

This country estate is bedecked with all the details that pronounce its French origins. The roofline, in particular, is an outstanding feature and allows high ceilings for interior spaces. Gathering areas are varied and large. They include a study, family room and keeping room. A large porch to the rear can be reached through the breakfast room or the master-suite sitting area. All three bedrooms have walk-in closets.

DESIGN BY
©Andy McDonald Design Group

DESIGN HPU040435

Square Footage: 3,032
Width: 73'-0" Depth: 87'-8"

DESIGN HPU040434

Square Footage: 3,230
Width: 94'-8" Depth: 88'-5"

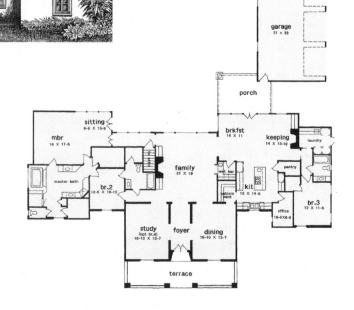

A mini-estate with French country details, this home preserves the beauty of historical design without sacrificing modern convenience. Through double doors, the floor plan opens from a central foyer flanked by a dining room and a study. The family room offers windows overlooking the rear yard and a fireplace. The owners bedroom suite features a sitting room and bath fit for royalty. A smaller family bedroom has a full bath nearby. A third bedroom also enjoys a full bath.

DESIGN BY
©Andy McDonald Design Group

DESIGN HPU040436

First Floor: 2,297 square feet
Second Floor: 977 square feet
Total: 3,274 square feet
Width: 67'-7" Depth: 98'-9"

DESIGN BY
©Andy McDonald Design Group

This comfortable French cottage is perfect to raise a family. Inside, the dining room is ready for easy entertaining with access to the front courtyard through a French door or via the foyer door. Nearby, warm up by the family-room fireplace, or watch nature unfold outside through a ribbon of windows. The kitchen enjoys an island workstation and a pantry. Adjoining the kitchen are a keeping room and a breakfast nook. A secondary bedroom with a private bath—perfect as guest quarters—has access to the keeping room. The owners wing ensures luxury and privacy, featuring a fireplace in the bedroom. Upstairs, two additional bedrooms share a bath and access to the game room.

European charm is written all over the facade of this lovely home. A paneled entry, a delicate balustrade and a hipped roof announce a thoughtful plan with an open interior and room to grow. A center island in the kitchen features a cooktop and space for food preparation. Privately located on the first floor, the master suite enjoys a luxurious bath. Three family bedrooms share a full bath on the second level.

DESIGN HPU040437

First Floor: 2,542 square feet
Second Floor: 909 square feet
Total: 3,451 square feet
Width: 74'-0" Depth: 84'-11"

DESIGN BY
©Andy McDonald Design Group

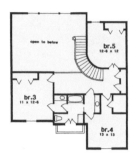

DESIGN HPU040438

Square Footage: 3,039
Width: 73'-8" Depth: 93'-3"

DESIGN BY
©Andy McDonald Design Group

A welcoming double-door glass entrance leads to a home reminiscent of a villa. The side-facing garage visually enlarges the home and provides extra storage at the back. Two fireplaces, in the keeping room and the family room, are a cozy touch. The smaller bedroom located near the luxurious master bedroom could be used for a home office. Two more bedrooms are found on the other side of the plan.

This grand French manor begins with the ultimate in privacy—a walled entry courtyard. Enter the home through double doors in the foyer, or in the study. The family room overlooks the courtyard and is open to the formal dining area. A keeping room, breakfast room and island kitchen form one large informal area to the back of the home. The keeping room has access to another walled courtyard. A large storage area separates the garage from the house. Bedrooms 3 and 4—and an optional Bedroom 5—on the second level share a full bath.

DESIGN HPU040439

First Floor: 2,556 square feet
Second Floor: 605 square feet
Total: 3,161 square feet
Width: 64'-4" Depth: 106'-8"

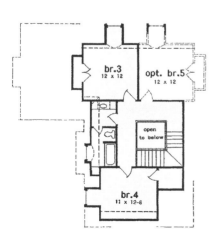

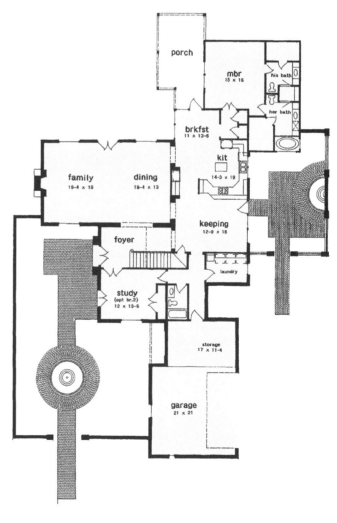

DESIGN BY
©Andy McDonald Design Group

351

m bath

mbr
15 x 17

study
12 x 14

br 2
12-5 x 11-8

br 3
14-3 x 11-4

balcony

keeping
17-8 x 14-10

brkfst
11 x 9-1

kit
14-10 x 11-6

porch

dining
13-10 x 15-8

family
26-1 x 23-4

foyer

pwdr

laundry

portico
10-2 x 10

garage
21 x 20

Looks are deceiving in this narrow design that enjoys plenty of room despite its small appearance. The living room opens from the front portico and accesses a covered porch to the rear overlooking the courtyard. A staircase from the family room leads up to two family bedrooms that share a bath but have separate vanities. Open to the family room, the kitchen provides a walk-in pantry, cooktop island and window sink. The study and master bedroom are to the rear of the plan.

DESIGN HPU040440

First Floor: 2,719 square feet
Second Floor: 618 square feet
Total: 3,337 square feet
Width: 47'-6" Depth: 119'-7"

DESIGN BY
©Andy McDonald Design Group

A steeply pitched French-style roof and an Italian-inspired, arched, double-door entry create an exterior with international interest. Inside is a thoroughly modern floor plan designed for active families. Upstairs, two family bedrooms share a bathroom. Each has a private vanity area. The children's den is an ideal place to play or study. An additional bedroom upstairs is a space-expanding option in this home. Downstairs, the island kitchen opens to the breakfast nook and keeping room. A nearby family room and dining room combination separates the casual areas from the master bedroom and another bedroom or a study.

DESIGN BY
©Andy McDonald Design Group

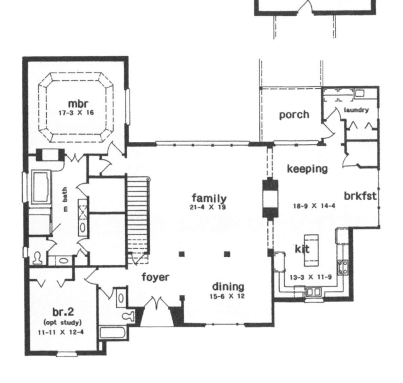

DESIGN HPU040441

First Floor: 2,345 square feet
Second Floor: 663 square feet
Total: 3,008 square feet
Bonus Room: 194 square feet
Width: 62'-10" Depth: 80'-11"

353

This charming home will have you hooked at first sight. An arch soffit invites guests to the great room. Enjoy the fireplace, built-in cabinets and enormous arched window overlooking the backyard from the great room. The kitchen provides a great use of space with a built-in desk, island and walk-in pantry. The master bedroom features built-in cabinets with French doors that open to the private bathroom.

DESIGN HPU040443

First Floor: 2,508 square feet
Second Floor: 960 square feet
Total: 3,468 square feet
Width: 79'-8" Depth: 70'-0"

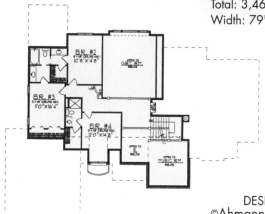

DESIGN BY
©Ahmann Design, Inc.

You are sure to fall in love with what this traditional French Country two-story design has to offer. The great room offers a fireplace surrounded by built-in cabinets, a two-story ceiling and striking arched windows. The study will provide you with a corner of the house to yourself with a view out the front and side. The master bedroom enjoys plenty of space and walk-in closets. The master bathroom features a welcoming arch over the bathtub and large shower.

DESIGN BY
©Ahmann Design, Inc.

DESIGN HPU040442

First Floor: 2,514 square feet
Second Floor: 975 square feet
Total: 3,489 square feet
Width: 74'-8" Depth: 64'-8"

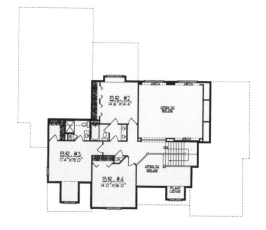

An attractive facade and amenity-filled interior make this home a showplace both outside and in. Immediately off the two-story foyer is the living room and formal dining room, both with interesting ceiling details, and the quiet library with built-in bookcases. The enormous gourmet kitchen features a large island work counter/snack bar, pantry, desk and gazebo breakfast room. Just steps away is the spacious family room with a grand fireplace and windows overlooking the backyard. Upstairs are three family bedrooms served by two baths and a luxurious master suite with a bay-windowed sitting room, detailed ceiling and skylit bath with a whirlpool tub.

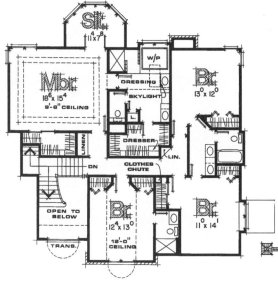

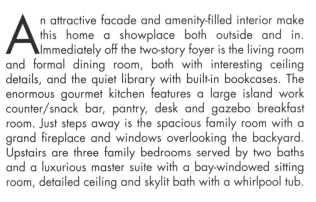

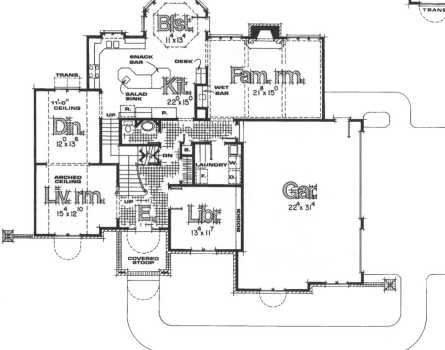

DESIGN HPU040444

First Floor: 1,709 square feet
Second Floor: 1,597 square feet
Total: 3,306 square feet
Width: 62'-0" Depth: 55'-4"

DESIGN BY
©Design Basics, Inc.

355

First Floor: 1,916 square feet
Second Floor: 1,256 square feet
Total: 3,172 square feet
Width: 59'-8" Depth: 60'-10"

DESIGN BY
©Living Concepts Home Planning

This home begins with a recessed cove entry and foyer open to an expanse of living area with views of the deck beyond. The living room features a fireplace with built-in bookcases on either side. The first-floor master suite has a walk-in closet and double vanity. The kitchen with a pantry is adjacent to a breakfast nook with a bay window and a formal dining room. On the second floor, two additional bedrooms share a bath and a recreation room.

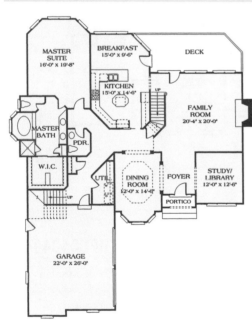

Stunning formal rooms highlight the front of this traditional design. An open foyer leads to a sizable family room, which provides a fireplace. The central gourmet kitchen serves an elegant dining room as well as a breakfast area bright with windows. The master wing features a garden tub, separate shower and double-bowl vanity. Upstairs, three additional bedrooms share a full bath and a hall that leads to a sizable bonus room.

DESIGN BY
©Living Concepts Home Planning

DESIGN HPU040445

First Floor: 2,264 square feet
Second Floor: 1,018 square feet
Total: 3,282 square feet
Bonus Room: 349 square feet
Width: 62'-8" Depth: 76'-4"

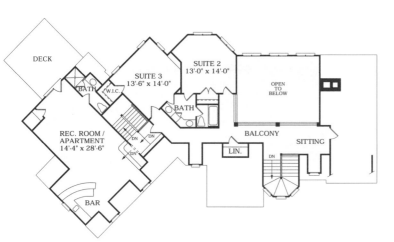

DECK

SUITE 2
13'-6" x 14'-0"

SUITE 3
13'-6" x 14'-0"

BATH

W.I.C.

OPEN
TO
BELOW

BATH

DN

DN

DN

BALCONY

REC. ROOM /
APARTMENT
14'-4" x 28'-6"

SITTING

LIN.

DN

BAR

If you've ever dreamed of living in a castle, this could be the home for you. Can't you just see Rapunzel leaning from one of those stepped windows in the turret? The stone-and-stucco exterior could easily come from the French countryside. The interior is also fit for royalty, from the formal dining room to the multi-purpose grand room to the comfortable sitting area off the kitchen. The owners suite has its own fireplace, two walk-in closets and a compartmented bath with dual vanities and a garden tub. Two stairways lead to the second floor. One, housed in the turret, leads to a sitting area and a balcony overlooking the grand room. The balcony leads to two more bedrooms and a recreation room (or apartment) with a deck.

DESIGN HPU040447

First Floor: 2,351 square feet
Second Floor: 866 square feet
Total: 3,217 square feet
Width: 113'-7" Depth: 57'-5"

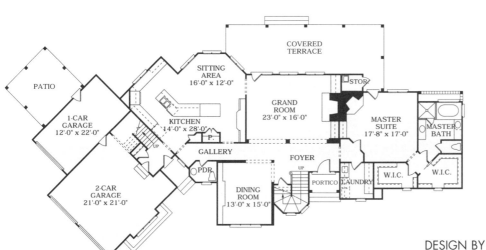

PATIO

1-CAR
GARAGE
12'-0" x 22'-0"

2-CAR
GARAGE
21'-0" x 21'-0"

SITTING
AREA
16'-0" x 12'-0"

COVERED
TERRACE

STOR

GRAND
ROOM
23'-0" x 16'-0"

KITCHEN
14'-0" x 28'-0"

MASTER
SUITE
17'-8" x 17'-0"

MASTER
BATH

P.

UP

GALLERY

FOYER

PDR.

W.I.C.

W.I.C.

UP

DINING
ROOM
13'-0" x 15'-0"

PORTICO

LAUNDRY

DESIGN BY
©Living Concepts Home Planning

357

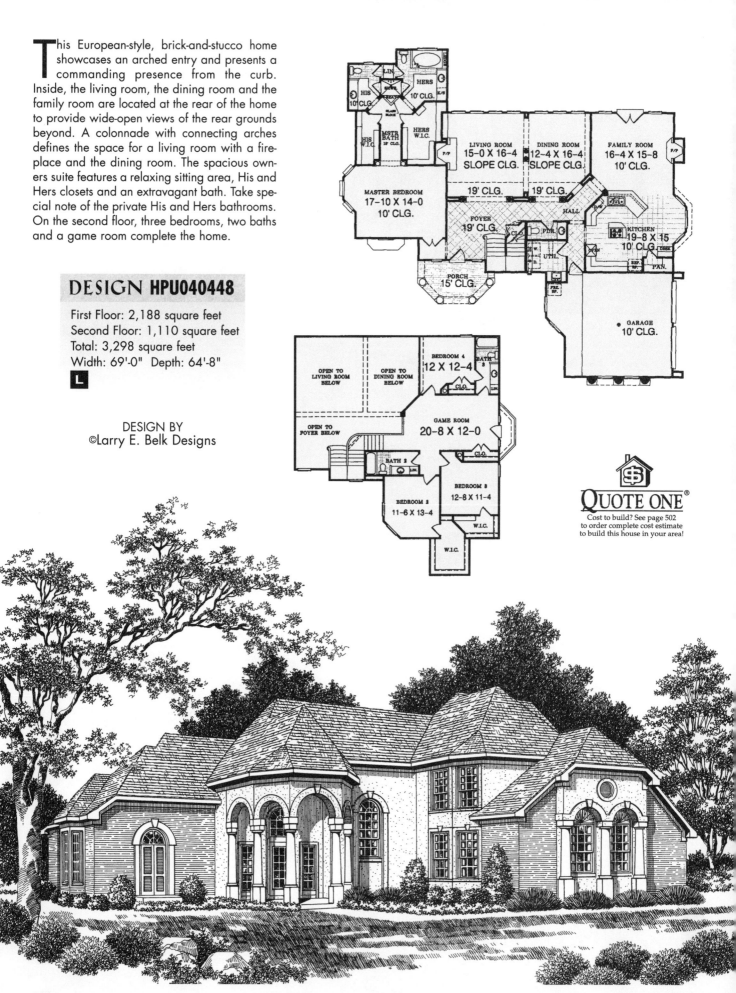

This European-style, brick-and-stucco home showcases an arched entry and presents a commanding presence from the curb. Inside, the living room, the dining room and the family room are located at the rear of the home to provide wide-open views of the rear grounds beyond. A colonnade with connecting arches defines the space for a living room with a fireplace and the dining room. The spacious owners suite features a relaxing sitting area, His and Hers closets and an extravagant bath. Take special note of the private His and Hers bathrooms. On the second floor, three bedrooms, two baths and a game room complete the home.

DESIGN HPU040448

First Floor: 2,188 square feet
Second Floor: 1,110 square feet
Total: 3,298 square feet
Width: 69'-0" Depth: 64'-8"

L

DESIGN BY
©Larry E. Belk Designs

QUOTE ONE®
Cost to build? See page 502
to order complete cost estimate
to build this house in your area!

358

An almost cathedral-like presence dominates this palatial facade. Its thick tower and the pointed glass above the front door inspire reverence. The floor plan is anything but church-austere, however. No luxury was left out. The large family room hosts both formal and informal gatherings and connects to the sheltered breakfast room and island kitchen. A bayed dining room rises to the more formal occasion. A master suite that you might have designed for yourself is secluded on the main level. Three family bedrooms are joined by a game room upstairs.

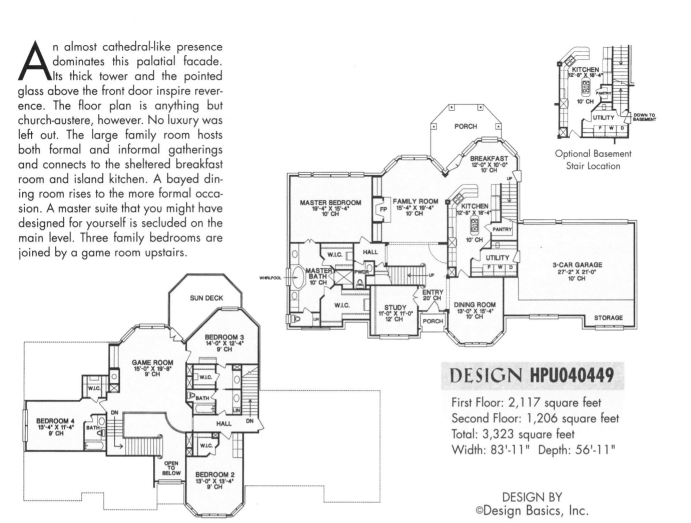

Optional Basement
Stair Location

DESIGN HPU040449

First Floor: 2,117 square feet
Second Floor: 1,206 square feet
Total: 3,323 square feet
Width: 83'-11"   Depth: 56'-11"

DESIGN BY
©Design Basics, Inc.

The informal ambience of English Tudor style is reflected in this European mini-estate. A brick, stucco and half-timber exterior, combined with shake shingles on a roof with dramatically curved eaves, provide the appropriate finish materials. Add to this the multi-pane windows and a pigeonnaire on the garage, and the beauty of this Old World-style home is complete. Elegance prevails inside as well, beginning with the wide entry gallery and continuing through the spacious living room, beam-ceilinged dining room, kitchen and morning room. The main-level master suite enjoys a quiet study nearby for reflective moments. Designed for a rear sloping lot, this home includes a lower-level game room, two bedrooms, a full bath and lots of storage space.

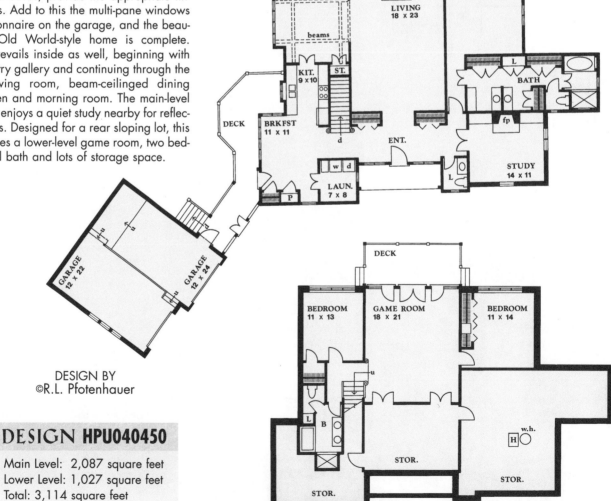

DESIGN BY
©R.L. Pfotenhauer

DESIGN HPU040450

Main Level: 2,087 square feet
Lower Level: 1,027 square feet
Total: 3,114 square feet
Width: 107'-2" Depth: 71'-9"

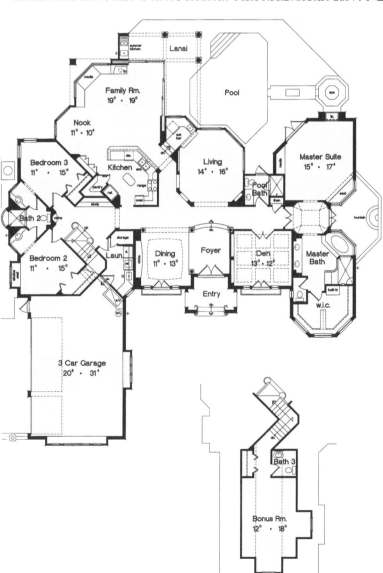

DESIGN HPU040451

Square Footage: 3,064
Bonus Room: 366 square feet
Width: 79'-6" Depth: 91'-0"

From a more graceful era, this 1½-story estate evokes the sense of quiet refinement. Exquisite exterior detailing makes it a one-of-a-kind. Inside are distinctive treatments that make the floor plan unique and functional. The central foyer is enhanced with columns that define the dining room and formal living room. A beam ceiling complements the den. An indulgent master suite includes a private garden with a fountain, pool access, a large walk-in closet and a fireplace to the outdoor spa. Family bedrooms share an unusual compartmented bath. The kitchen and family room are completed with a breakfast nook. Pool access and a lanai with a summer kitchen make this area a natural for casual lifestyles. A bonus area over the garage can become a home office or game room.

DESIGN BY
©Home Design Services, Inc.

361

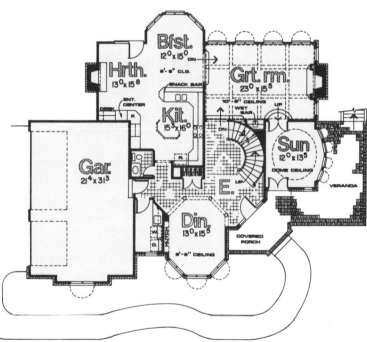

DESIGN HPU040452

First Floor: 1,719 square feet
Second Floor: 1,688 square feet
Total: 3,407 square feet
Width: 62'-0" Depth: 55'-4"

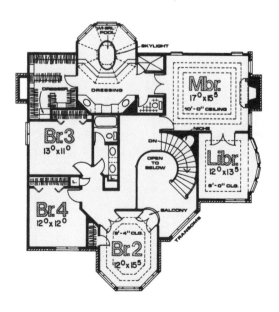

Two-story bays, luminous windows and brick details embellish this stately, traditional castle. Wouldn't you love to call it home? Inside, the soaring foyer is angled to provide impressive views of the spectacular curving staircase and columns that define the octagonal dining room. Although hard to choose, this home's most outstanding feature may be the sun room, which is crowned with a dome ceiling and lit with a display of bowed windows. This room gives access to the multi-windowed great room and an expansive veranda. A cozy hearth room, a breakfast room and an oversized kitchen complete the casual living area. The sumptuous master suite features a fireplace, a library and an opulent master bath with a gazebo ceiling and a skylight above the magnificent whirlpool tub. Three secondary bedrooms, one with a dramatic French-door balcony overlooking the foyer, and a full hall bath complete the second floor.

This two-story home features the old-fashioned look of a turn-of-the-century home mixed with a modern design. A courtyard is beautifully decorated with a combination of brick and stone for a traditional look. The great room has a two-story ceiling with a fireplace. The nook is open to the kitchen with a magnificent wood deck in front, and a screened porch to the right, ideal for enjoying the beautiful outdoor weather. The master suite has a wonderful bathroom, complete with a hot tub. Upstairs you'll appreciate the view of both the foyer and family room below as you cross the hall to any of the three bedrooms. You'll also enjoy the three-and-a-half-car garage, just right for your automobiles and recreational vehicles.

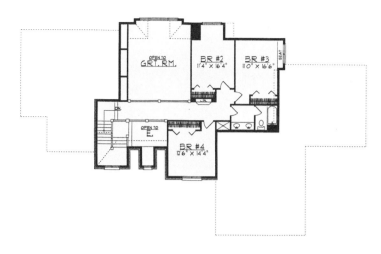

DESIGN HPU040453

First Floor: 2,224 square feet
Second Floor: 885 square feet
Total: 3,109 square feet
Width: 91'-8"   Depth: 66'-8"

DESIGN BY
©Ahmann Design, Inc.

DESIGN HPU040455

First Floor: 2,520 square feet
Second Floor: 836 square feet
Total: 3,356 square feet
Bonus Room: 354 square feet
Width: 94'-3" Depth: 71'-0"

Floor plan labels: SUITE 3 16'-0" x 12'-2"; BATH; W.I.C.; OPEN; BALCONY; SUITE 2 13'-4" x 12'-0"; BONUS ROOM 19'-10" x 11'-6"; STOR.

MASTER SUITE 15'-4" x 17'-10"; W.I.C.; MASTER BATH; DEN/ GUEST SUITE 13'-2" x 13'-6"; FOYER; LOGGIA; TERRACE; GRAND ROOM 18'-0" x 17'-8"; DINING ROOM 12'-10" x 13'-0"; FAMILY 15'-4" x 9'-2"; BREAKFAST 7'-6" x 11'-10"; KITCHEN 14'-4" x 17'-10"; LAUN.; GALLERY; PDR.; 2 CAR GARAGE 23'-0" x 23'-6"; 1 CAR GARAGE 19'-4" x 12'-0"

DESIGN BY
©Living Concepts Home Planning

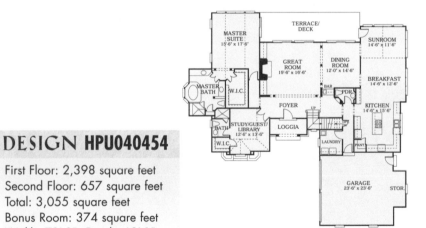

This stunning stucco exterior is enhanced by corner quoins and a two-story recessed entry accented with decorative stonework. The grand room and formal dining room form a large open area warmed by a fireplace and brightened by a metal-roofed bay window in front and windows and doors overlooking the rear terrace. Upstairs, two family bedrooms share a compartmented bath and a balcony overlook. A bonus room offers room for later expansion.

Floor plan labels: MASTER SUITE 15'-6" x 17'-6"; MASTER BATH; W.I.C.; BATH; STUDY/GUEST/ LIBRARY 12'-6" x 13'-6"; FOYER; LOGGIA; TERRACE/ DECK; GREAT ROOM 19'-6" x 16'-6"; DINING ROOM 12'-0" x 14'-6"; BAR; PDR.; SUNROOM 14'-6" x 11'-6"; BREAKFAST 14'-6" x 12'-6"; KITCHEN 14'-6" x 15'-6"; PANT.; LAUNDRY; GARAGE 23'-6" x 23'-6"; STOR.

OPEN TO BELOW; SUITE 4 12'-6" x 12'-6"; W.I.C.; BATH; BALCONY; SUITE 3 15'-0" x 11'-0"; W.I.C.; BONUS ROOM 14'-0" x 20'-0"

DESIGN HPU040454

First Floor: 2,398 square feet
Second Floor: 657 square feet
Total: 3,055 square feet
Bonus Room: 374 square feet
Width: 72'-8" Depth: 69'-1"

DESIGN BY
©Living Concepts Home Planning

European formality meets a bold American spirit in this splendid transitional plan. The library features a sloped ceiling and an arched window, and would make an excellent home office or guest suite. The deluxe owners suite uses defining columns between the bedroom and the lavish bath. Two secondary bedrooms share a bath upstairs. Please specify basement or crawlspace foundation when ordering.

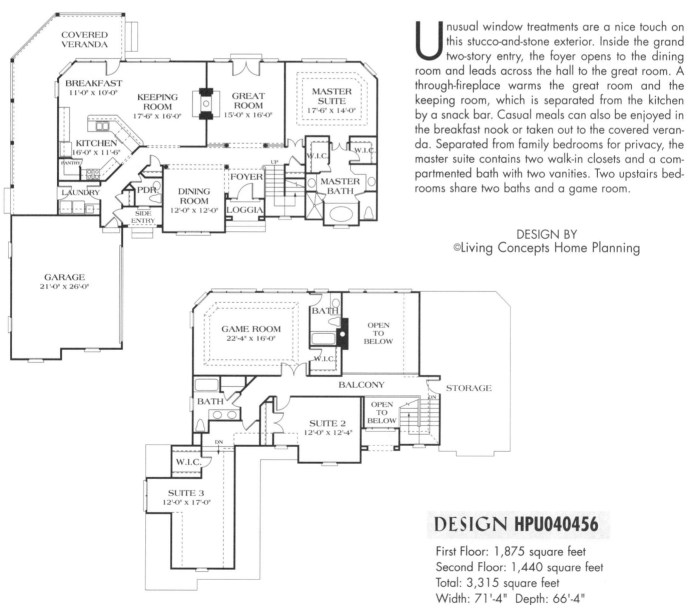

Unusual window treatments are a nice touch on this stucco-and-stone exterior. Inside the grand two-story entry, the foyer opens to the dining room and leads across the hall to the great room. A through-fireplace warms the great room and the keeping room, which is separated from the kitchen by a snack bar. Casual meals can also be enjoyed in the breakfast nook or taken out to the covered veranda. Separated from family bedrooms for privacy, the master suite contains two walk-in closets and a compartmented bath with two vanities. Two upstairs bedrooms share two baths and a game room.

DESIGN BY
©Living Concepts Home Planning

DESIGN HPU040456

First Floor: 1,875 square feet
Second Floor: 1,440 square feet
Total: 3,315 square feet
Width: 71'-4"   Depth: 66'-4"

A grand two-story entry, echoed on the garage, and a prominent chimney provide vertical accents to this massive stucco-and-stone home. A gallery hall follows the outline of the sunken grand room, which features a fireplace and access to a deck. Bedrooms include a guest suite on the first floor, a manor-sized master suite and two family bedrooms.

DESIGN HPU040457

First Floor: 2,085 square feet
Second Floor: 1,234 square feet
Total: 3,319 square feet
Bonus Room: 323 square feet
Width: 63'-10" Depth: 62'-11"

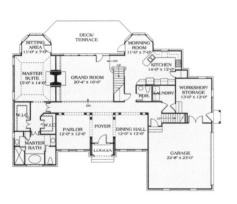

Designed for active lifestyles, this home caters to homeowners who enjoy dinner guests, privacy, luxurious surroundings and open spaces. The foyer, parlor and dining hall are defined by sets of columns. The grand room opens to the deck/terrace, which is also accessed from the sitting area and morning room. The left wing of the plan is dominated by the owners suite with its sitting bay, fireplace, two walk-in closets and compartmented bath.

DESIGN HPU040458

First Floor: 2,198 square feet
Second Floor: 1,028 square feet
Total: 3,226 square feet
Bonus Room: 466 square feet
Width: 72'-8" Depth: 56'-6"

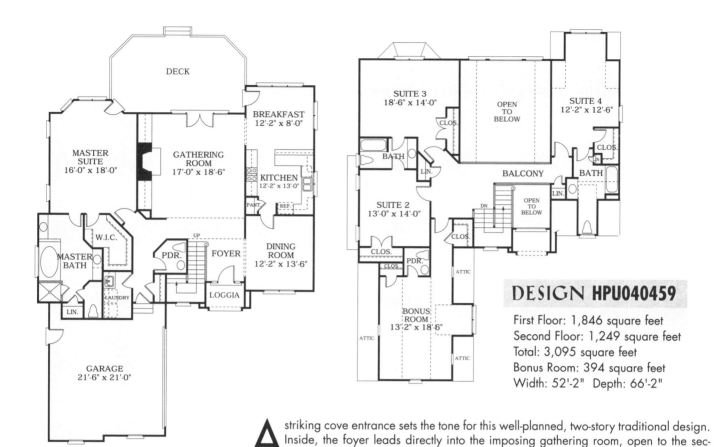

DECK

MASTER
SUITE
16'-0" x 18'-0"

GATHERING
ROOM
17'-0" x 18'-6"

BREAKFAST
12'-2" x 8'-0"

KITCHEN
12'-2" x 13'-0"

PANT.

REF.

W.I.C.

UP

MASTER
BATH

PDR.

FOYER

DINING
ROOM
12'-2" x 13'-6"

LIN.

LAUNDRY

LOGGIA

GARAGE
21'-6" x 21'-0"

SUITE 3
18'-6" x 14'-0"

CLOS.

OPEN
TO
BELOW

SUITE 4
12'-2" x 12'-6"

CLOS.

BATH

LIN.

BALCONY

LIN.

BATH

SUITE 2
13'-0" x 14'-0"

DN

OPEN
TO
BELOW

CLOS.

CLOS.

PDR.

ATTIC

CLOS.

BONUS
ROOM
13'-2" x 18'-6"

ATTIC

ATTIC

DESIGN HPU040459

First Floor: 1,846 square feet
Second Floor: 1,249 square feet
Total: 3,095 square feet
Bonus Room: 394 square feet
Width: 52'-2" Depth: 66'-2"

DESIGN BY
©Living Concepts Home Planning

A striking cove entrance sets the tone for this well-planned, two-story traditional design. Inside, the foyer leads directly into the imposing gathering room, open to the second floor, with double-door access to the large rear deck. To the right, the efficient kitchen is nestled between a formal dining room and breakfast nook. The master bedroom suite has a garden bath and large walk-in closet, plus direct access to the deck. Three additional bedrooms are arranged upstairs off the long balcony overlooking the gathering room. Two full baths and a large bonus room with a half-bath are also on this level.

DESIGN HPU040460

First Floor: 1,853 square feet
Second Floor: 1,342 square feet
Total: 3,195 square feet
Width: 68'-3" Depth: 50'-8"

DESIGN BY
©R.L. Pfotenhauer

The repetition of cornice returns and brick arches creates an appealing pattern, while numerous windows add an airy feel. A spacious family room with a fireplace and built-in shelves occupies the right side of the plan. To the left of the family room, the L-shaped kitchen with a cooktop island serves both formal and informal dining areas. Light will stream through the bay window in the breakfast nook. Upstairs, the owners suite provides two walk-in closets and a whirlpool tub. Also on the second floor, three family bedrooms share a full bath.

This brick two-story home makes an elegant statement with a full-facade entry, columns and keystone lintels. Inside, the two-story foyer greets guests with a formal dining room defined with columns. To the left of the foyer, double doors lead to the private library, and a short hallway nearby accesses the master suite. This suite enjoys its own private wing, with a striking bay-window view of the rear gardens and a lavish bathroom. The kitchen and breakfast room enjoy another bay-window view of the backyard, at the right of the plan. On the second floor, three secondary bedrooms, two full baths and a bonus room complete this design.

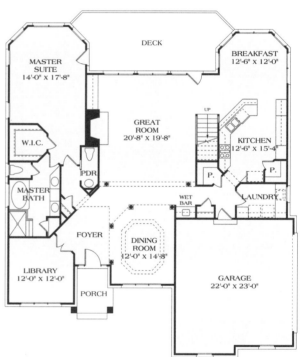

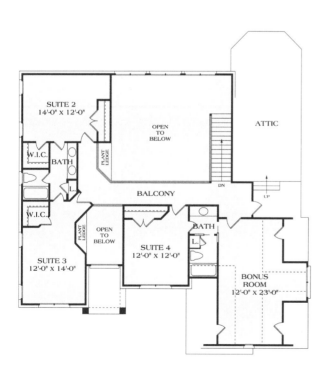

DESIGN HPU040461

First Floor: 2,048 square feet
Second Floor: 1,081 square feet
Total: 3,129 square feet
Bonus Room: 332 square feet
Width: 55'-0" Depth: 61'-8"

DESIGN BY
©Living Concepts Home Planning

369

ENT. CENTER
Fam. Rm.
20⁸ x 18⁶
ENT. CENTER

SNACK BAR   UP
Bfst.
12⁰ x 14⁰
Kit.
16⁸ x 14⁰
BUFFET
BENCH
STOOP
W. D.
RECYCLING
CENTER

HUTCH
SPACE
Din. Rm.
12⁰ x 16⁴
COVERED
STOOP

Gar.
22⁸ x 35⁸

13'-0" CEILING
Grt. Rm.
15⁴ x 20⁰

DN
12'-0" CEILING
E.
14'-0" CEILING
OFF MAIN

Sit.
10⁴ x 6⁰   COVERED
STOOP
UP
Mbr.
16⁴ x 14⁰
11'-0" CEILING

LINEN
CATHEDRAL
CEILING
WHIRLPOOL

DESIGN HPU040462

First Floor: 2,461 square feet
Second Floor: 1,019 square feet
Total: 3,480 square feet
Width: 74'-0" Depth: 79'-6"

DESIGN BY
©Design Basics, Inc.

A bay window, an arched entry and a single-story turret display the elegance shown throughout this plan. An elevated entry gives a view of the dining room past an open railing. French doors centered in the great room lead outside, and a second set of French doors opens to the family room, where twin entertainment centers encase the fireplace. An atrium door opens from this room to the outdoors. The functional kitchen offers a large cooktop island and snack bar and views the adjacent breakfast room through three arched openings. The owners suite, with a private bath in the turret, occupies the right side of the plan. A loft on the second floor works well as a computer center and features double doors that open to overlook the family room below. One secondary bedroom has a private bath, while two bedrooms share a bath.

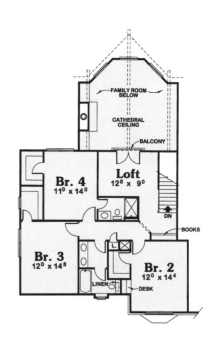

FAMILY ROOM
BELOW
CATHEDRAL
CEILING
BALCONY

Br. 4
11⁰ x 14⁰
Loft
12⁸ x 9⁰
DN
BOOKS

Br. 3
12⁰ x 14⁸
LINEN
DESK
Br. 2
12⁰ x 14⁴

Multi-pane windows and a massive arched entry welcome you to this attractive brick home. Inside, the foyer leads directly to the family room, with its eye-catching corner fireplace. Perfect for formal entertaining as well as family relaxing, this room is convenient to both the dining room at the front and the sunny bayed breakfast nook at the rear of the plan. The roomy patio will be a popular gathering place for guests and family alike. The island kitchen is ideally situated to serve all areas of the home. For privacy, a guest suite is set by itself to the left of the house, and a quiet study may be found at the front. Upstairs, the master suite beckons, with lots of windows, a massive walk-in closet and a pampering bath. Three family bedrooms and an unfinished area complete the plan. Please specify crawlspace or slab foundation when ordering.

DESIGN HPU040463

First Floor: 1,775 square feet
Second Floor: 1,345 square feet
Total: 3,120 square feet
Bonus Room: 262 square feet
Width: 62'-4"   Depth: 54'-10"

DESIGN BY
©Chatham Home Planning, Inc.

371

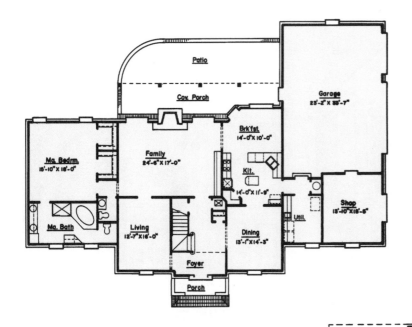

Patio

Cov. Porch

Garage
23'-2" x 35'-7"

Brk'fst.
14'-0" x 10'-0"

Family
24'-6" x 17'-0"

Ma. Bedrm.
15'-10" x 18'-0"

Kit.
14'-0" x 11'-9"

Ma. Bath

Living
12'-7" x 16'-0"

Dining
13'-1" x 14'-3"

Shop
13'-10" x 16'-6"

Util.

Foyer

Porch

Luxury is highly evident in this fine brick mansion. The master bedroom suite is one example of this, with its two walk-in closets, huge bedroom area and lavish bath. Another example of luxury is the four secondary bedrooms upstairs, with access to a private study. Take note of the spacious family room, complete with a fireplace and access to the rear covered patio. The island kitchen is sure to please, serving with ease the formal dining room or the sunny breakfast room. The three-car garage will easily shelter the family fleet.

Bedrm. 2
15'-0" x 11'-4"

Ba. 2

Bedrm. 3
15'-1" x 15'-0"

Ba. 3

Balcony

Bedrm. 4
12'-6" x 12'-10"

Bedrm. 5
13'-1" x 14'-6"

Study
12'-0" x 8'-10"

DESIGN HPU040464

First Floor: 2,190 square feet
Second Floor: 1,418 square feet
Total: 3,608 square feet
Width: 84'-10" Depth: 61'-10"

DESIGN BY
©Chatham Home Planning, Inc.

This stunning stucco mansion, with corner quoins and an elegant entrance, is sure to be a family favorite. The two-story foyer is flanked by the formal living and dining rooms and presents a graceful staircase to the upper level. A sunken family room features a fireplace and direct access to the rear sun deck. Light flows from bay windows into the breakfast room. Upstairs, a lavish master suite waits to pamper the homeowner, while three secondary bedrooms share two baths and access to a huge bonus room. Please specify basement, crawlspace or slab foundation when ordering.

DESIGN BY
©Jannis Vann & Associates, Inc.

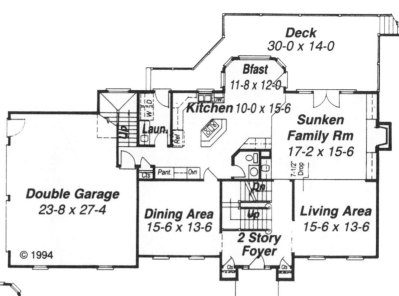

Deck
30-0 x 14-0

Bfast
11-8 x 12-0

Kitchen 10-0 x 15-6

Laun.

W D

Ref.

Cts   Pant.   Ovn

Double Garage
23-8 x 27-4

© 1994

Up

Sunken
Family Rm
17-2 x 15-6

7-1/2" Drop

Dn

Up

Dining Area
15-6 x 13-6

Living Area
15-6 x 13-6

2 Story
Foyer

Cts   Cts

Bdrm 2
11-4 x 15-6

Bdrm-3
11-4 x 11-6

Dn

Bath 2

M. Bath

KS

Bonus Room
14-4 x 27-4

Bath 3

Bdrm-4
13-2 x 13-6

Dn

Master
Bedroom
15-6 x 17-6

2 Story
Foyer

DESIGN HPU040465

First Floor: 1,553 square feet
Second Floor: 1,477 square feet
Total: 3,030 square feet
Bonus Room: 397 square feet
Width: 72'-4" Depth: 48'-0"

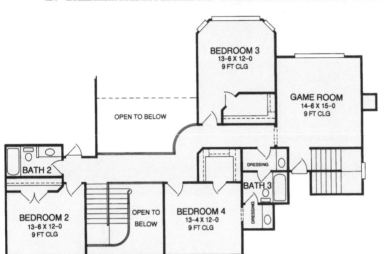

DESIGN HPU040466

First Floor: 2,055 square feet
Second Floor: 1,229 square feet
Total: 3,284 square feet
Width: 65'-0" Depth: 60'-10"

Colonial character mingles with country charm and Greek Revival elegance in this roomy four-bedroom home. A two-story foyer cheerfully introduces the elegant dining room with its tray ceiling. Across from the foyer, the light-filled living room features twin French doors accessing the rear yard. Located on the first floor, the master suite enjoys a luxury bathroom with a garden tub, a separate shower, His and Hers walk-in closets and twin vanity sinks. The kitchen, breakfast room and family room share an open area and access to a powder room near the garage. The second level includes three secondary bedrooms, two bathrooms and a game room.

DESIGN BY
©Larry E. Belk Designs

This two-story brick home is reminiscent of an early American design. From the efficiency of the extraordinary floor plan to the elegance of the custom trims and wood details, this home's timeless value is artistically showcased. The flow of the first floor creates ease of entertaining guests in the formal living room and dining room areas, while a comfortable and inviting atmosphere for family enjoyment exists in the kitchen and spacious hearth room. A fireplace, built-in entertainment center and custom wood ceiling treatment help to create a warm, cozy effect. Wood rails and newel posts decorate the stairs leading to a separate wing on the mid-level, offering children's bedrooms and a computer space. Continuing to the upper level, the master bedroom suite with its sitting area, fireplace and deluxe bath/dressing room combine to create a fabulous retreat.

DESIGN HPU040467

First Floor: 1,666 square feet
Second Floor: 1,779 square feet
Total: 3,445 square feet
Width: 71'-8" Depth: 38'-10"

DESIGN BY
©Studer Residential Designs, Inc.

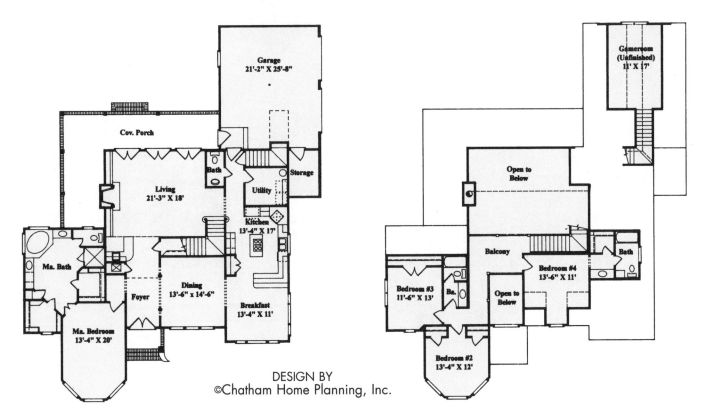

Garage
21'-2" X 25'-8"

Cov. Porch

Bath

Storage

Living
21'-3" X 18'

Utility

Kitchen
13'-4" X 17'

Ma. Bath

Foyer

Dining
13'-6" x 14'-6"

Breakfast
13'-4" X 11'

Ma. Bedroom
13'-4" X 20'

Gameroom
(Unfinished)
11' X 17'

Open to
Below

Balcony

Bedroom #4
13'-6" X 11'

Bath

Bedroom #3
11'-6" X 13'

Ba.

Open to
Below

Bedroom #2
13'-4" X 12'

DESIGN BY
©Chatham Home Planning, Inc.

A graceful tower enhances the facade of this delightful four-bedroom home. Once inside, columns define the formal dining room, while directly ahead is the spacious living room, complete with a fireplace and built-ins. The kitchen enjoys an island cooktop and a window over the sink. Light streams into both the kitchen and breakfast room from numerous windows. Luxury can be found in abundance in the master suite. Here, two walk-in closets, a separate tub and shower, and two vanities wait to pamper the homeowner. Upstairs is the sleeping zone, which includes three bedrooms—one with its own bath.

DESIGN HPU040468

First Floor: 2,095 square feet
Second Floor: 928 square feet
Total: 3,023 square feet
Bonus Room: 223 square feet
Width: 66'-0" Depth: 76'-3"

DESIGN HPU040469

First Floor: 1,812 square feet
Second Floor: 1,300 square feet
Total: 3,112 square feet
Width: 35'-0" Depth: 88'-0"

DESIGN BY
©Authentic Historical Designs, Inc.

Characteristics of Greek Revival architecture enliven the exterior of this four-bedroom home. The dining-room entrance is framed by a pair of square columns. The foyer leads to a large great room and also to a cozy keeping room off the kitchen. The kitchen has a large walk-in pantry and a sunny breakfast area that looks out onto a private courtyard. The downstairs master suite is tucked quietly away from the noise of family life. On the second level, a large sitting room and activity area overlooks the kitchen below, enabling the family cook to stay involved in the family fun. Three family bedrooms and two full bathrooms complete this floor.

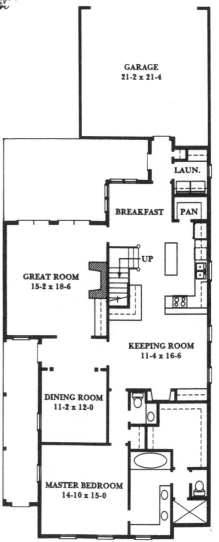

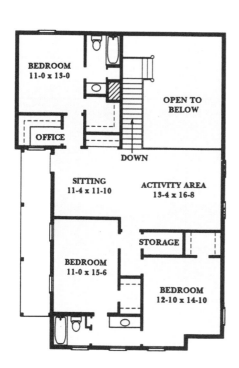

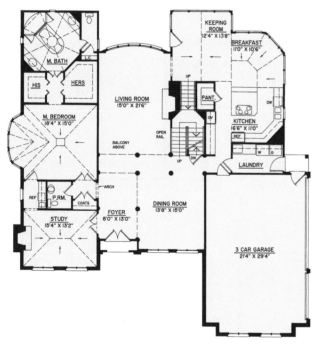

This grand Georgian home has a double-door entry topped by a beautiful arched window. Inside, the foyer opens to the two-story living room, which has a wide bow window overlooking the rear property. Double doors open to a study warmed by a fireplace. The kitchen features a walk-in pantry and serves both the formal dining room and the breakfast area, which adjoins the bright keeping room. The owners suite, secluded on the first floor, is large and opulent. Three more bedrooms and two baths are upstairs for family and friends.

DESIGN HPU040470

First Floor: 2,253 square feet
Second Floor: 890 square feet
Total: 3,143 square feet
Width: 61'-6" Depth: 64'-0"

DESIGN BY
©Archival Designs, Inc.

What better way to start—or even to end—your day than in the beautiful octagonal breakfast room within this masterful design? It opens to a curved island kitchen, with plenty of room for even the messiest of cooks and to the cozy family room, which provides access, via French doors, to the outside and shares a fireplace with the front parlor. A formal dining room and a powder room complete the fist floor. On the second floor, the master bedroom offers a romantic octagonal design, as well as a fireplace in the large sitting area. It also includes a luxurious master bath with twin walk-in closets. Two family bedrooms with walk-in closets share a full bath, while another bedroom features its own private bath.

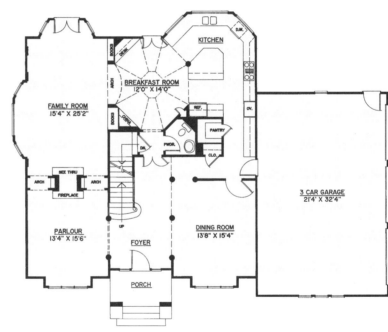

DESIGN HPU040471

First Floor: 1,597 square feet
Second Floor: 1,859 square feet
Total: 3,456 square feet
Width: 62'-0" Depth: 46'-0"

DESIGN BY
©Archival Designs, Inc.

379

DESIGN HPU040472

First Floor: 1,768 square feet
Second Floor: 1,436 square feet
Total: 3,204 square feet
Width: 77'-8"   Depth: 64'-8"

DESIGN BY
©Ahmann Design, Inc.

This exquisite, luxurious, brick two-story home is filled with dramatic amenities. You are welcomed by a uniquely shaped foyer that has ceilings that extend two stories. There is a formal living and dining room that flows into the amazing entryway. Double doors access the study. The kitchen is every chef's dream; it is spacious and well-designed, and it features a center island and nook where you can venture to the screened porch through splendid French doors. The family room is cozy and comfortable. The fireplace is surrounded by beautifully constructed built-in cabinets. A mud/laundry room is just off the garage. The second floor has three bedrooms and a master suite—all have detailed ceiling designs. There is a full bath with a double vanity, a whirlpool tub and a walk-in shower in the master suite.

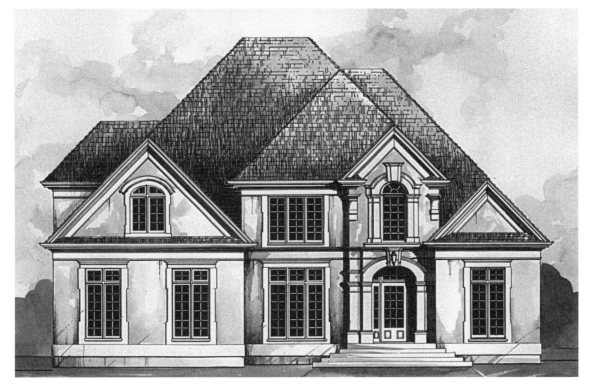

This narrow-lot design would be ideal for a golf course or lakeside lot. Inside the arched entry, the formal dining room is separated from the foyer and the massive grand room by decorative pillars. At the end of the day, the family will enjoy gathering in the cozy keeping room with its fireplace and easy access to the large island kitchen and the sunny gazebo-style breakfast room. The owners suite is located on the first floor for privacy and features a uniquely designed bedroom and a luxurious bath with His and Hers walk-in closets. Your family portraits and favorite art treasures will be well displayed along the upstairs gallery, which shares space with three family bedrooms and two full baths.

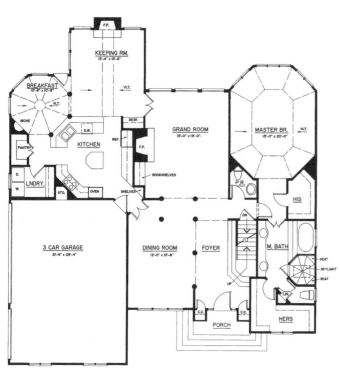

DESIGN HPU040473

First Floor: 2,032 square feet
Second Floor: 1,028 square feet
Total: 3,060 square feet
Unfinished Basement:
2,032 square feet
Width: 55'-8" Depth: 62'-0"

DESIGN BY
©Archival Designs, Inc.

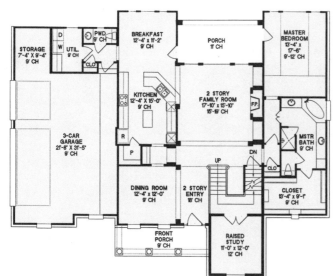

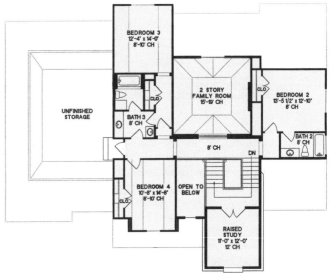

DESIGN HPU040474

First Floor: 2,060 square feet
Second Floor: 1,020 square feet
Total: 3,080 square feet
Bonus Room: 459 square feet
Width: 68'-3"   Depth: 55'-9"

DESIGN BY
©Design Basics, Inc.

The charm of this French country home begins with the hipped roof, brick facade and the arched and circle windows of the exterior. Upon entering, you will find a formal dining room to your left, which connects to the kitchen via a butler's pantry. A breakfast nook to the rear of the plan has views of the backyard and access to a half-bath and the utility room. At the center of the home is a beautiful two-story family room with a fireplace and access to the rear porch. The owners suite also accesses this porch and finds privacy on the right side of the first floor. The owners bath has a compartmented toilet, twin vanities and a huge walk-in closet. A raised study is found at the first landing of the staircase, which then continues up to three secondary bedrooms and two more baths.

Porch

Patio

Breakfast
13' x 10'5"

Laun.

Bath

Hall

stairs dn

Kitchen
17' x 13'2"

Garage
21'10" x 32'4"

butler's pantry

stairs up

Great Room
19'4" x 17'9"

Master Bedroom
13'8" x 17'9"

entertainment center

Dining
Room
13' x 12'9"

Foyer

Hall

tray ceiling

Porch

Bath

Bath

Dressing

walk-in closet

Bedroom
13' x 13'11"

Bath

Bonus Room
16'8" x 15

Balcony

stairs dn

Great Room
Below

Bedroom
13' x 13'4"

Multiple gables, a box window and easy maintenance combine to create a dramatic appearance for this two-story European classic home. The excitement of the great room begins with a wall of windows across the rear, a sloped ceiling and built-in entertainment cabinet. The kitchen offers an angled island that parallels the French doors and large breakfast room. The dining-room ceiling has a raised center section, and a furniture alcove is added for extra roominess. The luxury and convenience of the first-floor master bedroom suite is highlighted by His and Hers vanities, a separate shower and whirlpool tub. The second floor provides a private retreat for a guest suite and a bonus room offering the option of a fourth bedroom, library or hobby room. A balcony provides a panoramic view of the great room and foyer. The rear of this home is stepped for privacy and boasts a clever use of windows.

DESIGN HPU040475

First Floor: 2,192 square feet
Second Floor: 654 square feet
Total: 2,846 square feet
Bonus Room: 325 square feet
Width: 75'-0" Depth: 70'-0"

DESIGN BY
©Studer Residential Designs, Inc.

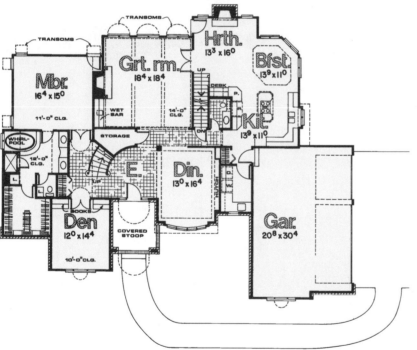

DESIGN HPU040476

First Floor: 2,252 square feet
Second Floor: 920 square feet
Total: 3,172 square feet
Width: 73'-4" Depth: 57'-4"

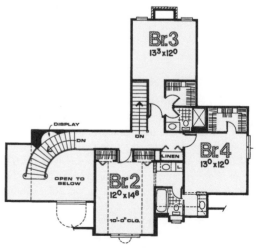

A curving staircase graces the entry to this beautiful home and hints at the wealth of amenities found in the floor plan. Besides an oversized great room with a fireplace and arched windows, there's a cozy hearth room with its own fireplace. The gourmet kitchen has a work island and breakfast area. A secluded den contains bookcases and an arched transom above double doors. The master bedroom is on the first floor, thoughtfully separated from three family bedrooms upstairs. Bedrooms 2 and 4 share a full bath, while Bedroom 3 has its own private bath. Note the informal stair to the second floor originating in the hearth room.

DESIGN HPU040477

First Floor: 1,631 square feet
Second Floor: 1,426 square feet
Total: 3,057 square feet
Width: 60'-0" Depth: 58'-0"

DESIGN BY
©Design Basics, Inc.

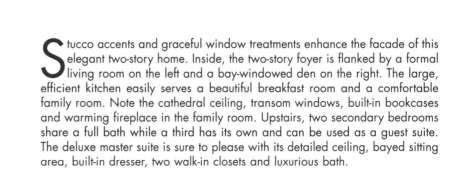

Stucco accents and graceful window treatments enhance the facade of this elegant two-story home. Inside, the two-story foyer is flanked by a formal living room on the left and a bay-windowed den on the right. The large, efficient kitchen easily serves a beautiful breakfast room and a comfortable family room. Note the cathedral ceiling, transom windows, built-in bookcases and warming fireplace in the family room. Upstairs, two secondary bedrooms share a full bath while a third has its own and can be used as a guest suite. The deluxe master suite is sure to please with its detailed ceiling, bayed sitting area, built-in dresser, two walk-in closets and luxurious bath.

DESIGN HPU040478

First Floor: 2,672 square feet
Second Floor: 687 square feet
Total: 3,359 square feet
Bonus Room: 522 square feet
Width: 72'-6" Depth: 64'-5"

DESIGN BY
Donald A. Gardner Architects, Inc.

A brick exterior mixed with cedar shakes creates an intriguing facade for this four-bedroom home with its dramatic hipped roof and dual chimneys. This home features formal living and dining rooms as well as a more casual family room and breakfast area. The living room is vaulted and overlooked by a second-floor balcony. A bedroom/study and the master suite are located on the first floor, while the second floor features two more bedrooms and a bonus room.

DESIGN HPU040479

First Floor: 2,372 square feet
Second Floor: 1,111 square feet
Total: 3,483 square feet
Bonus Room: 394 square feet
Width: 85'-4" Depth: 51'-3"

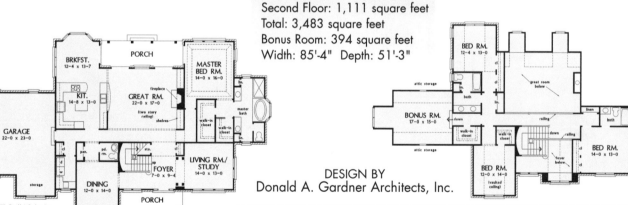

DESIGN BY
Donald A. Gardner Architects, Inc.

An exquisite brick exterior wraps this stately traditional home in luxury. An impressive two-story ceiling with clerestory dormers amplifies the great room with a fireplace, built-ins and access to the back porch. Topped with a tray ceiling, the master suite enjoys back-porch access, dual walk-ins and a luxurious bath. Upstairs, a balcony overlooks the foyer and great room. Two upstairs bedrooms feature vaulted ceilings, while a third boasts a private bath.

386

This brick two-story home has an ideal set-up for family or formal gatherings. When entering this home, you are greeted by a two-story foyer and a striking open staircase to the upper level. There are double doors just off the foyer to the formal living room. The formal dining room is spacious and a perfect place to serve holiday meals. The family room is astonishing with its two-story ceilings, fireplace and built-in cabinet. You can venture to the second level by either of the two staircases. There are four bedrooms on this level, which includes a cathedral-ceilinged master suite. The master bath offers a walk-in shower with a seat and double vanity.

DESIGN HPU040480

First Floor: 1,559 square feet
Second Floor: 1,713 square feet
Total: 3,272 square feet
Width: 64'-0" Depth: 54'-0"

DESIGN BY
©Ahmann Design, Inc.

DESIGN HPU040482

First Floor: 2,157 square feet
Second Floor: 956 square feet
Total: 3,113 square feet
Width: 71'-0" Depth: 62'-0"

Stucco, siding, shutters and class—all combine here to give this home plenty of curb appeal. A two-story foyer leads through an arched soffit to the formal living room on the left and offers a formal dining room to the right. A master bedroom suite is designed to pamper, with a large walk-in closet and a lavish, private bath. Upstairs, three family bedrooms share a large hall bath and a handy loft, good for studying, reading or computer work.

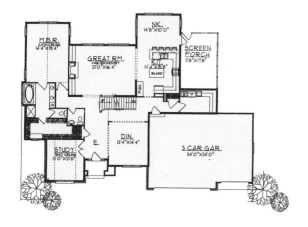

DESIGN BY
©Ahmann Design, Inc.

DESIGN HPU040481

First Floor: 2,174 square feet
Second Floor: 877 square feet
Total: 3,051 square feet
Width: 76'-0" Depth: 56'-0"

DESIGN BY
©Ahmann Design, Inc.

The two-story French country home will welcome you, and the amount of space in this home will give you plenty of room to grow. From the entry, the French doors open to a study with a tray ceiling. The great room with a two-story ceiling, fireplace, built-in shelves and stunning windows that overlook the backyard will amaze you. Also on the main floor of this home is a spectacular master bedroom.

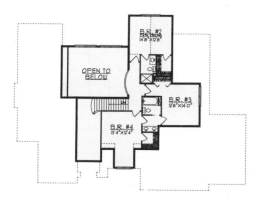

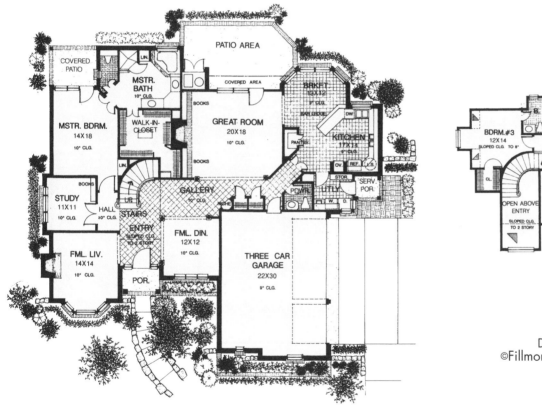

DESIGN BY
©Fillmore Design Group

Here's a cottage that would have provided plenty of room for Goldilocks AND the three bears! Wonderful rooflines top a brick exterior with cedar and stone accents—and lots of English country charm. Stone wing walls extend the front profile, and a cedar hood tops the large bay window. The two-story entry reveals a graceful curving staircase and opens to the formal living and dining rooms. Fireplaces are found in the living room as well as the great room, which also boasts built-in bookcases and access to the rear patio. The kitchen and breakfast room add to the informal area and include a snack bar. A private patio is part of the owners suite, which also offers an intriguing corner tub, twin vanities, a large walk-in closet and a nearby study. Three family bedrooms and a bonus room comprise the second floor.

DESIGN HPU040483

First Floor: 2,438 square feet
Second Floor: 882 square feet
Total: 3,320 square feet
Width: 70'-0" Depth: 63'-2"

Glass-filled, hipped dormers and corner quoins lend this four-bedroom home great curb appeal. Skylights illuminate the vaulted foyer and curved staircase. The formal dining room has a niche for a buffet and French doors leading to the rear deck. Decorative columns help define the living room, which offers a fireplace. A quiet den provides a bay window and a nearby full bath. The gourmet kitchen overlooks the family room, which has a hearth. A luxurious master suite and three secondary bedrooms fill the second floor.

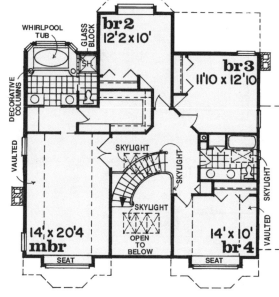

br 2
12'2 x 10'

br 3
11'10 x 12'10

WHIRLPOOL TUB

GLASS BLOCK

DECORATIVE COLUMNS

VAULTED

SKYLIGHT

SKYLIGHT

SKYLIGHT

SKYLIGHT

14' x 20'4
mbr

OPEN TO BELOW

SEAT

14' x 10'
br 4

VAULTED

SEAT

DESIGN BY
©Select Home Designs

DECK

brk
12'2 x 10'

SUNKEN

fam
14' x 15'

din
12' x 16'6

COUNTER

BUFFET

HALF WALL ARCHED

k
12'2 x 16'

ldr

W

D

DECORATIVE COLUMNS

P   B

23'6 x 23'
two~car
garage

SUNKEN

14' x 20'
liv

11'8 x 11'
den

DESIGN HPU040484

First Floor: 1,725 square feet
Second Floor: 1,364 square feet
Total: 3,089 square feet
Width: 64'-4"   Depth: 50'-4"

ecorative columns and gently curving arches welcome guests to this comfortable, brick, two-story home. Convenience is a hallmark within, with a second-floor laundry room for the three family bedrooms and a full-size stackable washer and dryer between the master bath and one of two walk-in closets. Continuing to put the homeowner first, this plan also features multiple built-ins and storage options. The great room features a beam ceiling, warming fireplace, entertainment center and built-in shelving. A tray ceiling adorns the master bedroom. The master bath is luxurious with a whirlpool tub and separate glass shower. Please specify basement, crawlspace or slab foundation when ordering.

DESIGN BY
©Michael E. Nelson,
Nelson Design Group, LLC

DESIGN HPU040485

First Floor: 1,974 square feet
Second Floor: 1,396 square feet
Total: 3,370 square feet
Width: 63'-0" Depth: 50'-4"

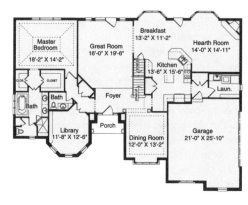

This gorgeous home combines fine exterior detailing with an exciting, functional floor plan. Three bay windows provide light and dimension to favorite family gathering areas. Columns define the formal dining room that enjoys easy access to the kitchen. An island, large pantry and wrap-around counter make cooking fun. The master bedroom pampers, while a second-floor balcony and three additional bedrooms complete this spectacular home.

DESIGN HPU040487

First Floor: 2,233 square feet
Second Floor: 853 square feet
Total: 3,086 square feet
Width: 67'-4" Depth: 50'-4"

DESIGN BY
©Studer Residential Designs, Inc.

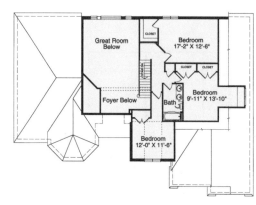

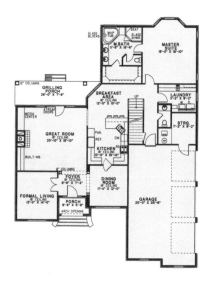

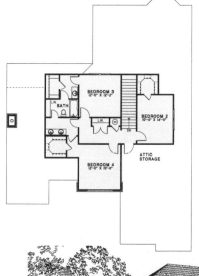

Quoins, keystone lintels and a Palladian window denote European influence in this charming, brick, four-bedroom home. A beautiful built-in media center and shelving system surrounds the fireplace in the great room. French doors in the great room access the grilling porch, extending the livable space outdoors. A bay window lights the master bedroom, and the sumptuous bath with its whirlpool tub adds elegance. Three secondary bedrooms featuring walk-in closets are located upstairs and share a full bath. Please specify basement or crawlspace foundation when ordering.

DESIGN HPU040486

First Floor: 1,597 square feet
Second Floor: 1,859 square feet
Total: 3,456 square feet
Width: 62'-0" Depth: 46'-0"

DESIGN BY
©Michael E. Nelson,
Nelson Design Group, LLC

Plenty of amenities are available within the brick-and-siding exterior of this two-story home. The covered porch invites guests and owners to relax and contemplate the scenery. The foyer elegantly invites guests to dinner in the formal dining room. Conveniently nearby, the kitchen has plenty of counter space, a snack bar and a walk-in pantry. The keeping room—complete with a corner fireplace—and the light-filled breakfast room provide plenty of informal eating and relaxing space around the kitchen. The great room also features a corner fireplace. Luxury is the keyword of the master suite. Adorned with a boxed ceiling and warmed by a gas fireplace with built-ins, the master suite enjoys a bath with a whirlpool tub and separate glass shower, His and Hers walk-in closets, and dual-vanity sinks. The second floor features a game room with built-ins around a window seat and two family bedrooms sharing a full bath. Please specify basement, crawlspace or slab foundation when ordering.

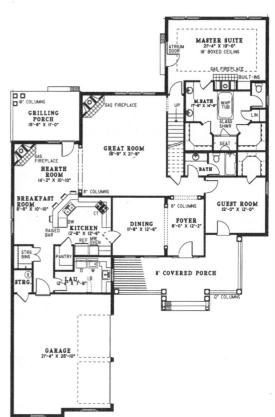

DESIGN HPU040488

First Floor: 2,257 square feet
Second Floor: 949 square feet
Total: 3,206 square feet
Width: 56'-0" Depth: 85'-7"

DESIGN BY
©Michael E. Nelson,
Nelson Design Group, LLC

esigned with your growing family in mind, this spacious two-story design is sure to be the home for you. The two-story entryway leads to the airy kitchen and breakfast nook. The kitchen, with a rectangular island for preparing and enjoying meals, looks into the family room. With a two-story ceiling and built-in cabinets surrounding the fireplace, the family room is ideal for family gatherings. A formal dining room and living room provide the perfect atmosphere for entertaining. Upstairs, the master bedroom has a generous walk-in closet and a master bath, complete with a spa tub and dual vanity. Three additional bedrooms share a full bath. Other amenities include a main-floor powder room and laundry room, which allows access to the three-car garage.

DESIGN HPU040489

First Floor: 1,746 square feet
Second Floor: 1,473 square feet
Total: 3,219 square feet
Width: 59'-0" Depth: 54'-0"

DESIGN BY
©Ahmann Design, Inc.

DESIGN HPU040491

First Floor: 2,096 square feet
Second Floor: 1,062 square feet
Total: 3,158 square feet
Width: 48'-0" Depth: 56'-0"

DESIGN BY
©Ahmann Design, Inc.

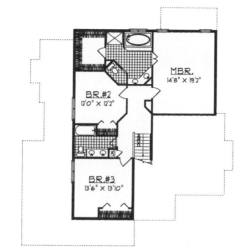

This two-story home features an eye-catching combination of brick and siding. Upon entering the foyer, you will take pleasure in the wide-open space the house provides. The copious feel of the living, family and dining rooms is great for social gatherings or comfortable nights around the fireplace. Upstairs, you'll find the spacious master bedroom with a large bathroom and walk-in closet.

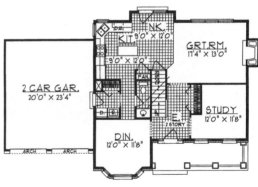

The two-story entryway leads to the cozy great room. Complete with a fireplace, the great room opens into the kitchen. The kitchen, with wraparound counters and a center island, is adjacent to the nook. A separate formal dining room is perfect for entertaining. Upstairs, the master bedroom has a cathedral ceiling and provides a private retreat, full bath and a roomy walk-in closet. Three additional bedrooms share a full bath.

DESIGN HPU040490

First Floor: 995 square feet
Second Floor: 1,125 square feet
Finished Basement:
995 square feet
Total: 3,115 square feet
Width: 56'-4" Depth: 35'-8"

DESIGN BY
©Ahmann Design, Inc.

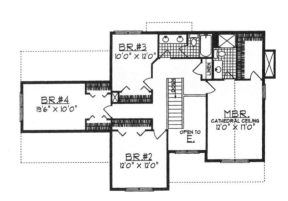

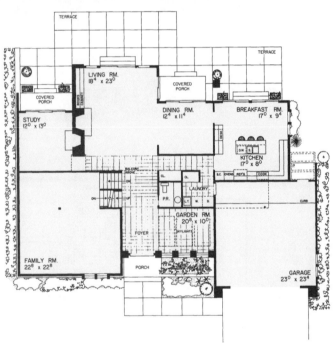

This attractive split-level contemporary home includes a skylit garden room just off the foyer. Note the large, sunken family room, great for entertaining a crowd. The living room features a fireplace with built-in shelves and access to the rear gardens. The study enjoys a cozy fireplace and a private covered porch. The gourmet kitchen enjoys a roomy island snack bar and a sunny breakfast room. The second floor includes the master bedroom with a whirlpool bath and walk-in closet, and two family bedrooms sharing a full bath.

DESIGN BY
©Home Planners

DESIGN HPU040492

Main Level: 2,070 square feet
Upper Level: 1,320 square feet
Total: 3,390 square feet
Width: 68'-4" Depth: 52'-4"

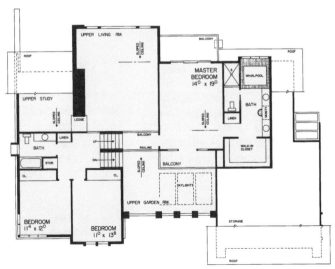

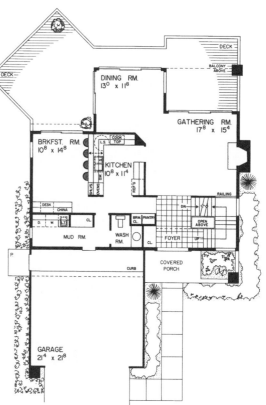

DESIGN HPU040493

Main Level: 1,096 square feet
Upper Level: 1,115 square feet
Lower Level: 1,104 square feet
Total: 3,315 square feet
Width: 40'-0" Depth: 58'-0"

L

DESIGN BY
©Home Planners

A splendidly symmetrical design, this clean-lined, open-planned contemporary home is a great place for the outdoor-minded. The gathering room—with a fireplace—dining room and breakfast room all lead out to a deck off the main level. Similarly, the lower-level activity room—with another fireplace—hobby room and guest bedroom contain separate doors to the backyard terrace. Upstairs are three bedrooms, including a suite with a through-fireplace, private balcony, walk-in closet, dressing room and whirlpool tub.

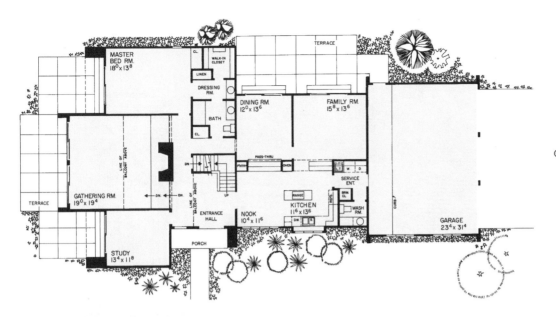

DESIGN BY
©Home Planners

QUOTE ONE®
Cost to build? See page 502
to order complete cost estimate
to build this house in your area!

DESIGN HPU040494

First Floor: 2,132 square feet
Second Floor: 1,156 square feet
Total: 3,288 square feet
Width: 90'-0" Depth: 46'-0"

L D

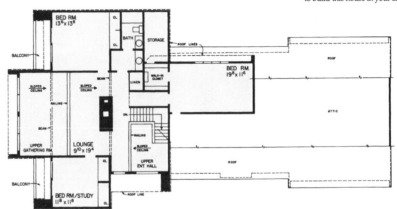

This beautifully designed two-story home provides an eye-catching exterior. The floor plan is a perfect complement. The front kitchen features an island range, adjacent breakfast nook and pass-through to a formal dining room. The master suite offers a spacious walk-in closet and dressing room. The side terrace can be reached from the master suite, the gathering room and the study. The second floor contains three bedrooms and storage space galore. The center lounge offers a sloped ceiling and skylight.

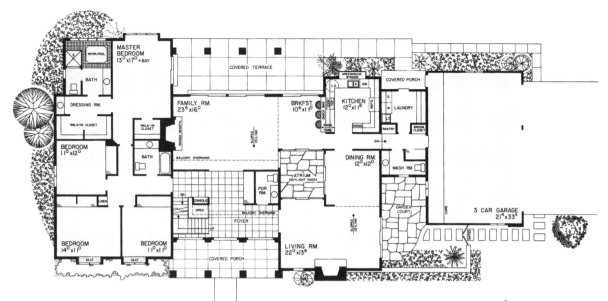

This lavish modern design has it all, including an upper lounge, family room and foyer. A front-facing living room with its own fireplace looks out upon a side garden court and the centrally located atrium. A large, efficient kitchen with snack-bar service to the breakfast room also enjoys its own greenhouse window. The sleeping area is situated at one end of the house downstairs to ensure privacy and relaxation. Here, a deluxe owners suite features a soothing whirlpool tub, dressing area and an abundance of walk-in closets. Three secondary bedrooms, two with window seats, share a full bath.

DESIGN HPU040495

First Floor: 3,173 square feet
Second Floor: 267 square feet
Total: 3,440 square feet
Width: 105'-0" Depth: 52'-8"

DESIGN BY
©Home Planners

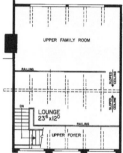

QUOTE ONE®
Cost to build? See page 502
to order complete cost estimate
to build this house in your area!

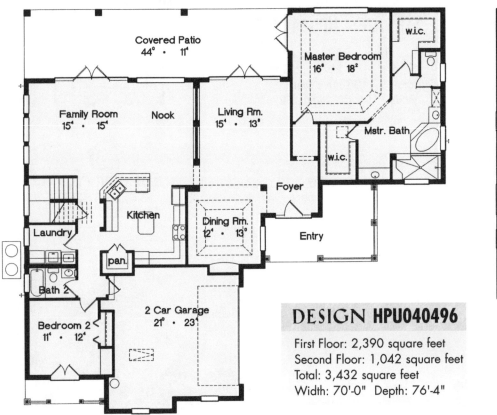

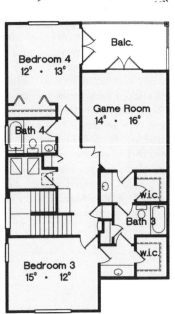

Covered Patio
44⁴ · 11⁴

Family Room
15⁴ · 15⁴

Nook

Living Rm.
15⁴ · 13⁰

Master Bedroom
16⁶ · 18²

w.i.c.

Mstr. Bath

w.i.c.

Kitchen

Laundry

Dining Rm.
12⁴ · 13⁰

Foyer

pan.

Bath 2

Entry

2 Car Garage
21⁰ · 23⁴

Bedroom 2
11⁴ · 12⁴

Bedroom 4
12⁰ · 13⁰

Balc.

Bath 4

Game Room
14⁰ · 16⁰

w.i.c.

Bath 3

w.i.c.

Bedroom 3
15⁰ · 12⁰

DESIGN HPU040496

First Floor: 2,390 square feet
Second Floor: 1,042 square feet
Total: 3,432 square feet
Width: 70'-0" Depth: 76'-4"

DESIGN BY
©Home Design Services, Inc.

A two-story farmhouse with a wraparound front porch and plenty of natural light welcomes you into this graceful, four-bedroom country classic. The large kitchen featuring a center island with a counter and a roomy breakfast area opens to the large great room for easy entertaining. There are plenty of interior architectural effects, with columns, arches and niches to punctuate the interior spaces. A separate dining room provides formality to this elegant home. The owners suite, privately situated on the first floor, features separate double vanities, a garden whirlpool tub and separate walk-around shower. A second bedroom on the main level would be a great guest room or maid's quarters with a private bath and direct access to the garage. Bedrooms 3 and 4 are tucked upstairs with a game room and two full baths.

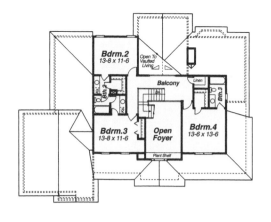

A combination of brick and siding and a raised metal porch roof create a stately look. This plan features the master bedroom on the main level, but also enjoys an optional fifth bedroom/library, allowing guests to remain on the first floor while three other bedrooms share the second floor. A dramatic entry features a two-story foyer looking past the U-shaped stairs into a vaulted living area with a dramatic rear window. The master suite enjoys a fireplace and bay-windowed sitting area, along with dual closets and vanities.

DESIGN HPU040497

First Floor: 2,047 square feet
Second Floor: 1,011 square feet
Total: 3,058 square feet
Width: 69'-8" Depth: 56'-5"

DESIGN BY
©Jannis Vann & Associates, Inc.

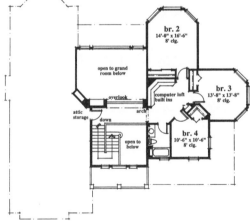

This romantic farmhouse, with its open living spaces and covered porches, is designed with gracious family living in mind. The grand room takes center stage with rear-porch access, a corner fireplace, a built-in media center and a pass-through to the kitchen. The master suite is lavishly appointed with a spa-style bath and a sitting area. Upstairs, a computer loft with built-ins serves as a common area to the three family bedrooms. Please specify basement or slab foundation when ordering.

DESIGN HPU040498

First Floor: 2,240 square feet
Second Floor: 943 square feet
Total: 3,183 square feet
Width: 69'-8" Depth: 61'-10"

DESIGN BY
©The Sater Design Collection

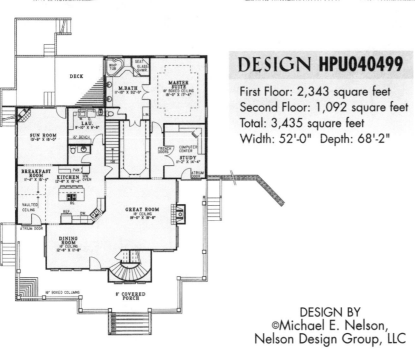

DESIGN HPU040499

First Floor: 2,343 square feet
Second Floor: 1,092 square feet
Total: 3,435 square feet
Width: 52'-0" Depth: 68'-2"

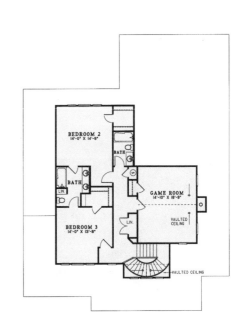

DESIGN BY
©Michael E. Nelson,
Nelson Design Group, LLC

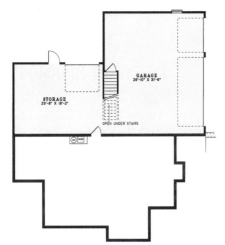

A wraparound porch and a Palladian window lend grace and charm to this three-bedroom farmhouse. Enjoy a moment of quiet contemplation on the front porch, or go inside to enjoy a warming fire in the great room. The open dining room and great room create a perfect entertainment area, with easy access to the kitchen—including a pass-through over the kitchen sink. The kitchen features a large island/snack bar. The nearby breakfast room has a vaulted ceiling, atrium-door access to the front porch and a view of the sun room. This room includes a corner fireplace, light-filled windows and access to the rear deck. A built-in computer center allows plenty of work space in the study. The master suite contains luxury amenities, such as a glass shower, whirlpool bathtub, walk-in closet and boxed ceiling. Two family bedrooms, two full bathrooms and a game room reside on the second level. Please specify basement, crawlspace or slab foundation when ordering.

With equally appealing front and side entrances, a charming Victorian facade invites entry to this stunning home. The foyer showcases the characteristic winding staircase and opens to the large great room with a masonry fireplace. An enormous kitchen features a cooktop island and a breakfast bar large enough to seat four. A lovely bay window distinguishes the nearby dining room. The master suite with a masonry fireplace is located on the first floor. The amenity-filled master bath features double vanities, a whirlpool tub, a separate shower and a gigantic walk-in closet with an additional cedar closet. The second floor contains two bedrooms—one with access to the outdoor balcony on the side of the home. The third floor is completely expandable. Please specify crawlspace or slab foundation when ordering.

DESIGN HPU040500

First Floor: 2,194 square feet
Second Floor: 870 square feet
Total: 3,064 square feet
Bonus Room: 251 square feet
Width: 50'-11" Depth: 91'-2"

L

DESIGN BY
©Larry E. Belk Designs

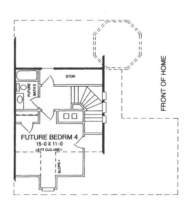

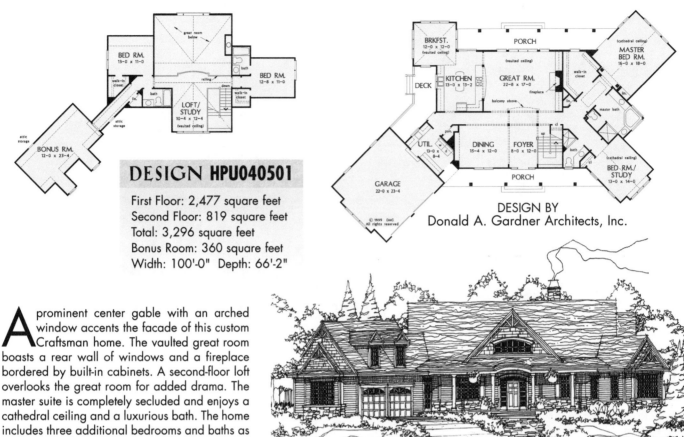

DESIGN HPU040501

First Floor: 2,477 square feet
Second Floor: 819 square feet
Total: 3,296 square feet
Bonus Room: 360 square feet
Width: 100'-0" Depth: 66'-2"

DESIGN BY
Donald A. Gardner Architects, Inc.

A prominent center gable with an arched window accents the facade of this custom Craftsman home. The vaulted great room boasts a rear wall of windows and a fireplace bordered by built-in cabinets. A second-floor loft overlooks the great room for added drama. The master suite is completely secluded and enjoys a cathedral ceiling and a luxurious bath. The home includes three additional bedrooms and baths as well as a vaulted loft/study and bonus room.

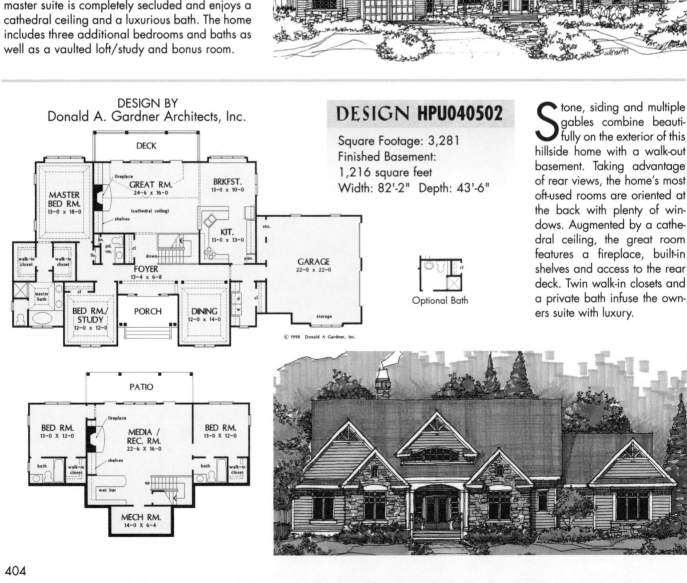

DESIGN BY
Donald A. Gardner Architects, Inc.

DESIGN HPU040502

Square Footage: 3,281
Finished Basement:
1,216 square feet
Width: 82'-2" Depth: 43'-6"

Optional Bath

Stone, siding and multiple gables combine beautifully on the exterior of this hillside home with a walk-out basement. Taking advantage of rear views, the home's most oft-used rooms are oriented at the back with plenty of windows. Augmented by a cathedral ceiling, the great room features a fireplace, built-in shelves and access to the rear deck. Twin walk-in closets and a private bath infuse the owners suite with luxury.

DESIGN HPU040503

First Floor: 2,755 square feet
Second Floor: 735 square feet
Total: 3,490 square feet
Bonus Room: 481 square feet
Width: 92'-6" Depth: 69'-10"

DESIGN BY
Donald A. Gardner Architects, Inc.

Dormers, gables with wood brackets, a double-door entry and a stone-and-siding exterior lend charm and sophistication to this Craftsman estate. Cathedral ceilings and fireplaces are standard in the living room, family room and main bedroom, while the living room, family room and study feature built-in bookshelves. The spacious kitchen with an island stovetop and walk-in pantry opens completely to the family room and breakfast area. The master suite excels with a private sitting room, access to its own porch, two oversized walk-in closets and a lavish bath. Overlooking both foyer and living room, the second-floor balcony connects two bedrooms, a library and a bonus room.

405

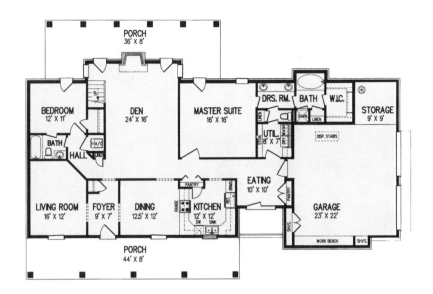

This four-bedroom design, though it has the quaint exterior of an older home, has all the features of modern-day life. A spacious den with a fireplace and rear-porch access provides the perfect gathering spot for quiet times; for more formal occasions, a living room and dining room are available. To the rear of the plan, a cozy bedroom with a roomy closet and porch access adjoins a full bath. The owners suite includes a walk-in closet and an opulent bath with a garden tub. Upstairs, two additional bedrooms feature private baths, walk-in closets and built-in bookshelves. A slope-ceilinged multi-purpose room—perhaps a game room, computer room or home office—completes the plan. Please specify crawlspace or slab foundation when ordering.

DESIGN BY
©Breland & Farmer Designers, Inc.

DESIGN HPU040504

First Floor: 1,925 square feet
Second Floor: 1,134 square feet
Total: 3,059 square feet
Width: 78'-0" Depth: 52'-0"

DESIGN HPU040505

First Floor: 2,042 square feet
Second Floor: 1,099 square feet
Total: 3,141 square feet
Width: 66'-0" Depth: 44'-6"

DESIGN BY
©Select Home Designs

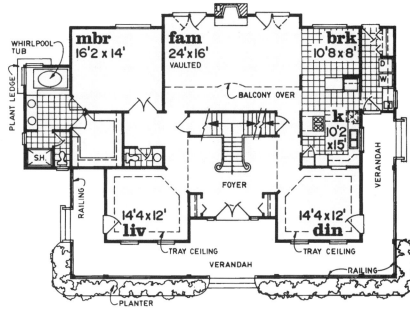

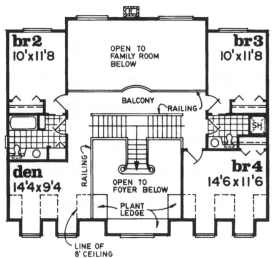

A wide, wrapping veranda graces the front of this design and is accessed from the living room and the dining room, as well as double doors at the entry. Both the living and dining rooms have tray ceilings. The family room is vaulted and has a cozy fireplace as its focal point. To either side of the fireplace are double doors to the rear yard. The kitchen has a center cooking island, spacious counters and a pass-through to the dining room. The breakfast room serves for casual occasions. The main-floor master suite features a lavish master bath with a roomy walk-in closet, whirlpool spa and twin vanity. A den or media center is found on the second floor with three family bedrooms and two full baths.

DESIGN HPU040507

First Floor: 2,033 square feet
Second Floor: 1,116 square feet
Total: 3,149 square feet
Width: 71'-0" Depth: 56'-0"

DESIGN BY
©Chatham Home Planning, Inc.

Tall columns march along the raised porch of this Southern-style home and frame a grand two-story foyer. In the great room, the fireplace stands between French doors leading to the rear porch and deck. The outstanding owners bedroom suite features a sitting room, a private porch and deck and a corner bath with a whirlpool tub. Upstairs a hall balcony connects three additional bedrooms and two full baths. Please specify crawlspace or slab foundation when ordering.

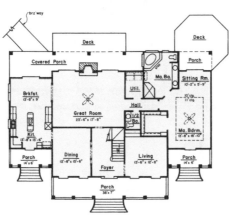

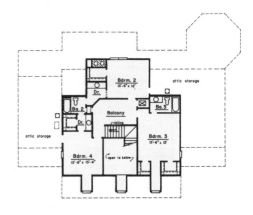

DESIGN HPU040506

Square Footage: 3,084
Bonus Room: 868 square feet
Width: 74'-0" Depth: 72'-0"

DESIGN BY
©Vaughn A. Lauban Designs

A gracious colonnade and three distinctive dormers set high on the roof give this home an elegant but homey appeal. Columns that separate and distinguish formal spaces flank the double-door entry. This home enjoys a split floor plan that allows for a secluded owners suite with pleasing appointments to the bath and bedroom. A guest suite or study can be found at the front left of the plan. Two additional bedrooms share a hall bath.

There's curb appeal galore in this stylish traditional home. Dormer windows extend gracefully from the steep roofline. A large front porch provides a comfortable retreat. Practical as well, this home provides storage space off the garage and in the attic. A game room upstairs, a computer alcove with a built-in desk under one of the dormer windows, and a downstairs study are functional for a variety of lifestyles. Three bedrooms—four if the study is used as a bedroom—three bathrooms and a powder room, and a terrific kitchen open to the hearth room and breakfast room, with a built-in entertainment center, complete this fabulous plan. Please specify basement, crawlspace or slab foundation when ordering.

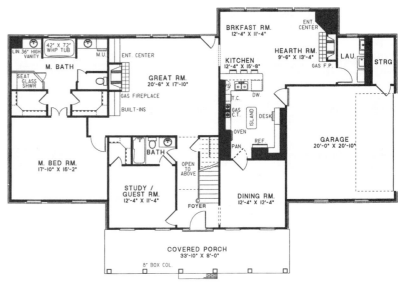

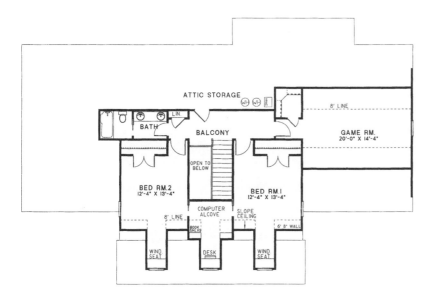

DESIGN HPU040508

First Floor: 1,977 square feet
Second Floor: 1,098 square feet
Total: 3,075 square feet
Width: 72'-4" Depth: 48'-4"

DESIGN BY
©Michael E. Nelson,
Nelson Design Group, LLC

DESIGN HPU040509

First Floor: 2,357 square feet
Second Floor: 995 square feet
Total: 3,352 square feet
Bonus Room: 545 square feet
Width: 95'-4" Depth: 54'-10"

DESIGN BY
Donald A. Gardner Architects, Inc.

From the two-story foyer with a Palladian clerestory window and a graceful stairway to the large great room with a cathedral ceiling and curved balcony, impressive spaces prevail in this open plan. The master suite, privately located at the opposite end of the first floor, features a sitting bay, an extra-large walk-in closet and a bath with every possible luxury. Three bedrooms and two full baths reside on the second floor.

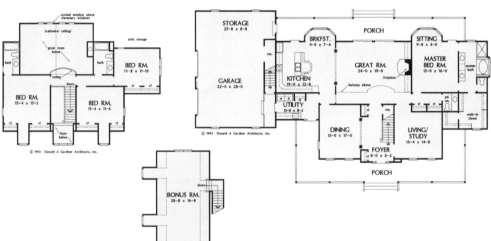

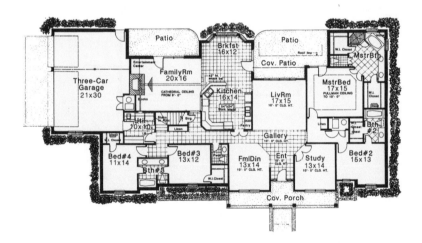

A distinctive exterior, a cathedral ceiling in the large family room, and room to expand make this country contemporary home a good choice. A study and formal dining room flank the entryway; three family bedrooms are across the front. The master suite offers plenty of seclusion, and a stairway leads to a future upstairs area.

DESIGN HPU040510

Square Footage: 3,270
Width: 101'-0" Depth: 48'-0"

DESIGN BY
©Fillmore Design Group

410

The definition of a transitional home is that it has space that can be converted as the family grows or as it moves out and less space is needed. This home is a perfect example. From its foyer, a study/bedroom opens to the left and features access to a bath. Another area worth noting is the basement. The rooms here can be used as either a garage/storage area and a bedroom, office or hobby room. As for the rest of the house, amenities abound in the master suite, efficient kitchen and hobby room off of the garage. Please specify crawlspace or slab foundation when ordering.

DESIGN BY
©Michael E. Nelson,
Nelson Design Group, LLC

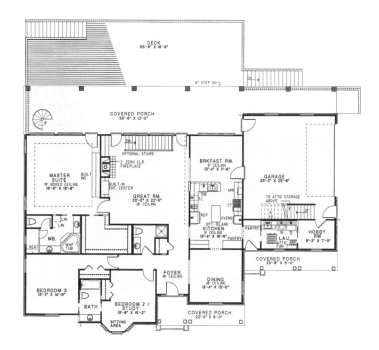

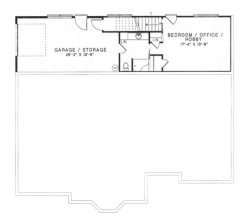

DESIGN HPU040511

Main Level: 2,650 square feet
Lower Level: 409 square feet
Total: 3,059 square feet
Width: 79'-0" Depth: 77'-8"

The splendor of this exciting two-story home begins with the solid brick exterior, multiple gables and soft wood trim. High ceilings in the foyer and great room showcase the wall of windows across the rear. The dining room is topped with a tray ceiling, and an alcove provides added space to display formal furniture. An expansive gourmet kitchen, island with seating, large breakfast area and cozy hearth room provide for today's active family lifestyles. From the garage, a hallway offers an orderly and quiet entry. Built-ins for a home computer and bookshelves are shown in the library. Relax and enjoy the master bedroom suite with its many luxurious amenities, including an exciting ceiling treatment and an expansive use of windows. The balcony of the second floor provides a dramatic view to the great room and leads to three additional bedrooms, creating a spectacular family-size home.

DESIGN HPU040512

First Floor: 2,297 square feet
Second Floor: 830 square feet
Total: 3,127 square feet
Width: 74'-8" Depth: 53'-0"

DESIGN BY
©Studer Residential Designs, Inc.

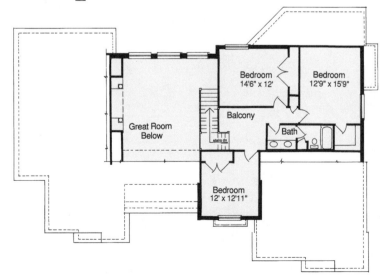

DESIGN HPU040513

Square Footage: 3,034
Width: 81'-4" Depth: 66'-8"

DESIGN BY
©Ahmann Design, Inc.

Truly a house one can call home—from its shingled and gabled exterior to its highly efficient interior—this design is sure to please. Stairs near the foyer lead to an optional finished basement. Directly ahead is an arched-ceiling great room, complete with a through-fireplace, built-in cabinets and a wall of windows. A lavish master bedroom suite offers two walk-in closets and a private bath. Two secondary bedrooms share a full bath.

Multiple gables, a boxed window and a brick-and-stone exterior combine to create an exciting front on this beautiful two-story home. A dramatic fireplace, sloped ceiling and built-in entertainment cabinet decorate the fashionable great room. The first-floor master bedroom with its tray ceiling, super bath and walk-in closet pampers homeowners with its size and luxury. Split stairs lead to a second-floor balcony that overlooks the great room for a dramatic effect. Three additional bedrooms top this spectacular home.

DESIGN HPU040514

First Floor: 2,181 square feet
Second Floor: 1,072 square feet
Total: 3,253 square feet
Width: 75'-0" Depth: 56'-9"

DESIGN BY
©Studer Residential Designs, Inc.

This four-bedroom brick home offers something extra special—though it looks like a ranch home, it's a two-story in reality! Designed for a hillside lot, this home offers two bedrooms, with bay windows, and a cozy recreation room with a fireplace on its lower level. On the main level, a formal dining room is at the front of the home, while the U-shaped kitchen easily serves the bayed nook via snack bar. A spacious living room warms those cool evenings with a fireplace. The lavish master suite comes complete with a walk-in closet and deluxe private bath. A secondary bedroom—or make it a study—finishes out this floor.

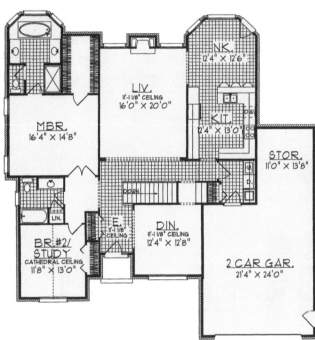

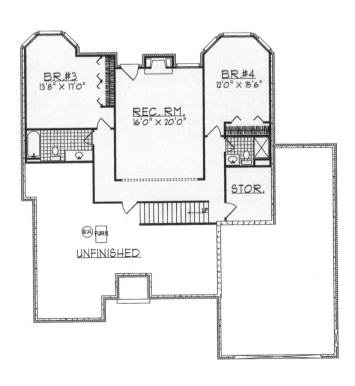

DESIGN HPU040515

Main Level: 1,930 square feet
Lower Level: 1,121 square feet
Total: 3,051 square feet
Width: 57'-0" Depth: 58'-10"

DESIGN BY
©Ahmann Design, Inc.

414

A delightful mix of styles combine to give this home plenty of curb appeal. From the foyer, a study, formal dining room and spacious great room are accessible. The gourmet of the family will enjoy the kitchen, with its work surface/snack-bar island and tons of counter and cabinet space. Two bedrooms are located on the right side of the home, each offering a walk-in closet and a private bath. The deluxe master bedroom suite is lavish in its amenities, which include a large walk-in closet, a fireplace and a sumptuous bath. Note the huge game room and extra bedroom over the garage—perfect for an in-law suite. Please specify basement, crawlspace or slab foundation when ordering.

DESIGN HPU040516

First Floor: 2,633 square feet
Second Floor: 752 square feet
Total: 3,385 square feet
Width: 75'-2" Depth: 89'-6"

DESIGN BY
©Michael E. Nelson,
Nelson Design Group, LLC

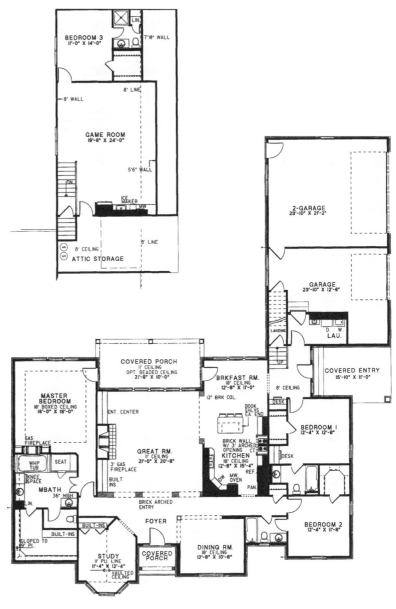

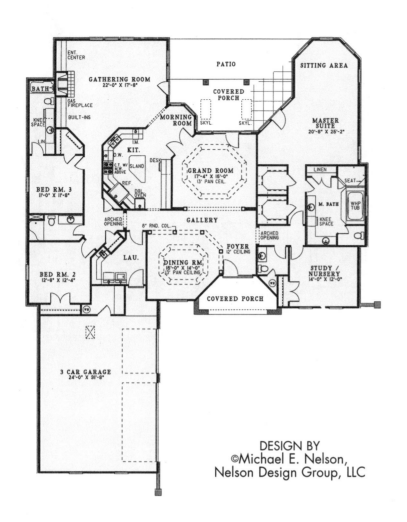

ENT. CENTER

GATHERING ROOM
22'-0" X 17'-8"

BATH

GAS FIREPLACE

BUILT-INS

KNEE SPACE

IN.

PATIO

COVERED PORCH

SITTING AREA

MORNING ROOM

SKYL

SKYL

MASTER SUITE
20'-8" X 26'-2"

BED RM. 3
11'-0" X 11'-8"

KIT.

I.M.

D.W.

ISLAND

C.T. W/ M.W. ABOVE

DBL OVEN

REF.

DESK

GRAND ROOM
17'-4" X 16'-0"
13' PAN CEIL.

LINEN

SEAT

M. BATH

WHP TUB

KNEE SPACE

ARCHED OPENING

GALLERY

8" RND. COL.

ARCHED OPENING

LAU.

FOYER
12' CEILING

DINING RM.
15'-0" X 14'-0"
13' PAN CEILING

BED RM. 2
12'-8" X 12'-4"

STUDY / NURSERY
14'-0" X 12'-0"

COVERED PORCH

3 CAR GARAGE
24'-0" X 31'-8"

DESIGN BY
©Michael E. Nelson,
Nelson Design Group, LLC

Gently curving arches and a grand covered porch liven up the facade of this palatial home. The foyer is flanked by columns defining the formal dining room and arched openings to other areas of the home. The grand room is situated beneath a thirteen-foot pan ceiling. Doors lead to the morning room and the rear skylit porch. The morning room enjoys spectacular views of the patio and separates the modern kitchen from the gathering room. Complete with built-in entertainment facilities and a gas fireplace, the family will be drawn to this warm room. Two family bedrooms are located nearby. The other side of the home holds the fantastic owners suite and the study/nursery. The suite features patio access, a roomy sitting area with bay windows, His and Hers walk-in closets and a luxurious private bath. A three-car garage with a storage room caps this design. Please specify crawlspace or slab foundation when ordering.

DESIGN HPU040517

Square Footage: 3,124
Width: 70'-0" Depth: 88'-2"

BEST AND BRIGHTEST

Luxurious homes that reflect elegant style

DESIGN BY
©Studer Residential Designs, Inc.

DESIGN HPU040518

First Floor: 3,087 square feet
Second Floor: 1,037 square feet
Total: 4,124 square feet
Width: 92'-2" Depth: 70'-10"

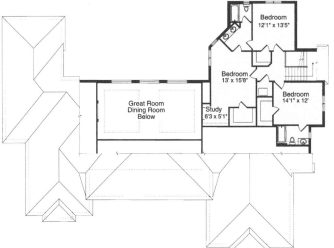

An elegant front porch, columns inside and out, various ceiling treatments and decorative windows create a spectacular home. An open floor plan provides large formal and informal spaces. The island kitchen with extensive counter space offers easy access to the formal dining and breakfast areas. Located for privacy, the impressive master bedroom suite showcases a deluxe dressing room with a whirlpool tub, dual vanities, an oversized shower and a walk-in closet. A library is located near the master bedroom. Split stairs are positioned for family convenience and lead to three bedrooms, each with a large walk-in closet and private access to a bath. A three-car garage and full basement complete this exciting showplace.

DESIGN HPU040519

Main Level: 3,570 square feet
Lower Level: 2,367 square feet
Total: 5,937 square feet
Width: 84'-6" Depth: 69'-4"

The stone-and-brick exterior with multiple gables and a side-entry garage create a design that will attract many passersby. The gourmet kitchen with an island and a snack bar combine with the spacious breakfast room and hearth room to create a warm and friendly atmosphere for family living. The luxurious master bedroom with a sitting area and fireplace is complemented by a deluxe dressing room and walk-in closet.

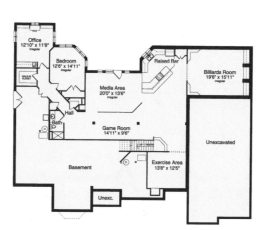

DESIGN BY
©Studer Residential Designs, Inc.

A brick-and-stone exterior with a tower and recessed entry creates a strong, solid look for this enchanting home. The large foyer introduces the great room with its beam ceiling and tall windows. The master bedroom with a sloped ceiling and spacious dressing area offers a relaxing retreat. Split stairs located for family convenience introduce the spectacular lower level, which is home to a wine room, exercise room, wet bar and two additional bedrooms.

DESIGN HPU040520

Main Level: 2,562 square feet
Lower Level: 1,955 square feet
Total: 4,517 square feet
Width: 75'-8" Depth: 70'-6"

DESIGN BY
©Studer Residential Designs, Inc.

T his exciting ranch-style home offers a floor plan to accommodate the lifestyle of a busy homeowner. The main floor offers a large open great room and formal dining room framed with an eleven-foot ceiling. A large kitchen with an island provides roominess for the cook and cook's helper. Pampering the homeowner with its luxury, the master bedroom suite has a coffered ceiling and deluxe dressing room. Two additional bedrooms and a first-floor laundry provide everything needed for comfortable living. The option of creating additional living space is available in the walkout basement.

DESIGN BY
©Studer Residential Designs, Inc.

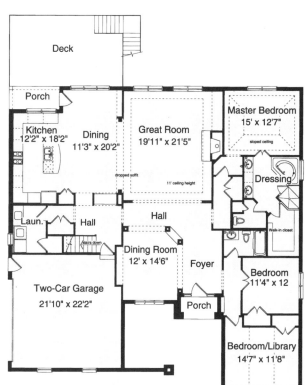

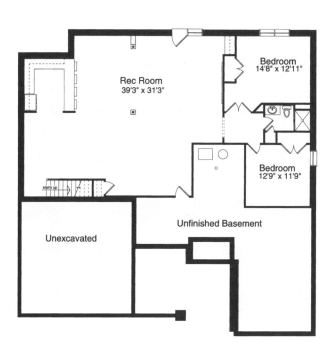

DESIGN HPU040521

Main Level: 2,469 square feet
Lower Level: 1,671 square feet
Total: 4,140 square feet
Width: 59'-0" Depth: 59'-6"

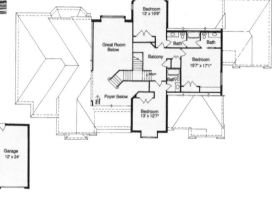

DESIGN HPU040523

First Floor: 3,364 square feet
Second Floor: 1,198 square feet
Total: 4,562 square feet
Width: 98'-6" Depth: 61'-5"

DESIGN BY
©Studer Residential Designs, Inc.

The richness of natural stone and brick set the tone for the warmth and charm of this transitional home. A deluxe bath and a dressing area with a walk-in closet complement the owners suite. The library retreat boasts built-in bookshelves and a fourteen-foot ceiling. A dramatic view greets you at the second-floor balcony. Two family bedrooms share a tandem bath that includes separate vanities, and a third bedroom holds a private bath.

DESIGN HPU040522

Main Level: 2,766 square feet
Lower Level: 1,882 square feet
Total: 4,648 square feet
Width: 81'-10" Depth: 50'-8"

DESIGN BY
©Studer Residential Designs, Inc.

A popular brick-and-stone exterior provides the rich, solid look to this beautiful home. Pampering the homeowner with its luxury, the master bedroom suite provides a deluxe bath with a whirlpool tub, separate shower, double-bowl vanity and spacious walk-in closet. Two bedroom suites on the lower level provide inviting accommodations for overnight guests or returning college students.

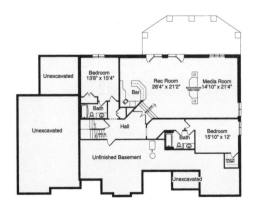

The combination of stucco, stacked stone and brick adds texture and character to this French country home. The foyer offers views to the study, dining room and living room. Double French doors open to the study with built-in bookcases and a window seat overlooking the rear deck. The breakfast room, family room and spacious kitchen make a nice backdrop for family living. The master suite is enhanced by a raised, corner fireplace and a bath with an exercise room. Upstairs, two family bedrooms—or make one an office—and a full bath are balanced by a large game room.

DESIGN BY
©Larry E. Belk Designs

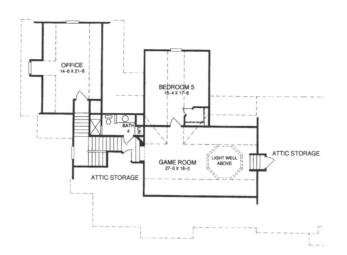

DESIGN HPU040524

First Floor: 3,328 square feet
Second Floor: 868 square feet
Total: 4,196 square feet
Width: 108'-2" Depth: 61'-6"

First Floor: 5,152 square feet
Second Floor: 726 square feet
Total: 5,878 square feet
Width: 146'-7" Depth: 106'-7"

From the master bedroom suite to the detached four-car garage, this design will delight even the most discerning palates. While the formal living and dining rooms bid greeting as you enter, the impressive great room, with its cathedral ceiling, raised-hearth fireplace and veranda access, will take your breath away. A gallery hall leads to the kitchen and the family sleeping wing on the right and to the study, guest suite and master suite on the left. The large island kitchen, with its sunny breakfast nook, will be a gourmet's delight. The master suite includes a bayed sitting area, a dual fireplace shared with the study, and a luxurious bath. Each additional bedroom features its own bath and sitting area. Upstairs is a massive recreation room with a sunlit studio area and a bridge leading to an attic over the garage.

DESIGN BY
©Fillmore Design Group

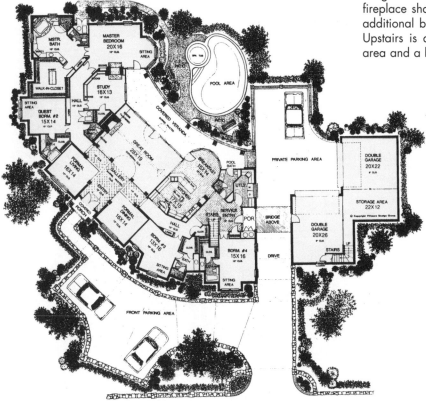

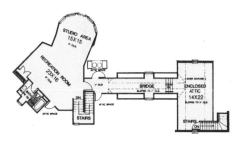

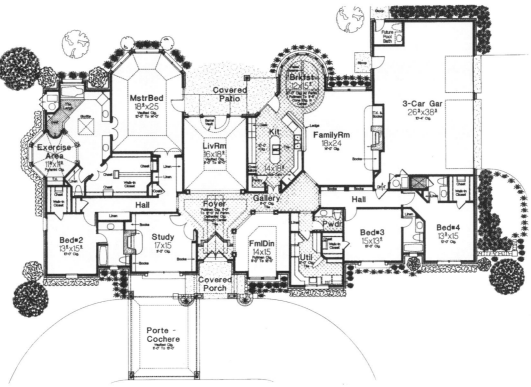

The hipped-roof, French-country exterior and porte-cochere entrance are just the beginning of this unique and impressive design. An unusual Pullman ceiling graces the foyer as it leads to the formal dining room on the right, to the study with a fireplace on the left and straight ahead to the formal living room with its covered patio access. A gallery directs you to the island kitchen with its abundant counter space and adjacent sun-filled breakfast bay. On the left side of the home, a spectacular master suite will become your favorite haven and the envy of your guests. The master bedroom includes a coffered ceiling, a bayed sitting area and patio access. The master bath features a large doorless shower, a separate exercise room and a huge walk-in closet with built-in chests. All of the family bedrooms offer private baths and walk-in closets.

DESIGN BY
©Fillmore Design Group

DESIGN HPU040526

Square Footage: 4,615
Width: 109'-10" Depth: 89'-4"

Interesting window treatments highlight this stone-and-shake facade, but don't overlook the columned porch to the left of the portico. Arches outline the formal dining room and the family room, both of which are convenient to the island kitchen. Household chores are made easier by the placement of a pantry, a powder room, a laundry room and an office between the kitchen and entrances to the side porch and the garage. If your goal is relaxing, the breakfast room, screened porch and covered deck are also nearby. The pampering owners suite is to the left of the main level, with three more bedrooms and a recreation room on the lower level. A bonus room above the garage receives natural light from a dormer window.

DESIGN BY
©Living Concepts Home Planning

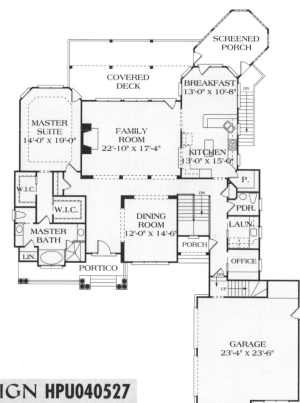

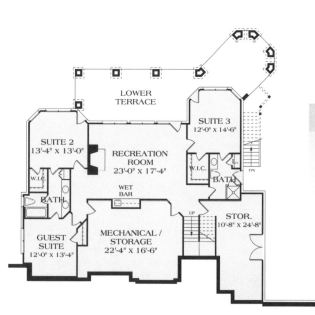

DESIGN HPU040527

Main Level: 2,213 square feet
Lower Level: 1,333 square feet
Total: 3,546 square feet
Bonus Room: 430 square feet
Width: 67'-2" Depth: 93'-1"

NOOK
13/0 X 11/8
(10' CLG.)

VERANDA

MASTER
13/0 X 16/2
(14' CLG.)

SITTING
10/2 X 14/2
(10' CLG.)

GREAT RM.
25/0 X 21/0
(17'-8" CLG.)

UNHEATED
SHOP
10/8 X 18/0

DINING
13/6 X 16/4
(10' CLG.)

DEN
11/0 X 14/8
(12' CLG.)

GARAGE
21/4 X 33/2

BR. 3
13/0 X 14/0

7/2 X 7/4

ATTIC
STORAGE

BR. 2
13/0 X 18/6

BONUS
16/10 X 16/6
(9' CLG.)

ATTIC
STORAGE

DESIGN HPU040528

First Floor: 2,698 square feet
Second Floor: 819 square feet
Total: 3,517 square feet
Bonus Room: 370 square feet
Width: 90'-6" Depth: 84'-0"

DESIGN BY
©Alan Mascord Design
Associates, Inc.

If you've ever traveled the European countryside, past rolling hills that range in hue from apple-green to deep, rich emerald, you may have come upon a home much like this one. Stone accents combined with stucco, and shutters that frame multi-pane windows add a touch of charm that introduces the marvelous floor plan found inside. The foyer opens onto a great room that offers a panoramic view of the veranda and beyond. To the left, you'll find a formal dining room; to the right, a quiet den. Just steps away resides the sitting room that introduces the grand master suite. A kitchen with a nook, laundry room and large shop area complete the first floor. The second floor contains two family bedrooms, two full baths and a bonus room.

DESIGN BY
©Living Concepts Home Planning

Gables, varied rooflines, interesting dormers, arched windows, a recessed entry—the detailing on this stone manor is exquisite! The foyer opens through arches to the formal dining room, an elegant stair hall and the grand room, with its fireplace, built-ins and French doors to the lanai. The informal zone includes a kitchen with an oversized work island and pantry, a breakfast nook and a family room with a fireplace and its own screened porch. An anteroom outside the master suite gives the homeowners added privacy and allows the option of a private entrance to the study. The master bath is loaded with extras, including a stairway to the upstairs exercise room. The second floor also offers a home theater and a home office, as well as four bedroom suites and a mother-in-law or maid's apartment. Note that there are four sets of stairs to aid in the traffic flow and a laundry room on each level.

DESIGN HPU040529

First Floor: 5,200 square feet
Second Floor: 4,177 square feet
Total: 9,377 square feet
Width: 155'-9" Depth: 107'-11"

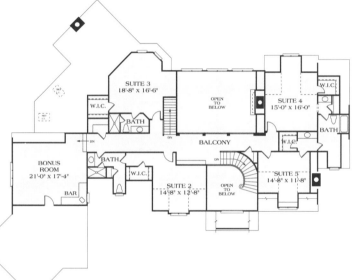

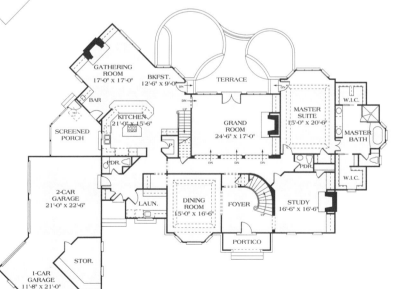

A stone-accented entrance welcomes you to this impressive French country estate. A sunken grand room combines with a bay-windowed dining room to create the formal living area. French doors open out to a multi-level terrace that links formal and informal areas and the master suite. A screened porch off the gathering room has a pass-through window from the kitchen to facilitate warm-weather dining. The master wing includes a study with a fireplace as well as a bayed sitting area and an amenity-laden bath. Two of the four bedrooms have private baths, while the others have separate dressing and vanity areas within a shared bath. A recreation room with a corner bar completes the plan.

DESIGN HPU040530

First Floor: 3,387 square feet
Second Floor: 1,799 square feet
Total: 5,186 square feet
Bonus Room: 379 square feet
Width: 110'-10"   Depth: 84'-6"

DESIGN BY
©Living Concepts Home Planning

427

brkfst
12-6 X 13-9

family
20 X 22-4

kit
15 X 16

dining
14 X 17

storage

study
17-6 X 11-8

foyer

garage
20 X 20

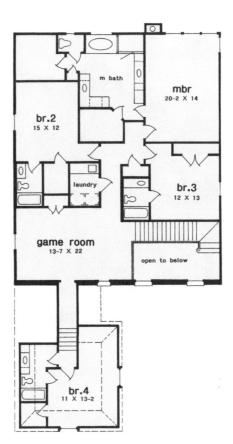

m bath

mbr
20-2 X 14

br.2
15 X 12

laundry

br.3
12 X 13

game room
13-7 X 22

open to below

br.4
11 X 13-2

A garage-top bedroom may be the perfect place for your teenager, offering privacy, a separate bathroom, a large walk-in closet and a view out of two arched dormer windows. There are plenty of great spaces for children and adults in this elegant home. A downstairs study and an upstairs game room are two extras that set this home apart. Four bedrooms each have a private bathroom, with an additional powder room located downstairs. Notice that there is lots of extra storage space in this home and that the laundry room is conveniently located near the cluster of bedrooms. An ideal home for growing families, for those who have frequent overnight guests or for use as a bed and breakfast, it offers true versatility with elegant styling.

DESIGN BY
©Andy McDonald Design Group

DESIGN HPU040531

First Floor: 1,909 square feet
Second Floor: 1,992 square feet
Total: 3,901 square feet
Bonus Room: 299 square feet
Width: 39'-9" Depth: 76'-10"

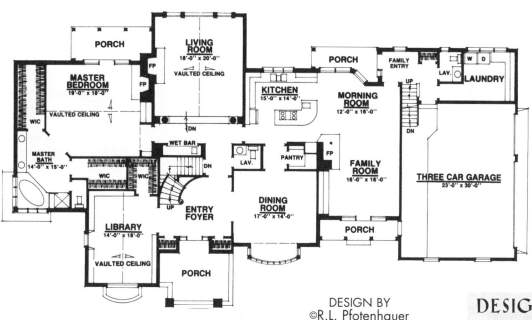

DESIGN BY
©R.L. Pfotenhauer

DESIGN HPU040532

First Floor: 3,182 square feet
Second Floor: 1,190 square feet
Total: 4,372 square feet
Bonus Room: 486 square feet
Width: 104'-0"   Depth: 60'-0"

In the Pays Basque region of rural France, you can find finished farmhouses such as this beauty. The steeply pitched roof drains water quickly, and the curved eaves push the water away from the wall, protecting the stucco. The two-story entry is graced with a beautiful curved stair, opening to a two-story living room with a vaulted ceiling. To the right is a formal dining room and to the left, a finely detailed library with a vaulted ceiling and an impressive arched window. The private master bedroom, with its vaulted ceiling, king-size bath and huge walk-in closets, will never go out of style. The second floor has two bedrooms with their own bathrooms and a bonus room for future use. Note the second stair that is convenient to the informal areas.

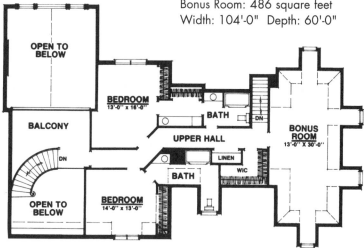

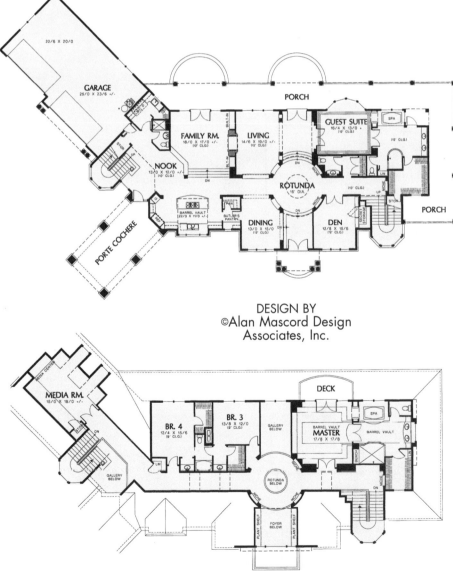

DESIGN BY
©Alan Mascord Design
Associates, Inc.

If it's space you desire, with a classy facade to further enhance it, this is the home for you! Inside, the foyer is flanked by a cozy den to the right and a formal dining room to the left. A lavish guest suite is loaded with amenities and is near the formal living room. The spacious kitchen will please any gourmet, with a cooktop island, walk-in pantry and a nearby sunken family room. Here, a fireplace, shared by the formal living room, will add warmth and charm to any gathering. Upstairs, two large bedrooms—each with walk-in closets and private lavatories—share a bath. A media room is just down the hall and is great for reading, studying or watching movies. The sumptuous master suite is designed to pamper, with such amenities as a walk-in closet, private deck, huge shower and separate spa tub. Note the tremendous amount of storage in the four-car garage.

DESIGN HPU040533

First Floor: 3,620 square feet
Second Floor: 2,440 square feet
Total: 6,060 square feet
Width: 139'-6" Depth: 91'-1"

DESIGN HPU040534

First Floor: 3,833 square feet
Second Floor: 2,133 square feet
Total: 5,966 square feet
Width: 125'-6" Depth: 80'-8"

GARAGE
27/4 X 22/4

GARAGE
23/2 X 21/2

COVERED PORCH

2 STORY
FAMILY
20/0 X 25/0

OFFICE
16/2 X 14/0
(10' CLG.)

COVERED PORCH

SITTING
16/8 X 11/2
(10' CLG.)

MASTER
14/2 X 14/6
(11' CLG.)

2 STORY
LIVING
15/0 X 20/2

2 STORY
FOYER

DINING
13/0 X 19/8
(10' CLG.)

NOOK
(10' CLG.)

STOR

BUTLER'S
PANTRY

COVERED PORCH

COVERED PORCH

DESIGN BY
©Alan Mascord Design
Associates, Inc.

VAULTED
BONUS
21/8 X 20/0

FAMILY RM. BELOW

VAULTED
GUEST BR.
13/0 X 12/0

LIBRARY

LINEN

BR. 3
14/4 X 15/8
(9' CLG.)

VAULTED
EXERCISE
10/0 X 9/0

STOR

FOYER
BELOW

LINEN

LIVING RM.
BELOW

BR. 2
13/0 X 14/6
(9' CLG.)

Stucco and stone details and multiple gables give this home a distinctive exterior. The striking glass-walled turret houses an elegant, octagonal, two-story living room with a fireplace. The dining room, across the foyer, is accessible to the gourmet kitchen through a butler's pantry. The kitchen opens to the large family room and a breakfast nook with access to a covered porch. The master suite takes up the left wing of the house with its bumped-out garden tub, room-sized walk-in closet and private covered porch. Two staircases—a beautifully curved one in the foyer and one in the family room—lead upstairs, where three bedrooms share two baths along with an exercise room and a large bonus room over the garage.

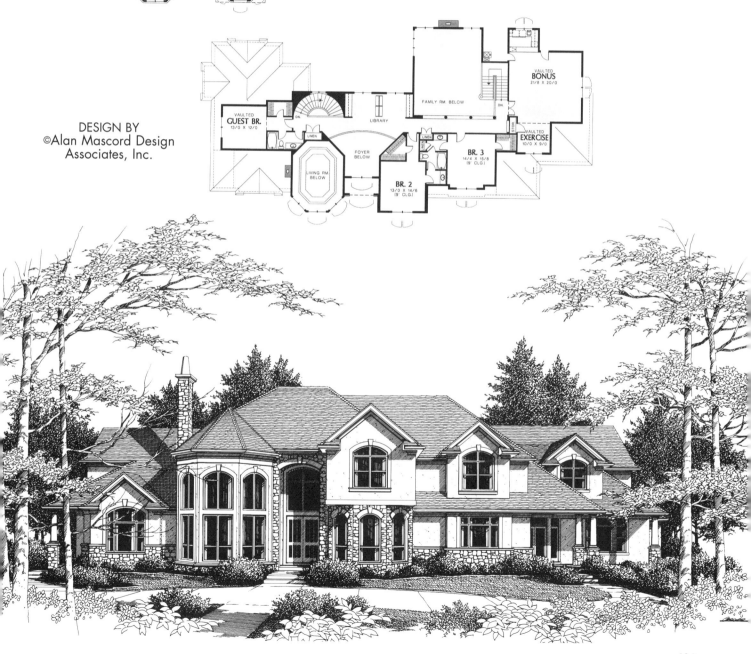

DESIGN HPU040535

First Floor: 2,518 square feet
Second Floor: 1,013 square feet
Total: 3,531 square feet
Bonus Room: 192 square feet
Width: 67'-8" Depth: 74'-2"

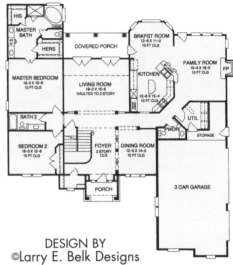

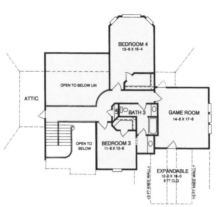

DESIGN BY
©Larry E. Belk Designs

Old World charm gives this design its universal appeal. The mixture of stone and brick on the exterior elevation gives the home a warm, inviting feel. Inside, an up-to-date floor plan has it all. Two living areas provide space for both formal and informal entertaining. The kitchen and breakfast room are open to the large family room. The owners suite and a secondary bedroom are located on the first floor. The second bedroom makes a great nursery, study or convenient guest bedroom. Upstairs, bedrooms 3 and 4 share a large bath, with private dressing areas. Please specify basement, crawlspace or slab foundation when ordering.

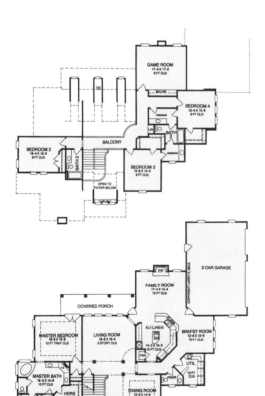

DESIGN HPU040536

First Floor: 2,666 square feet
Second Floor: 1,471 square feet
Total: 4,137 square feet
Width: 82'-2" Depth: 79'-10"

DESIGN BY
©Larry E. Belk Designs

A brick exterior, interesting window dressings and a multitude of rooflines lend this house eye appeal. Inside, a two-story foyer illuminates with natural light and leads past columns to the formal dining room and living room. To the left of the plan, the tray-ceilinged master bedroom enjoys private access to the rear porch, and features a luxurious bath. The second level includes three family bedrooms, two full baths and a game room.

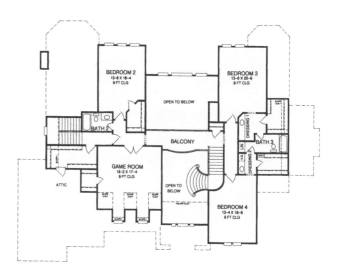

DESIGN HPU040537

First Floor: 3,261 square feet
Second Floor: 1,920 square feet
Total: 5,181 square feet
Bonus Room: 710 square feet
Width: 86'-2" Depth: 66'-10"

Elegantly styled in the French country tradition, this home features a well-thought-out floor plan with all the amenities. A large dining room and a study open off the two-story grand foyer that showcases a lovely flared staircase. A covered patio is accessed from the large formal living room. A more informal family room is conveniently located off the kitchen and breakfast room. The roomy master suite includes a sitting area, a luxurious private bath and its own entrance to the study. The second floor can be reached from the formal front stair or a well-placed rear staircase. Three large bedrooms and a game room are located upstairs. Bedrooms 3 and 4 feature private dressing areas and a shared bath. Bedroom 2 shares a bath with the game room. The walkout basement can be expanded to provide more living space. Please specify basement or crawlspace foundation when ordering.

DESIGN BY
©Fillmore Design Group

DESIGN HPU040538

First Floor: 2,778 square feet
Second Floor: 931 square feet
Total: 3,709 square feet
Bonus Room: 1,405 square feet
Width: 86'-0" Depth: 60'-1"

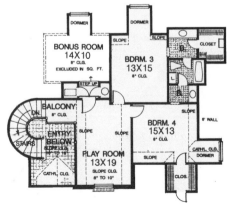

This brick-and-stone combination features a country-fresh look with a contemporary interior floor plan. Step into the gallery, and directly to your left is the sweeping staircase; to the right, you will find a large kitchen and breakfast area. The family room is enhanced with an entertainment center, fireplace and access to the rear patio. The first-floor master suite boasts a sumptuous bath. Along with two bedrooms, the second floor holds a playroom and a bonus room.

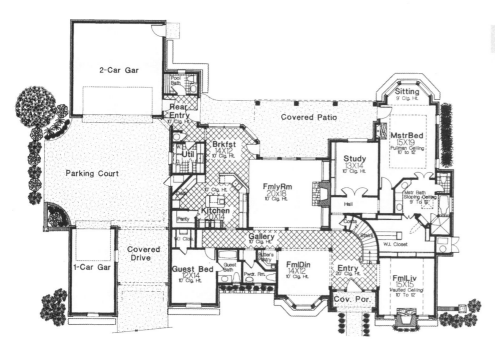

DESIGN HPU040539

First Floor: 3,248 square feet
Second Floor: 1,426 square feet
Total: 4,674 square feet
Width: 99'-10" Depth: 74'-10"

DESIGN BY
©Fillmore Design Group

Multiple rooflines, a stone, brick and siding facade and an absolutely grand entrance combine to give this home the look of luxury. A striking family room showcases a beautiful fireplace framed with built-ins. The nearby breakfast room streams with light and accesses the rear patio. The kitchen features an island workstation, walk-in pantry and plenty of counter space. A guest suite is available on the first floor, perfect for when elderly members of the family visit. The master suite, also on the first floor, enjoys easy access to a large study, a bayed sitting room and a luxurious bath. Private baths are also included for each of the upstairs bedrooms.

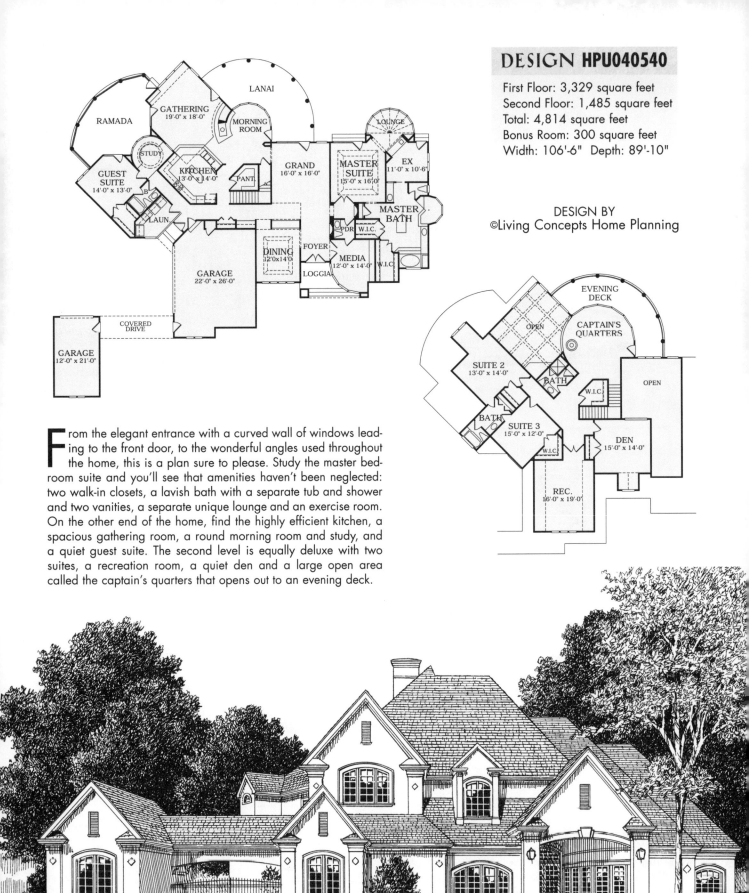

First Floor: 3,329 square feet
Second Floor: 1,485 square feet
Total: 4,814 square feet
Bonus Room: 300 square feet
Width: 106'-6" Depth: 89'-10"

DESIGN BY
©Living Concepts Home Planning

First Floor Plan Labels:

RAMADA

GATHERING
19'-0" x 18'-0"

LANAI

MORNING
ROOM

LOUNGE

STUDY

GUEST
SUITE
14'-0" x 13'-0"

KITCHEN
13'-0" x 14'-0"

PANT.

GRAND
16'-0" x 16'-0"

MASTER
SUITE
15'-0" x 16'-0"

EX
11'-0" x 10'-6"

LAUN.

MASTER
BATH

PDR.

W.I.C.

DINING
12'0x14'0

FOYER

MEDIA
12'-0" x 14'-0"

W.I.C.

GARAGE
22'-0" x 26'-0"

LOGGIA

COVERED
DRIVE

GARAGE
12'-0" x 21'-0"

Second Floor Plan Labels:

EVENING
DECK

OPEN

CAPTAIN'S
QUARTERS

SUITE 2
13'-0" x 14'-0"

BATH

W.I.C.

OPEN

BATH

SUITE 3
15'-0" x 12'-0"

DEN
15'-0" x 14'-0"

W.I.C.

REC.
16'-0" x 19'-0"

From the elegant entrance with a curved wall of windows leading to the front door, to the wonderful angles used throughout the home, this is a plan sure to please. Study the master bedroom suite and you'll see that amenities haven't been neglected: two walk-in closets, a lavish bath with a separate tub and shower and two vanities, a separate unique lounge and an exercise room. On the other end of the home, find the highly efficient kitchen, a spacious gathering room, a round morning room and study, and a quiet guest suite. The second level is equally deluxe with two suites, a recreation room, a quiet den and a large open area called the captain's quarters that opens out to an evening deck.

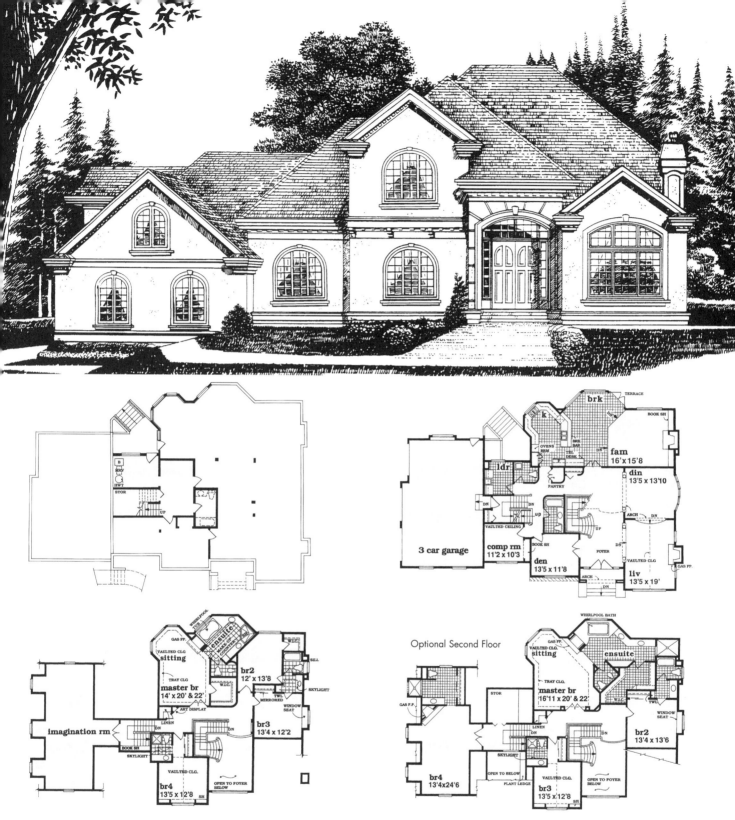

F inished in brick, with an elegant entry, this dramatic two-story home is the essence of luxury. Double doors open to a foyer with a sunken living room on the right and a den on the left. An archway leads to the formal dining room, mirroring the curved window in the living room and the bowed window in the dining room. The den and nearby computer room have use of a full bath—making them handy as extra guest rooms when needed. The family room, like the living room, is sunken and warmed by a hearth, but also has built-in bookcases. A snack-bar counter separates the U-shaped kitchen from the light-filled breakfast room. The second floor can be configured in two different ways. Both allow for a gigantic master suite with His and Hers vanities, an oversized shower, a walk-in closet and a sitting area.

DESIGN HPU040541

First Floor: 2,403 square feet
Second Floor: 1,684 square feet
Total: 4,087 square feet
Bonus Room: 644 square feet
Width: 77'-10" Depth: 55'-8"

DESIGN BY
©Select Home Designs

A graceful column and a multitude of windows define the entrance to this fine two-story home. Inside, a two-story foyer opens to a formal dining room on the left and directly ahead to the formal living room—complete with a warming fireplace. A cozy den, with a built-in desk and built-in cabinets, would work well as a home office. The spacious family room, with a second fireplace, built-in cabinets and snack bar into the kitchen, will be a favorite gathering place for your family. The homeowner will surely love the master bedroom suite on the second floor. Sunken down two steps, with two walk-in closets, a corner whirlpool tub, separate shower stall and two individual lavatories, this suite is designed to pamper. Three secondary bedrooms, two full baths and a bonus room complete this floor.

DESIGN HPU040543

First Floor: 1,931 square feet
Second Floor: 1,580 square feet
Total: 3,511 square feet
Bonus Room: 439 square feet
Width: 90'-3" Depth: 65'-8"

DESIGN BY
©Ahmann Design, Inc.

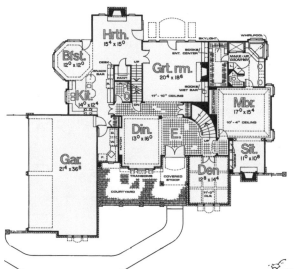

DESIGN HPU040542

First Floor: 2,603 square feet
Second Floor: 1,020 square feet
Total: 3,623 square feet
Width: 76'-8" Depth: 68'-0"

DESIGN BY
©Design Basics, Inc.

The stone facade of this traditional design evokes images of a quieter life, a life of harmony and comfortable luxury. The owners suite offers privacy on the first floor and features a sitting room with bookshelves, two walk-in closets and a private bath with a corner whirlpool tub. Three family bedrooms, each with a walk-in closet, and two baths make up the second floor.

QUOTE ONE®
Cost to build? See page 502
to order complete cost estimate
to build this house in your area!

Keystone lintels, an arched transom over the entry and sidelights spell classic design for this four-bedroom home. The tiled foyer offers entry to any room you choose, whether it be the secluded den with its built-in bookshelves, the formal dining room, the formal living room with its fireplace, wet bar and wall of windows, or the spacious rear family and kitchen area with its sunny breakfast nook. The owners suite offers privacy on the first floor and features a sitting room with bookshelves, two walk-in closets and a private bath with a corner whirlpool tub. Upstairs, two family bedrooms share a bath and enjoy separate vanities. A third family bedroom features its own full bath and a built-in window seat in a box-bay window. Note the four-car garage with plenty of room for the family fleet.

DESIGN BY
©Design Basics, Inc.

DESIGN HPU040544

First Floor: 2,813 square feet
Second Floor: 1,091 square feet
Total: 3,904 square feet
Width: 85'-5" Depth: 74'-8"

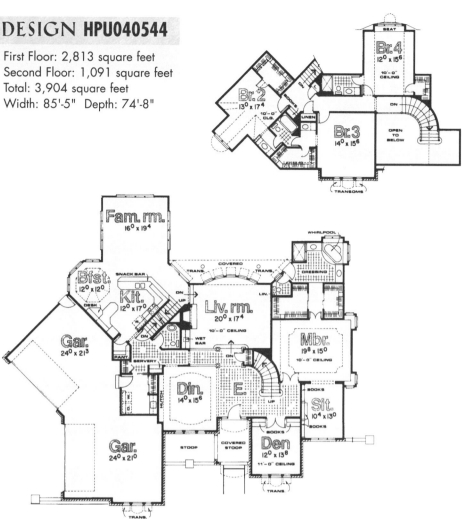

games rm

media rm

card rm

hobby rm/ br5

BUILT-IN MEDIA CENTER

WET BAR

UP

mech

HRV VACUUM HRV

ARCH HWT FURNACE

UP

STORAGE

wine

storage

exercise rm

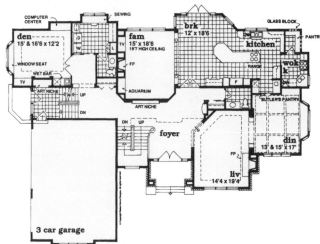

COMPUTER CENTER

SEWING

den
15' & 16'6 12'2

WINDOW SEAT

WET BAR

TV

ART NICHE

UP

fam
15' x 18'6
18'7 HIGH CEILING

TV

FP

AQUARIUM

ART NICHE

DN

brk
12' x 18'6

GLASS BLOCK

PANTRY

kitchen

RANGE

F

wok k

BUTLER'S PANTRY

DN UP

foyer

din
13' & 15' x 17'

FP

liv
14'4 x 19'4

3 car garage

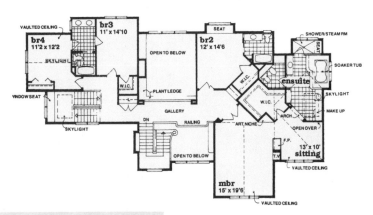

VAULTED CEILING

br4
11'2 x 12'2

br3
11' x 14'10

SKYLIGHT

WINDOW SEAT

SKYLIGHT

OPEN TO BELOW

W.I.C.

PLANT LEDGE

GALLERY

DN

RAILING

OPEN TO BELOW

SEAT

br2
12' x 14'6

W.I.C.

ART NICHE

mbr
15' x 19'6

VAULTED CEILING

SHOWER/STEAM RM

SEAT

SOAKER TUB

ensuite

W.I.C.

SKYLIGHT

MAKE UP

ARCH

OPEN OVER

F.P.

13' x 10'
sitting

VAULTED CEILING

T.V.

This grand, two-story European home is adorned with a facade of stucco and brick, meticulously appointed with details for gracious living. Guests enter through a portico to find a stately, two-story foyer. The formal living room features a tray ceiling and fireplace and is joined by a charming dining room with a large bay window. A butler's pantry joins the dining room to the gourmet kitchen, which holds a separate wok kitchen, an island work center and a breakfast room with double doors leading to the rear patio. The nearby family room enjoys a built-in aquarium, media center and fireplace. A den with a tray ceiling, window seat and built-in computer center is tucked in a corner for privacy. Served by two separate staircases, the second floor features a spectacular owners suite with a separate sitting room, an oversized closet and a bath with a shower/steam room and spa tub.

DESIGN BY
©Select Home Designs

PLAN HPU040545

First Floor: 2,596 square feet
Second Floor: 2,233 square feet
Total: 4,829 square feet
Basement: 2,012 square feet
Width: 81'-0"   Depth: 61'-0"

Quote One®

Cost to build? See page 502
to order complete cost estimate
to build this house in your area!

440

T his stunning traditional exterior combines brick and stucco for a dramatic look. Tray ceilings add architectural interest to both the living and dining rooms; the living room is further graced by a fireplace. Double doors off the vaulted foyer provide access to a den—or make it a guest room, if you wish. The kitchen is spacious and boasts a cooking island and an adjoining sunny breakfast room. A private media room is accessible from the family room through double French doors. The second floor features a large master bedroom with an enormous walk-in closet, a two-sided gas fireplace and an extensive luxury master bath. Three family bedrooms—one with a private bath—and a skylit bonus room over the garage complete the upper level.

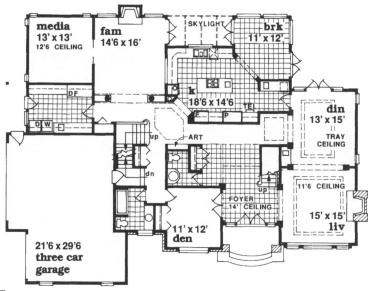

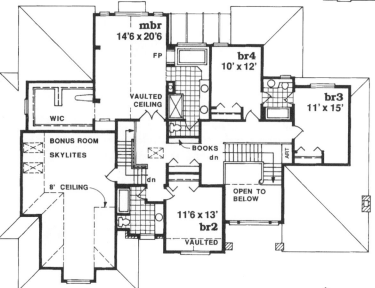

DESIGN HPU040546

First Floor: 2,389 square feet
Second Floor: 1,712 square feet
Total: 4,101 square feet
Bonus Room: 497 square feet
Width: 72'-0" Depth: 54'-0"

DESIGN BY
©Select Home Designs

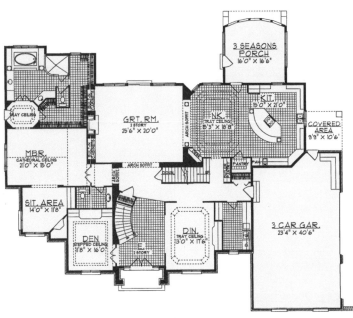

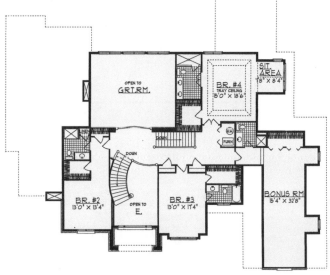

L avish, grand and luxurious—these words apply to this beautiful brick mansion with its expansive entrance. Inside, the two-story foyer leads to a formal dining room on the right and a cozy den with built-ins on the left. A curving staircase points the way to the upper level and the balcony overlooking the foyer and the great room. The huge kitchen is sure to please the gourmet of the family. It includes a large cooktop island with a snack bar, a walk-in pantry, plenty of counter and cabinet space, an adjacent nook and access to the three-seasons porch. Lavish is the word for the owners suite, which includes among its many amenities a separate sitting area with a fireplace. Upstairs, each bedroom has a walk-in closet and private bath. The bonus room is available for future expansion and features a full bath and large closet.

DESIGN HPU040547

First Floor: 3,536 square feet
Second Floor: 1,690 square feet
Total: 5,226 square feet
Bonus Room: 546 square feet
Width: 89'-8" Depth: 76'-0"

DESIGN BY
©Ahmann Design, Inc.

Multi-pane windows glimmer with sunlight, and corner quoins lend an established air to this five-bedroom plan. The foyer of this traditional-style home features a curved staircase. Amenities on the main floor include a sewing room, a separate wok kitchen and a butler's pantry. The kitchen boasts a walk-in pantry, expansive counter space and an island stove. On the second floor, the expansive master bedroom hosts a dramatic double-door entry and a large master bath. Three family bedrooms and two full baths complete this level. The basement enjoys a media room, a game room equipped with a fireplace, an exercise room, a storage area and a fifth bedroom with a bath.

DESIGN BY
©Select Home Designs

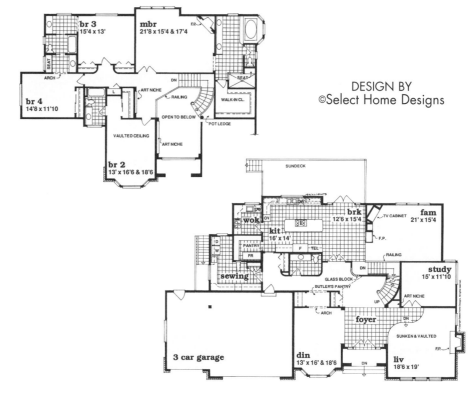

DESIGN HPU040548

First Floor: 2,555 square feet
Second Floor: 1,975 square feet
Total: 4,530 square feet
Width: 81'-8" Depth: 50'-4"

DESIGN BY
©Alan Mascord Design
Associates, Inc.

DESIGN HPU040549

First Floor: 2,813 square feet
Second Floor: 1,058 square feet
Total: 3,871 square feet
Width: 83'-0" Depth: 61'-0"

For an extra-luxurious hillside home, with unfinished space on the lower level, look no farther than this grand design. The main and upper levels have spacious living and sleeping areas, a service kitchen for the formal dining room, a den and gourmet kitchen. Two family bedrooms with a shared bath sit on the main level, while the master suite has the entire upper floor to itself. The master bath features twin vanity sinks, an oversized tub and a separate shower. The lower level holds the three-car garage, game room, shop and a full bath. Please specify basement or crawlspace foundation when ordering.

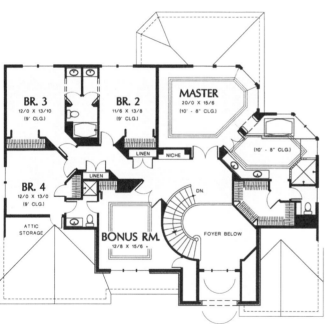

This grand traditional manor greets you with a two-story entry topped with a Palladian window. Inside, a beautiful curved staircase leads up to the sleeping quarters. The great room, the dining room and the breakfast nook provide plenty of windows. The open floor plan lets the kitchen serve every room with ease. A guest room with a full bath is tucked away in the back, while a study offers a private retreat at the front. The luxurious master suite features a bath with two sinks, a compartmented toilet and a large soaking tub.

DESIGN HPU040550

First Floor: 2,141 square feet
Second Floor: 1,724 square feet
Total: 3,865 square feet
Bonus Room: 249 square feet
Width: 64'-0" Depth: 59'-0"

DESIGN BY
©Alan Mascord Design
Associates, Inc.

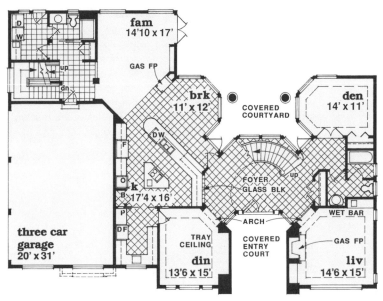

DESIGN HPU040551

First Floor: 2,240 square feet
Second Floor: 1,979 square feet
Total: 4,219 square feet
Width: 72'-0" Depth: 54'-6"

DESIGN BY
©Select Home Designs

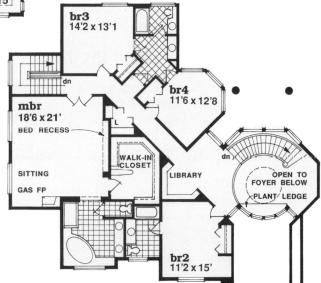

Enjoy regal splendor in a superbly detailed four-bedroom home. The entrance foyer creates a dramatic welcome with its curved staircase accented by a bayed wall of glass. This comfortable living room includes a gas fireplace and convenient wet bar. Featuring an innovative design, the kitchen boasts a triangular cooking island and an angled counter with a large seating area. A large bayed breakfast area is connected to the spacious family room by a double-sided gas fireplace. This beautiful, covered rear courtyard is framed with glass on three sides. The luxurious powder room with an adjoining bath is easily accessed by both the den and living room. The secondary rear stairs permit informal access to Bedrooms 3 and 4.

DESIGN HPU040552

First Floor: 2,006 square feet
Second Floor: 1,799 square feet
Total: 3,805 square feet
Width: 71'-8" Depth: 54'-2"

DESIGN BY
©Select Home Designs

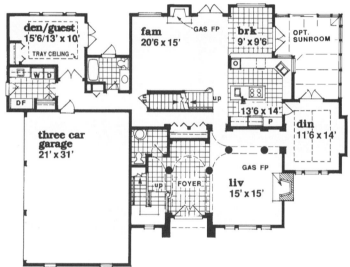

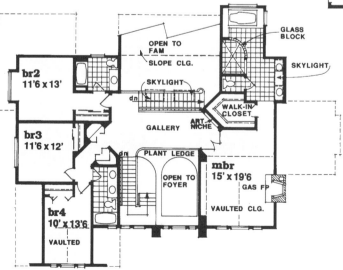

This beautifully detailed, luxurious four-bedroom home has an exterior of traditional brick. The two-story foyer opens to an impressive colonnade, creating a dramatic entry to this exclusive home. The pillars visually separate the living room, main foyer and hallway. The spacious kitchen, with a center cooking island, offers a large breakfast bar and corner sink overlooking the optional sun room. A private den or guest room with an adjacent full bath has rear access through double French doors. A railed gallery open to the vaulted family room and main foyer creates privacy for the master bedroom retreat. The elegant master bath features a skylit twin vanity, a large shower, a soaking tub and a compartmented toilet. A secondary rear stair provides access to the three family bedrooms.

This stately brick home offers a magnificent elevation from every angle, with a particularly impressive arched portico. The entry hall is highlighted by a majestic staircase ascending to an elegant balcony. The spacious formal dining room includes two built-in china cabinets and is easily reached from the living room with its cheery fireplace and attractive window seat. Between them is a handsomely appointed den with floor-to-ceiling cabinetry, a window seat and a spider-beam ceiling. An expansive gourmet kitchen with a walk-in pantry and an island cooktop/snack bar opens into a distinctive family room featuring a built-in rolltop desk, an entertainment center and a raised-hearth fireplace. The nearby breakfast nook offers panoramic views to the outside. Upstairs, a lavish master suite includes a sitting room with a fireplace framed by bookcases, a two-person whirlpool bath and two walk-in closets. Two of the family bedrooms feature flip-top window seats for added storage.

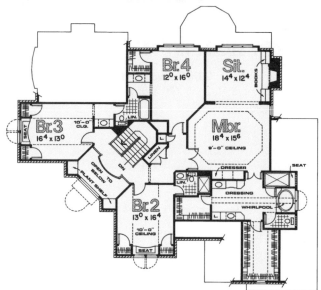

DESIGN HPU040553

First Floor: 2,040 square feet
Second Floor: 1,952 square feet
Total: 3,992 square feet
Width: 68'-0" Depth: 66'-0"

DESIGN BY
©Design Basics, Inc.

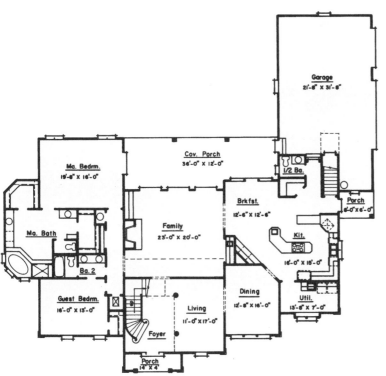

The vertical line of the two-story entrance is emphasized by stone quoins and echoed in the tall windows across the front of this impressive stucco home. The foyer, dominated by a graceful stairway, opens through decorative columns to the formal living and dining rooms. The family cook will appreciate the efficient kitchen, with its angled island cooktop and serving bar, walk-in pantry and sunny breakfast nook. A fireplace and built-in shelves are the focal point of the spacious family room, from which gatherings can easily spill out onto the rear covered porch. Two bedroom suites complete the first floor—a guest room with a private bath and a sumptuous master suite with access to the back porch and a pampering bath. Upstairs, two family bedrooms share a compartmented bath and a reading loft. A game room over the garage is reached by a separate staircase. Please specify crawlspace or slab foundation when ordering.

DESIGN HPU040554

First Floor: 3,002 square feet
Second Floor: 1,418 square feet
Total: 4,420 square feet
Width: 87'-10" Depth: 82'-0"

DESIGN BY
©Chatham Home Planning, Inc.

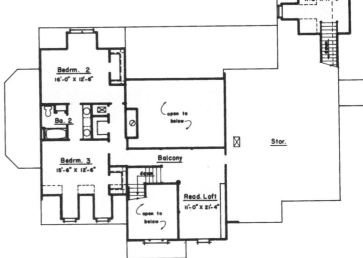

449

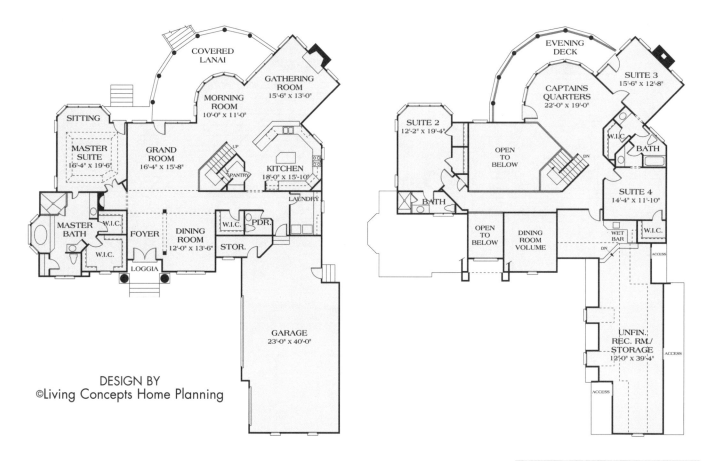

COVERED LANAI

GATHERING ROOM
15'-6" x 13'-0"

MORNING ROOM
10'-0" x 11'-0"

SITTING

MASTER SUITE
16'-4" x 19'-6"

GRAND ROOM
16'-4" x 15'-8"

UP

PANTRY

KITCHEN
18'-0" x 15'-10"

LAUNDRY

MASTER BATH

W.I.C.

FOYER

DINING ROOM
12'-0" x 13'-6"

W.I.C.

PDR.

STOR.

W.I.C.

LOGGIA

GARAGE
23'-0" x 40'-0"

DESIGN BY
©Living Concepts Home Planning

EVENING DECK

SUITE 3
15'-6" x 12'-8"

CAPTAINS QUARTERS
22'-0" x 19'-0"

SUITE 2
12'-2" x 19'-4"

OPEN TO BELOW

DN

W.I.C.

BATH

SUITE 4
14'-4" x 11'-10"

BATH

OPEN TO BELOW

DINING ROOM VOLUME

WET BAR

W.I.C.

DN

ACCESS

UNFIN. REC. RM./ STORAGE
12'-0" x 39'-4"

ACCESS

ACCESS

Double columns flank a raised loggia that leads to a beautiful two-story foyer. Flanking this elegance to the right is a formal dining room. Straight ahead, under a balcony and defined by yet more pillars, is the spacious grand room. A bow-windowed morning room and a gathering room feature a full view of the rear lanai and beyond. The owners bedroom suite is lavish with its amenities, which include a bayed sitting area, direct access to the rear terrace, a walk-in closet and a sumptuous bath.

DESIGN HPU040555

First Floor: 2,547 square feet
Second Floor: 1,637 square feet
Total: 4,184 square feet
Bonus Room: 802 square feet
Width: 74'-0" Depth: 95'-6"

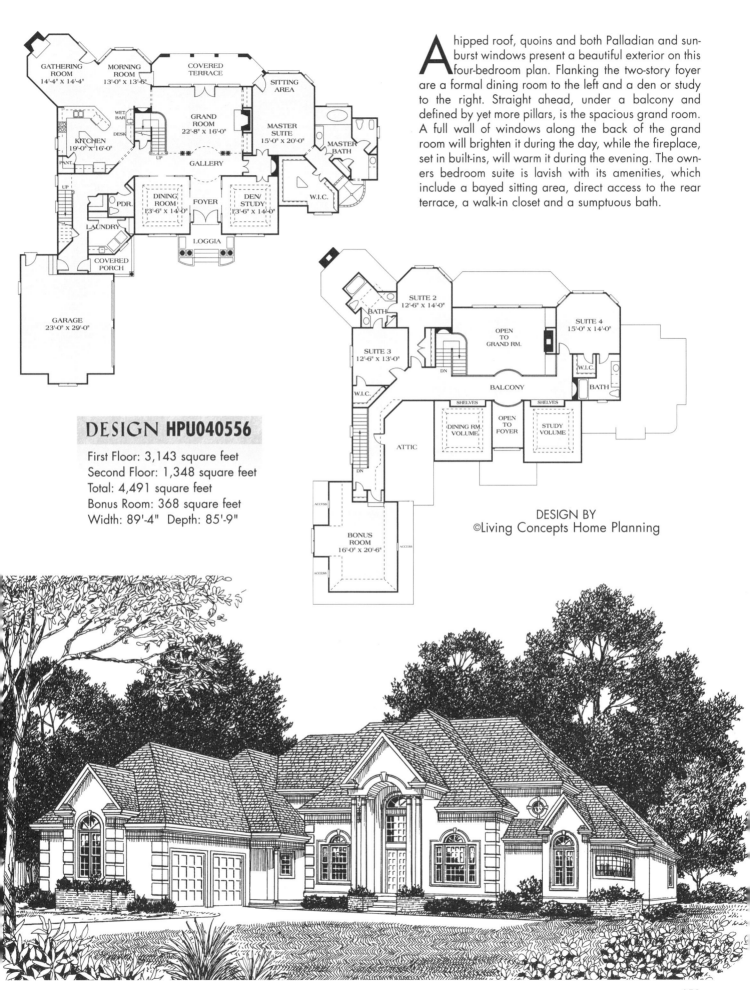

GATHERING ROOM
14'-4" x 14'-4"

MORNING ROOM
13'-0" x 13'-6"

COVERED TERRACE

SITTING AREA

WET BAR

DESK

GRAND ROOM
22'-8" x 16'-0"

MASTER SUITE
15'-0" x 20'-0"

MASTER BATH

KITCHEN
19'-0" x 16'-0"

PANT.

UP

GALLERY

W.I.C.

UP

PDR.

DINING ROOM
13'-6" x 14'-0"

FOYER

DEN/STUDY
13'-6" x 14'-0"

LAUNDRY

LOGGIA

COVERED PORCH

GARAGE
23'-0" x 29'-0"

A hipped roof, quoins and both Palladian and sunburst windows present a beautiful exterior on this four-bedroom plan. Flanking the two-story foyer are a formal dining room to the left and a den or study to the right. Straight ahead, under a balcony and defined by yet more pillars, is the spacious grand room. A full wall of windows along the back of the grand room will brighten it during the day, while the fireplace, set in built-ins, will warm it during the evening. The owners bedroom suite is lavish with its amenities, which include a bayed sitting area, direct access to the rear terrace, a walk-in closet and a sumptuous bath.

DESIGN HPU040556

First Floor: 3,143 square feet
Second Floor: 1,348 square feet
Total: 4,491 square feet
Bonus Room: 368 square feet
Width: 89'-4" Depth: 85'-9"

BATH

SUITE 2
12'-6" x 14'-0"

OPEN TO GRAND RM.

SUITE 4
15'-0" x 14'-0"

SUITE 3
12'-6" x 13'-0"

W.I.C.

DN

W.I.C.

BALCONY

BATH

SHELVES

SHELVES

DINING RM. VOLUME

OPEN TO FOYER

STUDY VOLUME

ATTIC

DN

ACCESS

BONUS ROOM
16'-0" x 20'-6"

ACCESS

ACCESS

DESIGN BY
©Living Concepts Home Planning

451

MASTER SUITE 15'-6" X 20'-0"

DECK WALK

OPEN TERRACE

GATHERING ROOM 22'-0" X 17'-0"

COVERED VERANDA

GALLERY 13'-0" X 6'-0"

W.I.C.

MORNING ROOM 10'-0" X 12'-0"

MASTER BATH

PDR.

KITCHEN 14'-0" X 14'-6"

CENTRAL HALL

UP

DN

LAUNDRY

PARLOR 14'-0" X 15'-0"

FOYER

DINING ROOM 14'-0" X 15'-0"

PORTICO

GARAGE 22'-0" X 37'-6"

G rand elegance is highly evident on the facade of this four-bedroom, two-story home. Note the details on the entrance portico—double columns, a balcony and a pediment. The elegance continues inside as seen with the formal dining room and formal parlor, which flank the foyer. An octagonal central hall leads to all other areas: a spacious gathering room, an island kitchen with an adjacent gallery and morning room, and a master bedroom suite. Upstairs, three large bedrooms—each with walk-in closets—share two full baths, access to a sitting area for reading, and a study area, which is perfect for the family computer.

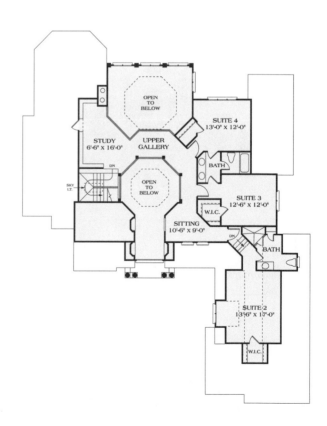

OPEN TO BELOW

STUDY 6'-6" X 16'-0"

UPPER GALLERY

SUITE 4 13'-0" X 12'-0"

BATH

DN

SKY L.T.

OPEN TO BELOW

W.I.C.

SUITE 3 12'-6" X 12'-0"

SITTING 10'-6" X 9'-0"

DN

BATH

SUITE 2 13'-6" X 17'-0"

W.I.C.

DESIGN HPU040557

First Floor: 2,716 square feet
Second Floor: 1,457 square feet
Total: 4,173 square feet
Basement: 1,290 square feet
Width: 69'-6" Depth: 101'-0"

DESIGN BY
©Living Concepts Home Planning

From the columned front porch to the curved patio in back, this house is filled with elegance and style. The foyer, featuring a graceful curving staircase, opens to the formal living and dining rooms. The focal point of the large family room is its fireplace, but windows will beckon you to the covered porch and patio outside. Multiple windows also highlight the kitchen, with its large work island, and the round breakfast room. The owners suite is in a private wing and has a large walk-in closet, an amenity-laden bath and its own entrance to the back porch. A nearby guest room could serve as a study or a library. Please specify slab or crawlspace foundation when ordering.

DESIGN HPU040558

First Floor: 3,117 square feet
Second Floor: 1,411 square feet
Total: 4,528 square feet
Width: 76'-10" Depth: 68'-10"

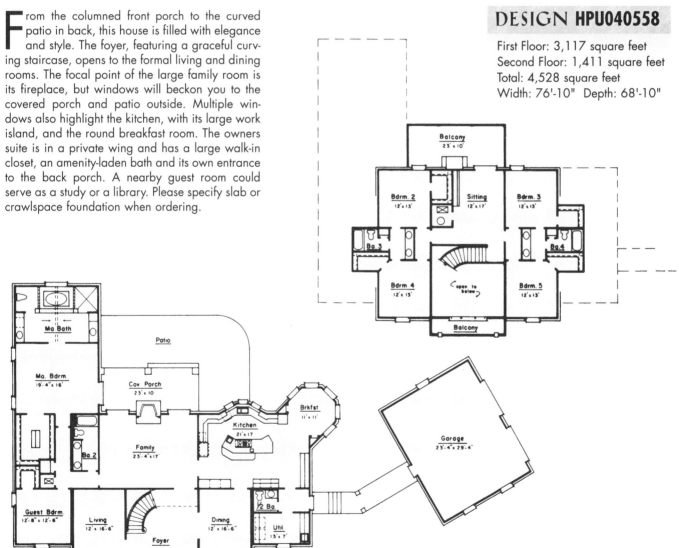

DESIGN BY
©Chatham Home Planning, Inc.

453

DESIGN HPU040559

First Floor: 1,741 square feet
Second Floor: 1,884 square feet
Total: 3,625 square feet
Width: 61'-9" Depth: 48'-10"

DESIGN BY
©Living Concepts Home Planning

Corner quoins, gabled rooflines and attractive shutters give this four-bedroom home plenty of curb appeal. Inside, the floor plan is designed for entertaining. For formal occasions, there is the living/dining room combination, separated by graceful columns. Casual gatherings will be welcomed in the spacious family room, which features a fireplace, built-ins and direct access to the rear deck. A sunny breakfast room is easily served by the efficient kitchen. A guest/study with a walk-in closet and a full bath complete this level. Upstairs, three bedrooms share two baths and access to a large playroom/loft. The master bedroom suite is sure to please with a tray ceiling, two walk-in closets and a luxurious bath.

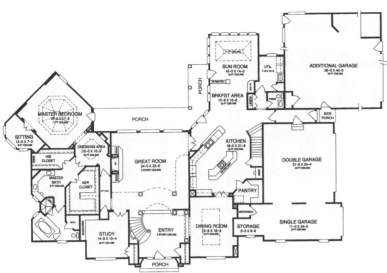

DESIGN HPU040560

First Floor: 3,722 square feet
Second Floor: 1,859 square feet
Total: 5,581 square feet
Width: 127'-10" Depth: 83'-9"

L

DESIGN BY
©Larry E. Belk Designs

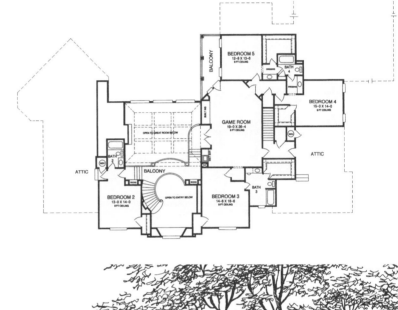

A richly detailed entrance sets the elegant tone of this luxurious design. Rising gracefully from the two-story foyer, the staircase is a fine prelude to the great room beyond, where a fantastic span of windows on the back wall overlooks the rear grounds. The dining room is located off the entry and has a lovely coffered ceiling. The kitchen, breakfast room and sun room are conveniently grouped for casual entertaining. The elaborate master suite has a coffered ceiling, private sitting room and a spa-style bath. The second level consists of four bedrooms with private baths and a large game room featuring a rear stair.

455

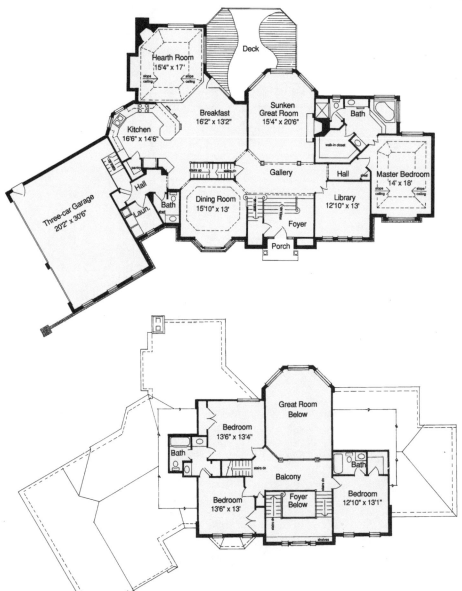

The diversity and strength of the exterior of this home reflects the excitement of the interior styling. Stairs in the foyer lead to a first-floor gallery, providing a panoramic view of the sunken great room. The two-story ceiling, along with the dramatic, rear-wall window arrangement and the elegantly faced fireplace, elevate this home into a phenomenal showplace. An extravagant kitchen/breakfast area with counter seating and a spacious pantry flows easily to the cozy hearth room. A second fireplace, furniture alcove, exciting ceiling treatment and multiple windows enhance the enjoyment of this family gathering place. Located on the first floor and positioned for privacy, an expansive master bedroom suite provides luxury, spaciousness and relaxation for the homeowner. Rounding out the first floor are the formal dining room and a private library/retreat. Three large bedrooms, two baths, service stairs to the kitchen and a balcony with a dramatic view of the great room top this exciting home.

DESIGN HPU040561

First Floor: 2,710 square feet
Second Floor: 964 square feet
Total: 3,674 square feet
Width: 101'-0"   Depth: 68'-8"

DESIGN BY
©Studer Residential Designs, Inc.

As one approaches this magnificent estate, he/she will be transformed back in time to the land of gentry. The opulence extends from the circular stairway that floats in front of the grand salon and floor-to-ceiling windows. The dining hall can easily seat twelve with additional furnishings. There is also a butler's pantry on the way to the oversized, octagonal kitchen, with a vaulted family room, vaulted breakfast area and an open stairway to the basement and second floor. To the left of the foyer is a master suite with all the finest appointments expected in a large home, from built-in dressers, cedar closets, study access, fireplace, built-ins and a massive column area over the bed. The second floor has a large stateroom with a sitting room and bath. Two additional staterooms feature private baths.

DESIGN HPU040562

First Floor: 3,102 square feet
Second Floor: 1,487 square feet
Total: 4,589 square feet
Bonus Room: 786 square feet
Width: 106'-0"   Depth: 56'-6"

DESIGN BY
©Archival Designs, Inc.

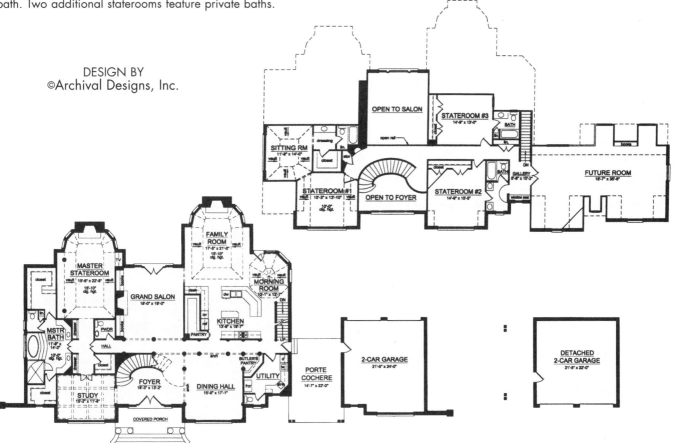

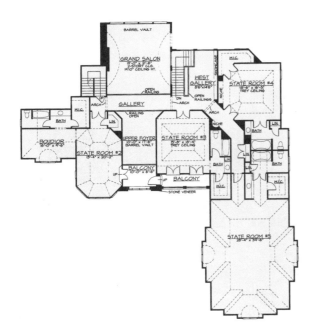

A stone-and-siding exterior, spires and interesting window details add to the elegance of this four-bedroom mansion. A keeping room with a pass-through to the kitchen and a fireplace with a built-in wood box, and a formal dining room with a fireplace on the first floor allow plenty of social possibilities. Separate guest quarters with a full bath, a lounge area and an upstairs studio, which is connected to the main house by a gallery, further enhance this home's livability. Four bedrooms with two full baths are found on the second floor, including the master suite with a fireplace.

DESIGN HPU040563

First Floor: 4,508 square feet
Second Floor: 3,322 square feet
Total: 7,830 square feet
Width: 83'-0" Depth: 116'-0"

VERANDA
19'-7" x 12'-0"

SCREENED
PORCH

STUDY
16'-0" x 13'-8"

KITCHEN

BRKFST RM
10'-0" x 13'-8"

DEN
14'-11" x 17'-4"

ARCH

DESK   C.C.

UP

GRAND RM
14'-8" x 21'-4"

UP   DN

P

UP

PWDR
ROOM

DN

VLT

VLT

BARREL

C.C.   C.C.

VAULT

DINING RM
15'-8" x 12'-9"

3 CAR
GARAGE
21'-4" x 32'-0"

FOYER
9'-4" x 12'-8"

WORK SPACE/
STORAGE

DESIGN HPU040564

First Floor: 1,950 square feet
Second Floor: 1,680 square feet
Total: 3,630 square feet
Width: 77'-0" Depth: 52'-0"

DESIGN BY
©Archival Designs, Inc.

SITTING
AREA
10'-0" x 14'-4"

MASTER
BEDROOM
15'-6" x 16'-4"

MSTR BATH

L.C.

OPEN TO DEN

OPEN TO BELOW

CLOSET

CLOSET

LAUND.

DN

UP

DN

CLO LIN

BEDROOM #2
12'-0" x 19'-6"

VAULT VAULT

BATH

SHELF

BEDROOM #3
14'-0" x 12'-0"

BEDROOM #4
12'-0" x 15'-0"

BATH

L.C.

CLOS.

SITTING RM
9'-6" x 9'-6"

ATTIC

WINDOW
SEAT

Interesting windows and rooflines give a unique character to this stucco facade. European influences are unmistakable. The study is highlighted by a beam ceiling, built-
ins and floor-to-ceiling windows. The grand room is to the
left of the plan and includes a bayed sitting area and a fireplace. Another bay window brightens the breakfast room,
which is found between the island kitchen and a den with
a second fireplace. The living room and a grand stair hall
complete the first floor. The elegant stairway leads up to
three family bedrooms and a sumptuous master suite.

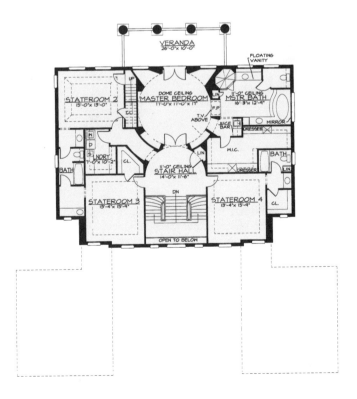

Simply elegant, with dignified details, this beautiful home is reminiscent of English estate homes. Two double garages flank a columned front door and are attached to the main floor by galleries leading to the entry foyer. Here a double staircase leads upstairs and encourages a view beyond the morning room, grand salon and rear portico. The gourmet kitchen has a uniquely styled island counter with a cooktop. For formal meals, the dining hall is nearby. The elaborate master suite and three staterooms reside on the second level. The master bedroom features a circular shape and enjoys access to a private lanai, a through-fireplace to the master bedroom, and numerous alcoves and built-in amenities.

DESIGN BY
©Archival Designs, Inc.

DESIGN HPU040565

First Floor: 2,175 square feet
Second Floor: 1,927 square feet
Total: 4,102 square feet
Basement: 1,927 square feet
Width: 74'-0" Depth: 82'-0"

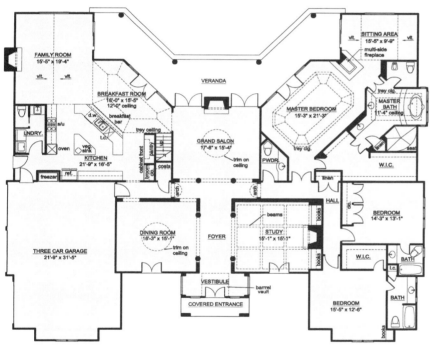

This Neoclassical home has plenty to offer! The elegant entrance is flanked by a formal dining room on the left and a beam-ceilinged study—complete with a fireplace—on the right. An angled kitchen is sure to please with a work island, plenty of counter and cabinet space, and a snack counter that it shares with the sunny breakfast room. A family room with a second fireplace is nearby. The lavish master suite features many amenities, including a huge walk-in closet, a three-sided fireplace and a lavish bath. Two secondary bedrooms have private baths. Finish the second-floor bonus space to create an office, a play room and a full bath. A three-car garage easily shelters the family fleet.

DESIGN BY
©Archival Designs, Inc.

DESIGN HPU040566

Square Footage: 3,823
Bonus Space: 1,018 square feet
Width: 80'-6" Depth: 70'-8"

461

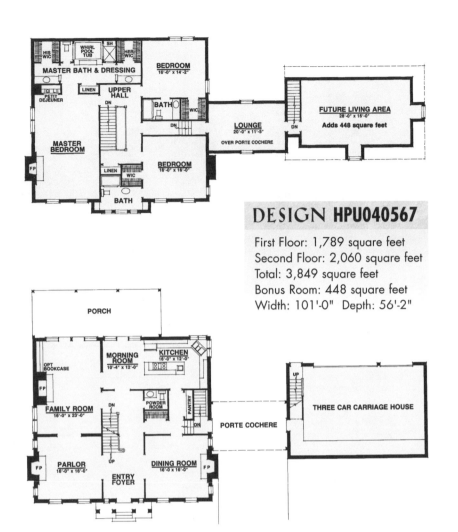

DESIGN HPU040567

First Floor: 1,789 square feet
Second Floor: 2,060 square feet
Total: 3,849 square feet
Bonus Room: 448 square feet
Width: 101'-0" Depth: 56'-2"

DESIGN BY
©R.L. Pfotenhauer

An abundance of amenities graces this two-story traditional design. Fireplaces warm both the formal dining room and the parlor, which connects to the large family room, also with a fireplace and an optional bookcase. The L-shaped kitchen, with its multi-purpose island, shares space with a cozy morning room. On the second floor, two family bedrooms feature walk-in closets and private baths, while the master bedroom features a fourth fireplace, a *petit dejeuner*, or kitchenette, and a His and Hers master bath with a whirlpool tub. A lounge located above the porte cochere will become a favorite getaway spot.

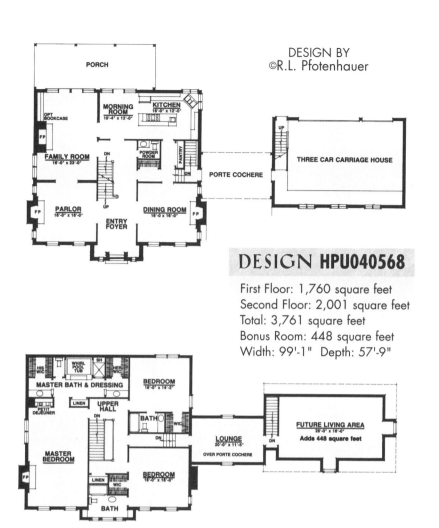

DESIGN BY
©R.L. Pfotenhauer

PORCH

MORNING ROOM
10'-4" x 12'-0"

KITCHEN
16'-0" x 12'-0"

OPT BOOKCASE

FP

FAMILY ROOM
16'-0" x 23'-0"

POWDER ROOM

PANTRY

DN

UP

THREE CAR CARRIAGE HOUSE

PORTE COCHERE

PARLOR
16'-0" x 16'-0"

DINING ROOM
16'-0" x 16'-0"

FP

FP

ENTRY FOYER

DESIGN HPU040568

First Floor: 1,760 square feet
Second Floor: 2,001 square feet
Total: 3,761 square feet
Bonus Room: 448 square feet
Width: 99'-1" Depth: 57'-9"

HIS WIC

WHIRL POOL TUB

SH

HER WIC

BEDROOM
16'-0" x 14'-2"

MASTER BATH & DRESSING

LINEN

UPPER HALL

PETIT DEJEUNER

DN

BATH

WIC

FUTURE LIVING AREA
26'-0" x 16'-0"
Adds 448 square feet

MASTER BEDROOM

DN

DN

DN

FP

LINEN

WIC

BEDROOM
16'-0" x 16'-0"

LOUNGE
20'-0" x 11'-5"
OVER PORTE COCHERE

BATH

WH

F

WIC

W D

UTILITY ROOM
42'-0" x 16'-3"

UP

BATH

TAP ROOM

STOR

BEDROOM/GUEST
16'-0" x 21'-0"

UP

RECREATION

FP

Stately gentility is a most appropriate phrase for this dignified Georgian design. The brick finish on the exterior is further enhanced by the cut-stone trim and the twin brick chimneys venting the multiple fireplaces. The large formal entry is an elegant setting for the four-foot-wide main stair—only one of three stairs that gives this home a well-thought-out traffic pattern. This home has all of the amenities that the most discerning homeowner could want. Note the generous family room, the island kitchen and the adjoining rear porch for comfortable informal living. The second floor has one of the most luxurious master suites. It features His and Hers dressing areas, a fireplace and even a *petit dejeuner* for late night snacks. Don't overlook the possibilities for the future living spaces in the lower level and over the carriage house.

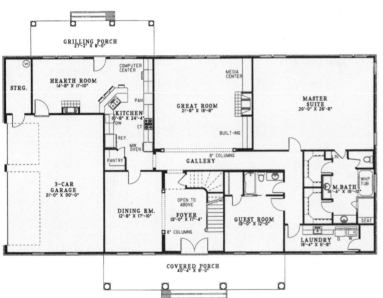

A two-story entry with striking columns and a pediment combine with a hipped roof to showcase this Neoclassical design. The dining room is conveniently near the entry foyer, perfect for formal entertainment. A beautiful wall of built-ins—including a media center—surrounding the fireplace adorns the great room. The kitchen is loaded with counter space, a built-in computer center, a walk-in pantry and a snack bar. The hearth room features a warming fireplace and access to the grilling porch. To the right of the plan, a guest room with a full bath, and a luxurious master suite enjoy privacy from entertainment zones. Indulge yourself with this sumptuous bath with His and Hers walk-in closets and a whirlpool tub and separate shower. A curved staircase leads to the second level and its three family bedrooms—or transform one into a game room.

DESIGN HPU040569

First Floor: 2,782 square feet
Second Floor: 1,173 square feet
Total: 3,955 square feet
Width: 82'-0" Depth: 58'-10"

DESIGN BY
©Michael E. Nelson,
Nelson Design Group, LLC

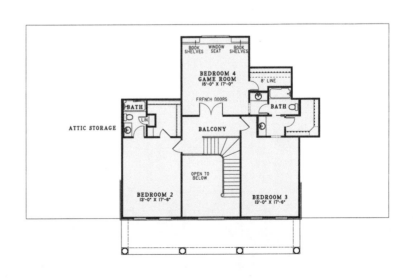

DESIGN HPU040570

First Floor: 4,528 square feet
Second Floor: 3,590 square feet
Finished Basement:
2,992 square feet
Total: 11,110 square feet
Width: 138'-2" Depth: 80'-10"

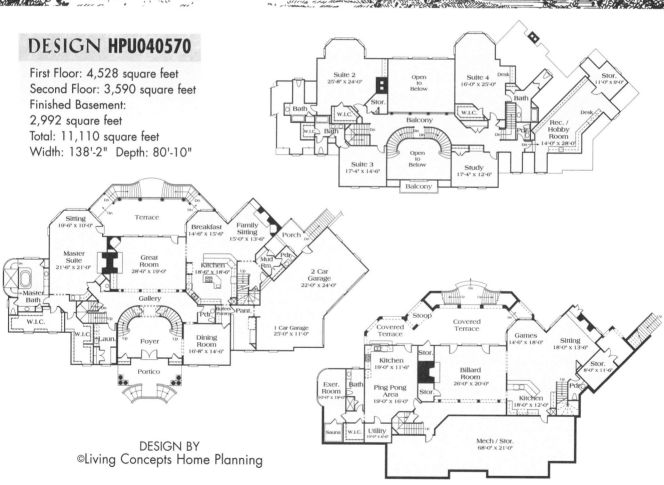

DESIGN BY
©Living Concepts Home Planning

If you're looking for a home that fits a sloping lot, yet retains a strength and character that matches that of our Colonial forefathers, you need look no further. The front elevation reflects a traditional style that incorporates design elements of an earlier period. However, the floor plan and the rear elevation provide a contemporary twist. Beyond the portico, you'll enter a two-story foyer framed by twin curving staircases. Straight ahead, a spacious great room separates the private owners suite to the left, and the formal dining room, kitchen, breakfast room and family/sitting room to the right. The second floor contains three suites—two with bay windows—three-and-a-half baths, a study and a recreation room. The basement sports a billiard room, two kitchens, an exercise room, a full bath, a game room and a sitting room.

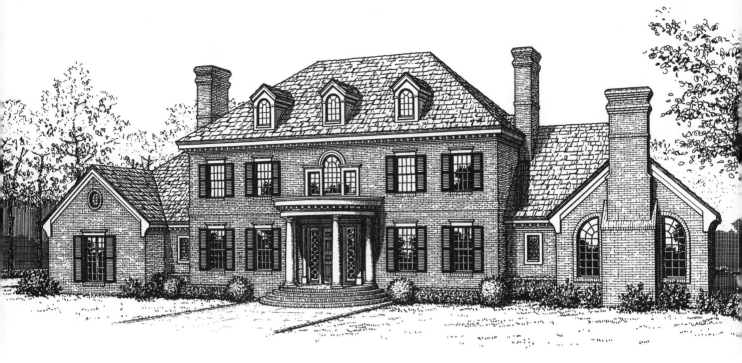

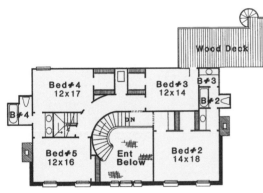

Wood Deck

Bed #4
12x17

Bed #3
12x14

B #3

B #2

Bed #5
12x16

Ent
Below

Bed #2
14x18

B #4

DN

DESIGN HPU040571

First Floor: 3,294 square feet
Second Floor: 1,300 square feet
Total: 4,594 square feet
Width: 106'-10" Depth: 52'-10"

The charm of the Old South is designed into this stately Federal manor. A round entry portico leads to the two-story foyer with a circular staircase. The formal living room, dining room and family room each feature a distinctive fireplace; the latter is also highlighted by a built-in entertainment center, walk-in wet bar, beamed cathedral ceiling, and access to a rear covered patio. Impressive ten-foot ceilings grace the entire first floor. The secluded master suite has a vaulted ceiling, three walk-in closets and patio access. Four additional bedrooms on the second floor share adjoining baths.

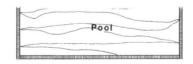

Pool

DESIGN BY
©Fillmore Design Group

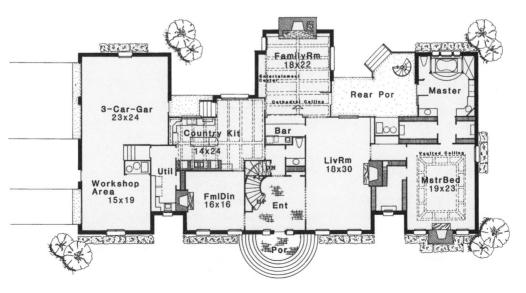

3-Car-Gar
23x24

Workshop
Area
15x19

Util

Country Kit
14x24

FmlDin
16x16

Ent

Bar

FamilyRm
18x22

Entertainment
Center

Cathedral Ceiling

Rear Por

Master

LivRm
18x30

Vaulted Ceiling

MstrBed
19x23

Por

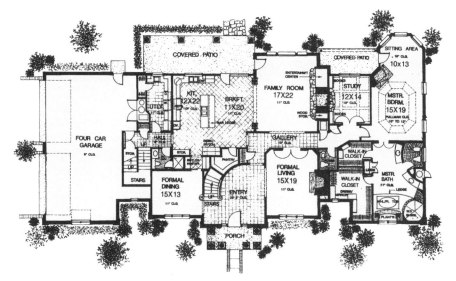

DESIGN HPU040572

First Floor: 3,599 square feet
Second Flloor: 1,621 square feet
Total: 5,220 square feet
Width: 108'-10" Depth: 53'-10"

DESIGN BY
©Fillmore Design Group

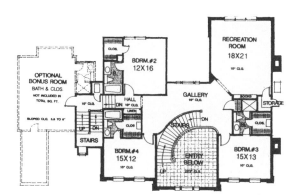

A grand facade detailed with brick corner quoins, stucco flourishes, arched windows and an elegant entrance presents this home and preludes the amenities inside. A spacious foyer is accented by a curving stair and flanked by a formal living room and a formal dining room. For cozy times, a through-fireplace is located between a large family room and a quiet study. The master suite is designed to pamper, with two walk-in closets (one is absolutely huge), a two-sided fireplace sharing its heat with a bayed sitting area and the bedroom, and a lavish master bath filled with attractive amenities. Upstairs, three secondary bedrooms each have a private bath and walk-in closet. Also on this level is a spacious recreation room, perfect for a game room or children's playroom.

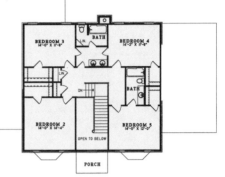

DESIGN HPU040573

First Floor: 3,209 square feet
Second Floor: 1,192 square feet
Total: 4,401 square feet
Width: 68'-8"   Depth: 76'-0"

DESIGN BY
©Michael E. Nelson,
Nelson Design Group, LLC

This two-story home has French flair on the exterior and modern comforts inside. The entry leads to the dining and living rooms at the front of the house, each enjoying a bay-window view of the front yard. The central great room features a fireplace framed with windows on each side. Escape to the secluded master suite with its luxurious bath, including a glass shower and separate whirlpool tub. To the left of the plan is a spacious kitchen with an island/snack bar, large pantry spaces, a built-in computer center and an adjoining breakfast room. Four secondary bedrooms and two full bathrooms complete the second floor. Please specify crawlspace, basement or slab foundation when ordering.

A graceful Palladian-style entry with fluted, two-story columns commands charm and respect for this Georgian homestead. Inside, a marble entry provides a traditional circular stairway and balcony. To the left lies an inviting living room and a family room that includes a fireplace and atrium doors leading to the deck area and beyond. The large kitchen, formal dining room with bay window, bar area and expansive sun room provide more than enough space for entertaining guests. An exercise room is featured for family fun and health. A luxurious master suite is positioned at the rear for seclusion, while a guest suite can be found just to the front. Five family bedrooms complete the second floor.

DESIGN HPU040574

First Floor: 4,082 square feet
Second Floor: 1,745 square feet
Total: 5,827 square feet
Width: 101'-7" Depth: 73'-0"

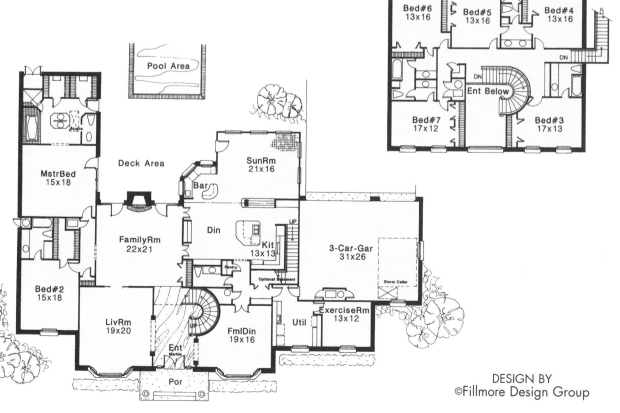

DESIGN BY
©Fillmore Design Group

DESIGN HPU040575

First Floor: 3,300 square feet
Second Floor: 1,170 square feet
Total: 4,470 square feet
Width: 87'-0" Depth: 82'-0"

The gracious exterior of this classic European-style home is accentuated by dual boxed windows, dramatically curved stairs and a glassed entry decorated with tall columns. A grand foyer showcases the dining room and great room, which offers a fireplace and French doors opening to a rear terrace. A gourmet kitchen adjoins the breakfast room, also open to the terrace; just beyond, a corner fireplace warms the hearth room. The luxurious owners suite provides a spacious walk-in closet and an opulent bath. Upstairs, a balcony overlooks the foyer and gallery. Three secondary bedrooms all provide walk-in closets; one offers a private bath.

DESIGN BY
©Studer Residential Designs, Inc.

470

Finished in brick veneer, this stately home has presence and a sense of permanence. The two-level entry opens to a bright foyer with a circular stair. On the right the living room features a box-bay window; on the left is a dining room with another box-bay window. The island kitchen, with a walk-in pantry and abundant counter space, easily serves the dining room. A breakfast room adjoins the kitchen and has a window seat and veranda access. It spills into the sunken family room with a fireplace. On the main floor, the master suite boasts a cozy sitting area, two walk-in closets and a master bath with a whirlpool spa and twin vanities. Each family bedroom has a spacious closet. A playroom on the second floor is graced by a coffered ceiling and a walk-in storage closet.

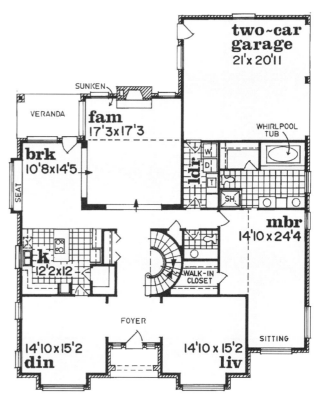

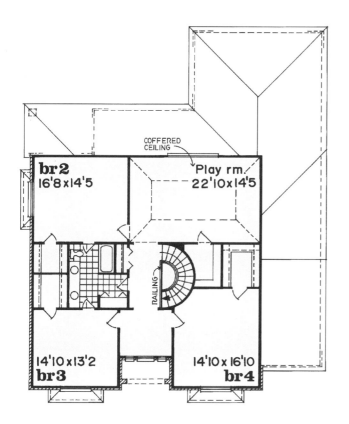

DESIGN HPU040576

First Floor: 2,177 square feet
Second Floor: 1,633 square feet
Total: 3,810 square feet
Width: 52'-0" Depth: 65'-0"

DESIGN BY
©Select Home Designs

DESIGN HPU040577

First Floor: 2,094 square feet
Second Floor: 2,169 square feet
Total: 4,263 square feet
Width: 76'-0" Depth: 70'-0"

DESIGN BY
©Studer Residential Designs, Inc.

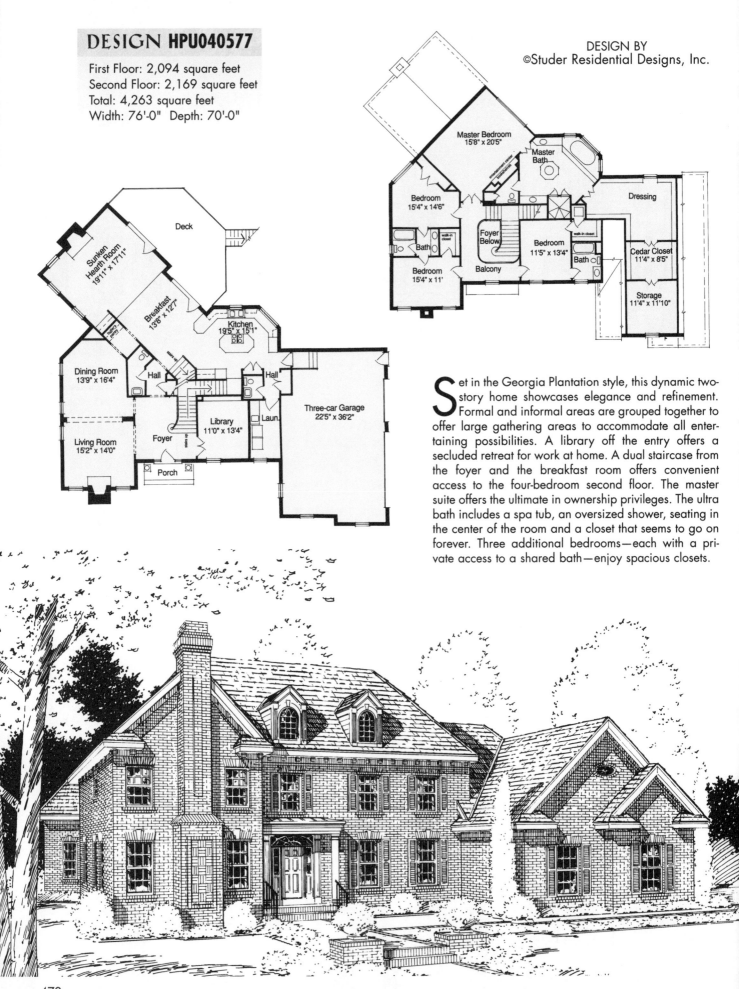

First Floor:
Sunken Hearth Room 19'11" x 17'11"
Deck
Breakfast 13'8" x 12'7"
Kitchen 19'5" x 15'1"
Dining Room 13'9" x 16'4"
Hall
Hall
Living Room 15'2" x 14'0"
Foyer
Library 11'0" x 13'4"
Laun.
Three-car Garage 22'5" x 36'2"
Porch

Second Floor:
Master Bedroom 15'8" x 20'5"
Master Bath
Bedroom 15'4" x 14'6"
Dressing
Bath
walk-in closet
Foyer Below
Bedroom 11'5" x 13'4"
walk-in closet
Cedar Closet 11'4" x 8'5"
Bath
Bedroom 15'4" x 11'
Balcony
Storage 11'4" x 11'10"

Set in the Georgia Plantation style, this dynamic two-story home showcases elegance and refinement. Formal and informal areas are grouped together to offer large gathering areas to accommodate all entertaining possibilities. A library off the entry offers a secluded retreat for work at home. A dual staircase from the foyer and the breakfast room offers convenient access to the four-bedroom second floor. The master suite offers the ultimate in ownership privileges. The ultra bath includes a spa tub, an oversized shower, seating in the center of the room and a closet that seems to go on forever. Three additional bedrooms—each with a private access to a shared bath—enjoy spacious closets.

ountry meets traditional in this splendid design. A covered front porch offers a place to enjoy the sunrise or place a porch swing. Gables, brick, stone and dormers bring out a comfortable appeal. With the formal areas flanking the foyer, an open flow is established between the column-accented dining room and the library with its distinguished beam ceiling. The two-story great room features a wall of windows looking out to the rear grounds. On the left, the gourmet kitchen serves up casual and formal meals to the breakfast and hearth rooms with the dining room just steps away. The master bedroom enjoys a sitting area with an array of view-catching windows, a spacious dressing area and an accommodating walk-in closet. Three family bedrooms—one with a private bath—complete the second level.

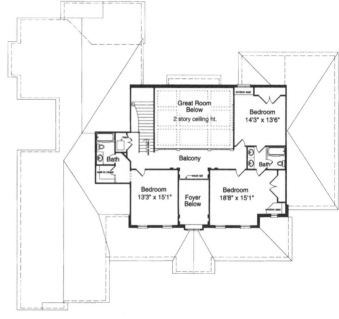

DESIGN HPU040578

First Floor: 3,414 square feet
Second Floor: 1,238 square feet
Total: 4,652 square feet
Width: 90'-6" Depth: 78'-9"

DESIGN BY
©Studer Residential Designs, Inc.

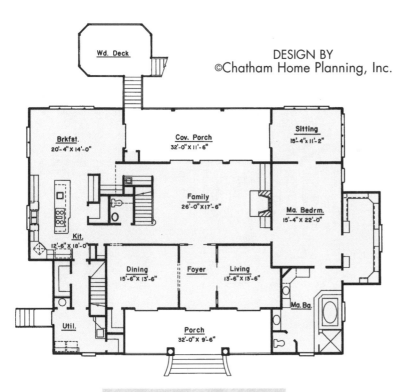

DESIGN BY
©Chatham Home Planning, Inc.

From its large front porch to its rear porch and deck, this lavish farmhouse bids welcome. The foyer offers entrance to both the formal living and dining rooms and opens into the heart of the home—the spacious family room, with its central fireplace and rear-yard access. A well-equipped kitchen features a desk, an island cooktop and a large breakfast area with views to the outside. The master bedroom boasts a separate sitting room, a huge walk-in closet and a luxurious bath with separate sinks and a whirlpool tub. All three of the upstairs family bedrooms include a walk-in closet and, while Bedrooms 3 and 4 share a full hall bath that includes dual sinks, Bedroom 2 features its own bath.

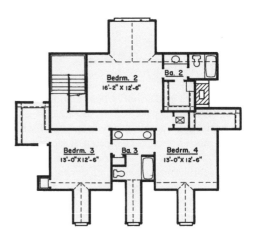

DESIGN HPU040579

First Floor: 3,045 square feet
Second Floor: 1,174 square feet
Total: 4,219 square feet
Width: 77'-0" Depth: 53'-0"

ormer windows complement classic square columns on this country estate home, gently flavored with a Southern-style facade. A two-story foyer opens to traditional rooms. Two columns announce the living room, which has a warming hearth. The formal dining room opens to the back covered porch, decked out with decorative columns. The first-floor master suite has His and Hers walk-in closets, an oversized shower, a whirlpool tub and a windowed water closet, plus its own door to the covered porch. A well-appointed kitchen features a corner walk-in pantry and opens to a double-bay family room and breakfast area. Upstairs, each of two family bedrooms has a private vanity. A gallery hall leads past a study/computer room— with two window seats—to a sizable recreation area that offers a tower-room bay.

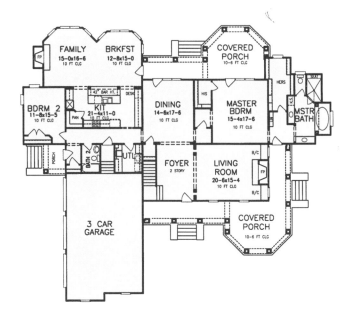

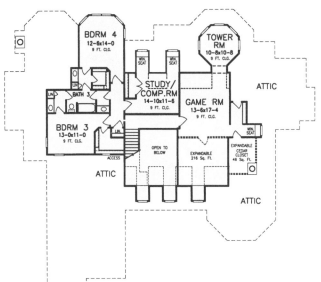

DESIGN HPU040580

First Floor: 2,687 square feet
Second Floor: 1,630 square feet
Total: 4,317 square feet
Bonus Room: 216 square feet
Width: 87'-1" Depth: 76'-7"

DESIGN BY
©Larry E. Belk Designs

Three classic dormers welcome you home. A covered porch and gabled roof offer country comfort. A formal dining room and informal eating area are located only steps away from the fully appointed kitchen. A spacious family room features a fireplace and a built-in entertainment center. The utility room is large enough to handle standard needs; there is even room for a hobby space. For those needing a home office, the bonus space with stairs accessed by an outside entrance is perfect for clients or customers. If it is to be used for a game room, noise will not be a factor because of its isolated location over the garage. The master suite boasts a large sitting area complete with a built-in entertainment center. Three large bedrooms and two full baths are located on the upper level. Please specify basement, crawlspace or slab foundation when ordering.

DESIGN BY
©Breland & Farmer Designers, Inc.

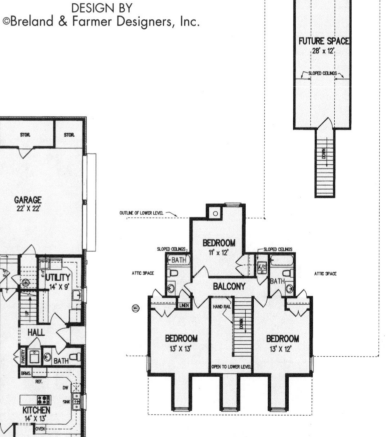

DESIGN HPU040581

First Floor: 2,702 square feet
Second Floor: 810 square feet
Total: 3,512 square feet
Bonus Room: 336 square feet
Width: 62'-0" Depth: 86'-0"

Reminiscent of the grand homes of the Old South, this elegantly appointed home is a beauty inside and out. A centerpiece stair rises gracefully from the two-story grand foyer and features Romeo-balcony overlooks to the foyer and living room. The kitchen, breakfast room and family room provide open space for the gathering of family and friends. The beam-ceilinged study and the dining room flank the grand foyer and each includes a fire-place. The master suite features a cozy sit-ting area and a luxury master bath with His and Hers vanities and walk-in closets. Three large bedrooms and a game room complete the second floor. Baths are effi-ciently designed with private dressing areas to give each bedroom a private bath. A large expandable area is avail-able at the top of the rear stair.

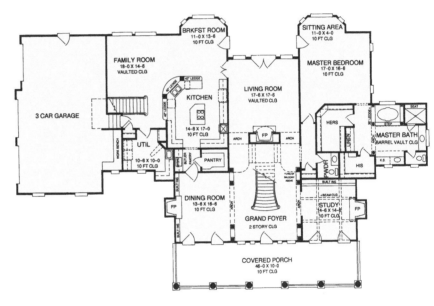

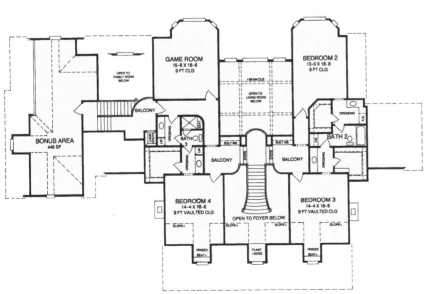

DESIGN HPU040582

First Floor: 3,170 square feet
Second Floor: 1,914 square feet
Total: 5,084 square feet
Bonus Room: 445 square feet
Width: 100'-10" Depth: 65'-5"

DESIGN BY
©Larry E. Belk Designs

477

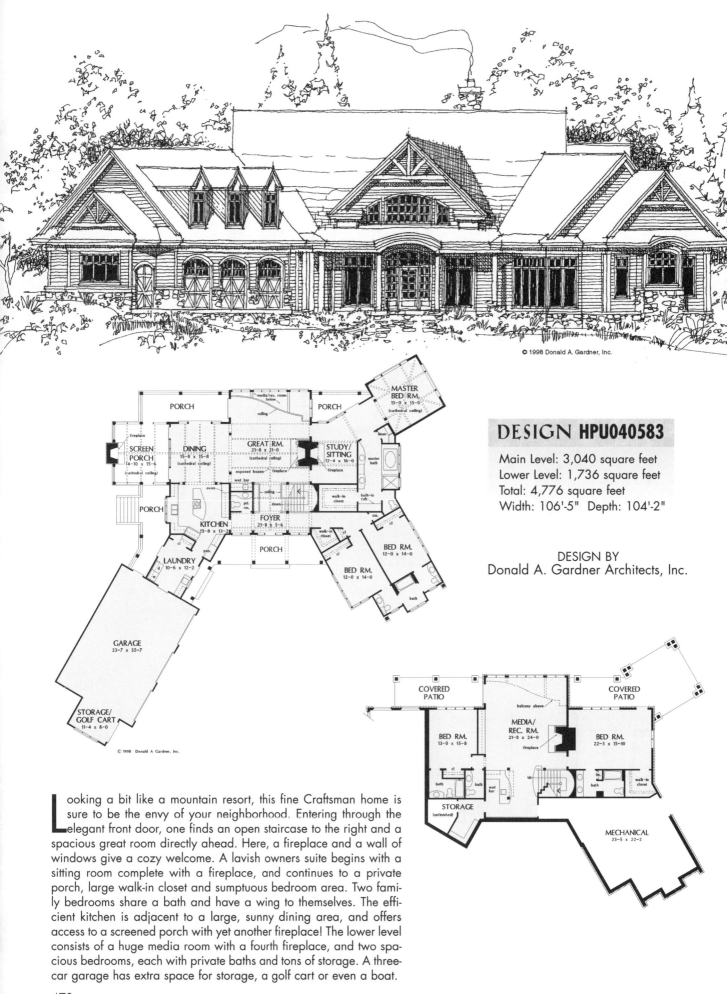

© 1998 Donald A. Gardner, Inc.

DESIGN HPU040583

Main Level: 3,040 square feet
Lower Level: 1,736 square feet
Total: 4,776 square feet
Width: 106'-5" Depth: 104'-2"

DESIGN BY
Donald A. Gardner Architects, Inc.

Looking a bit like a mountain resort, this fine Craftsman home is sure to be the envy of your neighborhood. Entering through the elegant front door, one finds an open staircase to the right and a spacious great room directly ahead. Here, a fireplace and a wall of windows give a cozy welcome. A lavish owners suite begins with a sitting room complete with a fireplace, and continues to a private porch, large walk-in closet and sumptuous bedroom area. Two family bedrooms share a bath and have a wing to themselves. The efficient kitchen is adjacent to a large, sunny dining area, and offers access to a screened porch with yet another fireplace! The lower level consists of a huge media room with a fourth fireplace, and two spacious bedrooms, each with private baths and tons of storage. A three-car garage has extra space for storage, a golf cart or even a boat.

This extraordinary four-bedroom estate features gables with decorative wood brackets, arched windows and a stone-and-siding facade for undeniable Craftsman character. At the heart of the home, a magnificent cathedral ceiling adds space and stature to the impressive great room, which accesses both back porches. Sharing the great room's cathedral ceiling, a loft makes an excellent reading nook. Tray ceilings adorn the dining room and library/media room, while all four bedrooms enjoy cathedral ceilings. A sizable kitchen is open to a large gathering room for ultimate family togetherness. The master suite features back-porch access, a lavish private bath and an oversized walk-in closet. A spacious bonus room is located over the three-car garage for further expansion.

DESIGN BY
Donald A. Gardner Architects, Inc.

DESIGN HPU040584

First Floor: 3,555 square feet
Second Floor: 250 square feet
Total: 3,805 square feet
Bonus Room: 490 square feet
Width: 99'-8" Depth: 78'-8"

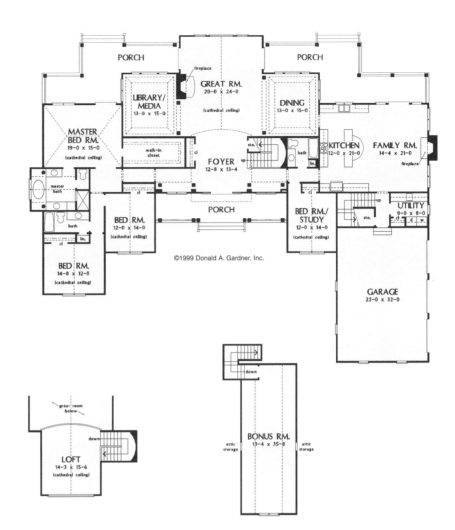

©1999 Donald A. Gardner, Inc.

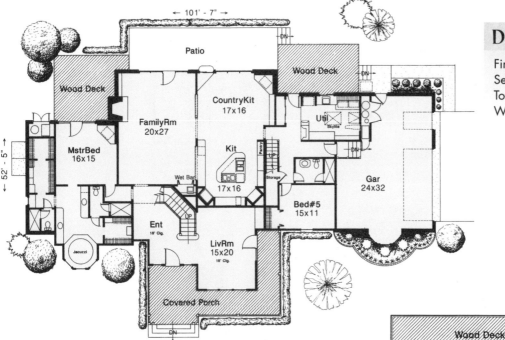

← 101' - 7" →

Patio

Wood Deck

Wood Deck

CountryKit
17x16

FamilyRm
20x27

Util
Skylite

52' - 5"

MstrBed
16x15

Kit
17x16

Pantry

UP

Storage

DN

Wet Bar

Bed#5
15x11

Gar
24x32

Ent
18' Clg.

LivRm
15x20
18' Clg.

Jacuzzi

Covered Porch

DN

DESIGN HPU040585

First Floor: 3,073 square feet
Second Floor: 1,230 square feet
Total: 4,303 square feet
Width: 101'-7" Depth: 52'-5"

Wood Deck

Bed#4
14x14

Bed#3
15x14

Attic Storage

DN

Bed#2
15x14

Balcony

Open To Entry Below.

Open To Living Room Below.

This large Victorian two-story home with brick and shingle siding has two unique bay windows with conical roofs and a covered porch. The expansive kitchen and country kitchen areas look to the rear patio, as does the family room, complete with a fireplace and wet bar. The owners suite accesses a private wood deck and is enhanced with two large walk-in closets, as well as a whirlpool tub. Two separate staircases lead upstairs to the sleeping quarters. Three bedrooms reside on the second floor; they share a full bath and a wood deck. A balcony looks down to the entry below.

DESIGN BY
©Fillmore Design Group

480

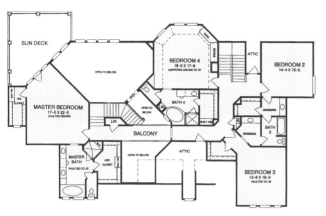

DESIGN HPU040586

First Floor: 3,359 square feet
Second Floor: 2,174 square feet
Total: 5,533 square feet
Width: 96'-5" Depth: 85'-6"

L

DESIGN BY
©Larry E. Belk Designs

A truly unique luxury home, this farmhouse has all the amenities. The fantastic covered porch surrounds three sides of the home and provides a wonderful area for outdoor living. A two-story foyer angles to draw the eye through double arches to the elegant living room with a fireplace flanked by built-ins and an area for the grand piano. The kitchen, breakfast room and family room join for casual living. Also on the first level are a home office, a game room and a cozy study. Upstairs, the master bedroom is luxuriously appointed and opens to a private sun deck. Three family bedrooms each have walk-in closets and private bath access.

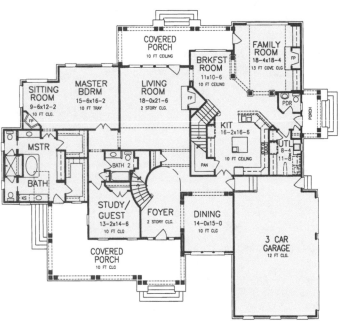

Timeless sophistication characterizes this lovely home designed for entertaining and family. A roomy wraparound front porch opens to the dramatic two-story foyer with a gracefully curved front stair. The large dining room and living room, with a beam ceiling and a striking two-story window wall, welcome all to this sensational home. The kitchen, breakfast room and family room are open to one another. A series of decorative columns defines the family room. The owners suite boasts a cozy sitting room with a corner fireplace. The private bath features His and Hers baths. Upstairs are two bedrooms, each with a private bath. A grand entryway welcomes visitors into this ageless wonder.

DESIGN HPU040587

First Floor: 3,219 square feet
Second Floor: 1,202 square feet
Total: 4,421 square feet
Width: 86'-1" Depth: 76'-10"

DESIGN BY
©Larry E. Belk Designs

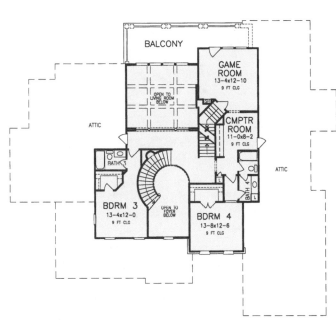

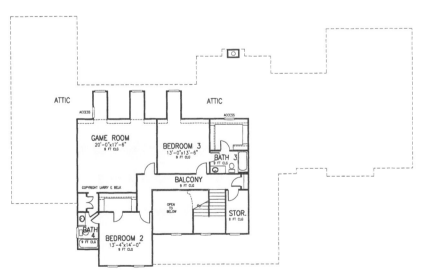

Brick and fieldstone adorn this two-story, four-bedroom home. A wraparound covered porch offers shelter from the elements and ushers you into a two-story foyer. Arches and columns separate the formal living and dining rooms, while the kitchen presents interesting angles and opens into the spacious family room via a snack bar. Note the direct access to the rear covered porch from the living room as well as from the family room. A secondary bedroom resides on the first floor and could be used as a guest suite or a cozy den. The master suite is sure to please with its many amenities, which include two walk-in closets, a lavish bath and access to a private porch. Upstairs, two family bedrooms are complete with private baths and large walk-in closets. A game room finishes this floor.

DESIGN HPU040588

First Floor: 2,931 square feet
Second Floor: 1,319 square feet
Total: 4,250 square feet
Width: 103'-7" Depth: 63'-9"

DESIGN BY
©Larry E. Belk Designs

483

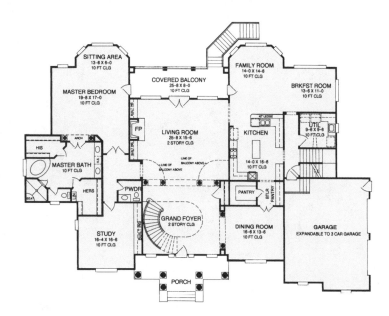

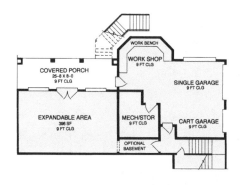

DESIGN HPU040589

First Floor: 3,413 square feet
Second Floor: 2,076 square feet
Total: 5,489 square feet
Bonus Room: 430 square feet
Width: 90'-6" Depth: 63'-6"

DESIGN BY
©Larry E. Belk Designs

Classic design combined with dynamite interiors make this executive home a real gem. Inside, a free-floating curved staircase rises majestically to the second floor. The enormous living room, great for formal entertaining, features a dramatic two-story window wall. The family room, breakfast room and kitchen are conveniently grouped. A large pantry and a companion butler's pantry serve both the dining room and kitchen. Privately located, the master suite includes a sitting area and sumptuous master bath. The second floor includes Bedroom 2, which has a private bath. Bedrooms 3 and 4 share a bath that includes two private dressing areas. A large game room is accessed from a rear stair.

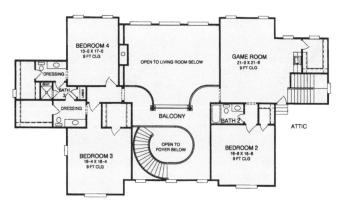

A distinctively French flair is the hallmark of this European-styled home. Inside, the two-story foyer provides views to the huge great room beyond. A well-placed study off the foyer provides an area for that much-used home office. The kitchen, breakfast room and sun room are adjacent to lend a spacious feel. The great room is visible from this area through decorative arches. A roomy utility room receives laundry from a chute above. A nearby built-in bench and desk help organize the rear entry of the home. The master suite includes a roomy sitting area and a lovely master bath with a centerpiece whirlpool tub flanked by half-columns. Upstairs, Bedrooms 2 and 3 share a bath that includes private dressing areas. An enormous game room is located upstairs and is reached by the convenient rear stair. Please specify crawlspace or slab foundation when ordering.

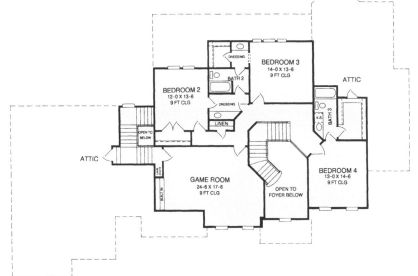

DESIGN HPU040590

First Floor: 2,608 square feet
Second Floor: 1,432 square feet
Total: 4,040 square feet
Width: 89'-10" Depth: 63'-8"

DESIGN BY
©Larry E. Belk Designs

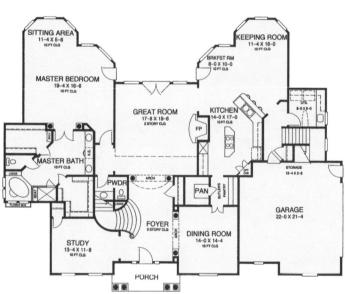

This home speaks of luxury and practicality and is abundant in attractive qualities. A study and dining room flank the foyer, while the great room offers a warming fireplace and double-French-door access to the rear yard straight back. A butler's pantry acts as a helpful buffer between the kitchen and the columned dining room. Double bays at the rear of the home form the keeping room and the breakfast room on one side and the owners bedroom on the other. Three family bedrooms and two baths grace the second floor. A game room is perfect for casual family-time. Please specify basement or slab foundation when ordering.

DESIGN HPU040591

First Floor: 2,639 square feet
Second Floor: 1,625 square feet
Total: 4,264 square feet
Width: 73'-8" Depth: 58'-6"

DESIGN BY
©Larry E. Belk Designs

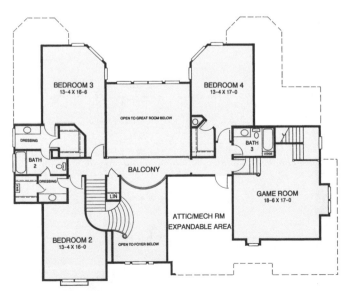

An impressive entry, multi-pane windows and mock balconies combine to give this facade an elegance of which to be proud. The grand foyer showcases a stunning staircase and is flanked by a formal dining room to the right and a cozy study to the left. The elegant sunken living room is graced by a fireplace, a wondrous piano bay, and a vaulted ceiling. The openness of the sunny breakfast room and the family room make casual entertaining a breeze. Located on the first floor for privacy, the master bedroom suite is lavish with its luxuries. A bayed sitting area encourages early morning repose, while the bath revels in pampering you. Upstairs, three bedrooms share two full baths and have access to a large game room over the three-car garage. Please specify crawlspace or slab foundation when ordering.

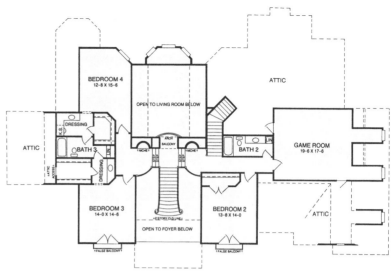

DESIGN HPU040592

First Floor: 3,264 square feet
Second Floor: 1,671 square feet
Total: 4,935 square feet
Width: 96'-10" Depth: 65'-1"

DESIGN BY
©Larry E. Belk Designs

DESIGN HPU040593

First Floor: 2,470 square feet
Second Floor: 1,360 square feet
Total: 3,830 square feet
Width: 77'-4"   Depth: 59'-8"

DESIGN BY
©Lucia Custom Home
Designers, Inc.

This design so well embraces the outdoors, it's almost difficult to distinguish where inside living areas end and outdoor spaces begin. Notice, for instance, the delightful dining garden, snuggled in between the formal dining room and the garage. Above it is a balcony adorning Bedroom 5. The family room has a curved glass view of the covered porch to the rear of the home; the living room echoes this option to the front. Even the dining room and master bedroom utilize curved glass accents. There is no lack of room in this design, either. Five bedrooms include a gallant master suite. Plus, the cozy study can become a guest bedroom as it is near a full bath. The second-level loft is a great place for quiet study or reading.

Blend the best elements of Spanish Colonial and contemporary design, and the result is an estate such as this. There are two ways to enter: through the main entry that separates the study and the dining room, or through the courtyard entry that leads directly into the eat-in kitchen. The living room is assigned columns and has a lovely gallery leading to the rear lanai. The family room is snug. It is a gateway to a private patio with a summer kitchen. A guest bedroom and master suite complete this level. The second floor holds three family bedrooms and access to two balconies (one with a nearby wet bar). Bonus space features a light-filled tower—make this hobby or study space.

DESIGN HPU040594

First Floor: 3,566 square feet
Second Floor: 1,196 square feet
Total: 4,762 square feet
Bonus Room: 479 square feet
Width: 85'-0" Depth: 81'-4"

DESIGN BY
©Lucia Custom Home
Designers, Inc.

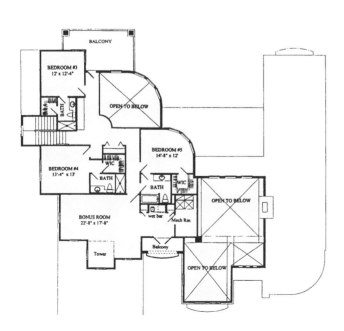

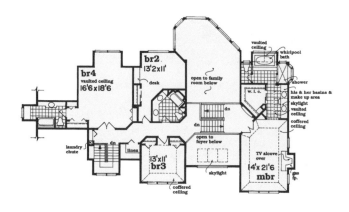

Three full levels of livability are contained within the floor plan of this design. The main level features formal living and dining areas, a family room with a vaulted ceiling, a breakfast nook and a study with a private terrace. The three-car garage is on this level and opens to the back of the plan. The upper level holds the bedrooms—three family bedrooms and a master suite. Bedroom 4 has a private bath, as does the master suite. Lower-level livability includes a game room, a home theater and an exercise area, plus a wine cellar for your private collection. A terrace at this level opens off the game room. Two large storage areas will be welcome.

DESIGN HPU040595

Main Level: 2,201 square feet
Upper Level: 2,034 square feet
Lower Level: 1,882 square feet
Total: 6,117 square feet
Width: 82'-6" Depth: 55'-8"

DESIGN BY
©Select Home Designs

This unusual stucco-and-siding design opens with a grand portico to a foyer containing a volume ceiling that extends to the living room. A multi-pane transom lights the foyer and the open staircase beyond. The living room has a fireplace and then proceeds up a few steps to the dining room with a coffered ceiling and butler's pantry, which connects it to the gourmet kitchen. Cooks will love the wet bar in the butler's pantry, the walk-in food pantry, a wine cooler, a built-in desk and the center island with a cooktop and salad sink. The attached hearth room has the requisite fireplace and three sets of French doors to the covered porch. The family room sports a coffered ceiling and fireplace flanked by French doors. The second floor boasts four bedrooms, including a master suite with a tray ceiling, covered deck and lavish bath. Two full baths serve the family bedrooms and a bonus room that might be used as an additional bedroom or hobby space.

DESIGN HPU040596

First Floor: 2,473 square feet
Second Floor: 2,686 square feet
Total: 5,159 square feet
Width: 57'-8" Depth: 103'-6"

DESIGN BY
©Select Home Designs

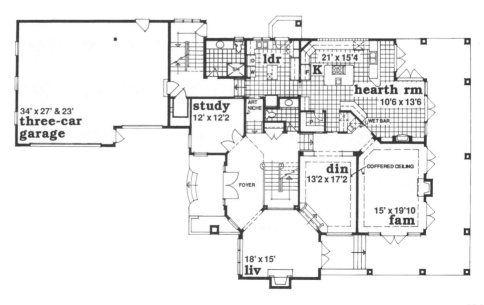

This elegant exterior blends a classical look with a contemporary feel. Corner quoins and round columns highlight the front elevation. The formal living room, complete with a fireplace and a wet bar, and the formal dining room access the lanai through three pairs of French doors. The well-appointed kitchen features an island prep sink, a walk-in pantry and a desk. The secondary bedrooms are full guest suites, located away from the private owner's wing. The master suite has enormous His and Hers closets, built-ins, a wet bar and a three-sided fireplace that separates the sitting room and the bedroom. The luxurious bath features a stunning, rounded glass-block shower and a whirlpool tub.

DESIGN BY
©The Sater Design Collection

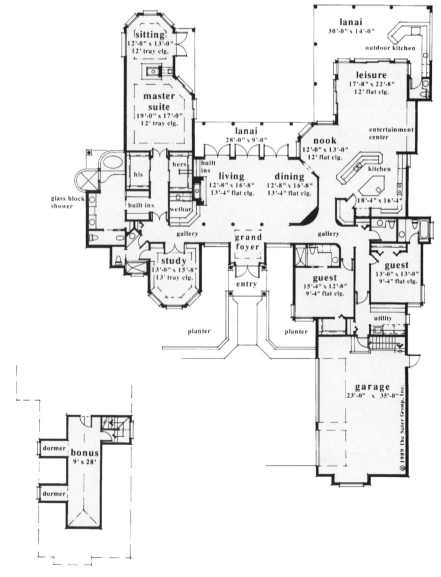

DESIGN HPU040597

Square Footage: 3,896
Bonus Room: 356 square feet
Width: 90'-0" Depth: 120'-8"

L

This grand traditional home offers an elegant, welcoming residence for the homeowner with luxury in mind. The grand foyer opens to a wonderful display of casual and formal living areas. Beyond the foyer, the spacious living room provides views of the rear grounds and opens to the veranda and rear yard through three pairs of French doors. An arched galley hall leads past the formal dining room to the family areas where casual get-togethers are enjoyed. Here, an ample gourmet kitchen easily serves the nook and the leisure room. The owners wing consists of a study or home office, and a grand master suite with an indulgent bath, offering the ultimate in comfort. The upper level contains three secondary bedrooms—each with a walk-in closet—and two with a private balcony. Please specify basement or slab foundation when ordering.

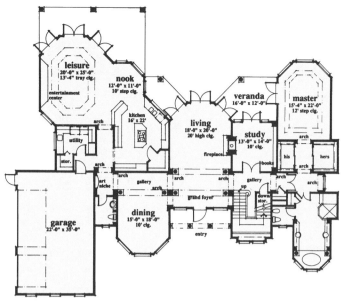

DESIGN HPU040598

First Floor: 3,546 square feet
Second Floor: 1,213 square feet
Total: 4,759 square feet
Width: 95'-4" Depth: 83'-0"

DESIGN BY
©The Sater Design Collection

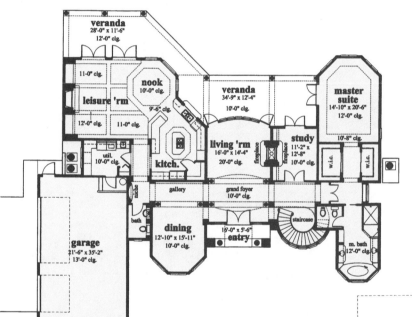

veranda
28'-0" x 11'-6"
12'-0" clg.

11'-0" clg.

nook
10'-0" clg.
9'-6" clg.

veranda
34'-9" x 12'-4"
10'-0" clg.

master
suite
14'-10" x 20'-6"
12'-0" clg.

leisure 'rm
12'-0" x 11'-0"

living 'rm
16'-0" x 14'-4"
20'-0" clg.

study
11'-2" x
12'-8"
10'-0" clg.

10'-8" clg.

util.
10'-0" clg.

kitch.

w.i.c.

w.i.c.

niche

gallery

grand foyer
10'-0" clg.

bath

dining
12'-10" x 15'-11"
10'-0" clg.

16'-0" x 5'-6"
entry

staircase

m. bath
12'-0" clg.

garage
21'-6" x 35'-2"
13'-0" clg.

DESIGN HPU040599

First Floor: 2,841 square feet
Second Floor: 1,052 square feet
Total: 3,893 square feet
Width: 85'-0" Depth: 76'-8"

DESIGN BY
©The Sater Design Collection

deck

deck

bedroom
12'-10" x 15'-2"
8'-8" clg.

guest
11'-2" x 19'-8"
8'-8" clg.

bath

open

bath

balcony
8'-8" clg.

STAIRCASE

bedroom
12'-10" x 15'-5"
8'-8" clg.

open

10'-0" clg.

This luxurious plan assures elegant living. A turret, two-story bay windows and plenty of arched glass impart a graceful style to the exterior, while rich amenities furnish contentment within. A grand foyer decked with columns introduces the living room, which boasts a curve of glass windows viewing the rear gardens. A through-fireplace is shared by the study and living room. The master suite fills the entire right section of the design and enjoys a tray ceiling, two walk-in closets, a separate shower and a garden tub set in a bay window. Informal entertainment will be a breeze with the leisure room, which adjoins the kitchen and breakfast nook and opens to a rear veranda. At the top of a lavish curving staircase are two family bedrooms sharing a full bath and a guest suite with a private deck.

DESIGN HPU040600

First Floor: 4,760 square feet
Second Floor: 1,552 square feet
Total: 6,312 square feet
Width: 98'-0" Depth: 103'-8"

As beautiful from the rear as from the front, this home features a spectacular blend of arch-top windows, French doors and balusters. Dramatic two-story ceilings and tray details add custom spaciousness. An impressive, informal leisure room has a sixteen-foot tray ceiling, an entertainment center and a grand ale bar. The large, gourmet kitchen is well appointed and easily serves the nook and formal dining room. The master suite has a large bedroom and a bayed sitting area. His and Hers vanities and walk-in closets and a curved, glass-block shower are highlights in the bath. The staircase leads to the deluxe secondary guest suites, two of which have observation decks to the rear and each with their own full baths.

DESIGN BY
©The Sater Design Collection

QUOTE ONE®
Cost to build? See page 502
to order complete cost estimate
to build this house in your area!

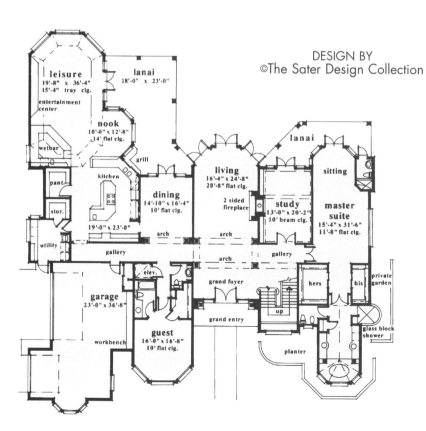

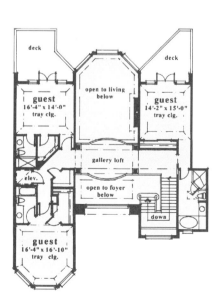

ontemporary styling coupled with traditional finishes of brick and stucco make this home a stand-out that caters to the discriminating few. The entry, with a two-story ceiling, steps down into an enormous great room with a see-through fireplace. A formal living room is open from the entry and begins one wing of the home. The bedroom wing provides three bedrooms, each with a large amenity-filled bath, as well as a study area and a recreation room. The opposite wing houses the dining room, kitchen, breakfast room and two more bedrooms. The kitchen offers a curved window overlooking the side yard and a cooktop island with a vegetable sink. A stair leads to a loft overlooking the great room and entry.

DESIGN BY
©Larry E. Belk Designs

DESIGN HPU040601

First Floor: 5,183 square feet
Second Floor: 238 square feet
Total: 5,421 square feet
Width: 93'-5" Depth: 113'-0"

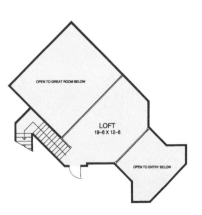

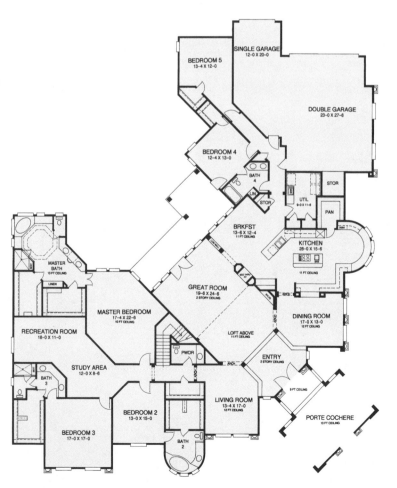

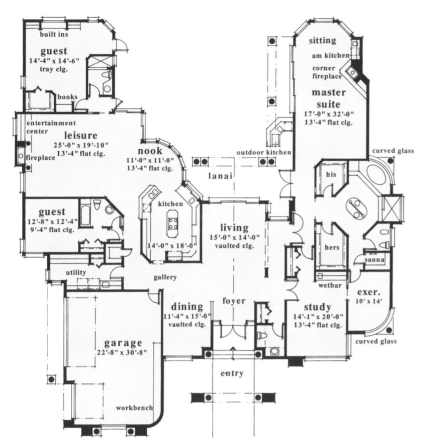

built ins

guest
14'-4" x 14'-6"
tray clg.

books

entertainment
center

leisure
25'-0" x 19'-10"
13'-4" flat clg.

fireplace

nook
11'-0" x 11'-0"
13'-4" flat clg.

guest
12'-8" x 12'-4"
9'-4" flat clg.

kitchen

14'-0" x 18'-0"

utility

gallery

sitting

am kitchen

corner
fireplace

**master
suite**
17'-0" x 32'-0"
13'-4" flat clg.

outdoor kitchen

lanai

curved glass

his

living
15'-0" x 14'-0"
vaulted clg.

hers

sauna

wetbar

exer.
10' x 14'

dining
11'-4" x 15'-0"
vaulted clg.

foyer

study
14'-1" x 20'-0"
13'-4" flat clg.

curved glass

garage
22'-8" x 30'-8"

entry

workbench

A free-standing entryway is the focal point of this luxurious residence. It has an arch motif that is carried through to the rear using a gabled roof and a vaulted ceiling from the foyer out to the lanai. High ceilings are found throughout the home, creating a spacious atmosphere. The kitchen, which features a cooktop island and plenty of counter space, opens to the leisure area with a handy snack bar. Two guest suites with private baths are just off this casual living area. The master wing is truly pampering, stretching the entire length of the home. The suite has a large sitting area, a corner fireplace and a morning kitchen. The bath features an island vanity, a raised tub with a curved glass wall overlooking a private garden, a sauna and separate closets. An exercise room has a curved glass wall and a pocket door to the study, where a wet bar is ready to serve up refreshment.

DESIGN HPU040602

Square Footage: 4,565
Width: 88'-0" Depth: 95'-0"

L

DESIGN BY
©The Sater Design Collection

HOME PLANNERS WANTS YOUR BUILDING EXPERIENCE TO BE AS PLEASANT AND TROUBLE-FREE AS POSSIBLE.

That's why we've expanded our library of Do-It-Yourself titles to help you along. In addition to our beautiful plans books, we've added books to guide you through specific projects as well as the construction process. In fact, these are titles that will be as useful after your dream home is built as they are right now.

BIGGEST & BEST

1001 of our best-selling plans in one volume. 1,074 to 7,275 square feet. 704 pgs $12.95 1K1

ONE-STORY

450 designs for all lifestyles. 800 to 4,900 square feet. 384 pgs $9.95 OS

MORE ONE-STORY

475 superb one-level plans from 800 to 5,000 square feet. 448 pgs $9.95 MOS

TWO-STORY

443 designs for one-and-a-half and two stories. 1,500 to 6,000 square feet. 448 pgs $9.95 TS

VACATION

465 designs for recreation, retirement and leisure. 448 pgs $9.95 VSH

HILLSIDE

208 designs for split-levels, bi-levels, multi-levels and walkouts. 224 pgs $9.95 HH

FARMHOUSE

200 country designs from classic to contemporary by 7 winning designers. 224 pgs $8.95 FH

COUNTRY HOUSES

208 unique home plans that combine traditional style and modern livability. 224 pgs $9.95 CN

BUDGET-SMART

200 efficient plans from 7 top designers, that you can really afford to build! 224 pgs $8.95 BS

BARRIER FREE

Over 1,700 products and 51 plans for accessible living. 128 pgs $15.95 UH

ENCYCLOPEDIA

500 exceptional plans for all styles and budgets—the best book of its kind! 528 pgs $9.95 ENC

ENCYCLOPEDIA II

500 completely new plans. Spacious and stylish designs for every budget and taste. 352 pgs $9.95 E2

AFFORDABLE

Completely revised and updated, featuring 300 designs for modest budgets. 256 pgs $9.95 AF

VICTORIAN

NEW! 210 striking Victorian and Farmhouse designs from today's top designers. 224 pgs $15.95 VDH2

ESTATE

Dream big! Twenty-one designers showcase their biggest and best plans. 208 pgs $15.95 EDH

LUXURY

154 fine luxury plans—loaded with luscious amenities! 192 pgs $14.95 LD2

EUROPEAN STYLES

200 homes with a unique flair of the Old World. 224 pgs $15.95 EURO

COUNTRY CLASSICS

Donald Gardner's 101 best Country and Traditional home plans. 192 pgs $17.95 DAG

WILLIAM POOLE

70 romantic house plans that capture the classic tradition of home design. 160 pgs $17.95 WEP

TRADITIONAL

85 timeless designs from the Design Traditions Library. 160 pgs $17.95 TRA

COTTAGES

25 fresh new designs that are as warm as a tropical breeze. A blend of the best aspects of many coastal styles. 64 pgs. $19.95 CTG

CLASSIC

Timeless, elegant designs that always feel like home. Gorgeous plans that are as flexible and up-to-date as their occupants. 240 pgs. $9.95 CS

CONTEMPORARY

The most complete and imaginative collection of contemporary designs available anywhere. 240 pgs. $9.95 CM

EASY-LIVING

200 efficient and sophisticated plans that are small in size, but big on livability. 224 pgs $8.95 EL

SOUTHERN

207 homes rich in Southern styling and comfort. 240 pgs $8.95 SH

SOUTHWESTERN

138 designs that capture the spirit of the Southwest. 144 pgs $10.95 SW

WESTERN

215 designs that capture the spirit and diversity of the Western lifestyle. 208 pgs $9.95 WH

NEIGHBORHOOD

170 designs with the feel of main street America. 192 pgs $12.95 TND

CRAFTSMAN

170 Home plans in the Craftsman and Bungalow style. 192 pgs $12.95 CC

COLONIAL HOUSES

181 Classic early American designs. 208 pgs $9.95 COL

DUPLEX & TOWNHOMES

Over 50 designs for multi-family living. 64 pgs $9.95 DTP

WATERFRONT

200 designs perfect for your waterside wonderland. 208 pgs $10.95 WF

PROJECT GUIDES

WINDOWS	STREET OF DREAMS	MOVE-UP	OUTDOOR	GARAGES	DECKS	HOME BUILDING	BOOK & CD-ROM

Discover the power of windows with over 160 designs featuring Pella's best. 192 pgs $9.95 WIN

Over 300 photos showcase 54 prestigious homes. 256 pgs $19.95 SOD

200 stylish designs for today's growing families from 9 hot designers. 224 pgs $8.95 MU

42 unique outdoor projects—gazebos, strombellas, bridges, sheds, playsets and more! 96 pgs $7.95 YG

101 multi-use garages and outdoor structures to enhance any home. 96 pgs $7.95 GG

25 outstanding single-, double- and multi-level decks you can build. 112 pgs $7.95 DP

Everything you need to know to work with contractors and subcontractors. 212 pgs $14.95 HBP

Both the Home Planners Gold book and matching Windows™ CD-ROM with 3D floor-plans. $24.95 HPGC
Book only $12.95 HPG

LANDSCAPE DESIGNS

SOFTWARE	EASY-CARE	FRONT & BACK	BACKYARDS	BUYER'S GUIDE	FRAMING	BASIC WIRING	TILE

      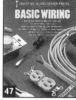

Home design made easy! View designs in 3D, take a virtual reality tour, add decorating details and more. $59.95 PLANSUITE

41 special landscapes designed for beauty and low mainte-nance. 160 pgs $14.95 ECL

The first book of do-it-yourself land-scapes. 40 front, 15 backyards. 208 pgs $14.95 HL

40 designs focused solely on creating your own specially themed backyard oasis. 160 pgs $14.95 BYL

A comprehensive look at 2700 prod-ucts for all aspects of landscaping & gar-dening. 128 pgs $19.95 LPBG

For those who want to take a more hands-on approach to their dream. 319 pgs $21.95 SRF

A straightforward guide to one of the most misunderstood systems in the home. 160 pgs $12.95 CBW

Every kind of tile for every kind of appli-cation. Includes tips on use, installation and repair. 176 pgs $12.95 CWT

BATHROOMS	KITCHENS	HOUSE CONTRACTING	VISUAL HANDBOOK	ROOFING	WINDOWS & DOORS	PATIOS & WALKS	TRIM & MOLDING

An innovative guide to organizing, re-modeling and decorating your bathroom. 96 pgs $10.95 CDB

An imaginative guide to designing the per-fect kitchen. Chock full of bright ideas to make your job easier. 176 pgs $16.95 CKI

Everything you need to know to act as your own general contrac-tor, and save up to 25% off building costs. 134 pgs $14.95 SBC

A plain-talk guide to the construction pro-cess; financing to final walk-through, this book covers it all. 498 pgs $19.95 RVH

Information on the latest tools, materials and techniques for roof installation or repair. 80 pgs $7.95 CGR

Installation tech-niques and tips that make your project easier and more pro-fessional looking. 80 pgs $7.95 CGD

Clear step-by-step in-structions take you from the basic design stages to the finished project. 80 pgs $7.95 CGW

Step-by-step instruc-tions for installing baseboards, window and door casings and more. 80 pgs $7.95 CGT

Additional Books Order Form

To order your books, just check the box of the book numbered below and complete the coupon. We will process your order and ship it from our office within two business days. Send coupon and check (in U.S. funds).

YES! Please send me the books I've indicated:

❏ 1:IKI $12.95	❏ 20:TRA $17.95	❏ 39:HBP $14.95
❏ 2:OS $9.95	❏ 21:CTG $19.95	❏ 40:HPG $12.95
❏ 3:MOS $9.95	❏ 22:CS $9.95	❏ 40:HPGC $24.95
❏ 4:TS $9.95	❏ 23:CM $9.95	❏ 41:PLANSUITE ..$59.95
❏ 5:VSH $9.95	❏ 24:EL $8.95	❏ 42:ECL $14.95
❏ 6:HH $9.95	❏ 25:SH $8.95	❏ 43:HL $14.95
❏ 7:FH $8.95	❏ 26:SW $10.95	❏ 44:BYL $14.95
❏ 8:CN $9.95	❏ 27:WH $9.95	❏ 45:LPBG $19.95
❏ 9:BS $8.95	❏ 28:TND $12.95	❏ 46:SRF $21.95
❏ 10:UH $15.95	❏ 29:CC $12.95	❏ 47:CBW $12.95
❏ 11:ENC $9.95	❏ 30:COL $9.95	❏ 48:CWT $12.95
❏ 12:E2 ....$9.95	❏ 31:DTP $9.95	❏ 49:CDB $10.95
❏ 13:AF $9.95	❏ 32:WF $10.95	❏ 50:CKI $16.95
❏ 14:VDH2 ....$15.95	❏ 33:WIN $9.95	❏ 51:SBC $14.95
❏ 15:EDH $15.95	❏ 34:SOD $19.95	❏ 52:RVH $19.95
❏ 16:LD2 ....$14.95	❏ 35:MU $8.95	❏ 53:CGR $7.95
❏ 17:EURO $15.95	❏ 36:YG $7.95	❏ 54:CGD $7.95
❏ 18:DAG $17.95	❏ 37:GG $7.95	❏ 55:CGW $7.95
❏ 19:WEP $17.95	❏ 38:DP $7.95	❏ 56:CGT $7.95

Canadian Customers Order Toll Free 1-877-223-6389

Additional Books Subtotal (Please print) $ _____
ADD Postage and Handling (allow 4–6 weeks for delivery) $ 4.00
Sales Tax: (AZ & MI residents, add state and local sales tax.) $ _____
YOUR TOTAL (Subtotal, Postage/Handling, Tax) $ _____

YOUR ADDRESS (PLEASE PRINT)

Name _____
Street _____
City _____ State _____ Zip _____
Phone (_____) _____—_____

YOUR PAYMENT

Check one: ❏ Check ❏ Visa ❏ MasterCard ❏ Discover ❏ American Express
Required credit card information:

Credit Card Number _____
Expiration Date (Month/Year) _____ / _____
Signature Required _____

HPU04

Home Planners, LLC
Wholly owned by Hanley-Wood, LLC
® 3275 W. Ina Road, Suite 110, Dept. BK, Tucson, AZ 85741

499

LET US SHOW YOU OUR HOME BLUEPRINT PACKAGE.

Building a home? Planning a home? Our Blueprint Package has nearly everything you need to get the job done right, whether you're working on your own or with help from an architect, designer, builder or subcontractors. Each Blueprint Package is the result of many hours of work by licensed architects or professional designers.

QUALITY

Hundreds of hours of painstaking effort have gone into the development of your blueprint set. Each home has been quality-checked by professionals to insure accuracy and buildability.

VALUE

Because we sell in volume, you can buy professional quality blueprints at a fraction of their development cost. With our plans, your dream home design costs only a few hundred dollars, not the thousands of dollars that architects charge.

SERVICE

Once you've chosen your favorite home plan, you'll receive fast, efficient service whether you choose to mail or fax your order to us or call us toll free at 1-877-675-4639. For customer service, call toll free 1-888-690-1116.

SATISFACTION

Over 50 years of service to satisfied home plan buyers provide us unparalleled experience and knowledge in producing quality blueprints.

ORDER TOLL FREE 1-877-675-4639

After you've looked over our Blueprint Package and Important Extras on the following pages, simply mail the order form on page 511 or call toll free on our Blueprint Hotline: 1-877-675-4639. We're ready and eager to serve you. For customer service, call toll free 1-888-690-1116.

Each set of blueprints is an interrelated collection of detail sheets which includes components such as floor plans, interior and exterior elevations, dimensions, cross-sections, diagrams and notations. These sheets show exactly how your house is to be built.

AMONG THE SHEETS INCLUDED MAY BE:

FRONTAL SHEET

This artist's sketch of the exterior of the house gives you an idea of how the house will look when built and landscaped. Large floor plans show all levels of the house and provide an overview of your new home's livability, as well as a handy reference for deciding on furniture placement.

FOUNDATION PLANS

This sheet shows the foundation layout including support walls, excavated and unexcavated areas, if any, and foundation notes. If slab construction rather than basement, the plan shows footings and details for a monolithic slab. This page, or another in the set, may include a sample plot plan for locating your house on a building site.

DETAILED FLOOR PLANS

These plans show the layout of each floor of the house. Rooms and interior spaces are carefully dimensioned and keys are given for cross-section details provided later in the plans. The positions of electrical outlets and switches are shown.

HOUSE CROSS-SECTIONS

Large-scale views show sections or cut-aways of the foundation, interior walls, exterior walls, floors, stairways and roof details. Additional cross-sections may show important changes in floor, ceiling or roof heights or the relationship of one level to another. Extremely valuable for construction, these sections show exactly how the various parts of the house fit together.

INTERIOR ELEVATIONS

Many of our drawings show the design and placement of kitchen and bathroom cabinets, laundry areas, fireplaces, bookcases and other built-ins. Little "extras," such as mantelpiece and wainscoting drawings, plus molding sections, provide details that give your home that custom touch.

EXTERIOR ELEVATIONS

These drawings show the front, rear and sides of your house and give necessary notes on exterior materials and finishes. Particular attention is given to cornice detail, brick and stone accents or other finish items that make your home unique.

SAMPLE PACKAGE

FRONTAL SHEET

FOUNDATION PLANS

DETAILED FLOOR PLANS

EXTERIOR ELEVATIONS

INTERIOR ELEVATIONS

HOUSE CROSS-SECTIONS

INTRODUCING EIGHT IMPORTANT PLANNING AND CONSTRUCTION AIDS DEVELOPED BY OUR PROFESSIONALS TO HELP YOU SUCCEED IN YOUR HOME-BUILDING PROJECT

MATERIALS LIST

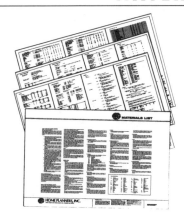

(Note: Because of the diversity of local building codes, our Materials List does not include mechanical materials.)

For many of the designs in our portfolio, we offer a customized materials take-off that is invaluable in planning and estimating the cost of your new home. This Materials List outlines the quantity, type and size of materials needed to build your house (with the exception of mechanical system items). Included are framing lumber, windows and doors, kitchen and bath cabinetry, rough and finish hardware, and much more. This handy list helps you or your builder cost out materials and serves as a reference sheet when you're compiling bids. A Materials List cannot be ordered before blueprints are ordered.

SPECIFICATION OUTLINE

This valuable 16-page document is critical to building your house correctly. Designed to be filled in by you or your builder, this book lists 166 stages or items crucial to the building process. It provides a comprehensive review of the construction process and helps in choosing materials. When combined with the blueprints, a signed contract, and a schedule, it becomes a legal document and record for the building of your home.

QUOTE ONE®

SUMMARY COST REPORT / MATERIALS COST REPORT

A new service for estimating the cost of building select designs, the Quote One® system is available in two separate stages: The Summary Cost Report and the Materials Cost Report.

The **Summary Cost Report** is the first stage in the package and shows the total cost per square foot for your chosen home in your zip-code area and then breaks that cost down into various categories showing the costs for building materials, labor and installation. The report includes three grades: Budget, Standard and Custom. These reports allow you to evaluate your building budget and compare the costs of building a variety of homes in your area.

Make even more informed decisions about your home-building project with the second phase of our package, our **Materials Cost Report.** This tool is invaluable in planning and estimating the cost of your new home. The material and installation (labor and equipment) cost is shown for each of over 1,000 line items provided in the Materials List (Standard grade), which is included when you purchase this estimating tool. It allows you to determine building costs for your specific zip-code area and for your chosen home design. Space is allowed for additional estimates from contractors and subcontractors, such as for mechanical materials, which are not included in our packages.

This invaluable tool includes a Materials List. For most plans, a Materials Cost Report cannot be ordered before blueprints are ordered. Call for details. In addition, ask about our Home Planners Estimating Package.

The Quote One® program is continually updated with new plans. If you are interested in a plan that is not indicated as Quote One, please call and ask our sales reps. They will be happy to verify the status for you. To order these invaluable reports, use the order form on page 511 or call 1-877-675-4639.

CONSTRUCTION INFORMATION

If you want to know more about techniques—and deal more confidently with subcontractors—we offer these useful sheets. Each set is an excellent tool that will add to your understanding of these technical subjects. These helpful details provide general construction information and are not specific to any single plan.

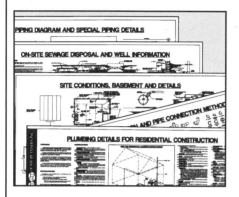

PLUMBING

The Blueprint Package includes locations for all the plumbing fixtures, including sinks, lavatories, tubs, showers, toilets, laundry trays and water heaters. However, if you want to know more about the complete plumbing system, these Plumbing Details will prove very useful. Prepared to meet requirements of the National Plumbing Code, these fact-filled sheets give general information on pipe schedules, fittings, sump-pump details, water-softener hookups, septic system details and much more. Sheets also include a glossary of terms.

ELECTRICAL

The locations for every electrical switch, plug and outlet are shown in your Blueprint Package. However, these Electrical Details go further to take the mystery out of household electrical systems. Prepared to meet requirements of the National Electrical Code, these comprehensive drawings come packed with helpful information, including wire sizing, switch-installation schematics, cable-routing details, appliance wattage, doorbell hookups, typical service panel circuitry and much more. A glossary of terms is also included.

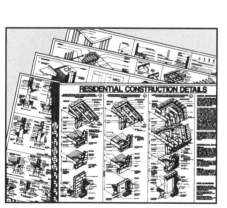

CONSTRUCTION

The Blueprint Package contains everything an experienced builder needs to construct a particular house. However, it doesn't show all the ways that houses can be built, nor does it explain alternate construction methods. To help you understand how your house will be built—and offer additional techniques—this set of Construction Details depicts the materials and methods used to build foundations, fireplaces, walls, floors and roofs. Where appropriate, the drawings show acceptable alternatives.

MECHANICAL

These Mechanical Details contain fundamental principles and useful data that will help you make informed decisions and communicate with subcontractors about heating and cooling systems. Drawings contain instructions and samples that allow you to make simple load calculations, and preliminary sizing and costing analysis. Covered are today's most commonly used systems from heat pumps to solar fuel systems. The package is filled with illustrations and diagrams to help you visualize components and how they relate to one another.

PLAN-A-HOME®

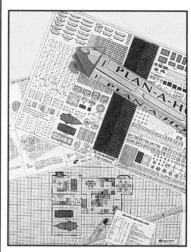

PLAN-A-HOME® is an easy-to-use tool that helps you design a new home, arrange furniture in a new or existing home, or plan a remodeling project. Each package contains:

✓ MORE THAN 700 REUSABLE PEEL-OFF PLANNING SYMBOLS on a self-stick vinyl sheet, including walls, windows, doors, all types of furniture, kitchen components, bath fixtures and many more.

✓ A REUSABLE, TRANSPARENT, ¼" SCALE PLANNING GRID that matches the scale of actual working drawings (¼" equals one foot). This grid provides the basis for house layouts of up to 140'x92'.

✓ TRACING PAPER and a protective sheet for copying or transferring your completed plan.

✓ A FELT-TIP PEN, with water-soluble ink that wipes away quickly.

Plan-A-Home® lets you lay out areas as large as a 7,500 square foot, six-bedroom, seven-bath house.

To Order, Call Toll Free 1-877-675-4639

To add these important extras to your Blueprint Package, simply indicate your choices on the order form on page 511. Or call us toll free 1-877-675-4639 and we'll tell you more about these exciting products. For customer service, call toll free 1-888-690-1116.

THE FINISHING TOUCHES...

THE DECK BLUEPRINT PACKAGE

Many of the homes in this book can be enhanced with a professionally designed Home Planners Deck Plan. Those home plans highlighted with a **D** have a matching Deck Plan, sold separately, which includes a Deck Plan Frontal Sheet, Deck Framing and Floor Plans, Deck Elevations and a Deck Materials List. A Standard Deck Details Package, also available, provides all the how-to information necessary for building *any* deck. Our Complete Deck Building Package contains one set of Custom Deck Plans of your choice, plus one set of Standard Deck Building Details, all for one low price. Our plans and details are carefully prepared in an easy-to-understand format that will guide you through every stage of your deck-building project. This page contains a sampling of six different Deck layouts (and a front-yard landscape) to match your favorite house. See page 506 for prices and ordering information.

EUROPEAN-FLAIR HOME
Landscape OLA088

WEEKEND-ENTERTAINER DECK
Deck ODA013

CENTER-VIEW DECK
Deck ODA015

KITCHEN-EXTENDER DECK
Deck ODA016

SPLIT-LEVEL ACTIVITY DECK
Deck ODA018

TRI-LEVEL DECK WITH GRILL
Deck ODA020

CONTEMPORARY LEISURE DECK
Deck ODA021

THE LANDSCAPE BLUEPRINT PACKAGE

For the homes marked with an **L** in this book, Home Planners has created a front-yard Landscape Plan that matches or is complementary in design to the house plan. These comprehensive blueprint packages include a Frontal Sheet, Plan View, Regionalized Plant & Materials List, a sheet on Planting and Maintaining Your Landscape, Zone Maps and Plant Size and Description Guide. These plans will help you achieve professional results, adding value and enjoyment to your property for years to come. Each set of blueprints is a full 18" x 24" in size with clear, complete instructions and easy-to-read type. Six of the forty front-yard Landscape Plans to match your favorite house are shown below.

Regional Order Map

Most of the Landscape Plans shown on these pages are available with a Plant & Materials List adapted by horticultural experts to 8 different regions of the country. Please specify the Geographic Region when ordering your plan. See pages 506-509 for prices, ordering information and regional availability.

Region	1	Northeast
Region	2	Mid-Atlantic
Region	3	Deep South
Region	4	Florida & Gulf Coast
Region	5	Midwest
Region	6	Rocky Mountains
Region	7	Southern California & Desert Southwest
Region	8	Northern California & Pacific Northwest

CAPE COD COTTAGE
Landscape OLA003

GAMBREL-ROOF COLONIAL
Landscape OLA004

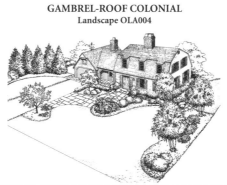

CENTER-HALL COLONIAL
Landscape OLA005

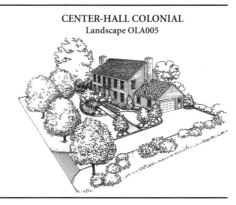

CLASSIC NEW ENGLAND COLONIAL
Landscape OLA006

COUNTRY-STYLE FARMHOUSE
Landscape OLA008

TRADITIONAL SPLIT-LEVEL
Landscape OLA029

HOUSE BLUEPRINT PRICE SCHEDULE

Prices guaranteed through December 31, 2001

TIERS	1-SET STUDY PACKAGE	4-SET BUILDING PACKAGE	8-SET BUILDING PACKAGE	1-SET REPRODUCIBLE	HOME CUSTOMIZER® PACKAGE
P1	$20	$50	$90	$140	N/A
P2	$40	$70	$110	$160	N/A
P3	$60	$90	$130	$180	N/A
P4	$80	$110	$150	$200	N/A
P5	$100	$130	$170	$230	N/A
P6	$120	$150	$190	$250	N/A
A1	$420	$460	$520	$625	$680
A2	$460	$500	$560	$685	$740
A3	$500	$540	$600	$745	$800
A4	$540	$580	$640	$805	$860
C1	$585	$625	$685	$870	$925
C2	$625	$665	$725	$930	$985
C3	$675	$715	$775	$980	$1035
C4	$725	$765	$825	$1030	$1085
L1	$785	$825	$885	$1090	$1145
L2	$835	$875	$935	$1140	$1195
L3	$935	$975	$1035	$1240	$1295
L4	$1035	$1075	$1135	$1340	$1395

OPTIONS FOR PLANS IN TIERS A1–L4

Additional Identical Blueprints in same order for "A1–L4" price plans ....$50 per set

Reverse Blueprints (mirror image) with 4- or 8-set order
for "A1–L4" price plans ....$50 fee per order

Specification Outlines ....$10 each

Materials Lists for "A1–C3" price plans ....$60 each

Materials Lists for "C4–L4" price plans ....$70 each

OPTIONS FOR PLANS IN TIERS P1–P6

Additional Identical Blueprints in same order for "P1–P6" price plans ....$10 per set

Reverse Blueprints (mirror image) for "P1–P6" price plans ....$10 per set

1 Set of Deck Construction Details ....$14.95 each

Deck Construction Package ....add $10 to Building Package price
(includes 1 set of "P1–P6" price plans, plus
1 set Standard Deck Construction Details)

1 Set of Gazebo Construction Details ....$14.95 each

Gazebo Construction Package ....add $10 to Building Package price
(includes 1 set of "P1–P6" price plans, plus
1 set Standard Gazebo Construction Details)

IMPORTANT NOTES

The 1-set study package is marked "not for construction."
Prices for 4- or 8-set Building Packages honored only at time of original order. Some basement foundations carry a $225 surcharge. Right-reading reverse blueprints, if available, will incur a $165 surcharge.

INDEX

To use the Index below, refer to the design number listed in numerical order (a helpful page reference is also given). Note the price index letter and refer to the House Blueprint Price Schedule above for the cost of one, four or eight sets of blueprints or the cost of a reproducible drawing. Additional prices are shown for identical and reverse blueprint sets, as well as a very useful Materials List for some of the plans. Also note in the Index below those plans that have matching or complementary Deck Plans or Landscape Plans. Refer to the schedules above for prices of these plans. All plans in this publication are customizable. However, only Home Planners plans can be customized with the Home Planners Home Customizer® Package. These plans are indicated below with the letter "Y." See page 511 for more information. The letter "Y" also identifies plans that are part of our Quote One® estimating service and those that offer Materials Lists. See page 502 for more information.

To Order: Fill in and send the order form on page 511—or call toll free 1-877-675-4639 or 520-297-8200. FAX: 1-800-224-6699 or 520-544-3086.

DESIGN	PRICE	PAGE	MATERIALS LIST	CUSTOMIZABLE®	QUOTE ONE®	DECK	DECK PRICE	LANDSCAPE	LANDSCAPE PRICE	REGIONS
HPU040001	A2	1								
HPU040002	A1	2								
HPU040003	A2	3								
HPU040004	A1	4	Y							
HPU040005	A2	5								
HPU040006	A1	6								
HPU040007	A1	7	Y							
HPU040008	A2	8								
HPU040009	A2	9b								
HPU040010	C2	9a	Y							
HPU040011	A1	10								
HPU040012	A4	11	Y							
HPU040013	A2	12a								
HPU040014	A3	12b	Y							
HPU040015	A2	13								
HPU040016	A2	14b	Y							
HPU040017	A2	14a	Y							
HPU040018	A2	15	Y							
HPU040019	A2	16	Y							
HPU040020	A1	17	Y							
HPU040021	A2	18b								
HPU040022	A2	18a								
HPU040023	A1	19								
HPU040024	A1	20								
HPU040025	A1	21								
HPU040026	A4	22	Y							
HPU040027	A2	23								
HPU040028	A2	24b	Y							
HPU040029	A2	24a	Y							
HPU040030	A2	25	Y		Y					
HPU040031	A2	26								
HPU040032	A2	27								
HPU040033	A2	28								
HPU040034	A2	29	Y							
HPU040035	A4	30a								
HPU040036	A4	30b								
HPU040037	A4	31								
HPU040038	A3	32	Y							
HPU040039	A2	33	Y							
HPU040040	A2	34	Y							
HPU040041	A2	35	Y							
HPU040042	A4	36								
HPU040043	A4	37								
HPU040044	A2	38	Y							
HPU040045	A2	39	Y							
HPU040047	A2	40b	Y							
HPU040048	A2	40a	Y							
HPU040049	A2	41								
HPU040050	A2	42	Y							
HPU040051	A2	43								
HPU040052	A2	44a	Y							
HPU040053	A2	44b	Y							
HPU040054	A2	45	Y							
HPU040055	A2	46b	Y							
HPU040056	A2	46a	Y							
HPU040057	A2	47	Y		Y					

DESIGN	PRICE	PAGE	MATERIALS LIST	CUSTOMIZABLE	QUOTE ONE	DECK	DECK PRICE	LANDSCAPE	LANDSCAPE PRICE	REGIONS
HPU040058	A2	48	Y							
HPU040059	A2	49	Y							
HPU040060	A2	50	Y							
HPU040061	A2	51a	Y							
HPU040062	A2	51b	Y							
HPU040063	A2	52a								
HPU040064	A2	52b	Y							
HPU040065	A2	53	Y							
HPU040066	A2	54a								
HPU040067	A3	54b								
HPU040068	A3	55								
HPU040069	A2	56b								
HPU040070	A3	56a								
HPU040071	A2	57								
HPU040072	A3	58a								
HPU040073	A2	58b	Y							
HPU040074	A3	59	Y							
HPU040075	A2	60a								
HPU040076	A4	60b								
HPU040077	A2	61	Y							
HPU040078	A4	62	Y							
HPU040079	A3	63								
HPU040080	A3	64a								
HPU040081	A3	64b								
HPU040082	A3	65	Y							
HPU040083	A3	66								
HPU040084	A3	67								
HPU040085	A4	68								
HPU040086	A4	69								
HPU040087	A3	70								
HPU040088	A3	71								
HPU040089	A3	72b								
HPU040090	A4	72a								
HPU040091	A4	73						OLA024	P4	123568
HPU040092	A4	74								
HPU040093	A4	75								
HPU040094	A3	76								
HPU040095	A3	77								
HPU040096	A3	78								
HPU040097	A3	79								
HPU040098	A3	80								
HPU040099	A4	81								
HPU040100	C1	24F			Y					
HPU040101	A3	82	Y							
HPU040102	A3	83								
HPU040103	A4	84								
HPU040104	A3	85								
HPU040105	A3	86								
HPU040106	A4	87	Y	Y	Y			OLA024	P4	123568
HPU040107	A4	88	Y							
HPU040108	A4	89	Y							
HPU040109	A3	90								
HPU040110	C1	91								
HPU040111	A3	92								
HPU040112	C1	93								
HPU040113	A3	94b	Y							
HPU040114	A3	94a	Y							
HPU040115	A3	95	Y							
HPU040116	A4	96a								
HPU040117	A3	96b								
HPU040118	A3	97								
HPU040119	A3	98	Y					OLA001	P3	123568
HPU040120	A3	99								
HPU040121	A4	100								
HPU040122	A3	101								
HPU040123	C1	102								
HPU040124	A4	103	Y							
HPU040125	A3	104b	Y							
HPU040126	A3	104a	Y							
HPU040127	A3	105	Y							
HPU040128	A3	106b	Y							
HPU040129	A3	106a								
HPU040130	A3	107	Y							
HPU040131	A3	108b								
HPU040132	A3	108a								
HPU040133	A3	109								
HPU040134	A4	110b								
HPU040135	A3	110a		Y						
HPU040136	A3	111		Y						
HPU040137	A3	112b	Y							
HPU040138	A3	112a	Y							
HPU040139	A3	113								
HPU040140	A3	114	Y					OLA001	P3	123568
HPU040141	A3	115	Y					OLA001	P3	123568
HPU040142	C3	116b	Y							
HPU040143	A3	116a								
HPU040144	A3	117								
HPU040145	A3	118	Y							
HPU040146	A2	119								
HPU040147	A3	120a	Y							
HPU040148	A3	120b	Y							
HPU040149	A4	121	Y							
HPU040150	A3	122b	Y							
HPU040151	A3	122a								
HPU040152	A3	123		Y						
HPU040153	A3	124a								
HPU040154	A3	124b	Y							
HPU040155	A3	125								
HPU040156	A3	126	Y							
HPU040157	C2	127								
HPU040158	A3	128								
HPU040159	A3	129								
HPU040160	A3	130	Y		Y			OLA001	P3	123568
HPU040161	A3	131						OLA004	P3	123568
HPU040162	A3	132						OLA004	P3	123568
HPU040163	A3	133	Y		Y			OLA005	P3	123568
HPU040164	A3	134b								
HPU040165	A3	134a								
HPU040166	A4	135								
HPU040167	A4	136b								
HPU040168	A4	136a								
HPU040169	A3	137								
HPU040170	A3	138	Y							
HPU040171	A3	139								
HPU040172	A4	140								
HPU040173	A3	141								
HPU040174	A3	142								
HPU040175	A3	143	Y							
HPU040176	A3	144	Y					OLA001	P3	123568
HPU040177	A3	145	Y							
HPU040178	A3	146								
HPU040179	A3	147	Y							
HPU040180	A3	148								
HPU040181	A4	149								
HPU040182	C1	150b						OLA012	P3	12345678
HPU040183	A4	150a	Y							
HPU040184	A4	151								
HPU040185	A4	152								
HPU040186	A4	153								
HPU040187	A4	154								
HPU040188	C1	155	Y		Y			OLA025	P3	123568
HPU040189	A4	156								
HPU040190	C2	157	Y		Y			OLA024	P4	123568
HPU040191	A4	158								
HPU040192	A4	159	Y							
HPU040193	A4	160	Y							
HPU040194	C2	161	Y							
HPU040195	A4	162	Y							
HPU040196	C2	163	Y							
HPU040197	C2	17F	Y							
HPU040198	C2	164	Y							
HPU040199	A4	165								
HPU040200	A4	18F	Y							
HPU040201	A4	166	Y							
HPU040202	A4	167	Y							
HPU040203	A4	168	Y							
HPU040204	A4	169	Y							
HPU040205	C2	170	Y							
HPU040206	A4	171								
HPU040207	A4	172	Y							
HPU040208	A4	173								
HPU040209	C1	19F								
HPU040210	A4	174	Y							
HPU040211	A4	175		Y						
HPU040212	A4	176								
HPU040213	A4	177								
HPU040214	A4	178		Y						
HPU040215	A4	179								
HPU040216	A4	180		Y						
HPU040217	A4	181								
HPU040218	C1	182	Y							
HPU040219	A4	183	Y							
HPU040220	C1	184	Y		Y					
HPU040221	A4	185								
HPU040222	C2	186	Y	Y	Y					
HPU040223	A4	187								
HPU040224	A3	20F	Y		Y					
HPU040225	A4	188								
HPU040226	A4	189								
HPU040227	A4	190a								
HPU040228	A4	190b								
HPU040229	C1	191	Y	Y	Y	ODA001	P2	OLA001	P3	123568
HPU040230	A4	192	Y							
HPU040231	A3	193		Y						
HPU040232	A4	194		Y						
HPU040233	A4	21F		Y						
HPU040234	A4	195	Y							
HPU040235	A4	196								
HPU040236	C1	197	Y							
HPU040237	C1	198b	Y	Y	Y	ODA011	P2	OLA008	P4	1234568
HPU040238	A4	198a	Y		Y					
HPU040239	A4	199		Y						

DESIGN	PRICE	PAGE	MATERIALS LIST	CUSTOMIZABLE®	QUOTE ONE®	DECK	DECK PRICE	LANDSCAPE	LANDSCAPE PRICE	REGIONS
HPU040240	A4	200	Y							
HPU040241	A4	201								
HPU040242	A4	202	Y							
HPU040243	A4	203	Y	Y	Y	ODA014	P2	OLA008	P4	1234568
HPU040244	C1	22F	Y							
HPU040245	A4	204			Y					
HPU040246	A4	205b	Y							
HPU040247	A4	205a	Y							
HPU040248	A4	206b	Y							
HPU040249	A4	206a	Y							
HPU040250	A4	207	Y							
HPU040251	A4	208a	Y							
HPU040252	A4	208b	Y							
HPU040253	A4	209	Y		Y					
HPU040254	A4	210a	Y							
HPU040255	A4	210b	Y							
HPU040256	A4	211	Y							
HPU040257	A4	212a	Y							
HPU040258	A4	212b	Y		Y					
HPU040259	A4	213	Y							
HPU040260	C1	214	Y	Y	Y					
HPU040261	C3	23F	Y	Y						
HPU040262	C1	215	Y	Y	Y	ODA012	P3	OLA010	P3	1234568
HPU040263	C1	216b	Y	Y	Y	ODA012	P3	OLA010	P3	1234568
HPU040264	A4	216a	Y	Y						
HPU040265	A4	217	Y							
HPU040266	A4	218b	Y		Y					
HPU040267	A4	218a	Y		Y					
HPU040268	A4	219	Y							
HPU040269	A4	220a	Y		Y					
HPU040270	A4	220b	Y		Y					
HPU040271	A4	221	Y							
HPU040272	A4	222a								
HPU040273	A4	222b	Y		Y					
HPU040274	A4	223	Y		Y					
HPU040275	A4	224	Y	Y	Y			OLA024	P4	123568
HPU040276	A4	225	Y							
HPU040277	A4	226a	Y	Y		ODA011	P2	OLA025	P3	123568
HPU040278	C1	226b	Y	Y	Y	ODA011	P2	OLA088	P4	12345678
HPU040279	C1	227	Y	Y	Y			OLA010	P3	1234568
HPU040280	A4	228	Y							
HPU040281	C1	229								
HPU040282	C1	230b	Y							
HPU040283	C1	230a								
HPU040284	A4	231	Y							
HPU040285	C1	232b	Y							
HPU040286	C1	232a	Y		Y					
HPU040287	C1	233	Y							
HPU040288	A4	234								
HPU040289	A4	235	Y							
HPU040290	C3	25F		Y						
HPU040291	C1	236	Y		Y					
HPU040292	A4	237	Y							
HPU040293	A4	238	Y							
HPU040294	A4	239								
HPU040295	A4	240								
HPU040296	A4	241								
HPU040297	C1	242								
HPU040298	C1	243								
HPU040299	C1	244								
HPU040300	C1	245								
HPU040301	C1	246								
HPU040302	C3	247								
HPU040303	C1	248b								
HPU040304	C1	248a								
HPU040305	C1	249								
HPU040306	C2	250	Y							
HPU040307	C2	251	Y							
HPU040308	C2	252a	Y							
HPU040309	C2	252b	Y							
HPU040310	C2	253	Y							
HPU040311	C1	254	Y							
HPU040312	C1	255								
HPU040313	C3	256								
HPU040314	C3	257								
HPU040315	C1	258a								
HPU040316	C1	258b								
HPU040317	C1	259								
HPU040318	A4	27F	Y							
HPU040319	C2	260	Y	Y	Y	ODA014	P2	OLA006	P3	123568
HPU040320	C2	261	Y	Y				OLA017	P3	123568
HPU040321	C1	262b	Y							
HPU040322	C2	262a	Y	Y	Y	ODA015	P2	OLA008	P4	1234568
HPU040323	C1	263	Y							
HPU040324	C2	264	Y		Y					
HPU040325	C2	265	Y		Y					
HPU040326	C2	266	Y							
HPU040327	C3	267			Y					
HPU040328	C1	268	Y							
HPU040329	C1	269								
HPU040330	C1	28F						OLA001	P3	123568

DESIGN	PRICE	PAGE	MATERIALS LIST	CUSTOMIZABLE®	QUOTE ONE®	DECK	DECK PRICE	LANDSCAPE	LANDSCAPE PRICE	REGIONS
HPU040331	A4	270	Y							
HPU040332	C1	271		Y						
HPU040333	C1	272a	Y							
HPU040334	C1	272b	Y							
HPU040335	C1	273	Y							
HPU040336	C1	274a	Y							
HPU040337	C1	274b	Y		Y					
HPU040338	C1	275	Y		Y					
HPU040339	C1	276	Y							
HPU040340	C1	277a	Y							
HPU040341	C1	277b	Y							
HPU040342	C1	278a	Y		Y					
HPU040343	C1	278b	Y							
HPU040344	C1	279								
HPU040345	C3	280b								
HPU040346	C1	280a	Y							
HPU040347	C1	281								
HPU040348	C1	282a		Y						
HPU040349	C1	282b	Y							
HPU040350	C2	283	Y	Y	Y	ODA012	P3	OLA024	P4	123568
HPU040351	C2	284		Y						
HPU040352	C1	26F								
HPU040353	C1	285								
HPU040354	C2	286b	Y	Y				OLA001	P3	123568
HPU040355	C2	286a	Y	Y		ODA015	P2	OLA013	P4	12345678
HPU040356	C2	287	Y	Y	Y	ODA011	P2	OLA025	P3	123568
HPU040357	C1	288b	Y							
HPU040358	C2	288a	Y							
HPU040359	C1	289	Y							
HPU040360	C2	290b								
HPU040361	C2	290a	Y							
HPU040362	C1	291	Y							
HPU040363	C2	292								
HPU040364	C2	293								
HPU040365	C2	294a	Y	Y	Y					
HPU040366	C3	294b	Y	Y	Y	ODA016	P2	OLA021	P3	123568
HPU040367	C3	295								
HPU040368	A4	296								
HPU040369	A4	29F								
HPU040370	C2	297								
HPU040371	C2	298								
HPU040372	C4	30F								
HPU040373	C2	299								
HPU040374	C3	300								
HPU040375	C1	301	Y							
HPU040376	C1	302								
HPU040377	C3	303								
HPU040378	C2	304	Y							
HPU040379	C2	305	Y							
HPU040380	C1	306								
HPU040381	C1	307								
HPU040382	C1	308								
HPU040383	C1	309								
HPU040384	C2	310b	Y	Y	Y	ODA006	P2	OLA004	P3	123568
HPU040385	C1	310a								
HPU040386	C2	311	Y	Y	Y	ODA012	P3	OLA018	P3	12345678
HPU040387	C1	312								
HPU040388	C1	313								
HPU040389	C3	31F	Y		Y					
HPU040390	C1	314								
HPU040391	C1	315								
HPU040392	C1	316								
HPU040393	C1	317								
HPU040394	C1	318b								
HPU040395	C1	318a								
HPU040396	C2	319								
HPU040397	C2	320b								
HPU040398	A4	320a								
HPU040399	C1	321								
HPU040400	C1	322b								
HPU040401	C2	322a								
HPU040402	C1	323								
HPU040403	C1	324a	Y							
HPU040404	C1	324b	Y							
HPU040405	C1	325								
HPU040406	C1	326b								
HPU040407	C1	326a								
HPU040408	C1	327								
HPU040409	C2	328								
HPU040410	A4	32F	Y							
HPU040411	C2	329								
HPU040412	C2	330	Y	Y	Y			OLA015	P4	123568
HPU040413	C2	331	Y	Y	Y			OLA038	P3	7
HPU040414	C3	332	Y	Y	Y			OLA016	P4	1234568
HPU040415	C1	333			Y					
HPU040416	C3	334	Y	Y				OLA001	P3	123568
HPU040417	C2	335						OLA017	P3	123568
HPU040419	C3	336								
HPU040420	C1	337								
HPU040421	C2	338a	Y							
HPU040422	C2	338b								

DESIGN	PRICE	PAGE	MATERIALS LIST	CUSTOMIZABLE	QUOTE ONE	DECK	DECK PRICE	LANDSCAPE	LANDSCAPE PRICE	REGIONS
HPU040423	C2	339								
HPU040424	C2	340								
HPU040425	C3	341								
HPU040426	C2	342	Y					OLA004	P3	123568
HPU040427	C2	343b								
HPU040428	C2	343a								
HPU040429	C2	344	Y					OLA001	P3	123568
HPU040430	C2	345								
HPU040431	C2	346a								
HPU040432	C3	346b	Y		Y			OLA008	P4	1234568
HPU040433	C3	347								
HPU040434	C2	348b								
HPU040435	C3	348a								
HPU040436	C3	349								
HPU040437	C2	350a								
HPU040438	C3	350b								
HPU040439	C3	351								
HPU040440	C2	352								
HPU040441	C3	353								
HPU040442	C2	354b								
HPU040443	C2	354a								
HPU040444	C3	355	Y							
HPU040445	C2	356b								
HPU040446	C2	356a								
HPU040447	C3	357								
HPU040448	C2	358	Y		Y			OLA008	P4	1234568
HPU040449	C3	359	Y							
HPU040450	C2	360								
HPU040451	C3	361								
HPU040452	C2	362	Y							
HPU040453	C2	363								
HPU040454	C2	364b								
HPU040455	C2	364a								
HPU040456	C2	365								
HPU040457	C2	366a								
HPU040458	C2	366b								
HPU040459	C2	367								
HPU040460	C2	368								
HPU040461	C4	369								
HPU040462	C2	370	Y							
HPU040463	C2	371	Y							
HPU040464	C4	372								
HPU040465	C2	373	Y							
HPU040466	C2	374								
HPU040467	C2	375								
HPU040468	C3	376								
HPU040469	C2	377								
HPU040470	C2	378								
HPU040471	C2	379								
HPU040472	C2	380								
HPU040473	C2	381								
HPU040474	C4	382	Y		Y					
HPU040475	C2	383								
HPU040476	C2	384	Y							
HPU040477	C3	385	Y							
HPU040478	C3	386a	Y							
HPU040479	C3	386b	Y							
HPU040480	C2	387								
HPU040481	C2	388b								
HPU040482	C2	388a								
HPU040483	C3	389								
HPU040484	C2	390	Y							
HPU040485	C2	391								
HPU040486	C1	392b								
HPU040487	C2	392a								
HPU040488	C2	393	Y							
HPU040489	C2	394								
HPU040490	C2	395b								
HPU040491	C2	395a								
HPU040492	C2	396	Y		Y					
HPU040493	C3	397	Y		Y			OLA030	P3	12345678
HPU040494	C3	398	Y		Y	Y	ODA022	P3	OLA031	P4	12345678
HPU040495	C3	399	Y		Y	Y				
HPU040496	C2	400			Y					
HPU040497	C2	401a			Y					
HPU040498	C2	401b								
HPU040499	C2	402								
HPU040500	C2	403						OLA004	P3	123568
HPU040501	C3	404a	Y							
HPU040502	C3	404b	Y							
HPU040503	C3	405	Y							
HPU040504	C2	406	Y							
HPU040505	C2	407	Y							
HPU040506	C2	408b	Y							
HPU040507	C3	408a								
HPU040508	C2	409								
HPU040509	C3	410a	Y							
HPU040510	C3	410b								
HPU040511	C2	411								
HPU040512	C2	412								
HPU040513	C2	413a								

DESIGN	PRICE	PAGE	MATERIALS LIST	CUSTOMIZABLE	QUOTE ONE	DECK	DECK PRICE	LANDSCAPE	LANDSCAPE PRICE	REGIONS
HPU040514	C2	413b								
HPU040515	C2	414								
HPU040516	C2	415								
HPU040517	C2	416								
HPU040518	C4	417								
HPU040519	C3	418a								
HPU040520	C4	418b			Y					
HPU040521	C1	419								
HPU040522	C3	420b								
HPU040523	C4	420a								
HPU040524	L1	421								
HPU040525	L2	422								
HPU040526	L1	423								
HPU040527	L1	424								
HPU040528	C3	425								
HPU040529	L4	426								
HPU040530	L3	427								
HPU040531	C4	428								
HPU040532	C4	429								
HPU040533	L2	430	Y							
HPU040534	L1	431								
HPU040535	C3	432a								
HPU040536	C4	432b								
HPU040537	L1	433								
HPU040538	C3	434								
HPU040539	C4	435								
HPU040540	L2	436								
HPU040541	L1	437	Y							
HPU040542	C4	438b	Y		Y					
HPU040543	C3	438a								
HPU040544	C4	439	Y							
HPU040545	L1	440	Y		Y					
HPU040546	C4	441	Y							
HPU040547	L1	442								
HPU040548	L1	443								
HPU040549	C3	444								
HPU040550	C3	445	Y							
HPU040551	C4	446	Y							
HPU040552	C4	447	Y							
HPU040553	C4	448	Y							
HPU040554	C4	449								
HPU040555	L2	450								
HPU040556	C4	451								
HPU040557	L1	452								
HPU040558	C4	453								
HPU040559	C3	454								
HPU040560	L1	455						OLA017	P3	123568
HPU040561	C3	456								
HPU040562	C4	457								
HPU040563	L3	458								
HPU040564	C3	459								
HPU040565	L2	460								
HPU040566	C3	461								
HPU040567	C3	462								
HPU040568	C3	463								
HPU040569	C3	464			Y					
HPU040570	L4	465								
HPU040571	L1	466	Y							
HPU040572	L1	467	Y							
HPU040573	C4	468	Y							
HPU040574	L2	469								
HPU040575	C4	470								
HPU040576	C3	471	Y							
HPU040577	C4	472								
HPU040578	C4	473								
HPU040579	C4	474								
HPU040580	C4	475								
HPU040581	C2	476	Y							
HPU040582	L1	477								
HPU040583	L1	478	Y							
HPU040584	C3	479	Y							
HPU040585	C4	480								
HPU040586	L1	481	Y					OLA017	P3	123568
HPU040587	L1	482								
HPU040588	C4	483								
HPU040589	L1	484								
HPU040590	C4	485								
HPU040591	L1	486						OLA008	P4	1234568
HPU040592	L1	487								
HPU040593	L1	488								
HPU040594	L1	489								
HPU040595	C4	490								
HPU040596	L1	491	Y					OLA017	P3	123568
HPU040597	C4	492	Y							
HPU040598	L2	493	Y							
HPU040599	L1	494			Y					
HPU040600	L4	495	Y		Y			OLA008	P4	1234568
HPU040601	L1	496								
HPU040602	C4	497	Y					OLA008	P4	1234568

BEFORE YOU ORDER...

OUR EXCHANGE POLICY

Since blueprints are printed in response to your order, we cannot honor requests for refunds. However, we will exchange your entire first order for an equal or greater number of blueprints within our plan collection within 90 days of the original order. The entire content of your original order must be returned to our offices before an exchange will be processed. If the returned blueprints look used, redlined or copied, we will not honor your exchange. Fees for exchanging your blueprints are as follows: 20% of the amount of the original order...*plus* the difference in cost if exchanging for a design in a higher price bracket or *less* the difference in cost if exchanging for a design in lower price bracket. (**Reproducible blueprints are not exchangeable.**) Please add $25 for postage and handling via Regular Service; $35 via Priority Service; $45 via Express Service. Shipping and handling charges are not refundable.

ABOUT REVERSE BLUEPRINTS

If you want to build in reverse of the plan as shown, we will include any number of reverse blueprints (mirror image) from a 4- or 8-set package for an additional fee of $50. Although lettering and dimensions will appear backward, reverses will be a useful aid if you decide to flop the plan.

REVISING, MODIFYING AND CUSTOMIZING PLANS

The wide variety of designs available in this publication allows you to select ideas and concepts for a home to fit your building site and match your family's needs, wants and budget. Like many homeowners who buy these plans, you and your builder, architect or engineer may want to make changes to them. Some changes may be made by your builder, but we recommend that most changes be made by a licensed architect or engineer. If you need to make alterations to a design that is customizable, you need only order our Home Customizer® Package to get you started. As set forth below, we cannot assume any responsibility for blueprints which have been changed, whether by you, your builder or by professionals selected by you or referred to you by us, because such individuals are outside our supervision and control.

ARCHITECTURAL AND ENGINEERING SEALS

Some cities and states are now requiring that a licensed architect or engineer review and "seal" a blueprint, or officially approve it, prior to construction due to concerns over energy costs, safety and other factors. Prior to application for a building permit or the start of actual construction, we strongly advise that you consult your local building official who can tell you if such a review is required.

ABOUT THE DESIGNS

The architects and designers whose work appears in this publication are among America's leading residential designers. Each plan was designed to meet the requirements of a nationally recognized model building code in effect at the time and place the plan was drawn. Because national building codes change from time to time, plans may not comply with any such code at the time they are sold to a customer. In addition, building officials may not accept these plans as final construction documents of record as the plans may need to be modified and additional drawings and details added to suit local conditions and requirements. We strongly advise that purchasers consult a licensed architect or engineer, and their local building official, before starting any construction related to these plans.

LOCAL BUILDING CODES AND ZONING REQUIREMENTS

At the time of creation, our plans are drawn to specifications published by the Building Officials and Code Administrators (BOCA) International, Inc.; the Southern Building Code Congress (SBCCI) International, Inc.; the International Conference of Building Officials (ICBO); or the Council of American Building Officials (CABO). Our plans are designed to meet or exceed na-

tional building standards. Because of the great differences in geography and climate throughout the United States and Canada, each state, county and municipality has its own building codes, zone requirements, ordinances and building regulations. Your plan may need to be modified to comply with local requirements regarding snow loads, energy codes, soil and seismic conditions and a wide range of other matters. In addition, you may need to obtain permits or inspections from local governments before and in the course of construction. Prior to using blueprints ordered from us, we strongly advise that you consult a licensed architect or engineer—and speak with your local building official—before applying for any permit or beginning construction. We authorize the use of our blueprints on the express condition that you strictly comply with all local building codes, zoning requirements and other applicable laws, regulations, ordinances and requirements. **Notice: Plans for homes to be built in Nevada must be re-drawn by a Nevada-registered professional. Consult your building official for more information on this subject.**

FOUNDATION AND EXTERIOR WALL CHANGES

Depending on your specific climate or regional building practices, you may wish to change a full basement to a slab or crawlspace foundation. Most professional contractors and builders can easily adapt your plans to alternate foundation types. Likewise, most can easily change 2x4 wall construction to 2x6, or vice versa.

DISCLAIMER

We and the designers we work with have put substantial care and effort into the creation of our blueprints. However, because we cannot provide on-site consultation, supervision and control over actual construction, and because of the great variance in local building requirements, building practices and soil, seismic, weather and other conditions, WE CANNOT MAKE ANY WARRANTY, EXPRESS OR IMPLIED, WITH RESPECT TO THE CONTENT OR USE OF OUR BLUEPRINTS, INCLUDING BUT NOT LIMITED TO ANY WARRANTY OF MERCHANTABILITY OR OF FITNESS FOR A PARTICULAR PURPOSE.

TERMS AND CONDITIONS

These designs are protected under the terms of United States Copyright Law and may not be copied or reproduced in any way, by any means, unless you have purchased Sepias or Reproducibles which clearly indicate your right to copy or reproduce. We authorize the use of your chosen design as an aid in the construction of one single family home only. You may not use this design to build a second or multiple dwellings without purchasing another blueprint or blueprints or paying additional design fees.

HOW MANY BLUEPRINTS DO YOU NEED?

A single set of blueprints is sufficient to study a home in greater detail. However, if you are planning to obtain cost estimates from a contractor or subcontractors—or if you are planning to build immediately—you will need more sets. Because additional sets are cheaper when ordered in quantity with the original order, make sure you order enough blueprints to satisfy all requirements. The following checklist will help you determine how many you need:

___ Owner

___ Builder (generally requires at least three sets; one as a legal document, one to use during inspections, and at least one to give to subcontractors)

___ Local Building Department (often requires two sets)

___ Mortgage Lender (usually one set for a conventional loan; three sets for FHA or VA loans)

___ TOTAL NUMBER OF SETS

Have You Seen Our Newest Designs?

At least 50 of our latest creations are featured in each edition of our New Design Portfolio. You may have received a copy with your latest purchase by mail. If not, or if you purchased this book from a local retailer, just return the coupon below for your FREE copy. Make sure you consider the very latest of what Home Planners has to offer.

Yes! Please send my FREE copy of your latest New Design Portfolio.

Offer good to U.S. shipping address only.

Name _____

Address_____

City_____ State _____ Zip _____

HOME PLANNERS, LLC
Wholly owned by Hanley-Wood, LLC
3275 WEST INA ROAD, SUITE 110
TUCSON, ARIZONA 85741

Order Form Key

| HPU04 |

ORDER FORM

 The Home Customizer®

"This house is perfect...if only the family room were two feet wider." Sound familiar? In response to the numerous requests for this type of modification, Home Planners has developed **The Home Customizer® Package**. This exclusive package offers our top-of-the-line materials to make it easy for anyone, anywhere to customize any Home Planners design to fit their needs. Check the index on page 506-509 for those plans which are customizable.

Some of the changes you can make to any of our plans include:

- exterior elevation changes
- kitchen and bath modifications
- roof, wall and foundation changes
- room additions and more!

The Home Customizer® Package includes everything you'll need to make the necessary changes to your favorite Home Planners design. The package includes:

- instruction book with examples
- architectural scale and clear work film
- erasable red marker and removable correction tape
- ¼"-scale furniture cutouts
- 1 set reproducible drawings
- 1 set study blueprints for communicating changes to your design professional
- a copyright release letter so you can make copies as you need them
- referral letter with the name, address and telephone number of the professional in your region who is trained in modifying Home Planners designs efficiently and inexpensively.

The Home Customizer® Package will not only save you 25% to 75% of the cost of drawing the plans from scratch with an architect or engineer, it will also give you the flexibility to have your changes and modifications made by our referral network or by the professional of your choice. Now it's even easier and more affordable to have the custom home you've always wanted.

 **ORDER TOLL FREE!**
For INFORMATION ABOUT ANY OF OUR SERVICES OR TO ORDER CALL

1-877-675-4639 OR **520-297-8200**
Browse our website:
www.eplans.com

BLUEPRINTS ARE NOT REFUNDABLE EXCHANGES ONLY

FOR CUSTOMER SERVICE,
CALL TOLL FREE **1-888-690-1116.**

HOME PLANNERS, LLC wholly owned by Hanley-Wood, LLC
3275 WEST INA ROAD, SUITE 110 • TUCSON, ARIZONA • 85741

THE BASIC BLUEPRINT PACKAGE
Rush me the following (please refer to the Plans Index and Price Schedule in this section):
___Set(s) of blueprints for plan number(s) _____. $_____
___Set(s) of reproducibles for plan number(s) _____. $_____
___Home Customizer® Package for plan(s)_____. $_____
___Additional identical blueprints (standard or reverse) in same order @ $50 per set. $_____
___Reverse blueprints @ $50 fee per order. Right-reading reverse @ $165 surcharge $_____

IMPORTANT EXTRAS
Rush me the following:
___Materials List: $60 (Must be purchased with Blueprint set.) Add $10 for Schedule C4–L4 plans. $_____
___**Quote One®** Summary Cost Report @ $29.95 for one, $14.95 for each additional,
    for plans _____ $_____
    Building location: City _____ Zip Code _____
___**Quote One®** Materials Cost Report @ $120 Schedules P1–C3; $130 Schedules C4–L4,
    for plan_____(Must be purchased with Blueprints set.) $_____
    Building location: City _____ Zip Code _____
___Specification Outlines @ $10 each. $_____
___Detail Sets @ $14.95 each; any two $22.95; any three $29.95; all four for $39.95 (save $19.85). $_____
    ❏ Plumbing ❏ Electrical ❏ Construction ❏ Mechanical
___Plan-A-Home® @ $29.95 each. $_____

DECK BLUEPRINTS
(Please refer to the Plans Index and Price Schedule in this section)
___Set(s) of Deck Plan _____. $_____
___Additional identical blueprints in same order @ $10 per set. $_____
___Reverse blueprints @ $10 per set. $_____
___Set of Standard Deck Details @ $14.95 per set. $_____
___Set of Complete Deck Construction Package (Best Buy!) Add $10 to Building Package
    Includes Custom Deck Plan _____ Plus Standard Deck Details

LANDSCAPE BLUEPRINTS
(Please refer to the Plans Index and Price Schedule in this section)
___Set(s) of Landscape Plan _____. $_____
___Additional identical blueprints in same order @ $10 per set. $_____
___Reverse blueprints @ $10 per set. $_____
Please indicate the appropriate region of the country for Plant & Material List.
(See map on page 505): Region _____

POSTAGE AND HANDLING	1–3 sets	4+ sets
Signature is required for all deliveries. **DELIVERY** No CODs (Requires street address—No P.O. Boxes)		
•Regular Service (Allow 7–10 business days delivery)	❏ $20.00	❏ $25.00
•Priority (Allow 4–5 business days delivery)	❏ $25.00	❏ $35.00
•Express (Allow 3 business days delivery)	❏ $35.00	❏ $45.00
OVERSEAS DELIVERY	fax, phone or mail for quote	

Note: All delivery times are from date Blueprint Package is shipped.

POSTAGE (From box above) $_____
SUBTOTAL $_____
SALES TAX (AZ & MI residents, please add appropriate state and local sales tax.) $_____
TOTAL (Subtotal and tax) $_____

YOUR ADDRESS (please print)

Name _____

Street_____

City _____State_____Zip _____

Daytime telephone number (_____) _____

FOR CREDIT CARD ORDERS ONLY

Credit card number _____ Exp. Date: (M/Y) _____
Check one ❏ Visa ❏ MasterCard ❏ Discover Card ❏ American Express

Signature_____

Please check appropriate box: ❏ Licensed Builder-Contractor ❏ Homeowner

 **ORDER TOLL FREE!**
1-877-675-4639 or 520-297-8200

Order Form Key

HPU04

511

Free with your blueprint order!

Order any set of blueprints from this book and Home Planners will include a complete window specification featuring Pella materials for your chosen design. Call **1-877-675-4639** or **520-297-8200** to speak to one of our experienced sales representatives who can help you in selecting and ordering your plans. For additional ordering information, refer to pages 500-511.

☎ ORDER TOLL FREE
1-877-675-4639 or 1-520-297-8200

Or, if you prefer, fill out the order form on page 511 and fax to 1-800-224-6699 or 1-520-544-3086.

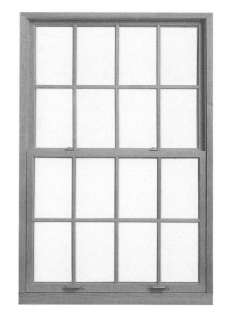